SOCIALIST
REGISTER
2 0 0 1

THE SOCIALIST REGISTER

Founded in 1964

EDITORS:
LEO PANITCH
COLIN LEYS

Visit our website at:

http://www.yorku.ca/org/socreg/
for a detailed list of all our issues, order forms and an online selection of
past prefaces and essays,

...and join our listserv by contacting
socreg@yorku.ca
for a discussion of the essays from this volume and issues relevant to socialists.

SOCIALIST REGISTER 2001

Edited by LEO PANITCH and COLIN LEYS
with GREG ALBO and DAVID COATES

MERLIN PRESS
FERNWOOD PRESS
MONTHLY REVIEW PRESS

First published in 2000
by The Merlin Press Ltd.
PO Box 30705
London
WC2E 8QD

British Library Cataloguing in Publication Data
1. The Socialist Register. —2001
I. Panitch, Leo 1945-   II Leys, Colin 1931-
355'. 005

Canadian Cataloguing in Publication Data
Main entry under title:
Working classes, global realities
ISBN 1-55266-031-1
1. Working class. 2. Labor, 3. Industrial relations. I. Panitch, Leo, 1945-,
II. Leys, Colin, 1931-   III Albo, Gregory.   IV Coates, David.
HX44.5.W67 2000   331.8   COO-950052-9

ISSN: 0081-0606

Published in Europe by The Merlin Press
0 85036 490 6 Paperback
0 85036 491 4 Hardback

Published in the USA by Monthly Review Press
1 58367 029 7 Paperback
1 58367 031 9 Hardback

Published in Canada by The Fernwood Press
1 55266 031 1 Paperback

Typeset by Jon Carpenter
Printed in Canada

CONTENTS

PREFACE

This thirty-seventh volume of the *Socialist Register*, 'Working Classes: Global Realities' follows naturally from last year's volume, *Necessary and Unnecessary Utopias*, which explored visions and strategies capable of transcending the pessimism prevailing on the Left and rekindling the socialist imagination. Socialist renewal remains, in our minds, inextricably linked with working-class emancipation. This must mean the working class in the broadest possible sense; and it must also mean transcending the limits of old forms of working-class organization and politics.

Hundreds of thousands of words have been written by Left thinkers over the past decade on the penetration of capital throughout the globe and the triumphs of the neoliberal project; and from Chiapas to the 'Battle of Seattle' much attention has also been devoted to the emergence of an 'international civil society' opposed to globalized capitalism—an opposition we heartily support. But the authors of this literature have too often accepted capitalist markets as the necessary organizing principle of modern economic and political life, or been too speculative and too minimally reformist in propounding ways in which capitalist markets might be managed, through taxes on financial speculation or international labour standards, for example. Such a truncation of political horizons was perhaps inevitable after the ignominious collapse of Communism and social democracy's embrace of 'third wayism', but seems to us profoundly misguided.

Against these intellectual and political currents it seemed to us important to devote the present volume to the state of the global proletariat at the beginning of the new millennium, since any serious reconstruction of the socialist movement must begin by confronting the realignment of class structures and the impasse of working-class politics that have taken place over the last quarter of the twentieth century. Class analysis as a mode of intellectual discourse, and social class as the pivotal axis of political mobilization, have both suffered marginalization, although certainly not complete collapse, in the face of the

casualization of work, trade-union decline and the fracturing of socialist political formations, not to mention the impact of neoliberal and post-modernist
ideas. This has undoubtedly been the case in the core capitalist countries, and
it is hard to avoid drawing similar conclusions for other parts of the world as
well.

Yet this period has also been marked by acute social inequalities 'growing
directly out of capitalist production itself', as Marx put it, a point conceded even
by the international agencies and states leading the drive for globalization, while
the absolute numbers of proletarians, and indeed workers in trade unions, have
never been greater. As a set of social relations, then, 'class' is as central to understanding the dynamics of contemporary capitalism as it ever has been. But class
as a political relation—in the sense of workers consciously forming a class 'in
so far as they engage in a common battle against another class', i.e., as an agency
advancing political and economic alternatives to neoliberalism and capitalism—
remains deep in crisis.

So it seems important and timely to try to assess as honestly as possible the
state of the global proletariat. One dimension of this is certainly to refresh class
analysis, developing the theoretical capacity to understand a world in which an
emerging 'cybertariat' coexists with 'peasantries', not to mention an increasing
number of factory workers worldwide. And if this means overcoming the
weaknesses of Marxist analysis, not least in relation to office workers and
farmers, it also means overcoming a tendency to take the class structure of the
'North' as a model for the 'South'. A second task, therefore, has been to try to
register the varied experiences of the contemporary working classes, and to do
this in a way, moreover, that not only recognizes the importance of spatial
differences and determinations, but also understands that this pertains to
workers' diverse 'ways of living' as well as to experiences at work. A third task
we set ourselves was to look at working-class organization, identity formation
and politics in various zones of the world, and assess their significance. Here
too, we have tried not only to note trends that are common, but also those that
have specific resonance for particular groups of workers and for particular
places.

Conceptually, this volume challenges at least two items of current academic
and political conventional wisdom. It challenges the claim—beloved of both
conservative thinkers and Third Way politicians—that we live in a post-class
age, that the working class no longer exists, and that to think in class terms is
to remain trapped in the mental furniture of the old millennium rather than the
new. It also challenges the tendency of much contemporary scholarship and
political discourse to treat globalization as simply a matter of the increased
mobility of capital. In our view this is to make three linked mistakes. It is to
think of capital in a fetishized form, to forget that capital is necessarily always
a social relationship, and to ignore the way in which the growth of capital in
general is possible only through the expanding extraction of value from labour
power. Capital is not suddenly more globally mobile because of the revolution

in information technology or the deregulation of financial markets; capital is more geographically diversified than it used to be because it now has more working classes to exploit. Those who declare that we live in an age without classes need to count the growing numbers of those sections of the world's producers who now depend—directly or indirectly—on the sale of their labour power for their own daily reproduction. The World Bank in 1995 put that number at 2.5 billion. The global proletariat is not vanishing but expanding at a rate that has doubled its numbers since 1975.

It is not the absence of proletarian numbers that is the defining feature of the age so much as the unprecedented combination of old and new proletariats in face of global capital. Throughout the history of modern capitalism, the proletarian experience has always been complex and many-layered; but never has it been as complexly structured as it is now. For within the modern global proletariat at least several new and complex forms of class construction and experience overlay each other. In the proletariats of the core capitalisms—in labour movements with their own long history—the current conjuncture is one of work intensification, class restructuring and growing employer and state offensives. Across each of the major economies of North America, Western Europe and Japan, differentially nuanced by national circumstance, the positions previously won by labour are now heavily under challenge. In each the work-effort bargain at the point of production is being intensified, job insecurity is rife, older and more unionized work groups are being replaced by newer and less organized ones, and the social settlement established by proletarian pressure in post-war capitalism's golden age is everywhere being eroded. In large swathes of the eastern and southern zones of what once was an undifferentiated Third World, no such social settlement exists to be defended, for there it is processes of early proletarian creation that are widely evident. There the working conditions, pay and social rights of the emerging labour forces share much in common with those typical of the core capitalisms earlier in the twentieth century: long hours for low pay, extensive use of child labour, the movement of workers from country to town, the denial of union and democratic rights and heavy state repression. Add to that the entry into the world labour market of 'Second World' workers hitherto sealed off by cold war divisions and whose experience of full-scale industrialization (in the case of the former Soviet Union) or initial industrial development (as in Vietnam and China) either was (or in the latter two cases, still is) mediated through the rhetoric and political structures of Communist regimes.

Old and new interact dramatically in the labour experience of the newly industrializing economies of the East and the South: where different groups of workers find themselves exposed, alongside one another, to a range of different but equally daunting material conditions: the rigours of advanced factory production, the demands of modern service employment, the insecurities of petty trade and the desperate poverty of marginalized employment. Old and new interact even within the labour experience of the core capitalisms, as migrant labour becomes progressively more important for the reproduction of capital in basic industries and service employment, and as the capacity of capital to relocate to ever cheaper and more exploited sources of labour ratchets down wages and conditions of even well-organized groups of workers.

The modern proletarian condition is thus more obviously a global one than at any previous time in the history of capitalism. It is also still one that fosters divisions as much as unity within the working class. The organizational questions of working-class politics remain as critical as ever. Class diversity and diverse class situations have also produced new kinds of struggle and new kinds of organization. Careful reflection on the promise and limitations of these has also been one of the main aims of this volume.

A stock-taking of the global proletariat obviously required contributors from a wide range of locations. Ursula Huws is a writer and researcher who is director of the independent social and economic research consultancy, Analytica, and Associate Fellow of the Institute for Employment Studies at the University of Sussex. Henry Bernstein teaches Development Studies at the School of Oriental and African Studies, London; and both Beverley Silver and Giovanni Arrighi are in the Sociology Department at Johns Hopkins University in Baltimore. Andrew Ross is Director of the American Studies Programme at New York University. Barbara Hariss-White teaches development studies, and Nandini Gooptu teaches South Asian History and Politics, both at Queen Elizabeth House, Oxford. Patrick Bond teaches in the Graduate School of Public and Development Management at Wits University in Johannesburg, and Greg Ruiters teaches Political Studies at that university; Darlene Miller, who is affiliated with the Sociology Department there, is also a doctoral candidate at Johns Hopkins University. Steve Jefferys has recently taken up a research chair in Employment Studies at the University of North London, and David Mandel teaches Political Science at the University of Quebec in Montreal. Haideh Moghissi and Saeed Rahnema teach Sociology and Political Science respectively at York University, Toronto. Huw Beynon is Director of the School of Social Sciences at Cardiff University in Wales; and José Ramalho teaches in the Department of Sociology at the Federal University of Rio de Janeiro in Brazil. Gerard Greenfield is a labour research activist based in Hong Kong; Rohini Hensman is a feminist labour activist and researcher working in Mumbai, India. Eric Mann is the Director of the Labour/Community Strategy Centre in Los Angeles; and Justin Paulson is a doctoral candidate in the Department of History of Consciousness at the University of California, Santa Cruz, and founder and Web-master of the ¡Ya Basta! Web page. Judith Adler Hellman teaches Social and Political Science at York University Toronto; and Peter Kwong teaches Political Science at Hunter College, City University of New York. Brigitte Young teaches in the Institut für Politikwissenschaft at the University of Münster in Germany; and Rosemary Warskett teaches in the Department of Law, Carleton University, Ottawa. Sam Gindin, recently retired as assistant to the president of the Canadian Auto Workers union, is now teaching in the Department of Political Science at York University, Toronto.

In thanking all the contributors, we should mention that for the first time in the *Register*'s history drafts of many of the essays for this year's volume were first presented at a workshop, held in Toronto in January 2000 and funded with the assistance of York University the Social Sciences and Humanities Research Council of Canada. We want to express our appreciation to those who participated, including the graduate students of the Political Science Department who acted as rapporteurs, while making it clear that neither they nor the contributors themselves necessarily agree with everything that appears in this volume. Marsha Niemeijer, the *Register*'s assistant at York University, played an especially important role in organizing this workshop for which we are very grateful, as we indeed are for all her excellent editorial and promotional work as well. As before, we have also been able to call on Alan Zuege's editorial skills in preparing the essays for publication, for which much thanks once again; and we also have to thank Vince Pietropaolo and Shuster Gindin for help with the photos used on our cover, as well as Louis Mackay for the cover design itself. And thanks again too to Tony Zurbrugg, and his staff at the new Merlin Press, who have brought enormous enthusiasm, skill and commitment to the production and distribution of the *Socialist Register*.

This has been one of the largest and most challenging volumes of the *Register* in many years, reflected in the sharing of editorial responsibilities by Greg Albo and David Coates alongside Leo Panitch and Colin Leys. But beyond this, without the further active support of the *Register*'s other contributing and corresponding editors in defining the theme, suggesting contributors and in a number of cases undertaking to write essays themselves, producing a volume on this scale would hardly have been possible. We thank them all. We want also to extend special thanks to George Ross and Reg Whitaker who have retired as contributing editors (but not, we want to assure our readers, as contributors of essays to future volumes). We are extremely pleased to welcome Ursula Huws and Alan Zuege as new contributing editors as well as Aijaz Ahmad as our new corresponding editor in New Delhi. Readers of the *Register* will already be aware of their contributions in recent years and will want to join us in welcoming them to the *Register* collective.

July 2000
L.P. C.L.
G.A. D.C.

THE MAKING OF A CYBERTARIAT? VIRTUAL WORK IN A REAL WORLD

Ursula Huws

It is possible to argue that in the aftermath of 1989 a single global economy is in formation. As the WTO dismantles any remaining checks on the free movement of capital, goods, services and intellectual property between countries, transnational corporations have an open field. With the terms of employment of a growing proportion of the world's population determined either directly or indirectly by these same corporations, the conditions would seem, at last, to have arrived to render possible the fulfilment Marx's injunction at the end of the Communist Manifesto: 'Workers of the world unite'. But are there in fact any signs that a global proletariat with a common consciousness is emerging?

This essay takes as its starting point a conception of capitalism as a dynamic force whose engine proceeds by the interrelated processes of commodification and accumulation. On the one hand it seeks insatiably for new commodities from the production of which surplus value can be extracted, and on the other for new markets to fuel its voracious expansion. New commodities arise either from the drawing into the cash economy of activities which were previously carried out by unpaid labour, for gift or exchange, or by the elaboration of existing commodities. Human activities and needs thus stand at either end of the process: production and consumption. The inevitable impetus is towards a complete industrialization of the globe, with the entire population involved on the one hand in contributing towards the production or circulation of commodities and the capital accumulation process in some capacity, and on the other in an ever-greater dependence on the purchase of these commodities for their survival.

The commodification process entails continuing seismic shifts in the social division of labour. This is not the place to describe in detail how, for instance, subsistence agriculture gives way to forms of farming locked into the market by the need to acquire such things as seeds, tools and fertilizer, as well as to sell its produce, or how in the process new social categories are created, such as the landless rural wage labourer or the plantation manager. Or how the resulting changes in a rural economy force peasants to send their children to the city as factory workers. Or how the automation of factories leads to a growing complexity in the division of labour which generates new groups standing between the paradigmatic proletariat and bourgeoisie: the foreman, for example, or the skilled draughtsman, or the purchasing manager. Or how these groups in turn are threatened or reconstituted at the next twist of technological development. Here it is enough simply to point out that their rise or demise affects not only the composition of the labour force—the organization of production—but also the structure of the market—the organization of consumption—since each of these groups buys commodities as well as selling its labour.

This point becomes particularly relevant when we come to discuss the current wave of technological change—the widespread use of information and communication technologies (ICTs)—because these, unusually in the history of automation, are technologies of both production and consumption. The possession or lack of these technologies is therefore likely to create a major new fault-line running through entire populations. The 'digital divide' is the currently fashionable term for this fault-line.

But before examining these new demographics in detail, it is necessary to take a step back and define what work it is we are talking about, by no means an easy task.

I

Whilst thinking about this essay, I wrote in a newsletter,

> Recent work has raised in a very acute form the problem of how to name the kinds of work which involve telematics. Even the traditional terms are unsatisfactory. 'White collar' implies a particular kind of male office worker who probably ceased being typical (if he ever was) sometime in the 1950s. 'Non-manual' denies the physical reality of pounding a keyboard all day. 'Office work' links it to a particular kind of location when the whole point of recent developments is that they mean such work can be done anywhere. And most of the newer terms are even worse. 'Telecommuter' applies only to those people who have substituted one kind of location (the home) for another (the city centre office). 'Teleworker' again tends to be restricted in practice to those workers who have relocated and cannot be applied to that whole class of workers

whose work is *potentially* delocalizable. Some commentators have come up with categories like 'digital analyst' or 'knowledge worker' but—apart from sounding rather pretentious—these tend to suggest a sub-category of work towards the top end of the skill scale. On the other hand 'information processor' falls into the opposite trap of suggesting that it applies only to the more routine work, like data entry. I notice that the European Commission's 'New Ways to Work' unit has lately taken to talking about 'e-work' and 'e-workers'. This is certainly in tune with the current fashion in New Labour Britain, where recent government statements on the 'Information Age' policy include reference to the appointment of an 'e-minister' to be in charge of 'e-business' and an 'e-envoy' to ensure that the policies are directed towards 'e-inclusion'. Perhaps 'e-work' is indeed the least bad option.[1]

I was interested to receive the following reply from Alice de Wolff, a researcher based in Toronto:

> I was amused by your discussion about what to call 'it'. We have had constant, very similar discussions about 'the' term ... Our experience is that there are two issues—one, to find an adequate description, and two, to find one that the workers involved relate to. We haven't managed to bring them together in any satisfactory way. When we use language other than 'office workers', or 'administrative professionals' (not my favourite), or 'administrative assistants', the people who do the work don't think it's about them. I am most comfortable with 'information workers', because I actually think it describes much of the work very well, and suggests a central location in the 'information economy'. I use it, and 'front line information workers' when I'm speaking with groups of office workers, and think it works well when used in context. But if we try to use it as a title of a document, event, etc., very few people relate'.[2]

This encapsulates very well the tension which underlies any discussion of class: between class as an analytical term (objective class position) and class as an aspect of personal identity (subjective class position). This in turn reflects the broader tension between structure and agency as conceptual frameworks for understanding the dynamics of social and economic change. I would not wish to minimize the difficulties of resolving these tensions in relation to other class categories, such as the 'working class' or the 'peasantry'. Nevertheless, the fact that such difficulties should arise so acutely in this context (which, for lack of a better term, I will call 'office work' for the moment) is indicative of a particular lacuna in the history of socialist thought.

With a few notable exceptions, the literature on office work leaves a distinct impression that on the whole socialists would rather not think about the subject at all and, when they have reluctantly had to do so, have been at a loss as to how to categorize office workers and whether to place them, with Crompton and Gallie, respectively, in a 'white-collar proletariat'[3] or 'new working class'[4]; to follow Lenin or Poulantzas[5] in locating them as part of a petty bourgeoisie whose interests lie with small employers and are opposed to those of manual workers; or to hedge their bets along with Wright, and regard them as occupying 'contradictory locations within class relations'.[6] Marx supplies a modicum of support for each of these positions. In his account, the inevitable proletarianization of the petty bourgeoisie (craft and own-account workers and small employers) sits side by side with an equally inevitable expansion in the numbers of employed clerical workers (whom he terms 'commercial wage workers'). However, he refuses the status of proletarian to the latter, stating that 'the commercial worker produces no surplus value directly' because 'the increase of this labour is always a result, never a cause of more surplus value'. Furthermore, he is of the opinion that 'the office is always infinitesimally small compared to the industrial workshop'.[7]

This is not the place for a detailed overview of debates about class. It is worth noting, however, that some degree of muddle about where to locate office workers seems to persist whether class is defined in relation to occupation (which corresponds, as Marshall et al. have pointed out, with categories defined by the technical relations of production[8]); to the social relations of production (the ownership or non-ownership of the means of production); to the social division of labour; to comparative income, to caste-based or other culturally constructed hierarchies (Weber's 'status-groups'); or to some empirically constructed stratification lacking any coherent conceptual underpinning, as in most official statistical categorizations.

II

During the nineteenth century there were reasonable empirical grounds for regarding 'clerks' as male. In the British Census of 1851, over 99% of people listed in this category were men. Despite an accelerating entry of women into the clerical work-force from the 1870s onwards, until the 1960s most theorizing about the class position of office workers continued to be rooted in the assumption that they were masculine. The two classic studies of office workers in the post-war period, Wright Mill's 'White Collar'[9] and Lockwood's 'the Black-Coated Worker'[10] reveal this assumption only too clearly in their titles which also, in their different ways, represent a sort of verbal throwing up of the hands in defeat at the problem of how to construct a conceptually coherent definition of office work. If there is no other feature which uniquely delineates office workers from the rest of the workforce, we can feel these authors thinking, then at least they have their clothing in common.

Although one can sympathize with the label problem, such blindness is staggering. Whilst these books were being written, women (clad, no doubt, in brightly-coloured New Look shirt-waisters or pastel twin-sets) were entering office work in unprecedented numbers, so that by the time of the 1961 census they represented about two-thirds of all clerical workers, in both Britain and the United States[11]—a proportion which had risen to three-quarters by the 1971 census. Wright Mills does in fact devote six pages of his 378-page opus to a discussion of the 'white-collar girl' but characterizes her mainly in terms of her love life. A discussion of gender plays no part in the formation of his bleak conclusion (essentially derived from Lenin) that white-collar workers will never develop distinctive forms of political agency and that even if they did, 'their advance to increased stature in American society could not result in increased freedom and rationality. For white-collar people carry less rationality than illusion and less desire for freedom than the misery of modern anxieties'.[12]

There is a blurred recognition in these authors' work that office workers cannot be regarded as a single homogenous entity. But this is combined with a strange reluctance to anatomize the differences within the broader category which can seem on occasion like a wilful refusal to see the obvious. This obliviousness offers a clue to the more general neglect of office work in socio-economic analysis, and, more specifically, in socialist discourse. It confronts the analyst in a particularly acute form with the unresolved 'woman question' which has been flapping about the attic of Marxist theory since its inception.

Most theories of class, at least until the 1960s, assigned women unproblematically to the class position of their fathers or husbands. If they were not economically dependent on these men and played an independent role in the economy (something with which some theorists were already uncomfortable) then this did not pose major problems because they would normally occupy positions in the same class as these fathers or husbands: the wives and daughters of factory workers would also work in factories; the wives and daughters of rentiers would also be rentiers, and so on (Marx's argument that domestic servants did not form part of the proletariat caused a few hiccups here, but not major ones, since servants were regarded as part of an obsolescent class and anyway merged into the reserve army of the lumpenproletariat from which there could be movement in and out of the proletariat without upsetting any important theoretical applecarts). In other words arguments could be developed on the assumption that peoples' class positions *as citizens* (in which the basic unit is the household) were the same as their class positions *as workers* (in which the basic unit is the individual); and, indeed, that the former derived from the latter. Whilst women are regarded simply as members of households no tension between these different identities need arise and movements between classes (for instance by 'marrying up' or 'marrying down') can be dealt with under the heading 'social mobility'.

The minute female office workers are treated *as workers*, however, this simple mode of analysis breaks down. One is forced to confront the awkward fact that office workers may occupy a different class position from their husbands or fathers. The most thorough empirical study of class position in the UK of which

I am aware concluded that 'fully half of the conjugal units in our sample are cross-class families, using the three-category version of Goldthorpe's class schema'.[13] Similar disparities arise using other classification methods, such as the Registrar General's categories used in UK official statistics, or Wright's neo-Marxist scheme.

This has implications not only for an analysis of the work-force but also for more general social analysis: if it is taken seriously, the household can no longer be perceived as a coherent political unit but must be recognized as fissured and complex; the atom must be split.

For the new generation of political analysts who came to adulthood in the 1960s and 70s a serious examination of office work *as work* posed enormous theoretical challenges and this may be the most charitable explanation of why it was, comparatively speaking, so neglected as a subject amongst those who were attempting to retheorize class politics at the time. There is perhaps another more personal reason, rooted in the class origins of this new generation of Left intellectuals. In the UK, at least, the post-war welfare state opened up new forms of upward mobility for men and women of working-class origin. Selection at the age of eleven filtered a high-achieving minority into grammar schools from which they could enter the expanding university system. The novels and plays of the period are full of the class guilt which ensued. The act of leaving one's father's class was experienced acutely as an act of betrayal but this was intertwined with an intoxication at the intellectual freedom of the new life of mental work. An oedipal delight at escaping from the authority of this father was combined with a romantic sense of loss and exile from the warmth and solidarity of a working-class community which was simultaneously both safe and claustrophobic, both politically revolutionary and morally oppressive.

These were the upwardly mobile sons of the blue-collar heroes of Sennett and Cobb's 'Hidden Injuries of Class',[14] the 'brainy' (and by implication effete) students who sat indoors revising for their university entrance examinations whilst their sneering mates who had left school at fifteen flaunted their new leather jackets and motorbikes and spent their weekly wages on taking bouffant-haired girl-friends down to the Palais to rock and roll on a Friday night. They felt both superior to and excluded from this new consumerist working-class culture and this, perhaps, inspired in them a permanent desire to earn the respect of these by-now-idealized working-class men. If they thought about women office workers at all it was most usually as class accessories of the bourgeoisie. One archetype of the period is the secretary who acts as a gatekeeper for her boss. With her crisply-accented 'I'm sorry but he's in a meeting right now' and her unattainable sexual attractiveness she can humiliate the working-class shop steward who is trying to gain access quite as effectively as the snootiest of head waiters. If any independent political agency is attributed to her at all it is (perhaps with some unconscious projection) as a traitor to the working class.

Only some explanation like this, it seems to me, can make sense of the subsequent political development of this generation of male left intellectuals: the romanticization and stereotyping of specific forms of working-class life long after many of their features had already passed into history; the almost fetishistic preoccupation with certain types of male manual work (coal-miners, auto workers, truck-drivers, dockers); the anxious and competitive display of their own working-class antecedents; the insistence that feminism was middle-class and alienating to 'real' working-class men.

In most cases it was not until the dawning of the 1980s that in their polit-ical imaginations these analysts were able to accept that proletarian men were as likely to be picking up the kids from school whilst waiting for their wives to get home from the office as to be coming home grimy from the pit or factory expecting to find a meal on the table.

III

Perhaps because he had enough direct experience of manual work to have no need to prove his political virility in this respect, it was Harry Braverman who constituted the honourable exception to this pattern and undertook, in his monumental *Labour and Monopoly Capital*,[15] the first serious theoretical engage-ment with white collar work which recognized the office as a differentiated locus of struggle between capital and labour. Braverman also demonstrated a link between technological change and change in the division of office labour. His (essentially Marxist) 'degradation' thesis was later challenged from a Weberian perspective by Goldthorpe who argued that the empirical evidence (derived from a study of census data) did not support the proletarianization hypothesis but that on the contrary what was taking place was the development of a new 'service class'.[16] Perhaps more importantly than whether Braverman was 'right' in the particulars of his analysis, this debate, coinciding as it did with a tremendous flowering of thoughtful feminist speculation about the relation-ship between class and gender, between paid and unpaid work, the nature of 'skill' and the explanation for gender segregation in the labour market,[17] opened up an immense and fertile field of enquiry.

The resulting literature covered an enormous range: agit-prop handbooks designed to rouse office workers to action, like those by Tepperman and Gregory in the United States or Craig in Britain; serious academic studies, like those by Crompton and Jones in Britain or Game and Pringle in Australia; and more journalistic overviews giving anecdotal support to the proletarianization thesis, like those by Howe, Howard, or Siegel and Markoff in the United States or Menzies in Canada.[18]

As well as raising a range of interesting questions, this added immeasurably to the store of empirical knowledge of the working conditions of office workers and the ways in which these were being transformed under the combined impact of the restructuring of markets, the ideological triumph of neoliberalism and the impact of technological change. Most of these studies, however, reflect the fact that they took place within specific geographical locales. The labour markets they analyse are generally national or regional ones, and the workers' positions are mapped against those of their compatriots in other industries or occupations within these national labour markets. Although there have been a number of studies of globalization of blue-collar work, little account is taken of the implications of the relocation of non-manual work across national boundaries. A partial exception is a series of small-scale empirical studies of data entry workers in developing countries[19] which implicitly follow Braverman's degradation thesis by drawing direct comparisons with the conditions of women workers in production work. What is missing is an analysis which examines the position of these office workers both in their own local labour markets and in relation to their comparators in other countries.[20] This is an enormous task which I do not dare to attempt here. Instead, what I will try to do in the next section of this essay is to clear away some of the underbrush which is currently impeding clarity of thought in order to specify the sorts of questions which researchers will need to address to produce the evidence which might render such an analysis possible in the future.

IV

Let us begin by outlining some of the dimensions of the problem. Office workers (to stick, for the time being, with this unsatisfactory term) can be defined in at least six different ways: in terms of the *functional relationship of their work to capital*; their *occupations* (their place in the technical division of labour); their *social relation to production* (the ownership or non-ownership of the means of production); their place in the *social division of labour* (including the gender division of labour in the household); their *comparative income* (and hence their market position as consumers); and their social '*status*'. Definitions constructed in these different ways are not necessarily coterminous and produce shifting and overlapping groups, riven with internal contradictions. And, of course, the structural categories thus created may not be recognized as relevant by the office workers themselves, who, in their upward or downward or horizontal trajectories across the boundaries between them may prefer to differentiate themselves by quite other criteria—their educational qualifications, for instance, or their consumption habits, or where they live, or, like Wright Mills and Lockwood, the clothes they wear to work.

Any analysis is further complicated by the fact that the empirical data, in the form of official statistics, are constructed using classification systems which do not map neatly on to any of these analytical categories. Nevertheless, let us recapitulate the evidence, such as it is, in relation to each of these approaches.

First, in terms of its *relation to capital*, office work can be regarded as covering the following functional categories: (a) design or elaboration of the content of products and services—including such things as software development, copy-editing, the design of Web-sites, product design, etc.; (b) purchase of inputs to these products or services and their sale—the army of clerks whose numbers, according to Braverman, multiply exponentially as the number of transactions increases, because of the need for the value of each transaction to be recorded by a 'mirror' in a system which 'assumes the possible dishonesty, disloyalty or laxity of every human agency which it employs';[21] (c) management of the production and distribution processes and of the workers themselves— descended from the eighteenth-century 'time-keeper', this class now includes a range of human resources management and supervisory functions as well as logistical tasks; (d) circulation—much of the banking and financial services sector falls into this category, as do some accounting and retail functions; (e) reproduction of the work-force—activities associated with teaching, child care, health care, social work, etc; (f) local, national or international government functions connected with the provision of infrastructure, market management and policing the population.

Of these categories, only (c) and (d) correspond to Marx's 'commercial workers' of whom he maintained that 'the commercial worker produces no surplus value directly ... the increase of this labour is always a result, never a cause of more surplus value'.[22] Category (a) makes an input to the product in the form of knowledge in much the same way that a craft worker contributed skill in the past. Its existence as a separate non-manual task is thus merely a reflection of an increase in the division of labour. Workers in this category, it can be argued, contribute directly to the creation of surplus value in so far as the product of their labour is appropriated from them by the employer.

Such a typology could have been sketched out at any time in the last two hundred years. However, applying it in any specific case has been rendered immeasurably more complicated as the years have gone by and the division of labour has grown more complex.

Perhaps the most important change which has taken place is the increasing commodification of 'service' activities. In the comparatively simple markets which Marx and Engels observed it was feasible to regard the archetypal capitalist commodity as a physical object made in a factory designed either to be sold to another capitalist as a means to produce other physical objects (for instance a loom, a vat or a printing press) or to be sold to a wholesaler or retailer for final consumption by the consumer (for instance a shirt, a bar of soap, or a newspaper). Since then, enormous elaborations have taken place. Each of the types of activity outlined above has itself become the basis of a host of new commodities, ranging from software packages to mind-controlling drugs, from electronic surveillance systems to credit cards, from educational CD-ROMs to baby alarms. Although the principles of economic analysis remain essentially the same,[23] breaking their production down into their component parts and plotting their interactions with each other and with the fulfilment of the primary functions outlined above is an intricate and time-consuming business. Indeed, in some cases the process can appear like zooming in on fractals, a descent into ever-smaller wheels within wheels, as with the seemingly inexhaustible inventiveness of capital each area of human activity becomes the basis for profitable new commodities.[24] Within the production process of each commodity, even if it is carried out within the a parent organization as a sort of sub-loop in the production process of another, the whole range of activities (design; management; execution; delivery to the customer), is reproduced in miniature. And the task of assigning workers according to their functional relation to capital is rendered even more difficult by the increasingly complex division of labour within functions.

Analysis is complicated still further by changes which have taken place in the ownership structure of corporations. The combined effects of privatization, the disaggregation of large organizations into their component parts, convergence between sectors, cross-ownership and 'vertical integration' have made a nonsense of the tidy traditional divisions between 'primary', 'secondary' and 'tertiary' sectors and between the 'public' and 'private' sectors of the economy as well as between the sub-sectoral categories within these devised by government statisticians. The new 'multimedia' sector, for instance, brings together organizations traditionally classified in many different places, including the public sector (state broadcasting corporations); metal-based manufacturing (computer companies, via their software divisions, and electronics manufacturers); printing and paper manufacturers (publishers); record and tape manufacturers; toy manufacturers (the ancestors of some computer game companies); business and financial services (independent software companies which are not branches of computer manufacturers); film distributors; and telecommunications companies. Convergence is taking place in many other areas of the economy too, for instance between banking and retailing and (thanks to biotechnology) between pharmaceuticals and agriculture.

Not only are the old sectors dissolving and new ones forming; there are also complex interrelationships between the corporate actors involved. Some have entered into shifting alliances to carve up particular markets or to collaborate in the development of new products;[25] others have bought stakes in each other (i.e., in firms which the public imagine to be their competitors), and mergers, de-mergers and take-overs are announced continuously. To make matters even more complicated, in addition to these external realignments, most companies are also involved in a continuous process of internal reorganization, whereby individual functions are transformed into separate cost or profit centres, or floated off as separate companies. Add to this the impact of outsourcing to external companies and we arrive at a situation where corporations can no longer be regarded as stable and homogenous. Rather they must be seen as mutually interpenetrating entities in constant flux, held together by an elaborate web of contracts which are in a continuous process of renegotiation. The sectoral classification of the 'employer' to which any given worker is assigned is an almost-accidental by-product of all these shenanigans, and this makes it impossible to use official statistics, at least in their present form, as a basis for serious analysis.

A second method of defining office workers is in relation to their *occupations*—the tasks that they carry out—or their labour process. Where workers have been able to organize effectively in the past and set up professional associations or trade unions, and especially where negotiation has succeeded in making recognized qualifications a basis for limiting entry to particular trades or professions, these occupations can be said to be largely socially defined, their boundaries made explicit in these negotiations and their practices defined by custom and by the vigilance of the actors who stand to gain from the continuation of these forms of closure (to use Parkin's Weberian term).[26] In most cases, however, the tasks carried out by any given group of workers are determined in large part by the technical division of labour and their labour processes are thus shaped by the design of the prevailing technology (which, it must be added, is itself shaped by the assumptions of those who commission it, and in which the existing social relations of production are therefore already embedded).

Even in the occupational groups which have defended their inherited working practices most strongly against the assaults of the last quarter-century it has been impossible to resist entirely the impact of information and communications technologies. Even doctors and lawyers, these days, not to mention telephone engineers, generally check their own e-mail from time to time, and the expectation of a personal secretary has all but disappeared amongst executives under the age of about forty-five, except for those who are very senior indeed. Meanwhile, across the rest of the work-force, an extraordinary and unprecedented convergence has been taking place. From tele-sales staff to typesetters, from indexers to insurance underwriters, from librarians to ledger clerks, from planning inspectors to pattern-cutters, a large and increasing proportion of daily work-time is spent identically: sitting with one hand poised over a keyboard and the other dancing back and forth from keys to mouse. Facing these workers on the screen, framed in pseudo bas-relief, are ugly grey squares labelled, in whatever the local language, 'file', 'edit', 'view', 'tools', 'format', 'window' or 'help', the ghastly spoor of some aesthetically-challenged Microsoft employee of the late 1980s. Gone are the Linotype machine, the rolodex, the card-index, the sheaves of squared paper, the mimeograph, the drawing board, the cutting-table, the telex machine, and all the other myriad tools of the mid-twentieth century, the mastery of which entitled one to a specific designation—the proud ownership of a unique skill. Gone too is the shared identity with other holders of that same skill. It must be remembered, of course, that the security bestowed by possessing these skills was often the security of the strait-jacket. Limited transferability meant increasing vulnerability with each wave of technological innovation, but specialist skill ownership did offer a basis for organizing and playing some part in negotiating the terms on which the newer technology would be introduced.

The skills required to operate a computer and its various communications accessories should not, of course, be mistaken for the totality of the requirements of any given job. They are often ancillary to other 'core' skills—the skills required to do 'the job itself'. However, these too may be undergoing a process of modification (which could take the form of routinization, or full commod-ification) which is changing their nature. Social workers, for instance, may find themselves filling out standard forms on-screen instead of writing, or delivering in person, more nuanced and qualitative professional reports on their clients; teachers may find themselves administering standard tests; insurance loss adjusters may have lost the discretion to decide what compensation a claimant should receive; Internet journalists may be required to write to tightly defined standard formats; whilst architects may be reduced to recombining standard components instead of designing freely 'from scratch'. Often these transforma-tions are disguised by a change in the division of labour. The job description of a professional may be stripped down to its core and the numbers of such staff reduced, whilst the former components of the job which are capable of routinization are transferred to lower-skilled workers. Thus, for instance, routine enquiries to a computer help-desk may be dealt with by the use of automated e-mail responses or by more junior staff, with only the really diffi-cult problems routed through to the more highly-paid 'expert'. Or sick people may be encouraged to call a call centre staffed by nurses before making an appointment to see a doctor, as in the UK's *NHS Direct*.

In general, it can be asserted that the number of tasks involving standard generic computer-related skills is growing rapidly, whether this is measured in terms of the numbers of people whose jobs involve these skills exclusively or in terms of the proportion of the time spent on these tasks by workers whose jobs also require other skills (or, indeed, both). This has curious and contra-dictory consequences. The fact that the skills are now generic has made it easier to skip laterally from job to job, company to company and industry to industry. But by the same token each worker has also become more easily dispensable, more easily replaceable; the new opportunities thus also constitute new threats. The combination of this new occupational mobility with the huge expansion of the potential labour pool has also made it much more difficult to build stable group identities based on shared skills. Attempts to construct barriers around skill groups are thwarted by the speed of change. Any invest-ment of time and effort in learning a new software package may be wiped out in a matter of months by the launch of a replacement. Existing hierarchies are challenged at precisely the moment that new fault-lines are created. At the head office, e-mail brings senior and junior members of staff into direct communi-cation with each other, cutting out middle layers of management, and a strange new camaraderie develops between colleagues of different grades as one shows the other how to eliminate a virus or unzip an obstinate attachment. But simul-taneously an unbridgeable gulf may have opened up between these same head office staff and their fellow-employees at a remote call centre, or data processing site.

When the only thing which can be predicted with certainty is that there will be more change it is difficult to generalize broadly about occupational trends: whilst some processes are Taylorized and deskilled, others become more complex and multi-skilled; whilst some groups are excluded, others find new opportunities opening up. An interesting empirical study recently completed in Canada by Lavoie and Therrien explored the relationship between computerization and employment structure. Following Wolff and Baumol[27] these researchers divided occupations into five categories: 'knowledge workers', 'management workers', 'data workers', 'service workers' and 'goods workers', and concluded that the category in which there was the greatest growth associated with computerization was not, as popular mythology would have it, the 'knowledge workers' but the 'data workers'—those who 'manipulate and use the information developed by the knowledge workers'.[28] This provides some support for the argument that the trend towards routinization outweighs, in numerical terms, the tendency for work to become more creative, tacit and multi-skilled.

The official statistics contain no categories labelled 'web-site designer' or 'call-centre operator' or any of the other new occupational categories which are emerging, although these figure in job advertisements and are clearly operational in the labour market. The question is, how permanent are they likely to be? And will they form the basis of new collective identities? Or will workers choose to group themselves in relation to some other variable, such as the employer they work for, or the site where they are based? The answer to this question will be a crucial determinant of the extent to which new class identities will develop independently of geography, and of the potential for organizing at a transnational level.

A third approach to characterizing office workers involves analysing their *relationship to the means of production*. Put crudely, in the classic Marxist formulation, if workers own the means of production, they are part of the bourgeoisie; if they are waged workers working for an employer who owns the means of production (and thereby produce surplus value), then they can be assigned to the proletariat. Self-employed workers and proprietors of small firms, in this model, belong to a petty bourgeoisie which will in due course be steadily squeezed out in the primary struggle between capital and labour, its members pauperized or proletarianized, except for a lucky few who become capitalists.

But this model too is becoming increasingly difficult to apply to office workers. First, the tendency of self-employment to die out has obstinately refused to take place. Although it has not expanded at the rate hoped for it by neoliberals during the 1980s, self-employment remains fairly constant, at least in most developed countries. Across the EU, for instance, the self-employed constituted a hardly varying 15% of the work-force over the two decades from 1975 to 1996.[29] This catch-all statistical category of course includes a range of different class positions. At one extreme are the self-employed with a few employees who can perhaps be regarded as petty bourgeois in the classic sense; then there are genuine freelances, who work for a range of different employers; and at the other extreme are casual workers whose self-employed status is a reflection of labour market weakness—people who lack the negotiating muscle to insist on a proper employment contract even though they are effectively working for a single employer. Despite the lack of change in their overall numbers, the evidence from the UK suggests that the composition of this group is changing, in the direction of the casual end of the spectrum. A study by Campbell and Daley found that the proportion of self-employed people with employees fell from 39% to 31% between 1981 and 1991,[30] whilst Meager and Moralee found that new entrants to self-employment were more likely than their earlier counterparts to be young, female, and entering relatively low value-added service activities. After analysing data from the British Household Panel Survey they concluded that the chances of a self-employed person being in the lowest earning category (the lowest 10%) were three times those of an employee. Even when an allowance was made for the under-reporting of income by the self-employed, the chances were still twice as high.[31]

Self-employment is not necessarily a permanent state, however. Another study by Meager and Moralee, based on a longitudinal analysis of European Labour Force Survey data, uncovered high rates of inflow and outflow.[32] This makes it difficult to regard self-employment as a stable marker of class identity; for some it might merely be a staging post between different jobs.

Another factor which makes it difficult to regard the self-employed as a separate category is the increasing tendency to manage employees 'as if' they are self-employed or, to use Rajan's phrase, to insist on 'mindset flexibility'.[33] Practices such as management by results, performance-related pay, and contracts in which working hours are not specified, combine with intensified pressures of work and fear of redundancy to produce a situation in which the coercive power of the manager is internalized. The pace of work is therefore driven by a self-generated compulsive drive rather than the explicit external authority of the boss. Closer to the piece-rates of the putting-out systems than the time-based pay (albeit with machine-paced work) of the factory, this method of management muddles the relationship between worker and employer, a muddle which is intensified when there is also a physical separation between them. One worker in seventeen in the British work-force, and a slightly higher proportion in North America, Scandinavia and the Netherlands (though less in the rest of Europe) now works from home at least one day a week using a computer with a telecommunications link to deliver work.[34] Of these, nearly half are formally self-employed. Since most of these workers own their own computers, it might be tempting to regard them as twenty-first-century equivalent of home-based hand-loom weavers, but can stand-alone personal computers really be regarded as the means of production? A loom can be used to produce cloth quite independently of any other loom, whereas in most cases the value of the computer to the employer rests on its being linked to others, in a system which is not owned by the worker.

This is a moot point, which there is no space to investigate further here. It relates interestingly, however, to another question which has some pertinence.

At least in a highly commodified economy, it is arguable that in order to make sense of the individuals' general relation to capital (and hence their class position) it is necessary to consider not only their relation to the means of production but also to the 'means of consumption' or 'means of reproduction'.[35]

The inexorable process of commodification has resulted in the decline of consumer service industries and their replacement by capital goods. In order to service themselves and their families, get themselves to work and otherwise function it is increasingly necessary for workers to invest in such capital goods, from cars to washing machines. In addition, the only way to achieve a decent standard of housing is to purchase their own homes. The need to pay for all these goods locks workers ever more tightly into the market. As Andrew Carnegie was shrewd enough to notice over a century ago, a working class which owns its own housing is the best possible protection against strikes and uprisings.[36] It is then at least arguable that the degree to which they have succeeded in purchasing these things might affect workers' subjective view of their own class position. Whether it could be said to constitute an objective difference is a matter for investigation. There may be an analogy between workers' relationship to the 'means of reproduction' and their relationship with the 'means of production' according to which the home-owner occupies a position analogous to that of the independent craft worker, or the proprietor of a one-man business. This analogy can be taken further: the division of labour in 'reproduction work' does not necessarily just involve householders themselves. Some workers may also employ cleaners, child-care workers or other servants,[37] thus occupying a place in the division of labour in reproduction work which is the equivalent of that of a small employer in production. This issue is especially important in considering the class position of the 'new' information workers in developing or newly developed countries, where the employment of servants, including live-in servants, is more common. In Hong Kong, for instance, Greenfield reports that it is usual for skilled manual workers, such as engineers, and lower-paid office workers, such as call-centre workers, direct sales persons, or mobile and paging company workers, living in low-rent accommodation, to employ a live-in domestic 'helper'. 'Working families whose incomes simply cannot accommodate a domestic helper still hire them, then exert extreme pressure on their helpers to minimize costs so that they can "get their money's worth." There is a even a growing tendency to hire "cheaper" Indonesian domestic helpers than Filipinas who number 350,000. It is interesting to note that in the aftermath of the Asian financial crisis the Hong Kong government intervened to alleviate the hardship of the average Hong Kong family by freezing the wages of domestic helpers!'.[38]

The use of non-occupational variables to assign workers to a class position is, to the best of my knowledge, untested and requires further analysis. It is particularly interesting in the context of the growth in homeworking, however, since the homeworker pays for many of the things more usually provided by the employer: the work space, storage space, heating, lighting, insurance, setting-up and putting-away time, management and monitoring (in the form of self-management, filling in reports and timesheets, etc.) as well as incurring various risks to health and security. The home computer plays an interesting and ambiguous role in this, since it is an instrument both of production and of reproduction, as likely to be used for ordering the groceries or doing the kids' homework as for the work itself.

Information and communications technologies play a pivotal role in blurring the boundaries between work and consumption, constituting as they do a shifting interface between server and served. An order for an airline ticket, for instance, may be transmitted over the telephone and keyed in by a call-centre worker or entered directly on to the airline's web-site by the customer; the labour of data entry may be either paid or unpaid. It is therefore difficult to separate a discussion of the division of labour in paid 'production' work from a more general discussion of the division of labour in unpaid, 'consumption' work, which, highly gendered as it is, brings one to the more general discussion of the *social division of labour*, the fourth category in our list, but one which is beyond the scope of this essay to address in detail.

Our fifth category is the simple empirical one of *relative income*. For those wishing to model society as a tidy hierarchical pyramid this has posed problems for over a century. The poor but genteel clerk who earns less than the vulgar navvy features in many nineteenth-century novels, from Dickens to Gissing, and survives well into the twentieth century, for instance in Forster's *Howards End*, Grossmith's *Diary of a Nobody* and some of Orwell's gloomier grubby-net-curtained novels. This clerk is presented as having traded money for a foothold (albeit precarious) in the middle classes and forms a male counterpart to the impoverished but well-educated governess hovering uneasily in an ambiguous social space between the servants' quarters and the drawing room (although his origins are likely to be humbler than hers, and his accent more suburban, his gender depriving him of the ever-latent potential for class elevation or downfall which constitutes the inherent inner drama of the feminine state).

The separation of status from income underlies most systems of class ranking, even the most empiricist and least theoretically grounded. It is explicit, for instance in the rationale for the Registrar General's Categories which are used for class analysis in the British official statistics. A paper written in 1928 by a senior official at the General Register Office argued against classification by income, asserting that 'any scheme of social classification should take account of culture ... (which) the occupational basis of grading has a wholesome tendency to emphasize'. In his opinion the criterion should be 'the general standing within the community of the occupations concerned'.[39]

Crompton and Jones note that there was parity between the earnings of male clerks and skilled manual workers from 1918 to 1936. For the next four decades, clerical workers' earnings declined in relative terms so that by 1978 they earned less than the average for all manual workers, with even the average wage for semi-skilled male manual workers exceeding that for male clerical workers. The earnings of female clerical workers were even lower, of course: rising from 42% of men's in 1913 to 57% in the mid-50s and 74% by the end of the 70s.[40] By the end of the 1990s, the hourly earnings of women clerical workers had reached 80% of men's across the EU.[41] Clerical workers clearly fall below most manual workers in terms of their purchasing power.

Now that much information-processing work can be moved from region to region and country to country using electronic links, it becomes necessary to compare earnings between countries as well as within them. Such comparisons are difficult to make with precision because of variations in the structure of taxation and benefit systems, but in the form of 'total labour costs' they figure prominently in the calculations made by employers when deciding what functions to locate where. And there are of course major differences. According to UNCTAD figures, in 1994 the average annual salary of a software programmer in India was US $3,975, compared with $14,000 in Malaysia, $34,615 in Hong Kong, $31,247 in the UK, $45,552 in France, $46,600 in the USA and $54,075 in Germany.[42] It is important, however, to be aware that such differences may be transient. The very success of the software industry in Bangalore, for instance, has resulted in a rapid inflation of local salaries which are now considerably higher than in other parts of India, such as Calcutta, where the supply of such skills still greatly exceeds demand, and in other parts of the world, for instance Russia, where routine programming activities, such as coding, are now subcontracted from India. Khilnani describes the impact on the local labour of the large-scale influx of foreign multinationals into Bangalore: 'These companies have transformed the wage structure of the Indian professional world. They are able to offer Indians in their late twenties salaries not even reached at the retirement points of Indian public enterprise salary scales'.[43]

It is possible that such developments may signal the beginning of a global convergence in wages for workers with such specific and definable IT skills in activities which are capable of being carried out independently of location. Such a convergence, if it were taking place (and so far too little empirical research has been carried out to substantiate this), would imply a substantial gain for workers in developing countries combined with a reining in of real wage increases (if not an actual decline) in developed countries. That such increases would trickle down into the rest of the local economy in the developing countries cannot, however, be taken for granted. New forms of polarization might well develop between the holders of delocalizable jobs and workers whose jobs are geographically fixed. The extent to which the delocalizable jobs will take root in any given geographical spot is also dependent on a number of variables. If they take the form of labour-only subcontracting, then their anchoredness is highly contingent. There is always a choice open to the ultimate employer whether to send the jobs to the people or bring the people to the jobs, in the process which is known in the software industry as 'body shopping'. For at least two decades it has been a common practice for planeloads of software engineers to be flown on demand from India to London, Frankfurt, Los Angeles or other sites where their skills are needed. Typically, in the 1980s and early 1990s they were employed by subcontractors. In 1992, liberalization of trade made it possible for the first time for software to be exported from sites in India, and a large-scale software export industry grew up based in Bangalore, and later in other centres such as Hyderabad, Poona and Chennai. However, employers still retain a choice, and both the United States and most European countries have recently loosened their immigration procedures to make it easy to get green cards for software engineers with scarce skills. Where there is a global market for skills, the employer's choice whether or not to relocate is therefore mirrored by the worker's decision whether to migrate or stay put.

Not all the new delocalized work involves technical software skills. In many developing countries there has also been a major growth in lower-skilled clerical work, such as data entry and typing, and in call-centre work. Here the earnings may well compare unfavourably with those of well-organized production workers. Gothoskhar describes how 'in the Indian context, the pay-levels of the younger call-centre workers may be much lower than those of middle-aged blue-collar workers'. However, she goes on to point out that a comparison based only on income may be misleading in terms of defining their class position: 'the very criteria of recruitment of these workers as of today are such that they are from two-income families, mostly from "white-collar" parents, people with an education in English and so on. This today at least excludes people from lower castes, people from the rural areas, and people whose parents are from what may be called the "traditional working-class" families'.[44]

This brings us to the sixth category, a class definition based on a notion of *status*. This term, in its Weberian sense, can be extended to cover a range of different variables including ethnicity, language-group, religion, skin-colour, caste or even the condition of slavery. The structure of most labour markets (and the history of most labour movements) bears powerful testimony to the force of such differences in creating patterns of inclusion and exclusion, privilege and deprivation. Labour markets are segmented along racial lines in North America, Europe, Australia and Japan quite as much as (if sometimes more covertly than) as they are in many developing countries. However, the fault-lines may fall somewhat differently. One important factor is language. Entry to the new world of information work is crucially dependent on the ability to understand, speak and write English, or, in some parts of the world, French, Spanish, German, Japanese or Arabic. In countries where this is not the native language, this is likely to be the prerogative of the highly-educated. Immediately, the threshold is raised above that required in the imperial parent economy. Relative wage levels and differences in the supply of and demand for labour and also play their part, of course. It is therefore not unusual to find the sorts of work which are carried out by school-leavers, or graduates from junior college, in the USA being carried out by graduates or post-graduates in a developing country. Sinclair Jones studied a medical transcription centre in Bangalore carrying out work for doctors in the United States. She reports that in the US the work was done by homeworkers, paid a piece-rate for the number of lines typed, who would normally be educated only to community college level, but that applicants in India generally arrive with a Master's Degree. Nevertheless, 'Even though there is a rather paradoxical disparity between the qualifications base of the US and Indian workers there are still huge cost advantages to undertaking this work in India. For graduates in India with, for example, a Master of Arts, there are limited options for employment. As an English teacher in Bangalore they might earn around Rupees 3,000 per month (approx. US $75)'. However, in the transcription centre, 'a good tran-scriptionist with two years' experience earns between Rupees 7,500 and 9,500 per month (US $190–$240) whilst some are earning over Rupees 12,000 (US $300) per month. This compares with workers in the US who earn between $1,800 and $2,400 a month. The experienced Indian medical transcriptionist is then about eight times cheaper than a US counterpart'.[45] Her social status in the local economy will nevertheless be quite different.

This has implications for how office workers identify their own interests and their potential for making common cause with other workers doing identical work in other countries. This question is complicated by another issue. Where workers are employed by foreign companies, the exploitation of labour by capital may not be regarded as such but rather as an imperial exploitation of natives by colonialists.[46] Instead of perceiving their interests as being aligned with those of other workers employed by the same multinational companies, they may see their interests as national ones, best served by aligning themselves with local capitalists against the imperializing outsiders. Such attitudes are likely to be reinforced by encounters with racist attitudes amongst the workers of the developed world.

We must conclude that although there is considerable potential for the emergence of a common class consciousness amongst information-processing workers, based in a common labour process, common employers and a common relation to capital, powerful counter-forces are present which seem likely to inhibit this development, the greatest of which, perhaps, is racism.

There is considerable evidence of successful organizing by the new 'e-workers' within countries, as indicated by the 1999 strike by call-centre workers at British Telecom in the UK and unionization amongst data entry workers in the Caribbean[47] and in Brazil.[48] There is also some evidence that when selecting locations employers consciously avoid areas where workers are likely to organize. In her study of the medical transcription centre in Bangalore, Sinclair Jones reports that 'the informant did comment that in the early stages they had considered establishment in Kerala on the basis that it has extremely high literacy levels. However, Kerala also has high levels of industrial organi-zation and the company decided not to take the risk. This kind of service provision is extremely vulnerable to stoppages given the commitment to rapid turnaround and the company management actively seeks to avoid becoming exposed to attempts at organizing labour'.[49]

However, examples of such organization across national boundaries are few and far between. One notable exception is the agreement covering call-centre workers jointly signed with Air Canada by the Canadian Auto Workers Union and their sister unions in the UK and the USA. In general, though, the evidence of resistance by these workers comes in more sporadic and anarchic forms, such as the writing of viruses or other forms of sabotage.

One factor which will undoubtedly influence the propensity of workers to organize and take militant action will be the extent to which this is likely to be in their own economic best interests. If low-level office work is perceived as the bottom rung of a ladder which can be scaled successfully by keeping on the right side of the boss, then hard work, keeping one's nose clean and sycophancy will offer the best route to advancement. If on the other hand no promotion prospects seem likely, for instance because the higher levels are located on another site halfway across the globe, or because only men, or only white people, or only people of a certain nationality or caste ever get promoted, then the best way to better one's income may well seem to lie in making common cause with one's fellow workers. Once again, we find that gender and race play a crucial role in determining class identity.

It is apparent that a new cybertariat is in the making. Whether it will perceive itself as such is another matter.

NOTES

1. *Analytica*, e-mail newsletter, March 2000.
2. E-mail from Alice de Wolff, April 2000.
3. Rosemary Crompton, and Gareth Stedman Jones, *White-Collar Proletariat: Deskilling and Gender in Clerical Work* (Macmillan, London and Basingstoke, 1984).
4. Duncan Gallie, *In Search of the New Working Class: Automation and Social Integration Within the Capitalist Enterprise* (Cambridge University Press, Cambridge, 1978).
5. Nicos Poulantzas, *Classes in Contemporary Capitalism* (New Left Books, London, 1975).
6. Erik Olin Wright, 'The Class Structure of Advanced Capitalist Societies' in his *Class, Crisis and the State* (Verso, London, 1979).
7. Karl Marx, *Capital*, Volume 3, (Lawrence and Wishart, London, 1974) pp. 299–300, quoted in Crompton and Jones, *White-Collar Proletariat*, p. 8.
8. Gordon Marshall, Howard Newby, David Rose and Carolyn Vogler, *Social Class in Modern Britain* (Hutchinson, London, 1988) p. 23.
9. C. Wright Mills, *White Collar: The American Middle Classes* (Oxford University Press, New York, 1951).
10. David Lockwood, *The Black-Coated Worker* (George Allen and Unwin, London, 1958).
11. Quoted in Harry Braverman, *Labour and Monopoly Capital: The Degradation of Work in the Twentieth Century* (Monthly Review Press, New York, 1974) p. 296.
12. Wright Mills, *White Collar*, pp. 352–353.

13. Marshall et al., Howard Newby, David Rose and Carolyn Vogler, *Social Class in Modern Britain* (Hutchinson, London, 1988) p. 68.

14. Richard Sennett and Jonathan Cobb, *The Hidden Injuries of Class* (W. W. Norton and Co., New York, 1972).

15. Harry Braverman, *Labour and Monopoly Capital*. (See note 11.)

16. John H. Goldthorpe, *Social Mobility and Class Structure in Modern Britain*, (Clarendon Press, Oxford, 1980) and 'On the Service Class: Its Formation and Future' in Giddens and Mackenzie (eds.), *Social Class and the Division of Labour* (Cambridge University Press, Cambridge, 1982).

17. I have discussed some of these ideas at greater length in Ursula Huws, 'Reflections on Twenty Years Research on Women and Technology', in Swasti Mitter and Sheila Rowbotham (eds.), *Women Encounter Technology* (UN University Institute of Technology, Maastricht, and Routledge, London, 1995).

18. Jean Tepperman, *Not Servants, Not Machines, Office Workers Speak Out* (Beacon Press, Boston, 1976); Judith Gregory, *Race Against Time* (9 to 5, Cleveland, 1981); Marianne Craig, *The Office Worker's Survival Handbook* (BSSRS, London, 1981); Rosemary Crompton, and Gareth Jones, *White-Collar Proletariat: Deskilling and Gender in Clerical Work* (Macmillan, London and Basingstoke, 1984); Ann Game and Rosemary Pringle, *Gender at Work* (Pluto Press, London, 1984); Louise Kapp Howe, *Pink Collar: Inside the World of Women's Work* (Avon, New York, 1977); Robert Howard, *Brave New Workplace* (Viking/Penguin, New York, 1985); Lenny Siegel and John Markoff, *The High Cost of High Tech* (Harper and Row, New York, 1985); Heather Menzies, *Women and the Chip; case studies of the effects of Informatics on Employment in Canada* (Institute for Research on Public Policy, Quebec, 1982).

19. These are discussed in Ursula Huws, Nick Jagger and Siobhan O'Regan, *Teleworking and Globalization* (Institute for Employment Studies, Brighton, 1999) and include Annie Posthuma, *The Internationalization of Clerical Work: a study of offshore office services in the Caribbean* (SPRU Occasional Paper No. 24, University of Sussex, Brighton, 1987); Antonio Soares, 'The Hard Life of the Unskilled Workers in New Technologies: Data Entry Clerks in Brazil' in H. J. Bullinger (ed.), *Human Aspects in Computing* (Elsevier Science Publishers, Amsterdam, 1991) and 'Telework and Communication in Data Processing Centres in Brazil' in U. E. Gattiker (ed.), *Technology-Mediated Communication*, (Walter de Gruyter, Berlin and New York, 1992); D. Pantin, *Export Based Information Processing in the Caribbean, with Particular Respect to Offshore Data Processing* (FIET, Geneva, 1995); Ruth Pearson, 'Gender and New Technology in the Caribbean: new work for women?', in J. Momsen (ed.), *Gender Analysis in Development* (Discussion Paper No. 5, University of East Anglia, Norwich, 1991); and Ruth Pearson and Swasti Mitter, 'Employment and Working Conditions of Low-skilled Information Processing Workers in Less Developed Countries' in *International Labour Review* (Geneva, April, 1993).

20. Exceptions to this are Christopher May's analysis in *The Rise of Web-Back Labour: Global Information Society and the International Division of Labour*, (Plymouth International Studies Centre, University of Plymouth, 1999) and the pioneering field studies of Jan Sinclair Jones, in various unpublished papers and in 'First you see it, Now you don't: Home based telework in the global context', Working Paper presented to the Australian Sociology Association Conference, Monash

University, Melbourne, 5–7 December 1999.

21. *Labour and Monopoly Capital*, p. 303.

22. Karl Marx, *Capital*, Volume 3, (Lawrence and Wishart, London, 1974) pp. 299–300, quoted in Crompton and Jones, *White-Collar Proletariat*, p. 9.

23. See my 'Material World: the Myth of the Weightless Economy', *Socialist Register*, 1999.

24. I have written about this process at greater length elsewhere. See, for instance, my 'Challenging Commoditization: producing usefulness outside the factory', in Collective Design (eds.), *Very Nice Work if you Can Get it: the Socially Useful Production Debate* (Spokesman Books, Nottingham, 1985) pp. 149–167.

25. Strategic alliances are discussed, *inter alia*, by John H. Dunning in *The Globalization of Business* (Routledge, London, 1993).

26. Frank Parkin, *Marxism and Class Theory* (Tavistock, London, 1979).

27. Edward Wolff and William Baumol, in Lars Osberg, et al. (eds), *The Information Economy: the Implications of Unbalanced Growth* (Institute for Research on Public Policy, 1989).

28. Marie Lavoie and Pierre Therrien, *Employment Effects of Computerization* (Human Resources Development Canada Applied Research Branch, Ottawa, 1999).

29. European Labour Force Survey data, Eurostat.

30. M. Campbell and M. Daley,'Self-Employment: into the 1990s', in *Employment Gazette*, London, June 1992.

31. Nigel Meager and Janet Moralee, 'Self-employment and the distribution of income', in J. Hill (ed.), *New Inequalities* (Cambridge University Press, Cambridge, 1996).

32. Ibid.

33. Amin Rajan and P. van Eupen, *Tomorrow's People* (CREATE, Kent, 1998).

34. I have explored this idea in greater depth in my 'Terminal Isolation: The Atomization of Work and Leisure in the Wired Society', in Radical Science Collective (eds.), *Making Waves: the Politics of Communications* (Free Association Books, London, 1985) pp. 9–25.

35. UK Labour Force Survey 2000, Office of National Statistics, UK, Analysis by Ursula Huws and Peter Bates, Institute for Employment Studies, July, 2000.

36. Quoted in Barbara Ehrenreich and Deirdre English, *For Her Own Good* (Pluto Press, London, 1979).

37. See Brigitte Young's essay in this volume.

38. E-mail from Gerard Greenfield, *Globalization Monitor*, Hong Kong, June 2000.

39. Quoted in Theo Nichols, 'Social Class: Official, Sociological and Marxist' in John Irvine. Ian Miles and Jeff Evans (eds.), *Demystifying Social Statistics* (Pluto Press, London, 1979) p. 159.

40. Crompton and Jones, *White-Collar Proletariat*, p. 27.

41. Eurostat data, 1999.

42. Source: UNCTAD and PIKOM data, quoted in Swasti Mitter and Umit Efendioglu, 'Relocation of Information Processing Work: Implications for Trade between Asia and the European Union', unpublished paper (UN University Institute of Technology, Maastricht, 1997).

43. Sunil Khilnani, *The Idea of India* (Penguin, Delhi, 1998) p. 148.

44. E-mail from Sujata Gothoskhar, June 2000.

45. Jan Sinclair Jones, 'First you see it, Now you don't: Home based telework in the

global context', Working Paper presented to the Australian Sociology Association Conference, Monash University, Melbourne, 5–7 December 1999.

46. This point is made by Peter Lloyd in *A Third World Proletariat* (George Allen and Unwin, London, 1982).

47. Pearson, 'Gender and New Technology in the Caribbean' (see note 19).

48. Soares, 'The Hard Life of the Unskilled Workers in New Technologies: Data Entry Clerks in Brazil' (see note 19).

49. Jan Sinclair Jones, 'First you see it, Now you don't: Home based telework in the global context' (see note 20).

'THE PEASANTRY' IN GLOBAL CAPITALISM: WHO, WHERE AND WHY?

Henry Bernstein

THE END OF AN ANACHRONISM?

In his *Age of Extremes*, Eric Hobsbawm declared that '*For 80 percent of humanity, the Middle Ages ended suddenly in the 1950s …*'. He was referring to peasants: '*the most dramatic change of the second half of this century, and the one which cuts us forever from the world of the past, is the death of the peasantry*' ('which had formed the majority of the human race throughout recorded history').[1]

Hobsbawm locates the disappearance of this truly world-historical anachronism in the 'revolution of global society' or 'global transformation' from the 1950s that extended industrial capitalism beyond its historic heartlands of Western and Central Europe and North America. This movement was registered in the 'spectacular figures' of the decline of the agricultural populations of Southern Europe, Eastern and South-eastern Europe ('ancient strongholds of peasant agriculture'), Latin America, 'western Islam' (North Africa and Western Asia), and the populous islands of South-east and East Asia. 'Only three regions of the globe remained essentially dominated by their villages and fields: sub-Saharan Africa, South and continental South-east Asia, and China'— although 'admittedly' these regions of 'peasant dominance' comprised half the world's population in the 1990s. The 'death of the peasantry' is thus somewhat exaggerated, even according to Hobsbawm's idiosyncratic demographic accounting, and 'even' though these regions 'were crumbling at the edges under the pressures of economic development' by the 1990s. What is clear is Hobsbawm's belief that the demise of the peasantry is long overdue, noting that in his student days in the 1930s 'the refusal of the peasantry to fade away was still currently used as an argument against Karl Marx's prediction that it would'.[2]

Did Marx predict this? And if so, what did he mean by 'the peasantry'? Questions of what and who 'peasants' are, where they are, and indeed *why* they are, in the world of global capitalism in the early twenty-first century, remain as difficult, elusive and contentious as they have been throughout the history of industrial capitalism, perhaps even more so. And not least because notions of 'the peasantry' are so encrusted with ideas, images and prejudices, ideologically both negative and positive, that attach to our core ideas of modernity. There is little doubt that for Marx (and successive generations of 'classic' Marxists, and Hobsbawm today) 'peasants' have indeed been emblematic of 'the world of the past', specifically as represented by the feudal (and 'Asiatic') agrarian formations of Europe and Asia and their classes of essentially parasitic (aristocratic and/or bureaucratic) landed property and of peasant labour exploited through rent and/or tax.

For 'classic' Marxism (i.e., that of nineteenth- and early twentieth-century Europe) both pre-capitalist landed property *and* peasantries confronted, and inflected, transitions to capitalism (and democracy) with material, social and cultural 'backwardness' and political reaction. Landed property is likely to be autocratic as well as parasitic, while 'family' or 'patriarchal' farming denies the advantages of economies of scale, development of the productive forces, and the technical division of labour (formation of the collective worker) in production on the land. Material and social backwardness generates reactionary culture and politics. Localism and stagnation in the countryside—a hermetic cultural space of custom, superstition and 'rural idiocy' (stuck in 'the Middle Ages'?)—contrasts with the expansive, indeed explosive, possibilities of bourgeois civilization as definitive of modernity: large-scale industry *and* urbanism and their culture of science and universality. The tenacious defence of small-scale property and its inheritance, if originally directed against feudal depredation, now contested the project of social ownership and production vested in the proletariat. By a profound irony of history, when classes of pre-capitalist landed property are swept away by bourgeois revolution (or national liberation) which confers or confirms, rather than dispossesses, peasant property, the latter becomes the principal, and problematic, manifestation of the past in the present.[3]

Such constructions of modernity thus view 'peasants' in the contemporary world as the great (if dwindling) residual of earlier historical epochs and modes of production. What alternative views and approaches are there? One alternative shares the position (albeit often implicitly) that peasant production is emblematic of 'backwardness' without, however, seeing it as anachronistic, as it performs the 'functions' for capital of cheapening the prices of agricultural commodities and/or labour power in accumulation on a world scale. An evident example is the idea of the 'articulation' of capitalism with other (pre- or non-capitalist) modes/forms of production, with its particular link to Rosa Luxemburg's theorization of imperialism. In this approach, the 'persistence' (*and* 'exploitation') of peasant production on a significant scale is part of, or especially representative of, the subordinate (and 'exploited') 'backward' capitalist economies of the imperialist periphery more generally.[4]

A different approach, followed here, is to investigate the constitution and reproduction of peasantries through the social relations, dynamics of accumulation and divisions of labour of capitalism/imperialism, without any assumption of either anachronism or 'backwardness'. This approach can deploy theoretical categories and methods used by Marx, Lenin and others, detached from the notions of peasant 'backwardness'/anachronism they held and that Hobsbawm clearly continues to hold.[5] Another advantage of this approach is that it brings 'peasants' within the same theoretical framework as 'family farmers' in the industrialized capitalist countries: both are situated at the intersection of two areas of major theoretical debate and contention concerning the specificities of agriculture and of petty commodity production in capitalism. What differentiates the 'peasants' of the South and the 'family farmers' of the North theoretically, then, might not be any intrinsic 'logic' of their forms of production or economic calculation (e.g., 'subsistence' and 'commercial') but how they are located in the international division of labour of imperialism and its mutations.[6]

CAPITALISM AND AGRICULTURE

A common assumption, inherited from classical political economy (and its roots in England's distinctive, indeed unique, path of transition to capitalism), is that the capitalist agricultural enterprise—the farm—is homologous with the mode of production, that it necessarily consists of capital and 'free' wage labour. By analogy with manufacturing industry, capitalist farming should increase its scale (concentration of capital), technical divisions of labour (formation of the collective worker), and productivity of labour (development of the productive forces), in line with the laws of motion of capitalism. Already in the late nineteenth century, this expectation was contested by reference to the strong 'persistence' of small-scale ('family') farming into the era of industrial capitalism: in Europe in the form of peasantries of feudal provenance (by contrast with the fate of pre-industrial artisans), and in the U.S.A. in the form of mechanized grain production in the prairies by farms employing family- (rather than wage-) labour.

The particular unevenness of the capitalist transformation of farming has thus long been remarked, and attempts to explain it in general terms typically start from the conditions of transforming nature that are peculiar to agriculture, and their implications. While manufacturing industry transforms materials already appropriated from nature, agriculture only transforms nature through the very activities of appropriating it, and thus confronts the uncertainties of natural environments and processes and their effects for the growth of plant and animal organisms.

Accordingly, it has been suggested that capital is inhibited from direct investment in farming for several reasons. One is that this tends to be more risky than investment in other branches of activity: the normal risks of market competition are compounded by the risks inherent in the environmental conditions of farming. A second reason, derived from value theory, is the non-identity of labour time and production time: the latter exceeds the former because of the growth cycles of plants and animals during which capital is 'tied up' and unable to realize profit. Another argument from value theory emphasizes the burden of ground rent which capital tends to leave to 'family' farmers to absorb (in the same way that they absorb risk and the delayed realization of surplus value). Yet other arguments centre on labour markets and labour processes. Capitalist agriculture is unable to compete for labour as economic development raises wage rates, giving family labour farms a 'labour-price advantage'. The labour process argument is that it is much more difficult, and hence costly, to supervise and control the pace and quality of wage labour in the field than in the factory.[7]

These are, of course, very general reasons advanced to explain a tendency, the accentuated unevenness of capitalist transformation of forms of production in farming. At the same time, they point to two features of agriculture in capitalism that are key to the formation and mutations of its international divisions of labour, especially in the era of globalization. The first is the drive of technical innovation to *simplify* and *standardize* the conditions of agricultural production: to reduce the variations, obstacles and uncertainties presented by natural environments to approximate the ideal of control in industrial production. This means producing yields that are as predictable as well as large (and fast maturing) as possible—by acting on soils (fertilizers, drainage), climate (irrigation, greenhouses), the attributes of organisms (improved varieties through selective breeding and now genetic engineering, hormonal growth stimulants), parasites and diseases (pesticides, veterinary medicines), weed growth (herbicides), and so on. Such technical innovations are conventionally classified as bio-chemical, raising the productivity of land (and often intensifying the quantum and quality of labour required), and mechanical, raising the productivity of labour (hence labour-displacing). The former are ostensibly scale-neutral (as claimed for the 'Green Revolution'), while the latter promote economies of scale, on *both* wage and family labour farms.

The second, and related, feature is the increasing *integration* of farming by capital concentrated upstream and downstream of production on the land. The former refers to capital in input production (above all chemical corporations which dominate seed development and production as well as fertilizers and other agricultural chemicals, but also farm machinery manufacturers), the latter to agrofood corporations in processing and manufacturing and the giant companies in food distribution and retailing. The provenance of such corporations is in the industrialized capitalist countries, and they tend to be the more concentrated the more developed the agricultural sector (and the economy in which it is located). Nonetheless, they are now engaged in a new wave of globalization (see below), in ways that affect the fortunes and prospects of many different kinds of farmers, including 'peasants' in the imperialist periphery. Of course, a strategic implication of the features of agriculture in capitalism outlined above is that the diversity of types of farming is much greater than that of the (increasingly globalized) branches which integrate the backward and forward linkages of farming. Farming enterprises in contemporary capitalism, *within* as well as across North and South, exhibit great diversity in their size, scale, social organization and labour processes (forms, and combinations, of family labour, free and unfree wage labour), their degree and types of capitalization and mechanization, and their forms of insertion/integration in markets and commodity chains.[8]

CAPITALISM AND PETTY COMMODITY PRODUCTION

The concept of petty commodity production specifies a form of small-scale ('family' or 'household') production in capitalism engaged in more or less specialized commodity production and constituted by a particular combination of the class places of capital and labour. The agents of this form of production are capitalists and workers at the same time because they own or have access to means of production and employ their own labour. 'Peasants' become petty commodity producers in this sense when they are unable to reproduce themselves outside the relations and processes of capitalist commodity production, when the latter become the conditions of existence of peasant farming and are *internalized* in its organization and activity. This historical moment is satisfied when 'forcible commercialization'[9] gives way to the reproduction of commodity reproduction through what Marx called 'the dull compulsion of economic forces':

> [To] suggest that a social formation is capitalist by virtue of being founded on the contradiction between wage-labour and capital is not to assert that all—or even the majority of—enterprises in this social formation will conform to a 'type' in which capitalists and wage-labourers are present ... what makes enterprises, and more generally social formations, capitalist or not, is ... *the relations which structurally and historically explain their existence* ... what has to be shown in order to 'prove' the capitalist nature of such social formations is that the social entities and differences which form [their] social division(s) of labour ... are only explicable in terms of the wage-labour/capital relation.[10]

It is contended here that the social formations of the imperialist periphery are capitalist in the sense specified, and that by the end of the colonial era in Asia and Africa the vast majority of farmers termed 'peasants' had been constituted as petty commodity producers within capitalism. Other aspects of the theory of petty commodity production also illuminate the character of peasantries in contemporary capitalism/imperialism. One is that 'spaces' for petty commodity production in the social division of labour are continuously [re]created as well as destroyed in processes of capitalist development (as noted by Lenin), a dynamic likely to be particularly accentuated in agriculture for reasons outlined above. This also points to a necessary distinction between the destruction of petty commodity production in particular *branches* of production as a result of capitalist development (e.g., the emblematic fate of hand-loom weavers, in both Britain and colonial India, in British industrialization), and the demise of *individual* petty commodity enterprises as a result of competition between petty commodity producers and the pressures on their reproduction as both capital and labour, which points to the vexed issue of class differentiation.

For Marx the development of agriculture in capitalism was charted above all through the *displacement* of peasant by capitalist farming (what might be called the enclosure model or effect). Lenin's emphasis on the tendency to class differentiation *among* peasants (and other petty commodity producers) was a fundamental addition to understanding paths of agrarian change, identifying the possibility of the *dissolution* of the peasantry through the formation of distinct classes of agrarian capital and wage labour from within its ranks.[11] Lenin's argument, contested at the time and ever since by agrarian populism, is often misunderstood theoretically (hence misapplied empirically). The tendency to class differentiation arises from the peculiar combination of the class places of capital and labour in petty commodity production, hence its 'exaggerated form of instability'.[12] *Poor peasants* are subject to a simple reproduction 'squeeze' as capital or labour, or both. Their poverty and depressed levels of consumption (reproduction as labour) express their intense struggles to maintain their means of production (reproduction as capital). Loss of the latter entails proletarianization. *Middle peasants* are those able to meet the demands of simple reproduction, while *rich peasants* are able to engage in expanded reproduction: to increase the land and/or other means of production at their disposal beyond the capacity of family/household labour, hence hiring wage labour.

Two additional theoretical aspects of class differentiation of the peasantry should be noted. One is that the class places of capital and labour which combine to constitute petty commodity production in capitalism are not necessarily distributed symmetrically within 'family' or 'household' production. Indeed, they are unlikely to be so as they typically follow the contours of gendered (and other unequal) divisions of property, labour and income in 'family' and kinship structures.[13] The other aspect is that class differentiation of peasants (*and* 'family farmers' in the advanced capitalist countries) can proceed via the increasing 'entry' or reproduction costs of petty commodity enterprise, resulting in the dispossession/proletarianization of weaker producers/poor peasants *without* any necessary formation of classes of rich peasants or capitalist farmers. This is emphasized because the presence/reproduction of 'family farmers' (in the U.S.A. and Europe) or middle peasants (in the imperialist periphery) is so often, and mistakenly, understood to signal an absence of class differentiation rather than being *one kind of outcome of class differentiation*, in which some petty commodity producers are unable to reproduce themselves as capital (often in conditions of particular kinds of relations with other capitals and/or technical change and its demands on investment). The point is relevant to the tendency towards fewer but larger (more highly capitalized) 'family' grain farmers in the U.S.A., for example,[14] and was also registered early in India's Green Revolution in the distinction between 'scale neutrality' and 'resource neutrality'. While the (bio-chemical) package of new hybrid seeds and fertilizers has no intrinsic scale economies and hence, in principle, can be adopted by all sizes of farms (a tech-nical proposition), its adoption in practice depends on a minimum level of resources, and a capacity to take risks, that poor peasants lack (a socio-economic reality reflecting and reinforcing class differentiation).[15]

The abstract ideas just presented are necessary to provide a theoretical point of entry and basis for considering 'peasants' in the capitalist mode of produc-tion, and in imperialism as its modern global form. The concepts used suggest and help explain the class differentiation of 'peasants' (as of other petty commodity producers) as a *tendency* within capitalism, not as an inevitable and uniform empirical trend. This tendency contains its own distinctive complex-ities and contradictions, some of which have been noted, and which are compounded by other more concrete observations.

First, that many—no doubt the great majority—of 'peasants' today are not exclusively engaged in farming but combine agricultural petty commodity production (including 'subsistence' in the sense noted above) with a range of other economic activities. That is to say, they rotate between different locations in social divisions of labour constituted variously by agricultural and non-agri-cultural branches of production, by rural and urban existence, and by the exchange of labour power as well as its combination with property in petty commodity production. Of course, these diverse combinations of farming with other activities are also structured by class relations: poor peasants are most likely to engage in wage labour and in the more marginal (and 'crowded') branches of non-agricultural petty commodity activity, in other words pursue 'survival' in conditions of extreme constraint; middle peasant households also typically diversify their sources of income (including from wage labour) to reproduce their means of agricultural production (including in those circumstances where the costs of their reproduction as capital increase, as noted above); rich peasants frequently pursue diversified accumulation strategies, with investment 'portfolios' in crop trading, money lending, rural transport, tractor renting, village shops and bars (which can help explain why agrarian accumulation does not proceed beyond certain limits).

A second and related concrete observation is that rural labour markets are pervasive in most areas of peasant production, and much middle peasant farming (as well as rich peasant farming) depends on hired labour.[16] The rural labour question is complicated by the fact that some middle peasant households sell as well as buy labour power (and even poor peasant households occasion-ally hire labour), and that the boundaries between the poor peasantry and the rural proletariat are often blurred (as the common and apparently paradoxical term 'landless peasants' suggests). Nonetheless, the prevalence and importance of labour hiring for peasant production is often overlooked, as is the intensity of the class struggle it generates in some areas of peasant capitalism.[17]

Third, if the poor peasantry is typically part of the reserve army of labour in the countrysides of the imperialist periphery (for capitalist estates and plantations where they exist, as well as for rich and middle peasant farms), all classes of the peasantry are likely to have links, albeit of different kinds, with urban centres and markets.[18]

The framework sketched here points to the great diversity of 'peasants' in the history and current period of capitalism/imperialism. Beyond the range of empirical variation and complexity we normally expect, there are specific structural sources of diversity (and instability) in the characteristics of both agriculture and petty commodity production in capitalism, hence in the ways that they intersect in 'peasant' production (as well as other 'family' farming). These sources of diversity include the 'obstacles' to capitalist farming presented by the conditions of agricultural production, both technical and social (e.g., rent, labour markets), and the tendencies to class differentiation of petty commodity production. And it should be clear that 'the peasantry' is hardly a uniform, or analytically helpful, social category in contemporary capitalism, whether by anachronistic reference (the survival of 'the world of the past') or in considering changes in agriculture and rural social existence generated by imperialism/globalization. The same stricture necessarily applies to any views of peasants as a (single) 'class' ('exploited' or otherwise).

The next two sections outline a periodization of imperialism and agriculture, first from the 1870s to 1970s and then since the 1970s (the era of 'globalization'), to indicate the differential locations of 'peasants' (in the South) and 'family' farmers (in the North) in international divisions of labour. This outline can only illustrate one source of determinations of agrarian formations and their dynamics within the imperialist periphery, the concrete analysis of which amplifies the wide range of diversity already noted, since such analysis necessarily introduces and integrates other determinants as well. The latter include pre-existing forms of agrarian structure and their specific modes of integration in international divisions of labour at different times; the forms and practices of both colonial and independent states in processes of agrarian change, and their effects; and, not least, the trajectories of class and other social struggles, in both countryside and town, and their outcomes for forms of agrarian property, labour and production.

IMPERIALISM AND AGRICULTURE, 1870s–1970s

The last three decades of the nineteenth century were as momentous in the formation of global capitalism as the period from the 1970s to the present; it was marked by the 'Second Industrial Revolution', by that wave of internationalization of investment emphasized in Lenin's analysis of modern (capitalist) imperialism, and by the formation of the first 'international food regime' identified by Harriet Friedmann's remarkable project on the international political economy of food.[19] The basis of that regime was the massive growth of grain (and livestock/meat) production on the vast internal frontiers of 'settler' states— Argentina, Australia, Canada, and above all the U.S.A.—combined with a (relatively) free trade order that made Europe increasingly dependent on grain imports.

> Settler agriculture cheapened agricultural commodity production, via the political appropriation and colonization of new lands. Subsequent technical changes, especially mechanized harvesting, adapted settler agriculture to labour shortages. Specialized commodity production ... [was] actively promoted by settler states via land and immigration policy, and the establishment of social infrastructure, mainly railways and credit facilities.[20]

Exports, especially of wheat, competed directly with the temperate agriculture of the European heartlands of industrial capitalism, by contrast with the complementary tropical agricultural production and exports of Asia and Africa whose colonial subordination and incorporation was completed in the same period. There were thus three distinct zones in the global division of labour in agricultural production and trade.

For the agrarian economies of the imperialist periphery this new period was marked by three broad types of change, the forms and effects of which remain pertinent to today's agrarian questions. One was the emergence of the 'industrial plantation' which replaced earlier types of plantation in Asia, the Caribbean, and parts of Latin America, generated new plantation 'frontiers' (in Indochina, Malaya, Sumatra), and greatly enlarged the scale and volume of this kind of highly specialized world market production of rubber, oil palm, sisal, sugar, cocoa, tea and bananas in what Stoler aptly described as a 'worldwide shift towards agribusiness'.[21] Latin America (mostly independent of colonial rule before the international hegemony of industrial capitalism) experienced a massive agricultural export boom—'a virtually unique combination in the nineteenth century of political independence and primary commodity-led incorporation into the international capitalist economy'[22]—through the new 'industrial plantation' and the second type of change: a new phase of commoditization of the colonial *hacienda*, involving further land grabbing from peasant communities and the expansion of a servile labour force.

The third kind of change, pervasive in much of Africa and most of Asia, where colonialism did not dispossess the varied peasantries it encountered, was the increased incorporation (in scale and intensity) of peasant farmers in the capitalist economy as producers of export crops (cotton, oil palm, coffee, cocoa, tobacco, groundnuts), of (sometimes new) food staples for domestic markets, and of labour power via migrant labour systems (including indentured and *corvée* labour) to build the railways and roads, and to work in the plantations, mines and ports. Of course—and as indicated above—there was a great variety of forms of land tenure and differential access to land, reflecting both diverse pre-colonial agrarian structures and the complex ways in which colonial rule and commoditization incorporated and changed them. Patterns of ownership and/or control of land were combined with a variety of labour regimes in Latin America, Asia and Africa, in both plantation production (with its drive to recruit and control a servile labour force) and peasant farming (not least in relation to changes in gender divisions of labour and their contestations).

Following the first 'golden age' of globalization (1870s–1914), the interwar period plunged the first international food regime into crisis. During the uneven recovery of the world economy in the 1920s, the basic branches of the most advanced (highest productivity) agriculture in Western Europe and the 'settler' economies again started to experience the effects of overproduction (later to become one of their defining features). This was especially so in the U.S.A. where 'the Depression for agriculture really began in the 1920s',[23] manifested in falling agricultural commodity prices and the falling value of land assets. With the advent of the Depression of the 1930s the major capitalist countries embarked on a course of agricultural protectionism: in Europe reviving and reshaping policy instruments improvised during the First World War to enhance self-sufficiency in food production, and in the U.S.A. initiating the comprehensive farm support policies of the New Deal. In the imperialist periphery, the decade of the 1920s in sub-Saharan Africa was (together with the 1960s) one of the two decades of greatest expansion of export crops in the twentieth century. In the 1930s, the instruments of agricultural protection and regulation introduced in Europe, such as marketing boards, were adapted to imperial purposes to extract the maximum transfers from the peasant agricultural export branches of the Asian and African colonies. In India the Depression intensified the long-standing colonial pattern of displacement of food staple production for domestic consumption by peasant-produced exports of cotton, jute, sugar, and fine grains.[24]

In the revival and accelerated growth of the world economy from the 1950s to the early 1970s a new and quite different 'international food regime' was established, under American hegemony and turning on the 'Atlantic pivot' of the U.S.A. and Europe. Its peculiarities, and the tensions it contained, are formulated as follows by Friedmann.[25] The regime maintained the farm support policies of the pre-war years in both the U.S.A. and the European Community (EC) which were integrated, however, by the use of American maize and soy products (the definitive field crops of the postwar 'second agricultural revolution') in processed animal feeds for intensive livestock/meat production. In fact, the production of meat and of high value-added manufactured foods ('food durables') for mass consumption became the leading international agribusiness sectors in the developed capitalist world as the postwar economic boom accelerated. In return for its openness to U.S. exports of raw materials for feedstuffs (and U.S. corporate investment in their manufacture in Europe) the EC was permitted to maintain high levels of protection for other branches, notably wheat and dairy products. In effect, this generated systems of national agricultural regulation by which European countries sought to replicate U.S. agricultural growth through a combination of import tariffs and export subsidies, without similar limits on the movement of agribusiness capital—an unstable combination of the freedom of capital with restriction on trade, as Friedmann puts it.

The U.S.A. also deployed its surpluses of subsidized grain (and soy oil) for strategic foreign policy purposes through foreign aid and export promotion (dumping), which stimulated dependence on (cheap) American wheat in many areas of the imperialist periphery which had hitherto been largely self-sufficient in staple food production. In turn this facilitated the further specialization of the latter in the production of industrial and (mostly non-staple) food crops for world markets, as did the ambitious development plans of the newly independent former colonies of Asia and Africa, for most of which the earnings of primary commodity exports (agricultural and mineral) were the principal source of foreign exchange for import-substituting industrialization (together with foreign aid; in Latin America foreign direct investment in manufacturing as well as extractive sectors was of particular importance). This created the conditions of a potential scissors effect for many poor, primarily agricultural, countries: one blade being increasing food import dependence, the other the fluctuating but generally declining terms of trade for their historic export crops. Friedmann emphasizes the contribution to the latter of the growth of industrially processed substitutes in the developed capitalist countries, notably high fructose corn (i.e., maize) syrup and soy oil substituting for sugar and (other) vegetable oils respectively (two of the principal tropical agricultural export commodities); we can add to this the substitution of synthetic for natural fibres, and the tendency to systematic overproduction of certain tropical crops like sugar or cocoa—the opening of virgin areas for plantations in South-east Asia overturned the long-standing dominance in world cocoa production of West African peasant farmers, for example.[26]

Agricultural production in the imperialist periphery thus became increasingly internationalized in a number of significant ways during the 'golden age'. One was through the international quasi-public investment of aid agencies, notably the World Bank, and their programmes to create more systematically commoditized and productive export-cropping peasantries in the name of 'national development' (which also built on the development plans of the late colonial state after 1945, notably in sub-Saharan Africa). Another was through American (and later European) strategic food aid and/or commercial dumping. A third example, reflecting postwar Malthusian fears of mass famine and starvation (hence pursued alongside population control), was international research and development of new high-yielding hybrid grain varieties (in order of importance, of rice, wheat and maize) to boost domestic food production capacity in peripheral countries.[27] Given the size of its population, India is the most celebrated example of such a 'Green Revolution', achieving national self-sufficiency in grain production in less than ten years by the mid-1970s.[28]

It was also during this period that major demographic shifts from rural to urban population occurred in the regions listed by Hobsbawm, resulting from industrialization and/or 'agricultural revolutions' (in his term) *whether such 'revolutions'—major advances in the productive forces in farming—occurred in those regions or elsewhere.* This of course, is a characteristic manifestation of the dynamics of 'uneven and combined development' within international divisions of labour, as noted if not explored by Hobsbawm in *Age of Extremes*, and in this instance at least partly explicable by the political economy of the 'second international food regime' as sketched above.

THE 1970s ONWARDS:
INTO THE ERA OF GLOBALIZATION

The conjuncture of the 1970s appears, in retrospect, to have been as definitive a moment of subsequent structural shifts in the world economy as that of the 1870s a century before (similarly manifested in a dialectic of global recession, adjustment, and massive expansion of international flows of money and commodities).[29] This applies to the collapse of the prevailing international food regime no less than to the end of international monetary stability and the declining competitiveness of U.S. industry. The proximate cause or trigger of the collapse was a brief episode of 'a sudden, unprecedented shortage and sky-rocketing prices'[30] in world grain markets, linked to enormous (and preferential) U.S. grain sales to the U.S.S.R.. This stimulated greatly increased borrowing by American farmers in the 1970s to expand production (on a scale equivalent to the growth of Third World debt in the same period), paving the way for the U.S. farm crisis of the 1980s.

Various U.S. governments applied (wholly ineffectual) embargoes on grain sales to the U.S.S.R. and China (in 1974, 1975 and 1980) before the structural nature of overproduction, and its attendant problems of surplus disposal, reasserted itself in the 1980s. By then U.S. grain exports, both for human consumption and animal feeds, faced increasing competition—in wheat from the EC (above all from France), and in soya, and especially processed soy products, from what Friedmann terms New Agricultural Countries (NACs), notably Brazil but also Argentina, Chile, India and China; while Thailand became a major exporter of cassava products for industrial starches as well as feedstuffs. In short, the basis of the relatively stable postwar international food regime—the export-oriented system of U.S. national agricultural regulation and its negotiated linkages with the EC around the 'Atlantic pivot'—was undermined as the EC and the NACs successfully *replicated* the American model, and in ways that 'modernized' and overtook it, according to Friedmann. The definitive end of the cold war, with the demise of the Soviet Union and its bloc, further undermined a key strategic rationale of the Atlantic pivot. As is well known, the Uruguay Round of 1986 established agricultural trade and its liberalization as central to the agenda of GATT under pressure from the U.S.A., which had hitherto blocked its subjection to GATT processes and rules. This started a fraught process, still far from complete, to bring international trade rules *and* national agricultural policies in line with 'what has already occurred structurally', as Friedmann puts it.

The most fundamental structural shift she points to—and one that is immediately recognizable in terms of debates about globalization—is the emergence, from the ruins of international (Atlantic-centred) regulation, of transnational agrofood corporations as 'the major (global) agents attempting to ... organize stable conditions of production and consumption which allow them to plan investment, sourcing of agricultural materials, and marketing'[31]—that is, *integrating* various sites of production and consumption through global private (corporate) regulation.[32] This occurs in a conjuncture in which the debt of the imperialist periphery, escalating since the 1970s, became the key lever of structural adjustment lending and trade liberalization, with a renewed emphasis—for the poorest countries—on their comparative advantage in agricultural exports as the principal means of economic recovery. Thus Friedmann formulates their position in a globalizing division of labour shaped by transnational agrofood corporations as debt-driven 'export platforms'. 'While feedstuffs, the heart of the food regime, are becoming globalized rather than merely internationalized, the completely new markets in "exotic" fruits and vegetables are global from the outset.'[33] The trade in such 'exotics' is often remarked as emblematic of contemporary globalization, manifesting a significant new wave of diversification of Northern diets (including 'designer' foods) through expanding consumer tastes and world-wide sourcing (including from 'peasant' farming) to satisfy them. Also suggestive of certain images of globalization is Friedmann's view of 'the subordination of the particularities of time and place to accumulation' by transnational agrofood corporations.[34]

As with many claims about globalization, those concerning the dynamics and mechanisms of the global restructuring of agriculture, food systems, and diets, require careful empirical and analytical consideration. In a recent (preliminary) assessment of globalization and export crop production in sub-Saharan Africa, Raikes and Gibbon call attention to the 'highly uneven extent of genuine globalization of (agricultural) raw material production, industrial processing/production and consumption', and suggest that concerning Africa the 'issue is not simply one of globalization, but of a more complex redefinition of economic role, whereby some of Africa's established links with the world economy are strengthened, others are weakened and disappear, and others are restructured.'[35] Their analysis is disaggregated in several pertinent ways over the period from the mid-1980s to the mid-1990s, including the dynamics of different commodity chains for most of Africa's 'traditional' export crops (including coffee, cocoa, cotton, tea, sugar and tobacco) and 'non-traditional' exports of fresh fruit and vegetables and cut flowers, and categories of producers of these various export crops. Commodity chains differ according to their forms of primary production and marketing, international trading, and distribution and retailing; to the types of degrees and locations of industrial processing and secondary manufacture they require; and to whether, how, and how much, each commodity chain is integrated and controlled by capitals concentrated at particular points in the chain. Raikes and Gibbon also distinguish four types of production systems: low-input and high-input smallholder (i.e., 'peasant') farming, large-scale commercial farming (mostly of European settler provenance in Kenya, South Africa and Zimbabwe), and multinational corporate plantations and estates. From the mid-1980s there have been important and interrelated changes that blur the boundaries between the first two and the last two categories: 'a steady increase of the extent of low-input smallholder production at the expense of its high-input counterpart, associated with the dissolution of parastatal- or quasi parastatal-led systems, and with trade liberalization' (i.e., effects of structural adjustment policies), and greater differentiation of large-scale commercial farming 'with part of it becoming more vertically integrated.'[36]

In addition to the agricultural 'export platform' dynamic, globalization also impacts on countries of the imperialist periphery with sufficient demand to attract agribusiness production for domestic markets, whether as an element of wage goods (e.g., certain parts of Latin America and North Africa) and/or luxury consumption. India provides a perhaps surprising, and hence instructive, example of the latter. Despite its levels of poverty, both rural and urban, the size of its population and the inequality of its income distribution have made India an arena of intense competition between transnational agrofood corporations since liberalization of its economy in the early 1990s. Jairus Banaji, who has documented this, suggests that globalization (in general terms) is principally about the restructuring of international investment patterns, with international firms 'attracted to large and expanding markets in the unsaturated regions of the world economy' (notably Asia) through 'a surge of investments in highly capital-intensive production facilities', including food processing and manufacturing plants.[37] In India many new factories are located in areas lacking histories of worker organization, where they can also be sourced by converting adjacent farm land to the production of the raw materials they require, often through contract farming arrangements.

The enhanced connections of the sites and forms of production and consumption in a globalization of agriculture driven by transnational corporations might seem a compelling manifestation of 'the pressures of economic development' on the 'peasantry' asserted (if not specified) by Hobsbawm, even allowing for the unevenness of such globalization emphasized by Raikes and Gibbon. The effects are likely to be uneven and contradictory for the kinds of reasons discussed. In some cases, particular forms of globalization generate expansions of capitalist agriculture that displace peasant farming (the enclosure effect)—for example, the development of large-scale mechanized cultivation of feed grains in Mexico at the expense of peasant land and production. In this instance, feed grain cultivation for direct export, and for feeding livestock destined for U.S. abattoirs and consumers, also combines with the increased exposure of Mexico's domestic markets to grain imports for human consumption. The latter exert pressure on peasant commodity production of food staples for domestic markets in many areas of the imperialist periphery, a feature of Friedmann's second international food regime (above) and one that continues and intensifies in the era of globalization and (selective) trade liberalization.[38]

Globalization can thus reduce or marginalize the contributions of their own farming to the incomes/reproduction of (especially poor but also many middle) 'peasants' and/or accelerate tendencies to class differentiation. In most of sub-Saharan Africa, the generalized economic and social crisis since the 1970s has depressed farm incomes and investment, as Raikes and Gibbon's observation of the shift from high-input to low-input smallholder agriculture suggests—a process compounded by the removal of subsidized inputs and credit, and the dismantling of the parastatal and state-managed co-operative organizations that channelled them to peasant farmers and marketed their crops (despite the ineffectuality of many such organizations).[39] The era of structural adjustment and liberalization has also generated new opportunities for land-grabbing at the expense of peasants in some parts of Africa, whether by local or foreign/international interests or alliances between them, and whether this represents *de jure* or *de facto* forms of privatization/enclosure. Another factor of interest is the apparently increasing difficulty, in these conditions of crisis, of recruiting labour for peasant farming, *including* that of younger men and women born into peasant households.[40] Not surprisingly, then, the costs of entry into such new activities as the contract farming of high value 'non-traditional' crops (fresh fruits, vegetables, cut flowers, decorative house plants) for global markets are beyond the reach of most peasant farmers, while expansion of these crops generally stimulates the demand for rural wage labour.

While it is impossible to generalize about the impact of uneven and diverse forms of globalization on (differentiated) peasantries, it is likely that in this current phase of imperialism most poor peasants confront an increasing simple reproduction 'squeeze'. Together with the landless rural proletariat, they form part of an expanding reserve army of labour in the countryside *and* in the cities and towns of large areas of the imperialist periphery, given the prevalence of rural–urban links which include, for many members of poor peasant households, regular migration in search of wage employment as 'footloose labour'.[41] This does not, however, indicate any uniform or linear route to an inevitable destination: the general or definitive demise of 'the peasantry'. The impulses to economic change generated by globalization, and how they are mediated by the diverse class structures and dynamics of the imperialist periphery, can consolidate certain spaces for agricultural petty commodity production, and create new spaces as well as destroy existing ones. Indeed, pressures on industrial and urban employment, and the immiseration that results, may generate tendencies to 're-peasantization' in some instances—one manifestation of how the growing numbers of the reserve army of labour straddle city and countryside in their pursuit of means of livelihood.

Any notion and possibility of 're-peasantization' no doubt affronts the view of the 'death of the peasantry' as definitive of modernity even more than either the facts or the explanation of the reproduction of agricultural petty commodity production in mature capitalism. It perhaps serves, though, as a useful reminder that the sociological (or phenomenal) features, hence boundaries, of the *urban* (as well as the rural) proletariat and the reserve army of labour are not as clear-cut as suggested by careless application of the abstract categories necessary to theorize their conditions of existence. This can be illustrated by the magnitude (as well as the enormous variation) of urban 'informal' sector self- and wage-employment, and by the fact that many urban working-class households in the imperialist periphery (and indeed in its core) depend on a range of petty commodity activities as well as wages for their reproduction.

In the era of globalization such processes are framed by the liberalization of international and domestic trade in agricultural commodities, the tendencies to regulation of global production and trade by new patterns of corporate agribusiness investment, and technical change in farming and food processing, manufacturing and distribution. All of these combine to affect the prospects and problems of agricultural petty commodity producers located differentially within the international division of labour.

The analysis of 'peasants' presented and illustrated here has concentrated on peasant production as an *economic form*, agricultural petty commodity production, constituted by the class relations (and contradictions) of capital and labour and located in the shifting places of agriculture in the imperialist periphery within international divisions of labour. If 'the peasantry' is thus constituted *and* differentiated by class relations, what implications does this have for the issues at stake in contemporary instances of 'peasant' politics, not least given the 'classic' Marxist presumption, referred to above, that those politics must be reactionary—anti-proletarian and anti-democratic?[42] To elaborate this question, and illustrate answers to it in particular circumstances, it is useful first to sketch, however schematically, some problematic aspects and characteristic tensions of the materialist analysis of politics more generally.

POLITICS: WORKERS AND 'PEASANTS'

Issues in political analysis

The starting point, already indicated at several points in this essay, is the proposition that the relation of wage labour and capital—the essential, hence definitive, basis of the capitalist mode of production—is neither self-evident nor experienced in 'pure' ways. Capitalist divisions of labour *necessarily* incorporate and generate social differences and divisions other than those of class (which does not mean that they lack effects for class relations and dynamics), of which Marx emphasized those between industry and agriculture, town and countryside, and mental and manual labour, to which (most) historical materialists today would add relations and divisions of gender and ethnicity. Furthermore, all such differences/divisions are inflected and overlaid by those generated by the international divisions of labour (and of property, income and power) of imperialism. If this is true of the economic forms and patterns of global capitalism today, requiring analysis adequate to their complexities, it applies just as (or more) forcefully to political and ideological dynamics and their determinations.

In short, and by extension, there is no (self-)evident or 'pure' phenomenal or concrete class subject given (or pre-given) by the essential social relation of the capitalist mode of production. Concretely, capitalism is structured through a variety of specific conditions and forms of exploitation and oppression (albeit linked by an underlying 'logic' of accumulation and class power), which are not experienced uniformly by those subject to different locations in its social divisions of labour. As Mahmood Mamdani observes, there are 'many ways in which power fragment(s) the circumstances and experiences of the oppressed', some of which are manifested as what Mao Zedong termed 'contradictions amongst the people'.[43]

What should be evident, then, is that such observations simultaneously enrich *and* complicate the demands of theory and practice on any socialist politics that abandons the ideal(ist) assumption of a 'pure' class subject (the proletariat), that recognizes the need to engage with popular and democratic struggles generated by and contesting the multiple forms of oppression within contemporary capitalism (including those manifested as 'contradictions amongst the people'), and that is open to new possibilities of practice, alliance and organization such struggles may disclose.[44] At the same time, this is not to yield to ideas that essentialize political subjects other than the working class, be they 'peasants', 'small farmers', 'indigenous people' or 'women' (as in so-called eco-feminism).[45] It is ironic that *because* a (collective) proletarian subject has often been essentialized in the socialist tradition, anti-proletarian ideological currents (sometimes quite explicit) find it easier to substitute for 'the working class' their own idealized (collective) subject of choice. The point is that socialist politics, in engaging with and contributing to a range of popular and democratic struggles, does so from the viewpoint of their class content and implications, in a sense embracing their contradictory impulses in order to assess their progressive character, rather than dismissing such struggles *a priori* for their class 'impurities' (according to an equation of class 'impurity' with reaction).

The question about 'peasant politics' posed above can be elaborated thus: how can the course of class and popular struggles generate more progressive forms of agrarian relations in the imperialist periphery, and otherwise contribute to progressive change including the broadening and deepening of democracy? And, of course, what does 'progressive' mean in particular circumstances of struggle, marked by specific forms of exploitation, by multiple types of oppression and their contradictions?

A first instance is the organization and struggles of agricultural workers (including those recruited from the poor peasantry) for better conditions of work and payment, for basic democratic rights, and to defend themselves against the class violence of landed property, agrarian capital and the state. This includes fighting against all forms of 'tied' labour relations based in personal dependence, debt bondage, and patronage—in short, any form of 'deproletarianization' that denies the one positive freedom of the proletarian condition in face of 'the dull compulsion of economic forces', namely mobility within labour markets and between employers.[46]

A second instance is struggles to establish and/or improve access to land (and other conditions of production) by landless workers and (poor and middle) 'peasants' against 'parasitic' forms of appropriation by landlordism and merchant's and usurer's capital, and/or by states that (variously) support individual accumulation by 'bureaucrat capital' or privileged sectors of capitalist farming at the expense of petty producers (who may be part of the reserve army of labour, as noted above).[47] This instance is more ambiguous than the first for reasons that should be evident from the preceding discussion. On one hand, 'accumulation from below' can have a democratic political dynamic, especially when agricultural petty producers (poor and middle peasants) and landless workers are subject to 'national' (ethnic, caste) as well as class oppression, and/or combine with workers (and perhaps the urban petty bourgeoisie) in democratic struggles against capital, and state policies and practices that favour it.[48] On the other hand, the success of such struggles *may* consolidate petty property in ways detrimental to workers' interests, especially when the 'agrarian interest' is defined by rich peasant ideology and rich peasant leadership of ostensibly encompassing rural ('peasant' or 'farmer') organizations and movements. These tensions can be illustrated briefly with reference to agrarian political movements in Brazil and India.

Brazil

James Petras has recently acclaimed the centrality of rural movements to Latin America's 'third wave' of radical politics in the postwar period, the most significant response so far to the advent of globalization and neoliberalism, which emerged and has developed independently of the electoral and sectarian parties of the Left (or their remnants) of earlier 'waves' of struggle. At the same time, this 'peasant resurgence' does not replicate 'peasant movements in the traditional sense, nor are the rural cultivators who comprise them divorced from urban life or activities.'[49] Petras' survey of this rural 'third wave'—in Brazil, Bolivia, Peru, Paraguay, Colombia, Chile, Argentina and Mexico—indicates specificities and differences due to variations in the agrarian histories and class structures, and the national political contexts, of these countries, but also suggests some common elements. These include 'the crises affecting industrial and urban areas, particularly growing unemployment and poverty', and how trade liberalization as above and increasing debt threaten the reproduction of poor peasant livelihoods. The 'basic class composition' of these movements in Brazil and more generally is 'rural landless workers' and the poor peasantry: 'impoverished peasants either … evicted from land or unable to subsist on tiny plots.'[50] In Bolivia the 're-peasantization' effect includes over 30,000 retrenched tin miners (the former vanguard of working-class struggle) who are now coca farmers and 'the most dynamic and influential sector in direct confrontation with the regime.'[51] The kinds of 'structural' or 'objective' factors noted here go together with a striking 'subjective' feature of the 'new peasantry' and its politics: 'a new generation of "educated" (primary or secondary school) peasant leaders ... with strong organizational capabilities, a sophisticated understanding of national and international politics, and a profound commitment to creating a politically educated set of cadres.'[52]

Together with the Zapatistas in Chiapas, Mexico, probably the internationally best known 'new' rural movement in Latin America is the MST in Brazil: the *Movimiento Rural Sem Terra* (Landless Workers Movement). This was started in the 1980s in the south and south-east of the country by the daughters and sons of European immigrant small farmers, and has since spread to most agricultural areas of the rest of Brazil. Its characteristic political tactic is land occupation and settlement, preferably followed by the formation of production co-operatives. Petras enumerates and explores regional variations in the activity and success of the MST, identifying a number of factors: the social origins of its activists; local histories of previous land occupations; proximity to big cities and mobilization of urban support by trade unions and municipal governments controlled by the Workers Party; the local balance of class forces as manifested in the (varying) ability of landowners to deploy state and extra-state violence and the capacity of the MST to defend itself; and the availability of land for occupation, together with concentrations of landless workers/poor peasants.[53]

Petras is aware of some of the problems and limits of these movements. He observes the 'heterogeneity' of the category of 'landless workers' and also its 'ambiguity' in relation to forms of production established on land seized by (re)occupation—whether this will consolidate agricultural petty commodity production (generate or strengthen a rural petty bourgeoisie?) or be able to sustain the political dynamic of the MST.[54] He notes too the difficulties of moving 'from protest to politics' in some instances (e.g., in Argentina), the organizational fragmentation strongly localized peasant politics are prone to (e.g., Mexico by contrast with the MST in Brazil), and that 'while this third wave represents intransigent opposition to the imposition of neoliberalism, it does not yet as offer a fully articulated plan for the seizure of power.'[55] However, these new rural movements lead the way in revitalizing mass democratic politics in much of Latin America; the MST is expanding its political work into the shanty towns of Brazilian cities; and, in Petras' view, this distinctive peasant resurgence exhibits creative forms of class analysis and political practice that connect with other sites of democratic struggle, including those of ethnic oppression.

India

India reveals substantial differences from Latin America. Its densely populated areas of irrigated cultivation contain no 'large uncultivated farms with fertile land near roads, markets and credit facilities' such as the MST targets for occupation in Brazil,[56] but display their own diverse and complex range of political processes and energies. The Indian counterparts to the MST of Brazil—in terms of significance and impact if not social character—are the 'new farmers' movements' that emerged in the 1970s in most of the major states of western India and peaked by the late 1980s, but remain politically significant in Maharashtra and the Green Revolution heartlands of the north-west (Punjab, Haryana, western Uttar Pradesh).[57] These movements claim, in one way or another, to represent *all* classes of farmers (and sometimes also the rural proletariat and rural women as a particular constituency) against particular government policies or the state more generally (and often urban-industrial society as well, including the urban proletariat). 'Their impact extends from demonstrations, blocking the food transportation system, denying officials access to villages, refusing to pay outstanding bills (tax arrears, electricity dues, bank loans) and withholding crops from local markets (which results in price rises) to an important role in the overthrow of Rajiv Gandhi's Congress government in the 1989 elections.'[58]

There is fierce debate about whether these movements are progressive, in what ways, and to what extent, starting with the claims to novelty signalled by the language of *farmers'* movements rather than peasant movements (which have specific associations with key processes and moments of struggle in India's colonial and independent history), their agitation over prices and subsidies (rather than land issues), and their declared autonomy from political parties. Similarly fiercely contested—in relation to the farmers' movements of particular parts of India as well as more generally—are explanations of their emergence and, above all, interpretations of their social composition and ideology, programmes and practices. At one end of the spectrum of debate Gail Omvedt, an activist intellectual in Maharashtra, supports what she sometimes calls the 'new peasant movement' in India as a progressive force for agricultural labour as well as peasant farmers, with an explicit critique of Marxist class theory and the way it has been used to justify industrialization financed by surpluses extracted from agriculture. She thus argues not only for increases in crop prices and rural wages, but for a national economic strategy that prioritizes investment in the countryside in the interest of rural development. She also rejects such charges as that the 'organized farmers' movement' is preoccupied with fertilizer subsidies, and that (religious and caste) communalism has specific rural roots in the rich peasantry: 'communalism has spread from the cities (the middle classes, the urban poor, *and* the organized working class) to the countryside, and ... farmers' organizations have a rather decent record on the issue.'[59]

At the other end of the spectrum are those like Brass and Banaji whose sophisticated analyses of rural class relations are far from the crude (but still common) Marxist positions targeted by Omvedt.[60] These critics of the new farmers' movements in India maintain that they are reactionary, not as a necessary consequence of their class membership, but because of their ideological and political impulse—'to reinforce the existing property rights and consolidate a broad-based and diversified rural capitalism'[61]—and their effect in obscuring capitalist development and its class divisions in the countryside. Factors adduced to explain the emergence of the new farmers' movements include shifts in the terms of trade between industry and agriculture, which began to move against the latter from the late 1970s; a slowing down in the rate of profit and accumulation of capitalist farmers and rich peasants, *and* pressures on the incomes of highly commoditized middle and small peasants, in the Green Revolution heartlands; loss of Congress Party hegemony in the countryside in the 1980s; and the interpenetration of urban and rural commercial capital. Possibly linked to the last is another contextual feature: the reduction of bonded and other servile labour relations in farming due to struggles by agricultural workers, facilitated by the increased availability of non-agricultural employment in the countryside, including rural towns.[62]

The class dynamics and trajectories of the new farmers' movements, as of rural politics in India more generally, are also inflected by ideologies and practices of caste oppression, how they are resisted, how issues of caste shape political parties and electoral competition at local, provincial and national levels, and how election outcomes affect rural class and caste relations. Jens Lerche provides a detailed analysis of the 'politics of the poor' in Uttar Pradesh with special reference to agricultural wage workers, trends in rural labour relations, and the role in the state government since 1993 of the low-caste BSP (Bahujan Samaj Party): 'for the first time in India a party headed by, run by and voted for by the lowly "untouchable" castes formed part of the winning coalition in a state election.'[63] The success of the BSP both reflects and catalyzes successful struggles by low-caste agricultural workers, whose support it gained through its focus on fighting caste oppression and exclusion while the Communist Party (CPI[M]) pursues a policy of broad alliances to attract middle and rich peasants and opposes the caste-based mobilization of workers. Even within the limits of the BSP programme that Lerche emphasizes—its 'utopian perspective of the creation of a largely untouchable petty bourgeoisie, and its refusal to tackle core class issues like land reforms'—he concludes that the fact of its electoral success (and consequent access to patronage in state administration and appointments, including the police) strengthens the position of agricultural workers in the countryside of Uttar Pradesh.[64]

CONCLUSION

To return to where this essay started: there is, of course, a rationale to Hobsbawm's view of 'the death of the peasantry' by the late twentieth century, but it is tautological at best: the peasantry (or better, peasantries) that inhabited 'the world of the past' (the greater and lesser agrarian formations of pre-capitalist eras) are indeed destroyed by capitalism and imperialism. At worst, however, it follows that 'peasants', 'smallholders', or 'small farmers' today are

then viewed as 'survivals' of that past, emblematic of 'backwardness', anachronistic, (explicitly or implicitly) reactionary, and doomed to extinction—a
position that precludes rather than encourages investigation and analysis of
exactly who, where and why 'peasants' are in contemporary global capitalism.
This essay has tried to suggest some of the theoretical means of such investigation and analysis, and to illustrate their applications.

Notwithstanding the brevity of the examples of agrarian political movements in Brazil and India, they serve to suggest the dynamic character of change
in the countrysides of the imperialist periphery, and the (different) places within
it of (differentiated) peasantries, both economically and politically. There is
nothing here to sustain inherited notions of 'the peasantry' as anachronism, or
as 'backward' in material, cultural or political terms: many 'peasants' occupy,
and reproduce themselves within, the economic 'spaces' for agricultural petty
commodity production in the divisions of labour of (a globalizing) capitalism,
and in processes of class differentiation, just as many fail to do so; they often
move between countryside and city and negotiate, and help shape, the cultural
worlds of both; they are clearly capable of effective collective action (for
different and sometimes contradictory class ends) in ways that can expand the
economic 'spaces' of their farming activity/reproduction and impact on
national political processes; they can be both militants and opponents of
progressive struggles that extend beyond their rural locales.

NOTES

Parts of this essay draw on and develop material presented in previous work, especially
Henry Bernstein, 'Agrarian Classes in Capitalist Development' in Leslie Sklair, ed.,
Capitalism and Development, London: Routledge, 1994. My debts to the work of others
like Harriet Friedmann and Peter Gibbon and his co-workers should be obvious. I am
grateful for comments on an earlier draft to comrades at the *Socialist Register* conference
in Toronto in January 2000, and to colleagues in the Agrarian Studies Program at Yale
University.

1. Eric Hobsbawm, *Age of Extremes: The Short Twentieth Century, 1914–1991*,
    London: Michael Joseph, 1994, pp. 288–9, 415 (emphases added).
2. Hobsbawm, *Age of Extremes*, pp. 291, 289.
3. On this Hobsbawm's perspective on land reforms in the twentieth century is
    instructive—Hobsbawm, *Age of Extremes*, pp. 354–7.
4. For example, Utsa Patnaik, 'Peasant Subsistence and Food Security in the Context
    of the International Commoditization of Production: the Present and History', in
    Peter Robb, ed., *Meanings of Agriculture. Essays in South Asian History and Economics*,
    Delhi: Oxford University Press, 1996.
5. As demonstrated by Peter Gibbon and Michael Neocosmos, 'Some Problems in
    the Political Economy of "African Socialism"', in Henry Bernstein and Bonnie K.
    Campbell, eds., *Contradictions of Accumulation in Africa. Studies in Economy and State*,
    Beverly Hills: Sage, 1985.
6. Two observations (whose rationale is explained below) may help demystify the

notion of 'subsistence' production by peasants (let alone its celebration). The first is that when commodity relations and circuits become internalized in conditions of peasant existence, the spaces and forms of 'subsistence' production (for own consumption) are determined by specific modes of insertion in commodity economy (agricultural and non-agricultural). The second is that the conditions of 'subsistence' production are themselves often commoditized, e.g., the purchase of inputs and labour hiring to cultivate food staples for one's own consumption, although the extent of this varies across different classes of peasants. On this see also Philip Woodhouse, Henry Bernstein and David Hulme, *African Enclosures? The Social Dynamics of Soil and Water*, Oxford: James Currey, in press.

7. On the non-identity of labour time and production time see S. A. Mann and J. A. Dickinson, 'Obstacles to the Development of a Capitalist Agriculture', *Journal of Peasant Studies*, vol. 5, no. 4, 1978, and for the rent burden argument: Gjoran Djurfeldt, 'What Happened to the Agrarian Bourgeoisie and Rural Proletariat Under Monopoly Capitalism? Some Hypotheses Derived from the Classics of Marxism on the Agrarian Question', *Acta Sociologica*, vol. 24, no. 3, 1981. See also the 'labour-price advantage' of family farms as formulated by Niek Koning, *The Failure of Agrarian Capitalism. Agrarian Politics in the United Kingdom, Germany, the Netherlands and the USA, 1846–1919*, London: Routledge, 1994, p. 172.

8. For important explorations of unfree labour, and related issues of class formation and struggle in agrarian production, see Tom Brass, *Towards a Comparative Political Economy of Unfree Labour*, London: Frank Cass, 1999.

9. The formulation of Krishna Bharadwaj in her seminal essay, 'A View of Commercialization in Indian Agriculture and the Development of Capitalism', *Journal of Peasant Studies,* vol. 12, no. 4, 1985.

10. Gibbon and Neocosmos, 'Some Problems', p. 169.

11. V. I. Lenin, *The Development of Capitalism in Russia*, Moscow: Progress Publishers, 1964 (first published 1899), ch. 2.

12. Gibbon and Neocosmos, 'Some Problems', p. 177.

13. Ibid., p. 177; Tom Brass, 'The Elementary Strictures of Kinship' in Alison McEwan Scott, ed., *Rethinking Petty Commodity Production*, special issue series of *Social Analysis*, vol. 20, 1986; Henry Bernstein, 'Capitalism and Petty-Bourgeois Production: Class Relations and Divisions of Labour', *Journal of Peasant Studies*, vol. 15, no. 2, 1988.

14. Grain (and other) production on 'family' farms in the U.S.A. provides a neat illustration of the theorization of petty commodity production presented here: are these farms family *labour* enterprises as well as family *property*? Many, in fact, are barely worked by family labour at all (except for a residual management function) in the sense that their ploughing, planting, spraying, and harvesting are done by specialized contractors. (Rich) peasant enterprises in some instances display analogous features.

15. Just as rich peasants are situated, both economically and politically, to gain disproportionate advantages from new technologies, including those that are supposedly scale-neutral; this was noted by perceptive observers of the early stages of India's Green Revolution.

16. The 1991 Indian census reported that of the agricultural workforce (about two-thirds of the total workforce) just under 60 percent were (owner) cultivators and just over 40 percent agricultural labourers, as cited in Gail Omvedt, '"We Want

the Return for Our Sweat": the New Peasant Movement in India and the Formation of a National Agricultural Policy', in Tom Brass, ed., *New Farmers' Movements in India*, London: Frank Cass, 1994, p. 144.

17. Emphasized for India by Jairus Banaji, 'Illusions About the Peasantry: Karl Kautsky and the Agrarian Question', *Journal of Peasant Studies*, vol. 17, no. 2, 1990.

18. Also noted by Hobsbawm, for whom such links are the channels through which modernity diffuses from city to countryside—Hobsbawm, *Age of Extremes*, pp. 364–9.

19. Harriet Friedmann, 'World Market, State and Family Farm: Social Bases of Household Production in the Era of Wage Labour', *Comparative Studies in Society and History*, vol. 20, 1978; 'The Political Economy of Food: the Rise and Fall of the Post-war International Food Order', *American Sociological Review*, vol. 88 (annual supplement), 1982; 'The Political Economy of Food: a Global Crisis', *New Left Review*, 197, 1993. As well as the juncture of the 'failure of agrarian capitalism', that is, a shift from the wage labour agricultural enterprise to the family labour farm in Britain, Germany, the Netherlands, and the USA, according to Koning's stimulating comparative study, 'The Failure of Agrarian Capitalism'.

20. Harriet Friedmann and Philip McMichael, 'Agriculture and the State System: the Rise and Decline of National Agricultures, 1870 to the Present', *Sociologica Ruralis*, vol. 29, no. 2, 1989, p. 101.

21. Ann Stoler, *Capitalism and Confrontation in Sumatra's Plantation Belt, 1870–1979*, New Haven CT: Yale University Press, 1985, p. 17; see also Valentine E. Daniel, Henry Bernstein and Tom Brass, eds., *Plantations, Peasants and Proletarians in Colonial Asia*, London: Frank Cass, 1992.

22. Eduardo P. Archetti, Paul Cammack and Bryan Roberts, eds., *Sociology of 'Developing' Societies: Latin America*, London: Macmillan, 1987, p. xvi.

23. S. A. Mann and J. A. Dickinson, 'State and Agriculture in Two Eras of American Capitalism', in F. H. Buttel and H. Newby, eds., *The Rural Sociology of the Advanced Societies: Critical Perspectives*, London: Croon Helm, 1980, p. 305.

24. Patnaik, 'Peasant Subsistence and Food Security', p. 210.

25. This section and the next draw heavily on Friedmann, 'The Political Economy of Food: a Global Crisis'.

26. There is a fuller and more nuanced discussion of issues of 'structural oversupply' of tropical agricultural export commodities in Philip Raikes and Peter Gibbon, '"Globalization" and African Export Crop Agriculture', *Journal of Peasant Studies*, vol. 27, no. 2, 2000.

27. The first systematic biochemical innovations applied to their food staples by western scientific research, by contrast with earlier extensive research efforts on export crops like sugar, rubber, and cotton.

28. Which does not mean that the Green Revolution was without its contradictions, which confounded the 'win-win' vision and claims of its architects. As is well known, among its other effects, it accelerated class differentiation of the peasantry in north-west India, displaced the cultivation of coarse grains and pulses essential to the diets of the poor with finer grains they cannot afford, distributed its productivity (yield) gains very unevenly across different parts of the country, and so on.

29. Explicit comparisons with the late nineteenth-century world economy in assessing globalization at the end of the twentieth century are made by, among others, Deepak Nayyar, *Globalization: the Past in our Present*, Chandigarh: Indian

Economic Association, 1995, and Paul Q. Hirst and Grahame Thompson, *Globalization in Question*, Cambridge: Polity Press, 1996.

30. Friedmann, 'Political Economy of Food: a Global Crisis', p. 40.

31. Ibid., p. 52.

32. P. McMichael and D. Myrhe, in 'Global Regulation vs. the Nation State: Agro-food Systems and the New Politics of Capital', *Capital and Class*, 43, 1991, present arguments for very strong and encompassing forms of globalization of agriculture, in contrast to the more cautious and differentiated approach of Raikes and Gibbon, 'Globalization'—see note 26 and below.

33. Friedmann, 'Political Economy of Food: a Global Crisis', p. 53.

34. Ibid., p. 55; this suggests a transposition to the global plane of features long estab-lished in the US meat industry, by 1900 the prototype of industrial food production: 'Geography no longer mattered very much except as a problem in management; time conspired with capital to annihilate space'—W. Cronon, *Nature's Metropolis. Chicago and the Great West*, New York: WW Norton, 1991, as quoted by Alexander Cockburn, 'A Short Meat-oriented History of the World. From Eden to the Mattole', *New Left Review*, 215, 1996, p. 27.

35. Raikes and Gibbon, 'Globalization', pp. 86, 53.

36. Ibid., p. 72.

37. Jairus Banaji, 'Globalization and Restructuring in the Indian Food Industry', in Henry Bernstein and Tom Brass, eds., *Agrarian Questions. Essays in Appreciation of T. J. Byres*, London: Frank Cass, 1996, p. 192.

38. Noted for Latin America more generally by James Petras, 'Latin America: the Resurgence of the Left', *New Left Review*, 223, 1997.

39. The negative effects of the withdrawal of fertilizer subsidies on maize production in East and Southern Africa are documented in Derek Byerlee and Carl K. Eicher, eds., *Africa's Emerging Maize Revolution*, Boulder CO: Lynne Rienner, 1997, where it provides one source of tension (among others) for the generally neolib-eral tenor of the analysis. This does not imply, however, that state support and regulation is all that sustains agricultural petty commodity production, which otherwise would ('naturally'?) succumb to the superior efficiency of capitalist farming. This lingering and problematic assumption—derived from 'classic' Marxism—continues to permeate much contemporary materialist analysis of agrarian questions. It is also very difficult to demonstrate empirically, given the wide range of subsidies, direct and indirect, that support large-scale (capitalist) farming in contemporary imperialism, in both core and periphery.

40. Noted by, among others, Sara Berry, *No Condition is Permanent. The Social Dynamics of Agrarian Change in Sub-Saharan Africa*, Madison WI: University of Wisconsin Press, 1993.

41. Jan Breman, *Footloose Labour. Working in India's Informal Economy*, Cambridge: Cambridge University Press, 1996.

42. As well as Marx's apparent view that peasants are incapable of effective collective action, expressed in the notorious 'sack of potatoes' metaphor in *The Eighteenth Brumaire of Louis Bonaparte* in Marx and Engels, *Selected Works*, Moscow: Progress Publishers, 1970.

43. Mahmood Mamdani, *Citizen and Subject. Contemporary Africa and the Legacy of Late Colonialism*, Cape Town: David Philip, 1996, p. 272.

44. Implicit here is the inadequacy, or historic redundancy, of adherence to the

Leninist party as the central, or even exclusive, form of organization of socialist politics, typically associated with 'purist' views of the proletarian subject.

45. Cecile Jackson, 'Women/Nature or Gender/History? A Critique of Ecofeminist "Development"', *Journal of Peasant Studies*, vol. 20, no. 3, 1993.

46. On processes of 'deproletarianization', their importance and effects see Brass, *Towards a Comparative Political Economy*.

47. On Latin America, see for example, Alain de Janvry, *The Agrarian Question and Reformism in Latin America,* Baltimore: Johns Hopkins, 1981, and with E. Sadoulet and E. Wilcox Young, 'Land and Labour in Latin American Agriculture from the 1950s to the 1980s', *Journal of Peasant Studies*, vol. 16, no. 3, 1989; on Africa, Mahmood Mamdani, 'Extreme But Not Exceptional: Towards an Analysis of the Agrarian Question in Uganda', *Journal of Peasant Studies*, vol. 14, no. 2, 1987; and Peter Gibbon, 'A Failed Agenda? African Agriculture under Structural Adjustment with Special Reference to Kenya and Ghana', *Journal of Peasant Studies*, vol. 20, no. 1, 1992.

48. For example, on Latin America, Petras 'Latin America', and Tanya Korovkin, 'Weak Weapons, Strong Weapons? Hidden Resistance and Political Protest in Rural Ecuador', *Journal of Peasant Studies*, vol. 27, no. 3, 2000; on Africa, Mamdani, 'Extreme But Not Exceptional', and Michael Neocosmos, *The Agrarian Question in Southern Africa and 'Accumulation from Below'*, Uppsala: Scandinavian Institute of African Studies, 1993; on South Africa specifically, Richard Levin and Daniel Weiner, 'The Politics of Land Reform in South Africa after Apartheid: Perspectives, Problems, Prospects', in Henry Bernstein, ed., *The Agrarian Question in South Africa*, London: Frank Cass, 1996, and Henry Bernstein, 'Social Change in the South African Countryside? Land and Production, Poverty and Power', *Journal of Peasant Studies*, vol. 24, no. 4, 1998.

49. Petras, 'Latin America', p. 21.

50. James Petras, 'The Political and Social Basis of Regional Variation in Land Occupations in Brazil', *Journal of Peasant Studies*, vol. 25, no. 4, 1998, p. 125.

51. Petras, 'Latin America', p. 27. Petras also notes the migration to the countryside of unemployed working-class households from provincial cities and towns in Brazil. There are some indications of similar movement from the mining areas of Central and Southern Africa to their historic rural zones of labour supply as mine-workers are retrenched on a large scale. The rural (black) townships of South Africa's highveld (the countryside of 'maize and gold') provided the hubs of massive (and still growing) shack settlements of evicted farm workers and retrenched miners in the 1990s. The politics of coca-growing 'class-conscious miners turned peasants' in Bolivia provides more than one interesting variation on themes of globalization. According to Petras,' Latin America', pp. 26–9, the radical politics of the *cocaleros* 'involves harnessing ancestral spiritual beliefs to modern forms of class and anti-imperial struggle. Marxist analysis is linked to pre-European values [concerning coca, H.B.] ... While the land issue continues to be impor-tant ... the main struggle is for free trade against the US-directed attempt to eradicate coca production'! It is often remarked that the organization of narcotics production and distribution (and laundering of its profits) is a particularly instruc-tive arena of globalization; domestically produced marijuana (mostly by small farmers) and the transit trade in cocaine (sourced in Brazil for European markets) and heroin (sourced in Thailand for European and North American markets),

provide probably the most dynamic and valuable commodities among Africa's 'non-traditional' exports and re-exports today—see Henry Bernstein, 'Ghana's Drug Economy: Some Preliminary Data', *Review of African Political Economy*, 79, 1999.

52. Petras, 'Latin America, p. 19.
53. Petras, 'Political and Social Basis'.
54. Ibid., pp. 125, 132.
55. Petras, 'Latin America', pp. 37, 43, 23.
56. Petras, 'Political and Social Basis', p. 130.
57. And that may re-emerge in one form or another as India's agrarian classes experience the effects of globalization, following liberalization of the country's economy from the early 1990s.
58. Tom Brass, 'Introduction' in T. Brass ed., *New Farmers' Movements in India*, London: Frank Cass, 1994, pp. 3–4.
59. Omvedt, 'Sweat of Our Brow', p. 158.
60. Brass, 'Introduction' and 'The Politics of Gender, Nature and Nation in the Discourse of the New Farmers' Movements', and Jairus Banaji, 'The Farmers' Movements: A Critique of Conservative Rural Coalitions', in Brass, *New Farmers' Movements*.
61. Banaji, 'Farmers' Movements', p. 239.
62. Although the decline in servile labour is also much debated, and its unevenness and gendered features widely acknowledged—see Terence J. Byres, Karin Kapadia and Jens Lerche, eds., *Rural Labour Relations in India*, London: Frank Cass, 1999.
63. Lerche, 'Politics of the Poor: Agricultural Labourers and Political Transformations in Uttar Pradesh', in Byres et al., *Rural Labour Relations*, p. 183.
64. Lerche, 'Politics of the Poor', p. 226; the progressive element or effect of BSP electoral successes in Uttar Pradesh is also noted by Banaji, 'Conservative Rural Coalitions', p. 240.

WORKERS NORTH AND SOUTH

Beverly J. Silver
and Giovanni Arrighi

One of the most puzzling developments of the closing decades of the twentieth century has been the precipitous decline of working-class consciousness and organization at a time of great numerical expansion of the world proletariat. What is most puzzling about this development is that it occurred in the wake of a deep crisis of global capitalism. It was not unreasonable to expect that the capitalist crisis of the 1970s would enhance rather than dampen the class consciousness of the expanding world proletariat. In the 1980s and 1990s, the crisis of capital turned instead into a crisis of labour, resulting in the destruction or fundamental restructuring of all the working-class organizations that had formed and consolidated over the preceding century.

The purpose of this paper is to highlight the relationship between the unevenness of capitalist development on a world scale and processes of working-class formation both before and during the current crisis. Our main argument is that, contrary to widespread opinion, the so-called North–South divide continues to constitute (as it has throughout the twentieth century) the main obstacle to the formation of a homogeneous world proletarian condition. In spite of the relocation of industrial activities from North to South typical of the current crisis, conditions of working-class formation remain thoroughly dependent on the huge and still widening gap that separates the wealth, status and power of a relatively small number of Western countries from those of the countries that contain the vast majority of the world's population. Any meaningful attempt to reconstruct socialist politics must put the overcoming of this gap at the centre of its theoretical and practical concerns.

THE RISE AND DEMISE OF THE WORLD LABOUR MOVEMENT

The basic facts of the world labour movement in the twentieth century can be summed up in six propositions:

(1) Workers' rebellions have been a constant of recorded world history. Only in the twentieth century, however, did labour movements become a force capable of having a distinct and significant impact on world politics. They became such a force through a long-drawn out process that began in the course of the Great Depression of 1873–96 and materialized more than half a century later in a fundamental restructuring of the dominant strategies, structures and mode of operation of world capitalism. This fundamental restructuring occurred with the establishment under US hegemony of what Aristide Zolberg has characterized as a 'labour friendly' international regime.[1] To be sure, the 'labour friendly' reforms instituted with the establishment of US hegemony—e.g., macroeconomic policies favouring full employment—went hand-in-hand with fierce repression of any sectors of the labour movement that sought a deeper social transformation than the postwar social contract offered. Nevertheless, the reforms instituted under US hegemony marked a significant transformation in comparison with the *laissez-faire* model of global regulation characteristic of the period of British world hegemony.[2]

(2) The labour movements that forced this metamorphosis upon world capitalism developed along two distinct and increasingly divergent paths. One was the predominantly 'social' path of movements that nested at the point of production and whose main weapon of struggle was the disruptive power that mass production puts in the hands of strategically placed workers. It originated in late-nineteenth-century Britain but assumed almost ideal-typical form in the United States. The other was the predominantly 'political' path of movements that nested in the bureaucratic structures of political parties and whose main weapon of struggle was the seizure of state power and the rapid industrialization/modernization of the states that fell under their control. It originated in Continental Europe, most notably in Germany, but assumed its ideal-typical form in the USSR.[3]

(3) The strengthening of labour movements along both paths occurred in the context of escalating inter-imperialist conflicts among the world's leading capitalist states. In the first half of the twentieth century the temporal profile of labour unrest in 'core' capitalist countries was thoroughly shaped by the two world wars. The world wars were part of a series of 'vicious circles' of domestic and international conflict which resulted in major waves of labour unrest and revolutions. Both world wars are characterized by a similar pattern: overt labour militancy rose on the eve of the wars, declined temporarily during the wars themselves, and then exploded in their aftermath.[4] The Russian Revolution took place during the First World War wave of labour militancy, while the aftermath of the Second World War was associated with the spread of the Communist world to Eastern Europe, China, North Korea and Vietnam. It was

the combined impact of the post–Second World War explosion of labour unrest in core capitalist countries and the spread of Communist revolution in more peripheral countries that brought about the establishment of the US-sponsored labour-friendly international regime.[5]

(4) Inter-imperialist conflicts created a favourable environment not just for the explosion of labour unrest in wealthier countries and the spread of Communist revolution in poorer countries. Equally if not more important, they created a favourable environment for a generalized 'revolt against the West'— in Geoffrey Barraclough's assessment 'the surest sign of the advent of a new era.'[6] Workers' struggles often played a key role in the revolt, including demands by Third World workers for the extension to the colonies of extant living and working standards in metropolitan countries.[7] But it became clear to both the colonizing powers and the emerging hegemonic power that such an extension of rights would be far too expensive. Thus, the 'labour friendly' international regime that emerged at the end of the Second World War was not meant to include the forming (or re-forming) nations of the colonial and semi-colonial world. High mass consumption and full employment—the touchstones of the welfare state—were said to be beyond the reach of their 'underdeveloped' economies. What the US promised these nations instead, in direct competition with the USSR, was 'national self-determination' (that is, juridical sovereignty in a greatly expanded interstate system) and 'development' (that is, assistance in catching up with the standards of wealth established by the core capitalist countries).[8] They were promised, in President Truman's words, a global 'Fair Deal' to be achieved through 'a wider and more vigorous application of modern scientific and technological knowledge.'[9]

(5) The 'labour-friendly' (for rich countries) and 'development-friendly' (for poor countries) international regime established under US hegemony was quite successful in staving off the multiple crises that had destabilized world capitalism ever since the outbreak of the First World War. For about twenty years—during the so-called Golden Age of Capitalism of the 1950s and 1960s—labour unrest in core countries and communist revolution in more peripheral countries were contained. According to Thomas McCormick this was 'the most sustained and profitable period of economic growth in the history of world capitalism.'[10] Whether or not this was indeed the case, the Golden Age of Capitalism, like comparable earlier periods of rapid growth of world trade and production, ended in a general crisis of over-accumulation. What was different in this crisis in comparison with analogous earlier ones is that the struggles of subordinate social groups (labour included) for a greater share of the pie was a driving force rather than a late development of the crisis. In earlier crises, the driving force was an intensification of inter-capitalist competition. This intensification, in turn, led to an intensification of social conflicts. In the late 1960s and early 1970s, in contrast, an explosion of social conflicts played a role in precipitating the crisis prior to the intensification of competition.[11]

(6) The deep capitalist crisis of the 1970s was first and foremost a reflection of the inability of world capitalism as instituted under US hegemony to deliver on the promises of a global New Deal—that is, as Immanuel Wallerstein has put it, to accommodate 'the combined demands of the Third World (for relatively little per person but for a lot of people) and the Western working class (for relatively few people but for quite a lot per person).'[12] Throughout the 1970s, these combined demands put considerable downward pressure on returns to capital. US attempts to counter this pressure through loose monetary policies backfired, leading to an escalation of inflation at home and a weakening of the US dollar in world financial markets. It was only between 1979 and 1982 that the crisis was partially resolved through a radical change in US policies. This radical change consisted of a liquidation of the labour- and development-friendly international regime of the preceding thirty years in favour of a capital-friendly international regime reminiscent of late nineteenth- and early twentieth-century *laissez faire* capitalism.[13] Under the new regime, the crisis of capitalism quickly turned into a crisis of organized labour and of the welfare state in rich countries, and the crisis of Communism and of the developmental state in poorer countries. The collapse of Soviet Communism was only an episode in this double crisis.

GLOBALIZATION, LABOUR RIGHTS AND DEVELOPMENT

Three years before the unravelling of the Soviet-centred Second World, Nigel Harris announced that the emergence of 'a global manufacturing system' was making the very notion of a Third World hopelessly obsolete.

> The conception of an interdependent, interacting, global manufacturing system cuts across the old view of a world consisting of nation-states as well as one of groups of countries, more or less developed and centrally planned—the First, the Third and the Second Worlds. Those notions bore some relationship to an older economy, one marked by the exchange of raw materials for manufacturing goods. But the new world that has superseded it is far more complex and does not lend itself to the simple identification of First and Third, haves and have-nots, rich and poor, industrialized and non-industrialized.[14]

Harris' contention that the spatial restructuring of industrial activities constitutes a fundamental departure from the real or imagined polarized structure of the world into 'First and Third, haves and have-nots, rich and poor, industrialized and non-industrialized' has gained credence, in one variant or another, among some of the best-informed observers of globalization.[15] According to this view, polarizing tendencies are still at work but *within* rather than between North and South, First and Third Worlds. 'Core-periphery'— in Ankie Hoogvelt's words—'is becoming a social relationship, and no longer a geographical one.'[16]

We are not sure exactly what this means, since 'core-periphery', as we understand it, is always a social relationship. It is a relationship between groups that nominally belong to the same social class (most notably, a world bourgeoisie or a world proletariat) but substantively are separated from one another by a radically unequal command over resources. The fact that, historically, political geography has been a major determinant of position in the core-periphery hierarchy does not mean that such a hierarchy was any less 'social'. It simply means that political geography (as summed up in such categories as First, Second and Third Worlds, North and South, East and West, etc.) constituted an essential dimension of class politics on a world scale. From this standpoint, Hoogvelt's (and Harris') contention can only be interpreted as claiming that class politics has now emancipated itself from all (or most) previous geopolitical constraints and determinations.

The political significance of this contention is vividly illustrated by the disputes and conflicts that culminated in the 'Battle of Seattle' and the World Trade Organization (WTO) débâcle. An editorial of *The Nation* hailed Seattle as 'a milestone for a new kind of politics'—the politics of 'the fabled red-green alliance' that had become quite prominent in Europe but had until now remained 'a leftist fantasy' in the United States.

> Splits between labour and environmentalists, young and old, were not merely forgotten. They were actively overcome. Ageing boomers marvelled at the intelligence, discipline and imagination of a generation they had written off as slackers. Labour shed its nationalism for a new rhetoric of internationalism and solidarity.[17]

The greatest achievement of this new kind of politics was its contribution to the last-minute implosion of the WTO talks:

> many dissident trade ministers, seeing the eroding support for the US agenda on Clinton's own streets, felt less compelled to comply with US unilateralism in the convention halls. (Other factors range from resentment over US anti-dumping laws to Clinton's call, quickly muted, to include labour rights in the agreement—which alienated many delegates from the Third World, where elites routinely exploit workers and ravage the environment.)[18]

This reading of the Seattle events implicitly concurs with the Harris/Hoogvelt contention that the North–South dimension of class struggle on a world-scale has for all practical purposes become irrelevant. From this point of view, Third World elites and multinational corporations are seen as close allies in the exploitation of workers and the ravaging of environments. At the same time, the WTO is seen as a key instrument of this alliance through its role in intensifying the worldwide competition that undergirds the heightened exploitation of workers and ravaging of environments. It follows from this imagery that the struggle of the new-born US red-green alliance against the WTO is an act of internationalist solidarity with Third World workers.

Yet this is not the only possible interpretation of the Seattle events and WTO débâcle. Indeed, much of the evidence supports the radically different view that the débâcle was primarily the result of a growing North–South split over the modalities of further trade liberalization. According to this view, the seeds of the débâcle were sown in Geneva in the weeks before Seattle.

> Developing countries voiced disappointment that five years after the WTO's creation they had not seen promised benefits. They put forward dozens of proposals, including changing some of the rules. Most of their demands were dismissed. The major economies pushed instead their own proposals to further empower the WTO by introducing new areas such as investment, competition, government procurement, and labour and environmental standards. Developing countries in general opposed these new issues, which would open up their markets more widely to the rich nations' big companies or would give these rich states new protectionist tools.[19]

These frustrations were heightened in Seattle when Third World delegates were excluded from key meetings held privately by rich countries. As William Finnegan put it: 'The leaders of the poorer countries, though often depicted as pawns of the major powers, content to offer their countries' workers to the world market at the lowest possible wages—and to pollute the air and water and strip-mine their natural resources in exchange for their own commissions on the innumerable deals that come with corporate globalizations—in reality, have to answer, in many cases, to complex constituencies at home, many of whom are alarmed about their own economic recolonization.'[20] For Finnegan, the revolt of the delegates from poorer countries 'echoed the fundamental questions being asked in the streets about the mandate of the WTO.'[21]

Nevertheless, Seattle also revealed a fundamental divide. Underneath the internationalist rhetoric of the protesters Third World delegates saw a national-protectionist agenda that US negotiators were ready to exploit in their attempts to extract more concessions from poor countries. Indeed, 'President Clinton had hoped that vigorous protests in Seattle—he had urged people to "get it all out of their system"—would move trade ministers to include concerns about the environment, labour and human rights.'[22] The fact that just a month before the big November 30 demonstration AFL–CIO President John Sweeney joined a group of business leaders in signing a letter endorsing the Clinton Administration's trade agenda for the WTO negotiations[23] provided additional evidence in support of this interpretation.

In sum, the forces that brought about the WTO débâcle had two radically different images of the confrontation. On the one hand, the loose alliance of labour and environmental groups that demonstrated in the streets saw themselves struggling against an alliance of multinational corporations and Third

World elites aimed at using the WTO as an instrument for increasing profits through the worldwide intensification of workers' exploitation and environmental destruction. In the words of Jay Mazur, Chair of the AFL-CIO International Affairs Committee: 'The divide is not between North and South, it is between workers everywhere and the great concentrations of capital and governments they dominate.'[24] On the other hand, the Third World delegates who torpedoed US attempts to launch a new round of trade liberalizing negotiations saw themselves as struggling against, among other things, an alliance of the US government and US labour and environmental groups aimed at using—in David Sanger's words—'higher labour and environmental standards to keep out their products, or at least to level the playing field by raising the costs of production in developing countries.'[25]

Taking issue with this characterization of poor countries as being fundamentally opposed to higher labour and environmental standards, William Greider has criticized the media for neglecting to mention that

> the AFL-CIO collected endorsements for its demands from more than one hundred labour federations from around the world, including struggling independent union movements in the poorest places, where labour is often brutally suppressed by force. They know they're on a hopeless treadmill without international protection, because their wages and working conditions will be undercut by the next poor country below them on the food chain, bidding for industrial jobs by sacrificing workers.[26]

This, of course, is a reiteration of the Harris/Hoogvelt contention that the North–South conflict has been superseded by a fundamental unity of the class interests of Northern and Southern workers. Moreover, on the other side of the barricade, Greider sees a fundamental unity of interests between Northern capital and Southern elites. In line with this contention, he goes on to criticize the media for ignoring also that

> India, Brazil and Pakistan could not prevail alone but were joined in opposition by the largest multinationals. Does Boeing support the idea of independent trade unions in China, where its workers are supervised and disciplined by CP cadres? ... No, of course not. In China, Mexico and many other low-wage production platforms, factory wages are effectively set by the government itself, not by free-market competition or collective bargaining. The companies like it that way. So, of course, do those governments.[27]

While reiterating the view of the 'Battle of Seattle' as the struggle of a potentially and embryonically united world working class against the alliance of multinational corporations and Third World elites, these passages highlight two closely related issues that constituted the subtext of the battle. The first is the issue of what mechanisms are most likely to ensure the universal protection of the rights of labour. And the second is the issue of what mechanisms are most likely to ensure a minimally equitable distribution of the costs and benefits of world trade and production. Let us briefly examine each issue in turn.

LABOUR RIGHTS AND THE RACE TO THE BOTTOM: MYTHS AND REALITY

As Greider puts it in the passages quoted above, the US red-green alliance's case for enshrining higher labour standards for poor countries in the WTO agreements rests on two main assumptions. The first is that, without international protection, Southern workers are 'on a hopeless treadmill ... because their wages and working conditions will be undercut by the next poor country below them on the food chain, bidding for industrial jobs by sacrificing workers.' The second assumption is that Southern governments set wages and working conditions at lower levels than free-market competition or collective bargaining would.

There is undoubtedly some truth in both assumptions. Nevertheless, both assumptions ignore important tendencies of labour-capital relations on a world-scale before and during so-called 'globalization'. First, the relocation of industrial activities from richer to poorer countries has often led to the emergence of strong new labour movements in the low-wage sites of investment, rather than an unambiguous 'race to the bottom.' Although corporations were initially attracted to particular Third World sites because they appeared to offer cheap and docile workers (e.g., Brazil, South Africa, South Korea), the subsequent expansion of capital-intensive mass-production industries created new and militant working classes with significant disruptive power.[28] This tendency is particularly evident if we focus on the leading industries of so-called Fordism such as the automobile industry,[29] but can be seen also in less propitious environments such as electronics.[30]

These labour movements not only succeeded in raising wages, improving working conditions, and strengthening workers' rights, they also often played a leading role in democracy movements.[31] Moreover, labour militancy pushed on to the agenda social transformations that went well beyond those envisioned by pro-democracy elites. Thus, a recurrent pattern is visible: while labour-repressive regimes have created the conditions for rapid industrialization and proletarianization ('economic miracles'), industrialization and proletarianization themselves unleashed processes that eventually undermined these same regimes.[32] In many of these cases international solidarity was non-existent. Liberation from labour-repressive regimes was generally brought about by workers' struggles on the ground. And even where vigorous solidarity movements existed (e.g., for South Africa), grass-roots militancy at home, rather than international solidarity, played the decisive role in the transformation.

This does not mean that all is well for the workers of the world. Far from it. Apart from the fact that the process of 'strengthening through industrialization' has affected only a small percentage of the Southern proletariat, the greater

freedoms that have accrued to labour through the liquidation of labour repressive regimes have not always translated into greater welfare. For the latest spread
of democracy has gone hand-in-hand with the liquidation of the development-
friendly regime and the resurgence of a labour-*unfriendly* international regime.
Under these circumstances, democratic governments are forced to make key
economic and social policy decisions affecting living standards with 'an eye at
least as much on pleasing the International Monetary Fund as appealing to an
electorate.'[33]

As for the position of Northern workers, while it is unclear whether or not
they have *on the whole* experienced a significant *absolute* worsening of their
working and living conditions, the gap between rich and poor has widened
rapidly, while conditions for those at the bottom of the wealth and income
hierarchy have stagnated or declined. In Western Europe, massive unemployment (especially among youth) has been the main (but not only) form that the
deterioration in conditions has taken since the 1980s. In the US, the portion
of national income going to profits (rather than labour) has grown over the
course of the past twenty years, erasing all of labour's gains from the 1960s and
1970s. And despite the long economic boom of the late 1990s, average real
wages remain lower than they were thirty years ago.[34]

Thus, while all is far from well for the workers of the world, any observable
worsening in their working and living conditions over the last 20–30 years *cannot*
be attributed primarily (if at all) to either repressive Third World elites or the
relocation of industrial activities from North to South. On the one hand, this
period has been characterized by successive waves of democratization at the
national level in the context of an increasingly labour-unfriendly international
environment. On the other hand, had relocation been the main thrust of the
ongoing restructuring of world capitalism, we would have most likely
witnessed a general structural strengthening of labour, and it is unlikely that we
would be speaking of a crisis of world labour today.[35] If we are speaking of such
a crisis, it is because the spatial relocation of industrial activities to lower income
countries—even the faster relocation made possible by the latest technological
developments—is not the most fundamental aspect of the capitalist restructuring
of the last 20–30 years.

As argued at length elsewhere,[36] the primary aspect of this restructuring is a
change in the processes of capital accumulation on a world scale from material
to financial expansion. This change is not an aberration but a normal development of the capitalist accumulation of capital. From its earliest beginnings 600
years ago down to the present, the capitalist world economy has always
expanded through two alternating phases: a phase of material expansion—in the
course of which a growing mass of money capital was channelled into trade and
production—and a phase of financial expansion, in the course of which a
growing mass of capital reverted to its money form and went into lending,
borrowing and speculation. As Fernand Braudel remarked in pointing out the
recurrence of this pattern in the sixteenth, eighteenth and nineteenth centuries,

'every capitalist development of this order seems, by reaching the stage of financial expansion, to have in some sense announced its maturity: it was a sign of
autumn.'[37]

As Braudel was writing, the great expansion of world trade and production
of the 1950s and 1960s began announcing its own maturity by turning into the
financial expansion of the 1970s and 1980s. In the 1970s, the expansion of
financial activities was associated with, and in many ways contributed to, an
expansion of capital flows from high- to lower-income countries. In the 1980s,
cross-border borrowing and lending continued to grow exponentially—the
stock of international bank lending rising from 4 percent of the total GDP of
all OECD countries in 1980 to 44 percent in 1991.[38] But capital flows from
high to lower income countries contracted sharply in the 1980s, from a net
inflow of almost US $40 billion in 1981 to a net *outflow* of almost $40 billion
in 1988.[39] In other words, the ultimate and privileged destination of the capital
withdrawn from trade and production in core locations has not been lower
income countries; rather it has been the locales and networks of financial speculation that connect high income countries to one another. It was this
withdrawal, rather than the relocation of production, that in the 1980s precip-
itated the crisis of world labour.

It cannot be emphasized too strongly that this crisis and the underlying
tendency towards the so-called financialization of capital were only in part due
to a spontaneous capitalist reaction to the crisis of over-accumulation that
resulted from the rapid expansion of world trade and production in the 1950s
and 1960s. Equally essential was the change in government policies—a drastic
contraction in money supply, higher interest rates, lower taxes for the wealthy
and virtually unrestricted freedom of action for capitalist enterprise—through
which between 1979 and 1982 the United States began to compete aggressively
for capital world-wide. This change initiated and has kept alive the intense
inter-state competition for mobile capital that has created the demand conditions for the great relocation of capital of the 1980s and 1990s from trade and
production to financial intermediation and speculation.[40]

This relocation, rather than the incomparably smaller relocation of industrial
activities from North to South, has been the main cause of whatever worsening
of working and living conditions Northern and Southern workers have been
experiencing over the past twenty years. More important, the world-wide relocation of capital to financial activities has benefited the North and South very
unequally. What is forgotten by those who base their analysis on the
North–South relocation of industrial activities is that the main direction of
capital flows in the 1980s and 1990s has not been from North to South but
from South to North (or wholly internal to the North). Crucial in this respect
has been the transformation of the United States from being the main source
of world liquidity and foreign investment—as it was through the 1950s and
1960s—to being the main debtor nation and largest recipient of foreign investment of the 1980s and 1990s.

This transformation radically changed the global context not just of labour–capital relations, North and South, but also and especially of Southern attempts to catch up with Northern standards of wealth. Contrary to Harris' and Hoogvelt's contention, the geographical dimension of core-periphery relations has become more rather than less marked, fully retaining its constraining and disposing influence on world-scale labour–capital relations. This brings us to the second issue raised by Greider in the passages quoted earlier on the issue of the inter-state distribution of the costs and benefits of world trade and production.

THE STRANGE DEATH OF THE THIRD WORLD

We have no dispute with Harris', Hoogvelt's and Greider's explicit or implicit contention that the Third World, as a political-ideological force, collapsed in the 1980s. But we question whether this has been accompanied by any levelling of economic opportunities. For the process of dispersal of industrial capacity that Harris and many others take at face value as 'development' has in fact been associated with a widening of the income gap that separates the vast majority of the population of the Third World from that of the First. The Third World has collapsed, along with the Second World, precisely because of a generalized failure to translate rapid industrial expansion into an advance up the value-added hierarchy of the world economy.

What is 'strange' about this collapse is that it occurred abruptly when Third World states were not just industrializing rapidly but were also wielding unprecedented power and influence in world politics. The Third World was primarily a political and ideological formation. Born out of the struggle for national self-determination of the peoples of Asia and Africa and of the parallel struggle for world hegemony between the US and the USSR, the 'Third World' experienced growing power and influence throughout the Vietnam War and its aftermath. Partly related to the US military effort in Vietnam, the economic conjuncture at this time also seemed to favour Third World countries. Their natural resources were in great demand, as was their abundant and cheap capital. Agents of First World bankers were queuing up in the antechambers of Third (and Second) World governments offering at bargain prices the over-abundant capital that could not find profitable investment in their home countries. Terms of trade had turned sharply against First World countries, and the income gap between the latter and Third World countries seemed to be narrowing.

Shortly after the oil shock of 1979, however, it became clear that any hope (or fear) of an imminent equalization of the economic opportunities of the peoples of the world was, to say the least, premature. US competition for mobile capital in world money markets to finance both a new escalation in the Cold War and the 'buying' of electoral votes at home through tax cuts, suddenly dried up the supply of funds to Third and Second World countries and triggered a major contraction in world purchasing power. Terms of trade swung back in favour of First World countries as fast and sharply as they had swung against them in the 1970s, and the income gap between the First World and the rest of the world became wider than ever. From 1982 onwards, it would no longer be First-World bankers begging Third World states to borrow their over-abundant capital; it would be Third World states begging First-World governments and bankers to grant them the credit needed to stay afloat in an increasingly integrated and competitive global economy. To make things worse for Third World states, they were soon joined in their cut-throat competition for mobile capital by Second-World states.

High finance is the arena where Third World solidarity, such as it was, was dissolved into cut-throat competition for mobile capital. This is the true significance of the Thatcher-Reagan counter-revolution. By shifting the terrain of the struggle to the arena of financial speculation, the counter-revolution threw the Third (and Second) Worlds into complete disarray and revived the fortunes of the First World, the United States in particular. This was not the only shift that enabled the First World to regain the upper hand. Militarily, for example, the Falkland/Malvinas War shifted the confrontation from the terrain of labour-intensive warfare to that of capital-intensive warfare, showing that, if Third World states could be drawn to fight on the latter terrain, all the disadvantages that had led to the defeat of the US in Vietnam would vanish. The validity of the lesson was confirmed most spectacularly by the Gulf War and again, though less spectacularly, in the 1999 war against Yugoslavia. But the most decisive weapon wielded by First World states under Anglo-American leadership in the destruction of the Second and Third Worlds was economic-financial rather than military-industrial. Third World states simply proved incapable of translating political-ideological power into economic-financial power.

This incapability had little, if anything, to do with deficiencies peculiar to Third World states. Rather, it had to do with law-like tendencies of the global capitalist system that buttress the existing hierarchy of wealth among countries. The durability of the global stratification of wealth has been documented for the 1938–1997 period in a series of studies.[41] Three findings deserve special attention. First, world population classified by the log of GNP per capita has tended to cluster into three strata (low-, middle-, and high-income) separated from one another by two low-frequency gaps. Second, while upward mobility of states across the two low-frequency gaps that separate the three strata occurred in the short run (one or two decades), it was rare for a country to be able to sustain an upward move in the long run (three or four decades)—a finding later replicated from a different perspective by Easterly et al.[42] As a result, only a few states have succeeded in consolidating their upward mobility from the low- to the middle-income stratum (Taiwan and South Korea) or from the middle- to the high-income stratum (Japan, Italy and, more recently, Singapore and Hong Kong as well). Moreover, owing to the faster demographic growth of the states in the lower-income strata, the relative demographic sizes of the three strata have remained roughly constant, in spite of these individual cases of upward mobility. Finally, starting in the 1960s, the difference in degree of industrialization between states in the high-income stratum and states in the other two strata (especially in the middle-income stratum)has decreased significantly. But whereas in the 1970s this tendency was associated with a narrowing of the income gap between the upper and the lower strata, in the 1980s and 1990s the continued narrowing of the industrialization gap was associated with a major widening of the income gap. In 1997, the average per capita GNP for countries in the middle-income stratum was only $2,465 or 12.5% of the average per capita GNP for countries in the high-income stratum; while the average per capita GNP of low-income countries was only $466 or 2.4% of the high-income countries.[43]

The image of development that emerges from the identification of these tendencies is one of a race in which low- and middle-income states attempted to move up in the value-added hierarchy of the world economy by internalizing within their domains one aspect or another of the 'modernity' of the wealthy countries (most notably, industrialization). As these attempts became general, however, they tended to defeat their purpose by activating interstate competition over resources that were made ever more scarce by the generalization of modernizing efforts—a competition, what's more, in which states in the high-income stratum were generally better positioned than states in the lower strata to come out on top. The idea that all states could catch up with the standards of national wealth of the high-income countries by internalizing the latter's modernity thus turned out to be an illusion. The spread of industrialization efforts, in other words, resulted more in the downgrading of industrial activities in the value-added hierarchy of the world-economy than in the upgrading of the low- and middle-income economies that were becoming more industrial.[44]

This stability of world income inequalities can be conceptualized in terms of Roy Harrod's and Fred Hirsch's notion of 'oligarchic wealth'[45]—a kind of long-term income that bears no relation to the intensity and efficiency of the efforts of its recipients and is never available to all no matter how intense and efficient their efforts are. Much of the political turbulence of the 1980s, and the related crisis of all variants of developmentalist efforts, can be traced to a situation in which a generalized attempt to attain oligarchic wealth through modernization left low- and middle-income states stranded with most of the costs and few of the benefits of industrialization.[46]

From this perspective, the 'retreat' of core capital into financial intermediation and speculation was a reaction to the intensification of competitive pressure in industrial activities as well as to the demands of both Northern workers and Third (and Second) World countries for a greater share of the pie. As previously noted, this retreat was not the outcome of spontaneous market forces acting on their own. Rather, both were the outcome of market forces acting under the direction and with the support of the US government. The simultaneous liquidation of the ideology and practice of the welfare and developmentalist states transformed the crisis of capital of the 1970s into the crisis of labour and of the Third (and Second) Worlds in the 1980s and 1990s.

Third World elites were not the passive victims of the US liquidation of the development project. At least some fractions of such elites were among the strongest supporters of the new Washington Consensus through which the liquidation was accomplished.[47] To the extent that this has been the case, Third World elites have been among the social forces that have promoted the liberalization of trade and capital movements.

But the same can be said of Northern workers' role in the liquidation of the welfare state. After all, it was a big swing in the US working-class vote (the so-called Reagan Democrats) that empowered the Republican Party to reverse New Deal policies in the United States and to escalate inter-state competition for mobile capital worldwide. And as the competition escalated, organized labour in Northern countries (the US in particular) generally supported their governments' efforts to out-compete one another (and especially poor countries) in attracting capital, thereby shifting competitive pressures onto workers elsewhere. While such efforts at 'self-protection' are hardly surprising, they do nothing to enhance the 'internationalist' credentials of Northern workers.

To be sure, such 'self-protection' efforts are not limited to Northern workers.[48] Nevertheless, it is difficult to place a significant share of the responsibility for the collapse of the developmental or welfare states on Southern workers. Indeed, if anything, the widespread and massive wave of anti-International Monetary Fund (IMF) protests carried out by Southern workers in the 1980s[49] slowed the transformation, well before the 'backlash' hit Paris in 1995[50] or Seattle in 1999.

In sum, it is plausible to conclude that both Third World elites and Northern workers have played some part in the success of the Reagan-Thatcher counter-revolution. The counter-revolution succeeded primarily because the welfare and developmental states had reached their limits in delivering on the promises of the global New Deal. But it also succeeded because the ruling groups of the United States managed to persuade Northern workers and Third World elites that, in order to break out of these limits, it was necessary to liquidate rather than preserve these two kinds of state.

The significance of Seattle is that Northern workers and Southern elites seem to have simultaneously realized that the dismantling of the welfare and developmental states benefited primarily Northern capital and did little or nothing in delivering on the unkept promises of the global New Deal. The positive outcome of this simultaneous realization has been to dramatize some of the limits and contradictions of the seemingly irresistible rise of US unilateralism in defining the rules of global competition. At the same time, however, this achievement was neither based upon, nor did it lead to the emergence of, a vision of labour-capital and core-periphery relations capable of constituting a more equitable alternative to US-sponsored globalization. On the contrary, Northern workers and Southern elites have so far seemed more inclined to pursue their own particularistic interests within the existing world order in opposition to one another, rather than join forces to figure out what alternative world order would make their interests converge.

THE CHINA SYNDROME

The issue of the universal protection of the rights of capital and the issue of the distribution of the costs/benefits of globalization between North and South were not the only issues that constituted the subtext of the Battle of Seattle. There was a third issue that, in a sense, encompassed the previous two. This is the issue of China's entry into the WTO. Although it was not even on the agenda of the WTO meeting, by most accounts this was the single most important issue in the back of many demonstrators' minds.

> 'China, we're coming atcha' yells Mike Dolan, the Nader group's organizer in Seattle, as he discusses the next item of business. 'There's no question about it. The next item of business is China.' Jeff Faux, director of the AFL-CIO-backed Economic Policy Institute, tells reporters that with China in the WTO it will be impossible to get labour and environmental standards installed, because China's too big ... 'The China vote is going to become proxy for all our concerns about globalization' says Denise Mitchell of the AFL-CIO.[51]

While conceding that 'there are Chinese elites oppressing Chinese masses inflicting dreadful working conditions and pay scales', Alexander Cockburn confesses that the sight of Western progressives execrating China makes him uncomfortable. It reminds him of how the century began—with 'the troops of the Western powers [breaking] the Boxer siege of the embassies in Peking, [looting] the Empress Dowager's summer palace and thus [destroying] for a time the valiant nationalist effort to halt colonial exploitation of China.' In the intervening hundred years China experienced a series of revolutions—part of the broader revolt against the West by the impoverished countries of Asia and Africa. Land and wealth were redistributed and an industrial base built in an attempt to foster internal demand and get a fair price for the commodities poor countries needed to sell abroad.

> The Western powers didn't care for that, any more than they liked the Boxers ... They never relented, never forgave. Some revolutions struggled on for several decades, in varying states of siege, boycotts, embargoes, economic sabotage ... The progressive intellectuals from the Economic Policy Institute who denounce China's 'state-controlled economic system' as 'market-distorting' ... aren't so far removed from those who have administered the siege of Cuba all these years. Many liberal NGO types are interventionist by disposition. The Somalia debacle, and to some extent the Kosovo nightmare, were their shows ... We don't need ... at the end of this imperial century to be signing on to a Yellow Peril campaign.[52]

The imperialist record of Western powers in dealing with China over the last 150 years is undoubtedly a good enough reason for feeling uncomfortable with Western progressives execrating China. There are nonetheless two further reasons that bear directly on the issues of 'universal labour rights' and 'greater distributional justice' discussed earlier. One concerns the position of the Chinese working class in the world labour movement, and the other concerns the position of China in the global economy.

The historical record of the labour movement in China and in the North/West in the twentieth century lends no support to the Seattle demonstrators' claim that Northern pressures on the Chinese ruling elites are an essential condition for the emancipation of the Chinese working class from oppression and exploitation. On the one hand, the record shows that the militancy of the Chinese working class can be and has been second to none. The explosion of labour unrest in China of the 1920s was probably the greatest such explosion of the century in any country at China's level of proletarianization.[53] The explosion was drowned in blood by the Western-backed Guomindang regime. But the experience initiated that fundamental reorganization and reorientation of the policies of the Chinese Communist Party that eventually led to the establishment of a regime that by all available indicators did more for the improvement of the condition of the working class in China than any previous regime.[54]

On the other hand, organized labour in the North/West in general (and in the US in particular) did little or nothing to support the struggles of the Chinese working class. While Western support for the Guomindang repression of the Chinese workers' movement of the 1920s went largely unchallenged, the US-led siege, boycotts, and embargoes of Communist China enjoyed the full support of the AFL-CIO. Nor should we forget that some of the biggest US strikes of the late nineteenth and early twentieth century had among their targets the exclusion of Chinese workers from the US labour market, while the American Federation of Labour actively fanned the flames of anti-Chinese sentiment. In a 1905 speech Samuel Gompers assured his (presumably Caucasian) audience that 'Caucasians are not going to let their standard of living be destroyed by Negroes, Chinamen, Japs, or others.'[55] Indeed, according to Alexander Saxton:

> Throughout the nineties and on into the twentieth century, the Federation [AFL] kept up a barrage, in openly racist terms, against the Chinese and other Orientals. Thus, [in 1893], the AFL convention resolved that Chinese brought with them 'nothing but filth, vice and disease'; that 'all efforts to elevate them to a higher standard have proven futile'; and that the Chinese were to blame for degrading 'a part of our people on the Pacific Coast to such a degree that could it be published in detail the American people would in their just and righteous anger sweep them from the face of the earth.'[56]

In light of all this, only a complete amnesia of the most basic facts of twentieth-century Chinese and world-labour history can give any credence to the claim that US labour's advocacy of the exclusion of China from the WTO is primarily, if at all, motivated by international workers' solidarity. Throughout the century—from the Boxer Rebellion, through the great strike wave of the 1920s and the Revolution of 1949—the Chinese working class had to rely primarily on domestic alliances to emancipate itself from poverty, insecurity, and oppression. Why, all of a sudden, should it have become so incapable of taking care of its own further emancipation as to require the assistance of Northern organizations that throughout the century have been part of its problem rather than of the solution? It is, of course, possible that the kinds of concessions that the United States has already extracted from China as a condition for its admittance to the WTO make exclusion rather than inclusion more beneficial for Chinese workers. But even if that were the case, on what grounds should Chinese workers interpret US labour advocacy of Chinese exclusion as an act of international solidarity? Have they not many more grounds for detecting some fundamental continuity between US labour action at the beginning of the twentieth century aimed at excluding Chinese immigrant labour, and US labour action at the end of the century aimed at excluding the products of Chinese labour?

The fact that the AFL-CIO, while formally endorsing the April 2000 anti-IMF/World Bank demonstrations in Washington, chose to concentrate its political energies for the season on a separate campaign to block normal trade relations between the United States and China[57] is the latest reason to suspect the depth and sincerity of US labour's new internationalism. Arguably, IMF structural adjustment and debt policies have had a far greater negative impact on the world's workers (including their indirect impact on workers in the North through intensification of labour market competition) than Chinese exports; yet the obsession with China is paramount.

This brings us to the second issue, that is, of global distributional justice. With this issue in mind, it is especially disturbing to note that the execration of China by Western progressives comes at a time when China appears to be emerging as the only poor country that has any chance in the foreseeable future of subverting the Western-dominated global hierarchy of wealth. China is not the only poor country that has escaped the ravages brought upon the Third and Second Worlds by the neoliberal counter-revolution of the 1980s. Several other states did much better than China, most notably South Korea, Taiwan, Hong Kong and Singapore. Nevertheless, these are small states, jointly accounting for an insignificant fraction of world population, whose upward mobility in the global hierarchy of wealth left the hierarchy itself as entrenched as ever. The far more limited economic advance of China, in contrast, involving as it does about one-fifth of the world population and more than one-third of the total population of low-income countries, threatens to subvert the pyramidal structure of the global hierarchy of wealth itself, and not just statistically, but economically, politically and culturally as well.

There is no denying that China's rapid growth raises in a particularly acute form the problem of absolute and relative scarcity of natural resources—a problem that the post-war world of oligarchic wealth accommodated through the exclusion of the majority of the world population from the mass consumption standards of the West. A new model of development that is less wasteful than the US-sponsored mass consumption model will be needed in a world of greater distributional justice. Unfortunately, there are few signs that China's ruling elites—any more than those of the West—are aware of the need to devise such an alternative model.

Granted this, directly or indirectly sabotaging China's further economic advance, as some Western progressives advocate, is not only morally untenable; it is in all likelihood a false solution of the problem. It is morally untenable because wealthy Western countries in general, and the United States in particular, have been and continue to be the world's leading polluters and destroyers of natural resources, both at home and abroad. And it is likely to be a false solution because the huge and growing disparities between the living standards of poor and wealthy countries are the single most important force that drives the elites of low- and middle-income countries into the adoption of the consumption norms and ecologically destructive practices of the wealthy countries.

For all the challenges it poses and continues to pose in this century, China's economic advance should be welcomed rather than feared and sabotaged by Western progressives, for two main reasons. One is that the advance is the most hopeful sign that the extreme global inequalities created under European colonial imperialism, and consolidated under US hegemony, will eventually give way to a more just and equal world. And the other is that its continuation is the best guarantee that a strong labour movement will emerge in China, capable of carrying one step further the 'long march' of the Chinese working classes towards their self-emancipation. Indeed, signs of such an emergent labour movement have grown together with China's industrialization/proletarianization.[58] Given the size and growing centrality of the Chinese working classes in world society, a strong Chinese labour movement would have a major invigorating impact on the world labour movement as a whole.

CONCLUSIONS

In a contribution to a forum on the 'Problems and Prospects of a Global Labour Movement', Dan Clawson chides left-academics for dismissing the protectionist strategy of 'most workers and many unions' as politically retrograde.[59] While acknowledging the potential affinity of protectionist strategies with racism and xenophobia (and hence its serious dangers), Clawson argues that 'workers also hold an important truth, and we need to take it seriously.'

> As an attempt to limit the impact of capital's internationalism, protectionism has almost invariably involved racist (e.g., anti-Japanese) and anti-immigrant stances ('they' are taking 'our' jobs; we need to keep 'them' out). But it is also an assertion that the economy should not be driven by an unfettered market, that limits need to be imposed on the

drive for profits, and that some means must be found to protect workers and the environment in order to put human needs above cost-benefit analysis.[60]

Clawson goes on to argue that we need a general theory of international labour solidarity that 'recognizes the need for local community built on planning and some degree of protection from the unfettered market', at the same time as it embraces international labour solidarity and rejects racism and xenophobia. How is such a balance to be struck?

In this essay we have argued that the crisis of labour was brought on by the massive shift of capital from investment in production and trade to finance and speculation, rather than by industrial relocation or most other phenomena associated with 'globalization'. We also argued that the current financialization of capital is not unprecedented, and that the last analogous period at the end of the nineteenth and beginning of the twentieth centuries led to two world wars, imperialism and fascism. Both financial expansions—past and present—have been associated with a tremendous polarization of wealth within and between countries, and with rapid transformations that unsettled established ways of life and livelihood. National-protectionist reactions have been strong, with racist and xenophobic overtones.[61]

Labour movements, as we know, played at best an ambiguous role in the rise of national-protectionism and imperialism. As E. H. Carr noted in discussing the collapse of the Second International on the eve of the First World War:

> In the nineteenth century, when the nation belonged to the middle class and the worker had no fatherland, socialism had been international. The crisis of 1914 showed in a flash that, except for backward Russia, this attitude was everywhere obsolete. The mass of workers knew instinctively on which side their bread was buttered ... International socialism ignominiously collapsed.[62]

To the extent that core labour movements once again decide that their 'bread is buttered' on the side of national-protectionism—that is, standing behind the power of their states to buttress global inequalities and divide the world's workers—our risk of descending into another lengthy period of systemic chaos and 'tribalism' is dramatically increased.

While the motivation for national-protectionism (and any attendant racism) may be rooted in the real insecurities experienced by workers, we should not repeat the mistake of pandering to working-class racism made by socialists in the late nineteenth and early twentieth centuries. Indeed, as Alexander Saxton points out: while it was socialists alone among labour activists who mounted any criticism of the anti-Chinese crusade of the late-nineteenth century, even they made a tactical decision to 'sail under the flag' of 'anti-coolieism' as 'a means of uniting and educating the working class.' Yet 'tactics ... have a way of becoming habits', and when the socialists sought 'to haul down the tactical flag' and raise instead the 'strategic flag of working-class unity', they were no longer able to affect the course of events. Moreover, by allowing anti-Chinese rhetoric to go unchallenged they helped pave the way not only for the exclusion of the Chinese and other immigrants, but for a general turn to an openly racist labour-movement policy towards blacks.[63]

While standing firm against racism, we also need to push for a new labour-friendly international regime in order to provide a climate in which, in Clawson's words, local communities can make plans, workers' livelihoods are protected from an unfettered market, and human needs are put above cost-benefit analysis. As we have argued here, the financial expansion is the result of conscious profit strategies of firms and conscious power strategies of core states, especially the United States. Therefore, 'there is an alternative.' Labour activists should be struggling against policies at the national and international level that 'boost' the speculative bubble as well as in favour of policies that 'burst' it. From this point of view, the speech by the president of COSATU (South Africa's trade union federation) at a recent mass rally in Johannesburg is to be applauded. He called for an end to the private sector's 'investment strike' and demanded that capital invest in jobs rather than stock exchanges.[64]

But the solution ultimately must include a transformation at the international level. The vicious circle of domestic and international conflict was brought to an end in the mid-twentieth century only with the establishment of the labour-friendly and development-friendly international regime under US hegemony that, at least in part, addressed the demands explicitly and implicitly being thrown up by the movements from below. Nevertheless, the solution cannot be a simple return to the main elements of that regime. For in promising to meet the aspirations of the mass movements, the US-sponsored regime fudged several issues. In particular, the ideology of unlimited growth ignored both the capitalist limits and environmental limits to the promise that all could and would enter the Age of High Mass Consumption.

Contrary to its promises, the American Century has resulted in a consolidation of world inequalities in income and resource use/abuse. Moreover, the overlap between the racial and wealth divides on a world-scale has been consolidated, while environmental degradation has proceeded at a pace and scale that is unprecedented in human history. Indeed, to the extent the 'strike of productive capital' comes to an end, the environmental limits of universalized, rapid growth will come to the fore, bringing with it renewed impulses to exclude some large percentage of the world's population from the enjoyment of those resources. Here, ultimately, lies the great challenge that will face workers North and South in the twenty-first century: that is, the challenge to struggle, not just against exploitation and exclusion, but for consumption norms and secure livelihood standards that can be generalized to all and for policies that actually promote this generalization.

NOTES

1. Aristide Zolberg, 'Response: Working-Class Dissolution', *International Labour and Working Class History*, 47, 1995, pp. 28–38.

2. Beverly J. Silver and Eric Slater, 'The Social Origins of World Hegemonies', in G. Arrighi and B. J. Silver et al., *Chaos and Governance in the Modern World System*, Minneapolis: University of Minnesota Press, 1999, pp. 202–7.

3. Giovanni Arrighi and Beverly J. Silver, 'Labour Movements and Capital Migration: The US and Western Europe in World-Historical Perspective' in C. Bergquist, ed., *Labour in the Capitalist World-Economy*, Beverly Hills: Sage, 1984, pp. 183–216.

4. Beverly J. Silver 'World-Scale Patterns of Labour–Capital Conflict: Labour Unrest, Long Waves, and Cycles of World Hegemony', *Review* (Fernand Braudel Centre), vol. 18 no. 1, Winter 1995, pp. 160–1.

5. Silver and Slater, 'The Social Origins of World Hegemonies', pp. 176–202; Silver, 'World-Scale Patterns', pp. 158–185.

6. Geoffrey Barraclough, *An Introduction to Contemporary History*, Harmondsworth: Penguin, 1967, pp. 153–4.

7. Frederick Cooper, *Decolonization and African Society: The Labour Question in French and British Africa*, Cambridge: Cambridge University Press, 1996.

8. Silver and Slater, 'The Social Origins of World Hegemonies', pp. 208–11.

9. Arturo Escobar, *Encountering Development: The Making and Unmaking of the Third World*, Princeton: Princeton University Press, 1995.

10. Thomas McCormick, *America's Half-Century: United States Foreign Policy in the Cold War*, Baltimore: Johns Hopkins University Press, 1989.

11. Silver and Slater, 'The Social Origins of World Hegemonies', pp. 214–6; Arrighi and Silver, et al., *Chaos and Governance in the Modern World System*, pp. 282–6; cf. Robert Brenner, 'The Economics of Global Turbulence: A Special Report on the World Economy, 1950–1998', *New Left Review*, 229, May/June 1998, pp. 1–264.

12. Immanuel Wallerstein, 'Response: Declining States, Declining Rights?', *International Labour and Working Class History,* 47, 1995, p. 25.

13. Giovanni Arrighi and Beverly J. Silver, 'Global Inequalities and "Actually Existing Capitalism"', paper presented at the conference 'Ethics and Globalization', Yale University, 31 March–2 April 2000.

14. Nigel Harris, *The End of the Third World: Newly Industrializing Countries and the Decline of an Ideology*, Harmondsworth, Middlesex: Penguin Books, 1987, pp. 200–2.

15. For recent examples see Ankie Hoogvelt, *Globalization and the Postcolonial World: The New Political Economy of Development*, Baltimore, MD: Johns Hopkins University Press, 1997, pp. xii, 145; David Held, Anthony McGrew, David Goldblatt and Jonathan Perraton, *Global Transformations. Politics, Economics and Culture*, Stanford, CA: Stanford University Press, 1999, pp. 8, 177, 186–7.

16. Hoogvelt, *Globalization and the Postcolonial World*, p. 145.

17. 'Democracy Bites the WTO' (Editorial), *The Nation,* 27 December 1999, p. 3.

18. 'Democracy Bites the WTO', p. 4.

19. Martin Khor, 'Take Care, the WTO Majority Is Tired of Being Manipulated', *International Herald Tribune*, 21 December 1999, p. 4.

20. William Finnegan, 'After Seattle: Anarchists Get Organized', *The New Yorker*, 17 April 2000, p. 46.

21. Finnegan, 'After Seattle', p. 47.

22. Timothy Egan, 'New World Disorder: Free Trade Takes On Free Speech', *New York Times,* 5 December 1999, pp. iv, 5.

23. Kim Moody, 'On the Eve of Seattle Trade Protests, Sweeney Endorses Clinton's Trade Agenda', *Labour Notes* (Detroit), no. 249, December 1999, p. 1.

24. Jay Mazur, 'Labour's New Internationalism', *Foreign Affairs*, January/February 2000, p. 92.

25. David E. Sanger, 'The Shipwreck in Seattle', *New York Times*, 5 December 1999, p. 14.

26. William Greider, 'The Battle Beyond Seattle', *The Nation*, 27 December 1999, p. 5.

27. Greider, 'The Battle Beyond Seattle', p. 5.

28. Silver, 'World-Scale Patterns', p. 182.

29. Beverly J. Silver, 'Turning Points of Workers' Militancy in the World Automobile Industry, 1930s–1990s', *Research in the Sociology of Work*, vol. 6, 1997, pp. 43–71.

30. Jefferson Cowie, *Capital Moves: RCA's Seventy-Year Search for Cheap Labour*, Ithaca, NY: Cornell University Press, 1999.

31. Ruth Berins Collier, *Paths Toward Democracy: The Working Class and Elites in Western Europe and South America*, Cambridge: Cambridge University Press, 1999, ch. 4; Gay Seidman, *Manufacturing Militance: Workers' Movements in Brazil and South Africa, 1970–1985*, Berkeley: University of California Press, 1995.

32. See also Beverly J. Silver, 'The Contradictions of Semiperipheral Success: The Case of Israel', in W. G. Martin, ed., *Semiperipheral States in the World-Economy*, New York: Greenwood, 1990; Beverly J. Silver, *Labour Unrest and Capital Accumulation on a World Scale*, Ph D Dissertation, Binghamton, NY: SUNY (Ann Arbor: University Microfilms International), 1992.

33. John Markoff, *Waves of Democracy: Social Movements and Political Change*, Thousand Oaks, CA: Pine Forge Press, 1996, pp. 132–5.

34. Robert Pollin, 'Globalization, Inequality and Financial Instability: Confronting the Marx, Keynes and Polanyi Problems in the Advanced Capitalist Economies', paper presented at the conference on'Globalization and Ethics', Yale University, 31 March–2 April 2000, table 5; Louis Uchitelle, 'As Class Struggle Subsides, Less Pie for the Workers', *New York Times*, 5 December 1999, Business Section, p. 4.

35. See the conclusions of Arrighi and Silver, 'Labour Movements and Capital Migration'.

36. Giovanni Arrighi, *The Long Twentieth Century: Money, Power and the Origins of Our Times*, London: Verso, 1994; Arrighi and Silver et al., 'Chaos and Governance'.

37. Fernand Braudel, *Civilization and Capitalism, Fifteenth–Eighteenth Century, volume 3. The Perspective of the World*, New York: Harper and Row, 1984, p. 246.

38. The Economist, 'World Economic Survey', *The Economist*, 19 September 1992.

39. UNDP, *Human Development Report 1992*, New York: Oxford University Press, 1992.

40. Arrighi and Silver, 'Global Inequalities'.

41. Giovanni Arrighi and Jessica Drangel, 'The Stratification of the World-Economy: An Exploration of the Semiperipheral Zone', *Review* (Fernand Braudel Centre), X, 1, Summer 1986, pp. 9–74; Roberto P. Korzeniewicz and William Martin, 'The Global Distribution of Commodity Chains', in G. Gereffi and M.

Korzeniewicz, eds., *Commodity Chains and Global Capitalism*: Westport, CT: Praeger, 1994, pp. 67–91; Arrighi and Silver, 'Global Inequalities'.

42. William Easterly, Michael Kremer, Lant Pritchett, and Lawrence H. Summers, 'Good Policy or Good Luck? Country Growth Performance and Temporary Shocks', *Journal of Monetary Economics*, 32, 1993.

43. Arrighi and Silver, 'Global Inequalities', based on World Bank data.

44. Arrighi and Drangel, 'The Stratification of the World-Economy'; Arrighi and Silver, 'Global Inequalities'.

45. Roy Harrod, 'The Possibility of Economic Satiety—Use of Economic Growth for Improving the Quality of Education and Leisure', in *Problems of United States Economic Development*, 1, New York: Committee for Economic Development, 1958, pp. 207–13; Fred Hirsch, *Social Limits to Growth*, Cambridge, Mass.: Harvard University Press, 1976.

46. Giovanni Arrighi, 'The Developmentalist Illusion: A Reconceptualization of the Semiperiphery', in W. G. Martin, ed., *Semiperipheral States in the World-Economy*, New York: Greenwood Press, 1990, pp. 11–42; Giovanni Arrighi, 'World Income Inequality and the Future of Socialism', *New Left Review* 189, 1991, pp. 39–64; Silver, 'The Contradictions of Semiperipheral Success'.

47. Lance Taylor, 'The Revival of the Liberal Creed—the IMF and the World Bank in a Globalized Economy', *World Development*, vol. 25, no. 2, 1997, pp. 145–52.

48. See the discussion of the South African textile unions' protectionist stance *vis-à-vis* Zimbabwean imports in Patrick Bond, Darlene Miller and Greg Ruiters, 'The Southern African Working Class: Production, Reproduction and Politics', in this volume.

49. John Walton and Charles Ragin, 'Global and National Sources of Political Protest: Third World Responses to the Debt Crisis', *American Sociological Review*, vol. 55, December 1990, pp. 876–7, 888.

50. R. Krishnan, 'December 1995: The First Revolt Against Globalization', *Monthly Review*, vol. 48, no. 1, May 1996, pp. 1–22.

51. Alexander Cockburn, 'Short History of the Twentieth Century', *The Nation*, 3 January 2000, p. 9.

52. Cockburn, 'Short History', p. 9.

53. Beverly J. Silver, Giovanni Arrighi and Melvyn Dubofsky, eds., 'Labour Unrest in the World Economy, 1870–1990', a special issue of *Review* (Fernand Braudel Centre), vol. 18, no. 1, Winter 1995, pp. 1–206; Mark Selden, 'Labour Unrest in China, 1831–1990', *Review* (Fernand Braudel Centre), vol. 18, no. 1, Winter 1995, pp. 69–86.

54. Selden, 'Labour Unrest in China'; Mark Selden, 'Yan'an Communism Reconsidered', *Modern China* 21, 1, pp. 8–44.

55. Quoted in Alexander Saxton, *The Indispensable Enemy: Labour and the Anti-Chinese Movement in California*, Berkeley: University of California Press, 1971, p. 273.

56. Saxton, 'The Indispensable Enemy', p. 271.

57. Finnegan, 'After Seattle', p. 49.

58. See for example, James Kynge, 'Riots in Chinese Mining Towns', *Financial Times*, 3 April 2000; Dorothy Solinger, *Contesting Citizenship in Urban China*, Berkeley: University of California Press, 1999, pp. 284–6.

59. Dan Clawson, 'Contradictions of Labour Solidarity', *Journal of World System Research*, vol. 4, no. 1, Winter 1998, pp. 7–8 [http://csf.colorado.edu/wsys-

tems/jwsr.html].

60. Clawson, 'Contradictions of Labour Solidarity', p. 8.
61. Silver and Slater, 'The Social Origins of World Hegemonies'; cf. Karl Polanyi, *The Great Transformation*, Boston: Beacon, 1957.
62. Edward H. Carr, *Nationalism and After*, London: Macmillan, 1945, pp. 20–1.
63. Saxton, 'The Indispensable Enemy', pp. 266–7.
64. Eddie Jayiya, 'Mass Action Brings Jo'Burg to Standstill', *The Independent*, 13 April 2000.

NO-COLLAR LABOUR IN
AMERICA'S 'NEW ECONOMY'

Andrew Ross

Advance waves of the new no-collar work first swept across Wall Street when office managers, conceding a barely-begun struggle, declared 'Casual Fridays' as the order of the day. Dress codes and other protocols of workplace formality were to be relaxed on the least industrious day of the work week. While starchy diehards growled about the abatement of the American work ethic, evangelists of 're-engineering' welcomed the custom as a bold innovation; workers would feel their personality was being acknowledged, and that their workplace was less alienating on the day it was most perceived to be so. Introduced by the employer, this new custom ironically evokes memories of Saint Monday, the pre-Taylorist working-class tradition of mass absenteeism at the close of the weekend. After all, Casual Friday was intended to energize white-collar workers by making them feel at home, rather than at work; all the more present for feeling like an absentee.

Far from spontaneous, Casual Friday is part and parcel of the new wave managerial ethos that preaches the levelling of workplace hierarchies. Employees are to feel empowered and individualized, workplaces are to feel fluid and recreational, and work is to be liberated from rigid, bureaucratic constraints. After several decades in which Americans were encouraged to find the true meaning of themselves in leisure time and consumption, work, according to this ideal, is once again the place where our identity is to be most deeply felt and shaped. Perhaps this is just as well. The U.S. boasts an economy where the amount of leisure time available to workers has been in steady decline since the early 1970s, and where chronic overwork, and not unemployment, is the primary feature of the labour landscape. Since there is no easy return to the days when a clear demarcation between work and leisure existed, the efforts of the new managerialism are aimed at dissolving the boundaries as much as possible.

For the most advanced and entrenched examples of this ethos, you would have to pay a visit to New York's 'Silicon Alley', where the Webshops of the New Economy have been at this game since the mid-1990s when start-up companies first began to colonize Manhattan's downtown manufacturing loft spaces. In those fledgling days, the physical culture of the New Media work-place was more or less an extension of the grungy artist's loft. When dot.com mania broke out, and the Alley was flooded with venture capital, ritzy designers were hired to create set piece interiors. Trophy environments at companies like Screaming Media, DoubleClick and Oxygen Media featured flexible, communal spaces, where cubicles were banished and walls were rendered translucent. The office was re-imagined as a giant, multi-purpose playroom for an ever-shifting team of workers. Cool, buzzworthy graphics are flung across the walls and ceilings. Pool tables in game rooms, basketball courts, and well-ness relaxation spaces are a relief and counterpoint to the omnipresent but deftly decentred computer workstations. Who would ever want to go home? Silicon Valley had pioneered an earlier version of the informal workplace, where whiz kids didn't have to grow up and leave the never-never land of adolescence where the thrill of exploration and invention was unsullied by the external, social world. Silicon Alley, the 'capital of content', upgraded the informality by adding all the hip features of an urban artist lifestyle.

THE RISE OF FREE AGENTS

For the New Economy's boosters, these environments are much more than real estate icons, they are the ultimate physical embodiment of all the 'flexi-bility' talk that has dominated corporate culture for the last twenty years. Indeed, they house Internet industries that sprang directly from the head of the restructured economy of flexible accumulation and which at the turn of the new century were pumping fresh, hot air into the wobbly, digital stock bubble. As numerous commentators have described, this economic restructuring, begun in the mid- to late-1970s, eliminated an enormous number of stable, high-wage union jobs, and resulted in the normalizing of low-wage temp work for a large segment of the labour force. The two decades between 1973 and 1993 showed a steady decline in full-time jobs, and a rise in part-time employment, from 16.6 percent to 18.8 percent of the general workforce, almost all of the increase resulting from *involuntary* contingent work, and most of it in temporary-help employment.[1] In the technically skilled echelons of the new information indus-tries, a de luxe form of temping emerged as the model pattern of employment, much hyped, and much overrated. Well-paid technicians, engineers, and designers became independent contractors, eschewing benefits, pension pack-ages and other forms of job security for the freedoms offered by contingent work. 'Employees without jobs', they moved from company to company, 'pollinating' the seeds of innovation, according to the new flexible style of corporate organization.[2]

Over the course of the 1990s, this model was much emulated. 'Consultant' became the fastest growing job description, if not the fastest growing job category, and segued into the phenomenon of the 'free agent'—in New Economy parlance a skilled but flexible worker with no enduring company loyalties beyond the terms of the contract. The corporate crusade to downsize and shed its permanent workforce seemed to have met its perfect love-match; workers who do not want a regular paycheck or any form of benefits from the companies for which they occasionally work. For the most fortunate, the freelance lifestyle is a heady potion, and their fantasies of autonomy (while still being paid by the Man) are seized on and glorified as a way to sell the profile of flexible labour in general. As a result, projected tallies for these 'free agents' are inflated, as many as 33 million according to some Internet industry boosters.[3] But who are these autonomous agents, and how voluntary is their employment condition?

According to the latest U.S. Bureau of Labor Statistics (BLS), for 1997, there were 5.6 million workers with contingent jobs (employment not expected to last for more than one additional year), most of whom are young and female, predominantly concentrated in low-wage temping, and 53 percent of whom would have preferred a job that was permanent. 'Workers with alternative arrangements' (numbers that overlap with those of contingent workers) include independent contractors, on-call workers, day labourers, temporary help agency workers, and workers provided by contract firms. The independent contractors (8.2 million, and 6.3 percent of the workforce), are concentrated in managerial, professional, sales occupations, and in the construction and services industries, and are more likely to prefer their employment arrangements than workers in other categories like on-call (2 million) and temps (1.1 million). Among these 8.2 million are the much heralded knowledge workers, labelled as free agents. Yet, between 1995 and 1997, when the knowledge industries were booming, there was a decline in the number of independent contractors, while all other categories, including those for contingent work, were little changed in those same two years.[4]

In March 2000 the *New York Times Magazine* devoted an issue to the 'new American Worker'. The issue focused on the concept of the free agent as a symptom of the shift away from the 'organization man' of post-war corporate culture, where company loyalty was regarded as a long-term two-way contract between employers and white-collar employees. With the replacement of conformity by innovation, and a large permanent workforce by temporary employee pools, a contract labour market is coming into its own, whereby free agents bid for jobs offered by employers on auction Web sites like Bid4Geeks.com and Monster.com. In the most breathless of these articles, Michael Lewis lumps together all of the categories of 'workers with alternative arrangements' to estimate the number of free agents at 12 million (out of a national workforce of 131 million), and avers that their typical mode of self-presentation usually includes

> piercing some highly unlikely body part and cultivating an air of total independence. Actually, what these people all were, or appeared to be, were artists. They kept artists' hours. They wore artists' clothes. They had persevered [in] the sort of odd habits that membership in any group—other than the group 'artists'—tends to drum out of people. Maybe the most interesting thing about them was their lack of obvious corporate attachments. Corporations usually paid for their existence, but otherwise seemed to have no effect on their lives. If forced to discuss the companies that paid the bills, these people tended to be dismissive, or at the very least, ironic.[5]

In another article, which debunks the romance of the free agent nation, Nina Munk cites a new media marketing consultant who, with her laptop and cell phone, is using an offbeat Greenwich Village cafe, Les Deux Gamins, as her portable office—'It makes me feel like I'm in Paris,' she says, 'Like Hemingway at Les Deux Magots.' Munk points out that more than 60 percent of these workers earn much less than full-timers in comparable jobs, and that the lure of liberation from routine work seems to result in people putting in more hours than they would at a regular, comparable job.[6]

THE LEGACY OF THE STARVING ARTIST

The references by Lewis and Munk to artists and writers are crucial. A large part of the attraction of the free agent profile draws on the appeal to Bohemian glamour. What are the consequences of this desire to assume the trappings of the artist? First of all, let us be clear that it is an invitation to underpayment. Artists' traditions of sacrificial labour are governed by the principle of the cultural discount, by which artists and other arts' workers accept non-monetary rewards—the gratification of producing art—as compensation for their work, thereby discounting the cash price of their labour. Indeed, it must be acknowledged that the largest subsidy to the arts has always come from workers themselves. The mythology of the 'starving artist' is rooted in the political economy of the creative professions, and the historical legacy of their emergence from the mould of aristocratic patronage.[7]

Just as important, however, is the serviceability of the artist's flexible labour. Since flexible specialization was introduced as a leading industrial principle the number of artists employed in the general labour force (defined in decennial Census data and annual Bureau of Labor Statistics reports as 11 occupations: artists who work with their hands, authors, actors and directors, designers, dancers, architects, photographers, arts teachers, musicians/composers, etc.) has swelled from year to year. According to the National Endowment for the Art's annual summaries of BLS tabulations, this number more than doubled from 1970 to 1990, showing an 81 percent increase in the course of the 1970s (while artists' real earnings declined by 37 percent), a 54 percent increase in the 1980s, a slight decline in the depression of the early 1990s, and a renewal of growth ever since, reaching a peak of 2 million in 1998. In 1997, artists were enjoying a growth rate in employment (at 2.7 percent) that far outstrips the general workforce (1.3 percent) and even that of other professional specialists (2.4 percent).[8]

These are impressive numbers, but they do not tell a simple story. To figure in the BLS survey, 'one must be working during the survey week and have described that job/work as one of eleven artist occupations.' Respondents are asked to describe the job at which 'they worked the most number of hours in the survey week.' Artists working more hours in other jobs outside the arts are classified as employed in those other occupations. By 1998, these amounted to an additional 330,000, for a total of 2,280,000 artists employed in the workforce.[9] Randy Martin points out that these requirements gloss over the verifiable existence of full-time jobs within that occupational sector: 'One works in an occupation, a sector, but has the flexibility to remain unattached. The artist can secure an identity for a day's wage, but the rest of the week remains unsecuritized.'[10] Because of the high degree of self-employment, and because they are most likely to have other jobs to support a creative trade that habitually employs them for only a portion of a workweek, employment and earnings data on cultural workers have always been unreliable. Even in the most highly unionized entertainment guilds, where the majority of members cannot find work on any given day, the dominant employment model is casual employment on a project-by-project basis. Loyalty is to the guild or craft or union, rather than to a single employer.[11]

There may be more going on here than the sleight-of-hand interpretation of statistics to paint a rosy picture of job creation in the arts. Whether or not we can verify a proliferation of new jobs, it is clear that the 'mentality' of artists' work is more and more in demand. In respect both to their function and the use of this work mentality, it looks as if artists are steadily being relocated from their traditional position at the social margins of the productive economy and recruited into roles closer to the economic centres of production. Indeed, the traditional profile of the artist as unattached and adaptable to circumstance is surely now coming into its own as the ideal definition of the post-industrial knowledge worker: comfortable in an ever-changing environment that demands creative shifts in communication with different kinds of employers, clients, and partners; attitudinally geared toward work that requires long, and often unsocial, hours; and accustomed, in the sundry exercise of their mental labour, to a contingent, rather than a fixed routine of self-application. A close fit, in other words, with the profile of the free agent.

NET SLAVES

In light of this artist profile, let us take a closer look at employment patterns in the New Media industries of New York City. The backbone of the Silicon Alley workforce in the pioneer phase of this new urban industry was staffed by employees—'creative content-providers', or digital manipulators in Web-site and software development—who had been trained primarily as artists. Deeply caffeinated 85-hour work-weeks without overtime pay are a way of life for Webshop workers on flexible contracts, who invest a massive share of sweat equity in the mostly futile hope that their stock options will pay off. Even the lowliest employee feels like an entrepreneurial investor as a result. In most cases, the stock options turn into pink slips when the company goes belly-up, or, in some cases, employees are fired before their stock options are due to mature. Exploitative manipulation of this mode of employee recruitment and retention has resulted in several major lawsuits that have rocked the industry. Yet the lure of stock options remains very strong, largely as a result of the publicity showered on the small number of employees who have struck gold in a high-profile 'IPO' (Initial Public Offering) among the new maze of new ones on the stock market.

Only 2.7 percent of workers in computer and electronics belong to unions (as compared to 56.2 percent in steel) and Webshop workplaces are entirely non-unionized.[12] For several fledgling years, about half of the jobs were filled by contract employees or perma-temps, with no employer-supported health care. With the explosive growth of the last two years, the number of full-time workers has increased noticeably (by 57 percent annually). Yet in the most recent industry survey, the expected rate of growth for part-time (30 percent) and freelance employment (33 percent) still competes with that for full-time job creation (38 percent). Evolving patterns of subcontracting in Silicon Alley are not so far removed from those that created offshore back offices for data-processing in the Caribbean, Ireland and Bangalore, or semiconductor factories in countries that also host the worst sweatshops in the global garment industry.[13] Most revealing, perhaps, is that in 1997 the average full-time salary (at $37,000) was well below the equivalent in old media industries, like advertising (at $71,000) and television broadcasting (at $86,000).[14]

As noted earlier, the Webshops physically occupy spaces filled by manufacturing sweatshops a century ago. Artists who took over these manufacturing lofts from the 1950s onwards enjoyed wide open floors where work space doubled as living space. This live/work ethos was embraced, to some degree, by the upscale, cultural elites who later consolidated 'loft living' as a real estate attraction, and it has been extended now into the funky milieu of the Webshops, where work looks more and more like play. In the most primitive startups, the old sweatshop practice of housing workers in the workplace has also been revived. Bill Lessard and Steve Baldwin, authors of *Net Slaves*, an exposé of industry working conditions, report on this phenomenon: 'We were up in Seattle on the book tour, and we visited a friend who's working for a startup that has installed beds in cubicles and is providing three meals a day. As if they were in a U-boat fighting a war! There are companies bragging about this kind of mistreatment!' Lessard and Baldwin sketch a portrait of an industry that benefits from the hagiographical 'myth of the 22-year-old code-boy genius subsisting on pizza and soda and going 36 hours at a clip.' Employees' quality of life approaches zero as a result, in 'the complete absence of a social life, a lousy diet, lack of exercise, chain smoking, repetitive stress disorders, and, last but not least, haemorrhoids. ... There's going to be a lot of sick people out there in a few years, and worse, they won't even have any health benefits.'[15]

All in all, the New Media workplace is a prescient indicator of the near future of no-collar labour, which combines mental skills with new technologies in nontraditional environments. Customized workplaces where the lines between labour and leisure have dissolved: horizontal networking among heroic teams of self-directed workers; the proto-hipster appeal of Bohemian dress codes, personal growth, and non-hierarchical surroundings; the vague promise of bounteous rewards from stock options; and employees so complicit with the culture of overwork and burnout that they have developed their own insider brand of sick humour about being 'net slaves', i.e., it's actually cool to be exploited so badly. Industrial capitalists used to dream about such a work-force, but their managerial techniques were too rigid to foster it. These days, the new wave management wing of the New Economy worships exactly this kind of decentralized environment, which 'liberates' workers by banishing constraints on their creativity, and delivers meaningful and non-alienated work for a grateful and independently-minded workforce.

At a time when this managerial revolution is 'liberating' employees, the workplace on the other side of the professional divide is more and more subject to automated forms of Taylorism. Worker monitoring, whether through keyboard strokes, e-mail and voicemail snooping, or surveillance cameras, is now standard practice on the part of the majority of American employers. Among service workers, human relations software is widely used for tracking, job timing, and to introduce speedup, yet the practice is also moving into white collar professions. The most infamous example is the regulation of physicians' schedules by health management organizations under the rubric of managed care. Alpha professionals, like doctors, are increasingly experiencing a loss of autonomy in the workplace, and are turning to union organizing as a result.

A VOLUNTEER LOW-WAGE ARMY

Labour history is full of vicious little time warps, where archaic or long foresworn practices and conceptions of work are reinvented in a fresh context to suit some new economic arrangement. The 'sweating' system of farming out work to competing contractors in the nineteenth-century garment industry was once considered an outdated exception to the rule of the integrated factory system. Disdained as a pre-industrial relic by the apostles of scientific management, this form of subcontracting is now a basic principle of almost every sector of the post-industrial economy and has emerged as the number one weapon in capital's arsenal of labour cost-cutting and union-busting. Where once the runaway shops were in New Jersey, now they are in Haiti, China, and Vietnam. So, too, the ethos of the autonomous artist, once so fiercely removed from industry's dark satanic mills and from the soiled hand of commerce, has been recouped and revamped as a convenient, even alluring, *esprit de corps* for contingent work in today's decentralized knowledge factories. Indeed, the 'voluntary poverty' of the *déclassé* Bohemian artist—an ex-bourgeois descendant, more often than not, of the self-exiled Romantic poet—may turn out to be an inadvertent forerunner of the discounted labour of the new industrial landscape.

In the academic sector in the U.S. we find a similar story about sacrificial labour. Indeed, the rapidity with which the low-wage revolution has swept through higher education in the last fifteen years was clearly hastened along by conditions amenable to discounting mental labour. For one thing, the 'willingness' of scholars to accept a discounted wage out of 'love for their subject' has helped not only to sustain the cheap labour supply but also to magnify its strength and volume.

The most obvious index of the changes in the academic labour force can be found in the rise of part-time employment, for that is how the payroll has been trimmed most dramatically. In 1970, the proportion of part-time faculty stood at 22 percent. By 1987, part-timers held 38 percent of faculty appointments, and ten years later, the proportion had risen to 42.5 percent. In addition, by 1988, the proportion of full-time faculty not on a tenure track, had risen to 20 percent.[16] Even among full-time faculty, the rate of compensation is depressed. Salary levels remain below those of 1971, and the gap between faculty salaries and those of other highly educated professionals has widened considerably. Faculty earned 13.8 percent less than professionals with a similar education in 1985, a gap that almost doubled by 1997, with faculty earning 24 percent less.[17]

Employers have long relied on maintaining a reserve army of unemployed to keep wages down in any labour market. Higher education is now in this business with a vengeance. In addition—and this is the significant element— its managers increasingly draw on a volunteer low-wage army. By this I do not mean to suggest that adjunct and part-timer educators eagerly invite their underpayment and lack of benefits or job security. Nor are they inactive in protesting and organizing for their interests. Rather, I choose the term to describe the natural outcome of a training in the habit of embracing non-monetary rewards—mental or creative gratification—as compensation for work. As a result, low compensation for a high workload becomes a rationalized feature of the job, and, in the most perverse extension, is regarded as proof of the worth of the academic vocation—underpayment is the ultimate measure of the selfless and disinterested pursuit of knowledge.

In some respects, the peripatetic regimen of the freeway flyer is germane to the eccentric work schedule of the traditional academic, who commonly observes no clear boundaries between being on and off the job, and for whom there is often little distinction between paid work and free labour. For the professionally active full-timer, this habitual schedule is bad enough. For the part-timer, desperate to retain the prestige of being a college teacher, the identity of being a switched-on, round-the-clock thinker, eager to impart knowledge, and in a position to freely extend her or his mental labour, feeds into the psychology of casualized work and underpayment. The industrial worker, by comparison, is not beset by such occupational hazards.

Again, what we see is the fabrication of a model 'flexible employee' out of the cloth of a customary training in the amateur ideals and irregular routines of mental labour which can be roundly exploited by cost-cutting managers in search of contingent labour. Because of the elective component of this situation, capital, it might be said, as part of its ceaseless search for ways to induct workers in their own exploitation, may have found the makings of a *self-justifying*, low-wage workforce, at the very heart of the knowledge industries so crucial to its growth and development.

THE MENTAL PRICE SYSTEM

My conclusion leaves us with some difficult questions. Are we contributing involuntarily to the problem when we urge youth, in pursuing their career goals, to place principles of public interest or collective political agency or creative expression above the pursuit of material security? In a labour environment heavily under the sway of neo-liberal business models, is it fair to say that this service ideal invites, if it does not vindicate, the manipulation of inexpensive labour?

Fifteen years ago, this suggestion would have seemed ludicrous. Labour freely offered in the service of some common benefit or mental ideal has always been the informal economic backbone that supports political, cultural and educational activities in the nonprofit or public interest sectors. Selfless labour of this sort is also a source of great pleasure. The world that we value most—the world that is not in thrall to market dictates—would not exist without this kind of volunteer discounted labour. But what happens when some version of this disinterested labour moves, as I have suggested here, from the social margins to core sectors of capital accumulation? When the opportunity to pursue mentally gratifying work becomes a rationale for discounted labour at heart of the key knowledge industries, is it not time to rethink some of our bedrock pedagogical values? Does the new landscape of mental labour demand more than the usual call for modernizing the politics of labour in the age of dot-com and dot-edu (the age of the Yale Corporation, the Microserf, and the consolidated push of Time Warner-Bertelsman-Disney-CNN-Hachette-Paramount-News Corp)?

On the one hand, there are sound reasons for retaining such ideals and traditions. Unpopular forms of intellectual, artistic, and political expression cannot and will not thrive unless they are independent of commercial or bureaucratic dictates. But these conditions of independence can no longer be 'defended' stubbornly and solely as a matter of humanistic principle, or as the free-standing right of a civilized society. When capital-intensive industry is concentrated around vast culture trading sectors, when media Goliaths feed off their control of intellectual property, and when the new Vested Interests routinely barter discount wages for creative satisfaction on the job, the expressive traditions of mental labour are no longer ours simply to claim, not when informal versions of them are daily being bought off and refined into high-octane fuel for the next generation of knowledge factories.

In so far as we participate in this economy as scholars, activists, or artists, there is a responsibility to recognize the cost of our cherished beliefs in political and educational ideals. These ideals come at a price, and managers of the New Economy are taking full advantage of the opportunities that exist for capitalizing on our neglect of that price. Our first challenge, then, could be to assess the special conditions for pricing wages for thought, under which 'free time' is systematically converted into un- or under-compensated labour (just as the hidden costs of the unwaged domestic labour of women have had to be acknowledged). Do such special conditions exist, or is pricing subject only to what the market will bear? As socialists, we know that the market does not function as an objective gauge of supply and demand—no more for sweatshop workers in an offshore Free Trade Zone than for CEOs in a tax-free zone of the Fortune 500. Ideas about the value of work and the worth of those who do certain kinds of work play a critical role in the price system, to use Veblen's pet phrase, and they must enter into our economic reckoning. Accordingly, we must remember that knowledge and rules of thumb passed on in a traditional craft are intellectual assets that will be stripped by managers looking for a comparative advantage. It was so in the steel mills where Frederick Taylor worked up his theories of scientific management, and it is little different in the knowledge factories of today.

Some part of the challenge also lies in organizing the unorganized, in this case those whose professional identity has been based on a sharp indifference to being organized. The sectors I have been describing here draw on an intimate and shared experience of the traditions of sacrificial labour. Yet they are divided by singular craft-like cultures, and by a tangle of class distinctions. Those most in denial (the most secure) will swear off any and every affinity. It will take more than a leap of faith to establish solidarity among mental labour fractions divided by the legacy of (under-the-table or above-the-salt) privileges passed down over centuries. Nevertheless, while the chief blight of these centuries had been chattel slavery, serfdom, and indentured labour (and we are not done with these), we must now respond to that moment in the soulful lullaby of 'Redemption Song' where Bob Marley soberly advises us: 'Emancipate yourself from mental slavery'.

NOTES

1. Lawrence Mishel, Jared Bernstein, John Schmitt, *The State of Working America,* Armonk, NY: M. E. Sharpe, 1997, pp. 258–73.
2. AnnaLee Saxenian, *Regional Advantage: Culture and Competition in Silicon Valley and Route 128,* Cambridge: Harvard University Press, 1994.
3. This notorious estimate is the work of Daniel Pink, operator of FreeAgentNation.com, and chief promoter of the concept in the dizzy pages of the industry rag, *Fast Company.* Nina Munk, 'The Price of Freedom', *New York Times Magazine,* 5 March 2000, p. 52.
4. Bureau of Labor Statistics, Report on 'Contingent and Alternative Employment Arrangements', December 1999.
5. Michael Lewis, 'The Artist in the Gray Flannel Pyjamas', *New York Times Magazine,* 5 March 2000, p. 46.
6. Nina Munk, 'The Price of Freedom', p. 54.
7. For a fuller analysis of this point and others in this essay, see Andrew Ross, 'The Mental Labor Problem', *Social Text,* Summer, 2000.
8. See the NEA Research Division Notes on 'Artist Employment in America' <www.arts.endow.gov.pub>.
9. NEA Research Division Note no. 73, April 1999.
10. Randy Martin, 'Beyond Privatization: The Art and Society of Labor, Citizenship, and Consumerism', *Social Text,* 59, Spring 1999, pp. 38–39.
11. Lois Gary and Ronald Seeber, *Under the Stars: Essays on Labor Relations in Arts and Entertainment,* Ithaca: Cornell University Press, 1996, p. 6.
12. David Bacon, 'Silicon Valley Sweatshops: High–Tech's Dirty Little Secret', *The Nation,* vol. 256, no. 15, 19 April 1993, p. 517.
13. Andrew Ross, 'Jobs in Cyberspace', in *Real Love: In Pursuit of Cultural Justice,* New York: NYU Press, 1998, pp. 7–34; and 'Sweated Labor in Cyberspace', *New Labor Forum,* 4, Spring, 1999, pp. 47–56.
14. Estimates based on annual reports on new media employment, Coopers and Lybrand/Price Waterhouse Cooper. New York New Media Industry Survey: Opportunities and Challenges of New York's Emerging Cyber-Industry, New York New Media Association, 1996, 1997 and 1999. There is no data on comparative compensation levels in the 1999 report, but Price Waterhouse confirmed to me that, without accounting for stock equity, the ratios for 1998 full-time employees are about the same as for previous years: $40k for new media; $83.5k for advertising; $84k for TV.
15. Bill Lessard and Steve Baldwin, *NetSlaves: True Tales of Working on the Web,* New York: McGraw-Hill, 2000, p. 246. For an active Web-site, see NetSlaves (Horror Stories of Working on the Web) at <www.disobey.com/netslaves>.
16. Data are from the 1987 and 1997 National Survey of Postsecondary Faculty (NSOPF) conducted by the National Center for Education Statistics of the Department of Education.
17. 'AUP, Annual Report on the Economic Status of the Profession 1999–2000', *Academe,* 86, 2 (March–April 2000).

MAPPING INDIA'S WORLD OF UNORGANIZED LABOUR

BARBARA HARRISS-WHITE AND NANDINI GOOPTU

If class struggle is first a struggle over class and second a struggle between classes, we can say that the overwhelming majority of the Indian work-force is still kept engaged in the first struggle while capital, even though stratified and fractured, is engaged in the second.

India's capitalist economy has a GDP about the size of Belgium's, but with a hundred times the number of people and of course a radically different history. Out of India's huge labour force, over 390 million strong, only 7% are in the organized sector. Even the term 'organized' is seriously misleading because only half of the 7% is unionized and in the vanguard of working-class politics.[1] The union movement, despite the efforts of workers, has been exposed to the exertions of political parties, machinations of the Indian state and onslaught of employers, so becoming fragmented and failing to represent consistently the interests of organized labour. 'Organized sector labour' means workers on regular wages or salaries, in registered firms and with access to the state social security system and its framework of labour law. The rest—93% of the labour force—works in what is known as the 'unorganized' or 'informal' economy.[2] Unorganized firms are supposed to be small. In fact they may have substantial work-forces, occasionally numbering hundreds, but where workers are put deliberately on casual contracts. There is actually no neat boundary between the two categories of labour. Some sectors, notably mining and dock labour, straddle the divide. In practically every 'organized' firm, including state-run corporations, unorganized labour is selectively incorporated into the labour process.[3]

Nowhere is this more evident than in manufacturing where the unorganized state of the work-force is overdetermined by a variety of converging forces. For most of the last century (and long before the era of flexible specialization or economic liberalization) a process of decentralized agro-industrial mercantile accumulation gave rise to a numerically powerful stratum of small-scale capitalists with low managerial costs and flexible labour practices, a stratum that was almost literally a law unto itself.[4] There, unorganized labour was and is unprotected by the regulatory regime of the state and deprived of any rights at work. In India, unlike in the West, state regulation of capital–labour relations was not imposed on capital after industrialization, but accompanied it. This meant that from the start, strong incentives were created for capital to evade these laws, while the state acted in the interests of capital whenever organized labour sought their enforcement. Employers' responses to radical trades unionism ensured *informalization* through subcontracting, putting out and casualization in 'organized' firms.

The massive unorganized sector, which contributes some 60% of GDP beyond the regulative and protective reach of the state, is one of the four most distinctive features of Indian capitalism. An audit of Indian labour must focus on the workers in this sector. A second feature is the unskilled nature of much work, with employers relying on casual labour and flexible employment practices, so attaching little importance to training and the development of skills.[5] A third distinctive feature is the absolute poverty of workers. While organized workers receive a third of all wages and incomes, 36% of the population survives on incomes below the stingy, nutrition-based official poverty line, a number far in excess of the official estimates of those un- or under-employed.[6] In 1995, an agricultural labouring household of 2 adults and 2 children earned about $130 a *year*. Two-thirds of all landless agricultural labour live below the poverty line. Fourth, most work may be unregulated by the state but the markets for their labour are far from 'unstructured'.[7] Work is organized through social institutions such as caste and gender. Capitalism is not dissolving this matrix of social institutions but reconfiguring them slowly, unevenly and in a great diversity of ways. The matrix still affects the tasks most people do, the kinds, terms and conditions of the contracts they are offered and either settle for or refuse. It also generates the volatile political forces—the struggles over class—which overlay the glacial development of the conflict *between* classes.

While the economy grew at 5% from 1977 to 1994, employment in the corporate sector was stagnant at 0.1%. Meanwhile, and despite a discourse of state compression, public-sector employment *grew* at 2.2% and that of the unorganized economy expanded at 2.6%.[8] Contrary to the beliefs behind the economic reforms, growth has become less and less labour-absorbing over time. The fastest-growing industries—engineering and software—are those with the highest labour productivity. The organized sector has shed and informalized up to half its labour force. Small-scale production has been adversely affected by a tight money policy and stagnant domestic demand. Agriculture, the construction industry, quarrying and petty trade are working as shock absorbers, but ones with ever weaker elasticities of employment.[9] Public infrastructure (irrigation, roads, stores, electricity, industrial estates) is known to work synergistically with private investment but has atrophied. Un- and underemployment are on the increase and of late the real wages of workers in the unorganized sector have stagnated and in some areas have declined. All this was clearly foreseen by the World Bank in 1989 which predicted some 8–10 million of extra unemployment from the stabilization phase alone.[10]

Cheek by jowl, even in rural India, a household with assets worth $200,000 these days has near-neighbours worth a mere $6. We agree with Sheila Bhalla that the new economic policy has been most successful in generating 'gross inequality—not the straightforward kind where most people get better off, ... (although) the benefits of growth accrue more to the rich than to the poor, but the really mean kind where the rich get richer and the poor get poorer, not just in relative terms but absolutely'.[11]

Indian capitalism has developed in distinctive eras, strata, sectors and regional blocks. The tiny minority of labour in the corporate and public sector—the so called 'commanding heights of the economy', increasingly confronting orogenies of global capital—accounts for 20% of GDP. Its fastest-growing and most publicized sector, software, amounts to 10% of India's exports yet it is a mere 0.1% of the global software trade. The brain drain has effectively deprived India of the engineers who drive software innovation. India's 'cheap labour' is not yet playing the role of global educated reserve army which has been attributed to it.[12] It relies in turn on wage goods produced by the altogether cheaper labour, which is the focus of our essay. Agriculture is still the largest single sector. While its share in the economy shrank from 41% in 1965 to 29% in 1994, during a period when both its technologies and its relations of production were transformed,[13] its share in total employment has hardly changed—from 73% to 67%. Its labour productivity remains stagnant, currently at around one-third of that in manufacturing and services.

The bulk of the Indian work-force consists of the catch-all category of the 'self-employed'. Although 'self-employed' may cover small family businesses, for the most part people classified this way are semi-independent peasants with small assets, petty commodity producers and traders. They exploit their own households and often both hire in and hire out labour according to seasonal peaks, their independence concealing 'sundry forms of wage labour'.[14] One recent estimate is that 56% of all Indian workers are 'self employed' in this guise, 29% are casual wage labourers and just 15% are in any kind of regular waged or 'salaried' employment whether organized or not.[15] 'Self-employed' people are entering labour markets in droves and being chosen for their experience by employers in preference to the third of the Indian population who have no assets at all.[16] The implication of having miniscule assets is the constant management of a trade-off between the calendar of demands of accumulation from petty production and trade and the compulsions of wage labour. The implication of being casual labour is that while employers will stop employing wage labour beyond the point at which marginal returns and costs are equalized, employees themselves will seek to maximize work days, a practice called 'self-exploitation'.

Attempts to model Indian workers as objects in a set of markets in which their prices vary according to supply and demand have proved to have a limited purchase on the real relations of labour, even when these relations are essentialized as money wages.[17] Indian labour is not competitively priced. It is highly heterogeneous. Not only its returns but also its politicization are shaped by the social construction of all the markets that make up Indian capitalism. In the struggle between classes, capital attempts to enforce its control of labour not only through the manipulation of various non-class social identities but also through the segmentation and fragmentation of labour markets. For instance, the blurred boundary between the organized and unorganized sectors is also a division across caste and gender.[18] The uneasy relationship between the struggle for, and that between, classes is central to the politics of Indian labour. The tactics by which the various fractions of Indian capital control labour are comprehensive and pervasive—not only at work but also outside work, and in the domestic as well as the public sphere. These tactics also operate through the state. Long before 'liberalization', capital has rained body blows on organized labour. However, the world of labour is not always what capital wills, for labour often reshapes and complicates that world. Employers' practices often undergo significant changes as a result of the efforts of labour, however limited or fragmented, to gain control over labour time and labour processes and increase pay.[19]

Both labour and capital are shaped for their routine encounters not only by class but also by gender, caste and point in the life cycle. The constant working of these relationships may involve aspects of life outside work which may distract from or compensate for class-based action. They also make for significant differences in the terms and conditions of work. In a recent study of two villages in West Bengal, twelve different types of wage-labour contract were found. There was no single village wage for casual labour. For any one kind of contract there was a great diversity of detailed terms and conditions, including pay. Households did not map onto types of contract such as 'casual labouring' or 'permanent labouring'. Labour contracts were affected by gender (more open-ended obligations and less power to choose for women), caste (which affects the tasks available to a household), age, and household composition. All these factors led to variations in the earnings of landless labourers.[20] Such axes of segmentation make for multiple solidarities which tend to make collective, class-based action harder to achieve.[21]

In the rest of this essay we try to map the dialectic between the way capital has manipulated labour relations embedded in Indian social institutions, and the politics of labour,[22] which will also lead us to examine the ability of the Indian state to respond to the needs and interests of labour. Moreover, the politics of labour does not remain confined only to responses to strategies of capital, but is also crucially shaped by the identities and perceptions of labourers themselves. Such politics, perhaps more appropriately identified as the politics of the poor than of labour, is a significant reality for labouring people. The transformation in labour conditions, be it through the agency of labour itself or capital and the state, cannot happen without initiatives and struggles by workers. Globalization and liberalization have intensified the need for these struggles.

THE SPATIAL UNIT FOR LABOUR

The social construction of the spatial unit for labour varies hugely in India. Rural workers have begun to migrate seasonally on a large scale. 'People who migrate this way are not "just" migrants. They may also be own-account farmers, petty traders, school students, gatherers and priests'.[23] Buses designed for 50 people can be found transporting 190 on peak days. New sources of demand for labour for harvests hundreds of miles away or in seasonal 'mud work' (construction) enable migrant labour to raise agricultural wages and to break free from debt relations and other demeaning practices in their villages of origin.[24] Nevertheless, the village still tends to be the key unit for the organization of labour, particularly for women workers who are stuck with housework and children. Familiarity counts in employers' decisions whether or not to spend time supervising operations. Both employers and employees have expectations about future work based on compliance and loyalty. The structures of differentiation in land relations, through which demand for labour is organized, vary village by village. So in the absence of highly developed rural transport (which is still rare), even if daily casual wages are known to be higher in the next village, labourers, especially women, often do not seek them. In turn this generates a fundamental lack of symmetry in the relations between agricultural employers and casual labour. While employers may not always maximize profit, they are able to use non-economic means to exploit workers; meanwhile workers are unable to maximize wages. Since those who do travel to get better wages are mostly men, it is hardly surprising either that the gender differential in wages is widening.[25]

Outside agriculture, even though the distribution of non-agrarian castes such as weavers (being based on networks, routes and towns rather than spatial territory) may still shape recruitment, in urban areas the geopolitical unit for a given labour market may be small.[26] Individual small capitalists set the terms and conditions of their labour contracts. Even when casual wages are 'agreed' across a sector within a town (in actuality usually imposed by associations of employers, often without any consultation with labour), the implicit terms for 'casual' labour (which may include hours, bonuses and perquisites) can be altered individually.[27] So also can the breakdown between the cash and kind (food) components of wages. Such practices prevent easy comparisons.

So the small-scale and fragmented nature of labour markets restricts collective action on the part of work-forces encompassing several villages or a segment of the non-farm or urban economy. The excess supply of labour also means that the threat of dismissal hangs over negotiations. Despite these constraints, small groups of workers do try to negotiate their terms of employ-ment at the level of the individual village or firm, and at times achieve wage increases or changes in employers' practices by 'formalizing' terms of employ-ment.[28] Their action is, however, focused on individual employers in the locality and is rarely of long duration, with the possibility of reversals and with few implications for the wider labour market. The anthropologist Jan Breman has argued that the movement of labour between firms or over short distances to get other jobs 'must be explained as a deed of protest', and that 'as employ-ment becomes less regular and wages lower, the intrepidity of the underdog seems to increase'.[29] Breman interprets such actions as expressions of proletarian class consciousness, showing workers' increasing refusal to accept their condi-tions passively. The fact remains that these attempts at wage negotiation or escape have no general impact on the relations between capital and labour, and fail to be enlarged into collective class-based resistance. The problem is not that workers lack political consciousness or the willingness to resist their exploita-tion, but that the structural constraints are too severe. Where resistance occurs, employers often resort to force and violence, often with the complicity of the local state and the police.

COERCION IN CONTRACTS:
PATRONAGE AND DEBT-BONDAGE

To reduce costs capital has a powerful interest in labour which is flexible. Flexibility is commonly achieved by capital through casualization and by labour through its physical movement. Yet many employers (rural and urban) want people to work at their literal beck and call: to work with cattle, irrigation, monitoring consignments of grain in town, shifting between workshop/firm and farm, between farm and family. Although outright, permanent, inheritable bondage is illegal and increasingly rare, labour is commonly tied not only by site but also by debt, by contracts which link in a single agreement terms and conditions for labour with those on land, money or product markets, and by the non-contractual obligations of patronage which may also require the work of the women and children of a male labourer. Such ties have thrived on the lack of symmetry of power associated with customary rights, particularly with rights of employers to command family labour and rights to terminate the rela-tionship. There is no archetype for such arrangements, and much regional variation in their incidence and intellectual contest on the left about their signif-icance in the process of capitalist transformation.[30] They are widely argued to be breaking down thanks to (i) migration which offers alternative work; (ii) new technology which reduces demand for labour; (iii) struggles by labour for contracts less encumbered by customary notions of dependence, inferiority and obligation; and (iv) other efforts towards emancipation, sometimes organized along lines of caste.[31] Yet the skein of patronage may uncoil only to recoil in the form of debt-bondage and labour attachment. Throughout South India for instance, the refusal by labourers to perform collective, unpaid irrigation 'duties' as 'clients' of a new stratum of lower-caste landowners—work their fathers performed for Brahmins who have since then sold their land—has contributed to ruining the longstanding system of tank-fed agriculture and forced landowners to invest in (or rent) private wells. The provision of accommodation and/or debt can then be used to force labour to operate electric pumpsets at night or whenever rationed electricity is available.[32] Farther north in Andhra Pradesh the refusal by men to accept this sort of contract means that women have graduated from being the assumed adjunct to permanently employed ('attached' or close to bonded) male labour to having such contracts in their own right.[33] In Jan Breman's region, Gujarat, 'neo-bondage is less personalized, more contractual and monetized, while also the elements of patronage have gone, which provided some protection and a subsistence guarantee, however meagrely defined, to bonded clients in the past'.[34]

The consequence of neo-bondage is that emancipatory politics has had to be focussed 'upwards' towards and against local patrons. Resistance usually consists in violating debt obligations and escaping, though it can also take collective forms.[35] Where bondage is now largely 'economic' (enforced with physical violence, when necessary) and not based on social (and indeed legal) legitimacy, or on workers' acceptance that employers are socially and ritually superior and have the right to extract labour, workers do resist coercive arrangements, even though they are still forced to enter into debt relations for job security or out of sheer penury. Some even choose the more risky option of wage labour on piece-rates, eschewing the security offered by debt-bondage. While this may not improve their economic condition, it 'might benefit the dignity of labour' and signal an emancipatory move, according to Breman.[36]

LABOUR-LAND RELATIONS

In the segmented labour and land relations in agriculture the detail of the labour process reflects local class configurations and the mode of appropriation and accumulation of surplus. Capitalist landowners set the terms and conditions of work, the most important of which is a socially determined wage. Their dominance is bolstered by caste authority and political clout. The size of their holdings, their production decisions (crops, technologies) and their investment decisions (particularly in irrigation and in the non-farm rural economy, in sectors like trade, finance, construction, mills, looms, processing industry and transport) determine the demand for labour.[37]

The technologically precocious region of north-west India is a case in point. The early stages of the green revolution were highly labour-absorptive. Large landowners responded by luring some labour into permanent contracts to tie them, while shifting others to piece-work and gangs ('contract' labour) to reduce labour costs. They also subdivided tenancies to reduce the costs of supervising labour and to ensure that unwaged family labour contributed to production. Later, employers started to mechanize to cram an extra season of rice or cotton into this wheat-producing region; the capacity of agriculture to mop up labour while production was growing fell, and labour even began to be displaced. Large landowners casualized their labour. Real wages fell. Employers turned to migrant labour, not to compensate for local shortages but to ensure control. A striking increase in reverse tenancy (in which small owners rent out land to large operators) was engineered to concentrate holdings and reap rents from economies of scale. Militant agitations in the name of all agrarian interests have consolidated gains for the local elites at the expense of landless labour which has been kept quiescent and controlled by threats to reduce demand for their work.[38]

By contrast small peasants and landless agricultural labourers who form the great mass of the rural work-force[39] are obliged to work by having dependent family members, by consumption needs, by debt (often at usurious interest) and, wherever there is no alternative, by the coercive power of dominant landowners to enforce rental contracts yielding low returns to tenants. They are effectively reduced to being wage-workers in thin disguise. Average land holdings have fallen dramatically. While small-size farms generally have small-size families, the smaller the holding the greater the proportion of the household which has to work for wages—including children, sick or disabled and elderly people.[40] Wage dependency is increasing inexorably in agriculture. In 1961 there were three cultivators for each landless labourer, by 1991 already the proportions were almost equal.[41]

The compulsions of labour have never gone without challenge, although the political agenda of the mass of labourers who are low caste may put food security (mediated through the state) and dignity (especially rights to use village space and public wells) ahead of contracts and pay. Labour scholars of northern India have recorded a flurry of strikes in the 1990s over wages, the length of the working day and humiliating treatment by employers; and the *dalit*-based Bhahujan Samaj Party has been voted into power in the state of Uttar Pradesh. ('Dalit', literally meaning the down-trodden, refers to untouchables and other low castes.) The counter-tactics of employers, including the formation of private armies to coerce labour through brutal suppression, reflect their power over aspects of life outside the wage relation. Employers have also denied recalcitrant labour access to common property resources and space, to force them into submission.[42]

THE GENDERING OF WORK

Domestic labour produces new labour-power for the wage-labour market and protects and sustains it when it is unemployed, incapacitated or past coping with the physical toil. This labour is female. It has long been appreciated that the process is not a straight subsidy between the genders because unpaid domestic labour cannot be compared to a money equivalent. Reproductive strategies also vary with class position. In households with few, if any, assets, people are compelled to work to reduce dependency, so it is not surprising that the highest proportions of female and child employment (called 'participation'!) are found here. By contrast, educated women in the propertied classes are frequently withdrawn and effectively secluded—thereby wasting the economic potential of their education—even to the extent of having adverse implications for the life chances of their girl children.[43] Where individual conditions are known, women own and control so remarkably less assets than men, are so much poorer and so significantly less educated that it has been suggested that their class positions are uniformly lower than men's.[44]

Though the gender division of *paid* work is more flexible than used to be thought, the division of domestic labour has proved extraordinarily rigid. The very rare case where an elderly man cares for children to liberate adult women for fieldwork is the exception that proves the rule that even disabled women must cope with the 'domestic' priorities: collecting fuel and water, washing clothes, cleaning the interiors of houses, child care, care of the elderly and sick, post-harvest processing and the preparation of food.

Women work longer and harder than men and their wage-work is what is available when these tasks are done. They face discrimination in every conceivable respect. Over two-thirds of women have no money returns from their work, though the proportion of wage workers among those working is higher than for men. Female labour is heavily concentrated in rural sites, in agricultural work, on casual contracts and at wages bordering on starvation.[45] Women's wages are practically everywhere lower than those of men irrespective of the tightening effect of male migration or of the development of male jobs in the non-farm economy. In agriculture in the 1990s women's wages were on average 71% those of men.[46] In non-farm work, women are likely to be concentrated in the lowest grades and stages, on piece-rates rather than time-rates and with earnings much lower than men's.[47]

Women's wage-work is not necessarily empowering for them either at work or at home. In Andhra Pradesh—as we saw—while the feminization of the gender division of tasks has enabled men to refuse work, their employers have been able to impose attached contracts on wives. Increases in women's absolute or relative income do not necessarily increase the power they have over domestic resources, budgets, decision-making and spending, despite—or because of—the fact that women's expenditure decisions are more likely to benefit the entire household.[48]

Whereas the work-force as a whole is becoming more masculine, the agricultural labour force becomes more feminine as women take on (or are forced by men to take on) most tasks except for ploughing and work with machinery. Despite serious under-reporting, many millions of women have entered the work-force over the last three decades. 'Participation'—largely distress-induced—went up from 16% in 1971 to 32% in 1988. With this proletarianization of women, however, comes female unemployment. As with domestic work, female unemployment is hidden. One careful study puts it at six to seven times that of men. One million jobs may have been lost in the 1990s. Female underemployment (women looking for more work) is also increasing at a faster rate than for men.[49]

The literature gives an overriding impression that women are as docile politically as they are reputed to be economically. But the support of women (taking the form of unpaid work, or even willingness to bond their own labour) has sometimes been important to struggles by men. In Bihar, women who are not bonded and who have employment options outside agriculture have taken the lead in strikes.[50]

AGE AND WORK CAPACITY

Child labour has always been part of the family labour force. Nearly two-thirds of child labour is of this sort. It is the continuity between this and paid work on the one hand, and the state's egregious neglect both of education and of any means of implementing the existing limited law banning child labour in hazardous industries on the other, which penalize the children of agricultural labourers.[51] The latest estimate is that while 40 million children work, 13 million or 6% of the 215 million children aged between 5 and 14 work for wages, the casual component (one-third) of which is slowly rising and being feminized. 'It is not that the economy cannot do without child labour, it is rather that many children cannot do without employment' comments Ajit Ghose. This begs questions about why. If they are orphans or escaping abusive families, or if their parents are sick or disabled, then they lack access to social security. If their parents are underemployed and looking for work then employers' cost-cutting may account for it. If their parents are employed then their low wages—and sometimes their 'selfish' consumption patterns (especially that of alcohol by men) explains why children labour. When adults are unemployed or mired in debt-bondage, children have to join the labour force.[52] Apart from domestic reproductive work, agriculture and animal husbandry, there are certain industries where children are extensively used in preference to adult labour, the Sivakasi match-making 'cluster' being a notorious case. Controlled by influential business families, it is organized at home or in sweat/work-shops. The state turns a blind eye in various ways—from exemption from the Factories Acts to not enforcing the Minimum Wages Act.[53] Child labour is only slowly on the decline as (non-mandatory) primary education diffuses at a snail's pace. Illiteracy and poor levels of education lead to casual labour, with predictable consequences generation upon generation.[54]

There is, of course, no age of retirement for 'unorganized' labour. Instead, people are incapacitated from the labour market by the physical insults of old age, by deteriorating eyesight and eye defects (in agriculture after decades of staring at the reflected sun in wet fields, in weaving by years of close work in dim light), and by occupation-related accidents and diseases. There is increasing evidence that employers will screen labour for physique and pay differential piece-rates according to workers' physical condition.

CASTE AND CLASS

Marxists have tended to avoid caste as an analytical category. On the one hand, to view caste as an allocator of occupations is to exaggerate since for the most part and for most of history most of the population has been confined to agriculture. On the other hand castes have become dynamic interest groups. There is also evidence of caste-occupational stratification, often enforced by workers themselves to maintain their hold over enclaves of the labour market or sectors of petty trade. Caste still shapes ideologies of work and status. It makes for compartmentalized labour markets, 'with non-competing groups whose options are severely constrained'.[55] It stratifies pay. Caste ideology also affects whether women work at all, what work they can do, how far from home they may move. In particular to be 'scheduled caste' (the lowest castes, mainly untouchables and 29% of the population) makes a person twice as likely to be a casual labourer, in agriculture and poor.[56] Scheduled caste women are also more likely to be in low-paid menial labour, thus reinforcing the gender division. In town, all the work connected with sanitation and public health infrastructure without which the economy cannot function is entrusted to scheduled castes. Even when employed by the state, these workers face routine harassment and contemptuous treatment. Elsewhere as labourers, they are often still found doing physically dirty jobs, or handling food still to be stripped of its protective husks and shells. As petty traders they have entered markets for commodities with certain physical properties, for example fruit with skins or vegetables—or recycled materials—that need further physical transformation before being consumed. In these cases, entry to even petty trade is a struggle: carving out and defending physical territory previously occupied by others or encroaching on congested public space.

Scheduled caste and tribal people are constitutionally entitled to positive discrimination ('reservations') in the public sector to redress their social and economic 'backwardness' and deprivation, but the consequences have been uneven and paradoxical.[57] Reservations have helped to entrench the importance of caste as a social institution for access to jobs, have reinforced the caste-based segmentation of the labour market and made the reserved castes into an interest group when the original intention had been to dissolve caste differences. Reserved jobs are limited (sometimes limited by retaliation from those implementing them) and commonly absorb only a fraction of those who qualify. The market for jobs for low-caste people is thus segmented between those who do and do not benefit from reservation. In the context of liberalization, the limited possibilities of expansion of public-sector employment raise new questions about the need for job reservation in the private sector if lower castes are to preserve their limited gains in employment.

Caste is also the basis from which urban, occupation-based trade associations have evolved. These are developing powerful corporatist regulative roles, substituting for the state and unambiguously supporting local capital in a way that limits class conflict. Their collective political agendas, focusing on claims and privileges from the state and on the control of derived markets (for instance, through negotiating and fixing the rates for lorry transport, by-products, credit, porters, cartmen and casual labour), push labour issues low down. Through collective action based on 'occupation', decisions are taken to lengthen working days, flout other aspects of the labour laws and ignore safety provisions. Even when employers and employees belong to the same caste, terms and conditions can be imposed on labour and attempts by labour to unionize can be collectively resisted by upholding caste solidarity. Ways of organizing labour can be encouraged which disempower workers: associations of 'textiles workers' are actually (caste-based) master weavers. We have also found organizations representing yarn twisters, market-place porters and handcart pushers entirely managed by bosses.[58]

Yet while caste is used by employers to exploit labour and keep it fragmented, labourers too deploy caste identities to organize and, often, to enhance their status and express dignity in the face of exploitation. Workers may emphasize caste linkages to maintain their hold over a particular enclave of the labour market (for a ubiquitous example, scheduled caste municipal workers). When employers and labourers belong to the same caste—e.g., in the diamond-cutting industry in Surat (Gujarat), or in the industrial district making cotton knitwear in Tiruppur (Tamil Nadu)[59]—labourers often emphasize their caste solidarity with employers, thereby ensuring the exclusion of other caste groups. This has ambivalent effects. While such a monopoly benefits labourers, their reliance on vertical caste ties undermines their ability to challenge exploitation by employers. (There has never been a strike in the Surat diamond industry, despite extreme exploitation and physical abuse.)[60]

No less importantly but far less instrumentally, however, caste plays another role in labour politics. It has provided an idiom for many sections of the labouring poor, especially lower castes, to organize politically, although not always within the context of work or labour relations. Social movements and the political mobilization of untouchables (or *dalits*) in India in recent years have gained momentum in their search for dignity and social status. They have turned to the state for protection of their rights and for preferential access to public employment and education. Caste-based social movements have developed synergies with the work-place based politics of lower castes. For instance, scheduled caste municipal sanitary workers have organized to improve working conditions and wages, and at the same time have established caste associations for the internal reform of their caste, demanded recognition and dignity and challenged the legitimacy of ritual subordination. Lower-caste groups have also attempted to forge horizontal linkages with cognate castes of labourers and thus expanded the scope of mobilization. That lower-caste labourers in both rural and urban contexts now more actively contest the power of their employers cannot but be understood within the context of a wider process of political mobilization. In rural Bihar, the struggles of scheduled caste/untouchable landless labour, at times in alliance with radical left-wing political organizations, against their 'clean' upper- or middle-caste landowners-employers, have led to violent confrontations, caste battles reflecting class conflict.[61]

It would be wrong to interpret such political mobilizations of labour and expressions of collective identity in the language of caste as a form of false-consciousness, not least because caste and class exploitation interpenetrate in the strategies deployed by employers, and because exclusion from or inclusion in particular sectors of the labour market rests very significantly on caste status. If caste, as a social institution, continues to configure the labour market and determine relations between labour and capital, then it would be too restrictive an interpretation to exclude 'caste' politics, outside the work-place, as being irrelevant to the politics of labour. In fact, the former is central to the latter. Caste consciousness and class consciousness are not mutually exclusive, but can reinforce each other. Notions of class inflect other languages of politics (such as caste) and are expressed in terms not based exclusively on perceptions of economic antagonism. The growing power of lower-caste politics, including its growing institutionalization in political parties and successful electoral participation, may have little direct impact on labour relations. It does, however, form a very significant aspect of the politics of the labouring poor, even if not of the politics of labour qua labour, and it also enhances the capacity and willingness of labour to contest the power of upper-caste employers and their exclusion from various segments of the economy and the labour market.

WORKFORCE INSECURITY

Workers in India are insecure. Open unemployment (rigid at 12%) is not such a feature of work as intermittent, insecure, poorly productive underemployment. The coexistence of open unemployment with positive wages has proved hard to explain unless the continual resistance by employees to any reduction of the real food-equivalence of the wage is factored in. Over a quarter of the casual labour force at any given moment is looking for more work and the proportion is growing. Seasonal unemployment and employment overlap and coexist. Even industrial and commercial capital operates seasonally, and periods of idleness dot the weeks of peak labour demand. Employers are wily in making labour insecure. Payments are withheld. Contracts and debt are manipulated so as to ensure the availability of labour at peak periods of demand (at below the going rate) while at other times labour is dumped or made to work at below market rates.[62]

These tactics are not confined to agriculture. In small towns dominated by agro-processing there are not one but several fault lines in the security of labour which materially affect its power struggles. The typical 'unorganized' firm (tightly controlled by hierarchized male family members in order to concentrate accumulation) has a labour force divided by its extent and kind of security. Being part of the permanent labour force is here a condition to be aspired to, in contrast to being permanent labour in agriculture. Labourers are selected by origin (local), caste (usually not scheduled), and gender (male). Permanent work offers a diversity of livelihoods ranging from the night watch to accountancy, but all requiring individual trust. Contracts are individualized and verbal. They vary in their periods of payment and of notice of dismissal, the one delayed (sometimes pay is yearly) and the other instant. Some permanent jobs can be part-time, some seasonal. Many bosses agree to time off for employees to work their own land or to do periodic trade, or they make working on the owner's land integral to the factory or workshop 'contract'. A primitive form of occupational welfare is usually extended to this part of the labour force. Employers will give loans and also 'gifts' of petty cash for purposes such as medical expenditure, education and marriages. At one and the same time these acts parody state social protection and reveal how capital acts opportunistically to tie up labour it does not wish to lose. In stark contrast, the casual labour force is characterized by low and fluctuating pay, higher turnover and no security. While labour recruiters may be given annual bonuses and lent small sums of money, attempts are made to turn labour over so as to reduce its customary entitlement to annual gifts and to avoid protective obligations.

Male casual labour is occasionally unionized.[63] Yet the multiplicity of unions invites the political mediation of disputes, which are rarely resolved in favour of labour. The labour laws tend not to be enforced by unions but by the state. Factories Acts inspectors with huge territories to cover and few resources with which to enforce the law are more often than not found to be implicated with bosses in a nexus of corruption around the evasion of labour protection laws and the erosion of labour rights. Female casual labour is subjected to extremes of casualization, negligence and harassment and to unsafe and unsanitary working conditions, their wages often being reported by bosses as 'pocket money'. In such firms, work has for decades been subcontracted, often exported to rural sites to avoid inspection and to profit from cheap or unwaged family labour, from low rents and from the ease of evasion of any 'welfare' obligations and taxes. So capital uses informal practices and the idiom of social protection highly selectively so as to render the majority of the work-force insecure and a small minority less insecure. But the latter works in ambivalent ways which not only protect but also bind the beneficiaries. As a result the micropolitics of labour within a firm may be complex.

THE STATE AND LABOUR

India has two forms of state-mediated social protection. In the first, the state favours its own employees. 'Public employees are served best, or rather have ensured that they are best served', with respect to pensions, provident funds, sickness, maternity and unemployment benefit.[64] Twelve percent of the work-force is covered, overwhelmingly male. The state also gives persistent subsidies to the highly regulated 'market' for social insurance—covering at best 8% of (male) lives—and experiments endlessly (but with few successes) with ways and means of increasing the coverage of insurance. Granted this jungle, the idea that a welfare state or 'protective social security' is a luxury India cannot afford is contested by few. It then becomes possible to argue that the ramshackle and leaky raft of anti-poverty policies, targeted development schemes, employment guarantees and food security measures managed through the public distribution of grain (all of which have their own histories and politics) are the appropriate, 'promotive' forms of social security.[65] Certainly they are the unsystematic ways in which the state 'protects' labour. They are all that capital allows the state to achieve in this direction. Critics have retorted that rather than promote labour they subsidize it for capital.[66]

The second system of social security, set up in Tamil Nadu in 1989 and copied in New Delhi in 1995 (so that the legal framework exists for other states to implement[67]), is a major departure from this orthodoxy. Consisting of pensions for the aged, widows, agricultural labourers and physically handicapped people, survivor benefit, maternity assistance, marriage grants and accident relief (to those under a poverty line set by local states and in this case twice the national level), it amounts to 1.5% of state expenditure.[68] It is not a luxury. In the state where it was first implemented, old age and widows' pensions were most consistently claimed, with one evaluation showing that a third of those eligible were included after five years of operation. The pension is $2.50 per month plus one free meal a day and two sets of clothing a year. Many old people are found unsupported by their relatives, contrary to widespread assumptions. Local discretion proves kinder than the official eligibility guidelines which have proved harsh and restrictive. Even so the majority of those eligible are not covered, particularly women. Long delays and bribes also diminish this benefit. While the impact of this rough but unready safety net on the lives of claimants may be very significant, its all-India impact on the security of workers' lives is negligible.

The work of the Labour Ministry may also have a limited, or even backhanded, impact on workers. Take the labour laws.[69] Their loopholes are big enough for the proverbial bus to be driven through them. The Trades Union Act *allows* registration but does not require recognition of trade unions as agents of collective bargaining. While the Industrial Disputes Act curbs the rights of employers, their powerful tool—the lock-out—is hardly penalized and the state is empowered to conciliate through a judicial maze which makes workers dependent on highly qualified, legally knowledgeable representatives. Any union, however small, can intervene in labour disputes, thereby creating a field day for manipulation by employers.[70] The Minimum Wages, Contract Labour and Child Labour Acts declare entitlements which actually have to be struggled for by labour organizations. Further, without reforms to give access to the courts and make their decisions binding, these laws are toothless. Labour organizations asserting claims to entitlement are, moreover, often dealt with under criminal procedure. At best, all these laws have a normative role: to raise expectations and act as a rallying point for mobilization.[71] At worst the very laws supposedly protecting labour encourage capital to informalize it.

The state-in-action also reveals itself as profoundly ambivalent towards outright proletarianization. On the one hand it lends support to capital at labour's expense, all the way from the ring-fencing of unorganized labour to the love affair between the promoter families dominating big business and the nationalized banking institutions. Elsewhere there are mighty subsidies for property, however 'small scale', in the shape of cheap electricity, fertilizer, credit and food, all ineluctably resistant to blandishments from Washington. The first three can intensify the pace of differentiation, while cheap food slows it. The public distribution system of subsidized foodgrains (and up to 59 other essential commodities) is broad-based, broadly redistributivist and very hard to fine-tune.[72] In Kerala and West Bengal leftist parties have achieved land reforms and laws securing tenancies, thereby consolidating a decentralized base for petty accumulation. Throughout India, the gains won by capital in a 'shadow state', through a racketeering nexus of tax evasion and bribery, are larger and broader than the gains won in this same nexus by labour, in the form of a large army of petty livelihoods.[73] Yet on the other hand, the beneficiaries from land or tenancy reforms, from the distribution of house sites and from periodic amnesties on encroachment, are but drops in the ocean. State-directed commercial credit to enable landless people to join the propertied classes is deliberately denied them. The negligent enforcement of the social wage also weakens labour. The river of revenue from tax on liquor is at the expense of widespread domestic violence, pauperization and food scarcity in the households of drinkers. And the many nutrition and employment schemes, fuelled by the massive buffer stock of food-grains which the Government of India is obliged to replenish (as much for technical as political reasons), often do little more than subsidize (female) labour for capital. Only in those rather rare places where the wages on employment schemes exceed the ruling swathe of rates for agricultural labour may such schemes have an empowering knock-on effect on claims for wage increases. Further, if the public works created by them prove to be really useful public goods then the spatial and social mobility of workers—out of bondage and into towns and the non-farm economy—may be given a boost.[74]

LABOUR ORGANIZATION

By now it is evident why unorganized labour remains so weak *vis-à-vis* capital in India, and why the politics of class among Indian labour—especially unorganized labour—is so fettered. The possibility of resistance or protest at the work-place, let alone collective, class-based mobilization on a mass scale, is fraught with difficulties for informal-sector labour faced with fluidity and insecurity of work, migration and circulation of labour, localized and segmented labour markets with heterogeneity of employment practices, the extensive use of coercive contracts and debt-bondage, and the preponderance of social institutions (especially caste and gender) in structuring the labour market and determining the relations of capital and labour.

So, how does unorganized labour contest the power of capital? The ways in which labour seeks to reshape and contest the world envisaged by capital constitute a key element of work-place politics. At one end of the spectrum, 'everyday forms of resistance' prevail, encompassing non-cooperation with employers in periods of peak demand for labour, reneging on debt repayment, or simply escaping and leaving a job; at the other end, wage bargaining, protests and strikes.[75] Yet while instances of labour agitation are not hard to find, they are often exceptions to the general trend. Labour protests tend to remain localized, small-scale, and focused on immediate employers—reflecting the structural characteristics of the labour market and employment relations. The possibility of an enlargement of scope remains severely restricted. Moreover, with frequent changes in employment and employers, politics at the work-place often becomes irrelevant.

It is hardly surprising, then, that the political expression of much of Indian labour is to be found outside the context of work, in non-class modes and in the arena of democratic politics and social movements. The political mobilization of lower castes—those usually located at the lowest end of the labour market and landless workers—has already been mentioned. The labouring poor also forge solidarities in the locality and neighbourhood, albeit sporadically. Their experience of control or exploitation does not remain confined to the work-place. Labour discipline is also achieved through the branches of the state, notably the police, especially in urban areas, where the labouring poor are the most direct targets of police action and brutality. Increasing urban violence and the mobilization against the police of poor people in urban neighbourhoods reflect state control over labour's public spaces. The exploitation of labour also happens indirectly through the lack of urban housing, essential services, utilities and infrastructure. In this, the local and national states and the local propertied elites are all complicit. Not only is there no provision of public housing to speak of, but local councils also fail to raise taxes from the propertied to extend the provision of services. Capital has a conflict of interest. On the one hand, it is in the interest of employers to ensure housing for workers so as to reproduce the labour force. On the other, when labour is in excess supply, and indeed in order to reinforce its mobile and flexible character, local capital helps to prevent the creation of permanent habitats for labour by avoiding investment in housing directly and by evading taxation. The direct exploitation of labour at the work-place is thus not entirely separate from the indirect exploitation of labour through the lack of provision of essential infrastructure. Problems of housing and lack of urban services for workers have crucially shaped their politics, with violent clashes in urban neighbourhoods over space, territory and services, both among the poor themselves and between the poor and local propertied classes or agents of the local state.[76] While the shortage of housing and infrastructure is a predicament shared by all workers, the competition for these undermines class solidarity.

The 'struggle between classes' through formal unionization, while by no means a negligible element of Indian labour politics, still only involves a section of organized sector workers and a small fraction—4%—of the total labour force. It is fragmented. The All-India TUC was founded in 1920 and has been controlled since 1929 by the Communist Party of India; the INTUC was created by the ruling Congress Party in 1947 deliberately to challenge Communists and establish the role of government in the control of labour. The Hind Mazdoor Sabha was formed by socialists in 1948, splitting in 1964. The Bharatiya Mazdoor Sangh (BMS) was created in 1955 by the right-wing Hindu nationalist Rashtriya Swayamsevak Sangh (RSS) to suppress class conflict; and the Centre of Indian Trades Unions (CITU) by the Marxist Communist Party in 1970 after the Communist parties split. Other union movements have been created by regional political parties, pioneered by the Tamil Dravida Munnetra Kazhagam, when it came to power in 1967 in the (then) Madras State. As parties have split, so have their unions. Parties influence unions rather than vice versa. Others have been formed in the corporate and public sectors and by individual charismatic leaders. There is an increasing tendency for unions to be based on regional, communal or caste lines. Labour unions, with some notable exceptions, have historically concentrated on advancing the interests of those whom they represent in organized industry, on whom the law confers the right to engage in industrial action, and have ignored unorganized workers without this right.[77] Attempts to include unorganized workers in their constituency have been perceived by unions to pose a danger to the meagre benefits that they have succeeded in wresting for their own members. The existing form of the labour movement thus remains irrelevant to the large majority of Indian workers. Trade unions have even failed to protect the more vulnerable sections of unionized labour, such as women or lower castes, when they have come under threat of retrenchment or have been unable to secure the benefits to which they are legally entitled.

The union movement has also suffered from many external pressures. The Indian state, even while it instituted a panoply of laws to regulate the relations between capital and labour, has in practice upheld the interests of capital. Indeed, it can be argued that the elaboration of a regulatory regime for labour by the nascent independent state, committed to industrialization and the nurture of private capital, was motivated by the need to relieve capital from the pressure of organized labour and to contain labour militancy within the straitjacket of legal and bureaucratic negotiations. Indian labour unions emerged under the umbrella of various competing political parties, which has fragmented the trade union movement and fostered rivalry among trade unions.[78] Labour unions affiliated to political parties are often torn between the need to further party political agendas and the responsibility to advance the interests of labour. When unions linked with political parties have failed to uphold these interests, workers have bypassed such unions and rallied around charismatic leaders or organizations on caste, regional or sectarian lines. Alternatively, they have formed semi-independent unions based in individual industrial units. The latter have been more consistent in representing labour and have been in the vanguard of militant agitations.[79] They have also borne the brunt of the onslaught by management, often with the connivance of the state. The most radical employees' unions, including those affiliated to Communist parties, have been marginalized by the state and debarred by bureaucratic fiat from representing workers in industrial disputes. Political parties given to moderation have also sponsored rival unions to undermine the influence of militant labour organizations and not infrequently acted in concert with employers.[80]

A trade union movement beset with internal difficulties, external constraints and fragmentation has more recently, since the 1980s, come under a major onslaught from capital and faced a new ruthlessness on the part of managers.[81] Trade unions in the 1970s and early-80s were able to launch major strike actions, notably in Bombay, in the context of changing patterns of labour recruitment. The consequence was a major managerial offensive, both a frontal assault and a war of attrition, against employees' unions in particular. Companies were determined to secure flexibility and impose control over pay and over work schedules and work loads, which set the terms of collective bargaining. In a drive to beat the unions into submission, lock-outs of factories were declared by employers following strikes, thus severely trying the staying-power of labour. Rival unions, acting in concert with employers, were deployed to fracture workers' solidarity. Where unions did succeed in forcing settlements in favour of workers, companies showed no compunction in violating them, backed with lock-outs to prevent further agitation. Employers also had recourse to Voluntary Retirement Schemes, refused to fill vacant jobs, and unilaterally changed the nature of employment contracts, including the conversion of bargainable grades into non-bargainable grades, not only to deny workers the rights of organized sector employees, but also to redefine them as *not* being 'workers' under the Industrial Disputes Act. In addition, production units were relocated to geographically dispersed sites, and out-sourcing or subcontracting became increasingly commonplace for large industries or factories. In this way, the organized sector itself came under threat with an expansion in the ranks of unprotected labour which severely undercut the social constituency of the trade-union movement.

In Mumbai, for instance, the impact of voluntary retirement schemes has to be set in the context of a co-ordinated attack which involved interlocking strategies, all centred on the progressive and systematic erosion of the bargaining unit. The ability of companies to sub-contract was the single most powerful weapon in this arsenal of strategies. It is clear that management had finally decided to de-unionize labour and to press for de-unionization even at the cost of large-scale destruction of jobs and closure of factories. Liberalization has added considerable impetus to the employers' offensive, but is clearly not the cause of it. In this current climate, the creation of a vast pool of unprotected labour is viewed to be integral to the (largely imaginary) pursuit of competitive advantage, even though this is in complete violation of the social and legal foundations of modern democracy.

EMANCIPATING FUTURES?

We envisage at least three vectors as being crucial to the development of a politics of emancipation. First, the union movement urgently needs renewal so as to encourage the rise of a pro-active, co-ordinated and self-governing trade unionism, which invests substantially more resources in training and strives to recover collective bargaining initiatives through inroads into company decision-making. The remarkable examples of some Bombay-based employees' unions such as the Hindustan Lever Employees' Union, the Philips Employees' Union and the Kamani Employees' Union need noting in this respect.[82] Renovation means the formulation of wider political and social perspectives, from issues relating to control over employee pensions, or work-place exposure to toxic substances and the threat of hazardous production to local communities,[83] to active opposition to the repeated and ubiquitous violations of human rights and labour law that pervade India. Yet, these initiatives are more likely to emerge from the local independent employees unions. The central trade union leaderships have even sometimes endorsed positions that are diametrically opposed to them, e.g., their willingness to buy into 'national sovereignty' arguments, reinforcing sovereign nation-state control over domestic jurisdictions such as child labour, political repression and labour standards.[84] The seeds of such a renovated unionism lie both in the past lessons and experiences of movements like the employees' unions, and in the growth of new work-forces in productive sectors that have sprung up since the nineties.

The second vector of change must be a set of clear public policy choices which expand and give teeth to the legal rights available to workers regardless of gender. A charter of rights would need the broadest possible remit, to cover every sector of a complex and segmented labour market where, through deliberate lack of regulation, the bulk of the labour force is reduced, *de facto*, to a condition of near-servitude; while, at the opposite end, elite or strategic groups of salaried personnel are deprived of bargaining rights by arbitrary legal devices which construe 'bargainable labour' in ways at complete variance with international best practice or ILO Conventions.[85] Such a charter would mean a political attempt to alter the background legal rules which affect the distribution of power and advantage in labour markets and society as a whole.[86]

Much of the thrust of economic liberalization in India in the nineties has been an application precisely of such normative choices, but one based on the assumption that freeing markets from regulation necessarily means greater freedom for business *from* organized labour. In fact, throughout the nineties, de-regulation has gone hand in hand with re-regulation, since no market exists in a regulatory vacuum and rules are essential to the construction of efficient and orderly markets. Labour is the remarkable exception to this process. But this politics of liberalization is simply a construction of capital and the state's economic agenda, not an inevitable, much less absolute, expression of some 'essence' of liberal economic reforms. The second needed vector is thus a progressive revamping of corporate and labour laws to give substantial bargaining rights to the unorganized sector, treating all employees on a par, without the conscious legal discrimination which currently holds the bulk of the labour force in a sort of thraldom; and to give to organized labour corporate governance rights, so that employees and unions can recover some control over the management decisions which are currently decimating their ranks. Enabling legislation and mechanisms to translate law into claim and claim into enforcement (for these and related laws including social and food security, child labour, equal opportunities, health and safety, etc.) is crucial to a democratic renewal of society in India.

However, while the first two vectors lack significant social and political forces to drive them, the third, that of democratic politics, has potential to give the poor some clout. If poor people emerge as significant political constituencies of the large number of political parties that now compete for power in India, their needs and interests, including legal protection for labour and social security measures, which are already insinuated into the policy agendas of the constituent states, might heave themselves upwards. After all, despite the retrenchment of public expenditure (in relative if not absolute terms), no state government has had the courage to ignore the imperatives of electoral politics and to mess very much with the food subsidies for the poor. Quite the reverse. When the central government aspires to reduce foodgrains subsidies, state governments have lately been allowed to get themselves severely indebted to protect this longstanding, leaky but redistributivist measure to guarantee food and contain open market prices for this most basic of wage goods.

While there is no evidence yet for any rebalancing of public policy in favour of the poor or of labour, there is overwhelming evidence of increasing democratic electoral participation by lower castes and the poor. This has been hailed as the 'participatory upsurge of the oppressed'[87] and characterized as the 'plebianization of public culture'.[88] Electoral turnouts in India have steadily increased since independence, but far more significantly, the composition of those who vote has registered a sea change. While in the years after independence the more affluent, the educated, the upper castes and urban residents formed the majority of voters, in the 1990s, comparatively, the lower castes, the illiterate, rural people and those with low incomes have started to vote in far larger numbers.[89] The reasons for the increasing democratic engagement of the poor are yet to be explained and it is far from clear that concerns about labour relations have a bearing on electoral participation. Yet the acceleration of democratic participation suggests that poor people have an increasing urgency to shape the contours of wider democratic politics and to engage with state power and public policy. Whether this might also have any impact on the working and living conditions of Indian labour is an imponderable.

The question of labour, however, is not at all incidental to current democratic struggles in India. For the 'democratic upsurge' has elicited from the propertied, upper- or middle-classes, and upper castes a 'conservative revolution',[90] the most dominant institutional expression of which is the Hindu nationalist political party—the Bharatiya Janata Party. Psephological analysis has conclusively confirmed that the poor and lower-castes rarely support the BJP, whose core constituency consists of upper- and middle-classes and castes. Sociological studies have indicated the strong participation of commercial communities and rural and urban capitalist classes in the activities of the BJP and its affiliate organizations. They are drawn to the party because it pledges its commitment to the increasingly expansionist ambitions of Indian capital and because it espouses ideologies of caste and patriarchal subordination as well as a strong, militarized state, one capable of enforcing political stability, public order and discipline. In quest of a world safe for capital where the democratic political mobilization of the poor can be tamed, the propertied now look to the BJP. Arguably, capital's fear of labour and its need to further subordinate labour, and make it more flexible and even less politically organized, consolidates its support for the BJP. Not only did the assault on unions coincide with the rise of the BJP and its affiliate political organizations, there is also ample direct evidence that militant, Hindu-chauvinistic, right-wing organizations, like the Shiv Sena in Bombay, were instrumental in undermining labour militancy and strikes in the 1980s, with their own trade unions acting in cahoots with employers to emasculate militant employers' unions. The politics of the Hindu Right can justly be interpreted in terms of a wider struggle between capital and labour in India, being played out in the arena of democratic politics.

Both employers and government authorities are currently working on the short-sighted assumption that India's comparative advantage lies in the undisputedly low cost of labour. But large reserves of cheap labour cannot constitute the foundations of a modern, globally competitive economy. Not only does such a strategy entail the suppression of political and trade union rights for the majority of wage-earners, and the deliberate fragmentation of the labour force, but also it presumes a poorly educated, semi-literate and badly nourished mass of labourers who are constantly vulnerable to exploitation—hardly one that can sustain mass demand for the goods and services produced by a modern economy integrated into the global system. At a time when Indian employers are pressing for wholesale deregulation of the labour market, in the pursuit of short-term profitability, it is clearly in the long-term interest of the economy to have a labour force with the requisite levels of training and job security. This presupposes an expansion of the laws protecting and regulating labour together with large-scale public investment in what is known in development circles as 'human capital' (health, education, social and food security) and infrastructure (housing, sanitation, electricity and water), as well as a concerted political drive to create the social and legal conditions under which workers feel free to organize without fear of reprisal or caste atrocities.

The point, of course, is not that the state is likely to undertake any such programme of its own accord, but that the 'making' of a modern working class has to be the core of any vision that struggles to modernize social and political conditions in the country, and the central interest of progressive political forces. Moreover, a genuinely democratic vision of the Indian polity would have to be a politics of totalization, given the embeddedness of labour in the whole matrix of institutions which sustains the numerous trajectories of accumulation in the country, from caste, communal and gender oppression to the various forms of authoritarianism which exclude workers from citizenship and citizens from democracy. It would no longer be possible for a democratic politics in India to replicate the atomized and fragmented forms of reasoning and imagination which counterpose politics to economics, trade unionism to political parties, or democracy to socialism.

NOTES

We are very grateful to Jairus Banaji and Rohini Hensman without whose helpful advice, critical response and active contributions, particularly to the final section, this essay would never have been written; to Gerry and Janine Rodgers who supplied useful literature and to Danny Sriskandarajah who gathered statistical information.

1. Sharit Bhowmik, 'The Labour Movement in India: Present Problems and Future Perspectives', *The Indian Journal of Social Work*, vol. 59, no. 1, 1998, pp. 147–66.
2. Agriculture is included, even though land is registered, because of the small and fluctuating size of labour forces on the vast bulk of individual holdings.
3. One recent study of corporate capital put the proportion of unorganized labour in different corporations at between 40% and 85%. S. Davala (ed.), *Employment and Unionization in Indian Industry*, Delhi, Friedrich Ebert Stiftung, 1992, quoted in Bhowmik, 'The Labour Movement'.
4. Nandini Gooptu, *The Urban Poor and the Politics of Class, Community and Nation: Uttar Pradesh between the Two World Wars*, Cambridge, Cambridge University Press, forthcoming; Christopher Baker, *An Indian Rural Economy, 1880–1955: The Tamilnad Countryside*, New Delhi, Oxford University Press, 1984; Barbara Harriss-White, *A Political Economy of Agricultural Markets in South India; Masters of the Countryside*, New Delhi, Sage, 1996.
5. Kiran Desai, 'Secondary Labour Market in India—a Case Study of Workers in Small Scale Industrial Units in Gujarat' in Maya Shah (ed.), *Labour Market Segmentation in India*, Mumbai, Himalaya, 1999, pp. 13–28.
6. Poverty varies according to harvests and foodgrains prices. Two-thirds of those said to be living on under $1 a day in the world today are in South Asia. Ninety percent of India's poor live in the poverty belt covering east and central India, inland Maharashtra and eastern Madhya Pradesh, a diverse and scarcely urbanized region. The official Indian poverty line is set and revised at a rural income allowing for the consumption of 2,200 calories per day together with 20% for shelter, clothing and medicine. By this account poverty was at its minimum (34%) in 1989. The intransigent persistence of poverty masks a massive increase in inequality. Sheila Bhalla, 'Liberalization, Rural Labour Markets and the Mobilization of Farm Workers: the Haryana Story in an All-India Context', *Journal of Peasant Studies*, vol. 26, nos. 2/3, 1999, p. 30.

7.   Pace Bhowmik, 'The Labour Movement', p. 149.
8.   S. Guhan and K. Nagaraj, 'Adjustment, employment and equity in India', *International Labour Office*, Employment Programme Paper, no. 4,Geneva, 1995. Organized employment for women grew at three times that for men, fastest in the urban tertiary sector. See Nisha Srivastava, 'Striving for a Toehold: Women in the Organised Sector', in T. S. Papola and Alakh Sharma, *Gender and Employment in India*, New Delhi, Vikas, 1999, pp. 181–205.
9.   Ajit Ghose, 'Current Issues of Employment Policy in India', *Economic and Political Weekly*, vol. XXXIV, no. 36, 4 Sep, 1999, pp. 2592–2608; Wendy Olsen, *The Limits to Conditionality*, Oxford, Worldview, forthcoming; Bhalla, 'Liberalization', pp. 36–9.
10. World Bank, *India: Poverty, Employment and Social Services*, Washington, World Bank, 1989.
11. Bhalla, 'Liberalization', p. 63.
12. Sunil Mani, 'A Survey of Deregulation in Indian Industry', in Mitsuhiro Kagami and Masatsugu Tsuji (eds.), *Privatization, Deregulation and Economic Efficiency*, Cheltenham, Edward Elgar, 2000; Raphie Kaplinsky, 'Is Globalization all it is cracked up to be?', *Bulletin of the Institute of Development Studies*, vol. 30, no. 4, 1999, pp. 106–15.
13. Terence Byres, 'The new technology, class formation and class action in the Indian countryside', *Journal of Peasant Studies*, vol. 8, no. 4, 1981. The distribution of employment between sectors of the economy has hardly changed in the last two decades.
14. Jan Breman, *Footloose Labour: Working in India's Informal Economy*, Cambridge, Cambridge University Press, 1996, p. 12.
15. Ajit Ghose, 'Current Issues'.
16. Sheila Bhalla, 'Liberalization'.
17. Maya Shah (ed.), *Labour Market Segmentation*.
18. In 1991 a mere 4% of the female work-force was in the organized sector. Women were 12% of the organized work-force but 33% of the unorganized work-force, and that is likely to be a gross underestimate. Scheduled caste workers are heavily concentrated in the unorganized work-force. Sheila Bhalla, 'Liberalization'.
19   See Geert de Neve, 'Asking for and giving *baki*: neo-bondage, or the interplay of bondage and resistance in the Tamil Nadu power-loom industry', in Jonathan Parry, Jan Breman and Karin Kapadia (eds.), *The Worlds of Indian Industrial Labour*, New Delhi, Sage, 1999, pp. 379–406; Dilip Simeon, 'Work and Resistance in the Jharia Coalfield', pp. 43–76 in the same book; Chitra Joshi, 'The Formation of Work Culture: Industrial Labour in a North Indian City, 1890s–1940s', *Purusartha*, no. 14, 1992, pp. 155–72; and Rajnarayan Chandavarkar, *Imperial Power and Popular Politics: Class Resistance and the State in India, c.1850 –1950*, Cambridge, Cambridge University Press, 1998, pp. 66–68.
20. Ben Rogaly, 'Agricultural Growth and the Structure of "Casual" Labour-hiring in Rural West Bengal', *Journal of Peasant Studies*, vol. 23, no. 4, 1996, pp. 141–166.
21. See Jean Dreze and Naresh Sharma, 'Palanpur: population, society, economy', in Peter Lanjouw and Nicholas Stern (eds.), *Economic Development in Palanpur over Five Decades*, Oxford, Clarendon, 1998, pp. 66–76.
22. This cannot be a literal mapping, for the work on India's regions of accumulation has not yet been done. It is a daunting task because India's regions are an amalgam

of agro-ecological, agro-structural and politico-administrative. There are huge regional variations in the composition of capital which affect options for labour. While in the so-called *Bimaru* states (after the Hindi for 'sick') less than 20% of rural jobs are not in agriculture, 54% are not in agriculture in the rural non-farm sector in Kerala and 30% in West Bengal. Yet the latter relatively advanced states—and those with active Communist parties—have high levels of unemployment, while the reverse applies to Bimaru states. It is the persistence of petty production and artisanal work in poor states together with the decline of petty production as a safety net coupled with the inability of the economy to absorb labour at the wages offered, which explains this paradox. Other states such as Maharashtra have developed with relatively low levels of unemployment, relatively tight labour 'markets' and an employment guarantee scheme run by the state. See K. Nagaraj, 'Labour Market Characteristics and Employment Generation Programmes in India', in Barbara Harriss-White and S. Subramanian (eds.), *Illfare in India: Essays on India's Social Sector in Honour of S. Guhan*, New Delhi, Oxford University Press, 1999, pp. 77–80; and Jairus Banaji's review of Daniel Thorner's *Atlas of the Agrarian Regions of India*: 'Metamorphoses of Agrarian Capitalism', *Economic and Political Weekly,* vol. XXXIV, 2 Oct., 1999, pp. 2850–58.

23. Ben Rogaly et al., 'Seasonal Migration, Welfare Regimes and Adverse Incorporation: A Case Study from East India', paper for the Global Social Policy Regional Workshop, DfID, Koitta, Bangladesh, March, 2000, p. 2.

24. Gerry Rodgers and Janine Rodgers, 'Semi-feudalism meets the market: A report from Purnia', *Economic and Political Weekly,* forthcoming. Most rural migrants, especially women, remain within the same district.

25. Though *within* the agricultural sector it is converging, see Jeemol Unni, 'Women Workers in Agriculture: Some recent Trends', in Papola and Sharma, *Gender and Employment*, pp. 99–121.

26. For linear and network territoriality, see Mattison Mines, *The Warrior Merchants*: *Textiles, Trade and Territory in South India*, Cambridge, Cambridge University Press, 1984. Even in the organized sector 'sheer physical concentration or dispersal affects the capacity of workers to sustain strikes and the aggressiveness of employers': Jairus Banaji and Rohini Hensman, 'Outline of an Industrial Relations Theory of Industrial Conflict', *Economic and Political Weekly,* vol. XXV, no. 34, 25 August 1990, p. 135–6.

27. Perquisites include clothing, loans of cash, help towards the school fees of children, medicines and medical fees, see Harriss-White, *A Political Economy*, p. 255.

28. Breman, *Footloose Labour*, pp. 248–54. The *Labour File,* vol. 5, no. 12 noted four large co-ordinated protests against the state and landlords in 1999 (pp. 26–28).

29. Breman, *Footloose Labour*, pp. 255–56.

30. See the debates summarized in Jan Breman, 'The study of industrial labour in post-colonial India—the informal sector: a concluding review', in Parry et al., *The Worlds*, pp. 407–432.

31. Jens Lerche, 'Politics of the Poor: Agricultural Labourers and Political Transformations in Uttar Pradesh', *Journal of Peasant Studies,* vol. 26, no. 2/3, 1999, pp. 182–241; in the important special issue edited by Karin Kapadia and Jens Lerche, *Rural Labour Relations in India*.

32. David Mosse, 'The symbolic making of a common property resource: History,

ecology and locality in a tank-irrigated landscape in south India', *Development and Change*, vol. 28, no. 3, 1997, pp. 467–504; S. Janakarajan, 'Village Resurveys: Issues and Results', in Jan Breman, Peter Kloos and Ashwani Saith (eds.), *The Village in Asia Revisited*, Delhi, Oxford University Press, 1997, pp. 413–425.

33.   Lucia Da Corta and Devaluri Venkateshwarlu, 'Unfree Relations and the Feminization of Agricultural Labour in Andhra Pradesh, 1970–95', *Journal of Peasant Studies*, vol. 26, no. 2/3, 1999, pp. 71–139.

34.   Breman, *Footloose Labour*, p. 169.

35.   Workers have attempted to turn debt relations to their advantage. In the power loom industry in Kumarapalayam town in Tamil Nadu, for example, employers debt-bonded labourers when they were in scarce supply but soon found that workers proceeded to dictate terms of employment, realizing that employers were not in a position to dismiss them while the latter still owed money to the former (Geert de Neve, '*Baki*').

36.   Breman, 'Industrial labour', pp. 423–5; Breman, *Footloose Labour*, pp. 237–9.

37.   When they enter local agribusiness, their pre-harvest loans can be interlocked with post-harvest sales, thereby indirectly controlling the markets which shape the production of their creditors.

38.   P. K. Jha, *Agricultural Labour in India*, New Delhi, Vikas, 1997; Sheila Bhalla, 'New Relations of Production in Haryana Agriculture', *Economic and Political Weekly*, vol. 1, no. 13, 27 March, 1976 and 1999, 'Liberalization'.

39.   Some 60–80% in one study of northern Tamil Nadu.

40.   See Jha, Table 3. On and off-farm work is not directly substitutable. Either work on the small plot owned comes first and so wage-work is a residual, irrespective of the pay, or off-farm activity determines the crop choice and labour inputs on a small farm and cultivation is the residual; Krishna Bharadwaj, 'A View on Commercialization in Indian Agriculture and the Development of Capitalism', *Journal of Peasant Studies*, vol. 12, no. 1, 1985, pp. 7–25.

41.   Ajay Varma, Poonam Chauhan and M. M. Rehman, *Indian Labour: A select statistical profile*, Noida, Giri National Labour Institute, 1997.

42.   Ravi Srivastava, 'Rural Labour in Uttar Pradesh: Emerging features of subsistence, contradiction and resistance', *Journal of Peasant Studies*, vol. 26, no. 2/3 1999, pp. 263–315; Jens Lerche, 'Politics of the poor'.

43.   Alice Clark (ed.), *Gender and Political Economy: Explorations of South Asian Systems*, New Delhi, Oxford University Press, 1993; Barbara Harriss-White, 'Gender, Capital and Co-operative Control' (Cambridge Commonwealth Lectures, ch. 4), *Working Paper Series*, http://www.qeh.ox.ac.uk, 2000.

44.   T. S. Papola and Alakh Sharma, 'Introduction', in Papola and Sharma (eds.), *Gender and Employment*, pp. 1–23; da Corta and Venkateswarlu, 'Unfree relations'.

45.   The average daily wage for rural women is 47% of the official nutritional poverty line. For urban women it is 44%. For men it is 66% and 79%, respectively; see Ghose, 'Current Issues'.

46.   Ghose, 'Current Issues'; the data are the latest for 1994. The logic of wage-work may differ according to gender, with women having a target income still prepared to work until their marginal productivity approaches zero (and therefore to accept very low wages) while men strenuously resist attempts to lower wages below a 'reservation'. The question is whether women are low-paid because forced into tasks of low productivity consistent with their prior obligations (which are the

result of patriarchal power relations within households), *or*, because jobs bear social meanings, low-status jobs pull low-status people and women are ascribed with low status as people, *or* because women's wage work is also at the mercy of patriarchal discrimination on the'market'. The jury is still out. The facts that women can be paid less than men where tasks are directly comparable, that women are being forced into attached contracts and that employers regularly refer to women's wages as 'pocket money' need setting against the successful struggle for gender parity in minimum wages in parts of the rice bowl of West Bengal and in Kerala.

47. Sudha Deshpande, 'Gender-based Discrimination in Segmented Labour Markets in India', in Shah, *Labour Market Segmentation,* pp. 118–129; Ramesh Iyer, 'Labour Market Segmentation and Women's Employment and Earning Differentials in India', in Shah, *Labour Market Segmentation,* pp. 130–151.

48. Male consumption has been shown in a number of studies not only to be biased towards the provision of investment goods but also towards male adult goods: liquor and narcotics. Jayati Ghosh, 'Macro-economic Trends and Female Employment', in Papola and Sharma, *Gender and Employment,* pp. 318–350.

49. Ghose, 'Current Issues'; Varma et al., 'Indian Labour'; da Corta and Vankateshwarlu, 'Unfree Relations'. In urban areas, while men are casualized, the proportion of women workers on regular wages has actually increased, though there is little opportunity for upward mobility and regular work is now threatened again by 'flexibilization'. See Pravin Visaria, 'Level and Pattern of Female Employment, 1911–94' and Amitabh Kundu, 'Trends and Patterns of Female Employment', both in Papola and Shah, *Gender and Employment* , pp. 23–51 and 52–71.

50. Kalpana Wilson, 'Patterns of Accumulation and Struggles of Rural Labour: Some aspects of agrarian change in central Bihar', *Journal of Peasant Studies,* vol. 26, no. 2/3, 1999, pp. 316–355; Karin Kapadia and Jens Lerche, 'Introduction', *Journal of Peasant Studies,* vol. 26, no. 2/3, 1999, pp. 1–9.

51. Education is still not mandatory and in the only state where it was made mandatory (Tamil Nadu in 1995) it has not been implemented. The law on Child Labour is the Child Labour (Prohibition and Regulation) Act of 1986. See Vasudha Dhagamwar, 'The Disadvantaged and the law', in Barbara Harriss-White, S. Guhan and Robert Cassen (eds.), *Poverty in India: Research and Policy,* New Delhi, Oxford University Press, 1992, pp. 433–448.

52. C. P. Chandrasekhar, 'The Economic Consequences of the Abolition of Child Labour: An Indian Case Study', *Journal of Peasant Studies,* 24, 3, 1997, pp. 137–179.

53. The carpet industry in Uttar Pradesh and Jammu and Kashmir is another example. It is known that many of the children here are virtual slaves, purchased with lump sum payments to parents by agents for carpet manufacturers. Most of these children come from the scheduled caste and tribes, agricultural labouring families in Bihar, subject to fierce oppression from private armies of upper-caste landowners.

54. Yet secondary education produces a peculiar paradox for workers because it behaves as a luxury good, fitting young educated people, especially women, *not* to enter the labour market See Ghose, 'Current Issues'.

55. John Harriss, 'Vulnerable workers in the Indian urban labour market', in Gerry Rodgers (ed.), *Urban Poverty and the Labour Market,* Geneva, International Labour Office, 1989.

56. 'Scheduled' in the constitution to receive positive discrimination. This is a term

for untouchables, Gandhi's *harijans* ('children of god') and now self termed 'dalits' (the oppressed). For analyses of work-force data and data on the many dimensions through which scheduled caste and tribal people are still viciously discriminated against, see K. Nagaraj, 'Labour Market Characteristics', p. 84; D. Jayaraj and S. Subramanian, 'Poverty and Discrimination: Measurement and Evidence from rural India', in Harriss-White and Subramanian, *Illfare in India*, pp. 196–226; Sarah Ahmed, 'Occupational Segregation and Caste-based Discrimination in India' in Maya Shah, *Labour Market Segmentation*, pp. 67–92.

57. Oliver Mendelsohn and Marika Vicziany, *The Untouchables: Subordination, Poverty and the State in Modern India,* Cambridge, Cambridge University Press, 1998, ch. 4.

58. Elisabetta Basile and Barbara Harriss-White, 'The Politics of Accumulation in Small Town India', *Bulletin of the Institute of Development Studies,* vol. 30, no. 4, 1999, pp. 31–9.

59. Saurashtra Patels are owners, commission agents and traders, and they employ labour from the same caste. In Tiruppur a significant part of the entire cluster, owners and workers, are Vellalar Gounders.

60. For the Surat case see Miranda Engelshoven, 'Diamonds and Patels: A report on the diamond industry of Surat', in Parry et al. (eds.), *The Worlds,* pp. 353–378. For Tiruppur, see Sharad Chari, 'The Agrarian Question comes to Town', Ph.D. Thesis, UC Berkeley, 2000 and see also Philippe Cadene and Mark Holmstrom (eds.), *Decentralized Production in India: Industrial Districts, Flexible Specialization and Employment,* New Delhi, Sage,1998.

61. Gail Omvedt, *Reinventing Revolution: New Social Movements and the Socialist Tradition in India,* New York, M. E. Sharpe, 1993, pp. 58–61. Clean castes are those not ritually polluted.

62. Karin Kapadia, 'The Profitability of Bonded Labour: the Gem Cutting Industry in Rural South India', *Journal of Peasant Studies,* vol. 22, no. 3, 1995, pp. 446–83.

63. Workers in the unorganized sector are under 1% of all members of trade unions.

64. S. Guhan, 'Social Security in India: Looking one step ahead', in Harriss et al. (eds.), *Poverty in India* pp. 282–300.

65. Etisham Ahmed, Jean Dreze, John Hill and Amartya Sen, *Social Security in Developing Countries,* Oxford, Clarendon, 1991.

66. Wendy Olsen, *The Limits to Conditionality.*

67. This was in a highly opportunistic last-ditch attempt by the then ruling Congress Party to drum up pre-electoral support.

68. This amounts to 0.4% of state domestic product. See Barbara Harriss-White, 'State, Market, Collective and Household in India's Social Sector' in Harriss-White and Subramanian (eds.), *Illfare in India,* p. 316.

69. The 1926 Trades Union Act; the 1947 Industrial Disputes Act; the 1948 Factories Act and Employers' State Insurance Act; the 1961 Maternity Benefits Act; the 1965 Payments of Bonus Act; the 1972 Employees' Provident Fund and Miscellaneous Provision Act and the Payment of Gratuity Act; not to mention those affecting the unorganized sector: the 1970 Contract Labour (Regulation and Abolition Act) and last and least the 1986 Child Labour (Protection and Regulation) Act; see Bhowmik, 'The Labour Movement'.

70. Bhowmik, 'The Labour Movement'.

71. Dhagamwar, 'The Law and the Disadvantaged'.

72. Jos Mooij, *Food Policy and the Indian State: The Public Distribution System in South*

India, New Delhi, Oxford University Press.

73. See Mooij, *Food Policy* for the PDS; Ron Herring, *Land to the Tiller: the Political economy of Agrarian reform in South Asia,* New Haven, Yale University Press for land reforms and Barbara Harriss-White, 'The Local State and the Informal Economy' (Cambridge Commonwealth lectures, ch. 6), *Working Paper Series* http://www.qeh.ox.ac.uk, 2000 for the state.

74. Srivastava, 'Rural Labour in UP'; da Corta and Venkateshwarlu, 'Unfree Relations'.

75. Breman, *Footloose Labour,* ch. 8; Gail Omvedt, *Reinventing Revolution.* A case in point is the unionization of informal-sector women workers through SEWA discussed by Rohini Hensman elsewhere in this volume.

76. Cadene and Holmstrom, *Decentralized Production.*

77. Bhowmik, 'Labour Movement', pp. 158–9.

78. Bhowmik, 'Labour Movement', p. 153, pp. 160–62 and International Labour Office, *World Labour Report,* Geneva, 1992.

79. These paragraphs draw heavily on Jairus Banaji and Rohini Hensman, *Beyond Multinationalism: Management Policy and Bargaining Relations in International Companies,* New Delhi, Sage, 1990.

80. Bhowmik, 'Labour Movement'. However, when it comes to *strikes* there is evidence that it is the history and experience of bargaining at the plant level which explains industrial conflict. See Banaji and Hensman, 'Outline'.

81. See Banaji and Hensman, 'Outline' and Jairus Banaji and Rohini Hensman, 'A short history of the employees unions in Bombay, 1947–1991', paper presented to the First Annual Conference of the Association of Indian Labour Historians, 16–18 March, 1998, New Delhi.

82. Banaji and Hensman find that multinational managements integrate finance and technology but deliberately isolate labour on its various sites. However, as a result, *some* Indian labour has more power in collective bargaining than either the work-forces of national capital or those in the HQs of MNCs. See Banaji and Hensman, *Beyond Multinationalism.*

83. Or their collective opposition to the country accepting the WHO Framework Convention on Tobacco Control. See Tara Jones, *Corporate Killing: Bhopals Will Happen,* London 1988.

84. See 'Tobacco and TUs: wrong end of stick', *Economic and Political Weekly,* XXXV, no. 16, 15 April 2000, p. 1329.

85. E.g., the ability of scientific and technical personnel to join unions (in the UK, for example), or the various ILO conventions which secure such rights for higher grades of employees; see also ILO, *Decent Work,* Geneva, 1999.

86. Cf. Katherine Van Wezel Stone, 'Labour markets, employment contracts, and corporate change', in J. McCahery, S. Picciotto and C. Scott (eds.), *Corporate Control and Accountability: Changing Structures and the Dynamics of Regulation,* Oxford, Oxford University Press, 1993.

87. CSDS Team, in *Frontline,* 26 Nov., 1999.

88. Thomas Blom Hansen, *The Saffron Wave: Democracy and Hindu Nationalism in Modern India,* Princeton, Princeton University Press, 1999.

89. On changing voting patterns, see Yogendra Yadav, 'Understanding the Second Democratic Upsurge: trends of Bahujan participation in electoral politics in the 1990s', in Francine Frankel, Z. Hasan, R. Bhargava and B. Arora (eds.),

Transforming India: Social and Political Dynamics of Democracy, New Delhi, Oxford University Press, 2000; Yogendra Yadav, 'India's Third Electoral System, 1989–99', *Economic and Political Weekly,* vol. XXXIV, nos. 34–35, Aug. 21–27, Aug. 28–Sep. 3, 1999; J. Alam, 'What is happening inside India's democracy', *Economic and Political* Weekly, vol. XXXIV, no. 37, 11–17 September, 1999.

90. Hansen, *Saffron Wave.*

THE SOUTHERN AFRICAN WORKING CLASS: PRODUCTION, REPRODUCTION AND POLITICS

Patrick Bond, Darlene Miller and Greg Ruiters

Southern Africa is probably the world's most extreme site of uneven capitalist development.[1] Inequality within and between the region's countries is severe, with race and gender domination largely undisturbed by the post-colonial experience, with the environment taking enormous strain, and with South Africa—and its 40 million of the region's 102 million citizens—responsible for $130 billion of Southern Africa's $160 billion in 1998 output. Yet, while it is logical to anticipate an uneven, fragmented evolution of working-class power and political strategy, given the area's different modes of class struggle, levels of consciousness, organizational capacity, militancy, and relations with political parties and other social forces, developments in one country do act as major reference points for others. Southern Africa's rich radical traditions—including once-avowed 'Marxist-Leninist' governments in Mozambique, Zimbabwe and Angola, and mass-movements and powerful unions—owe much to revolutionary socialism and nationalism, yet this never gave rise to an explicit regional class project.

Drawing upon a legacy of regional class formation that goes back to the nineteenth century, can a coherent, cross-border vision emerge to counteract the unevenness? Will 'globalization' provide this opportunity, given the 1999 upsurge in international working-class consciousness in reaction to the multinational corporate agenda, and a new round of parasitic South African corporate investment in the region? Or will fragmentation prevail, as already reflected in a late 1990s upsurge in South African working-class xenophobia?

Certain aspects of working-class experience are, of course, regionally universal or at least comparable, in part reflecting the importance and homogenizing effect of migrant labour. The counterpart of the current regeneration of urban–rural linkages caused by the desperation of many unemployed workers—including more than a million laid off during the 1990s—is the rural–urban drift to the region's rapidly-growing urban slums. Also common to all these countries are issues of perpetual concern to workers: the HIV/AIDS pandemic; the prevalence of child labour; ongoing farm labour-tenant exploitation; low skills levels and inadequate training; rising privatization pressures and controversies over other public sector restructuring measures; periodic refugee inflows and debates over immigration policy; the emerging Export-Processing Zone threat (based on prototypes in Botswana, Lesotho and Swaziland) to occupational safety/health and wages; and mass poverty. These broader social concerns, and other reflections of daily struggle, benefit little from the traditional corporatist (big government + big business + big labour) relationships still favoured by some of the region's union leaders.

Yet the concentration and centralization of Southern African capital—from a geographical anchorage in Johannesburg—is providing the whole region's workers with opportunities to challenge the same employers through cross-border solidarity. If a free trade agreement aiming to reduce interregional barriers is brought to fruition, a gradual homogenization of regional economic conditions has been predicted. But it could just as easily intensify the region's polarizing tendencies, given the parallel process of South African capital's expansion and the linkage of the region to Europe and North America through unfavourable free-trade deals. A variety of other compelling reasons have also emerged, since the end of apartheid, for action on a regional scale to be taken up more enthusiastically by workers and their allies. Cross-border social and cultural connections have intensified; long-term migration patterns have begun to solidify (since permanent residence was granted to long-term guest workers by the South African government in 1995); controlling arms, drugs and other illicit traffic needs regional co-operation, as does the management of regional resources (such as water); the artificiality of nation-states sired at Berlin's colonial Africa carve-up conference in 1885 is more readily questioned as post-colonial nationalism fades. There is wider recognition of the worsening unevenness of development (and related ethnic tensions) between the rich and poor areas of the region.

Our scan of regional prospects driven not by Washington and its proxies, but by popular forces in the region, necessarily begins in the core industrial sites (mainly South Africa's and Zimbabwe's large cities, as well as their now-declining mining regions) where black workers established the first organizational roots of class power already in the 1920s, often in the face of opposition from higher-skilled white workers and artisans. The ebb and flow of black working-class power was heightened by impressive industrial unrest during the 1940s, followed by a downturn associated with intensified state repression, the formal establishment of apartheid in 1948, and the banning of trade unions or their leaders in many of the colonial regimes. Later, from the 1950s, working-class power was overlaid by the rise of nationalist political movements. As these movements gained progressively greater access to state power across Southern Africa—and yet soon proved themselves hostile to working-class interests and ambitions—workers had to decide whether and how to strive for a post-colonial, post-nationalist and post-neoliberal future.

In the immediate future, as Southern Africa remains mired in sustained economic crisis, the logic of neoliberalism will have to be contested not only through defensive protest but through a new regionalism and by forging more effective international solidarity, to serve working-class and poor people's interests. There exists a broad and not necessarily socialist framework for this line of argument, namely a United Nations World Institute for Development Economics Research project whose leading African proponent, Samir Amin, advocates 'regionalization aiming at the building of a polycentric world', in part grounded in 'grassroots labour-popular social hegemonies'.[2] It is with this potential project in mind that we attempt to document lines of cleavage between and within the region's working classes and state/capital alliances.

Hence the five main sections of this essay interrelate: (1) the historical colonial-capitalist origins of the region and its working classes; (2) the contemporary economic crisis; (3) the strength and organizational state of the Southern African working class today; (4) the potential contestation of regionalism, between workers and the region's states/capitals (dominated as they tend to be by South African bureaucrats and corporations); and (5) divergent perspectives on major international economic issues. With this information, existing regional and even global strategies and tactics can be assessed and new ones proposed.

1. ORIGINS OF THE SOUTHERN AFRICAN PROLETARIAT

To understand the region's working class in the twenty-first century requires considering, however briefly, its formation in the late-nineteenth. There we find durable aspects of class-race-gender-environmental power serving a process of capital accumulation in more than a dozen major urban centres, with capital ultimately flowing to London, New York and Lisbon. Over the course of the past century or so, diverse international and intraregional connections were forged through trade, transport and communications links, customs unions, South African corporations' regional investment strategies, conflict over natural resources (especially water), and labour migration. Early commercial imperialism was codified by the 'Scramble for Africa', the Berlin conference of 1885 at which national boundaries were demarcated by Britain, Portugal, France, Germany and Belgium.

The region's partial, disarticulated proletarianization occurred initially through mining and related industries, not only on the Johannesburg reef, but also in patches of Zimbabwe (termed 'Southern Rhodesia' until 1965 and then 'Rhodesia' until 1979) and the copper-fields of Zambia ('Northern Rhodesia' until independence in 1964). Of greatest interest, of course, is the fate of indigenous black African people under the compulsion of new wage-labour disciplines. Yet even earlier, many white workers in and around the Kimberley diamond mines, the Johannesburg gold fields and the railways imported European traditions of trade unionism and mutual aid (e.g., building societies) as early as the 1880s; and by the 1910s a brand of imported 'communism' (racist and sexist) flared brightly prior to the famous 1922 white mineworkers' strike (with the egregious slogan 'Workers of the world, unite for a white South Africa!'). In the wake of effective state repression, a co-opted white Labour Party then allied with other disaffected social layers within the South African government, as did a similar group of unionized white artisanal populists in Southern Rhodesia just to the north. A 'whites-only' welfare state—providing job-creation programmes, pension schemes, health benefits, housing and the like, especially to Afrikaners who represented 'the poor white problem'—emerged in both these rapidly-industrializing countries during the 1930s. With the impressive rise of inward-oriented manufacturing and development-finance systems, many white workers evolved into middle-class managerialism, while black workers found labour markets increasingly attractive as local growth raised black wages in relation to white wages by an unprecedented (before or since) 50% during the 1930s–40s.

How, in the process, were indigenous African people disenfranchised and (partially) proletarianized? Once the colonial spoils were divided at Berlin, the British government mandated the Cape governor Cecil John Rhodes and his British South Africa Company to seize a vast area stretching north from Lesotho. The British military beat back resistance from the region's Africans (most decisively in Southern Rhodesia during the 1890s) and from Afrikaners (in the South African Anglo–Boer War of 1899–1902). British settlers thereby gave birth to the socio-political construct of Southern Africa. Using traditional techniques to strip land from indigenous peoples—'hut taxes', debt peonage systems and fees for cattle-dipping and grazing, as well as other more direct forms of compulsion—the settlers drew African men from the fields, into the mines and emerging factories.[3]

But it took more than geopolitical influence and investment to form a regional working class. Radicalized capitalism throughout Southern Africa also came to depend heavily upon extraordinarily 'cheap' migrant labour and various forms of extra-economic coercion. The Johannesburg mining houses soon organized a Chamber of Mines in order to establish recruitment offices in far-flung parts of the region. Northern Rhodesia's transnational-controlled copper-mines and various Southern Rhodesian enterprises also followed the migrant labour model. The system's profitability and durability relied quite simply on a subsidy—from household production by the migrant workers' families back home on the land—that allowed wages to be set well below the cost of reproduction of labour power. In short, white capital and states in the region spent next to nothing on black education in rural areas, on black workers' and their families' health care, or on black workers' pensions. The subsidy came partly from exhausting the ecology of the 'bantustan' (homeland) labour reserves, where land and water were degraded over time due to over-population pressure (millions of people having been forcibly removed from 'white' parts of South Africa and Rhodesia). But the subsidy was mainly provided by the household production of rural women; without jobs they were denied pass-books, and without pass-books they were denied access to the white settlers' major cities, even for conjugal visits to their partners working there. To find male workers at home in the rural areas for only a couple of weeks a year was not uncommon.

Migrant labour remains a core element of the surplus extraction process today, but with cash remittances from the cities now balancing the rural–urban subsidy. One indication of how badly South African capital required cheap immigrant workers is the way the 1986 decision of the South African apartheid ruler P. W. Botha to expel several hundred thousand Mozambican workers (as part of his regional destabilization initiative) was reversed after pressure from the Chamber of Mines, whose members still require 200,000 foreign workers for gold production alone.[4]

Over the course of a century, resistance by black workers to this diabolical system has been often violent and decisive, but sporadic. Sometimes, everyday-life survival strategies generated defensive mutual aid societies, such as the 'burial' societies and social clubs (especially based on dancing, and oriented to 'homeboy' networks) which emerged at the turn of the century. Yet militancy was not far away, and under the difficult conditions of the 1920s—inflation, stagnant incomes, tightening racial restrictions and increasing hardship—the Industrial and Commercial Workers of Africa (ICU) flourished as a general-workers' union straddling urban and rural workers across the region, drawing members from as far as Rhodesia and Nyasaland. The ICU called for defiance of the pass laws, negotiated with municipalities over worker grievances, and campaigned for minimum wages. But ultimately the movement failed to match its fiery rhetoric with action. Formed during a 1919–1920 dock-workers' strike, over time the ICU's 250,000 members became demoralized as internal strategic differences widened. White communists were expelled in 1926, and due to leadership conservatism—exemplified in the slogan 'hamba kahle' (go carefully)—various provincial branches seceded, until during the early 1930s the ICU faced demise.[5] Likewise the Communist Party of South Africa fell into a deep internal ideological crisis during the 1930s over the race/class debate, and even vibrant new 'red unions' could not sustain strikes. Revolutionary social-ists led by Max Gordon (a close associate of Leon Trotsky) were somewhat more successful, grouping six unions with a combined membership of 15,700 into a joint committee. But the black political field was left mainly to the African National Congress (ANC), which from its founding in 1912 until the mid-1950s was dominated by petit-bourgeois leaders championing extremely moderate strategies.[6]

During the high-growth period of the late 1930s and early 1940s, black worker militancy increased (in 1942, for example, 58 strikes involved over 13,000 workers). Communists helped launch the Congress of Non-European Trade Unions, yet neither they nor the ANC gave effective support to the crucial African mineworkers' strike of 1946. Though nearly 100,000 black miners struck for five days, it ended in bitter defeat, with thirteen of their number killed and 1,000 arrested. Black workers would struggle another thirty years before basic trade union and negotiating rights would be won, because the whites-only election of 1948 introduced formal apartheid. During the same year a general strike in Bulawayo and Salisbury also surprised the nationalist and communist movements, but was likewise severely repressed by a powerful white state.

In the 1940s and 1950s, even the region's poorest white families had graduated from 'poor white' status to being masters of a 'house girl' or 'boy'. But even with over half a million African women servants by the 1940s, all attempts to organize domestic workers failed, even in South Africa. Women were associated in the white media with illegal beer brewing, hawking and prostitution. 'Surplus' women in urban areas were hounded by the state, and whether 'illegal', deserted, widowed or unmarried, found security only in squatter communities on the periphery of towns. Township social movements like Soweto's Sofasonke and Alexandra's bus-boycotts grew strong and gave rise to successful land invasions thanks to the solidarity and desperation of women activists.

Yet labour and community struggles seldom overlapped during the 1950s and 1960s, for South Africa's shanty town struggles were abandoned or diffused by middle-class leaders. However, the ANC became progressively radicalized by the youth wing, led by Nelson Mandela, Oliver Tambo and Walter Sisulu. ANC leaders encouraged workers to join the South African Congress of Trade Unions (SACTU), but moulded the unions to fit the nationalist agenda. Banned along with black liberation movements during the early 1960s, SACTU lost most of its leading activists to ANC underground work, demoralization or exile. Moreover, the rapid growth of mass production industry changed the relative weight, numerical power and locations of black workers.[7] A similar process unfolded in Southern Rhodesia, with numerous bannings of parties interspersed by the rise of important links between trade unions and nationalists, illustrated by the railroad union organizer Joshua Nkomo's rapid ascent to the status of 'father of the nation'.[8]

The deepening of proletarian class formation relations changed the character of politics, but only once a new round of more general anti-apartheid protest was kick-started across the region during the 1970s. Between 1950 and 1980 the number of black workers in South Africa's manufacturing sector rose from 360,000 to 1,103,000 and in mining from 450,000 to 768,000. Increasingly strident forms of worker organization were catalysed by the 1973 dockworker strikes in Durban. By 1976, trade unionism paralleled Steve Biko's Black Consciousness Movement and the student-led revolts that began in Soweto. At the time of the launch of the Congress of South African Trade Unions (Cosatu) in 1985, some 12,000 black shop stewards represented an advanced guard of self-sacrificing militants, combining action within work-places, schools, townships and cities. In contrast to the sterile organizing of the 1950s, the mid-1980s witnessed trade unions' metamorphosis into nerve centres of informal resistance across the political spectrum. At the height of P. W. Botha's 1985–1989 state of emergency, for example, commuter trains in Johannesburg's industrial heartland became transmission belts of political mobilization and education. Industrial area committees sprouted up and workers occupied factories in a rash of sleep-in strikes. Anti-apartheid political mobilization found new channels of expression.[9]

The unprecedented growth in Cosatu's membership and power in the 1980s was not an isolated phenomenon. Similar processes were evident across the whole semi-periphery, from Brazil and the Philippines to Poland and South Korea, besides other Southern African countries. Cosatu served as a regional role model and gave direct assistance to unions in Namibia, Zambia, Zimbabwe and Swaziland. In Namibia, a decade after the severe repression of the 1970s, unionism made a comeback when mass stayaways won support of 70 percent of workers (in sympathy with school boycotts and opposition to South Africa's role in Namibia). But relations between nationalists and the unions were often tense, as the former feared that too successful a union movement would displace the national liberation movement. Namibian mineworkers leader Ben Ulenga faced bruising encounters with the South West Africa People's Organization, which summoned him to Europe during a strike at Rossing Uranium mine to tell him that workers had no right to decide when strikes should be called.[10]

Across the region during the 1960s–90s, nationalist politics dictated that workers tone down or repress class demands, in the process undermining internal democracy.[11] During the early 1980s, 'workerists' within the South African labour left—the Federation of South African Trade Unions (Fosatu, later to become Cosatu)—saw their movement not only in terms of trade unionism but also as a potential political alternative to the ANC's 'populism'. According to the Fosatu general secretary, Joe Foster, nationalists 'would destroy the unity of worker organization. Our concern is with the very essence of politics and that is the relation between the major classes in South Africa, being capital and labour. We should not hesitate to attack those who are impeding the development of a working-class movement'.[12] The ANC/SACP writer Mzala had other priorities and contended: 'It is impossible for South Africa to advance to a socialist future without the elimination of national inequality'.[13] Under pressure by the mid-1980s, key workerists quietly made peace with nationalists, whose township and rural prestige was immensely greater. Yet throughout the region, powerful tensions between nationalism and socialism remained. When occasionally, as in Zimbabwe, Mozambique and Angola, the unified Marxist-Leninist-nationalist project graduated from oppositional discourse to state power, the working classes were inevitably disappointed.

Nationalism was not the only political mobilizing challenge to working-class politics. The sensibility of Southern African labour transcends the boundaries of factories, fields and mines, merging with broader social movements to spawn a host of popular protest activities. Another challenge faced by workers in South Africa comes from market ideologues who regularly blame labour militancy for the stagnation of the country's economy. Yet as we discuss next, working-class organization and political orientation are hardly responsible for the region's structural decline.

2. SOUTHERN AFRICA'S STRUCTURAL DECLINE

The systemic class exploitation and race-gender domination outlined above continued until the last quarter of the twentieth century. Then a long-term crisis began. During the two decades from 1960 to 1980, black nationalist movements north of South Africa intensified the momentum of liberation, but then presided over a degeneration into debt, dependency and neo-colonial subjugation. The terms of trade moved decisively against mineral and agriculture exports after 1973; real international interest rates on borrowed money soared from –4% in the 1970s to +4% in the 1980s; and 'globalization' revealed most of the region's manufacturing to be uncompetitive, particularly after 1990. From economic crisis and material desperation follow many of the geopolitical dilemmas of the 1980s–90s, seriously aggravating violent regional conflicts (civil war and strife in Angola, the DRC, Lesotho, Mozambique, South Africa, Zambia and Zimbabwe, which killed as many as two million people and set nationalist rulers against each other), and growing arms traffic.

With a few exceptions—namely Mauritius and Botswana, for very specific, non-reproducible reasons—Southern African economic conditions have been depressed since the mid-1970s, especially since the early 1980s in gold-producing countries (the price of an ounce fell from a high of $850 in 1981 to just above $250 in mid-1999). Dividing the most recent periods for which reliable data are available into an immediate post-colonial 'developmental' era (1965–80) followed by generalized 'structural adjustment' (1980–95), even official statistics reveal the decay. If we add to the ten core Southern African countries (see Table 1) high-growth Mauritius and Seychelles on the one hand, but also (declining) Tanzania and the DRC on the other (the two pairs effectively offsetting each other), we find that the SADC 14-country average annual per capita GDP growth—corrected for currency fluctuations through the 'Purchasing Power Parity' measure[14]—was 3.0% from 1965 to 1980 and –0.7% from 1980 to 1995. The latter period saw foreign debt servicing double from 5 to 10% of export earnings, with Zambia, Mozambique, Zimbabwe and Malawi paying more than 20% by 1995. The largest economy, South Africa, declined from 3.2% per capita annual GDP growth in the first period to –1.0% in the second.

Table 1: Southern African Socio-Economic and Labour Market Conditions (mid–late 1990s).

Country	GDP per capita	Agric as % of	Industry as % of	Gini coefficient	Human Devel.	Population 000s	Labour force 000s [% female]	Formal jobs 000s [%civil service]	Union members	Union density
ANGOLA	1,839	12	59	n.a.	.344	11,099	5,103 [46]	n.a. [138]	n.a.	n.a.
BOTSWANA	5,611	5	56	53.7	.678	1,533	528 [46]	288 [98]	59	20
LESOTHO	1,290	10	46	56.0	.469	2,023	825 [37]	250 [n.a.]	36	14
MALAWI	773	42	27	62.0	.334	10,016	4,848 [49]	558 [48]	75	14
MOZAMBIQUE	959	33	12	n.a.	.281	18,028	9,145 [49]	450 [63]	190	42
NAMIBIA	4,054	14	30	70.0	.644	1,584	435 [41]	260 [67]	106	41
S. AFRICA	4,334	5	31	58.4	.717	37,859	9,787 [37]	5,708 [1,562]	3,202	56
SWAZILAND	2,954	14	45	n.a.	.597	926	327 [37]	57 [na]	21	44
ZAMBIA	986	22	40	46.2	.378	8,275	3,854 [45]	469 [151]	280	60
ZIMBABWE	2,135	15	36	56.8	.507	11,247	4,948 [45]	1,497 [175]	350	23

Most years 1995 (consistency throughout ensured in SADC Regional Human Development Report).

PPP = Purchasing Power Parity.

Industry includes mining and manufacturing.

Union density = union members as a % of formal sector jobs.

Sources: *UNDP Human Development Report 1998*, *SADC Regional Human Development Report 1998*, Torres 1998, *World Labour Report, 1997/98*, *Trade Unions of the World 1996*, *Africa Competitiveness Report 1998*.

Southern African economic prospects were perhaps most adversely affected by South Africa's skewed historical industrialization process and recent de-industrialization. South Africa's economy is itself characterized by severe disarticulations. A 'minerals-energy complex' still comprises the core quarter of the economy, encompassing gold, coal, petrochemicals, electricity generation, processed metals products, mining machinery and some other, closely-related manufactured outputs.[15] Intermediate capital goods (especially machines that make other machines) remain underdeveloped, while luxury goods are produced locally at close to world standards (if not prices), thanks to high relative levels of (traditionally white) consumer demand based on extreme income inequality, decades of protective tariffs and the presence of major multinational corporate branch plants. Meanwhile, basic needs industries are extremely sparse, as witnessed by the grossly inadequate output of low-cost housing, dangerous and relatively costly transport, and the underproduction of cheap, simple appliances and clothing (which are increasingly imported), at the same time that social services and the social wage have been set at extremely low levels for the country's majority.[16]

Reflecting the local over-accumulation crisis, South African manufacturing average profit rates fell steadily from 40 percent during the 1950s to less than 15 percent during the 1980s, and reinvestment dropped by 2 percent each year during the 1980s. By the trough of the 1989–93 depression, net fixed capital investment was down to just 1 percent of GDP, compared with 16 percent during the 1970s. From 1994–96, fixed investment picked up but then settled back into malaise, and the country consistently recorded bottom-tenth rankings in World Economic Forum competitiveness surveys. Post-apartheid trade liberalization all but demolished several key South African industries, including electronics, appliances, footwear, clothing, and textiles.[17]

The regional situation was even worse. Between 1992 and 1994 alone, Zimbabwe's largest textile firm and more than 60 clothing firms collapsed.[18] The country became little more than a re-export platform for (technically 'dumped') South and East Asian textiles and second-hand clothes from European aid agencies. Zambia's clothing and textile industries likewise suffered dramatically during the early 1990s trade liberalization, with 90% of garment and more than a quarter of weaving jobs lost.

Accompanying and contributing to the structural decline in the regional economy was the simultaneous failure of orthodox structural adjustment policies. Notwithstanding vocal labour protest, South Africa adopted its *Growth, Employment and Redistribution (Gear)* strategy in 1996. But over the period 1996 to 1999, virtually all *Gear's* targets were missed; to illustrate, formal sector (non-agricultural) net job losses from 1996–99 amounted to 500,000 instead of anticipated net employment gains of 950,000 new jobs. Zimbabwe suffered similarly at the hands of a 1991–95 'Economic Structural Adjustment Programme' (ESAP) which, against all evidence to the contrary, the World Bank's Project Completion Report gave the best possible final grade: 'highly satisfactory'.[19] Zimbabwe failed to achieve its macroeconomic objectives. Over the years 1991 to 1995 manufacturing output fell in absolute terms by 40% while the share of manufacturing in GDP dropped from a peak of 32% in 1992 to 17% in 1998. The same was true of virtually every adjustment programme in the region. Subsequently, at the end of the 1990s, there was somewhat higher growth, from a very low base, in some countries (notably Mozambique and Malawi). Yet such growth self-evidently failed to trickle down to most people, as poverty worsened and inequality rose sharply. In 1999 real wages in many African countries were at levels similar to many decades ago, particularly when changing consumption norms following currency crashes, the lifting of subsidies and price controls, and the destruction of local manufacturing by import liberalization are taken into account. Officially-set minimum wages dropped far below the starvation line in most countries in the region.

Even if a small group of state elites, merchants, financiers, compradors and other rentier-types have benefitted from regional economic restructuring, the vulnerable in Southern African societies have paid most for the stagnation and decline of the past quarter-century. To illustrate, the daily per capita supply of calories across the region fell from 2,122 in 1970 to 2,108 in 1995 (with Malawians, Zambians and Zimbabweans all suffering additional 20–25% per capita declines in daily protein consumption during the 1970–95 period). In the health sector—with its particularly important impact on women, children, the elderly and disabled—SADC-wide conditions deteriorated during the mid-1990s to levels among the world's worst for under-five mortality (140 per 1,000 children); maternal mortality (888 per 100,000 live births); life expectancy (52); malnutrition (20% of children under five under weight, and 36% suffering stunting); measles immunization (just 68% of 1-year olds); contraceptive use (just 28% of women from 15–45 years); and incidence of the deadly diseases malaria (5,550 per 100,000 people), tuberculosis (149 per 100,000 people), and HIV-AIDS (30 AIDS cases per 100,000 people and a 12% prevalence for adults under 49 years in 1995, worsening dramatically by decade's end as the pandemic spread through South Africa).[20]

State services could not keep up, even in a country as wealthy as South Africa (the site of the world's first-ever heart transplant, but where most rural black people still have no primary health care) let alone one as poor as Mozambique (where World Bank conditionality for meagre debt relief in 1998 included a fivefold increase in user-charges for public health services). The health crisis was just one of the features contributing to regional workers' growing sense of desperation—and in some cases to their willingness to organize not only for immediate economic demands but also to change society, or at the very least, the government.

3. SOUTHERN AFRICAN WORKERS, ORGANIZATIONS AND CLASS POLITICS

In what condition have these multiple and interlocking economic and social crises left Southern African workers? For brevity's sake, we focus upon the concentrated sites of commodity production—formal and informal—in which workers come into contact with each other, and with the direct surplus extraction system. Across Africa, organized labour's reactions have in part flowed directly from the crisis conditions noted above.[21] Yet even in the advanced

South African economy, work-place trends incorporating flexibilization, labour-outsourcing and the subcontracting of union jobs have together made the documentation of class relations very difficult. In general, conflict and consent do not correspond directly and easily with the contours of core and periphery. Permanent work-forces are not necessarily more militant or co-opted than contingent work-forces, despite these inequalities in material conditions.

The numbers tell at least some of this story. Of around one hundred million people living in the ten core countries of Southern Africa, the potential 'labour force' is estimated at less than one-third (32 million); but more importantly, only about one in ten people is 'formally' employed. Approximately 40% of these are now organized, however. Although employment in non-agricultural sectors has been declining since the mid-1980s, Southern African trade unions have claimed growing membership over the past decade (contrary to waning unionization rates in most parts of the world); in some sectors organizing of workers only became legal over the past two decades, so that for example domestic and commercial agricultural workers are having some success with nascent unions. Namibia, South Africa, Swaziland and Zimbabwe are recording impressive increases in union membership, although extensive privatization in Zambia has led to a contraction. Continuous organizing drives by the region's stronger unions maintain membership at high levels, withstanding the effects of even mass retrenchments. These figures show substantial union power.

Over time, working classes across the region began to adopt progressive positions in opposition to their governments. As Herbert Jauch puts it, 'With the SADC divided along political lines, trade unions have achieved a higher degree of unity than ruling nationalist parties'.[22] A regional perspective and discourse may, indeed, override a variety of national limitations. Fred Cooper argues, 'The tension between workers' claims to globally defined entitlements and Africans' assertions of political rights as Africans was, during the 1940s and early 1950s, a creative and empowering one'.[23] In contemporary struggles, though, a regional and more universalist paradigm potentially allows workers to raise demands for higher standards of socio-economic rights more forcefully. In contrast, the trap of nationalist-corporatism, and the national competitiveness framework, have generated only slim gains for workers as liberation movements have moved sharply right.[24]

Politically, Southern African unions spent some hard years in the post-independence era breaking away from ruling party tutelage and explicit state repression (although Mozambican and Malawian unions are still heavily influenced by their governments). In countries with relatively robust political-party divisions that take place in the electoral sphere (or, as in Angola, on the battleground), the political alliances of trade unions become an issue (e.g., in Botswana, Mozambique, Namibia, South Africa and Zimbabwe). But party politics and union politics are uneasy bedfellows. In Zambia, a trade unionist (Frederick Chiluba) was elected president as leader of a multi-class Movement for Multiparty Democracy in 1991 following 27 years of (Kenneth Kaunda's) nationalist misrule—and then even more forcefully implemented structural adjustment during the 1990s. In contrast, in Zimbabwe, the ruling ZANU regime (led interminably by the autocratic Robert Mugabe) continued to give lip service to socialism while carrying out unrelenting neoliberal policies; political opposition rallied around left-leaning trade union leaders (Morgan Tsvangirai and Gibson Sibanda) whose Movement for Democratic Change became the main (or at least second biggest) party in parliament in the June 2000 elections. Likewise in Namibia, where rampant presidentialism prevents serious internal party debate, the SWAPO-affiliated National Union of Namibian Workers charged that the ruling party had scant regard for workers: 'if reconciliation is understood as the perpetuation of apartheid and is equated with exploitation, then workers will no longer tolerate this'.[25] A similar post-nationalist movement—the Congress of Democrats—led by a former trade unionist (Ulenga) became the official opposition after 1999 elections, while several individual unions expressed a desire to end their affiliation with Swapo.[26]

In South Africa, more durable left-leaning politics were generally associated with trade unions, but by the late 1990s debates raged about whether an alliance with the ruling ANC liberation movement (decidedly neoliberal in economic policy terms) was helping workers, or stunting their further mobilization and development. In practice, however, the union movement has increasingly lost internal vibrancy and has become more of an appendage of the ANC. Public sector strikes against job cuts and inadequate pay rises and large-scale anti-privatization demonstrations by municipal workers reflect widespread grassroots antipathy to ANC policies. But in the absence of alternative political parties or a credible set of options, workers still place pragmatic value on the alliance as a means of pressuring the ANC, even if so far, according to Glenn Adler and Eddie Webster, such 'pressure has objectively eroded the position of workers'.[27] Cosatu leaders condemned the ANC government—specifically, the Minister of Public Administration Geraldine Moleki-Fraser (who was also deputy SA Communist Party chairperson)—for

> trying to isolate and undermine workers demands by posing the dispute as being about 'general' interest versus 'sectoral' ('selfish', 'economist') interests of public sector workers. The 'dirty tricks' campaign [entailed] disinformation, and statements released to the press without consulting with the unions, and conducting the dispute in the media. The actions of the government are not in accord with spirit of the Tripartite Alliance, and indicate a greater concern to appease international capital than to enhance workers' rights and speed up delivery.[28]

Cosatu is also a part of the National Economic Development and Labour Council, a corporatist arrangement in which business, state and labour jointly formulate policy on labour and economic issues. But nearly two-thirds of workers surveyed had no knowledge of the council.[29] Cosatu is increasingly vulnerable to both bureaucracy and careerism, as leaders successfully seek paths to more lucrative government jobs. On the other hand, this is a process reserved for a few, as many local-level corporatist efforts in the same vein— 'work-place forums' mandated under the post-apartheid Labour Relations Act to edge unions into local co-determination of productivity issues—have failed to take off.

Elsewhere the story has not advanced so far. In Botswana and especially Swaziland, labour has become the basis for a progressive political-party and pro-democracy activism which may pose substantial challenges for neocolonial governments, while in Malawi trade unions played a role in unseating a neocolonial dictator (President Banda) during the 1990s but did not replace him with a leader of their own. In Mozambique, nascent unions were by the late 1990s showing a capacity for militancy. Working-class movements in Lesotho (drawing on traditions of mine labour) and Angola (still bedevilled by war) were slow to gather pace. The point, perhaps, is that a major breakthrough for workers cannot occur in one country without the rest of the regional working class seeing some possibility of also gaining power in their own respective states, and also simultaneously developing a regional perspective that transcends the artificial boundaries drawn up by colonialists. That possibility we return to shortly.

However, simply counting union membership and estimating labour influence over local politics is only the beginning. The ability of federations and individual unions to embark upon major strike action is just as vital an indicator of strength. In Zimbabwe, autonomous, shopfloor-based actions outran the ability of national union bureaucrats to control or direct the membership and the corporatist strategy mistakenly pursued by the ZCTU during the mid-1990s quickly became irrelevant. And in South Africa, despite the country's deep economic woes, union militancy increased as the state's attack on public sector workers intensified.

Regionally-co-ordinated actions and growing class consciousness also reflect progress. In Swaziland, for example, an eleven-day general strike in 1996 and further strikes in 1997 led to solidarity in the form of a border blockade organized by sister unions in South Africa and Mozambique, which forced the anachronistic monarchy to concede worker rights. Indeed, new sections of workers across the region are demanding similar rights to those won by South African unions.

International and regional solidarity is probably the only real hope for many of the less-resourced union movements, as well as the relatively weak Southern African Trade Union Co-ordinating Council (SATUCC) itself. But given the difficult material conditions faced by regional unions and enormous tactical and strategic differences over international economic policy (see Section 5), it may be more realistic to begin by enquiring whether there exists a basis for a regional working-class consciousness as opposed to giving priority—as South African workers have so far been under heavy pressure to do—to retaining ties with nationalist allies.

4. REGIONAL CAPITAL ACCUMULATION, RESISTANCE AND GEOGRAPHICAL VISION

Can workers establish a regional class consciousness in coming years? Notwithstanding cross-border solidarities associated with three decades of anti-colonial and nationalist liberation struggles (1960–90), notions of Southern Africa remain for the most part contained within dominant global conceptions of regionalism: namely a sub-imperial South Africa as the gateway for capital accumulation in Africa as a whole, but organized on a regional scale between Pretoria and the global institutions (using Thabo Mbeki's notion of an 'African Renaissance' as cover). This has required new, post-apartheid institutional processes that take for granted a conception of the Southern African region as a 'capital-catchment' area undergoing ever-amplifying uneven development. It remains to be seen whether there can be an alternative, working-class regional vision, and whether class practices may emerge to turn Southern African workers into agents for historical change.

What would a potential working-class regional solidarity have to contend with? We see two aspects of contemporary politics and economics that threaten the universal class interests of Southern African workers. The first is the power of the multinational corporate/banking free-trade/finance agenda. But as discussed below, events in 1999 proved that the apparent power of US-centred neoliberalism is also pock-marked with vulnerabilities, even if the international working class remains confused over whether to try 'fixing' or 'nixing' neoliberalism's core institutions.

Second, elite-nationalists are contemplating an interlocking of South–South interests, with workers left out of the equation. This is not merely a matter of Robert Mugabe's oft-stated envy of the Malaysian exit-option from volatile international currency speculation (late 1999 saw Mahathir Mohamad giving seminars to Southern African leaders not only in a resort near Kuala Lumpur, but also, at Mugabe's insistence, at Victoria Falls). More to the point, a recent ANC/Alliance discussion document, 'Global Economic Crisis and its Implications for South Africa', explicitly asked, 'Can we forge a Brasilia-Pretoria-Delhi-Beijing Consensus in the absence of any Washington Consensus?'[30] Likewise in the wake of breakdown of the Seattle World Trade Organization (WTO) talks in November 1999, South Africa's trade and industry minister Alec Erwin regularly proposed restarting negotiations on the basis of an alliance between Mexico, Brazil, Nigeria, Egypt, India and South Korea.

But looking beyond occasional statements of Southern African and South–South interstate solidarity, to where capital is actually flowing, we may see a hint of a more realistic regionalism, and also of worker resistance. Sub-Saharan Africa has witnessed a renewed ebb and flow of South African corporate penetration since around 1993. Privatization and liberalization of African parastatal firms were critical points of contact, as were banking, services, retail activity and mining firms.[31]

What are the implications? To consider one example hyped loudly and regularly by Pretoria, it now transpires that 'public-private partnerships' in geographically-concentrated ('corridor'-aligned) infrastructure projects between South African investors and the region's states are unprofitable, for the primary reason that affordable state finance is virtually unavailable, given Southern Africa's huge residual liabilities to northern creditors. Thus Erwin castigated the North for its 'criminal, just criminal' lack of substantive debt relief shortly after the 1999 G-8 Summit in Cologne. (That this public outburst against a US official occurred at the primary site of regional elite-pacting, the Davos-based World Economic Forum's Southern Africa conference, was all the more telling.)

Under Erwin, after all, South Africa's Department of Trade and Industry (DTI) had taken practical responsibility for the regional restructuring required for a particularly neoliberal, export-oriented, accumulation process. Behind the DTI strategy is faith that 'Spatial Development Initiatives' (SDIs) will add a rich fabric of 'development' along and within a corridor linking key nodes of accumulation (especially Johannesburg–Maputo) which embody features of 'Export Processing Zones' (EPZs).[32] The DTI project methodology seeks first to identify potential port/rail/EPZ complexes in an underdeveloped target area that might be of interest to investors, and then help local stakeholders plan and promote infrastructural investments which improve access.[33] By the end of 1999, only two of the fourteen proposed SDIs were operative. But the official consensus around the SDI strategy—spatially-fetishized, environmentally-destructive, capital-intensive and lacking appropriate backward-forward linkages as it surely is[34]—shows how far a regional version of the Washington conception of globalization enjoys hegemony amongst Southern African policy-makers.

Such a regional strategy requires institutional frameworks, such as SADC, an institution initiated by northern donor governments during the 1980s to help combat apartheid which morphed uneasily—with a major 1999 hiccup due to staff corruption, requiring an entirely new secretariat—into an organization for free-trade deals under the rubric of regional integration, co-operation and harmonization. As early as 1989, SADC committed the region to becoming a free-trade area by 2006, but progress has been slow, including steps backward when during the mid-1990s Zimbabwe and Zambia imposed tariffs on imported South African manufactures that were threatening entire domestic industries.

Aside from SADC, other parallel and occasionally competing institutional arrangements for the region (most of which will probably be merged or fade over time) include the Common Market of Eastern and Southern Africa, the South African Customs Union (a long-standing free trade deal between SA, Lesotho, Botswana, Swaziland and Namibia) and the Common Monetary Union, while WTO membership will open up other regional and bilateral relationships (e.g., bringing in Angola and Mozambique, which otherwise are not involved in non-SADC free-trade arrangements). All such bilateral and multi-

lateral deals are premised, it is clear, upon export-orientation not inward industrialization, and upon increasingly 'flexible' and competitive labour markets.
Southern African labour understands this, implicitly, even if SATUCC and the
federations of each country have not yet established an alternative vision. To
this end, SATUCC advisor Dot Keet has proposed that to 'deglobalize' from
neoliberal, multinational corporate and financial influence, requires not only
alliances with those in the North seeking 'innovative alternatives to over-
producing/consuming capitalism', but also a proactive, internally-oriented
regionalism.[35]

If the elaboration of such an alternative regional-global strategy—based not
only upon regional delinking from neoliberal imperialism in alliance with
Northern social and labour movements, but also relinking along South–South
axes—is in the interests of poor and working people in Southern Africa, it
could also be the basis for a global working-class strategy. However, such a
strategy must first confront some extremely serious contradictions within the
labour movement itself and in its relations with national governments.

5. DIVERGENT NATIONAL–GLOBAL INTERESTS, RHETORIC AND STRATEGIES

SADC trade unions' politico-ideological orientation towards the world
market is of interest to the rest of the international working class, because virtually all the world's unions are struggling with how to respond to debilitating
global economic processes. But by no means have Southern African workers
found a unified or unifying approach to what clearly should be universal,
namely the multifaceted struggle against neoliberalism. Just two examples of the
divergent, sometimes contradictory, processes currently underway must suffice:
resistance to structural adjustment (especially the role of the IMF/World Bank),
and the debate over 'Social Clauses' in trade agreements.

The IMF and World Bank played substantial macroeconomic policy-making
roles in Southern Africa during the period of economic crisis. We can consider
the experiences of the two most important union movements—those of South
Africa and Zimbabwe—for illustrations of the dangers and possibilities to which
this influence gave rise. As noted above, South Africa's *Gear* policy was a
resounding failure in all except two areas: fiscal discipline and a low inflation
rate. At the press conference announcing *Gear*, the then Deputy President
Thabo Mbeki confirmed: 'Just call me a Thatcherite'.[36] Although the SACP
initially endorsed *Gear*, Cosatu reacted critically: 'We have serious reservations
over conservative fiscal policies that the document intends to implement'. After
a month, Cosatu general secretary Mbhazima Shilowa said, quite simply:
'Something has gone terribly wrong'.[37] A year later, the SACP formally
condemned *Gear*, and by mid-1998 Mandela and Mbeki very publicly rebuked
the SACP at its national congress, in the midst of another currency crisis (and
in doing so were understood to be addressing the domestic and international
financial markets as much as the activists).

By the end of 1999, in his 'Millennium Message', Cosatu's new general secretary, Zwelinzima Vavi, complained of the 'deepening unemployment crisis and massive inequalities growing at catastrophic proportions ... The interventions made by the democratic government have failed to stem the characteristics of the apartheid economy'. Referring to the ongoing public-sector wage dispute (in which government rejected a stalemated bargaining forum and instead unilaterally imposed a below-inflation increase), Vavi warned that collective bargaining was 'under threat' and that in particular 'bureaucrats in the Finance Department want to ... fragment [the] centralized bargaining we won during the dark days of apartheid'.[38]

But if Cosatu's reactions to structural adjustment, World Bank policies and fiscal tightening at the expense of workers were admirably critical in their rhetorical tone, this did not translate into a practical or even sustained ideological challenge in reality. There were no strategies or tactics for beating the Department of Finance bureaucrats or the conservative forces in the ANC more generally, notwithstanding a major show of force in the form of a national strike in May 2000 endorsed (at the cost of a day's pay) by half of the eight million work-force. *Gear* continued to be implemented without substantive challenge, aside from discrete strikes against particular aspects of neoliberalism (e.g., municipal privatization)—even when at the worst point of the East Asian crisis in 1998, the Washington Consensus was attacked by the leading intellectual Joel Netshitenzhe (writing with Shilowa and SACP intellectual Jeremy Cronin) in the ANC Discussion Document referred to above:

> The present crisis is, in fact, a global capitalist crisis, rooted in a classical crisis of over-accumulation and declining profitability ... As the depth and relative durability of the crisis have become apparent, the dominant economic paradigm (the neoliberal 'Washington Consensus') has fallen into increasing disrepute.[39]

Known locally as 'talk-left, act-right' politics, this sort of alliance discourse contrasts with the potentially more radical, if softer-spoken, reaction of the Zimbabwe Congress of Trade Unions (ZCTU) to that country's dismal 1991–95 Economic Structural Adjustment Programme (ESAP) and subsequent policy drift, a dissonance which should be explained. For ZCTU statements may initially give an equally, though opposite, misleading impression of the underlying balance of forces and political dynamic.

At the beginning of the 1990s, the ZCTU under Tsvangirai's leadership broke out of the paternalist grip in which the Zimbabwe African National Union (ZANU) government had held the federation since its 1981 founding (when Albert Mugabe, brother of Robert, served as secretary), and through which union strategies, tactics and politics were controlled during the 1980s. As general secretary in 1989, Tsvangirai even found himself in jail for two weeks simply for supporting left-wing students' criticism of ZANU's rapid right-wing drift towards structural adjustment. Quickly identifying neoliberalism as one of the most important issues (along with corruption) dividing the Zimbabwe government from the masses, Tsvangirai predicted a difficult period ahead at a time when bourgeois commentary was universally optimistic.[40]

And ESAP's failure did indeed generate unprecedented 'IMF Riots' in 1993 and 1995 (see section 1 above). Yet the ZCTU was not well-placed to take advantage of this opening, and instead zigzagged between a front-building strategy and a desire for corporatist technical solutions. This can probably be explained by the movement's initial political marginalization, its weak shopfloor base, and the ZANU government's divide-and-conquer strategy. As the ZCTU retreated into an aspirant-corporatist mode, even Tsvangirai sought an accommodation with neoliberalism.

To this end, in 1996 the ZCTU issued an important policy advocacy document, *Beyond ESAP*. Blinkered by the desire to remain relevant to reforming ESAP in potential tripartite settings (including sectoral fora dealing with housing, social security and other social policies), *Beyond ESAP* in fact codified many of the Mugabe regime's worst conceptual errors and policy recommendations. Tsvangirai himself wrote in the foreword that 'While acknowledging that SAPs are necessary, the study shows that they are insufficient in fostering development'; a more militant political strategy would have generated the affirmation that ESAP was unnecessary and indeed that it underdeveloped Zimbabwe during the 1990s.[41]

The basis for such concessionary language was a protracted but fruitless attempt to establish a broad 'social contract' that would, as Tsvangirai put it in the mid-1990s, 'involve the three parties reaching a consensus where workers agree to restrain wage demands on the one hand and employers agree to control price increases for commodities, invest surpluses to create more jobs and train workers on the other. For government, you would expect them to cut spending'.[42] However, in the wake of a year-long wave of worker militancy in 1997–98 (including previously docile public sector employees and even the chronically atomized plantation workers) and two successful national mass strikes against Mugabe's policies, Tsvangirai suddenly moved to the left: instead of joining a National Economic Consultative Forum in January 1999, as expected, he led a ZCTU walkout on the grounds that Mugabe's government could not be trusted; a few weeks later, he convened a broad-based National Working People's Convention (a significant name) which issued quite radical resolutions;[43] he led a civil-society 'National Constitutional Assembly' process that in 1999 garnered sufficient popular support to force Mugabe to set up his own constitution-rewriting commission; and when in mid-1999, he announced the formation of the 'labour-backed' Movement for Democratic Change (MDC, often termed the 'workers' party'), a founding manifesto balanced its overall good governance orientation with quite expansive socio-economic visions.[44]

The best indication of the potential for Zimbabwe workers' leftward momentum in 2000 and beyond—in the wake of the conservative discourses of the 1990s—may simply be Mugabe's own confused and confusing reaction: a resurgence of leftwing rhetoric.[45] By late 1999, Mugabe publicly told the IMF to 'shut up!', amongst other outbursts reported in the international press, and after losing a national constitutional referendum to the MDC in February 2000, he stage-managed land invasions of white-owned commercial farms. But again and again, throughout its history, ZANU had shown a remarkable capacity to talk-left, act-right, with Mugabe reserving his most revolutionary-sounding rhetoric for those occasions when leftwing political threats appeared.

In the June 2000 election, the MDC took 46% of the vote in an election characterized by massive intimidation of MDC supporters, to become the official opposition, setting up a close contest for the presidency in 2002 (Mugabe would by then have appointed his successor). Could the outcome be as bad as Zambia's—where former trade union leader Chiluba was influenced by neoliberal advisers as well as by aspirant-bourgeois political allies prior to taking power? Given the MDC's need to contest ZANU in rural areas with a progressive programme and alliances, this is not a foregone conclusion. Time will tell whether talking right—as in *Beyond ESAP*—becomes the actual electoral platform and programme of governance, or whether a mass-democratic, populist instinct can find space to grow within the MDC, ensuring that the leaders must continue looking leftward for popular support.

Beyond these fluid, disparate and contradictory national struggles, can internationalist strategies and tactics reconfigure class struggle in a more favourable way? In the case of trade agreements, the interests of the world's workers *appear* to lie in a concerted programme to raise the standard of living (including gender and environmental protections) of those at the bottom of the global hierarchy, by attaching clauses to trade agreements enforced by the WTO. Yet the debate on the inclusion of social, labour, governance and environmental clauses in trade agreements to this end became extremely thorny during the 1990s, serving as a divisive 'wedge issue' within the international movement.

Divisions were also found in Southern Africa. From Johannesburg, Vavi and other Cosatu leaders pushed for such clauses to be applied against regional trading partners. In contrast, many progressive African social movements, NGOs, churches and women's groups, development agencies, technical think-tanks and intellectuals—some of them gathered in the Ghana-based Africa Trade Network—condemned the imposition of conditions on what they argue is already a terribly unequal trade, investment and financing relationship with the South. A November 1999 workshop of SATUCC and regional social movement activists issued a 'Statement on the Seattle Ministerial' rejecting 'the widening of the ambit of issues under the WTO through the inclusion of the Social Clause'. The potential value of such clauses was outweighed, in the activists' view, by the damage done to power relations through amplifying the legitimacy and power of the WTO. But Cosatu's Vavi—who did not attend—immediately disassociated SATUCC (over which he presided) from the workshop statement. Instead, in Seattle a few days later, Vavi joined forces with the South African government and local big business, to demand less-protectionist trade rules, but nevertheless including the Social Clause. The delegation gained prized access to Green Room deliberations, though it returned empty-handed (and Erwin soon dropped his support for the Social Clause).[46]

The Social Clause strategy thus appears discredited. If we take as a first principle that labour internationalism is violated by promoting the interests of an oppressor nation over those of an oppressed nation, above all when the wishes of the latter have not been consulted, then this is no loss. On this basis it is easy to support boycotts against apartheid-era South Africa and SLORC-run Burma—for whom sanctions called for by popular, democratic movements translate into a strategic attack on local oppressors—but difficult to justify 'humanitarian' interventions in the sphere of trade via Social Clauses enforced by the WTO, where economic interests are imperialist or at best narrowly protectionist, and where *status quo* power relations are only exacerbated.

Just how visionary can regional and international labour and social solidarity be, in the early twenty-first century? We retain optimism, for as Gramsci put it, 'It is absurd to think of a purely objective prediction. Anybody who makes a prediction has in fact a programme for whose victory he is working, and his prediction is precisely an element contributing to that victory'.[47] Our examples from Southern Africa's national labour movements, from uneasy regional integration and regional visions, and from international economic policy and institutional contestation, suggest strategic orientations that can promote unity and avoid divisive tactics. Against TINA—'There Is No Alternative'— Southern African radicals have long counterposed the Zulu word for 'hope', THEMBA: 'There Must be an Alternative'. In sum, there must be, as a South African mineworker said at the Seattle labour rally, a basis, perhaps beginning on a regional scale, to have 'workers of the world unite'.

NOTES

1. To establish our boundaries, the Southern African Development Community (SADC) comprises both strong and frail nation-states: Angola, Botswana, the Democratic Republic of the Congo (DRC), Lesotho, Malawi, Mauritius, Mozambique, Namibia, South Africa, Seychelles, Swaziland, Tanzania, Zambia and Zimbabwe. The large, well-populated but impoverished island of Madagascar also belongs, geographically, but is generally excluded due to its isolation and Francophone heritage. For the purposes of this essay, we mainly consider the capital flows, labour movements and regional linkages within the ten most southern, mainland countries (i.e., omitting the DRC, Mauritius, Seychelles, and Tanzania.)

2. Samir Amin, 'Regionalization in Response to Polarizing Globalization', in Bjorn Hettne, Andras Inotai and Osvaldo Sunkel (eds), *Globalism and the New Regionalism*, London, Macmillan, 1999, p. 77.

3. Similar imperatives were introduced in Portuguese-controlled Mozambique and Angola, and in Namibia (the German-run former South West Africa until South

Africa took over after World War I). But such accumulation was mainly based upon extractive (rather than settler-oriented) economics, via control of plantation labour.

4. Liv Torres (ed.), *One out of Ten: The Labour Market in Southern Africa*, Oslo, Fafo, 1998, p. 56. Nearly half of these workers are from Lesotho, with another third from Mozambique and the balance from Swaziland and Botswana. The definitive work on migrancy is David McDonald (ed.), *On Borders: Perspectives on International Migration in Southern Africa*, New York, St Martin's Press, 2000.

5. Edward Roux, *Time Longer than Rope*, Madison, University of Wisconsin Press, 1964.

6. Dale McKinley, *The ANC: A Political Biography*, London, Pluto Books, 1997.

7. Robert Fine and Dennis Davies, *Beyond Apartheid*, London, Pluto Press, 1991.

8. Brian Raftopoulos and Ian Phimister (eds), *Keep on Knocking: A History of the Labour Movement in Zimbabwe, 1900–1997*, Harare, Baobab, 1998.

9. Greg Ruiters, 'Urban Struggles and Urban Defeats in the 1980s', *Urban Forum*, 11, 2, 2000; Mzwanele Mayekiso, *Township Politics*, New York, Monthly Review, 1996.

10. Colin Leys and John Saul, *Namibia's Liberation Struggle: A Two-edged Sword*, London, James Currey, 1995, p. 84.

11. John Saul, 'Liberation without Democracy', in Jonathan Hyslop (ed), *African Democracy*, Johannesburg, Witwatersrand University Press, 1999, p. 167.

12. *Fosatu Workers News*, April 1982, p. 2. See also Dave Lewis, 'Capital, Trade Unions and Liberation', *South African Labour Bulletin*, 11, 4, 1986, p. 35.

13. Cited in John Saul, 'Class, Race and the Future of Socialism', in William Cobbett and Robin Cohe (eds), *Popular Struggles in South Africa*, London, James Currey, 1988, p. 216.

14. Without such corrections, the per capita GDP collapse is enormous, leaving Southern Africa with six of the world's sixteen poorest countries: the DRC ($110), Mozambique ($140), Malawi ($210), Tanzania ($210), Madagascar ($250) and Angola ($260), according to *The World Bank Atlas 1999*.

15. Ben Fine and Zav Rustomjee, *The Political Economy of South Africa: From Minerals-Energy Complex to Industrialization*, London, Christopher Hurst and Johannesburg, Wits University Press, 1996.

16. Patrick Bond, *Cities of Gold, Townships of Coal: Essays on South Africa's New Urban Crisis*, Trenton, Africa World Press, 2000.

17. Patrick Bond, *Elite Transition: From Apartheid to Neoliberalism in South Africa*, London, Pluto Press, 2000.

18. Zimbabwe Congress of Trade Unions, *Beyond ESAP*, Harare, p. 48.

19. World Bank, *Project Completion Report: Zimbabwe: Structural Adjustment Programme*, Country Operations Division, Washington, DC, 1995, p. 23.

20. Southern African Political Economic Series, *SADC Regional Human Development Report*, Harare, 1998.

21. Thomas Callaghy and John Ravenhill (eds), *Hemmed In: Responses to Africa's Economic Decline*, New York, Columbia University Press, 1993.

22. Herbert Jauch, 'Building a Regional Labour Movement', *South African Labour Bulletin*, 23, 1, 1999, p. 85.

23. Frederick Cooper, *Decolonization and African Society: The Labour Question in French and British Africa*, Cambridge, Cambridge University Press, 1996, pp. 468–471.

24. Carolyn Bassett and Marlea Clarke, 'Class Struggle', *Southern African Report*, March 2000.

25. Leys and Saul, *Namibia's Liberation*, p. 167.

26. Roseline Nyman, 'An Overview of Namibian Unions', in Torres, *One out of Ten*, p. 162.

27. Glenn Adler and Eddie Webster, 'South Africa: Class Compromise', *Southern Africa Report*, March 2000.

28. Cosatu Press Statement on Public Sector Strike, http://www.cosatu.org.za.

29. Vishwas Satgar and Conrad Jardine, 'Cosatu and the Tripartite Alliance', *South African Labour Bulletin*, 23, 3, 1999, p. 8.

30. ANC/Alliance, 'Global Economic Crisis and its Implications for South Africa', Discussion Document, reprinted in the *African Communist*, 4th quarter 1998, p. 5. However, to understand the limits of the South–South discourse, it is worth reminding ourselves that the South African government occupied a host of crucial positions during 1998–99—the headship of the Non-Aligned Movement, the presidency of the UN Conference on Trade and Development, the chair of both the Commonwealth and the Organization of African Unity, the host of the Southern African Development Community, UN Security Council member, the Governing Board chairmanship at the IMF and World Bank—and did virtually nothing to change global power relations and economic processes.

31. Fred Ahwireng-Obeng and Patrick McGowan, 'Partner or Hegemon? South Africa in Africa', *Journal of Contemporary African Studies*, 16, 1, 1998.

32. Herbert Jauch and Dot Keet, *A SATUCC Study on Export Processing Zones in Southern Africa: Economic, Social and Political Implications*, Cape Town, International Labour Research and Information Group, 1996.

33. Paul Jourdan, Ketso Gordhan, Dave Arkwright, and Geoff de Beer, 'Spatial Development Initiatives (Development Corridors): Their Potential Contribution to Investment and Employment Creation', Working Paper, Development Bank of Southern Africa, Midrand, October, 1996.

34. Emblematic is the Coega SDI, as described in Patrick Bond, 'Economic Growth, Ecological Modernization, or Environmental Justice?: Conflicting Discourses in Post-Apartheid South Africa', *Capitalism, Nature, Socialism*, 11, 1, 2000.

35. Dot Keet, 'Globalization or Regionalization: Contradictory Tendencies? Counteractive Tactics? Or Strategic Possibilities?', Institute for Global Dialogue Working Paper, Johannesburg, June 1999.

36. Associated Press, 14 June 1996.

37. For analysis, see Hein Marais, *South Africa: The Political Economy of Change*, London, Zed and Cape Town, University of Cape Town Press, 1998.

38. Zwelinzima Vavi, 'Cosatu Millennium Message', Johannesburg, 22 December 1999.

39. ANC Alliance, 'The Global Economic Crisis', p. 1.

40. *Southern Africa Report*, July 1991.

41. *Beyond ESAP*'s neoliberal policy prescriptions are critiqued in Patrick Bond, *Uneven Zimbabwe: A Study of Finance, Development and Underdevelopment*, Trenton, Africa World Press, 1998, Chapter 12.

42. Cited in Lloyd Sachikonye, 'Trade Unions: Economic and Political Development in Zimbabwe since Independence in 1980', in Raftopoulos and Phimister, *Keep on Knocking*, p. 127.

43. 'National policies should prioritise the mobilisation and organisation of resources to meet people's basic needs ... The country should aim to reduce its dependency on foreign loans and the loss of sovereignty that this brings ... The right to a minimum standard of health inputs (food, water, shelter) and health care must be defined and entrenched in the constitution, guaranteed and funded on an equitable basis by the state through its mobilization of national resources'. (http://www.samara.co.zw/zctu/position.htm)

44. http://www.mdc.co.zw/intro-frames.html. Nevertheless, in February 2000, Tsvangirai appointed a charismatic (white) official of the Confederation of Zimbabwe Industries as MDC economic secretary to lead the MDC economic desk, generating expectations that once in power, Zimbabwe would follow Zambia's post-Kaunda experience. Coverage of the ambiguities is found in *Southern Africa Report*, May 2000.

45. Further background is provided in Patrick Bond, 'Zimbabwe's Political Reawakening', *Monthly Review*, 50, 11, 1999.

46. Workshop on Trade and Investment in Southern Africa, 'Statement on the Seattle Ministerial', Johannesburg 11–13 October 1999; SATUCC, 'Communique', Johannesburg, 5 November 1999; for more on the debate, see http://www.aidc.org.za.

47. Antonio Gramsci, *Selections from Prison Notebooks*, London, Lawrence Wishart, 1971, p. 185.

WESTERN EUROPEAN TRADE UNIONISM AT 2000

STEVE JEFFERYS

Tuesday, 30 November 1999, was not 'business as usual' in France. That day saw between 80,000 and 120,000 French bank workers—more than at any time since 1974—staging a national one-day strike. Their aim was to force the main high-street banks to renew a national collective agreement and, according to the unions, 30,000 of them demonstrated in Paris alone with smaller demonstrations in all French cities.[1] The same Tuesday saw some nine hundred miners riot outside the Prefecture in Metz in Eastern France to force the government to make the loss-making nationalized French coal company increase its 2000 wage offer above 0.5%. At Marseille's Prefecture it was the same tune but a different song. There, another 30,000 people demonstrated peacefully for a Christmas bonus for the unemployed before blocking one of the city's major roads. Meanwhile, in Paris and another twenty cities, several thousands more were also demonstrating for a tougher 35-hour-week law.[2]

This illustration does not prove that most French or European workers and their unions are returning to their former militancy. As we shall see this is very far from the case. But this one day of mobilization simply reminds us that Europe's working classes are far from being at an all time low and that Europe's socio-political future remains contested. There are huge and growing pressures for Western Europe to adapt to the practices and mores of American managerial and financial capitalism. Yet the positive political consequences of the mid-century defeat of European authoritarian capitalism, of the restraints that this subsequently imposed on Europe's capitalist classes, of the experiences of Christian Democratic and/or Social Democratic governments vying to attract workers' votes, and of the wave of collective worker mobilizations of the 1970s are still present.

The survival of restraints on neoliberalism in most European countries owes much to their institutionalization after the Second World War and to Europe's divided post-war history. The latter particularly influenced the largely dominant Christian and Social Democratic parties to try to counteract the Stalinized rhetoric of workers' rights that emanated from Eastern Europe with substantial reforms which have by no means yet been completely undone. One clear result has been that unlike during the depressions of the 1880s and 1890s or the 1930s, the deep and scarring economic recession and transformations of the 1980s and 1990s did not witness rising working-class mortality. Indeed, for the first time Europe's response to a major capitalist crisis was not to go to war but instead, despite the continuous protests of sections of the capitalist class, to effect some small redistributions of income (albeit generally between workers rather than by taking from the capitalist class) to offset the worst effects of joblessness. Of course, in the 1990s, particularly since the defeat of Soviet Communism and re-emergence of American hegemony, international capital's remote power over European workers has been growing. Yet, while the glow of social and economic democracy is dimmer in Western Europe than a quarter of a century ago, by comparison with the first half of the century—and with virtually the whole of working people's previous history—it cannot seriously be said to have been completely extinguished. Enough light remains, certainly, to show the way ahead to those who want to see.

In focusing this essay on Western European trade unionism we are obviously leaving out much. The European Union's (EU) fifteen states, even with their population of 369 million and employed labour force of 152 million people,[3] nevertheless only account for half the states that lie west of the Urals. And we are well aware that trade unionism is only one element within the complex process by which the working-class presence makes itself felt at the end of the millennium. Moreover, even in the EU, each country's class structures, and the articulations between social classes, are almost all so different that it is difficult to convey an idea of the evolution of these relations in any overall sense.[4] All we want to do here is provide some sense of the experience of the Western European working classes through observations of the evolution of their trade union movements.

We will look most specifically at four cases, each reflecting the main European types of trade union movement which are often distinguished from each other: the 'Latin' confrontational model (France), the liberal-voluntarist model (UK), the social-democratic model (Sweden) and the neo-corporatist-conservative model (Germany).[5] But we shall especially concentrate on a comparison of only two labour movements: the French, which could be viewed as one of those which has changed least over the last twenty-five years, and the British, which, now currently experiencing the lowest levels of strike action since records began, can be seen to have changed most.[6] The British and the French trade-union movements may be seen as being at opposite ends of a trade-union spectrum ranging from those most influenced by market or business unionism to those where class struggle unionism remains strongest. It would be wrong, however, to see a simple bipolar trade-union ideological spectrum in Europe. Richard Hyman is right to call for greater sensitivity to the complexities of trade-union ideological orientation, and to the pluralistic and contested character of European trade unionism. He points to the continuing existence of a distinct ideological dimension associated with social integration, which embraces commitments to social justice, 'fairness' and class harmony, and notes that all three (market, social integration and class struggle) ideological orientations are present in all movements, and combine in varying alliance patterns.[7] My own recent comparative study of bank trade-union activists, for instance, found that British trade unionism predominantly combines market and social integration orientations, while French mainly combined those based on class-struggle and social-integration ideologies.[8]

We shall begin with an examination of the processes of occupational and organizational transformation that have restructured European workers' lives over the last quarter-century, the products of the common responses of European capitalisms to the world economic slowdown since the 1970s, and of the fragmentation of the industrial manual working class and the growth in the service sector and white-collar working classes. We will then look at the broad lines of the trade-union crisis that resulted. Nearly one-half of Western Europe's employed workers were unionized twenty-five years ago, but today only roughly one-third are, half of whom work in the shrinking public sector. In a slowly growing labour market the consequence has been a loss of influence over governments and employers, and a marked overall decline in mobilizing capacity, particularly over national sectoral employment regulation.

Yet the ebbing of trade union influence is a complex process. We shall illustrate this in terms of the processes of change in France and Britain. In France, while trade-union membership has fallen significantly since the decade of militancy after 1968, the mass public sector strike wave of 1995 confounded the pundits who had predicted the end of class-struggle in France.[9] This has been followed by an increase in private-sector strikes in 1999 and the first quarter of 2000 in response to growing pressure from capital to eliminate the 'French exception' shown starkly in the comparatively low share of profits within French GDP. By contrast, the British trade unions seem not yet to have recovered from their significant defeat in the miner's strike of 1984–5 and remain diminished as a social force in terms of numbers as well as ideologically. Socialists, we shall suggest in conclusion, need to reflect on the different experiences of France and the UK in terms of their implications for future patterns of control and conflict, and of the possible contributions Europe's working classes can still make to fundamental political and social change.

THE EUROPEAN WORKING CLASS AND THE CHANGING NATURE OF WORK

The work carried out by Europeans has changed considerably over the last quarter-century. Four main trends are worth emphasizing here, in the context of trying to better understand the processes of working-class formation. First, work has tended to become physically lighter and less dangerous to the health. In part this is reflected in the virtual disappearance of agricultural employment and the shift from jobs in mining and heavy industry to jobs in service industries. Whereas a quarter of a century ago one in ten worked in agriculture and four out of ten in industry, two out of every three jobs in Europe today are in the service sector. These changes are captured in Table 1.

Table 1: Structural Change in Work, 1974–1998 (ranked by the size of the agricultural work-force in 1974).

Percentage of persons in civilian employment

	Services		Industry		Agriculture	
	1974	1998	1974	1998	1974	1998
UK	55.1	71.4	42.0	26.6	2.8	1.7
Sweden	48.3	71.0	37.0	25.9	6.7	3.0
Germany★	46.3	62.8	46.7	34.4	7.0	2.8
France	49.9	69.2	39.4	26.4	10.6	4.4
EU15	48.9	65.5	40.4	29.6	11.7	4.7

★Germany in 1974 was just West Germany; in 1998 it is reunified Germany.

Sources: for 1974 see OECD, *Historical Statistics: 1960–1994*, Paris: OECD, 1996; for 1998 see Eurostat, *Enquête sur les forces de travail: Résultats 1998*, Luxembourg: Eurostat, 2000.

This change obviously affected the kinds of jobs being done. It is often forgotten that both white-collar and manual workers are essential to virtually all production and service tasks. But Table 2 shows how much more dependent Europe's service sector is upon white-collar jobs than is its industrial sector.

The shift from industry to services has huge consequences on the nature of work and on the socialization processes into work. One of the effects for working-class formation arising from the shift from industry to services and to lighter work was that the classic communities associated with male manual workers, of dockers, steelworkers and miners, disappeared. At the same time service-sector work sites tended to be smaller than industrial sites, which in any case were shrinking in size. By 1992 only one third of the total EU work-force was still employed in companies with 250 or more workers, those traditionally most closely associated with high levels of union density and working-class collectivism generally.

Table 2: Occupational Composition of Salaried Employment in EU Manufacturing and Services, 1995.

	Manufacturing (%)	Services (%)
Managers, legislators and senior officials	4.8	8.3
Professionals	6.4	17.4
Technicians	10.2	15.9
Clerks	11.2	17.2
Total 'White-collar' occupations	**32.6**	**58.8**
Service workers	3.1	19.0
Craft and related trades	33.3	6.2
Plant & machine operators and assemblers	22.3	5.5
Elementary occupations	8.8	10.5
Total 'Manual' occupations	**67.5**	**41.2**

Source: European Commission, *Panorama of EU Industry*, 1997, Luxembourg: European Commission, 1997.

The second significant trend is that a growing proportion of this changing composition of collective work is now being carried out by women. Strongly implanted in Europe's informal economy a century earlier, the last quarter of the century has seen a significant return of women to active economic participation. Table 3 charts these changes between 1974 and 1994.

Table 3: Women's Share (%) of the European Labour Force, 1974–1994 (ranked by level of participation in 1974).

	1974	1994
France	37.0	43.8
UK	37.4	43.7
Germany★	37.5	42.4
Sweden	41.8	48.0
EU15	34.8	41.6

★Germany in 1974 was just West Germany; in 1998 it is reunified Germany.

Source: OECD, *Historical Statistics: 1960–1994*, Paris: OECD, 1996.

By 1998 women made up 22.6% of all EU industrial employment, and 48.8% of all service sector employment.[10] The implication of the trend towards equal participation in paid employment for the processes of working-class formation are twofold: first, the ideology of the 'male breadwinner' is becoming less materially based, with continuing tensions and collective struggles around gender inequalities (and a growing alienation of young male manual workers); while second, paid work itself is increasingly sharing space at the centre of the process of working-class formation with the family and wider non-work social experiences (like education, old age and the processes of consumption of goods and services), around which women have traditionally mobilized.

Table 4: Employment Structure (%) in France, the UK, Germany and Sweden, 1998.

	France	Germany	Sweden	UK
Directors, senior managers	7.7	5.7	4.9	15.0
Professional, intellectual, scientific (highly skilled)	10.4	12.9	15.1	15.4
Intermediate professions	17.1	19.9	20.1	8.5
Administrative staff	14.2	12.7	10.8	16.3
Personal services and sales staff	12.3	11.3	17.7	14.7
Largely white-collar %	**61.7**	**62.5**	**68.6**	**69.9**
Artisans and skilled workers	13.5	18.2	12.0	12.1
Drivers and assembly workers (semi-skilled)	10.9	7.5	10.9	8.2
Unskilled manual and white-collar workers	7.8	7.5	5.2	8.1
Largely manual %	**32.3**	**33.2**	**28.1**	**28.4**
Total numbers in employment (million)	**22.5m**	**33.5m**	**3.9m**	**26.9m**

Source: Eurostat, *Enquête sur les forces de travail: Résultats 1998*, Luxembourg: Eurostat, 2000.

The third important trend for working-class formation is that work has tended to become more 'managerial'. Much larger proportions of the work-force are now engaged in co-ordinating tasks within capitalism (in administration, buying, sales, marketing, the media, consulting, supervision, etc.) rather than in direct production. Thus in France whereas employers and senior managers (*cadres supérieurs*) were just 7.6% of the work-force in 1975, these same two categories comprised 12.8% by 1998.[11] If the definition is widened to include both 'management' and 'professional and related supporting management and administration' occupations in the UK, their proportions rose from 12.3% in 1979 to 17% by 1988, and after a decade of supposed 'managerial delayering' in 1998 were still at 16%.[12] The structure of European employment in our four target countries confirms both the dominance of white-collar occupations in national employment, and the high proportions of the combined categories of managers and highly-skilled white-collar workers. The evidence is displayed in Table 4.

In all four countries the numbers of managers and highly-skilled white-collar workers either equalled (as in Germany) or exceeded the numbers of skilled workers—who constitute a major traditional organizing centre of trade unionism. One estimate suggests that by 2000 some sixteen million 'managers' were employed within the fifteen EU states, and where they have received training it has been largely in American-style managerialism. While it is the case that for some of these managers, as with many highly-skilled white-collar workers (including this writer), new technology and the diversification of work has actually made it more intellectually interesting and engaging that twenty-five years ago, for many others this is at best only partly true. These 'managers' frequently have little direct autonomy, as the new technologies have increasingly permitted their jobs to be 'Taylorized'.[13] By some accounts their experiences of exploitation are not that different from those of less-skilled and less-well-rewarded workers with much less autonomy. A national survey of 20,000 managerial and professional workers in BT, Britain's flagship telecommunications giant, for example, found in 1999 that 50% worked over 46 hours a week (10% more than 55), 40% said they suffered from stress and 23% had experienced or witnessed bullying at work (a further 7% were unsure).[14] Yet the lack of any clear alternative to the ideology of competitiveness, means that most of these managers simply accept the longer hours and greater stress and pressure that is being imposed on them. Moreover, managers in the private sector have fairly consistently supported Europe's flirtation with new right politics in the 1980s and 1990s, and have looked to sectional market-ideology trade unionism to defend their privileges rather than to broader alliances involving other white-collar or even manual workers. On the other hand, managers in public sector jobs, particularly in Sweden and most spectacularly in France in December 1995, have been more ambivalent as to market ideology and what it means in terms of their collective identity.

The fourth change in work is a trend towards increased job insecurity and 'atypical' work schedules—on shifts, at night, at weekends, part-time, seasonally, on fixed-term contracts and on call-out. A minimum fixed-term contract where a worker signs a 'new' contract every 30 minutes has even been adopted by a sub-contractor of France Télécom to provide temporary call centre cover for peak traffic.[15] This in some ways represents a return to the liberalism of the end of the nineteenth century. Large and growing proportions of European workers (particularly women and the ethnic minority workers) do not have permanent, standard hours jobs. Many managers and skilled white-collar workers, too, now experience job insecurity, although it is of a substantially different nature to that experienced by intermediate professionals, administrative workers and semi-skilled and unskilled workers who (as we see from Table 4) together make up 50% of French employment, 47.6% of the German, 47% of the Swedish and 41.1% of the British.

The expansion in part-time working is highlighted in Table 5. While the rise in the proportion of those working part-time should, arithmetically, have enabled the century-long decline in average working hours worked to continue over the last quarter-century, the reality is more complex.

Table 5: EU Part-time Working by Persons in Employment, 1979–1998, (ranked by 1998 part-time proportion) and Average Part-time Employee Hours.

	Part-time employment (% of all employment)		Average weekly part-time hours
	1979	1998	1996
UK	16.4	24.9	17.8
Sweden	23.6	23.2	23.9
Germany	11.4	18.3	18.8
France	8.2	17.3	22.7

Sources: for 1979 see Eurostat, *Labour Force Survey: 1979 Results*, Luxembourg: Eurostat, 1981; for 1996 part-time hours see Eurostat, *Labour Force Survey: 1996 Results*, Luxembourg: Eurostat, 1998; for 1998 see Eurostat, *Enquête sur les forces de travail: Résultats 1998*, Luxembourg: Eurostat, 2000.

Despite rising unemployment the decline has really continued only in Germany, where part-time working increased considerably but where the unions also made a priority of responding to the recession by work sharing. Elsewhere, the experience generally followed that of the US, where the impact of the growth of part-time working was more than offset by the longer hours being worked by full-time workers. Table 6 shows that many European full-time workers were working longer hours in the mid-1990s than in the mid-1980s.

The growth in less secure forms of employment and in particular in socially disruptive forms of working—at night and on weekends—in the context of the shift from industrial to service-sector employment implies that many of the methods associated with continuous production flows are now being applied in the service sector. The logic of 'just-in-time' now dominates the provision of services ranging from rubbish collection to travel or life insurance. From the point of view of working-class formation the effects of the more extensive use of 'flexible' work schedules are ambiguous. On the one hand the generalization of precarious work, and in particular its concentration among women and ethnic minority workers, can permit greater understanding of the need for a collective response. On the other hand, 'flexibility' is a highly divisive and sophisticated labour-control system that often targets the most vulnerable, or renders the better organized more vulnerable, and frequently makes the physical organization of a collective identity extremely difficult.

While the four trends sketched above are having important consequences for

Figure 1: Share of GDP of OECD Europe Going to Workers (compensation) and to Capitalists (operating surplus), 1970–1996

Source: OECD, *National Accounts, Main Aggregates, 1960–1996*, Paris: OECD, 1998.

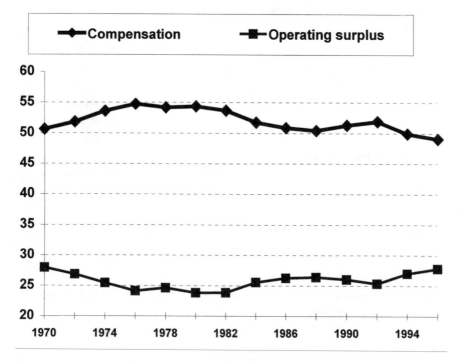

the occupational and class identities of Europe's trade unions, one other experience largely overwhelmed them during the 1980s and/or 1990s: the return of high levels of unemployment. Partly this was associated with economic restructuring away from industry, partly too, it was linked to the emergence of labour-saving technologies; but above all it was politically constructed. Europe's political parties, of right and left, adopted more or less monetarist strategies for coping with the slower rates of growth that followed the revaluing of commodity prices in the oil crises of the 1970s. Figure 1 traces the consequences of the new politics. It shows the changing class balance of GDP distribution in Western Europe's OECD member states between 1970 and 1996 as the operating surpluses available to Europe's capitalist classes first fall and then recover their 1970 levels, while the share of GDP going as compensation to European workers first rises to around 55% and then falls to under 50%, below where it stood in 1970.

In this readjustment, labour market flexibility, deregulation, privatization and deflation were all measures that were recommended (or required) by the IMF, OECD and eventually by the European Union itself. Table 7 provides a measure devised by Milton Friedman to assess over a range of fifteen policy areas the extent to which individual countries moved towards 'economic freedom'.

Table 6: Average Working Hours in Selected European Countries and the US, 1970–1997 (ranked by increases in full-time workers' weekly hours, 1983–1993).

	Average hours actually worked per person in full-time or part-time employment per year				Changes in hours of full-timers
	1970	1979	1990	1997	1983–1993
US	1,836	1,905	1,943	1,966	+4.7
UK	1,821	1,773	1,731	+3.8	n/a
Sweden	1,641	1,451	1,480	1,552	+1.8★
France	1,962	1,813	1,668	1,656	+0.4
Germany§	1,885	1,699	1,557	1,503	−6.1

★ = 1987–1994.

§ = Average hours actually worked per *employee* per year.

Sources: OECD, *Employment Outlook*, Paris: OECD, 1991 and 1998.

Table 7: Scores on Friedman's 'Economic Freedom' 1–10 ratings (ranked by extent of 'freedom' in 1995).

	1995 Rating	Initial Rating★
US	7.9	6.1a
Switzerland	7.4	7.0a
UK	7.3	4.6b
NL	6.5	5.5b
Ireland	6.5	4.1a
Germany	6.4	5.9a
France	6.1	3.6c
Denmark	5.9	3.7c
Sweden	5.9	3.5b
Italy	5.5	3.6c

★ = Initial Ratings are for (a) 1975, (b) 1980 or (c) 1985.

Source: D. Henderson, The Changing Fortunes of Economic Liberalism: Yesterday, Today and Tomorrow, Occasional Paper 108, London: Institute of Economic Affairs, 1998.

Among the policies sacrificed along the road towards 'economic freedom' were those promoting full employment. This was not just an economic goal. The notion that Western European society had responsibilities to provide employment and incomes arose during the shift to the left that occurred in the 1940s, and had been deeply embedded. However, at one point or another after 1980 the goal of full employment as the principal aim of macroeconomic policy was everywhere replaced with the target of low levels of price inflation. The result was that not only did the unions confront the four trends discussed above, they also confronted a massive rise in levels of European unemployment, as shown in Table 8.

Table 8: Standardized Average Unemployment Rates in Western Europe (% of total labour force), 1974–1997 (ranked by unemployment in 1974).

	1974–79	1980–89	1990–97
UK	5.0	10.0	8.8
France	4.5	10.8	11.2
Germany	3.2	5.9	7.9
Sweden	1.9	2.5	7.5

Source: OECD, *Unemployment Outlook*, Paris: OECD, 1991, 1998.

Conditions of exploitation and alienation clearly have not been eliminated for European workers. The 'new' capitalisms of Western Europe have not changed their spots. In this sense the 'old' working class has also not gone away. The relations of nearly three-quarters of the work-forces of Western Europe to capital remain distinct, inherently conflictual and are often disputed. However, the changing nature of work, its feminization, its managerialization and its increasing precariousness have had significant impact on working-class identities, posing severe problems for European trade unions.

THE IMPACT OF CHANGE ON EUROPEAN TRADE UNIONS

How then did Europe's trade unions respond to the four trends discussed above delivered in a political climate where flexibility, deregulation, privatization and higher unemployment were all political weapons used to achieve increases in the share of GDP disposable to its capitalist classes? The unions had, after all, shifted to the left in the 1970s, as had society as a whole. It is important to remember that voting for left-wing parties across thirteen Western European countries only reached its postwar high of 36.8% in 1976–1980, up from its average 33.6% share in 1961–1965.[16] Union movements that had traditionally been quite close to narrower, occupational business unionism, had been challenged from within by newer and broader visions. Common union demands throughout Western Europe in the 1970s included those for 'workers' control', directly-elected workers' directors, workers' participation via union-controlled investment funds, for more protection against dismissal for workers' representatives, for extensive regulation of multinational companies (the International Labour Organization even published a declaration on good multinational corporation practice) and of employment conditions generally, and for extensions of nationalization.

The harsher contexts of the 1980s and 1990s largely, but not entirely, effaced all of these aspirations. The few new progressive reforms already introduced into national laws were either left languishing or repealed by right-wing administrations, and the unions largely abandoned the advocacy of those reforms not yet realized. Trade-union tactics that had worked in periods of low unemployment seemed increasingly ineffective virtually everywhere. Only in Sweden did trade-union membership rise in the new era. Political pressure on the Social Democratic government ensured that government employment initially expanded to fill the gap created by contractions in the private sector, but even here unemployment in the 1990s was allowed to rise to 7.5%—nearly as high as in Germany and the UK. Nevertheless, the robust role played by the Ghent system in Sweden, whereby the unions were largely responsible for the administration of unemployment insurance, ensured that workers (manual, white-collar, skilled and unskilled) responded rationally to the rising threat of unemployment by joining unions. By 1995, 91% of Swedish wage and salaried workers were union members compared to 84% ten years earlier.[17]

Elsewhere the dimensions of the ensuing trade union crisis were similar not only in terms of falling union membership and density, but also in terms of an ageing membership, difficulties in feminizing in proportion to the rising share of women workers, problems of unionizing in smaller work-places and especially in the fast-expanding private service sector of the economy. The unions generally became less representative of the work-force, and often much less capable of mobilizing workers, either in terms of voting or in terms of strike action. According to ILO figures, union membership as a percentage of wage and salary earners had by 1995 fallen in the UK to 33% (from 46% in 1985), in the reunited Germany to 29% (from 35% in 1991), and in France to 9% (from 15% in 1985).[18] In Britain's private sector, where firms increasingly decided against recognizing trade unions, the proportion of work-places of more than twenty-five workers which had at least one work-place union representative fell from 38% in 1980 to 17% in 1998.[19] Table 9 shows these changes in union membership; strike rates (which fell everywhere apart from Germany where it remained at a very low level despite a small blip upwards after reunification), and collective bargaining coverage (which remained surprisingly resilient except in the UK).

But while formal national or sectoral collective agreements remained in place, their content tended to leave more and more of the detail to decentralized local enterprise bargaining. More European firms (at least outside the Scandinavian countries) are managing without unions. In larger establishments where unions cannot be avoided employers have increasingly embraced human resource management techniques for involving the unions in the processes of company policy legitimation, and for persuading local union representatives to embrace a form of enterprise unionism. Thus in both Germany and France in the 1990s many works councils, although formally without negotiating rights on issues concerned with collective bargaining, have gradually become a conduit for 'agreements' that permit greater enterprise-level 'flexibility' than laid down in the nationally or regionally established collective agreement. In Britain the trade-union movement has officially embraced 'partnership' with the employers as a means of trying to secure continued recognition for its representative role.

Table 9: Trade Union Density, Strike Rates and Collective Bargaining, 1980–1994.

	Change (%) in trade union density, 1980–1994	Change (%) in strike rate, 1980/4–1990/3	Change (%) in collective bargaining, 1980–1994
France	−9	−41	+10
Germany	−7	+14	+1
Sweden	+11	−83	+3
UK	−16	−81	−23

Sources: OECD, *Employment Outlook*, Paris: OECD, 1997; Aligisakis, *International Labour Review*, 1997.

Not surprisingly, given these responses to the membership crisis, the unions also faced growing organizational problems. Levels of participation in the unions generally fell, although by how much is difficult to tell. Many unions offered discounted membership to part-time or young workers, and established women-only structures to try and increase their participation. In Belgium, Denmark, Italy, the Netherlands and Britain, packages of financial services, such as credit cards and insurance, were offered as incentives to join. In Germany, Denmark and Britain union leaders frequently responded to the gathering crisis by seeking to take over smaller unions or to merge. This process, of course, did little to appeal to those whose union membership reflected an occupational identity rather than the need for particular services. Membership has fallen but membership heterogeneity has increased, creating greater challenges for effective representation. In Britain between 1982 and 1994 the numbers of Trade Unions Congress (TUC)-affiliated unions fell from 105 to 68 and the total of their memberships fell from 11 million to 7.2 million (1.9 million of these members belonged to unions swallowed up in the 17 mergers between TUC affiliates).[20]

The evidence to date is that, while these mergers may have guaranteed the pensions of the full-time officials of the unions concerned, they have not made a significant difference to resolving the trade-union crisis. They do, however, have one important and potentially negative aspect: the muting or even suppression of traditions of dissent and pluralism within the merging unions. The Left inside the trade unions have (except in France) broadly supported mergers on the grounds of 'solidarity' and in the hope that they could strengthen union bargaining power. But they have then found themselves in a still more isolated minority situation in a larger union whose main post-merger purpose appears to be to try and survive the culture shock and power struggles brought on by the merger.

The decline in union membership appears to have slowed or stopped around the mid-1990s. This may be explained by three factors: first, the greater emphasis the unions are starting to place on organizing and recruitment and, related to this, a technological boost from the establishment of direct debit systems of receiving union dues which keeps those who are union members paying more regularly; second, a (possibly temporary) less unfavourable political climate for trade unionism, with most (and briefly in 1998 as many as thirteen) of the EU countries governed by left or centre-left parties; and third, the impact of the general economic recovery in Western Europe which helped lower unemployment and slow the job losses in union-strong industrial sectors.

One further element should be added to the outline of a defensive and weak European trade-union response to the open assault being made upon it by capital over the last twenty-five years. This is the European Union dimension. This is not the place to debate whether Europe itself is a possible forum for mobilization, or how effective European social law is in terms of restraining capital. But it is necessary to record that one of the responses of the nationally weaker trade union movements to the crisis was to invest a little more in terms of resources and lobbying in trying to create a European social framework of employment regulation. Partly as a result, watered-down laws have been passed on a range of issues, among which the most significant are measures covering workers' redundancy rights, equal pay rights, consultation rights, working time, health and safety, part-time and temporary working conditions. Rights to organize or to strike have so far been rejected, and most of the substantive law that has been passed has had very little real effect because it is so minimal. However, a bottle can either appear half-empty or half-full, and Europe's unions are still committed at the official level of the European Trade Union Confederation (ETUC) to trying to extend workers' rights through the highly institutional, remote and often non-democratic processes that are available.

CHANGE IN FRANCE AND BRITAIN

The French and UK cases are representative in their own ways of the two extremes of union responses to the changes in Europe of the last twenty-five years. A common lament from French employers is about how little employment relations and government intervention have changed in France since the 1970s. Politically the reason for their concern is fairly obvious. After twenty-three continuous years of right-wing government, from 1958 to 1981, in the

Figure 2: **The Growth (000s) in French Public Sector Employment, 1980–1996**
Source: INSEE, *Tableaux de l'économie Française: Edition 2000,* Paris: INSEE, 2000.

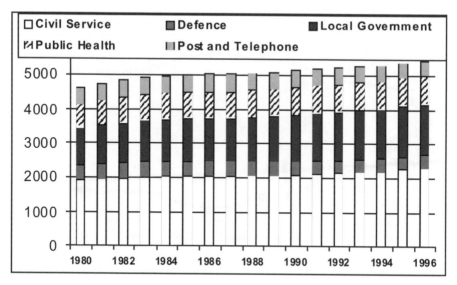

following twenty years France either had a left or centre-left president or parliament governing for all but two years, and for a third of these eighteen years the Communist Party has even been included as a coalition partner. Little wonder, then, that the open adoption of neoliberal policies has been eschewed, and that the employers have felt they lacked allies. For in the same way that New Labour embraced aspects of Thatcherism, the French right (a cross between Gaullist nationalists, Christian Democrats and political liberals) has adopted or retained major aspects of Mitterrandism (many of which were inherited, in any case, from De Gaulle's *dirigisme*).

There were two critical political moments in France since 1981 from the employers' point of view. The first significantly slowed down the pace of deregulation in France. It was the 1988 presidential election, when to most commentators' surprise, Mitterrand was elected for a second term of office. This slowed down the advance of neoliberalism and persuaded the largest component of the right, the Gaullist Party, that this was not an effective political platform on which to run. Immediately France's privatization programme was put into cold storage—from which it re-emerged only with the election of another right-wing parliament in 1993—and although Mitterrand's centre-left Socialist governments of 1988–93 continued to apply monetarism and to encourage employers to increase work-place flexibility, they made no major attack on French welfare and actually increased public sector and in particular female employment in an attempt to counter high unemployment. By 1996,

**Figure 3: French Capital's Operating Surpluses and Workers'
Compensation as a Share of GDP, 1960–1996**
Source: OECD, *National Accounts, Main Aggregates, 1960–1996*, Paris:
OECD, 1998.

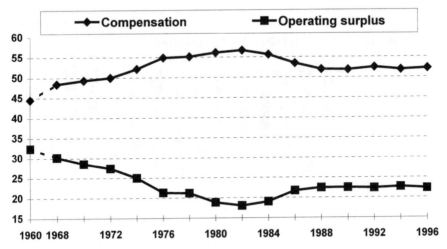

56% of civil servants and 60% of local government officers were women
compared to a private sector female participation rate of 45%. Civil service
numbers also rose after 1988, and these increases continued under the right-
wing Balladur government from 1993. Figure 2 shows how overall government
employment (including the post office and the now partly-privatized France
Télécom) has risen throughout the last two decades, from 4.8 million in 1982
to 5.4 million by 1996, by when it had risen from 20.5% of the active population to 21.3%, but was actually one in four of those in a job.

The second critical moment in recent French history was the public sector
strike wave of 1995. This occurred just six months after the Gaullist candidate
Jacques Chirac had been elected President on a highly opportunistic platform
that included defending French social security rights and supporting wage
increases. The result of his government's subsequent attack on French public
sector workers' pension arrangements was devastating. More workers came on
to the streets to demonstrate than had done so in 1968, a month-long railway
strike virtually ground the economy to a halt, and in the end the continued
popular support for the strikers meant the government was forced to back
down.[21] Not only did this workers' mobilization postpone any serious attempt
to reform the pension system, but it also led directly to the 1997 parliamentary
election defeat suffered by the right. This election was won by the Socialist
Party in coalition with the Greens and the Communists, and on a political
programme whose core remained social democratic. It included commitments
to introducing a shorter working week to help create new jobs, and to regulating capital movements in and out of France.

The French employers could thus be said to have a point. Since 1988 in particular the resilience of French workers' pensions within GDP has meant that although real wages have not risen, French workers' overall compensation has not continued to fall, and French capital's operating surplus has stopped rising, as illustrated in Figure 3. By 1996 both were still far from recovering their positions of 1968, before the decade of conflict that marked the 1970s.

The argument here is not that French capital is weak. Far from it. As the world's fourth largest economy (after the US, Japan and Germany), its capitalist class has done and is doing well. The argument is that the French state, under pressure from political and industrial representatives of the working class, actually does restrict capital's ability to exploit French workers in various ways. At the lowest level, this means a labour code which states that workers cannot eat their lunches where they actually work, thereby providing a 'legal' reinforcement of the culturally-powerful French lunch 'break', that has virtually ceased to exist for many equivalent British workers. At a higher level it also means that dismissing workers takes much longer and is generally much more expensive than almost anywhere else in Europe. While some suggest this may create a disincentive to invest in France, this factor, if it exists, is probably more than compensated for by the additional costs attached to disinvesting from France or being absent from the French market. Certainly none of a series of econometric studies by the OECD have been able to provide clear evidence that high levels of collective bargaining coverage, high minimum wage rates or employment protection are associated with low economic performance.[22] The French unemployment replacement rate (the average income maintained during the first year of unemployment), for example, currently stands at 75% for low-paid workers falling to about 50% of higher-paid workers, compared to an average of just 30% in the UK. Yet from the French employers' viewpoint their freedom to secure 'normal' European levels of profit is being denied by the average 48% non-wage labour costs of employment, compared to the 45% in Germany, 41% in Sweden and 29% in the UK.[23]

It is these comparisons with other European and US experiences, the fact that a quarter of the work-force is involved in productive and service activity not under the direct control of the market, and their sense that a strong protectionist and dirigiste state will no longer be the best guarantor of their future prosperity that makes French employers more combative in the current resurgence of industrial relations conflict in France. After the Gaullist and right political parties split again in 1999, the employers have largely given up hoping in the short-term that the right will be re-elected on a neoliberal platform. So, drawing on the anger generated among smaller firms at the 35-hour week laws passed by the Socialist coalition government passed in June 1998 and January 2000, the main French employers' association relaunched itself in 1998 as the 'Movement' of French enterprises (the *Medef*). In 1999, capitalizing on the larger employers' strategic sense of trade-union weakness, the *Medef* threatened to pull out of the social security, unemployment and pension funds that it jointly runs with the unions unless they accept radical changes. The threat, of course, may successfully split the unions and lead to a new settlement much less favourable to French workers as a whole. But it may also be a bluff that if called could have a reverse effect to that intended: namely it might help reforge a sense of working-class unity and identity between French manual and white-collar workers. Whatever happens, the conflict illustrates the extent to which French employers feel distanced from state power and influence.

Does this mean that the numerically weak trade-union movement feels much closer to the French Socialist Party? Unlike the British Labour Party there have never been organic links between the French unions and socialists. Far from giving money to political parties, the French union confederations tend to be the recipients of benefits in terms of cheap or no-cost accommodation for offices or conferences, provided by local government authorities being run by friendly politicians. If anything, although always secretive and much denied, the strongest links were between the Communist Party (PCF) and the Confédération Général du Travail (CGT) trade union confederation—although these too now can be said to no longer exist in any real form, since the CGT on two occasions in 1999 and early 2000 refused to appeal to its members to support demonstrations called by the PCF. On the other hand, the plurality of linkages between the five state-'recognized' trade-union confederations and the government, has meant that informal contacts do occur on a very regular basis. Some socialist ministerial advisers are known to be former trade unionists, and although they lack a formal stature, these avenues all continue to offer ways of exercising pressure on the state as it attempts to secure a social settlement between capital and labour.

More important, however, is the French union movement's mobilizing capacity. It still has the power, as shown in 1995, to confront a government and play a part in its downfall. Part of this strength lies in the postwar settlement, which constructed the social welfare system that has been run ever since by the employers and trade unions, thereby legitimating the latter's presence, often directly funding union full-time officials and institutionalizing trade-union pluralism. Because at the time the government did not wish to reward the majority Communist-controlled CGT, it created a situation which formally gave nearly as many rights to minority unions as to majority ones.Unlike the situation in the UK, this encouraged the elaboration of and eventually the preservation of discrete political identities around the trade union ideologies of the market, social integration and class struggle discussed above. In turn, the fact that at virtually all negotiations there was at least one union represented that would criticize proposals from a class perspective (however distorted by Stalinism) meant that the others, too, would often be forced to make their arguments in broad class terms. In 1988, when the Confédération Française Démocratique du Travail (CFDT) ceased to espouse a bottom-up conflict perspective, and started a major shift towards the ideologies of market 'realism', the loose federal structure of French trade unionism allowed a new formation,

SUD (Solidaires, unitaires, démocratiques) to emerge, first in the nationalized post and telecommunications, and later in most of the rest of the public sector.[24] Its growth during the 1990s to a position where it is now the second or third strongest union in terms of votes for public sector works council representatives, testifies to the continued links between the processes of trade-union organization, the wider political perspective of working-class struggle, and the institutional characteristics of the French industrial relations and welfare systems. Indeed, the union legitimation (and the numbers of full-time union posts provided) resulting from their social welfare role is one important reason the *Medef* is now targeting the post-war settlement that brought it about; the other is its desire to bring this potentially highly profitable insurance business into the private domain.

A still more important reason for the survival of union power lies in the fact that although they now persuade fewer than one in ten of all workers to pay union dues, in most larger work-places trade unionists still receive more than three-quarters of all votes cast in works council elections; and on the right issue, when the unions issue a strike call, they can be followed by anywhere between one in five and two out of three workers. Non-unionists in work-places where there are union representatives will almost always say, as frequently as unionists, that it is vital for a union to be present and that the union makes a difference.

The way in which the trade unions represent the working class in Britain is totally different. As we have seen, the British unions have a larger (although declining) membership, but have also always been much more occupationally-rooted and are recognized not as a result of any legal right but by employer acquiescence. In the last two decades the political context has been the near opposite to that of France: instead of two decades of centre-left government, there have just transpired nearly two decades of overtly ideologically right-wing government. This gave virtually unlimited rein to management to reverse the earlier defeats it had experienced over anti-union laws and miners' wage rises in 1972 and over the general election of 1974. In contrast to the continuing influence of French unions as the economy adjusted to the world economic slowdown, the British trade unions were totally excluded by the Conservatives. One outcome was a decisive shift towards increased inequality in Britain. While Sweden and France (where multi-employer bargaining was not dismantled) managed the processes of change in the 1980s and early 1990s without significantly changing income inequalities for those at work, the UK experience tended to mirror (although less extremely) that of the US.[25] Moreover, as Figure 4 shows, by 1996 British capital had succeeded not merely in returning to its 1970 level of operating surplus as a proportion of GDP, but in surpassing it by 25%, while simultaneously reducing the share of employee compensation (wages and pensions) since 1980 by over 5%.

There were three key events in the right's successes in Britain. The Falklands War of 1982 proved a godsend to a deeply unpopular Conservative adminis-

**Figure 4: UK Capital's Operating Surpluses and Workers'
Compensation as a Share of GDP, 1960–1996**
Source: OECD, *National Accounts, Main Aggregates, 1960–1996*, Paris:
OECD, 1998.

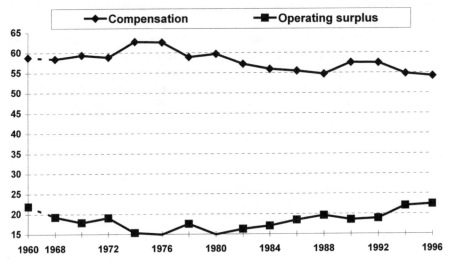

tration, which wrapped itself in the Union Jack and decisively won the 1983
General Election. More strategically, however, there was the historic defeat of
the miners' strike of 1984–5 and the context of a 15-year-long period of high
unemployment. These bit deeply into union membership and confidence.
Between 1980 and 1998 the proportion of work-places with 25 or more
employees that reported 100% union membership fell from 18 to 2%; while
those reporting no union members at all rose from 30 to 47%; among private
sector work-places union density fell from 56 to 26%. By 1998 a national
survey of work-places with 25 or more employees found that only 52% of
unionized workers felt that the unions were taken seriously by management,
and only 46% felt that unions make a difference to what it is like at work.
Among *non-unionized* workers views were still much more critical: only 30%
felt the unions made a difference.[26]

The third key event that helped configure late-twentieth-century British
trade unionism was the Conservative's fortuitous election victory of 1992. This
followed two years after a mass popular class rebellion against the Thatcher poll
tax reform had temporarily forged a new vision of 'us' against 'them', where
the 'us' embraced wide sections of white-collar middle class as well as manual
workers, and had led to Thatcher's removal as Tory leader. Yet the Labour
Party failed to capitalize on this broad resurgence of a working-class presence,
notably in proposing to raise income taxes on significant elements of the 'new'
middle classes, including groups like primary school head teachers, rather than
focusing on taxes on the rich and the wealthy. The following five years then

saw the Labour Party fall into the hands of the 'Third Way' Blairites. Under its leadership 'New Labour' rapidly rejected the core social democratic promises of redistribution, of tackling structural inequality and of empowering independent employee representation, all of which had featured in the 1992 election programme, and adopted instead a Clinton-style 'New Democrat' modernizing and liberalizing managerial platform.

Where for nearly a century craft unionism, US-style business unionism and class-oriented unionism (whether of the reformist or revolutionary variety) had flourished hand in hand in Britain, by the mid-1990s the latter had been marginalized. The proud National Union of Miners that had still had a quarter of a million members in 1984 saw its membership drop below 25,000 and Arthur Scargill reduced to a minor sectarian figure—a caricature of the great political and union miners' leader of the 1970s and 1980s. The earlier pluralistic ideology of labourism was largely replaced by a new language stressing 'partnership' and the end of adversarialism. While its core was nothing new—this form of business unionism had been the subject of the Mond-Turner talks after the defeat of the 1926 General Strike—the particular discourse was taken from continental Europe. There it is essentially based on a blend of Christian democracy with human resource management ideology, but in a context where 'partnership' is enforced by a series of constitutional and institutional rights established in the late 1940s when the balance of class forces was much more equal. In the UK, in a voluntaristic industrial relations system, and as an accompaniment of a defensively-motivated union merger movement and of the virtual disappearance of a coherent publicly-articulated socialist critique of capital within the trade-union movement, the adoption of the 'partnership' approach has encouraged a marked homogeneity of trade-union discourse. The old political divisions between 'left' and 'right' in most major unions where politics had been contested for generations virtually disappeared in the late 1990s, and in the few unions where the left has still been able to mount candidates for high office left votes have rarely exceeded 30%. Where has the Labour 'Left' gone? Some of its components have been attracted to the Blairite project. This provides an ideological justification for the shift towards the advocacy of 'third way' employer partnerships that has been embraced by the Britain's recently merged engineering and electrical union (the AEEU). Others have chosen to remain silent in face of the New Labour machine which has so successfully centralized the Labour Party as to place near-complete power over its internal life in the hands of Blair's inner cabinet. This process has been resisted and above all resented by many Labour Party activists, who were thus ready in both Wales and London to support anti-Blairite candidates in the cautious moves Labour is making to restoring or creating some forms of regional and local government. In London, the former Greater London Council leader and virtually the only remaining Left parliamentary critic of New Labour, Ken Livingstone, won the Mayoral election in May 2000 with the support of huge numbers of angry Labour supporters, as well as with the votes of Conservatives and others just wanting to attack Labour. However, the most important signal from this local election was the massive abstentions by traditional Labour voters angry that New Labour was not representing their interests effectively.

Largely unchallenged, important parts of the trade-union movement are openly seeking to sustain their existence through transforming themselves from bargainers over universal, basic sectoral or occupational labour-market conditions into the providers of services to 'enterprise unionism'. Table 10 illustrates the declining importance of multi-employer collective bargaining in Britain in the Conservative era.

Table 10: The Decline of Multi-employer Collective Bargaining in Different Sectors of the British Economy, 1980–1998.

	1980	1998
Distribution of employees		
Private sector manufacturing	38	25
Private sector services	26	44
Public sector	36	32
Multi-employer collective bargaining with recognized unions		
Private sector manufacturing	57	25
Private sector services	54	12
Public sector	81	47

Source: M. Cully, S. Woodland, A. O'Reilly and G. Dix, *Britain at Work as depicted by the 1998 Workplace Employee Relations Survey*, London: Routledge, 2000.

The strategy of embracing single-employer bargaining will, its advocates contend, make them acceptable as interlocutors, not only to workers seeking independent and adversarial representation but also to company human resource management departments. Its implementation is likely to draw British trade unionism still closer to the American model, where bargaining pressure is exercised essentially on individual firms and not on the basic standards within the wider labour market at the sectoral or national levels. In adopting this approach, 'partnership' supporters are effectively redefining the purpose of trade unionism much more narrowly around market unionism than it has been in the past. Whether this strategy can succeed in providing a meaningful focus for working-class representation at the level of the individual firm in a context where the common trends in work discussed above have become more predominant, and are demanding an increasingly general political response, is, however, far from assured. There is little enough in the American example to give rise to confidence that this is a viable recipe for trade-union influence over twenty-first-century capitalism.

WORKING CLASS CHANGE AND THE FUTURE

We have attempted to provide a broad-brush view of current trends in European working-class formation and trade-union response. In part the range of responses sketched reflect the countries' different political fortunes. During the 1980s and 1990s Britain experienced eighteen years of radical right-wing governments, consistently ready to use the state's power against the unions and in favour of private enterprise. By contrast in France, although a government elected in 1981 on a radical socialist platform had by 1983 given way even on Keynesian reformism, neoliberalism was nevertheless held in check by the strength of the Gaullist Christian Democratic and *dirigiste* traditions, by the electoral intervention of the neo-fascist National Front whose substantial support effectively denied the democratic right the monopoly of political power it might otherwise have enjoyed, and by an electoral system that sustains coalitions, debate and political diversity. The result was twofold: first, French social democracy was not significantly pulled to the right other than by the 'natural' effects of running a successful capitalist economy in an era of monetarism; and second, the presence of Communist and Green parties and others to its left meant the Socialist Party at least retained its rhetorical commitments to redistribution of wealth and regulation of capital. The decline of the Communist Party from about 20% of the vote in the 1970s to 6–8% today has been 'compensated' by the emergence of the Greens with about 8–10% and of the Far Left with 4–6%. The *de facto* political consensus which ensued meant that despite rising and then high French unemployment, and despite significant changes in the balance of class forces in favour of capital, the French state continued to support the welfare and industrial relations social partnership and regulatory systems established after the Liberation and not only retained but actually increased its employment share during the 1980s and 1990s. In Britain where no such political mediation occurred to soften, regulate and protect the working class from global market intervention, and where the political system allowed majority governments to be elected on a minority of votes, labour legislation was rewritten to totally undermine effective trade-union action, and virtually all the industries and services nationalized by Labour after 1945 were privatized or obliged to surrender key parts of their activities to private-sector contractors.

These different political experiences account for a great deal in terms of the range of potential the different movements now possess. In Britain, where union mergers seem to be further disorienting the membership, the crisis has fostered still further depoliticization, alongside a real retreat by the Left. The election of one Socialist Alliance candidate to the Scottish Parliament, the achievement of votes of between five and ten percent for Socialist Alliance candidates in three of London's twenty-five London regional seats, and the two small but militant anti-WTO demonstrations in 1999 and 2000 confirm that there is a Left potential, but also that it is very weak indeed. In France, on the other hand, the crisis has led to a considerable political debate among the activists about how to proceed at a time of considerable organizational difficulty and challenge from the employers. In turn, in the absence of traditions of all-embracing union formations, disagreements about how far to 'go along with' or 'oppose' the new trends have led both to the very rapid growth of SUD (now a part of the Group of Ten independent trade-union organizations) and to the establishment of several new political-union networks (linking unemployed, anti-racist, Tobin tax campaigns and anti-WTO movements with union activists). Also, and with perhaps even greater implications for the future, outside these often professionally-driven 'formal' protest channels, in November 1998 French 16–18-year-olds staged a massive series of strikes and 200,000-strong demonstrations for more teachers and resources that won significant government concessions. This was followed in the winter of 1999–2000 by a wave of teacher strikes that eventually forced the resignation of the minister of education.

With suitable caution, the discussion and examples from France and Britain suggest certain arguments in the general debate about the direction of Western European trade unionism. First, there is the very obvious point that in order to maintain its genuine claim to representation, the trade-union movement must bring its agenda more closely in line with the aspirations and fears of the changing work-force. Above all, the contrasting experience of Britain and France suggests this means defending by all means necessary and available the concept of *labour market-wide* regulation of employment conditions. This is both a *class* project and one which is probably the only effective way of preventing the 'race to the bottom' which is commonly, and rightly, seen as a consequence of enterprise unionism. It is one which involves unions taking the initiative, as Richard Hyman argues, in establishing a 'worker-oriented meaning of flexible working time', in developing policies for 'enhanced individual entitlements to education and training ... for more effective (and workers-oriented) provisions both by employers and by education and training institutions ... for demand-side policies to encourage employment growth', and in mobilizing to create 'a genuine and favourable structure of opportunities ... necessarily a collective project, one which challenges both employers' discretion and the anarchy of market forces.'[27] Collective bargaining needs to be maintained, strengthened or re-established with an agenda that offers across-the-board benefits to all workers.

Second, given the trends towards greater influence of global capitalism within national borders (that we have not had space to discuss here, but by which we mean the increasing share of global capital in, for example, French and German companies and their adoption of American accounting and reporting procedures), it is more likely that the most successful ways of achieving labour market-wide regulation in the future will be *politically* rather than through traditional collective bargaining. This may mean political lobbying of governments, national and European, to pass laws regulating capital and laying down minimum conditions; or it may mean mobilizing workers and consumers in boycotts of particular companies; or it may involve the defence of immigrant workers' rights to enter the labour market; or it may mean the support for—or the formation of—political parties that will still represent workers' interests. It also involves unions associating themselves more clearly with the objectives of the environmental, anti-genetically modified food, anti-racist, feminist and anti-globalization movements. Their activities question the legitimacy of the contemporary distribution of power and capitalism's priorities for the world's resources, the same ideological starting point for union resistance to individual managements. Above all, the shift of trade unionism towards a more political focus encompasses a broad vision conception of trade unionism and of its responsibility to play a progressive role in society.

These first two objectives imply a third: the need to reshape the texture of collective adversarialism from its current stereotype based around ageing white male manual workers to fit the current dominant model of a feminized flexible white-collar labour force. This involves unions investing in their 'new' activists—through training and research—to provide an organizational underpinning to a critical independent approach both to their companies and to capital. It involves developing new and imaginative ways of struggling, many of which will involve the new technologies that paradoxically permit both greater managerial control, while enabling broader and more sophisticated vistas of employee resistance. By taking the sense of political independence that is still retained by significant minorities of French trade unionists, and generalizing this out, the political will to maintain and develop these independent forms of working-class organization into the new millennium can not only be sustained, but also, clearly, can make a difference.

Europe's working classes are thus faced with two major questions at the start of the new millennium: can their unions continue to provide effective interest representation of working people, and can their social democratic parties (or any other) remain (or become) distinct expressions of a critical approach to capitalism that programmatically and in practice attempts to curb workers' exposure to market forces? We have argued that by 2000, after twenty-five years of attrition, working-class identities are fragmenting and working-class interests are losing ground to capital. However, they are still far from being counted out. This is much clearer in France, Germany and Sweden than it is in the UK. Indeed, and paradoxically for many, the result of the extension of certain minimum working rights under European Union social legislation driven by social democratic and Christian democratic pressure from continental Europe is that UK workers today have access to more employment rights than they have ever had before, and are increasingly exercising them. It should not be imagined, though, that the retention of worker influence in France, Germany and Sweden resulted simply from incorporationist strategies adopted by their capitalist classes. In each of these countries there were higher levels of conflict in the 1990s than in the second half of the 1980s, as the employers kept testing for concrete evidence of worker demobilization. The broad retention and even partial extension of some elements of protection from 'free' market forces is important as an indicator of the degree of articulation of working-class interests. Essentially they testify to the complexity of running capitalist societies where the owners of capital have to secure some form of legitimation for policies aimed at increasing their operating surpluses at the expense of workers' compensation. European differences and in particular the contrast between the UK and France thus suggest that although facing similar pressures, there is no single monolithic trend sweeping all before it in a headlong rush towards Milton Friedman's 'economic freedoms'. Europe's working classes still have voices and they are still being exercised.

NOTES

1. The employers' estimate of strikers was 20% below that of the unions, but was still substantial at 31.5% of the total labour force. In some cities the banks admitted that between 70% and 80% had been involved.
2. *Le Monde*, 2 December 1999.
3. Eurostat, *Enquête sur les forces de travail: Résultats 1998*, Luxembourg: Office des publications officielles des Communautés Européennes, 2000.
4. For a whole book that attempts to monitor these changes see Mick Carpenter and Steve Jefferys, *Management, Work and Welfare in Western Europe: A Historical and Contemporary Analysis*, Aldershot: Edward Elgar, 2000.
5. See Jelle Visser, *Industrial Relations and Social Dialogue*, Geneva: International Labour Organization, 1999, pp. 1–60.
6. This comparison is additionally of interest since both these two countries entered the new millennium under 'socialist' governments elected in 1997, thereby posing important questions about the contemporary political reach of the different trade unionisms.
7. See Richard Hyman, 'Union identities and ideologies in Europe', in P. Pasture, J. Verberckmoes and H. de Witte, eds., *The Lost Perspective? Trade unions between ideology and social action in the New Europe: Significance of Ideology in European Trade Unionism*, Aldershot: Avebury, 1996, pp. 60–89.
8. See Steve Jefferys, 'A Tale of Two Conferences: British and French bank trade union activists compared', *Industrial Relations Journal*, forthcoming.
9. See Steve Jefferys, 'Down but not out: French Unions after Chirac', *Work, Employment & Society*, vol. 10, no. 3, 1996, pp. 509–527; Steve Jefferys, 'France 1995: the backward march of labour halted?', *Capital and Class*, no. 59, pp. 7–21.
10. Eurostat, 'Enquête sur les forces de travail'.
11. INSEE, *Tableaux de l'économie Française: Edition 2000*, Paris: INSEE, 2000.
12. HMSO, *Labour Force Survey 1979*, London: HSMO, 1981; HMSO, *Labour Force Survey 1988-1989*, London: HMSO, 1991, ONS, *Labour Force Survey Quarterly Supplement 2*, London: HMSO, 1998.
13. See Carpenter and Jefferys, *Management, Work and Welfare in Western Europe*, chapter 6, for a discussion of these trends.
14. Society of Telecomms Executives, *Stressing Performance VIII*, Wimbledon: STE, 1999.
15. *Le Monde*, 22 April 2000.
16. Bartolini, 1989.
17. International Labour Organization, *World Labour Report*, Geneva: ILO, 1997.

18. Ibid.

19. M. Cully, S. Woodland, A. O'Reilly and G. Dix, *Britain at Work as depicted by the 1998 Workplace Employee Relations Survey*, London: Routledge, 2000.

20. See J. Waddington, R. Hoffman and J. Lind, 'European trade unionism in transition? A review of the issues', *Transfer*, no. 3, 1997; and R. Undy, 'The British movement: the importance of the "aggressive" unions', *Industrial Relations Journal*, vol. 30, no. 5, 1999.

21. For two complementary accounts of the strike see Jefferys, 'Down but not out' and Jefferys, 'France 1995'.

22. See the continuing failure of attempts to 'prove' the economic case for neoliberalism in the OECD's *Employment Outlook* since 1994.

23. See A. Hassel, and B. Ebbinghaus, 'Concerted reforms: Linking wage formation and social policy in Europe', International Conference of Europeanists, Chicago, 30 March 2000.

24. Annick Coupé and Anne Marchand, eds., *Sud: syndicalement incorrect: Sud-Ptt une aventure collective,* Paris: Syllepse, 1998.

25. OECD, *Employment Outlook*, Paris: OECD, 1997, p. 68. The income gap between the bottom decline and median earnings increased by 0.11% and 0.06% per year respectively for US men and women between 1979 and 1989, and by 0.05% per year for all UK workers of both genders.

26. Cully et al., 'Britain at Work'.

27. Richard Hyman, 'Trade unions and interest representation in the context of globalization', *Transfer*, vol. 3, no. 1, 1997.

'WHY IS THERE NO REVOLT?
THE RUSSIAN WORKING CLASS
AND LABOUR MOVEMENT

DAVID MANDEL

'Why is there no revolt?' People sympathetic to Russian workers naturally pose this question when faced with accounts of impoverishment, mass unemployment, unpaid wages, wholesale dismantling of social programmes, the pillaging of national wealth and destruction of the country's human and economic potential, and an illegitimate government that has made contempt for the law the centrepiece of its policy. Russian workers have suffered tremendously over the past years of capitalist restoration, even if their situation was far from ideal to begin with. While they have resisted, the resistance has obviously been ineffective. This was unexpected by most observers, given that the working class formed the vast majority of the Soviet population, was relatively well-educated, socially quite homogeneous, concentrated in giant enterprises, massively organized in trade unions, thoroughly exposed to socialist ideas (if not reality), and enjoyed a standard of living well above Third World levels.

This essay offers elements of an answer to the question 'Why don't they revolt?' It presents them under three headings: the legacy of the Soviet past; the current economic and political situation; and, finally, the strategy and practice of the unions, the main organized form of the labour movement today. The argument, briefly, is that the Soviet system, both because of its repressive nature and the contradictory nature of its social relations—neither capitalist nor socialist but an incoherent amalgam of both—prevented the emergence of an independent working class practice and consciousness. This began to develop under Perestroika, as the system collapsed. But the form that collapse assumed—a 'revolution from above' in which the popular movement played a subordinate role—and the unprecedentedly deep economic crisis that immediately followed, have held back and, to some extent, reversed this process, giving a new lease on life to the old corporatist practice. A final section discusses the independent, minority current in the labour movement and its prospects. By way of illustration, the essay focuses on unions in the auto and agricultural machine-building sectors (ASM in the Russian acronym), which are in most ways typical but have also often been on the cutting edge of labour movements in Russia as elsewhere.

THE LEGACY

The Soviet economy formally 'belonged' to the people, whose legal title was consecrated in the constitution. In practice, the people's ownership rights—the rights to decide collectively what and how to produce and how to use the surplus—were usurped by the managers, the *nomenklatura*. Soviet workers did not face a class of owners, who could buy and sell the means of production and distribution. To the very end, the bureaucracy exercised its power as usurpation and enjoyed its material privileges—exclusively privileges of consumption—as corruption. The ruling elite was forced to hide behind a socialist facade of democracy and egalitarianism that was in sharp contradiction with real social relations.

This system could obviously not tolerate independent social organization, especially of workers, the state's official social base. The totalitarian character of the state was necessary to compensate for the fragile social and ideological foundations of the ruling bureaucracy, a power élite without property or legitimacy. The bureaucracy had reason to fear the working class. Labour revolts in Eastern Europe and in the Soviet Union (Novocherkassk 1981, the miners' strikes in 1989 and 1991, the Belarussian general strike in April 1991) demonstrated the relative ease with which workers under this system could mobilize spontaneously on a large scale and translate initially economic grievances into demands for democracy, once the fear of repression had been overcome. Several factors favoured this: the state as unique employer, centralized economic management, the relatively homogeneous character of the working class, its concentration in giant enterprises, and, above all, the regime's fragile legitimacy.

On paper, unions had considerable power in the enterprises. Though they did not negotiate wages, they monitored the application of wage policy and of the Labour Code, participated in periodic revision of output norms (often vigorously resisted by workers), negotiated and monitored local agreements covering health and safety, housing construction and standards, catering, etc. They also ran the Health-and-Safety Inspectorate, with powers to investigate, issue binding orders, fine and even shut down facilities. They took part in administering social benefits such as sick leave, pregnancy and maternity leave, pensions, health care, vacation subsidies, child care, leisure activities. They formally had considerable power in resolving grievances, and could even remove managers for violating collective agreements or the Labour Code.

Yet Soviet trade unions were undemocratic and notoriously subservient to management and political authorities. After Stalin's death, they were cut a somewhat longer leash, but the bias in favour of meeting production targets, hence in favour of management, remained very strong. Basic decisions affecting wages, social benefits, and labour rights were made by central party-state authorities, unions playing at most a consultative role. The national union apparatus had little political clout within the bureaucracy. Its meetings followed closely on those of the party Central Committee so that they could take the appropriate decisions. The union bureaucracy was widely known as a 'grave-yard' for 'non-perspective' party and state cadres.

There were some courageous, dedicated—and unambitious—union leaders who tried to assert workers' rights against management or political authorities. But the norm was subservience. The union chairperson was one corner in the enterprise 'triangle' along with the director and party chairperson. When the coal miners negotiated during their strike of July 1989, the union leaders quite naturally sat facing them alongside government officials and managers.

It would be wrong to say that unions did not defend workers' interests, but they did so only to the extent this did not bring them into conflict with management or political authorities. It could not have been otherwise. Except sometimes at the lowest levels, union leaders were appointed and removed from above. To mobilize workers against management would have violated a basic tenet of the system. The merciless repression of the general strike in Novocherkassk in 1962 was not simply a nervous overreaction. Strikes did occur from time to time in individual shops, but any union leader who dared to lead them would lose his or her job and party card and have to deal with the KGB. During one of the state's periodic campaigns to inject life into the unions, *Trud*, the national union newspaper, accurately characterized them as '"semi-defenders" of the workers'.[1] Not surprisingly, these campaigns always failed.

But the repressive political framework is not the whole explanation of union subservience. While Soviet workers had a sense of 'us', the powerless and unprivileged, against 'them', the bosses, other aspects of the system muted this antagonism and confused the lines of opposition. For one thing, the ruling group was not a class of owners, but a group of administrators organized in a hierarchy of power and privilege, each one under the thumb of his or her supe-riors. Workers could see themselves as merely the lower rungs of a continuous ladder of power and privilege. Moreover, even towards the end, the bureau-cracy was still a relatively open group in terms of its members' social origins.

More important were the paternalistic social relations that bound workers to the bureaucracy. While workers were indeed powerless, they did enjoy impor-tant social rights, notably job security, a guaranteed job, and a 'social wage' that included free health care and education at all levels, pensions, subsidized housing, communal services, leisure and cultural activities, public transport, basic foodstuffs, etc. In 1984 this was equal to two-thirds of the money wage and gave workers a solid level of economic security.[2] Official propaganda aside, there was a material basis for workers to view this state as a protective father, albeit an authoritarian and corrupt one. The father-state also defended them against a hostile capitalist world.

Paternalism, or 'corporatism', was especially pronounced at the enterprise level, where the director played a dual role as representative of the state as well as lobbyist for and defender of his or her 'work collective' (a Soviet term including management). Profit maximization and reducing labour costs were not goals of Soviet managers. What mattered was meeting production targets. Doing this in the inherently uncertain conditions of the 'planned' economy required a relatively large and flexible work force. To secure this when labour was chronically in short supply, management tried to keep wages relatively high and was flexible with work schedules and discipline during slack periods. Moreover, to the degree that bonuses and social benefits depended on enterprise performance, workers did share an interest in meeting plan targets. When management, seconded by the union, appealed to workers to 'consider the situation of the enterprise', that is, to agree to periodic massive overtime and sub-standard conditions, they generally responded positively. Fear was part of it, but there was also a sense that their interests were linked to those of 'their' enterprise.

Gorbachev's liberalization, the political tangent of his market reform, opened space for an independent labour movement. Strikes over wages and work time became more frequent, at times embracing whole enterprises and lasting several days. But until the coal miners' strike of July 1989, there were no mobilizations involving several enterprises. During the strike movement of the spring of 1991 (at first, mainly miners, but with scattered support from other branches; then a general strike in Belarus) protest again went beyond the isolated enterprise. The movement was thus gradually expanding, but at the time of the collapse of the old regime, the majority of workers had not yet been drawn into collective actions.

Gorbachev rebuked the unions for dancing in step with management, but they did not become independent, despite the radical decentralization of power within their organizations after 1990. There were some exceptions, mainly where there had been spontaneous rank-and-file mobilizations, but these were rare. After their 1989 strike, many of the miners' strike leaders were elected to union posts, but most soon left in frustration. The Independent Miners' Union (NPG) was formed in 1990 on a platform of union independence and was followed by other 'alternative' or 'free' unions, the most successful being in the transport sector (stevedores, locomotive engineers, pilots, etc.). Elsewhere, notably in auto, where alternative unions existed, they represented (and continue to represent) small minorities in conflict with the large 'traditional' unions.

As part of his reform, Gorbachev created self-management bodies (STKs), granting them limited, ambiguous powers. Most STKs were easily dominated by management. A genuine movement arose, however, in 1990 when Gorbachev's attempted to get rid of the STKs as part of his conversion to capitalism. This movement advocated enterprise autonomy and a shift in power to the 'work collective'. But it never won much active rank-and-file support; nor did its leaders seriously try to mobilize it. Moreover, although the STK movement opposed the bureaucratic system it lacked its own economic vision, apart from enterprise autonomy. As such, and because it looked more for support from above than below, it was easy prey for liberal forces. Its leaders in Russia gave their support to Yeltsin, who promised great things, but then privatized in a way that in practice excluded workers from power and ownership. As for the unions, they saw the STKs as rivals and accepted privatization as inevitable.

Despite certain openings to real progress by the labour movement that appeared under Gorbachev, Russian workers on the whole failed to develop independent organizations and their own programme of social transformation. There were several reasons for this. The most obvious is that they needed time to overcome the legacy of totalitarian rule: fear, cynicism, atomization, subservience to and complicity with arbitrary authority, and, not least, a weak sense of rights and dignity. The capacity for self-organization and solidarity develop through struggle, but most workers had not been drawn into the movement. Change would have proceeded faster had the political opening been the result of struggle from below rather than a gift from above. While the workers' movement did help to push things well beyond what Gorbachev had intended, it also let itself be used by liberal forces hostile to workers' interests. To some extent, the inability to develop an independent labour programme was a legacy of the 'Communist' past, which had discredited not so much socialist values—workers remained attached to its ideals of democracy, equality, and social justice[3]—but the institutional arrangements necessary to realize them. After sixty years of bureaucratic 'socialism', workers had a hard time believing that central planning of any kind could be democratic and efficient. This allergy to centralism played into the hands of the liberal forces, who presented the market as freedom.

But labour's inability to develop its own vision was also a reflection of the international situation. The bureaucratic regime broke down in a period when labour and socialist movements around the world were in retreat. Soviet workers saw no attractive socialist models: the other 'Communist' systems were restoring capitalism or stagnating. With the notable, but distant, exceptions of Brazil and South Africa, there were no labour movements fighting for socialism as a real, immediate goal. Even victorious defensive struggles against the neoliberal onslaught were rare. To Russian workers, who had little understanding of capitalism, it seemed—as the liberals constantly reminded them—that capitalism alone was 'normal'. Moreover, liberal forces inside Russia enjoyed the political and financial backing of international capital in the form of the G-7 and their financial institutions. Without this support at major crisis points, 'shock therapy' could not have been pursued so single-mindedly and for so long. In contrast, the little aid foreign unions offered their Russian counterparts was aimed at helping them adapt to capitalism not to fight for a workers' alternative. The AFL-CIO, which had the biggest foreign labour presence, actively fostered business-unionism and helped draw the most militant elements into the Yeltsin camp.

THE PRESENT SITUATION

Two aspects of the present situation in particular weaken workers' capacity to resist: acute economic insecurity and, for lack of a better term, the growing social decomposition of the working class. Both are the consequence of prolonged economic depression, itself largely the result of state policy. Russia's GNP is today between 50 and 60 percent of its 1990 level; industrial output is around 45 percent.[4] In the ASM sector, production of agricultural machines, buses, trolleys, and trucks has dropped by about 90 percent. Car production, the one outstanding exception in the vast machine-building sector, is at 80 percent of predepression levels. The main factors behind the decline are the contraction of internal demand—presently about a third of the 1990 level[5]— and the critical financial situation of enterprises, which lost their operating capital in the 1992 price liberalization, have no access to affordable credit and are burdened with high taxes and costs of raw materials and energy. Investment has fallen every year since 1990; in 1998 it was at less than a sixth of its 1990 level.[6] Net investment is negative: Russia's capital stock is shrinking.

The government's transition strategy involved rapid privatization and exposure of enterprises to market discipline, forcing them to sink or swim. After six decades of a centrally administered economy, prices were freed overnight, government subsidies and social spending slashed, the economy opened to the world, the money supply severely restricted. The reformers apparently intended to restructure through destruction of a large part of existing industry, since the enterprises were given no chance to adapt. Amidst the chaos of such lightning changes from above, Russian capitalism at its present stage displays a number of particular traits. Property rights are quite fragile, and owners cannot count on the state to defend them. (The big owners have private armed forces.) Most of the population does not consider the private owners of enterprises as legitimate. Legal title itself is often in dispute and does not guarantee the owners control. Where workers are united and determined and have taken over their enterprise or imposed control over management, neither owners nor the state have been able to dislodge them by force, though, in the end, workers' control in isolated enterprises has little hope of success. In most cases, it is the director who wields absolute power, unrestricted by law, owners, or workers. The distinction between legitimate and illegitimate business can be made only in theory.[7] When criminal elements do not directly control enterprises (according to the government, the mafia controls 50 percent of the non-state and 60 percent of the state sectors),[8] management is paying tribute to them or to corrupt state officials, or stealing on its own. It is usually a combination of all these things.

Another feature is demonetization of the economy: at the end of 1998, an average of 52 percent of transactions of industrial enterprises were in kind.[9] Of most concern to workers are wage arrears: in the auto and truck sectors in March 1999 they averaged 4.2 months; in the agricultural machine-sector—7.4.[10] These are, in fact, forced loans to management at negative interest since wage arrears are not indexed. But probably the most striking feature is the system's cannibalism: it is consuming the country's accumulated wealth, destroying its very capacity to produce wealth. Depreciation allowances exceed 30 percent of GDP.[11] An estimated US$136 billion poured out of Russia between 1993 and 1998, far exceeding capital inflows from foreign investors and international loans.[12] Research and development spending has fallen 15-fold; spending on science—50-fold. Many scientists have emigrated or abandoned their professions. The most skilled workers and engineers were among the first to leave dying enterprises for the new private sector, where their skills are rarely used.[13]

But not only skills: the labour force itself is being destroyed as a result of declining living standards, cuts in health care, stress caused by the depression and social dislocation. Births have fallen dramatically, and male death rates are at levels of the end of the nineteenth century.[14] According to a prominent demographer, the most probable scenario over the next half-century is a population decline of 45 percent. (US population is expected to grow by 45 percent over the same period.)[15]

There is no consensus in the labour movement on the nature of management's interests, but one thing is clear: almost all directors are much better off today than they were under the old regime, while almost all workers are much worse off. As the perspective of change in economic policy and a recovery receded, managers came to view their enterprises as sources of rent or simply objects to be pillaged. While they do not necessary want to destroy them outright, as they are sources of personal enrichment, there is little incentive to make the effort—probably futile anyway—to restore them to health. As noted, managers enjoy broad freedom from control—from owners and the state, as well as the unions. They are also relatively free of market forces too, since the bankruptcy law is 'soft'. Management can also count on free loans in the form of unpaid wages. Pro-management unions and parties, like the Communist Party, cite overstaffing as evidence that many directors are still 'red' and want to 'preserve the work collective'. But it is the workers alone who bear the cost of this 'excess' labour in the form of abysmally low wages.

The restoration of capitalism has had a big impact on the structure and composition of the working class, the majority of whom now work in the private sector or in enterprises where state ownership is mainly formal. Commercialization and privatization have led to strong differentiation in the situation of enterprises and workers, among and within sectors and regions. For example, in the ASM sector, the VAZ auto plant, which has kept most of its labour force, pays an average wage six times higher than Rostsel'mash (agricultural machinery), which has lost three-quarters of its workers.[16] Wages also vary widely within enterprises, even sometimes for the same work and skill level. Labour itself is 'free', but movement into big cities, where jobs are more plentiful, is restricted by local (unconstitutional) regulations and by the absence of affordable rental housing.

In 1998, 38.6 percent of the employed labour force was in industry, construction and transport; 45.6 percent in trade and services; and 13 percent in agriculture. The proportion of women was unchanged at 48.5 percent since 1992. There are no reliable figures on union membership, but in 1998 the 'traditional' Federation of Independent Trade Unions (FNPR) claimed 40 million members. (The employed labour force was 63.6 million.) Although this figure is probably inflated, union density is high. Probably over 90 percent of employees of large and medium enterprises, as well as almost all public service workers, belong to an FNPR affiliate.[17] The ASM Union claimed about 800,000 workers or 88.6 percent of the sector's work force in 1998. The rest are not union members or belong to an alternative union.[18] There are virtually no unions in the newly created private sector (mainly small enterprises in services and trade), where arbitrary managerial power has full sway.

Industrial employment declined from 29.6 percent of the work force in 1992 to 22.2 in 1998, but in absolute numbers the drop was 42 percent.[19] The ASM sector itself has lost 70 percent of its jobs since 1992.[20] Mostly this took the form of workers leaving 'of their own volition' to seek a living wage. The first to leave were younger workers as well as the more skilled, bolder and more adaptable. These categories of workers had been at the forefront of the labour upsurge under Gorbachev. The average age of those who remain in industry is close to 50. They tend to be more subservient, fearing for their jobs and pensions. In addition, periodic 'administrative leaves', the irregular work cadence, the uncertainty of the wage and its small size not only undermine discipline but also demoralize. Garden plots and second jobs drain energy and commitment away from struggles in the enterprise. Laid-off workers are hard to assemble. The stress and demoralization caused by the economic crisis has affected men especially strongly; alcoholism is pandemic.

Unemployment has climbed from zero under the Soviet system to a real rate of close to 30 percent (including the involuntarily partially employed and those earning less than minimum subsistence). The state puts the rate at around 12 percent.[21] The very weak social safety net does nothing to allay fear of unemployment. But employment does not provide even temporary security, since at the start of 2000, wages of two-fifths of Russia's workers were below the very low official subsistence minimum for one person (US$41 a month), while the average wage was equal to only 1.7 subsistence minima.[22] Average pensions are also below the subsistence minimum, and savings were wiped out by hyperinflation in 1992.

Some workers supplement their wages with second jobs in the 'grey economy', but such opportunities are quite limited in the smaller towns, and they require good health and usually special skills or a car. Garden plots (usually 600 square metres) play a significant role, especially in smaller towns. There is also considerable mutual aid within families. A more important cushion to low wages and pensions is the still relatively modest, though rapidly rising, cost of housing (workers inherited their apartments from the Soviet period) and of utilities and municipal transport. Basic medical care is generally free, but scheduled hospital stays, operations and drugs can entail serious outlays. Lower levels of education are free, though parents are constantly being asked to contribute. Finally, pilfering from enterprises, when there is something of value, is quite widespread.

For most workers, the chief positive aspect of the transition has been the maintenance of freedoms of association and speech, no small matters when viewed from a Russian perspective. Unions are relatively unrestricted by the state. So far at least, the state has rarely resorted to coercion, even when faced with acts of civil disobedience, like blocking railway lines. Although the government is bent on weakening the labour code, legislation still compares favourably on several counts with Western codes, thanks to hold overs from the Soviet period. But the practical value of these rights is very limited. The new constitution, introduced in 1993 through a rigged referendum, gave virtually absolute power to the President. The bloody suppression of the Supreme Soviet a few months earlier was a warning to all oppositional forces to respect the bounds of the new pseudo-democracy, something that parties and unions have done. The Russian government in practice has declared a moratorium on legality. Anyone with sufficient power or money can ignore the law, unless, of course, he or she attracts the ire of someone with more power or money. The government has set the tone. Official corruption is endemic at all levels. Fiscal policy is itself based on theft: public sector wages and pensions are withheld for months and without indexation; money for budgeted expenses is 'sequestered'; enterprise orders placed by the state go unpaid. Privatization was probably the most massive theft in history. Finally, underfinanced and often politicized courts offer little recourse to unions, except in the case of individual grievances, such as wrong dismissal. But decisions can take years.

UNION STRATEGY: FROM 'TRANSMISSION BELT' TO 'SOCIAL PARTNER'[23]

Both the legacy of the Soviet past and the current economic and political situation strongly condition and limit the options of unions. Nevertheless, unions have choices, and the predominant choice is 'social partnership', a strategy based on subordination of union strategy to the aims of management at the enterprise and political levels. Other key aspects of union practice, especially the absence of democracy and of solidarity, are closely bound up with that strategic choice. Union strategy and practice are the third part of the answer to 'Why Don't They Revolt?'

Partnership

The basic premise of 'social partnership' is that workers and management share a fundamental interest in the health of 'their' enterprise that creates a solid basis for co-operation. By implication, shared interests with other workers—and so solidarity—are secondary. So is the need for an active committed membership based on broad democracy, since the strategy is one of co-operation, not confrontation. Some lip service is paid to the need to be strong in order to be accepted as a partner, but in practice 'partnership' is treated as a magic formula that eliminates social contradictions and frees unions of any concern with the correlation of forces.

With the transition to capitalism, the Russian government, seconded by the International Labour Organization, as well as some foreign unions, forcefully began to promote the ideology and trappings of 'social partnership'. Union leaders did not need much persuading, since the new formula served to legitimate their traditional practice, dressing it up in phraseology appropriate to a market economy. It makes little difference that the material bases of the old corporatism—the repressive state, guaranteed employment, job and wage security, and the social wage—are gone or seriously undermined. Nor has evidence of widespread managerial corruption affected union strategy significantly.

To some extent, the depression, the threat to jobs and the very survival of the enterprises has replaced socialist ideology, job security and the social wage as the main argument for union subservience. As one union leader put it, 'If there is no plant, there is no union'. Any union must consider the threat of job cuts and even closure when formulating its demands or its response to management's concession demands. However, when union leaders typically argue that the alternative to 'partnership' is permanent class war, destructive to all sides, this presents a false choice, since even the most militant worker recognizes that a factory cannot function without minimal co-operation between union and management. The real choice is not between social peace and permanent all-out war but between union independence and subservience to management's goals, between the union acting as 'salesperson' for management goals and adopting an independent strategy based upon analysis of the membership's interests.

Today, as in Soviet times, when management asks workers to 'consider the situation of the enterprise', the union generally takes management's side, whether the issue is unpaid wages, unsafe conditions, temporary layoffs or reduced hours (which by law require the worker's agreement), job cuts, or dropping indexation. Union subordination to management goals has reached the point that, with the blessing of the national leadership, many local ASM unions are restoring 'labour competition' (formerly 'socialist competition'), including the awarding of bonuses and certificates to the most productive shops.

'Some perhaps would like to see the union on one side and the administration on the other', said a department union president at the Gorky Auto Plant. 'But, thank God, that isn't the case here. We all live as one family; we all depend on each other. Simply put, the plant is doing well, and that means that its union is also doing well: it can send more people on subsidized vacations, give them material help, etc. ... We are all together, a collective, and that includes the administration, the union leaders and the workers.'[24]

The traditional unions have not broken with the Soviet practice of including managerial personnel (often even the general director) in their ranks, despite the message this sends to workers. The typically strong presence of administrators at union conferences gives them a determining influence on the discussion and voting, especially in this period of heightened insecurity. Asked how unions can defend workers when they count management among their members, an FNPR secretary admitted that it was perhaps undesirable but he justified the practice by the transitional nature of the period: 'First of all, certain traditions exist. Secondly, there is no clearly defined stratum of entrepreneurs (employers), conscious of their interests. Many directors have worked for decades at the enterprise and feel themselves part of the work collective.'[25]

'Is there a class of employers to whom I can make demands?' wondered the union president at a Yaroslavl truck parts factory. 'Our director-general is a union member. We don't have a workers' movement because we don't have a class of employers, real bosses with clear interests and powers opposed to ours.' This typical complaint is based upon the idea that unions in 'normal' capitalist countries can make demands and win them through economic pressure because they face 'real employers'. However, the problem of Russian unions is not the absence of 'real employers'. It is the economic crisis that undermines the effectiveness of withholding labour. But it does not logically follow that 'partnership' is the answer.

Effective action in the economic crisis calls for co-ordination of local union struggles thereby raising them up to the national level, where economic policy is made. But here too the strategy is 'social partnership'. In June 1997, ASM and two other machine-construction unions organized a big conference with directors to develop joint actions for resolving the crisis. The meeting subjected government policy to withering criticism and adopted a list of emergency measures, but there was no discussion of strategy to force the government to adopt the measures, which would have meant the abandonment of shock therapy. Indeed, at the request of management, the very word struggle was dropped from the resolution. The resolution further stated that 'In resolving social-labour conflicts, the participants of this conference appeal against extreme methods of struggle—strikes and acts of civil disobedience.'[26]

Most of the unions' political actions, in fact, have the tacit agreement, sometimes even the open support, of management. At the October 1998 FNPR protest, the Kirov Factory workers were treated to the spectacle of their director-general and the city governor marching alongside the presidents of their union and the Leningrad Federation of Trade Unions. It is said that Yeltsin himself expressed sympathy for the protesters, though they were demanding his ouster. As usual, the demonstrators' demands were ignored, and the unions soon forgot them too. Apart from such spotty participation in FNPR protests and picketing government buildings, the political action of the ASM Union has consisted principally of lobbying and supporting 'centrist' political parties, whose electoral lists are heavily weighted with directors and entrepreneurs, with a few union leaders for good measure.

Early attempts to create a democratic socialist party based on the unions failed to win the active support of union leaders. In the December 1999 parliamentary elections, most FNPR unions, including ASM, supported the 'centrist' Moscow boss Luzhkov's party. As always, the 'centrists' did poorly. A union member asked the leader of the FNPR's political wing: 'Unions are workers' organizations. Luzhkov is a representative of the recently formed bourgeoisie. What can these opposites have in common?' He received this answer:

> If you insist on discussing in classical Marxist terms, let me remind you that there are periods when the classics themselves told workers and representatives of the bourgeoisie to act together, for example, during bourgeois-democratic revolutions. The essence of our present situation is that the labour movement and nationally-oriented capital have powerful common enemies: the financial-bureaucratic oligarchy, living exclusively from the sale of resources, and the forces in the West that are interested in transforming Russia into a semi-colony for the extraction of raw materials. We also have common goals: to restore the real economy of the country, raise popular living standards, defend the political and economic independence of Russia. These goals create the possibility of a firm and, I believe, long-lasting union of the labour movement and entrepreneurs engaged in the real economy of Russia. And the natural leader of that union, in my view, is Yurii Luzhkov.[27]

Putin has now inherited the mantle of 'natural leader' and the FNPR supported him in his successful presidential bid.

Why this the stubborn attachment to a failed strategy? On one level, 'partnership' is a response to weakness. Union leaders reject strategies based on independence because they do not believe they can shift the balance of forces by mobilizing their members, who are passive, fearful, and lack confidence in their ability to change things. Demoralization is a fact, but this argument skirts the role that 'partnership' plays in reinforcing it. It is very rare for union leaders to make a serious effort to build a rank-and-file base for independent action (which as we shall see, is possible, even if difficult, in present conditions).

'Partnership' is attractive to union leaders because it is a less risky, and certainly less onerous, strategy from the vantage point of their own personal interests. From the vantage point of their own personal interests, 'partnership' does work. In conditions of generalized poverty, unemployment and lawlessness, confronting management promises little personal reward but presents much risk. Managers have many ways of forcing union leaders out of their elected position and out of the plant. Most of them are engineers who have become deskilled after years in union office and would have trouble finding equivalent work elsewhere. On the other hand, a co-operative relationship with management offers considerable rewards. Except for the unlikely case of a spontaneous rank-and-file mobilization, management's support ensures the union leader's re-election. It is also not uncommon for union leaders eventually to cross over into top management posts. The former national president of the ASM Union is now an assistant plant director. Career prospects aside, management can offer material perks, and outright corruption of union leaders is not unheard of.

In present conditions, for a union leader to break with 'partnership', he or she has to be exceptionally bold, committed and principled, and preferably also have marketable skills. Or else he or she has to have been elected on the wave of a more-or-less spontaneous rank-and-file revolt. Of course, it also helps if the enterprise in question is working and making money. These conditions are rare today.

Weak Solidarity

Workers form unions because collectively they are in a stronger bargaining position. Solidarity is not simply an ideal but the key resource of labour. 'Partnership', which teaches that workers' basic interests are linked to the well-being of 'their enterprise' (as defined by management), tends to undermine solidarity. For the same reason, national unions have a hard time developing an effective strategy, since the pursuit of common goals usually requires some sacrifice of short-term, local interests. In a society that promotes individualism in a myriad of ways, most workers learn the importance of solidarity only through participation in struggle, when solidarity becomes their fundamental resource. However, Russian unions avoid confrontation, even at the price of making important concessions. They strive to resolve problems without involving the membership, through concertation with management behind closed doors. Not only do they not need members' active involvement; from their point of view, it is an encumbrance and threat. Most union leaders describe their function as 'buffers', muting protest and directing it into less threatening channels. This is one of the reasons union density remains high—neither management nor the state are interested in dismantling the unions. Something more threatening might take their place.

The absence of solidarity is a particularly serious handicap in present economic conditions, when isolated action cannot be effective. Over the past decade, though much less in the past two or three years, various local ASM unions have engaged in bitter, prolonged strikes, usually provoked by wage arrears accumulated over many months. These strikes sometimes brought partial relief and even resulted in the director's ouster, but they could not fundamentally change the situation. Even the limited victories often owed more to civil disobedience aimed at political authorities than to economic pressure on management.

The radical decentralization of power in a union like the ASM was probably inevitable, and would have been healthy, if the local unions were prepared to delegate a minimal amount of power and resources to the national union. But discipline in the ASM Union is very weak, and the national union is starved for resources. Its real share of dues is less than two percent, an indication of the low level of solidarity.[28] Instead, local unions spend a good part of their dues on 'material support' for individual members to help pay for medicine, operations, funerals, weddings, etc. and on socio-cultural and sports activities. Even when money is not involved, local unions often ignore the national office, failing to send reports and copies of collective agreements or to comment on proposals.[29] The result is a magic circle: the national office cannot provide services, while local unions say that it must prove itself before they will give more resources.

Of course, the national leadership is weak, even relative to its limited resources. The president of the Yaroslavl region, which has moved a considerable distance from 'partnership', complains that the Central Committee 'has no economic programme; there is no discussion of the future of our sector ... [The President] could do a lot more to unify the union. Each plant is stewing in its own juices. There is no critical analysis of the FNPR's strategy. The problem is that they are conciliators.' But a weak national union obviously suits most local leaders. As a result, unlike its Belarussian and Ukrainian counterparts, the Russian ASM makes no serious attempt to enforce the sectoral agreement that sets minimum standards or to mobilize local unions for participation in political protests. It is therefore somewhat of an exaggeration to speak of a national union. It is little more than a meeting place for local leaders and an office for relaying and collecting information. It does represent the member unions in international forums and in the FNPR and lobbies the government on their behalf, but without a national strategy or co-ordinated action to back it up.

Solidarity, however, is not much stronger at the plant level, where one shop might strike over wage arrears or threatened job cuts and not receive even symbolic support from the others or from the plant committee. Conversely, one shop might pull out of a strike over wage arrears after getting paid, while the others are left waiting. In large factories, workers have only the vaguest idea about the plant committee and no direct contact with it. Shop committees often ignore the plant committee's requests for input into drafting the collective agreement. Wages for the same work can vary sharply from shop to shop.

Obviously, one cannot blame weak solidarity entirely on the leaders. As we have shown, the leaders' penchant for 'partnership' has objective causes. Workers' poverty and insecurity induce them to seek individual survival strategies. The point, however, is that the union leadership has adopted a policy that reinforces this tendency rather than fighting it.

Alienated Membership

The main beneficiaries of the ending of state control of unions and their decentralization are not the members but the local presidents at the plant level. Regional and central union officers are now accountable to them. But they themselves are not really accountable to the membership, whose level of participation in decision-making is minimal. Union leaders complain about the indifference and passivity of the rank-and-file, their 'consumerist' attitude toward the union. At one seminar, a plant president reputed for her militancy composed a poem comparing the membership to neglected pigs who abandon the thought of revolt the minute the farmer tosses them some slop.

Such contempt may be shocking and undeserved, but rank-and-file passivity is a real obstacle to union democracy, which requires at least a significant minority of active members. It is a fact that workers often continue working for months without being paid before they take action; they acquiesce to work in unheated shops in winter; they tolerate the petty tyranny of administrators who could be ousted at seemingly little risk. Ineffective, subservient union leaders usually have little trouble getting re-elected, because 'there's no alternative', no credible alternative leader prepared to present him or herself.

Poverty, insecurity and an ageing work force mean workers have less time, energy, and inclination to fight for collective goals. People are reluctant to run for unpaid union office, and unions cannot compensate most officers. More important are the psychological consequences of the depression and the accumulated defeats. Cynicism and a profound sense of powerlessness are widespread. The sense of dignity, always critical in mobilizing workers, is weak.

But this is only one side of the picture. The following are typical remarks of ordinary members: 'I don't know anything about what the plant committee is doing. There are annual meetings. The chairman doesn't talk to ordinary workers. Maybe he feels it's below his dignity. Or else he's afraid.' 'The leaders keep to themselves. In practice, they've got their own organization, separate from ours. The two cross paths only when it comes to dues.'

Leaders justify 'partnership' by citing the workers' passivity: any leader who confronts management will end up alone and be crushed. It is better, therefore, to keep on the director's good side, so that he or she will 'show understanding'. But 'partnership' actually moves leaders to actively discourage rank-and-file activism, since the union's main bargaining chip is its value as a 'buffer' to keep the work force under control. 'Thank God', said the union president of Moscow's ZIL truck factory, 'that we avoided a social explosion!' He had only praise for the workers' patience in the face of massive jobs cuts and months of unpaid wages. And the president who compared her members to pigs had spent the previous morning persuading them to abandon a wildcat (but legal) strike over unpaid wages. Even when these leaders mobilize their members, their goal is not to force management's hand but to 'attract its attention' and to allow workers to let off steam.

This is also how the FNPR views its protests. In the lead-up to its

November 1997 protest, its paper came out with an editorial entitled 'A Letter to Our Evil-Wishers'. It conceded the ritual character of the protests, when workers demonstrate, the government makes promises, and nothing changes. Call us naïve, it went on, but would you rather have desperate workers blocking roads and stopping trains? We, at least, are doing our duty, trying 'to save the fragile social peace in our half-ruined country'.[30] What is surprising is not that most workers do not participate in these protests but that hundreds of thousands nevertheless do! This indicates a real potential for mobilization.

Even when there is no outright corruption, 'partnership' puts union leaders in an ambiguous position *vis-à-vis* their members. At one plant, a dissident group was planning to run an alternative slate in coming elections. The incumbent president was unperturbed: 'With the general director sitting up front [at the conference], they won't so much as squeak.' Of course, in her view, these were irresponsible, self-seeking troublemakers, who would ruin the co-operative relations she had established with management. She was not in the least embarrassed to make this statement to an outsider. This is a leader who bases her power on management's power, not the membership's. She has no interest in rank-and-file activism; it is threatening.

Information is the life-blood of democracy, but little is done to facilitate its flow. There are almost no rank-and-file activists or even shop-level officers at national congresses or in the Central Committee. Of the 80 delegates at the Third Congress of the ASM Union in 1997, 52 were plant presidents or vice-presidents; 21 were regional presidents. There were only 16 women, though they are half of the membership. Seventy-one delegates had higher education, indicating few workers.[31]

Democracy does not fare better at lower levels. Most unions do not even produce a newsletter or occasional bulletin. And there is little person-to-person contact. A worker at the Kirov Tractor Factory said of his president: 'From his office to his car; from his car to his office. He never appears in the shops.' Local unions have cut drastically the number of full-time shop presidents—a crucial link to the rank and file, and many have done away altogether with group leaders. As a result, shop presidents tend to be recruited from office staff whose jobs leave them time for minimal union duties. But these people are distant from workers' concerns, dependent on management, and have little commitment to the union. This is a question of union priorities more than poverty, since significant sums are spent on individual 'material aid' and socio-cultural activities. Union officials spend most of their time on routine administration and devote little time to education and mobilization, to discussing strategies with the membership. A shop president explained: 'There are a lot of tasks. We deal with workers' problems from birth to death. We take care of the person up to and including the funeral. One of the main tasks is to find money for all that. On the whole, it is the resolution of 'small' problems that you can't entrust to the employer, who is busy organizing production. This everyday work takes up most of my time.'[32]

Leaders rarely consult the membership on the major issues of low and unpaid wages, layoffs, deteriorating health and safety conditions. Their approach is routinely administrative, and they accept as gospel management's references to 'objective conditions'. When job cuts are ordered, leaders limit themselves to checking that no one in a protected category (e.g., pregnant women) is on the list and that the required payments are made. The issue is not put before the membership. The possibility of resisting is not even entertained, though resistance has been known to limit the damage. Membership participation in negotiating collective agreements is also minimal. As one plant president explained: 'We met with the director. He issued an order to set up a joint commission with the union. We took last year's agreement as the basis. We sent it around to the shops for suggestions. They were supposed to hold meetings, but there weren't many suggestions. People are passive. Then we held a conference. All the managers and specialists were present. It was adopted unanimously.'[33] It did not occur to him that the managers' presence and membership's passivity are linked.

BUILDING AN INDEPENDENT MOVEMENT

Some unions have moved beyond 'partnership' in an effort to overcome the weakness that characterizes 'traditional' unions. While they are too few and dispersed to fundamentally change things, they give an idea of the possibilities as well as limits of union action in present conditions.

The Kirov Tractor-Assembly Shop

This shop has been the militant core of the giant metallurgical and metal-working factory since Perestroika. Assembly lines, which bring together large numbers of people working at similar tasks and situate them strategically to paralyze the entire production process, were the main breeding grounds of militancy in the machine-building sector before the depression. Aleksandr, an assembler, was the shop's informal leader and co-founder of the factory's workers' committee in 1990. This committee, which acted outside the framework of the bureaucratized union, led a number of successful campaigns, including a reform of the wage system which, in typical Soviet fashion, made workers bear the cost of management's failings. The committee scored a coup in bringing Yeltsin to the factory at a time when he was a political pariah and viewed by workers as a fighter for democracy and social justice. In 1992, when public opinion was still behind Yeltsin and the labour movement was dazed by the sudden profound change brought on by shock therapy, the shop struck for wage indexation and sent a collective letter to the Supreme Soviet demanding it stop the government's policy of 'economic genocide'. It also appealed to other plants to join it in a regional strike committee.[34] This was just one of the shop's numerous attempts to organize a broader opposition movement, all of which failed.

As activism declined, Aleksandr decided to give the union a try and was easily elected shop president. But the market for tractors collapsed, and the work force shrunk rapidly. Having found little support outside the shop, exhausted and disappointed, Aleksandr announced he would not run for re-election, but waited to see if the plant president would persuade him to stay. After all, he was the leader of the active core of the whole union. But the president was happy to be rid of this 'white raven'. The only candidate willing to run for shop president was an office worker. Things were all set to return to 'normal', but at the election meeting the workers balked and proposed Svetlana instead, a 47-year-old assembler. She resisted mightily ('I have kids, I have to work. When will I find time for the union?' [The position is unpaid]). But years of struggle had created militant tradition, and she gave in. Svetlana set to work developing a core of activists, 'all who are not completely dead'—as it turned out, mainly women. She adopted a policy of total transparency, with committee meetings open to all, held directly in the shop. All key decisions are made by the general assembly. Each morning before work she and her activists visit each work place.

In most ways, the practice of the shop committee is the opposite of the plant committee. And it clashes with the plant committee almost as much as with management. Svetlana considers union independence so important that she will refuse a drink offered by management because of how it might be viewed. Management has more than once threatened to get rid of her. The shop committee is constantly raising new issues with management. This is not activism for its own sake. The union has won real victories over work conditions, wages and jobs, where other unions are passive, citing 'difficult objective conditions'. The victories are necessarily small and precarious, but they have cemented the workers around the shop union, which instils fear and respect in management well beyond its numerical and economic weight in the factory.

One such conflict arose over the temperature, which in most Russian production facilities hovers around freezing in winter. This is justified as a cost-saving measure, and workers accept it as a fact of life. In this shop, the workers burned wood in steel drums to warm their hands from time to time. But management ordered the drums removed as a hazard and because workers destroyed factory property for firewood. The workers seemed prepared to submit, but Svetlana countered by demanding that heat and lighting conform to health-and-safety norms, that the leaky roof be repaired and that management distribute clean work clothes, all provided by law or the collective agreement. The shop superintendent refused even to read the demands and threatened to fine the workers. The plant president berated Svetlana for once again acting independently of him, though he himself did nothing. In the end, management finally backed down in the face of the workers' refusal to obey. It also fixed the roof and improved the lighting.

The assembly shop was the main force in the 'tractor war' of 1999, pitting the union against the government which was preparing to sign a multi-billion-dollar deal with US farm-machinery companies that would have completely finished off the Russian industry.[35] With the assembly shop breathing down its neck, the plant committee drew up a plan of action that included lobbying, media exposure, demonstrations and civil disobedience. It tried, but failed, to draw other factories into the struggle. It did, however, finally wake up the director, who exerted a definitely moderating influence on the campaign. As the struggle was gathering force, mass picketing was planned, along with giant tractors, around the governor's office to coincide with the Prime Minister's visit to St Petersburg. Alarmed, the regional government agreed to send the Minister of Agriculture to the plant. The director asked the union to call off the action which had been set for the next day, and the plant president acceded. When Svetlana refused to call off her members, the plant committee telephoned them at their homes. 'We needed the action,' she explained, 'regardless of the minister's promises. The workers had never been so united—people even came in from their vacations; they were ready to fight. They wanted to speak for themselves, to feel that they are people, that they count for something. And the union stifled them, used them as a bogey.' The minister, who claimed to have been unaware that the plant made cheaper but fully equivalent tractors to those to be imported, promised to exclude Kirov tractors from the deal and to finance a leasing programme for farms to purchase them. Production has since picked up, but sentiment in the shop is that they were thrown a sop to shut them up while the deal went through, and that nothing has been resolved.

Keenly aware of the limits of isolated struggles, the shop committee has been active beyond the factory. It regularly brings out a remarkable 80 percent of its workers to political protests and it was one of the city's rare unions actively to support 1998 the miners' protest camp in Moscow. Svetlana has made the rounds of the various left parties to see what they have to offer workers. But her shop union remains quite isolated, even within its own factory.

Edinstvo

This union at the VAZ auto plant in Togliatti (120,000 employees) is the most successful of the alternative (non-FNPR) unions outside of the transport and coal mining sectors. Its success has been facilitated by the relatively strong market for its compact cars. Employment levels have not fallen, and wages are relatively high. VAZ played an important role in the self-management (STK) movement of Perestroika, but no visible trace of that remains. (The leader left in 1992 to join a mystical sect.)

Edinstvo was founded at the end of the period of heightened labour activism unleashed by Perestroika. It soon attracted 2,000 members, aided by a series of partial, mostly spontaneous strikes, whose leadership it assumed. The last one occurred on the main assembly line in 1994 over delayed wages, and was met with unusual severity, including a disguised general lockout, dismissals and the stationing of riot police in the shop. Management's show of force and the deepening depression halted Edinstvo's growth, but over the past year and a half it has grown to 3,500.

Edinstvo is subject to severe harassment and discrimination by management, which refuses to negotiate with it, ignoring a court decision. Workers who join Edinstvo tend, therefore, to be more active and committed than the members of the traditional union. The latter too has some good activists and even a few militant shop committees, but their work is constantly undermined by the plant committee, whose leaders generally end up in management jobs. Corruption is rampant in the administration, which has been the object of several criminal investigations (that typically yielded no results). The factory has incurred huge losses through dealings with intermediary firms, many of which were set up by management personnel or their relatives. Edinstvo's president was twice wounded in armed attacks, which remain unsolved.

Edinstvo's practice stresses independence from management, who cannot be members of the union. In 1998–99, it actively opposed management's concession demand to eliminate indexation, which Edinstvo had won for all the workers in a 1992 strike. Already in 1996, the traditional union had agreed to limit indexation to 72 percent of inflation, citing the plant's serious financial situation. Predictably, in 1998 management returned to demand the complete end of indexation and its replacement with a bonus dependent upon profits. Although rejected at a first union conference, the demand was finally accepted on the second try after much arm-twisting in which the traditional union leadership itself participated, brandishing the threat of job losses. Edinstvo's president was not even allowed to speak at the conference. Edinstvo's position was that workers have no say in running the plant and so should not be made to pay for its poor performance. To drop indexation would, in fact, only reduce management's incentive to run the plant efficiently. The market for cars is strong, management's salaries are huge, and corruption is a major source of losses.

Edinstvo functions openly and democratically. As a matter of principle, it has only one full-timer, its vice-president, a worker fired for participation in the 1994 strike. Any officer can be recalled by a 10 percent vote of the relevant constituency. The proceedings of the executive's meetings are posted and distributed in leaflets. Decisions to send members to seminars and meetings in other cities or abroad are taken by vote and explained in order to avoid an appearance of favouritism, the rule in the traditional union. Detailed reports on these trips are made at meetings and are published. In contrast to the traditional unions, Edinstvo has a strike fund (20 percent of dues) and spends relatively little on material aid and cultural-recreational activities.

Edinstvo leaders devote a lot of time to face-to-face education, agitation, recruitment, grievance handling, and defending members against harassment. Much effort is devoted to informing workers of their rights—a concept weakly developed in Russia—and to showing that arbitrary authority can successfully be challenged. For example, after an Edinstvo member, a woman, refused to undergo a physical search at the gates, the union began a campaign to end this illegal and degrading practice. 'Why go to the trouble of installing electronic controls at the exits,' asked a leaflet, 'why think about the rights and dignity of the rabble, when it is so much easier to degrade a thousand honest workers to catch one thief.' This concern for dignity is rare in Russia, but of critical importance in building an effective labour movement.

Like most alternative unions, Edinstvo also spends a lot of time on legal action (the former president earned a law degree), although that tends to exclude ordinary members and is not very effective. It can, however, have an educational function, which Edinstvo fully exploits. The emphasis on courts is a response to the general decline of rank-and-file activism, which affects Edinstvo too. Although VAZ is doing relatively well, management is at pains to remind workers of the disastrous situation that surrounds them.

Edinstvo's membership is not politically homogeneous, but most of its leaders supported Yeltsin, at least until his last few years. Subsequently, they shifted to ex-general Lebed, who, according to the union president, could deliver a badly needed strong state. Clearly, support for union independence does not always mean support for working class independence. However, in the 1999 parliamentary elections, Edinstvo ran its president as an independent labour candidate, rejecting invitations to join party lists. With almost no money, he won, a mark of the standing of the union in this factory riding. At the same time, however, he joined Putin's local campaign committee.[36] Unlike the traditional union, whose horizon stops at the factory gate (it did partially finance Togliatti's first church in the 1990s), Edinstvo has given active support to numerous outside labour struggles.

Yaroslavl Motor Builders

Yaroslavl has four diesel plants employing about 40,000 workers—down from 55,000, though production has fallen by 70 percent. The largest plant, the Yaroslavl Motor Factory, was the scene of the first major worker protest of Perestroika—a week-long strike against Saturday work.[37] However, activism dropped quickly thereafter. The unions stood by passively as shock therapy slashed real earnings. Even the start of wage arrears in 1994 did not provoke an immediate response, despite the efforts of individual activists.

The shift came in 1995 with the strike movement at the Tutaev Motor Factory, about an hour outside of Yaroslavl. Of Tutaev's 49,000 inhabitants, 8,400 work at the plant and cannot leave it because there is no other employment in town and no buyers for their apartments for them to move away. In 1995, a few activists were finally able to mobilize the workers over wages arrears (six months' worth) and managerial corruption. A strike committee was elected, which over the next two years led three strikes, one lasting five weeks and which included blocking highways. The old union committee was replaced with people from the strike committee, and a new director acceptable to the workers was appointed. Temporary relief was obtained on wages, though the problem soon returned.

The mood gradually shifted in the other factories too. In 1995, rank-and-file activists formed alternative unions at the Motor and Fuel-Apparatus

Factories. In 1996, the other plants also finally struck briefly and blocked roads over wage arrears. The strike committees, which have become quasi-permanent, act as mobilizing committees for the unions but also as an organized opposition to prod the union leadership. The Yarosavl factories have the lowest union density in the ASM sector (50–70 percent), and so the strike committees are the only elected bodies that represent all workers.

The failure of isolated protests to bring more than fleeting relief led to the creation in the fall of 1996 of a joint council of strike committees, an initiative supported by the regional president. The council developed a strategy of escalating actions that went beyond the usual demand to 'pay us our wages': the workers demanded a joint development plan for the four plants and state investments to upgrade the motors to meet export standards. A campaign of civil disobedience spurred the regional governor to press Moscow, which acceded, at least on paper, to the workers' demands. Although the federal government reneged on its signed commitment, it gave some relief by allotting credits to the Minsk Truck Factory, the main buyer of Yaroslavl's motors.

In 1998, the four plants initiated the creation of a region-wide co-ordinating committee for collective actions. Inspired by the coal miners' example in Moscow, it set up a workers' camp alongside the railway tracks, presenting a permanent threat to rail communications between Moscow and the northeast.[38] In September 1998, hundreds of autoworkers brought rail traffic to a stop for three hours. The regional co-ordinating committee, with the support of the regional union federation, organized a conference of representatives of enterprises and popular organizations from across Russia's central regions to prepare a general political strike. (The FNPR and the Communist Party had called a one-day strike for October 7 separately, but both had since given their support to Primakov's new 'leftist' government, formed in the wake of the August financial collapse.) The committee's demands were Yeltsin's resignation, a new economic policy, and constitutional reform to subject the government to democratic control.

The ultimate goal of the Yaroslavl workers was to create a 'ring of anger' in the central regions surrounding Moscow on the day following the general strike in order to block rail traffic to the capital and press home the demands of the strike. But though participation across Russia in the October 7 protest was the largest ever, only Yaroslavl's workers blocked the rails on October 8. Even so, they forced their governor and regional legislature to endorse their demands, to admit on a permanent basis three representatives of their co-ordinating committee into the regional government with a consultative voice, and to give the unions television time. The governor also established a commission with union participation to develop an anti-crisis programme and eliminate wage arrears. The labour movement became the predominant political force in the region.

PERSPECTIVES

But Russia has many regions. These examples are exceptional, and in each case one can point to special conditions that favour them: a 'culture of struggle', a relatively good economic situation, an unusual concentration of plants in the same subsector in a relatively small town where 'there is nowhere else to go'. The main problem that they all face is isolation. All these organizations realize that alone they cannot affect the basic causes of their members' condition and they have made serious efforts to reach out.

The acutely felt need for the 'live elements' of the labour movement to break out of their isolation explains the remarkable resonance that the miners' 'picket', a tent camp pitched in front the 'White House' in Moscow in the summer of 1998, had in the working class. On the face of it a modest and some-what bizarre initiative—about 200 coal miners baking in the summer sun for weeks on end with no response from the government—became a powerful magnet for worker activists from all over Russia, a rallying point and meeting place for the exchange of experience, for mutual support, and potentially for practical co-ordination. Such a place they could not find in the official union structures, which are, in practice, obstacles to solidarity and co-ordination. The FNPR, and most of its affiliated unions, essentially ignored the 'picket'.

But conditions in 1998 were not yet ripe. And they were made worse by the financial crash and devaluation of July, which dealt a further blow to real wages and employment. While the October 7 protest was the biggest ever, it entailed little risk for its participants. However, even in Yaroslavl, the much more dangerous rail blockade of October 8 brought out only a few hundred workers, mainly Tutaev women (who faced down over a thousand armed troops), this after 25,000 workers on the previous day had voted unanimously for the blockade. Another complicating factor was the formation in August of a 'left' government, including Communists, under Primakov. This did, in fact, mark a temporary retreat of the Yeltsinite forces, utterly discredited by the financial collapse. But Primakov had no intention of breaking with interna-tional capital, which would have required a radical democratization of power and policy. Under Primakov, the workers continued to bear the full brunt of the crisis and of Russia's debt payments. And so, once the government had stabilized the situation, Primakov and the Communists were easily removed to make way again for the Yeltsinite forces, and eventually Putin.

The 'picket' itself ended in betrayal by the leaders of the alternative miners' union (NPG), who had solemnly pledged that this time they were fighting for the interests of the entire working class and would not abandon their political demands for economic concessions. But that is exactly what they did, without bothering to consult the 'picketers', only a few days before the October 7 national protest. But the point is not so much the leaders' betrayal as that it provoked no serious reaction among miners or other workers.

All the same, the experience was widely viewed as positive among activists.

There has been growth, though painstakingly slow, of solidarity and a willingness to confront enterprise and state authority. A recent military-style assault on a worker-occupied-and-managed pulp-and-paper mill near the town of Vyborg evoked an unprecedented outpouring of support from unions and individual workers all over Russia. But in the end, the mill workers were defeated, though not by violence. This was one of a number of conflicts in Russia over workers' control and property rights. But workers have even less chance of winning these than traditional union struggles, so long as their actions are uncoordinated and state power is in hostile hands.

There is thus still a long way to go. In the meanwhile, many workers will be tempted by strong men 'saviours' like Putin, who appeal to misplaced national pride and the hunger for security of a people stripped of all dignity by the forces the strong man really represents. Decisive change that could lead to an independent, militant, and effective labour movement will probably have to await at least the first stages of an economic recovery, which would help to allay the widespread insecurity and bolster workers' readiness to take risks. There are signs that the depression has bottomed out and that recovery is beginning, though it is tenuous, since investment has not increased.

Another factor that would provide a powerful boost to the Russian labour movement is a clear turn away from neoliberalism in North America and Western Europe, and labour's passing to the offensive in these heartlands of capitalism. Such an offensive would have a contagious effect, raising morale among Russian workers. It would undermine the positions of Russia's new ruling class and its international backers as well as those of the 'patriotic left' that supports a mythical 'patriotic bourgeoisie', and thus open political space for democratic alternatives.

NOTES

1.   V. Mozhaev, *Nezavisimaya gazeta*, 11 November 1994.

2.   V. M. Rutgaizen and Yu. E. Shevnyakov, 'Raspredelenie po trudu', EKO, 3, 1987.

3.   D. Mandel, 'A Market Without Thorns', *Perestroika and the Soviet People*, Montreal: Black Rose Press, 1991, pp. 91–116.

4.   S. Shenfield, 'On the Threshold of Disaster: The Socio-Economic Situation in Russia,' 1999 (unpublished), FNPR web site (http://www.trud.org/index7-4.htm); *Sovetskya Rossiya*, 4 November 1999 (State Statistics Committee reports).

5.   Ekonomicheskii fakul'tet MGU, *Ekonomicheskii almanakh*, vyp. I, TEIS, Moscow, 1997, p. 97, p. 31; *Informatsiya o sotisal'no-ekonomicheskom polozhenii Rossii, yanvar'-aprel' 1999g*, Moscow, 1999, p. 54.

6.   *Ekonomicheskii almanakh*, 1997, pp. 11, *Bank Austria E-W report 1/99*, p. 22; Goskomstat Rossii, web site (http://www.gks.ru/osnpok.htm).

7.   *Financial Times*, 29 August 1999.

8.   *Izvestiya*, 11 November 1999.

9.   S. Menshikov, 'Russian Capitalism Today,' *Monthly Review*, July–August 1999, p. 95.

10. 'Report of the Vice-President to the Eleventh Plenary Session of the Central Committee of the ACM-Workers' Union,' 15 April 1999, p. 12, unpublished.
11. Menshikov, 'Russian Capitalism Today', p. 82.
12. *Financial Times*, 21 August 1999.
13. Shenfield, 'On the Threshold of Disaster'.
14. Ibid.
15. M. Feshbach, 'A Comment on Recent Demographic Issues and a Forbidding Forecast', David Johnson's Russia List (davidjohnson@erols.com), 4 August 1999.
16. ASM-Holding, *Analiticheskii obzor, yanvar'-oktyabr' 1998g*, Moscow, 1998, pp. 44–45.
17. *Le Devoir* (Montreal) 7 October 1998; Goskomstat, *Informatsiya o sotsial'no-ekonomicheskom polozhenii Rossii*, 4, 1999, pp. 60–61.
18. *Golos profsoyuza*, 3, 1999, p. 2, and no. 2–3, 1998, p. 4.
19. Goskomstat Rossii, *Rossiiskii statisticheskii ezhegodnik 1996*, Moscow, Logos, 1996, p. 84; Goskomstat, *Rossiya 1999*, 1999, p. 28; Goskomstat, *Russia in Figures, 1999*, table 7.3 (http://www/gks.ru).
20. *Golos profsoyuza*, 3, 1999, p. 2; 'Report of the President to the Third Congress of the Union of ASM Workers', October 1997, p. 20 (unpublished).
21. FNPR's estimate. *Solidarnost'*, 15 April 1999.
22. *Izvestiya*, 26 February 2000.
23. Most of what follows is based upon direct observation, interviews or discussions at union seminars.
24. *Golos profsoyuza*, March–April 1996.
25. FNPR web site (http://www.trud.org/archive).
26. Resolution of the All-Russian Conference of Machine Builders 'On Joint Actions of Employers and Trade Unions,' 4 June 1997 (unpublished).
27. FNPR web site (http://www.trud.org/archive).
28. *Golos profosyuza*, 2–3, 1998.
29. V. Gorenkov, 'Information on the Sectoral Tariff Agreement in 1998 and 1999 and the State of Work on Collective Agreements' 16 March 1998 (unpublished); *Golos profsoyuza*, 4, 1999, p. 1.
30. *Solidarnost'*, October 1997.
31. *Golos profsoyuza*, October 1997, p. 1.
32. B. Maksimov, 'Legko li byt' liderom?', 1999 (unpublished).
33. Maksimov, 'Legko li byt' liderom?'
34. D. Mandel, *Rabotyagi: Perestroika and After Viewed from Below*, New York: Monthly Review Press, 1994, pp. 262–3.
35. *Kommersant*, 23 December 1998, p. 8. This is based upon interviews with S. Vasilieva and on B. Maksimov's, 'Na polyakh bitvy "traktornoi voiny"', 1999 (unpublished).
36. *Rabochaya politika*, 24 December 1999; *Samarskoe obozrenie*, 31 January 2000.
37. Mandel, *Perestroika and the Soviet People*, pp. 26–29.
38. Some published information can be found in *Sovetskaya Rossiya*, 30 July, 3, 9, 19, 22, 24 September 1999, and *Rabochaya politika*, 4, 1999.

THE WORKING CLASS AND THE ISLAMIC STATE IN IRAN

HAIDEH MOGHISSI AND SAEED RAHNEMA

In all the major political developments in twentieth-century Iran, from the constitutional revolution of 1906–11 and the nationalization of the oil industry in early 1950s to the political upheavals of early 1960s and the 1979 revolution, workers were major participants and demonstrated a high level of militancy. However, governments of diverse persuasions, from the Pahlavis' modernizing dictatorial monarchy to the liberal nationalists, and the Islamists' pre-modern theocracy, have ignored workers' legitimate demands and suppressed their dissent. Many factors account for this failure, not least of them being the qualitative and quantitative weaknesses of the working class—a result of the specific nature of capitalist development and industrialization in Iran. Because of its own internal weaknesses, the workers' movement has depended historically on left social democratic and communist movements both organizationally and intellectually. In fact, socialist and communist ideas about the workers' right to form unions and emancipate themselves preceded the emergence of the working class itself. Yet dependence on external leadership made Iranian workers susceptible to the theoretical and political wavering and internal conflicts of the country's left intelligentsia. As well, the continuous suppression of the left by successive dictatorial regimes inevitably also affected the militancy and organizational efficacy of the working-class movement.

In this context, it is reasonable to argue that the progress of the working-class movement has been and continues to be directly linked to the movement for democracy and social change. Removing the political obstacles standing in the way of independent trade unions and other forms of labour organization remains the working-class movement's most immediate task. But this is not possible without achieving other democratic advances, including full freedom of expression and association and a free press, and other constituent elements of political and economic democracy. Without this the left intelligentsia cannot develop effective communicative and political links with the workers' movement, and that movement, in turn, will be confined to sparse, sporadic actions at the factory-level, as it is today.

EVOLUTION OF THE WORKING-CLASS MOVEMENT

Ideas about workers' rights and organizations emerged in last decades of the nineteenth century.[1] Several Iranian intellectuals formed the first Social Democratic Party in 1903; its programme called for, among other things, the right to unionize and strike, and an eight-hour working day.[2] They also tried to make connections with socialist leaders in Russia. This was exemplified by the 'Iranians' Letter' sent by Chalangarian to Kautsky in 1908 and the latter's response.[3] Initial efforts to establish trade unions began in 1906, at the peak of the Constitutional Revolution (1905–1911), with the formation of the printers' union in Tehran. The return to power of the supporters of the absolutist monarch in 1908, and their defeat by the constitutionalists in 1910, predictably led first to the suspension and then the resumption of trade union activities. The first decade of the twentieth century marked the actual organization of the printers' trade union and the publication of its newspaper, Unity of Labour (*Ettehad-e Kargaran*); their successful strike has been called 'the first manifestation in Persia of a collectivist or socialist movement.'[4] Encouraged by the printers' success in improving their working conditions, including an eight-hour day and overtime pay, between 1910 and 1922 several other unions were formed including a bakers' union and unions of postal workers, shoemakers and dressmakers. In the 1920s Iran's first Communist Party, *Edalat* (Justice), was also started.

In this period, both trade union activities and the political movement for national independence got their inspiration from revolutionary developments in Russia. Socialist and labour activists among the Iranian diaspora in Russian Azarbaijan, and the formation of Iran's first communist party in Baku, played a determining role in the upsurge of labour activism in the homeland. The first congress of the party held in Anzali in 1920 emphasized the rights of 'Iranian toilers' to organize their own trade unions and urged the party's local branches to work in that direction. This led to the emergence of the all-Union Council of Tehran (*Showray-e Etehadiehay-e Tehran*), consisting of three representatives from each union and representing 20 percent of all workers in Tehran.[5]

Reza-Khan's British-backed military coup d'état of 1921, his eventual seizure of the throne in 1925, and his brutal suppression of left activists struck severe blows to the primordial labour movement. Yet Reza Shah's reign also marked the emergence of modern industries and a significant increase in the size of the industrial working class. This eventually led to the second major period of labour activism which, with the direct involvement and support of the

Iranian communists, came about after Reza Shah's removal from power in 1941. In fact, the period 1941–1953 was perhaps the most important period in the history of the labour and trade union movement in Iran. The oil workers syndicates, led by the Yousef Eftekhari group, achieved enormous success in organizing workers in the oilfields of southern Iran.[6] Workers constituted 80 percent of members of the newly formed Tudeh Party (the pro-Soviet Communist Party); by 1942, the Central United Council (CUC) (*Showray-e Motahedeh Markazi*), organized and led by the Tudeh Party, claimed a membership of 400,000 workers through 186 affiliated unions.[7]

The state's response to the growing demands and political influencs of the unions and the Tudeh in the post-war period was essentially coercive. In 1949 the CUC was banned and many of its leaders were detained. But the period also saw the rise of the nationalist movement against the Anglo-Iranian Oil Company and the coming to power of Mossadeq's nationalist government. This was a period of constitution-based government and a free press, leading to greater political awareness and activism on the part of large sections of the middle- and lower-middle classes and working classes, and the growing appeal of the socialist ideas and programs promoted by the left. But the Tudeh Party turned the labour unions into appendages of the party in the service of its short-term agenda, influenced mainly by the Soviet Union's foreign policy.

The return to power of Mohammad Reza Shah through the 1953 CIA-induced coup d'état, and the brutal suppression of the Tudeh Party and labour leaders, once more forced a retreat of the labour and left movements. The Tudeh Party was declared illegal, socialist publications were banned, and all independent unions were disbanded and replaced by state-run syndicates. At the same time, there was major drive toward industrialization. In the absence of a strong domestic entrepreneurial class the government played a dominant role in directing industrialization, working closely with multinational corporations. The Shah's drive toward the industrialization and modernization of Iranian social and economic structures, however, did not permeate the political arena where no independent, voluntary institutions within civil society were allowed. Between 1953 to 1978, for twenty-five years, the working class remained effectively unorganized and lived under close surveillance by the SAVAK (the secret police). Of course, there were still sporadic struggles for improving pay and working conditions, and in the 1970s, after several major 'illegal' strikes, industrial workers achieved some of their economic demands. But the demands for the right to establish independent unions and to participate in management had to be put on hold until 1978, when the tide of the anti-Shah revolution swept away the state's coercive apparatuses and its agents.

With the weakening of government control and police surveillance industrial plants again became sites of labour activism. Strikes, particularly by the most privileged segments of the Iranian working class in key industries such as oil, communications, heavy industries and power plants, had a severe impact on the Shah's regime and brought the country to a virtual economic halt.[8]

Becoming aware of its own power and potential for united struggle, and influenced by left organizations that had resumed their activities, the working class rearranged and enlarged its demands. Initially limited to pay and working conditions, under the influence of the left its demands now included political and anti-imperialist measures such as the nationalization of the key industries and expulsion of foreign employees.

The establishment of united front organizations, such as the Workers and Employees Councils (*Showra-ye Kargaran va Karmandan*), during and immediately after the 1979 revolution provided a unique experience in self-management and democratic participation and had an enormous political and ideological impact on workers and the left organizations. The councils, one of the most fascinating outcomes of the revolutionary movement, were thought at the time to be an instrument for consolidation of political democracy in Iran. In various factories and plants they ventured to assert control over production, management and distribution, as well as enabling workers to participate in the country's political process. But these ambitious goals proved illusory. The divided ideological and membership configuration of the councils made them the locus of the hard struggles and conflicting agendas of workers and salaried employees. Both categories had membership in the councils. In addition, the councils were beset by constitutional and organizational ambiguities. The three major political currents in contemporary Iran, the socialists, the nationalists, and the Islamists, each to varying degrees tried to mould the workers' movement and bring it under their control. Lacking its own internal ideological and organizational cohesion, the Iranian working class was hampered by these diverse and hostile tendencies. Constant infighting within the councils added to the ideological confusion.

The gradual takeover of the councils by Islamic activists and functionaries of the Islamic state, and the expulsion and eventual suppression of secular left activists and their replacement with Islamic *Showras*, ended a major period of independent labour activism in Iran. Whatever their achievements, the divisive atmosphere of the early councils exhibits clearly the political and organizational weaknesses of the Iranian working class and the left generally. The causes of these weaknesses are manifold. In this essay we focus on three: the configuration of the working population; emerging mechanisms of Islamic state control; and the troubled relationship between workers and left political groups and organizations.

THE CONFIGURATION OF THE WORKING POPULATION

The relatively small number of industrial workers employed in large modern industries is a factor which inhibits the formation of a strong and united working class. Intense work segmentation and a weakly developed division of labour has not only created a highly fragmented working class within the manufacturing sector, but pre-capitalist crafts still continue to live side by side with capitalist industrial enterprises. The vast majority of the latter are very small firms, while the larger enterprises, mostly established through licensing agreements with MNCs, are predominantly government-owned and controlled and have been the main arena for worker activism. However, this activist core is under constant intensive surveillance not only by the police but also by fellow workers of the factories' Islamic associations. Two decades after the establishment of the Islamic Republic, which promised to install 'the rule of the toilers' (*mustaz'afan*) and to create a strong, independent industrial sector and sustained industrial development, the new regime has failed to break the cycle of industrial weakness which is reflected also in weaknesses in the working-classes' organizational abilities.

Table 1: Configuration of Working Population (aged 10+) by Employment Category, 1996 ('000s):

Employers	Self-employed	Wage/salary earners private sector	Wage/salary earners public sector	Unpaid family workers	Co-ops and others	Total
528	5199	3270	4258	797	520	14572
3.6%	35.6%	22.4%	29.2%	5.4%	3.5%	100%

Source: Adapted from Statistical Centre of Iran, *Statistical Yearbook: 1996–97*, Tehran, 1998, p. 79.

As in other developing countries, the traditional left in Iran has tended to lump together all working people (with the exception of the peasants) and to call them the working class or proletariat. This conceals the heterogeneity of the living and working conditions and demands of a very diverse population and is theoretically meaningless and politically misleading. A closer look at the employment categories show that wage and salary earners constitute about half of the working population. According to the latest census data (1996), out of a total population of over 60 million, 14.5 million people aged ten or over are working. Of these about 3.2 million, or 22.4 percent, are wage and salary earners in the private sector, and about 4.2 million, or 29.2 percent, are wage and salary earners in the public sector. The five million self-employed are the still largest category, constituting 35.6 percent, not counting the over 5 percent (just under a million) who are unpaid family workers (see Appendix and Table 1).[9]

Even among those who sell their labour as wage and salary earners, moreover, there are enormous differentiations in economic, social, political and cultural conditions with very real consequences in terms of alliances and combined political actions. Indeed, the working population really falls into three distinct class categories. First, there are the 40 percent of the working population who are traditionally petit bourgeois, or old middle class, made up of the self-employed and unpaid family workers, the majority of whom work under pre-capitalist relations.[10] Then there is the diversified and problematic 'new middle class', which technically includes everyone from managers to professionals, and to salaried clerical and retail employees. We may exclude the 2 percent who have senior executive occupations who clearly fall within the capitalist class, or are directly in the service of value extraction.[11] The rest, which we estimate at 3.5 million people or no less than 24 percent of the working population, properly constitute a new middle class which needs to be differentiated from the working class, especially in a less developed country like Iran, because of their higher level of education, job security, income and social status. Only 27 percent of the total working population, 4 million out of 14.5 million, are wage workers. They are also differentiated in terms of skills, income and working environment, of course, but their similar overall condition and relation to capital justifies grouping them under the single category of the wage workers (see Appendix and Table 2).

Table 2: Configuration of Working Population (aged 10+) by Occupational Category, 1996 ('000s):

Senior officials Executive	Profes- sionals	Tech- nicians	Clerical	Service, sales workers	Agricultural and fishery	Craft and trade workers	Plant and machine operators	Elementary occu- pations	Others
325	1263	457	614	1480	3043	2942	1303	1931	1213
2.2%	8.6%	3.1%	4.2%	10.1%	20.9%	20.15%	8.9%	13.2%	8.3%

Source: Adapted from Statistical Centre of Iran, *Statistical Yearbook: 1996–97*, Tehran, 1998, p. 80.

In addition to its small size, the Iranian working class is highly differentiated and segmented. For example, the industrial (manufacturing) workers, the most politically significant section of the Iranian working class, are scattered in over 360,000 industrial establishments, 91.6 percent of which are workshops of less than five workers and employees. Of the 1.2 million wage and salary earners in the manufacturing sector, over 269,000 work in these small workshops alongside hundreds of thousands of unpaid family workers. Over 279,000 work in small-/mid-sized factories of 6–49 workers and employees, and about 69,000 in factories of 50–99 workers and employees. At the other pole, however, over 1,200 factories and plants have over 100 workers and employees and in total employ over 580,000 wage and salary earners.[12] These workers form the core of the Iranian working class and are the focus of attention of labour activists, and as such are the main targets of the Islamic regime's ideological and repressive apparatuses.

A further significant aspect of the situation of the Iranian working population relates to the millions of unemployed. The latest sample data of the 15- to 64-year-old working population show the percentage of the unemployed to be

13.1,[13] which is far below the actual number. The vast majority, or 57.9 percent of the unemployed, are in the 15 to 24 age category. This fact partly explains the continued youth unrest and activism in present day Iran. There is, additionally, a large 'sub-proletariat' of shanty town dwellers, the '*zaghe-neshinan*', mostly made up of the displaced rural population who live under precarious conditions. During the revolution Khomeini and the Islamists, unlike the left that almost solely focused its activities on industrial workers, successfully mobilized this large population of urban poor by addressing their specific concerns.[14] All these factors—the high percentage of the traditional middle class, the existence of a sizable new-middle class, the relatively small percentage of wage workers and their dispersion in large number of small and medium workshops and factories, as well as the persistence of millions of unemployed and the growing size of the shanty town sub-proletariat—have serious implications for the kind of political agenda that can be credibly put forward by and for different social classes, including workers.

Table 3: Configuration of Female Working Population, 1976–1996 ('000s):

	1976	1986	1996
Female Population	16,352	24,164	29,164
Economically Active Population*	9,796	12,820	16,027
Females Economically Active	1,449	1,307	2,037
Employed Female Population	1,212	975	1,765
Senior Officials/managers	5	13	16
Public Sector Wage and Salary Employees	245	407	698
Private Sector Wage and Salary Employees	322	99	249
Self Employed	130	181	347
Unpaid Family Workers	495	212	366
Co-ops and Unspecified	12	70	87

* This includes unemployed seeking work.

Source: Calculated on the basis of the population census results, Iran Statistical Centre, *Iran Statistical Yearbook*, 1977, 1987, 1997, Tehran, pp., 29, 31, 58, 70, 80, and 81.

Another major aspect of the configuration of the working population relates to gender. The sexual segregation of the work force is a persistent policy of the Islamic state, and under Islamic rule the share of women in the total economically active population dropped from the pre-Revolutionary figure of 14.8 percent in 1976 to 10.2 percent in 1986.[15] Although this percentage increased in the mid-1990s to 12.7 percent, the female participation rate remains below the pre-revolutionary figure (see Table 3). Much of the increase in female employment relates to the government sector. Female employment in the public sector as a proportion of total female employment increased from 20 percent in the pre-revolutionary period to 31 percent in the mid-1980s and 39 percent in the mid-1990s. Two factors explain this increase. First, dramatic population growth, which sharply increased the demand for new female teachers. Women are overwhelmingly dominant in the staff of sexually segregated educational institutions (82 percent). Ideological and political considerations also account for new female hiring. Employed in the public sector are large numbers of female family members of government officials, martyrs (*Shohada*), veterans (*Janbazan*), and the war disabled (*Ma'lulin*). To these, we should add an even larger number of women who since the revolution have been recruited into such institutions as the all-female morality squads, Islamic associations of government and semi-government agencies, the *Pasdaran* Corps, the Society for Islamic Propaganda (*Howzeh-ye Tablighat-e Eslami*), the Martyr's Foundation (*Bonyad-e Shahid*), the militia (*Basij*),[16] and the special women's committees in neighbourhood Mosques—all charged with disseminating Islamic values through indoctrination and intimidation. Thus, most of these women are employed in state and para-state apparatuses designed to control and police other women.

In the industrial manufacturing sector, women comprise only 5.2 percent of all wage workers and salaried employees.[17] In the post-revolutionary period, the number of female self employed and unpaid family workers increased dramatically. This trend has both economic and ideological causes. First, in many cases, men have replaced female workers whose employment, otherwise, would add to day-care costs. But beyond this, ideologically, the Shari'a-based Iranian Civil Code, by recognizing the man as family head and putting him in charge, has enforced his responsibility 'for providing for the wife' (Article 1106) and has promoted the perception that women's paid employment is not necessary for the family's upkeep. This and other legal provisions, such as the husband's right to prevent his wife from working in jobs which he considers 'against the family's interest' (*Masaleh-e Khanevadegi*, Article 1117) are 'anti-female-labour force participation messages.'[18] Of course such messages do not prevent women from doing paid work without which increasingly family's survival is impossible. Yet, the messages work to legitimize women's inferior status in work and pay hierarchies. The combined impact of economic and ideological factors has increasingly pushed female workers out of the large urban industries which are covered by the provisions of the Labour Law. Female industrial workers at present are found in three different categories: large industries, small workshops with less than ten workers and women working at home (piece-workers). The last category, according to one study, comprises the majority of female urban workers, who are excluded not only from the provisions of the Labour Law, but from work statistics as well.[19] Obviously, this situation negatively affects the organizability of the employed female population.

The segmentation of the working population on the basis of class, gender and work is intensified further by the ideological and religious differentiation imposed by the Islamic state. From its inception, the regime's indoctrination and manipulation of the people's (including the workers') religious beliefs drove an ideological wedge between them. Earlier decades of dictatorial rule and anti-socialist propaganda had already helped to inoculate the vast majority of workers against infection by socialist ideas. The organizational splintering and intellectual and political isolation of the left movement made the workers even more vulnerable to Islamic ideology. Through intimidation and deceptive rhetoric the Islamists managed to construct a wall separating both the working poor and organized labour from socialist ideas and projects. The Islamic regime turned the 'opium' of the masses into the steroid of the masses. But responding to overpowering demands for social justice, promoted by the left, the Islamic regime, while violently attacking the 'atheistic' language of the socialists, nevertheless appropriated some of the ideas and jargon of the outlawed groups. One faction of the ruling bloc even started to identify itself as 'left' to differentiate itself from the conservatives, which they identified as the 'right'. Parallel to the creation of separate students' associations, women's organizations and professional groups, each faction has established its own workers' association whose main task has been to support its parent faction when the need arises. The formation of the Association of Islamic Councils, the House of Labour, and an Islamic Labour Party (*Hezb-e Eslamiy-e Kar*), with the pretext of facilitating 'the participation of productive forces in political power'[20] are cases in point.

Despite this ideological manipulation, however, objective realities and the harsh conditions of life which Iranian workers must endure began to strip away illusions about the Islamic regime. During over two decades of Islamic rule industrial workers, the unemployed and the urban poor have confronted the regime through sporadic protests, sit-ins and strikes, demanding an improvement in wages and working conditions. Workers suffered most in the early post-revolutionary period, particularly during the harsh working conditions imposed by the regime as a result of the long war with Iraq. Such measures as the extension of the working day, reduction of wages, forced fund-raising for the war by the Islamic workers councils and associations, involuntary transfer of workers to the front, and inadequate bunkers during bombardments of the factories are cases in point. The workers resisted these measures as best as they could through such actions as signing petitions to the authorities and organizing sit-ins and protests within the confines of their factories. In many cases they boycotted the general meetings of the Islamic councils, demonstrated against the Islamic associations in the factories and in some cases resorted to strikes. Workers' protest would reach its height whenever the news of war casualties involving a fellow worker on the front was received in the factory.[21]

With the war ending, the workers became bolder in their demands, and moved their demonstrations to the nearby streets or highways. Major issues for the workers in the post-war period have been delayed wages and benefits, lack of occupational safety standards, job classification schemes, and layoffs. Labour activists have recorded about 90 cases of strikes in large industries alone in 1998, including strikes in the Isfahan Steel plant, Behshahr Textiles, the Hamedan Glass manufacturing plant, and most important of all several strikes and demonstrations by workers in the oil industry at the Abadan Refinery, and in Gachsaran. Most of these protests involved the blockages of major highways, followed by brutal responses by the police and military.[22] Other examples of such actions include the co-ordinated strike of thousands of workers from the National Industrial Groups, General Tyre and Arak Industrial Groups.

In other cases, workers have used the regime's rhetoric and celebrations against it. For example, under pressure from workers the 1999 May Day celebration was organized by the House of Workers and the Ministry of Labour with the participation of parliamentarians from the regime's pragmatic faction as speakers, in defiance of an explicit ban by the Ministry of Interior. At the rally staged in Tehran (which started with a recital of the Quran and concluded with the Shi'i ritual of chest beating), the workers seized the opportunity to protest against a new bill which had been introduced in the parliament. This bill, initiated by the conservatives, exempted small workshops with fewer than three workers from provisions of the Labour Law but, faced with such severe resistance, it was postponed. However, the outgoing conservative majority, even after its overwhelming defeat in the parliamentary election in February 2000, later passed the bill, now amended to exclude workshops with less than five workers and employees from the provisions of the Labour Law.

MECHANISMS OF CONTROL UNDER THE ISLAMIC STATE

The Islamic government replaced the Shah's regime at a time when all the major industrial plants and public and private institutions were under the control of the workers' and employees' councils (*showras*). The councils were the outcome of strike committees that had emerged during the 1979 revolution, and which in the absence of the owners and managers were in control of these institutions. The major councils, in many cases, were either formed by or were under the ideological influence of the sympathizers of different left organizations, or the Islamist Mujahedin.[23] Early in the post-revolutionary period the councils were supportive of the new regime. All of them followed Khomeini's back-to-work decree. However, confrontation with the Provisional Government, headed by the liberal nationalist/Islamist Bazargan, was inevitable. The government's policy was to try to preserve the *status quo* in the industrial sector, while the councils had radical demands including the immediate improvement of working conditions and wages, the nationalization of industries, and workers' participation in management. The liberals in government were too slow in responding to the demands of the councils; the councils had no patience for waiting for gradual reforms. After the hostage crisis, the fall of the Provisional Government and the consolidation of the clerics' monopoly of power, the situation changed. The regime tried to bring the pluralist and independent Showras under its control, and failed. This failure led to the suppression of the councils and the establishment of the yellow 'Islamic Showras'. The role of these councils, along with the 'Islamic associations' which mushroomed in most major plants and institutions, was similar to the *Arbeitsfronts* in Nazi Germany and the *Sampo* in Japan during wartime fascist rule. While creating an atmosphere of terror in the workplace, they moved towards a thorough-going ideological indoctrination of workers and employees.[24]

The new regime's labour policy was one of its most contentious preoccupations, second only to the clerics' gender crusades. Under intense pressure from the left organizations and workers in the early months of the revolution, the regime annulled the *ancien régime's* Labour Law. With the demise of the councils and workers' militancy, the first version of a new Islamic Labour Law, based on a fundamentalist interpretation of Islam, was designed by an arch-conservative Labour minister. This draft, among others, implicitly envisaged the worker (*kargar*) as a semi-slave who 'rents' himself/herself to the employer (*karfarma*), and who must therefore remain under the almost absolute control of the employer. The draft created such an uproar that it was shelved after intense infighting within the ruling bloc. Faced with the realities of a society that had experienced capitalist market relations and associated impacts, the regime had to retreat and make some concessions with regard to the rights of workers—as it also did in its gender politics. Even in the absence of the left and pro-workers opposition which, by then, it had already brutally suppressed, the regime's rhetoric of being a government of the dispossessed could be manipulated by workers and the ruling populist faction to force the government to come up with a less outrageous law. In the end, it took about twelve years for the Islamic Republic to devise and approve its Labour Law.

As in other social and political domains, pragmatists in the regime, responding to internal and international pressures, had learned to adopt seemingly acceptable legislation knowing that they are not bound to implement it. After years of going back and forth between the Parliament and the Council of Guardians, the new draft was eventually approved by the Expediency Council in 1990.[25] Cleverly drafted, the new Labour Law is not only far more advanced than the pre-Revolutionary Law, but in many of its provisions it is among the most progressive labour laws in the Middle East. For example, the law makes layoffs very difficult and increases compensation at termination (Articles 21–33). This had been one of the workers' major concerns. It also reduces working hours from 48 to 44 hours a week and to 36 hours for hazardous jobs (Article 51, 52). The minimum working age was increased to 15 (Article 79). Annual paid leave was increased to 30 days (Article 64).

The pre-Revolutionary provision of 'equal wages' for men and women 'for performing work of equal value' (Article 38) was confirmed, with an added proviso prohibiting wage discrimination on the basis of 'age, gender, race, ethnic origin and political and religious convictions.' Pregnancy leave was increased from ten weeks (six weeks before and four weeks after child-birth) to ninety days (Article 76).[26] These provisions are more woman-friendly than the pre-Revolutionary Labour Law, at least on paper. However, actual practice, as also seen in the case of promised but not delivered day-care provisions, effectively cancels out the progressive legislation. In fact, many employers would stop hiring women if they had to be paid the same wages as men. Studies conducted by researchers in both the pre- and the post-revolutionary periods show that, intimidated by the employers' layoff power, female workers hesitate even to disclose their wage and working hours to researchers.[27] Pregnancy leave, amounting to two-thirds of the last wage, as in the past, applies only to workers who have paid the employees' share of insurance. It needs to be borne in mind, moreover, that only a tiny minority of female workers are employed in industries which are covered by the Labour Law.

The area where the new law deliberately and significantly falls far short of the old law is in its attempt to restrain workers' right to organize. In fact, with regard to the right to form labour unions and to negotiate collective agreements as well as the right to strike—that is, in the most important three areas for guaranteeing workers' rights—the Islamists' Law is more reactionary than the Labour Law enforced by the Shah. Fearful of labour unions, their legacy and their historical links with the left, the new Law has even avoided using the familiar terms of *Sandika* (syndicate) or *Etehadieh* (union). Instead, it has invented 'Guild Societies' that workers 'may establish' to 'protect the legitimate and statutory rights and interests of workers and employers (sic) ...' (Article 131). To add to the confusion, two other types of organizations are seen as representing workers; one, the notorious 'Islamic associations', whose aim is '... to propagate and disseminate Islamic culture ...' (Article 130), and the other, the 'Islamic workers councils', the yellow councils that replaced the genuine workers' and employees' councils. Each factory or plant can choose only one of the three types of organizations, each of which can only be established under strict supervision of the Ministry of Labour and Social Affairs. The irony, however, is that even these rudimentary and strictly controlled organizations, as a result of intense pressure of the workers, have come to create problems for the regime. Because of the provisions that are favourable to workers the Labour Law has become a major source of tension between the populist and hard-line factions of the ruling bloc. Both public and private sector managers have called for major revisions of the Labour Law. They want easier provisions to facilitate layoffs.

The Islamic republic's other 'progressive' legislation included a Social Security Law (which on paper expanded the coverage of the insured), as well as a law compelling the sale of a total of 43 percent of the government's shares in public companies to their wage workers and salaried employees (financial support for the purchase of shares was provided through the creation of co-operatives but, notably, most of the purchases have been of shares in money-losing companies).[28]

But overall the Islamic State's policy in relation to the Iranian working class has been in line with its overall repressive political strategy. In its over two decades in power, the regime has developed the most powerful and intricate array of coercive, ideological, and economic apparatuses to suppress dissent. It is not an overstatement to claim that no other type of state, including fascist regimes, has ever succeeded in establishing and employing such diverse apparatuses of control over a deliberately weakened civil society. In addition to apparatuses typically available to other states, such as the police, the army, the courts, the mass media and the educational system, the Islamic regime in Iran has incorporated its traditional Shi'i structures, and a range of new institutions, at various levels of civil society.

In the early years of the post-revolutionary period, particularly during the eight-year Iran–Iraq war, the mosques became multi-functional. Residents in each neighbourhood had to maintain good relations with its clerics and functionaries. Apart from their traditional function of being a place for prayers and religious propaganda, the mosques distributed coupons (*bon*) for subsidized and rationed food on which the vast majority of the people depended for their survival. A certificate of good morals was also needed by job applicants, and receiving it depended on their participation in prayers and other activities. Although their non-propaganda functions have since diminished, the mosques—now estimated to number 50,000—continue to be a base for the regime in every neighbourhood. In addition to the mosques there have been Islamic revolutionary committees, one of the most feared and repressive institutions of the regime, formed by the lumpen proletariat and bullies of the neighbourhoods (these committees were later incorporated into the regular 'law-enforcing' bodies). At work places also, each plant and institution has an Islamic association. The larger organizations have a resident cleric, and, if necessary, a resident representative of the Supreme Leader, who makes sure that there is no deviation from the 'revolutionary' line. For major confrontations there are the elite Islamic revolutionary guards, *Pasdaran* and the Islamic militia, *Basiji*, in addition to the regular police, gendarmes and army. The Islamic Republic also has a most extensive set of ideological apparatuses, combining the traditional Shi'i institutions such as regular sermons delivered in mosques and the Friday prayers with modern mass media and the Internet. The most significant players are the clerics themselves, whose number has grown more than any other occupation and profession, as has the number of seminary schools in the holy cities of Qum and Mashhad.[29] Graduate clerics are employed in public and private organizations as prayer leaders or work in the growing number of mosques and prayer houses in factories and other institutions.

In addition to massive propaganda and ideological indoctrination, the clerics maintain control over their followers through economic means and the provision of social welfare. The largest fund of this type belongs to the late Ayatollah Khomeini, known as 'Imam Khomeini's Aid Committee'. Established in 1979 and now secured through more than 1130 branches throughout Iran, it provides a vast array of social and financial services to needy followers. Over 1.7 million people are 'permanent' beneficiaries of this fund, mostly the working poor and the unemployed. The aid committee also provides health services through clinics, covering over 4.3 million people. It provides educational grants to over 769,000 students and has created over 850 youth centres in urban and rural areas to provide 'education, ideological guidance, and physical education'. It also gives allowances for the construction and repair of dwellings, marriage allowances, and interest-free loans.[30]

In addition to clerics' funds there are also several extremely powerful religious/para-statal organizations, including the Mostaz'afan and Janbazan Foundation, the Martyrs Foundation, and the Fifteenth Khordad Foundation, which run the lucrative confiscated properties of the last Shah's Pahlavi Foundation and those of the richest families of the previous regime. The Mostaz'afan Foundation, one of the largest corporations in Iran,[31] is the richest cash cow of the clerical establishment outside the oil-rich government itself. With links to the powerful bazaar, the traditional economic base of the clerics, this foundation has helped create a new bourgeoisie out of the Islamic elite, while at the same time providing assistance to poor followers, including disabled or sick veterans. Over 325,000 people receive 'permanent' allowances from the Mostaz'afan Foundation, and over 230,000 families are covered by the Martyr Foundation.[32] The use of religious economic institutions and the provision of welfare to recruit or sustain followers has always been an effective way of maintaining and expanding followings in Shi'ite tradition, a policy now effectively used by many other Sunni and Shi'i fundamentalist groups in the region, notably HAMAS in the occupied territories, and Hizbollah in Lebanon. The difference in Iran, though, is that the Islamic clerics have amassed enormous wealth in their religious funds, endowments, and foundations, and at the same time are in control of the government and its enormous oil revenues.

Had it not been for the economic, social and political crises to which the clerical regime has repeatedly been subject, the existence of such extensive apparatuses of state control would destroy all hope for the liberation of the country from fundamentalist rule. But the same interrelated factors which account for these crises also prompt hopes for future change. First, this gigantic machine lost its leader: it could not replace Ayatollah Khomeini with an equally charismatic and powerful figure capable of maintaining a balance between different clerical factions within the ruling bloc. Second, unlike most post-revolutionary regimes, the ruling bloc has not been able to resolve its internal conflicts by the physical or ideological elimination of one faction by another. With the Ayatollah's death political differences continuously widened on economic, social, political and moral issues. These differences, moreover, represent less the contending opinions of clerics and their conflicts over the prescriptions of the Quran, than irresolvable contradictions stemming from the realities of running a society whose social and economic structures have undergone dramatic changes over several decades prior to the revolution. In establishing its ideal state, a regime modeled after the Islamic golden age of the seventh century had to swim against the historical current. It confronted a society which had experienced a degree of modernization and modernity, and had had a long, though unsuccessful history of struggle for democracy and political freedoms, and could not easily be governed through a pre-modern political and legal system and an Islamic moral order.

Above all, in over two decades in power the Islamic government 'of the dispossessed' has failed to provide for the most deprived section of the population. The ever-widening gap between the working poor and newly rich, the evident corruption, outright mismanagement of the economy and the indisputable abuse of power by the clerics to accumulate wealth, which accompany their hypocritical moral crusades aimed particularly at women and youth, have severely discredited the regime in the eyes of a growing number of people. Continued and intensified political repression (which now affects even the Islamists within the system), and particularly the cold-blooded murder of intellectuals and writers (referred to as the 'chain assassinations') directly at the hands of high ranking officials who have gone unpunished, has done much to discredit the Islamists' projects and to delegitimize the regime.

THE LEFT AND THE WORKING CLASS: THE STRUGGLE FOR CHANGE

The left, historically the strongest supporter of the workers' movement in Iran, suffered a terrible defeat at the hands of the Islamists. This was partly a result of its own weaknesses and mistakes and its tendency to underestimate the robust mass-based coercive power of the Islamic state, and to overestimate the numerical and organizational capacity of both the left and the working class. Theoretical and analytical confusions led to fatal mistakes in formulating the immediate priorities of the left movement as well as a faulty agenda of demands under the Islamic state.

Almost from the inception of the post-revolutionary period, organizations in the highly diverse Iranian left exhibited two distinct orientations towards the Islamic regime. The first, represented by the Tudeh Party, and the Fedayeen *Axariat* (Majority), which was quite popular immediately after the revolution,[33] was characterized by a certain infatuation with the Ayatollah's 'anti-imperialism', and sought to ally itself with 'progressive' and 'revolutionary democratic' elements within the Islamic regime, hoping to direct it towards a 'socialist orientation'.[34] The other orientation, made up of smaller, more radical left organizations, such as the *Fedayeen Aghaliat* (Minority), *Rah-e Kargar* (Workers Path),[35] *Peykar* (Struggle),[36] *Etehadieh Komunistha* (Communist Union),[37] and *Komeleh*,[38] chose open confrontation with the regime, hoping to 'overthrow' it and to 'elevate' the revolution to the socialist stage. Both approaches have failed. The groups who sought an alliance with the 'progressive' clerics were discredited by excusing, and eventually even colluding with, the regime's brutal and anti-democratic policies; the organizations seeking the regime's overthrow facilitated their own annihilation by confrontation with a ruthless, but, at the time, popular regime. In the end, both were brutally suppressed. Thousands of left activists were executed, imprisoned, maimed, or driven into exile. One devastating result of the left's defeat has been its loss of contact, perhaps even credibility, with the working class.

These two distinct political lines still dominate the discourses of the surviving left organizations in exile. The disgraced first group continues to seek an alliance with the 'moderate faction' within the ruling bloc, embodied in the person of President Khatami. It fails to appreciate the simple fact that so long as the clerical regime enjoys a monopoly of power it does not need and will not seek an alliance with any other force. It will concede such an alliance only when it faces a serious crisis of authority, and in any case, the alliance will include only the political forces ideologically and politically closest to the Islamic regime. That means, at most, a connection with moderate Islamist and liberal nationalist forces. Even if, as a result of a strange turn of events, the clerics were to look to the compromising faction of the left as an ally, it will not be treated as a major player (given the left's organizational weakness and its lack of credibility). Instead, it will be used in the service of the state. Similarly, the radical segments of the left who call for the overthrow of the regime in favour of establishing a socialist workers' state do not explain their strategies for achieving socialism or who their potential allies are. Their approach is obviously based on the assumed homogeneity and numerical predominance of the proletariat within the working population who are going to lead the socialist revolution. They do not seem prepared to recognize either their own organizational weakness and lack of linkage with the working class, or the strength of the present regime.

Organizationally weak, mainly based in exile, and having a minimal presence in political events inside Iran, the left, despite some name changes and new coalitions, remains sharply divided. The organizations inclined to compromise, such as the People's Democratic Party of Iran,[39] the Organization of People's Fedayeen-Majority, and the remnants of the Tudeh Party, retain hopes for reform within the clerical regime. Others such as the Left Workers Union, the Union of Peoples Fedayeen, the Communist Party of Iran, and the Workers Communist Party of Iran, herald an impending proletarian revolution. They emphasize their 'proletarian' character by adding an adjective, *Kargari* (of workers) to their names to differentiate themselves from the 'bourgeois communists'. Except in a few cases, the left movement appears to be operating within the old theoretical and organizational framework, without making serious efforts at self-assessment or self-criticism even when the Islamic regime is facing a serious political crisis and popular resistance is on the rise.

That such popular resistance is developing there can be no doubt. Frustrated by over two decades of political and cultural repression, corruption and economic deprivation, and benefiting from the Islamists' crippling factional divisions and in-regime conflicts, the Iranian people are learning how to resist the regime in ingenious ways. The remarkable resistance of women, youth and various sections of the professional strata and intellectuals, as well as several major riots over 'illegal' building in shanty towns and ceaseless strikes and sit-ins in the industrial sector, suggest that, perhaps for the first time in modern Iranian history, the people have taken political initiatives without co-ordination and organized leadership. A good example is the 1997 presidential elections, in which voters participated enthusiastically and elected Khatami to the presidency, despite both the conservatives' fierce propaganda in favour of the other candidate, and the radical left's plea to boycott the elections. After this election, the people continued to force the regime to play according to the rules of its self-invented democratic game, taking advantage of the shifting forces among the Islamists and the emergence of a new coalition calling for a free press and democracy. On two other occasions—the 1998 elections to the city councils, and particularly the 2000 parliamentary elections—the people actively participated and voted in favour of less conservative candidates.

Yet the people's remarkable resistance, despite the human sacrifices it has involved, will not guarantee social and political change. For one thing, it is devoid of an organized, unified and clear-sighted leadership, and the opposition in the diaspora, including the left, is as divided as ever. In the absence of a democratic left alternative, debates over modernity versus tradition, democracy versus authoritarianism, social justice versus Islamic justice and the need for the separation of religion and state are carried out by a new breed of Muslim intellectuals, many of whom previously served in the repressive physical and ideological apparatuses of the Islamic state. These disillusioned Islamists who (unlike the secular intellectuals) have access to their own 'alternative' papers have become household names for their bold criticism of the repression, corruption and despotism of the conservative clergy. The danger, once more, is that the left, the working class and other progressive forces will lose the opportunity to mobilize the massive discontent around a secular democratic alternative.

The fact remains that despite the bloody suppression of the secular left opposition, and extensive negative propaganda by the regime, socialist and secular ideas are still influential. That they have become recurring themes in the oppositional Islamic liberal discourses prompts optimism that the left has a chance to emerge as an active part of the opposition and gain the support of the working classes for building a progressive alternative united front against the Islamists. The immediate goal of such a united front must be to remove the sacred halo around a corrupt and brutal regime and to fight for the transfer of power to a secular democratic state. It must represent the interests and the voices of various social classes, including new-middle-class professionals and the working poor alike. The segmentation of the working class by work and ideology has had a serious impact on the level of its involvement in the movement for democracy and social change. Thus it becomes clear why the main challenges to the Islamic regime in the last two decades have come from the women's movement, youth, university students and from middle-class intellectuals, writers and professionals. If these movements are joined by the working class, they will become more effective. Only through such a broad, focused, organized, and co-ordinated struggle will the left prevent yet another interpretation of Islam embodied in the 'moderate clergy' and 'Muslim intellectuals' from emerging as the effective alternative to the faction of the clergy which now rules. Only by establishing the rights of all citizens to participate in political processes and to form their own voluntary organizations will the working class regain the confidence to represent its own interests which in a democratic system will be the interests of the most oppressed and the most deprived sections of the population.

APPENDIX

The 1996 census provides separate figures for employers, the self-employed and unpaid family workers, but does not distinguish between wage workers and salaried employees. However, it is possible to estimate roughly the numbers and percentages of these latter categories using the data of occupational categories, shown in Table 2, and the data of wage and salary employees in different sub-sectors of the economy, shown in Table 1. By looking at the detailed sub-categories of ISCO (International Standard Classification of Occupations) on the basis of which the data of Table 2 have been calculated, most of the occupational categories can be grouped under the three categories of social classes, the traditional middle class, the new middle class and the wage workers.

Aside from the Senior Officials and Executives, the Professionals (who include engineers, scientists, computing professionals, medical doctors, nurses, teachers, academics, accountants, social workers, writers, artists) and Technicians (who include electronic and communication technicians, draughts-persons, photographers, medical assistants, building inspectors, faith healers, real estate agents) as well as the Clerical employees belong to the new-middle classes. Non-wage Agricultural and Fishery workers are mostly traditional middle classes, while the vast majority of Machine Operators (roughly 90 percent), and all the Elementary Occupations, form the wage workers. However, even within the category of Operators there are occupations, such as taxi drivers and truck drivers, that cannot be considered as wage workers, as many of them are the owners or co-owners of their vehicles.

The two categories of Service and Sales workers, and Craft and Trade workers, are more differentiated and fall under more than one social class category. Since detailed data for each of these categories are not available, by considering the descriptions of each of the occupational sub-categories we have assumed that the majority (80 percent) of Service/Sales workers, including travel attendants, transport conductors, restaurant services workers, to hairdressers, fire fighters, police officers, etc., fall under the new-middle class, and the rest under Workers. The majority (80 percent) of Craft and Trade workers ranging from the non-wage quarry workers and bricklayers to carpenters, roofers, plumbers, welders, motor vehicle mechanics, and electrical and electronic mechanics belong to the traditional middle classes; the rest fall under the working class.

To cross-check the estimates of separate figures and percentages of wage workers and salaried employees, another set of data dealing with the wage and salary employees in different sub-sectors of economy was used. Of the 4,258,000 workers and employees of the public sector, 2,759,000, or 64.7 percent, are in the public administration sub-sector. The vast majority or 90.4 percent of this sub-sector are salaried employees, and only 9.5 percent are wage workers.[40] For other sub-sectors of both the public and the private sectors, such as agriculture and fishing, manufacturing and mining, construction, utilities, and commercial services, we have used the 20/80 'administrative ratio' for salaried employees and wage workers respectively. This is a low ratio for salaried employees in a third-world setting like Iran, which as a result of lower organizational efficiency has a higher administrative ratio or intensity than more advanced countries.[41] On this basis, the total number of wage workers in both the public and the private sectors amounts to over 3,871,000, or about 26 percent of the total employed population, similar to the figure using the data of Table 1. The wage workers (WW) figure is calculated on the basis of the following: Public Sector WW = Agriculture (0.8 * 57,000) + Manufacturing (0.8 * 619,000) + Construction (0.8 * 63,000) + Service (0.8 * 586,000) + Public Administration (0.095 * 2,759,000) = 1,255,855. Private Sector WW (0.8 * 3,270,000) = 2,616,000; Public WW + Private WW = 3,871,855.

NOTES

1. The oldest (handwritten) document in this regard is Khan-e Khanan, *Political Treatise*, 1894, in which the author refers to the need for '*majma'ha*' (associations), and labour 'rules' for regulating working conditions. See Fraidoun Adamiat, *Ideologi-ye Nehzat Mashroteh (Ideology of the Constitutional Movement in Iran)*, Tehran: Payam Publishing, 1976, p. 282.

2. Saeed Rahnema, *Tajdid-e Hayat-e Social Democracy Dar Iran? (Re-birth of Social Democracy in Iran?)*, Stockholm: Baran Publishers,1996, p. 17.

3. See J. Riddle, ed., *Lenin's Struggle for a Revolutionary International*, New York: Monad Press, 1984, pp. 60–65. Thanks are also due to Mehrdad Vahabi for his helpful comments.

4. Tarbiyat, cited in Habib Ladjevardi, *Labor Unions and Autocracy in Iran*, Syracuse: Syracuse University Press, 1985, p. 3.

5. Asnad-e Tarikhi-e Jonbesh-e Kargari, *Social Demokrasi va Kommonisti-e Iran 1903–1963 (Historical Documents: The Workers, Social Democratic and Communist Movement in Iran)*, vol. 6, Florence: Mazdak Publisher, not dated, pp. 107–8.

6. See Kaveh Bayat, and Majid Tafreshi, *Memoires of Yousef Eftekhari*, Tehran: Ferdows Publishing, 1991.

7. Fred Holliday, *Iran, Dictatorship and Development*, Harmondsworth: Penguin, 1997, pp. 199–200.

8. Ali Rahnema and Farhad Nomani, *Secular Miracle*, London: Zed Press, 1990, p.12.

9. Iran Statistical Centre, *Statistical Yearbook, 1996–97*, Tehran, 1998, Table 3–7, p. 79.

10. These relations, to use Olin Wright's distinction, may entail both relations of domination and appropriation in the form of individual appropriation by the self-employed under his/her self direction and control, yet the individuals involved are not capitalistically exploited. The same is true of unpaid family workers who, despite the fact that their labour is appropriated and dominated by someone else, usually the family patriarch, are not exploited in the capitalist sense. See Erik Olin Wright, *Classes*, London: Verso, 1985, pp. 50–51.

11. This is true whether we consider Poulantzas' distinctions of ownership and/or possession, Olin Wright's notions of degrees of ownership and contradictory class location, or Carchedi's two-fold division of capitalist management and the unity-in-domination of the labour process and the production of surplus value. See Nicos Poulantzas, *Classes in Contemporary Capitalism*, London: *New Left Review*, 1975, p. 180; Erik Olin Wright, 'Classes', pp. 42–51; Guglielmo Carchedi, *On the Economic Identification of Social Classes*, London: Routledge & Kegan Paul, 1977, p. 8.

12. Iran Statistical Centre, 'Statistical Yearbook,1996–97', pp. 200, 206.

13. Iran Statistical Centre, *Employment and Unemployment Data*, Tehran, 1997, p. 22.

14. Bijan Jazani, the founder and leader of the Fedai movement, writing from his jail cell, was the first left theorist to recognize the significance of the shanty town dwellers. See section by Mehrdad Vahabi in *On the Life and Works of Bijan Jazani*, Paris: Khavaran publishers, 1999.

15. For controversies over the decline or increase in female employment after the revolution, see Haideh Moghissi, *Feminism and Islamic Fundamentalism: The Limits of Post-modern Analysis,* London and Islamabad: Zed and Oxford University Press, 2000, pp. 111–115.

16. By 1994 over 300,000 militia (*Basiji*) were recruited to push back the 'West's cultural invasion' and 300,000 more were to be hired for ordering good and preventing evil (*Amr-e Be Marouf Va Nahy-e Az Monkar*). See *Iran Times*, 28 October 1993.

17. Iran Statistical Centre, 'Statistical Yearbook, 1996–1997', p. 206.

18. Mehrangiz Kar, *Eliminating Discrimination Against Women: Comparing the Convention on the Elimination of All Forms of Discrimination Against Women With Iranian Laws*, Tehran: Parvin Publication, 1999, p. 252.

19. Maryam Mohseni, 'Kargaran-e Zan-e Khanegi' (Women Home Workers) in *Negah-e Zan*, Tehran: Touse'e Publishers, no. 1, 1998, pp. 9–14.

20. *Salam*, Tehran: 11 Ordibehesht 1378/1(May) 1999.

21. For a detailed account of workers' reactions during the war, see *Rah-e Kargar*, nos. 37–48, 1987.

22. See, *Kargar-e Kommunist*, no. 1 (September) 1999, pp. 36–38, and various issues of *Rah-e Kargar*, and *Etehad-Fadaian*, 1999.

23. Mujahedin-Khalq originated from a radical Islamic guerrilla group fighting against the Shah's regime. After the revolution they followed their eclectic ideology, mingling some socialist ideas with their interpretation of Islam, were brutally suppressed by the clerical regime, and were reduced to a religious cult based in Iraq but with a large following in other countries outside Iran.

24. For workers councils in Iran, see Saeed Rahnema, 'Workers Councils in Iran: The Illusions of Workers Control', in *Economic and Industrial Democracy: An International Journal*, Vol. 13, No. 1, February 1992. See also Asaf Bayat, *Workers and*

Revolution in Iran, London: Zed Press, 1987.

25. The Council of Guardians is a twelve-member body of Islamic jurists and lawyers that acts as an upper chamber and oversees the decisions of the parliament. The conflicts between the two, representing different factions of the regime had created a stalemate that led Khomeini to order the establishment of a new extra-parliamentary body, the Council of Expediency, to resolve the disputes and come up with final decision. See Saeed Rahnema and Sohrab Behdad, eds., *Iran After the Revolution: Crisis of an Islamic State*, London: I. B. Tauris, 1996, Appendix.

26. Labour and Social Security Institute, *Labour Law of the Islamic Republic of Iran*, Tehran, 1993.

27. See *Huquq-e Zan Dar Iran (Women and the Law in Iran (1967–1978))*, 1994. Compiled by Mahnaz Afkhami, Women's Centre of the Foundation of Iranian Studies.

28. Labour and Social Security Institute, *Law of Transfer of Government Shares To Workers*, Tehran, 1996.

29. The Shi'i hierarchy works through recruiting young seminary students (*tolab*) as the tutees of a senior cleric or Ayatollah, who pays their *shahrieh* (allowance). A cleric's major financial source is the donations, *Sahm-e Imam*, that he receives from his followers. The *Sahms* are a sort of tax that Muslim believers must pay to the Imam of their choice. One of the functions of the tutee, acting as a sort of spiritual labourer, is to recruit new followers for the cleric by preaching in the rural areas and working class neighbourhoods. The more followers he finds, the higher will be his own allowance. The top clerics compete with each other to attract more tutees by paying higher wages, and use part of the income received for charities to help their followers. See, Sayed Ali Akbar Mohtashemi, *Khaterat (Memoir)* Volume I, Tehran: Hoseh Honary, 1997, pp. 112–19.

30. The figures are for 1996, Imam Khomeini's Aid Committee Activities, cited in Iran Statistical Centre, 'Statistical Yearbook, 1996–1997', pp. 486, 487.

31. S. Michel, 'Les Déshérités sont à vendre', *Le Point*, no. 1420, 3 December 1999, p. 41.

32. Iran Statistical Centre, 'Statistical Yearbook, 1996–1997', pp. 488, 489.

33. The Iranian Peoples Fedayeen Guerrillas was the leading left underground organization during the time of the Shah. After the revolution the organization dropped its armed struggle strategy and changed its name to Organization of the People's Fedayeen. Soon a split divided the organization into a radical hard-line Minority and a pro-Soviet Majority. Several other splits occurred in both groups. Details of the splits are discussed in Saeed Rahnema, 'Re-birth of Social Democracy in Iran'.

34. On some of the populist positions of the Tudeh and Fedayeen *Axariat* (Majority) on political democracy, a free press and the democratic rights of women and ethnic and religious minorities, see Haideh Moghissi, *Populism and Feminism in Iran: Women's Struggle in a Male-defined Revolutionary Movement*, London: Macmillan, 1994 and 1996.

35. Workers Path was formed by a group of prominent political prisoners after the revolution, advocating an immediate move towards socialism. It is still active in Kurdistan and elsewhere outside Iran.

36. An extreme radical pro-Maoist organization that evolved out of the religious radical Mujahedin-e Khalq. The organization does not exist any more, though

some of the founding members are active.

37. This Maoist organization was formed by Iranian students abroad, mostly in the United States, who returned to Iran after the revolution. A section of the organization launched a rural guerrilla action which failed completely and was eliminated.

38. A radical Iranian Kurdish left organization advocating socialism for Kurdistan and Iran. After the revolution it joined several smaller groups and formed the 'Iranian Communist Party'. A group split off from within the organization and formed the 'Iranian Workers Communist Party'. The former is active in Kurdistan and the latter mostly outside Iran.

39. This party emerged out of a split in the Tudeh Party in 1987, rejecting Leninist policies and advocating political democracy and social justice.

40. Iran Statistical Centre, 'Statistical Yearbook, 1996–1997', p. 88.

41. See R. L. Daft, *Organization Theory and Design*, New York, 1992, pp. 160–161, and Saeed Rahnema, *Organization Structure: A Systemic Approach*, Toronto: McGraw-Hill/Ryerson, 1992, pp. 44–45.

DEMOCRACY AND THE ORGANIZATION OF CLASS STRUGGLE IN BRAZIL

HUW BEYNON AND JOSÉ R. RAMALHO

In Brazil it is still appropriate to talk in terms of a workers' movement. Alone in the states of Southern America, the trade unions in Brazil still have a capacity to organize workers and to exert a powerful influence upon workplace activities. The main trade union federation is linked to a new political party—the Workers' Party (PT—*Partido dos Trabalhadores*)—that retains a commitment to a socialist programme. And, more generally, the fact that land reform has emerged as a major political issue (as a consequence of an innovative and radical social movement of the landless) indicates that class struggle—in the fullest sense of the term—is very much alive in Brazil.

Brazil is a country of many economic and social contrasts which makes it difficult to talk of a working class with a uniform profile. In a real sense the situation in Brazil can best be understood as a process of combined and uneven development within which the working class is in the process of 'making' and being made. Given the characteristics of the Brazilian social formation, any consideration of class and politics needs to focus on class formation, a process with a spatial and temporal dynamic which is very different from the advanced capitalist countries.

THE BRAZILIAN SOCIAL FORMATION

Brazil's GDP (US\$ 777.1 billion in 1998) ranks it among the richest countries in the world, and its economic and political elites benefit enormously from this. Corporate executives in Brazil are amongst the most highly paid in the world. But it is also one of the most unequal societies, with an income distribution ratio that is rarely matched for its extremity. The size and geographical scope of its territory (fifth in the world by land mass, sixth by population at 161 million in 1998) and the pattern of its economic development has resulted, moreover, in sharp contrasts among its states and regions.

Most of the past forty years in Brazil have been dominated by massive internal migration. These enormous flows of people have largely been from the poorer rural areas (especially the North-east) to the industrialized South-east where they have contributed to the country's rapid urbanization. Today, some 73% of the Brazilian people live in towns and cities. Here the urban complexes of São Paulo and Rio de Janeiro stand apart. These cities have been central to the massive engine of economic growth established in the South and South-east. The São Paulo state is an extraordinary symbol of this change. It has a widely diversified economy with advanced manufacturing processes operating in many of its factories and a highly innovative intensive agricultural system— the latter dominated by Japanese-Brazilian proprietors. This region's economy has a GDP that is comparable to that of Argentina or Spain. Its centre—São Paulo—is the site of enormous wealth, poverty and violence. Here, in a city of 17 million people, twenty percent of the population lives in the most primitive conditions in *favelas* while the rich live in the opulent surroundings of the Jardins. Over 8,000 people are murdered every year in this city and local social workers often refer to life there as 'an undeclared civil war'. The city's infamous Carandiru prison has 7,200 inmates, many living fifteen to a cell.

Similar processes are at work in Brazil's 'second city', the old imperial capital of Rio de Janeiro. Here, workers who were employed in the building industry of the sixties and seventies (and who transformed the structure of the city) could only find a place to live in the *favelas* that fill the steep hillside area within Rio. As these areas became overpopulated millions of people relocated, occupying the lowland areas of the *baixadas* some fifty miles from the city centre. These places were built on the basis of mutual labour; drainage and sewerage is primitive at best and where there is electricity it is mostly illegally tapped from overhead cables. A quarter of the city's population live here, in these very basic conditions. Here, life is lived on the edge and political practice is linked to the operation of 'death squads' and drug dealers who inflict punishment of transgressors and opponents.

In sharp contrast with these two enormous cities of the South-east, which dominate the economy, the states of the North-east have a very different social form. These mainly rural areas were the centre of the slave plantation and latifundia agriculture that dominated imperial Brazil. Dominated by patriarchal forms of politics, they still play an important role in the political economy of the federal Brazilian state. Economically too, their role is changing. In the past ten years, the region has attracted a group of manufacturing industries based on intensive labour which takes advantage of very low wages in this region. A textile industry was established in Pernambuco with costs comparable to those of China. More recently these developments have accelerated, with these states vigorously adding fiscal incentives to compete for capital projects with the

South-east, in what has been described as 'fiscal warfare' between the Brazilian states. The most recent, and dramatic, example of this was the decision of the Ford motor company to reconsider its decision to locate a new assembly plant in the South-east. The plant was planned for location in Rio Grande do Sul, a state controlled by the Workers' Party. However, Ford began to feel uneasy with this choice and, in 1999, announced its plan to shift production to the state of Bahia in the North-east.

The situation becomes more complex when we add Amazonia and the undeveloped West to the picture. In the 1970s many workers migrated to these regions. In the absence of any meaningful land reform, rural workers were attracted by the idea of new farming opportunities. Often these developments were associated with the reintroduction of forms of forced labour. Others (in search of fortunes) were attracted to the variety of mining operations that became established in these regions. Many were prospectors who often came into conflict with the indigenous peoples of the area. These activities contrast remarkably with the highly organized operation of Brazil's largest mining corporation Compagne Vale do Rio Doce at Carajás. Here in the South of Para the company established an enormous estate, surrounded by a policed boundary—a state within a state. It mines millions of tons of iron ore a year, transported directly by rail to its terminal at São Louis and then off to the steel mills of Japan. The Carajás complex involves a new town built on a grid system. With its schools, medical service, shops and sports arena, it resembles a town in the US mid-West. Many of the managerial and clerical staff we talked with there in 1995 had moved to Carajás to'get away from Brazil'. They admired the order, the policing and the absence of crime. Many of the workers, however, disliked the regimentation and more and more of them had been given permission to live outside the perimeter in a town established earlier by gold prospectors.

Across these spatial divides, Brazil's industrialization has had a number of powerful distinguishing features. Historically, it had always been strongly associated with state regulation. This was especially pronounced in the populist period of Vargas and the emergence of the *new state (estado novo)* through which economic activities were directed and managed. For over fifty years capitalist development in Brazil took place through this highly-regulated corporatist system within which trade unions were established and received their membership dues as a direct tax. This persisted through periods of dictatorship and has only recently been weakened under the neoliberal reforms of the Cardoso government.

A second feature that stands out is the high percentage of the population and the labour force earning a living through work in the informal sector of the economy. This has been a persistent feature and as neoliberal policies tightened up the formal labour market the jobless flowed into this sector. In this informal economy women, who today make up 40% of the Brazilian labour force, play an especially important part. A new feature, which has increasingly accompanied the new neoliberal phase of accumulation, is a strong downward trend in the quality of jobs and in the strength of labour within the work-place as the formal sectors are restructured. As Pochman has documented: 'through to the early 1980s, eight out of ten new job opportunities were wage-paying. This ratio is very different today: eight out of ten new jobs do not pay regular wages, leaving only two wage-earners with workbook registration'.[1] Within this restructuring context, the situation is worse for the rising number of women in the labour market. Lena Lavinas has shown how the restructuring process moved rapidly from manufacturing to the service sector, reducing the availability of employment and pushing many women into unemployment,[2] and this has occurred just at a time when women were increasingly seeking to move out of the informal sector and into registered paid employment.

The emergence of a free trade zone in the southern cone has further encouraged the massive transfer of capital investment into Brazil through the operations of major transnational corporations. Labour migration from north to south that fueled previous economic booms has slowed down enormously, and in its place we are beginning to witness the footloose capital that has been familiar to Northern economies over the last twenty years. This takes place in a context of class struggle from below, however, which has also made Brazil a very different place than it used to be.

THE NEW TRADE UNIONISM

In the 1970s, and in ways that were affected by the pattern of capital formation, trade unionism in Brazil took on new characteristics, adopting a stance critical of the corporate ideology that had dominated labour relations since the 1930s. This soon grew into one of the main centres of political resistance to the military dictatorship.

It was in the region most heavily industrialized by foreign investments in Brazil—the belt of industrial towns that had grown up around São Paulo known as the ABC Region (Santo André, São Bernardo and São Caetano)—that the 'new trade unionism' emerged in its most radical form. This movement challenged the dictatorial administration then in office, publicly violating trade union legislation and anti-strike regulation and triggering a revolution within the trade union structure by questioning the links between trade-union leaders and the Ministry of Labour. At the same time, it was building up its legitimacy through factory-floor representation in the work-place. This movement flourished mainly among the metal-workers, most of whom were employed in the auto-assembly sector concentrated in this region. One manager in the early VW plant reflected that in this period, the trade unions 'civilized the companies'.[3]

This radical trade unionism, although it had initially established itself within the 'official union' arrangements of corporate collectivism, was deeply critical of the dense web of corporatist regulation. In its stead, it offered a trade unionism of the factory floor that reshaped collective action, not least by encouraging militant workers who sought to extend the range of demands made in collective bargaining talks. These new militants (many of them migrants from the North-east) began to raise very new demands regarding working conditions. [4]

The struggles of these workers against authoritarianism in the factories was, remarkably, transformed into a more general struggle for democracy. As such the major strikes of 1978, 1979 and 1980 received enormous popular support. At that time, these workers and their leaders came to symbolize a broader-based struggle for democratic freedoms and human rights, which represented a powerful demonstration of solidarity. During the 1980 strike, for example, the military police placed all of the trade union leaders in jail and made a point of severely harassing the São Bernardo Trade Union. In spite of this the strike continued and the workers won most of their demands. This strike, the release of the trade union leaders and the victory took on iconographic significance in Brazil in the 1980s. It was seen as an example of courage and of an alternative source of legitimate power within the society—a critical event in the destabilization of the dictatorship and the emergence of democratic politics in Brazil.

The leaders of the new trade unionism (having observed the variety of collaborations during the dictatorship period) had become deeply suspicious of traditional politics, including the existing parties of the Left. They explicitly rejected the union-party relationship that had characterized populism, but what to replace it with was a major issue. Equally pressing was the fact that their great strength had been built in one small corner of Brazil; albeit the one most deeply involved in advanced capitalist manufacture. This posed the question of how this fraction of the working class could maintain the momentum and extend its organizing capacity beyond the ABC district. Out of the many discussions on these questions in this period came the establishment of the Unified Workers Confederation (CUT—*Central Unica dos Trabalhadores*), a leftist organization concerned to extend the example of the 'authentic' trade unionists from the ABC factories more generally throughout Brazil. The driving forces behind this new union were these very ABC militants, who had in their struggles built alliances with militants from the progressive wing of the Roman Catholic Church as well as Leninist and Trotskyist groupings.

These activists had a common strategy that could be identified through three key elements:[5]

1. The rejection of capitalism as a model for social organization, at the same time as they rejected the Communist aspects of socialism, basically embodied in the experiences of the countries of Eastern Europe;

2. A relatively critical view of the corporate trade union structure, of state interventionism in capital/labour relationships, and the associated bureaucratization of trade unions;

3. A strong emphasis on grassroots and shop-floor organization and mobilization for trade union actions.

Although each of these principles were commonly held among working-class activists in the advanced capitalist states in the 1960s and 1970s,[6] in Brazil in the 1980s they not only stood in remarkable contrast to a history of statist politics that dominated all memory, they became the basis for the foundation of the new workers' organizations that have become the leading working–class institutions in the country. In the context of the break–up of the military government, the new trade unionism challenged both the populist practices of the past and the idea of any new form of social democratic politics. In its stress upon direct democracy (and the importance of workers and the working class within this) the alliance that produced the CUT was attempting to turn the struggles of the ABC into a revolutionary movement that would transform Brazil.

The immediate outcome of this was the establishment of a solidly-based nation–wide workers' organization whose political actions had marked repercussions on the life of the country. During the economic crises of the 1980s when Brazil experienced an inflation rate of 40% a month it called a number of important strikes in different sectors over wage issues. These strikes and national stoppages saw an extension of 'authentic' trade unions beyond the ABC district and the car and engineering workers. It now involved bank workers and public sector workers; blue collar and white collar and blouse. In the transitional period that followed the dictatorship, the CUT played a critical role in placing the experiences and viewpoints of workers centrally and (for the first time) directly on the political agenda.[7]

These developments took place alongside the construction of a new political party, the Workers' Party (PT—*Partido dos Trabalhadores*). The PT was founded in 1980, and widened the social constellation that produced the CUT to include human rights activists, socialist intellectuals and groups from within both Roman Catholic and Protestant churches that supported workers' struggles. It maintained the core support of sectors of the left that broke away from the centralism and bureaucratic approach of the Brazilian Communist Party. Attracting supporters from such a broad spectrum, the Workers' Party remained remote from traditional leftist organizations, and was critical of what it saw to be the centralized nature of these organizations. As with the CUT, democracy and participation were the central pillars upon which the new party was constructed.

This meant that, whereas historically most of Brazil's political parties had been established at the initiative of the ruling classes, reflecting state strategies, the Workers' Party broke new political ground by seeking to establish its structure on grassroots bases. In this respect it benefitted from the democratic experience of the trade unions and the social movements that sprang up during the late 1970s. Like the CUT, the PT needed to proceed simultaneously on a number of different fronts. On the one hand, as the dictatorship unravelled, it needed to organize for political representation in the new democratic state. On the other, it needed to maintain its links with the activities of the CUT. The complex reality of the Brazilian social formation made any simple form of 'trade union party' quite inadequate to the task of seriously building a socialist platform. The PT prioritized a policy of widening its base beyond the direct concerns of waged workers and deliberately created a novel political conduit for social movements associated with the rights of women, cultural and ethnic minorities, and the environment—all without losing its identity as a party of the working class.[8] As a result the PT took on a distinctive political and ideological form: at one time an electoral machine, at another, organizer of social protest, at yet another supporter of workers on strike.[9] The complexity of this form was stretched further by the variety of different political viewpoints that were attracted to the party and encouraged within it. Whilst social democratic parties like the Labour Party in the UK purged or marginalized their leftist elements, the PT encouraged their active involvement in the party. In this way too it acquired a representative dimension that extended beyond the trade unions. Although the influence of the CUT has from the beginning been strong, it has not been in a position to define the political programme or standpoint of the party.

Yet there is no denying the presence of workers throughout this entire process, participating at various levels of the party, running for office and being elected to political positions in parliament and also for executive jobs in the party's administration. The most outstanding example of this is the party's 'Chairman of Honour' (*Presidente de Honra*) Luiz Inácio da Silva, better known as Lula. A worker involved in shop-floor organization in São Bernardo, Lula became the unchallenged leader of the trade union movement in the ABC districts, and was one of those imprisoned in 1980. Lula came to symbolize the emergent presence of the workers in the evolving political process of democracy in Brazil. In a way that was quite novel, he was able to establish a credible political stance that rejected the solutions presented by the traditional political elites to the problems of social inequalities and poverty. He has explained his understanding of the politics of PT as follows:

> Here in Brazil the government will have to improve living conditions for the mass of people for they know that, if they don't, the PT will go on expanding and the working classes will get more and more organized. Even if I fail to reach power, so long as they improve social conditions that will be an important achievement.[10]

Such impact had it made on Brazilian political life by 1989, that although the PT was one of twenty-one parties that contested the county's first democratic presidential election since the fall of the dictatorship, it came second in the first ballot with Lula as its candidate. Amidst enormous excitement and political campaigning, the contrast in the final round between Lula and Collor could not have been more complete. They represented in a dramatic fashion alternative social and political options for the new Brazil. On the one hand, Lula, a migrant from the North-east, was an imaginative thinker at the head of the world's newest socialist party. On the other hand, Collor, also from the North-east, had been governor of one of the poorest states, and although he presented himself as a new type of anti-corruption politician, he was still a legitimate heir of the established political elites as well as the ancient landowning families. Lula was narrowly defeated in the final ballot on a 52%–48% vote. Such was the balance of forces within the fledgling democracy. It gave optimism to those who saw in Lula and the PT the beginnings of a new kind of political praxis. But it also confirmed the depth of authoritarian and reactionary traditions in Brazil and the capacity for these to mobilize in the new context.

NEOLIBERALISM IN BRAZIL

Collor, from the political right, appreciated that Brazil could not maintain its Balkanized existence within a world economy being transformed by globalization. He was poised to embark on a neoliberal project (with an important degree of popular support, building as it did upon dissatisfaction with many of the excesses of the state-regulated regime) before he was impeached for embezzlement of public funds. Collor was replaced by his vice president— Itamar Franco—who recruited to his administration key figures from within the universities and from the old parties of the left. Most notable amongst these was Fernando Henrique Cardoso who had been an outspoken critic of the military regime. As finance minister and then as president, Cardoso pushed forward a succession of financial and political reforms that produced remarkable changes throughout the economy in the 1990s.

Fernando Henrique Cardoso was an ally of Lula's in the seventies and eighties when he was a professor of Sociology at the University of São Paulo. Cardoso represented a very different kind of left strategy, however, and it was one that deeply split the intellectual left that had flocked to support Lula in 1989. In the context of Brazil, Cardoso's strategy could be seen as a clear attempt to establish an ordered approach toward a social democratic politics of the European type.[11] But in order to achieve the changes that were demanded from neoliberal structural adjustment policies, Cardoso chose not to make an alliance with the left and centre left, but with centre and far right of the political spectrum. His majority in parliament was held in place by some of the most reactionary political forces of the country. Yet the radicalism of the neoliberal project (presented through a social democratic discourse of reform and transformation) was such that it enabled Cardoso to emerge as a far more formidable foe of the left than Collor. In subsequent elections he portrayed Lula and the PT as 'defenders of the old, against needed reforms'.

The neoliberal transformation of the Brazilian economy in the 1990s under Cardoso's leadership has been remarkable. The stabilization of the currency (by tying it to the US dollar) dramatically reduced inflation. The tariff wall that had protected the industrial structure of the Brazilian economy was gradually taken down and the massive state-owned industries were put up for sale. In its corporatist phase, the Brazilian state had sheltered domestic and foreign companies from competition from abroad. In return, the international companies were obliged to purchase components and service from within Brazil. The rapid removal of this supporting framework produced a wave of bankruptcies amongst Brazilian-owned firms and with it a series of mergers and take-overs initiated by foreign-owned capital. As a consequence, the economy became significantly more open[12] and this was associated with an upsurge in industrial productivity. Initially, these improvements were due to idle capacity being brought back into use, although this was also associated with a pruning of the labour force. By the mid-nineties, however, as the economy shifted to positive growth, the challenges of international competition saw deliberate attempts being introduced to boost efficiency at the factory-floor level.[13] This involved many of the practices (e.g., out-sourcing; delayering; just in time; re-engineering) that had earlier been introduced in Europe and the USA.[14]

The establishment of a South American Common Market—MERCOSUL—linking Argentina, Brazil, Paraguay and Uruguay served to extend these processes. Trade flows among these countries rose steadily in the nineties,[15] to be upset by Brazil's foreign exchange crisis in early 1999. The linking of this new market with the deregulation and stabilization of the South American economies attracted vast amounts of international capital. These investments were associated with the privatization of the telecommunications, steel, transportation, mining, electricity, and petrochemicals sectors among others. Equally significant was the flow of new investment into private manufacturing, especially the automobile industry which (with companies like Ford and Volkswagen operating in Brazil since the 1950s) had fuelled the Brazilian boom in the 1960s and laid the basis for the ABC district's industrial strength. With the new investment, this industry has maintained a strategic position in the economy, accounting directly for 12% of Brazil's industrial GDP and, due to the characteristics of its production chain, extending its influence strongly into other sectors of the economy.

In the late 1990s this sector went through some remarkable changes.[16] The Brazilian-owned auto-parts industry was virtually wiped out through a process of sales and mergers that left the industry dominated by multinationals associated with global auto-assembly projects.[17] Furthermore, there was a radical change in the spatial configuration of both the component and assembly ends of the industry. New investment in plant was made away from the powerful ABC district. This decentralizing strategy was clearly linked with the need to control the spread and strength of trade unionism while taking full advantage of tax incentive wars for new investment that sprang up with the federal state. VW, for example, located all of its new assembly operations outside the ABC district. One of the first of these was a truck plant, opened in Resende in up-state Rio de Janeiro in 1996. In moving to Resende, the company did not attempt to hide the fact that part of its plan focused on the establishment of labour relationships different to those of the ABC region of São Paulo. Its industrial director, Luiz de Luca, was particularly determined on its new green-field site to avoid 'the bad habits of São Bernardo', where the unions make it 'not possible to negotiate'.[18] His claim that 'everyone was getting out of the

ABC region' was confirmed as each of the major world automobile assemblers opened (or planned to open) new plants in Brazil at the end of the nineties in new green-field locations, taking advantage of low wages, skilled labour and somewhat inexperienced trade unions. In this way production doubled to two million vehicles in 1997, whilst employing just half the workers of the earlier period.

THE TRADE UNIONS UNDER NEOLIBERALISM

Neoliberal policies in Brazil created major new problems for militant trade unionism. Privatization, for example, created new problems for CUT members and the restructuring of state employment drew the organization into potentially unpopular struggles. In its home base of the ABC its members faced lay-offs, possible plant closures and unemployment. In the new green-field areas it faced competition from other trade union associations. Of these, *Forca Sindical* was the most significant, both in terms of its growth and the political challenge it posed to the CUT. Adopting a more cautious and politically conservative approach it achieved the backing of some important local unions, including the São Paulo Metal-Workers' Union.

In the face of these developments the CUT began to ease itself away from its militant stance. This was made most clear in the decision of the ABC Metal-Workers' Union to participate in the newly established consultative committees (the sectoral chambers). As the unions adjusted to the changed circumstances 'the clamouring demands of the previous decade'[19] were reformulated through involvement by the trade-union representatives in the discussion of broadranging proposals for sectoral development. In explaining the shift in CUT policy Jácome Rodrigues and others have emphasized 'the sweeping economic and social crisis'. However, they have also drawn attention to an ongoing process of bureaucratization within the union federation, which has led to 'a more contractual and pragmatic stance in negotiations with the business sector and the government, shedding much of the discourse that shaped the origin of the CUT'.[20]

Nevertheless, the CUT (partly as a result of the protection that trade unions retain under the old corporatist umbrella) weathered this storm better than might be expected. Its position of industrial strength linked with wider popular support managed to continue through the eighties and nineties. In 2000 the organization had 2,600 affiliated trade unions representing some eighteen million workers located in the centres of economic and political power in Brazil.[21] What is in question therefore is the CUT's capacity to use the political capital stockpiled over the recent past to defend labour rights within a context of rising unemployment, and an interventionist IMF. Undoubtedly, this new situation demands new thinking and new tactics. It seems that in many ways they have been successful. For example, in the ABC industrial area, the experience built up by the metal-workers and their factory-floor power of representation endows them with considerable negotiating power. Their experience of the sectoral chambers has been a contradictory one. In a way it smacks of a collaborationist approach that contrasts with their earlier aggressive militancy. However, viewed in the context of Brazil's authoritarian past they have a contrary significance. Ample evidence suggests that, for the first time in Brazil, negotiations between trade unions and companies are being conducted on the basis of legitimacy and respect in contrast to the attitudes of earlier decades when despotic factory systems simply imposed targets and production organization systems.[22] In this new context the local activists operate with a sophisticated and 'open-eyed' approach to their circumstances. On the one hand they bargain, they argue and they negotiate. So, in the view of Luiz Marinho, the leader of the ABC Metal-Workers' Union,

> the plants are modernizing and cutting jobs regardless, with or without trade union participation. Our role is to negotiate the pace of modernization for companies. If we do nothing, they will shut down the companies here and assemble the automobiles someplace else. The difference is that, if we were there, we could at least avoid some lay-offs and preserve some jobs. We either attempt to hang on to something, or we will be left with nothing.[23]

On other occasions they retain the capacity to strike and to mobilize popular support in highly imaginative ways. This was the case, for example, at Ford in São Bernando in 1998. As part of its general restructuring of its operations in Brazil, the company indicated that it intended to close the plant. The trade union immediately called for a strike and production was stopped. Quickly the strike took on a wider dimension. Many of the workers invaded and camped inside the factory with their families. They symbolically reframed the issue of the closure of the factory in terms of its general effect upon the life of people who lived in the area. This was enhanced by the picketing of the chain of Ford dealerships throughout the country, with workers and their supporters wearing a blue and white sash, similar to those in Ford advertising, but the logo 'Ford' was replaced by 'Fome' (which means hunger in Portuguese). These events had a great visual impact and were picked up by television. In their interviews the workers and their trade union representatives turned the localized problem of the ABC into an example of the failures of neoliberal policies and the cruelty of unemployment.

The impact of these new corporate strategies has been so threatening that it has encouraged joint action between the two rival trade union federations. In 1999, CUT and *Forca Sindical* jointly petitioned for a national wage agreement to cover all workers in the car assembly plants. Corporate executives summarily dismissed this demand. They insisted that there could be no such wage agreement, as it would threaten the very existence of the industry in Brazil. In response, the unions called for a 'strike festival'. This represented the first attempt at building a national strike of workers across the many states of Brazil where auto-assembly now takes place. One day stoppages were called in sequence across the states where the national leaders of the two federations met with the strikers and explained the unions' plans to eradicate the enormous wage differentials that had been established between workers in different car plants across the country.

More worrying, however, are the more general effects of neoliberalism upon employment and work relationships. Outside of the state and the major manufacturing sectors, there has been a gradual slide towards insecure work, undermining the collective organization of the workers. In contrast with their poised and successful approach in the highly organized sectors of employment, the trade unions seem all at sea when faced with the problems of the growing informal sector. The marked presence of women in the labour market, for instance, is causing problems for trade unions whose members consist largely of men and whose policies are designed for a male labour force. On two separate occasions we have talked to members of the CUT's metal workers at their educational school in São Paulo. On both occasions the audience was predominantly male and both uneasy and uncertain about the issues posed to the union by the increasing proportion of women in the labour force. They have been clearer about the problems posed by the industrial relocation strategies, particularly in the automotive sector, and the need for fresh efforts to set up trade unions in these newly industrializing areas.

This points to a critical dilemma for trade unions that relates directly to the complex processes of class formation under way in Brazil. In his considered summation of these issues, Oliveira has concluded that Brazil's trade unions, in their attempt to formulate new strategies that blend defensive actions with more general policies aimed at improving the general condition of workers in the non-organized sectors, have been 'greatly concerned with democracy as the starting-point for reworking the current labour relation system and redefining the course of the country'. Nevertheless, 'the exclusion of more than one-third of the economically active population from the formal labour market—subject to all types of informal practices or chronic unemployment—limits the scope of the trade unions and makes it almost impossible to represent a significant contingent of workers'.[24] Oliviera's observation that trade unions have become acutely aware of how their 'range of action remains restricted to only a portion of the working class' was reinforced in the late nineties as large numbers of Brazilians became involved in a social movement that had *land* as its central concern.

THE NEW LANDLESS MOVEMENT

Among countries with relatively well-developed manufacturing sectors, Brazil stands unique in having managed to industrialize without agrarian reform. Agricultural land remains highly concentrated in the hands of a class that can be traced back to the owners of the slave plantations. In spite of massive out-migration to the urban centres in the sixties and seventies, the rural economy remains characterized by harsh inequalities and acute poverty. This has given rise to a new and important social movement that was communicated around the world in Sebastião Salgado's photographic exhibition *Terra—Struggle of the Landless*.

This landless movement sprang up in Southern Brazil in 1984, and has been spreading throughout the country ever since. It has developed a militant strategy of occupying and settling unproductive lands; a strategy it pursues in a highly organized and disciplined manner. By the early 1990s, the movement had created its own clearly recognizable identity reflected in its own flag, music, leaflets, posters and documents.[25] Its success can be measured in hundreds of settler camps that have sprung up across the country. It is no surprise, for example, to see one of them as you travel along one of the main roads. The encampments are easily identifiable. They are quite large and in them very poor people have established new homes in precarious tents made of cheap black plastic sheeting. Always there are signs of garden agriculture—the first activity of the settlers. In established camps, the agriculture is more developed and produce is sold at local markets. If no markets exist, settlers have set up agricultural and industrial co-operatives. Some of these were successfully producing meat and milk products by the end of the decade.[26] All of these camps fly the flag of the movement—a red flag with white circle. Inside the circle is a green map of Brazil inside of which is a depiction of a man and a woman, the man with a machete in his raised hand. On the flag the sign—Movimento dos Trabalhadores Sem Terra. Dotted around the perimeter of these places are other colourful banners with other graphic slogans: 'land is not earned but conquered' or 'occupy and produce'.

The political aims and rhetoric of this movement differ enormously from those of the trade unions and also the political parties. Its uniqueness lies in the clear determination of its leaders to remain independent of the trade unions, political parties and the Roman Catholic Church. This deep suspicion held by the Brazilian poor for Brazilian institutions of all sorts is the source of considerable strength. Tactically, its leaders realize that it will be difficult for these organizations to refuse it support without incurring political losses. The charismatic quality of some of its leaders, combined with the fairness of their demands, has drawn support to it. This is amplified by the incredible power of its demonstrations. These use visual imagery to convey the conditions of the poor and landless in Brazil.

In 1997, for example, in its most spectacular action to date, the landless movement organized a march on the capital city of Brasilia. Thousands of representatives marched across the country from the north, the south, the northeast and the south-east. Esterci has described this event and its significance:

> after two months, walking more than six hundred miles, holding their red banners and sickles, the tired and sweated faces of the workers of the march cheered and the eyes of some became full of tears when they saw the city's main avenue, with all the ministries' buildings, the entrance of the town, the place of the three powers. Under a rain of 'ticker tape' that

came from the windows of the buildings, they arrived to the main avenue and thirty thousand people were there to receive them. City dwellers brought them flowers and baskets with food; trade unionists and militants of opposition parties waved their banners.[27]

The success of this demonstration—the fact that the people had marched so far and had so captured the imagination of the population of the city—unsettled the government. The president found it impossible to avoid a meeting with the representatives of the movement to discuss land reform. For the first time therefore the government spoke directly to the leadership of the landless movement and some of the organized opposition that had been built around it. That meeting was attended by, among others, a Xavante chief, a metalworker and a Catholic bishop.

The 'marches on Brasilia' were tremendously successful, and had widespread repercussions. To begin with, they attracted enormous media attention. In a society where the television dominates all other forms of communication (parabolic aerials appear in the most unlikely of places), the marches placed the case of the rural poor and the iniquities of concentrated land ownership on the political agenda. It was brought into the living rooms of the well to do, and also into the homes of the very poor. In the countryside and in the cities the imagination of many poor people was stirred by the prospect of a new life. The families of small farmers who own their land wanted the same chance for their children. The rural unemployed wanted land to plant crops. In the sprawling slums of São Paulo demands for work began to be transformed into calls for a plot of land where children could be brought up in safety, away from drugs and violence. To many people the demands seemed both reasonable and realizable. As a result, and against all expectations, a spontaneous 'back-to-the-land movement' emerged in Brazil in the nineties. The MST has encouraged this development. It has set up detailed arrangements that facilitate the movement of the urban unemployed into the countryside. The MST is investing heavily in young people who are able to learn and rapidly disseminate the movement's credo.

It became clear in the 1990s that the MST was a movement to be reckoned with and that its determination to resocialize the rural populace and reinvent community life was a real, if extraordinary, political development. According to Lerrer,

> when a family moves into a MST settlement or camp, it faces very tough survival conditions. In order to ensure internal structuring, its members must participate directly in the organization in some sector: health care, safety, education, negotiation, hygiene, food. They must also obey rigid rules that are discussed and decided at meetings by their fellow settlers. There are constraints on alcohol, the length of time spent in the camp, work, respect for women, etc. Generally, dwellers in these camps help underwrite their maintenance by offering a percentage of their pay as

rural workers. All these regulations shaping daily life are only put in practice when approved by the majority.[28]

The movement's main leader, João Pedro Stédile has outlined its three key characteristics: the first is that it is a grassroots movement which welcomes the entire family: the elderly, women and children. He writes:

> On this point, it differs from trade unions, because traditionally only adult men attend union meetings. We feel that our strength lies here because, in addition to being macho, men tend to be conservative and individualistic. As this movement includes all members of the family, it acquires incredible potential.[29]

Stédile also writes of the movement's second characteristic—its 'trade union component' in the corporate sense:

> The possibility of getting its own patch of land is the motive prompting a family to settle on vacant land or camp out for an unspecified period. Initially, this is a struggle to meet an economic claim. We have also learnt that the fight for land cannot be restricted to its corporate nature, the trade union element, it must go further, if a family struggles only for its own patch of land and loses its links to the larger organization, the battle for land has no future.

The political element is the third characteristic. Here the coherent ideology of the movement's leadership becomes especially clear. It its view:

> The MST has only managed to survive because it has matched private, corporate interests with class interests ... We were aware that although the struggle for land and agrarian reform has a peasant-based social core, it will only progress if it forms part of the class struggle. Right from the start, we were well aware that we were not fighting against *grileiros* illegally taking over unclaimed or ownerless lands for re-sale. We were fighting against an entire class, the large-scale land owners. We were not battling merely to apply the Land Act, but rather against a bourgeois state.

Leaving aside the possible propaganda-like nature of these comments, the main outcome noted during the 1990s is that this movement has grown into a major political force in Brazil, taking the lead in terms of its political demonstrations, media presence, and even in the oppositional negotiations with the government. In 2000, urban trade union leaders and the leadership of the PT have been adapting their calendars to fit in with the emerging strategy of this new mobilizing agency.

THE WORKERS' PARTY AND THE FUTURE OF BRAZILIAN DEMOCRACY

During its twenty years of existence, the Workers' Party has given credibility to the view that it could both support strikes and the struggles of the social movements *and* take political office through the electoral process. Despite Cardoso's consistent ability to defeat Lula in the presidential elections, the PT has chalked up some important ballot-box triumphs. It expanded its seats in Congress from 1.7% in 1982 to 11.7% in 1998 with fifty-eight Federal congressmen. There were also seven PT senators by this point. The 1998 Congressional election showed a trend towards the generalization of the PT vote nation-wide. The party has been successful in mayoral elections in some of Brazil's largest cities, including São Paulo, Porto Alegre, Belo Horizonte, Santos and Belém; and it has won governorships of Rio Grande do Sul, the Federal District, Espírito Santo, Mato Grosso do Sul and Acre. Perhaps the greatest achievement of PT is that for the first time the parliament in Brazil contains elected representatives who are drawn from the working classes—a woman like Benedita da Silva for example. Now senator for the state of Rio, this gifted black woman was brought up in the *favelas* of the city and speaks powerfully with the voice of the urban poor. In an earlier period, São Paulo elected Luiza Erundina, another black woman, born in the north-east, as its mayoress, albeit on a minority vote. Although subsequently defeated, to have such a figure at the head of a radical administration in the very heart of Brazil's powerhouse was an emphatic symbolic statement. More permanently successful have been the PT's activities in Rio Grande do Sul where the people recently elected Olivio Dutra, one of the CUT's founders, as its governor.

The PT has proved that a party which operated originally in a 'symbolic mode' as a political mobilizer can develop a serious programme for governing states and cities while at the same time using its occupation of governmental office as a basis for its mobilizing politics to be expanded and developed. Most significant of these administrative departures has been the 'participative budget' though which the citizens of a city like Porto Alegre have been involved in meetings and discussions over budgetary and programmatic alternatives. In her observations of these developments, Hilary Wainwright has observed:

> What is crucial is the creation of a democratic socially conscious force, independent of the state but in close negotiation with it. This new source of democratic power effectively counters the pressures of undemocratic or corrupt business. It both expresses, and puts power behind, the democratically negotiated needs and priorities of the people.[31]

Less discussed, but equally important, has been the party's commitment to ideas of 'basic income' as a means of alleviating poverty and developing the citizenship potential of the very poor. Brazil's city streets are full of children—begging, hassling, cajoling, acting—working for money. The level of school attendance amongst the poorest is negligible. One of the interesting achievements of the PT administration in the Federal District of Brasilia related to this problem. Developing ideas of basic income, families were granted 100 Reais (about $50) on condition that they kept their children at school. This successful intervention in social policy proved popular as it removed a perceived 'social nuisance' and also improved the educational standards of the poorest.

Of course, since Lula's near victory in 1989, the electoral fortunes of the PT at the presidential level have been meagre, as Lula has been opposed by Cardoso, a man originally himself of the left and far different from Collor. This most remarkable twist of fate expresses in its clearest form the significance of the PT being still regarded as an invader in the developing democratic polity of Brazil. Brazilian society is unique in the seamless way in which it conjoins the informal (as seen in the ways in which presidents are known by their first names—hence FH or Fernando Henrique) with the hierarchical. Here, everyone is equal, but everyone is expected to know their place. This is especially evident in relation to skin colour and racism. The PT broke this mould in a way which many of the intellectual elite found difficult to cope with. Cardoso is a good example of this. A university academic with few links to workers' organizations, he would have found it impossible to be in a subordinate role to a man like Lula.

In a country such as Brazil, democracy must be viewed as a strategy guaranteeing the existence and continuation of various forms of worker and peasant organization. The history of Brazil indicates a strong tradition of resolving political problems through force. The nation's recent political history includes military dictatorships which gagged the basic freedoms to speak, disagree and organize political groups. As a prospect, it is not possible to consider political alternatives for the Brazilian working class other than through democratic means, building up enough clout to impose alternative pressures. In this case, democracy should be seen as a necessary enabling process through which class construction can take place.

The PT can be seen to have intervened decisively in the democratic process in ways which effectively allow workers to express their views and impose pressures upon the system. The party has interpreted 'democracy' in a radical sense, extending it beyond the formal requirement to vote in elections as affirmed in the Constitution. Here PT and the trade unions and social movements have succeeded in stretching the democratic process, acting out the right to free assembly and the right to march and demonstrate. These activities can be seen to contribute to a process of working-class formation in Brazil. More prosaically, they can be seen as the source of power with which to deal with a burgeoning international capital and one of the most deeply entrenched agrarian interests in the world.

We can leave the concluding words of this essay to Tarso Genro, formerly the Mayor of Porto Alegre in southern Brazil, and a leading PT strategist, who has expressed with remarkable clarity the role that the party needs to play in the context of a deeply deformed political culture:

> it is necessary to respond to the decadence of traditional political representation by seeking new political forms that strive to politically re-unify formal and informal society. The inclusion in democratic political actions and work of those subsisting in informal society, or involving them in self-affirmation activities reflecting their human dignity constitute the new Utopian benchmark of the Left.[32]

NOTES

1. *Folha de São Paulo* and *O Globo*, April 23, 1998.
2. *O Globo*, March 8, 1998.
3. A.L. Negro, (1997) 'Servos do Tempo', G. Arbix and M. Zilbovicius (eds), *De JK a FHC—A reinvenção dos carros*, São Paulo: Scritta, 1997.
4. See A. Cardoso, *Sindicatos, Trabalhadores e a Coqueluche Neoliberal*. Rio de Janeiro: FGV, 1999, pp. 34, 5; I. Jácome Rodrigues, *Sindicalismo e Política: a trajetória da CUT*. São Paulo: Scritta, 1997.
5. A. Comin, (1994) 'A experiência de organização das centrais sindicais no Brasil', M. Oliveira, et al. (eds.), *O Mundo do Trabalho—crise e mudança no final do século*, São Paulo: Scritta/Cesit/Mtb-PNUD, 1994, p. 367.
6. H. Beynon, *Working for Ford*, London: Penguin, 1973; Hilary Partridge, 'Italy's Fiat in Turin in the 1950's', Theo Nichols (ed) *Capital and Labour: A Marxist Primer*, London: Fontana, 1980.
7. Rodrigues, *Sindicalismo*, p. 230.
8. N. Esterci and J. R. Ramalho, 'Votes and Violence', *Red Pepper*, 30, November 1996, pp. 28-29
9. R. Meneguello, *PT—a formação de um partido*, São Paulo: Paz e Terra, 1989 .
10. Interview in S. Branford and B. Kucinski, *Brazil—carnival of the oppressed*, London: Latin America Bureau, 1995 .
11. See Paul Cammack, 'Cardoso's Political Project in Brazil: The Limits of Social Democracy', *Socialist Register 1997*, pp. 223-44.
12. Amman, E. (1995) 'Defensive modernisation: Brazilian industry responds to the challenge of market liberalisation'. Manchester Brazililan Research Group, The University of Manchester, Manchester, UK, p. 3.
13. Ibid., p. 4.
14. See, for example, L. Gitahy, M. Leite and F. Rabelo, 'Relações de Trabalho, Política de Recursos Humanos e Competitividade', em Estudos da Competitividade da Indústria Brasileira, 1993; M. Leite, 'Reestruturação produtiva, novas tecnologias e novas formas de gestão da mão-de-obra', Oliveira, *O Mundo,*1994.
15. T. Vigevani and J. P. Veiga, 'A Integração Regional no Mercosul', Arbix and Zilbovicius, *De JK a FHC*, pp. 348-50.
16. A. Abreu, L. Gitahy, J. Ramalho and R. Ruas, 'Industrial Restructuring and Inter-Firm Relations in Brazil: a study of the Auto-Parts Industry in the 1990s', *Occasional Papers No 21*, Institute of Latin American Studies, University of London,

London, 1999.

17. See the essays by A. Posthuma, C. Addis and G. Arbix, Arbix and Zilbovicius, *De JK a FHC*, 1997.

18. H. Beynon and J. R. Ramalho, 'Transforming Production/Transforming Society: The case of the Brazilian Automobile Industry', M. Harvey and H. Beynon (eds), *Changing Capitalisms*, Manchester: Manchester University Press, 2000.

19. Comin, A. 'A experiência', 1994, pp. 386-88.

20. Rodrigues, *Sindicalismo*, p. 235.

21. *Folha de São Paulo*, October 17, 1999.

22. N. Castro, 'Modernização e trabalho no complexo automotivo brasileiro—reestruturação industrial ou japanização de ocasião', N. Castro (ed.), *A Máquina e o equilibrista— inovações na indústria automobilística brasileira*, São Paulo: Paz e Terra, p. 42.

23. *Veja* magazine, March 25, 1998.

24. M. Oliveira, 'Avanços e limites do sindicalismo brasileiro recente', Oliveira, *O Mundo*, 1994, p. 510.

25. D. Lerrer, 'Movimento Sem Terra no Brasil: a nova cara da luta secular pela terra', M. S. P. Castro and A. Wachendorfer, (orgs), *Sindicalismo y Globalización* Caracas: Nueva Sociedad, 1998, p. 171.

26. Neide Esterci, 'Forward March', *Red Pepper*, 37, June 1997, pp. 24-25.

27. Ibid.

28. Lerrer, 'Movimento', pp. 173-4.

29. J. P. Stedile and B.M. Fernandes, *Brava Gente—a trajetória do MST e a luta pela terra no Brasil*, São Paulo: Editora Perseu Abramo, 1999, pp. 32-35.

30. *Folha de São Paulo*, November 8, 1998.

31. H. Wainwright, *Reinventing Democracy*, Rio de Janeiro: UFRJ, 2000

32. T. Genro, *O futuro por armar—democracia e socialismo na era globalitária*. Rio de Janeiro: Vozes., 1999, pp. 40, 61, 62.

ORGANIZING, PROTEST AND WORKING CLASS SELF-ACTIVITY: REFLECTIONS ON EAST ASIA

GERARD GREENFIELD

The resurgence of working-class militancy in East Asia in the last decade has inspired the radical imagination and offered us renewed hope in the struggle against capitalism. This was most clearly expressed in the mass protests and strikes by workers at the height of the Asian economic crisis in 1997–98 which appeared to challenge the logic of the capitalist 'globalization' project, while demonstrating the power of (re)emerging independent workers' organizations in the face of ongoing state repression. Precisely because of this ongoing repression and the social destruction wrought by the economic crisis, these strikes and protests were all the more significant for their courage, commitment and sacrifice. In this sense every strike and every protest may be viewed as a victory, with the historical accumulation of these fragments bound up in some way in the project of working-class emancipation. For example, in an essay published in *Monthly Review* in September 1998, David McNally concluded: 'East Asia has become the focal-point of the international class struggle. Out of these struggles a new "Asian model" may emerge—a model of working–class resistance to capitalist globalization. We have much to learn from these struggles. And we owe them our solidarity and support'.[1]

There is no doubt that we have a great deal to learn from these struggles and that international solidarity and support is necessary. Yet if we really are to learn from these struggles then it is also necessary to take a sober look at the substance of this resurgent militancy and to examine more closely the nature of these new, independent workers' organizations and their politics of protest. Of course, such an assessment must not be based on a pre-determined model of what 'real' working-class militancy should involve, or how working-class organizations should be organized. Insisting on conformity to a 'correct' model serves to extinguish rather than inspire creative organizing and radical struggle. My purpose in this brief essay is not to dismiss the importance of these workers' organizations and their strategies, but to share some critical reflections on the contradictions within them. A critical understanding of these contradictions is all the more important if we recognize that many of these workers' organizations—even those engaged in militant struggles—were not created *by* workers, but *for* them.

Organized labour in East Asia has long been characterized by the dominance of unions and workers' organizations created and controlled by the state to repress genuine working-class activity. Organizing in defiance of this state-controlled unionism is precisely what defines the rise of 'independent' unionism. Despite this challenge, the persistence of state-controlled unionism has benefitted greatly from the collusion of other states (particularly the US) and international institutions, as well as extensive political and financial support by social democratic parties and national trade union centres overseas. In the aftermath of the Asian economic crisis this support has substantially increased, facilitating union 'democratization' based on the re-ordering of official union bureaucracies and a shift from authoritarian state unionism to pro-business or 'social contract' unionism. In a broader sense the mainstream current in international solidarity involves a mutually reinforcing rhetoric of compromise, where tripartitism, social pacts and 'the rule of law' underlie a strategy of containment of working-class militancy and an attempt to suppress it from 'within'.[2]

In Indonesia, for example, prior to the resignation of Suharto on 21 May 1998, the International Confederation of Free Trade Unions (ICFTU) and several overseas trade union centres and social democratic parties provided political and financial support to the state-controlled *Serikat Pekerja Seluruh Indonesia* (SPSI, All-Indonesia Workers' Union).[3] This support continued even while the ICFTU campaigned for the release of imprisoned trade unionists such as the head of *Serikat Buruh Sejahtera Indonesia* (SBSI, Indonesian Prosperous Workers' Union), Muchtar Pakpahan, and the head of the more radical *Pusat Perjuangan Buruh Indonesia* (PPBI, Indonesian Centre for Labour Struggle), Dita Sari. When several SPSI unions renamed themselves *Reformasi* SPSI (Reform SPSI) following Suharto's resignation, this change in name (but not in structure, policies or relations with the military) was welcomed by the ICFTU and overseas trade-union centres as sufficient grounds for providing greater financial aid. Part of the reason was that the ICFTU and powerful national centres such as the AFL-CIO and Japan's Rengo were demanding 'unity' based on the formation a single national trade-union federation centred around the 'reformed' SPSI which continued to collude with the authoritarian political regime and the military. Ironically, this international manoeuvring coincided with the mass movement of workers out of SPSI at plant-level. By refusing to pay dues, denouncing SPSI officials, or forming their own unions, workers directly challenged this system of repression and organizational displacement from above. Despite this challenge from below, consolidation from above was secured through increased overseas financial and political support. This external legitimation, combined with continued military intervention in strikes and labour disputes and state repression of freedom of association, enabled official union bureaucracies to consolidate their power while introducing more effective means of control over their rank-and-file membership.

The continued dominance of state-controlled unions in Indonesia and other parts of East Asia also raises questions about the uncritical use of unionization rates as a measure of the 'growth' or relative 'strength' of working-class organization. If workers are compelled to join unions created by the state and are prevented from genuine self-organization, then high unionization rates—and indeed the notion of union membership—is put in question. What is really happening is the *organizational displacement* of working-class self-activity. This displacement not only involves the suppression of genuine self-organizing among workers but also the appropriation of the language of working-class politics and organization. The very meaning of what a 'union' is and its purpose is fundamentally distorted and may continue to influence workers' perceptions and expectations long after the struggle against state-controlled unionism is won. In Indonesia, for example, while collaboration with management was the primary role of the SPSI unions, they were also expected to fulfill a paternalistic duty of assisting workers (individually, not collectively) in exercising limited legal claims by putting their cases to the labour department and labour courts. This pursuit of narrowly defined legal rights and dependence on assistance by authority figures still shapes workers' understanding of unions, including independent unions.

While these new, independent unions and workers' organizations are engaged in militant strikes and street protests, they remain to a large extent under the leadership and control of (former) student activists and are dependent on the charity and assistance of middle-class non-governmental organizations (NGOs). This dependence reinforces the notion of unions as vehicles for *helping* rather than *organizing*. Furthermore, the politics of these independent unions and workers' organizations is often characterized by the subordination of workers' knowledge and experience to elite expertise and technocratic rationality, further displacing workers' self-activity from within their own organizations. Moreover, while fighting for democracy and waging militant struggles these independent unions did not—and still do not—hold direct, democratic elections of their leaders. Most of the leaders and representatives in unions and workers' organizations such as SBSI, PPBI and its later incarnation, *Front Nasional Perjuangan Buruh Indonesia* (FNPBI, National Front of Indonesian Workers' Struggle) are not directly elected by the rank-and-file, but are appointed by a central executive committee which itself is not elected but is decided through closed discussions among an elite core of activists.

To some extent this is a reflection of their historical legacies. As illegal organizations forced to operate underground, organizing was based on secretive networks and the delegation of authority through personal contacts and trusted friends. Under these conditions the openness required for direct democratic elections often did not exist. However, more than two years after these organizations were legalized and their leaders released from prison, top-down structures and closed decision-making processes continue. The appointment of student activists and NGO staff as leaders of union affiliates and branches continues in Muchtar Pakapahan's SBSI and—despite its radical language and militant protests—also in the FNPBI led by Dita Sari. It could be argued that these organizations are still in transition, and that time is needed before the leadership can be directly elected without prior agreements and deals among the incumbent leaders. However, the leadership of these organizations claim to already be democratically elected (or more accurately, 'chosen'), and so the need for change and debate about such change is not acknowledged. Given these developments, it would seem that the journey from state-controlled unionism to more a radical, independent unionism will be longer than imagined.

This raises an important question concerning the relationship between acts of worker militancy and the prospects for working-class self-emancipation, particularly where there is an absence—or outright suppression—of workers' direct involvement in the determination of protest actions and their objectives. The fact is that the majority of strikes and protests which constituted this working-class militancy in Indonesia—as an essential part of what some claim was a 'revolution'—were organized and led by student activists with limited direct involvement in leadership and organization by workers themselves. Moreover, the way in which protest action and strikes were organized and carried out often reproduced hierarchies of authority and control and reinforced specific kinds of external expertise and elitist forms of leadership. Therefore, the mass mobilization of workers in militant protests and strikes tended to articulate political demands for democracy and democratic reform in society at large but without promoting democratic processes within the collective action or organization itself.

Take for example the struggle at the Hong Kong-owned textile factory PT Tyfountex in Solo at the end of June 1998. A five-day strike by 1,700 workers brought production to a halt, affecting all 7,000 workers at the plant. Strike demands centred on wage increases to keep up with high inflation, payment for overtime work and other allowances, and better working conditions. In organizing the strike workers directly challenged the authority of the SPSI union and rejected its claim to represent their interests. The struggle intensified when the management locked-out then fired several hundred workers. On 24 August, over 800 workers travelled from Solo to Jakarta and held a series of demonstrations at the Labour Department over a period of several days. When the workers attempted to take their protest to the representative office of the International Labour Organization (ILO) they were blocked by the military and police, and in the violent clash which followed 20 workers were injured. In the following months 200 workers returned to Jakarta on several occasions to continue their protest. However, by early 1999 the struggle was in the hands of lawyers, ending with a ruling by the labour court that none of the 800 dismissed workers were entitled to reinstatement or compensation.

The strike was clearly of great importance in terms of the length of the struggle and its escalation from a factory strike in Solo to street protests in Jakarta. Yet many observers saw it as much more. Writing on the Indonesian 'revolution' in the September 1998 issue of *International Socialism*, Clare Fermont cited the Tyfountex strike as an example of a new wave of mass mobilizations among workers in the aftermath of the May uprising that overthrew Suharto. The uprising itself, as Fermont points out, was largely a student movement: 'During the protests that led up to 21 May, the workers were relatively passive'.[4] The example of the Tyfountex strike thus implies an end to this perceived passivity and the consolidation of the working-class basis of this 'revolution'.[5] Although Fermont assumed the participation of all 7,000 workers at Tyfountex in the strike, the point is less the number of workers than the qualitative transformation the strike underwent:

> Some 7,000 workers at the Tryfountex [sic] Indonesia factory in Solo went on strike between 30 June and 4 July to demand higher wages and other fringe benefits. After management threatened mass sackings, workers set up an independent Workers' Committee for Reform (Komite Reformasi Kaum Buruh), which among other things called for their factory to be nationalized. The committee also declared that workers should not confine themselves to immediate economic demands, and invited student leaders to address the workforce.[6]

The transformation in demands from wage increases to nationalization is explicitly linked to the formation of the *Komite Reformasi Kaum Buruh* (KRKB, Working Class Committee for Reform). It is also implied that the KRKB politicized the struggle by inviting student leaders to address the striking workers. However, the KRKB was not organized by the Tyfountex workers but by student activists, and the act of inviting students leaders to speak to the workers was less a political move on the part of militant workers than an expression of the basic function of KRKB and its student-activist agenda. Moreover, while the most militant workers were involved in the KRKB's activities, in the following months it continued to be led by the student activists who created it. It was also the latter who decided to take the protest to Jakarta, taking the strength out of the picket line and allowing the management to replace all of the workers and resume production. In addition, the opportunity was left open to the SPSI union to propagandize against the strike among the remaining workers and new recruits.

When the workers went to Jakarta the student-led KRKB made no preparations for food and other logistics, relying instead on charity organizations and volunteers. The workers slept on the floors, stairs and grounds of the office of YLBHI, a legal aid foundation, and were constantly without enough food or water. While hundreds of workers tried to find food or lined up to receive aid packages distributed by charity organizations, the student leaders discussed plans and strategies behind closed doors. Workers were informed of the day's plan of action only moments before. In fact, when they attempted to march to the ILO office and fought with the military and police, the vast majority of workers still had no idea of where they were headed or why. The possible relevance of the ILO to their struggle was not explained and the matter of going there was not even discussed.

My point here is not that the action was poorly planned or that it was a failure. Faced with mass dismissal and military repression, the courage and commitment expressed in these protests was of great significance to the workers and students themselves and to the wider labour movement. On the surface the image of workers marching down the street shouting militant slogans expressed their collective strength, and that is how it appeared in the mass media. But behind this something very different was taking place, with workers' frustration and uncertainty growing each day. When they returned to the YLBHI office each evening and waited for further instructions from student activists, their collective strength quickly dissipated. It was an important struggle and it was militant. But the question remains as to what exactly this has to do with revolution. 'The outbreak of the revolution in Indonesia raises a number of crucial theoretical questions',[7] reads the opening line of an essay by Tony Cliff entitled 'Revolution and counter-revolution: lessons for Indonesia' (later published as a pamphlet in Indonesian). Yet the most critical question is whether or not it was *really* a revolution. In the same essay Cliff actually reminds us that: 'The heart of Marxism is that the emancipation of the working class is the act of the working class'.[8] Yet if we juxtapose this claim with the strikes and protests like the Tyfountex struggle, then the contradiction between the way in which the protest action was organized and working-class self-activity is apparent.

Of course, there are hundreds of other strikes which could be analysed to reveal a different political dynamic and very different consequences from the one I have chosen to discuss. The point is that if we are to take seriously the project of working-class emancipation as *self*-activity, then we must undertake a critical examination of the collective capacities and processes through which acts of protest are organized and carried out, rather than uncritically accepting these acts as militant or revolutionary in themselves. The Tyfountex workers were not in control of the protest action, the determination of their demands or the strategies for achieving those demands. The shift in demands from wage increases to nationalization could only be revolutionary if the workers were involved in making that shift. However, so long as student activists organized and led the KRKB and workers had no organization of their own, then the issue of nationalization is far less radical than it appears. If the factory *were* nationalized, who would be in control?

Another example of this dynamic between student activists and worker militancy concerns the strike by workers at PT Walet Kencana, a pesticide factory in Surabaya, East Java, which operated as a subcontractor for the German-based TNC, Bayer. At the end of September 1998 over 2,500 workers began a strike demanding wage increases which led to the destruction of parts of the factory and its closure. After smashing the offices and destroying equipment the protest shifted to the local parliament. The destruction of the factory is not really the issue. As unexciting as it may seem, if the workers discussed, debated and collectively decided this course of action—a long and complex process—then it would have some direct relationship to the process of working-class self-emancipation. Like the Tyfountex protests, the reality was that the course of action was decided by student activists on the workers' behalf. Therefore, while it was militant it was far from revolutionary. Once the factory was closed and the protest outside parliament dispersed, the student activists went on to organize other protests or went back to their campuses. What the workers did after that is unclear. Most likely they found themselves among the ranks of 20 million other unemployed workers.[9] I am not suggesting that strikes and protest action be avoided for fear of unemployment. My argument is that whether this outcome is the consequence of workers' own collectively-determined action, organized and led by themselves, or whether it is the result of student activists' notions of radicalism, has important implications for the relationship between these acts of militancy and working-class emancipation. Over the past few years it is precisely this kind of mobilization from above by student activists which has alienated workers from the labour movement, creating distrust of workers' organizations and working-class politics.

As the Tyfountex and Walet Kencana strikes indicate, much of what is deemed as militant and radical often involves taking the struggle from the factory to the streets. Clearly this is important if workers' struggles are to move beyond issues such as wages and job security. However, what also occurred was that the issue of workers' control over production and workers' collective capacity to exercise that control was obscured. The possibility of long-term factory occupations and production control struggles were replaced with short-term street protests and rallies. Only a week in the seven-month life of the Tyfountex struggle was spent at the factory itself, while the rest of this time was dedicated to sporadic street demonstrations which expressed militant slogans and increasingly less radical demands outside the offices of the labour department in Jakarta.

A very different lesson may be drawn from peasant struggles in Indonesia—struggles which have received much less attention in the literature on the Indonesian 'revolution', yet nonetheless point to more radical processes and practices. From the early 1990s there have been widespread land occupations by peasant-farmers and villagers seeking either to reclaim land appropriated from them in the past or to establish control over new farming land necessary for the survival of their communities. This included the take-over of agro-industrial plantations where export-oriented cash crops such as tobacco and coffee were destroyed and replaced with corn and basic foods necessary to feed the community. The take-over of several golf courses in East and West Java and North Sumatra in 1997–98 (some of which remain under occupation today) combined the planting of subsistence crops with a direct challenge to the privilege and wealth of the ruling class. Although these collective survival strategies met with forced removal by the military, the self-organized strength of these movements and their emphasis on control continues to shape their politics of protest and resistance. Sadly, the possibility of extending this experience to the labour movement is limited by the division of labour and territorial politics of NGOs and student activists which serves to isolate rather than unify the workers' and peasant movements.

The possibility of the *radical* organizational displacement of working-class self-activity, and the contradictions within the democratic aspirations of independent workers' organizations and their anti- or non-democratic practices, both suggest that the situation is far more complex than it seems. In the case of Indonesia, unraveling this complexity involves acknowledging both the importance and the limitations of student activists' contributions to mass protests and the radicalization of workers' struggles. For example, nationally co-ordinated campaigns against the Indonesian military (ABRI) have been effective in linking work-place confrontations with the military to wider popular opposition to the 'dual function' of ABRI in society and its excessive political and economic power.[10] Faced with intimidation, threats, and beatings, workers' daily experience of military intervention in labour disputes was linked to the 'back to barracks' campaign organized by student activists and more progressive NGOs. The slogan 'back to barracks' was built upon a programme of popular education, pamphleting, and community organizing, which included teaching a critical popular history of the relationship between the labour movement and military repression under three decades of the Suharto regime. In contrast to other student-led mass protests (such as opposition to the IMF), it was not only the slogan that was radical but the very process of building a critical consciousness.[11]

What this also suggests is that there *is* an important role for student and NGO activists in workers' struggles, but that this role should be carefully defined. Obviously, work-place struggles and strikes must be broadened to address wider political issues and to link up with other social movements and community-based struggles. This kind of radicalization may involve student activists active in trade-union education committees, study circles, critical-analytical research groups, as well as publishing popular education material such as newsletters, bulletins and pamphlets. However, there is a significant difference between contributing to these struggles by radicalizing them through clearly defined popular education strategies on the one hand, and assuming leadership roles and decision-making power which shape the politics and actions of workers' organizations on the other. In other words, radicalization should not be based on external *intervention* to define workers' struggles, but on a critical *contribution* to the conditions under which workers' self-organized struggles are possible. The aim is to strengthen workers' collective power, not to supplant it. Such an approach also recognizes the fact that student activists and others have much to learn from workers and worker-activists, reasserting the importance of workers' knowledge and experience as central to these struggles rather than being reduced to 'testimonies', 'evidence', or 'case studies' situated within students' own radical agenda.

These issues relate to the wider contradiction evident in the emergent trade-union movements in the region—that independent unions supporting the struggle for democracy are not necessarily democratic organizations in themselves. This is evident not only in the absence of democratic elections and decision-making in these organizations, but also in the reproduction of paternalistic and patriarchal relations of authority and elitist notions of knowledge and expertise. While this observation is certainly not new, it suggests that the radical aspirations and revolutionary potential which many socialists attribute to these movements deserve deeper, more critical reflection. The reality is that, for all their exciting potential, the nature of these militant protests is such that they may inhibit the further development of workers' own capacities for self-emancipation. If they are not to perpetuate the organizational displacement of working-class self-activity (if only in a different form), then their organizational focus must more clearly locate radical 'events' in the broader and more fundamental context of building the kind of class capacities that can realise new possibilities for truly revolutionary change in East Asia.

NOTES

1. David McNally, 'Globalization on Trial: Crisis and class struggle in East Asia', *Monthly Review*, 50 (4), September 1998, p. 13.
2. Elsewhere I have discussed the case of the ICFTU in East Asia. See Gerard Greenfield, 'The ICFTU and the Politics of Compromise', in Ellen Meiksins Wood, Peter Meiksins and Michael Yates (eds.), *Rising from the Ashes? Labour in the Age of 'Global' Capitalism*, New York: Monthly Review Press, 1998, pp. 180–9.
3. A useful historical background on the SPSI is provided in Vedi Hadiz, *Workers and the State in New Order Indonesia*, London and New York: Routledge, 1997, pp. 76–82; 92–104.
4. Clare Fermont, 'Indonesia: the inferno of revolution', *International Socialism*, 80, Autumn 1998, p. 30.
5. According to John Rees' analysis of the demonstrations outside the People's Consultative Assembly (MPR) in Jakarta in November 1998: 'The forces of the revolution are stronger than in May because the working class played a larger role in the demonstrations in November'. John Rees, 'After "Bloody Friday": What's next for the Indonesian revolution?', http://www.internationalsocialist.org/pubs/indonesia/indonesia-e.html#rees.
6. Fermont, 'Indonesia', p. 27.

7. Tony Cliff, 'Revolution and counter-revolution: lessons for Indonesia', *International Socialism*, 80, Autumn 1998, p. 53.
8. Ibid., p. 60.
9. Several months later PT Walet Kencana reopened and continued production for Bayer. The workers now employed there know nothing of the strike and protests two years' earlier.
10. 'Indonesia: Military intervention in labour disputes', *Asian Food Worker* 28 (2), April–September 1998, pp. 4–6.
11. Yet even here there were important contradictions. Despite this campaign to demilitarize society and restrict the role of ABRI, student activists from radical organizations such as KOBAR created 'command headquarters' on university campuses and appointed their own 'commanders' to organize and lead demonstrations. Thus hierarchical structures of authority and control were produced which often mimicked the very military structures they were opposing.

ORGANIZING AGAINST THE ODDS: WOMEN IN INDIA'S INFORMAL SECTOR

Rohini Hensman

It is estimated that less than 8 percent of the work-force in India belongs to the formal sector, leaving more than 92 percent—well over 350 million people in a labour force of almost 400 million—in the informal sector.[1] This is partly due to non-implementation of existing legislation, but mostly a result of the inadequacy of these laws. For example, the Factories Act, 1948, which covers working conditions, health and safety, basic amenities like toilets, working hours, creches and much else, does not apply to work-places with fewer than ten workers using power-driven machinery or less than twenty workers without such machinery; similarly the Employees' State Insurance Act, 1948, providing for sickness, accident and maternity benefits, also does not apply to work-places with less than twenty workers without such machinery, nor to workers earning more than a fairly low wage, above which unions have to negotiate their own schemes with employers. Thus employers have a variety of ways to evade these laws: for example, splitting up an establishment into smaller units which are supposedly independent of one another, putting out work to homeworkers, employing large numbers of contract workers (on site) who are supposedly employees of labour contractors and therefore do not appear on the payroll of the company, or subcontracting production to smaller work-places. The Contract Labour (Regulation and Abolition) Act, 1971, forbids the employment of contract labour for work of a perennial nature, but the way this legislation has been formulated leaves gaping loopholes which have been exploited by unscrupulous employers, including the government itself.

One of the biggest obstacles to organization of informal sector workers is the fact that they are not covered by provisions of the Industrial Disputes Act, 1947, which prevent arbitrary closure of the enterprise and provide redress for workers subjected to dismissal for trade union activities. This means that although workers in theory have the right to unionize, in practice this means very little, because employers can either dismiss individual workers who join a union, or close down an entire unit and reopen it with new, non-unionized workers, and there is no redress for workers who are victimized in this way.

The other factor which must be taken into account when looking at the background against which women workers have had to work out their organizational strategies is the extreme social discrimination against women and girls, which begins even before birth with selective abortion of female foetuses, and carries on with female infanticide and less nutrition and health care for girls, so that India has fewer females than males in the population. The undervaluation of girls resulted in a female literacy rate of only 39.4 percent in 1991, one of the lowest in the world, as against 63.9 percent for males. This in turn affects the ability of women to get any employment except the worst, and makes it easier for employers to force them into adverse conditions.[2]

The problems are most acute for homeworkers, the vast majority of whom are women. Even their status as workers is not recognized without a struggle, and the lack of any formal employer–employee relationship makes it only too easy for employers to get rid of workers who are seen as trouble-makers by denying them work. Decentralization of production enables employers to evade labour legislation covering working conditions, hours of work, paid leave, weekly off-days and holidays, Provident Fund payments, etc. Organization in this sector is rare, and it is therefore worth looking at a some of the strategies that have been employed.[3]

THE NAVAYUGA BEEDI KARMIKA SANGAM

The production of beedis (Indian cigarettes) is a clear illustration of the employer strategy of decentralization in order to evade labour legislation. Beedi production used to take place in factories, but these were closed down in the 1970s, and the work put out to women homeworkers. This made the entire employer–employee relationship extremely hard to regulate. However, the Beedi and Cigar Workers (Conditions of Employment) Act, 1966, had extended the definition of the employer–employee relationship to include contract workers and homeworkers. Along with the Minimum Wages Act, 1948, this is one of the few labour laws applicable to homeworkers.

The Navayuga Beedi Karmika Sangam is a beedi workers' union in the city of Hyderabad, Andhra Pradesh, with a membership consisting entirely of women homeworkers. Here the struggle was, first and foremost, to be recognized as workers at all. When the Progressive Organization of Women (POW) and the All-India Federation of Trade Unions (AIFTU) began to organize these women, government statistics showed only a few hundred workers in the city; in fact, when the Labour Department was pressurized to investigate in 1986, they found there were approximately 10,000! The union contacted the women by going from house to house; holding meetings was difficult because the only time they came together was when they were delivering the completed beedis and collecting fresh raw materials. Moreover, initially women were scared to be known to belong to the union, because they could easily be victimized and quite often were. Nonetheless, the union was registered in 1987, and by 1994 the membership had grown to around 5,000.

At the time the union was started, the rate of pay was about Rs 8.00 for rolling 1,000 beedis—a long day's work for a skilled worker, and many needed help from children in order to reach this target. The union organized strikes, but even more effective, perhaps, were the demonstrations and other agitations which obtained city-wide publicity for the plight of the workers. They succeeded in getting the rate increased, but it still lagged behind the minimum wage, which kept increasing as inflation eroded its value (e.g., in early 1995, when the minimum wage was Rs 28 per day, the union won an increase to Rs 20 per 1,000 beedis). The struggle to regularize employment was less successful. Although employers were required to issue identity cards and appointment letters to the workers as proof of employment, hardly any of them were doing so. However, the workers did succeed in getting welfare cards from the government after a long, hard struggle. These entitled them to maternity benefit of Rs 250 for each of two births and scholarships for their children from the central government. Paid holidays, leave and weekly off-days were not given anywhere; it was strictly a matter of 'no work, no pay'.

There were also domestic problems. Many of the women were beaten by their husbands, and often encountered as much opposition to their union activities from their homes as from employers. In some of these cases the women subsequently dropped out of union activities, but sometimes other workers and the POW intervened to put pressure on their husbands to allow them to participate actively in the union.

One factor which seems to have been crucial to the success of the union is the existence of legislation which applies to this section of workers, which provided both a legal resource which could be used against recalcitrant employers, and a psychological source of strength to the women. However, many problems remained. The level of their earnings was still barely at subsistence level, and they had no paid leave or other benefits. Worst of all, they were still extremely vulnerable to victimization for trade union activities. This undermined their bargaining position *vis-à-vis* employers, and also left them with an underlying sense of insecurity.

SARBA SHANTI AYOG

Sarba Shanti Ayog (SSA), based in Calcutta, West Bengal, was started in 1978 as a development organization to promote artisan/craft producer groups. Subsequently, the Sasha Association of Craft Producers separated out as a specifically marketing organization. The Sasha shop was set up in 1981 in Calcutta, and sales in other parts of the country are handled through regular exhibitions and a wholesale unit supplying to craft shops in different cities. A significant export market has also been built up through Alternative Trade Organizations like Oxfam and Traidcraft. Marketing is carried out on a professional basis, and this has been crucial to the survival of the project.

By 1995, SSA consisted of a network comprising approximately fifty craft groups and fifteen communities. The majority of craft groups ranged in size from four or five to a hundred people and were involved in a wide variety of activities, including weaving, printing, embroidery, batiks, garments, terracotta, leather, toys, musical instruments, etc. The groups would come to SSA seeking help in setting up production units and SSA would find out if they had any skills which could be built on. Once an activity had been identified, SSA would carry out a skills training programme, usually provided by people from other groups. SSA also provided guidance on financial and production management and group functioning; in some cases this involved training not only in accountancy but even in basic literacy. The network would provide the new group with an advance of up to 75 percent—in exceptional cases 100 percent—to stock raw materials if they were cheaper in bulk.

Once the group is set up SSA continues to provide assistance with product design and development, partly through specialized designers, partly through workshops in which there is interaction between the groups. It provides continuing support of other types too, and, most crucially, assistance with marketing. Other community activities sometimes branch out from the producer groups. The health programme was most in demand and had developed furthest; health workers—mainly women—had been trained in preventive health. Education, child care and environment programmes were also in operation, often started on the initiative of producer group members or their relations.

The Self Help Handicrafts Society was a group producing garments, with a membership of forty-five women. Most were earning Rs 6–700 per month in early 1995, but some earned less and a few earned more, the maximum being about Rs 1000 per month. Sunday was an unpaid off-day, but the workers had decided to give themselves casual leave of 10 days and annual leave of 10 days per annum, paid at the rate of Rs 16 per day. They also had sixteen public holidays annually, paid at the rate of Rs 9 per day. Medical allowance was Rs 180 per annum, and they got three months maternity leave which they could not as yet afford to pay for. If there was an accident at work, treatment was free. Bonus was according to profit, and there was an Internal Savings Scheme, to which members contributed 10 percent of their wages and Self Help made a matching contribution. Normally this would be made available to members on retirement, but they had the option of taking loans out of it in an emergency. The women clearly had much greater control over their own working conditions and remuneration than most women workers in the informal sector.

However, problems still remain, the main one being that earnings are still at the low level characteristic of the informal sector. The most likely reason for this is the very low productivity of the work done in the groups, much of which is handicrafts; it would probably not be possible to break through to a substantially higher level of earnings unless more sophisticated technology and mass production are used. One experiment of this sort was in progress, namely the manufacture of herbal cosmetics using modern machinery.

SELF EMPLOYED WOMEN'S ASSOCIATION (SEWA)

SEWA, begun in 1972 and based in Ahmedabad, Gujarat, was registered in 1972 as a trade union under the Trade Union Act, 1926, and combines the functions of a bank, trade union and co-operatives. SEWA co-operatives are registered under the Co-operatives Act, and each one elects its own executive committee. All members of co-operatives are also members of SEWA. The link with SEWA is important in many ways. SEWA provides the co-operatives with training in skills and business management, initial working capital and help with tackling policy issues; it also helps them with design and marketing, including market research and assistance with attempting to keep up with changing market demand by adapting designs to it. Apart from handicrafts SEWA also has co-operatives performing services like cleaning, cooking and childcare.

The existence of SEWA as an umbrella organization provides co-operatives with a medium through which they can interact with one another. Thus artisan co-operatives can share skills and designs while service co-operatives can provide one another with services. More interestingly, the link has proved very useful to the trade union constituents of SEWA. Since the women in these belong to the informal sector where legal protection is virtually absent, the attempt to organize themselves and demand even minimum wages is often met by victimization and loss of employment. After a number of such experiences, 'The workers realized that unless alternative sources of work were provided their bargaining power would always remain low'(*SEWA in 1988*, p. 49). Thus co-operatives were seen as complementing the union function and strengthening the bargaining power of the workers.

The experience of the *chindi* workers illustrates this very well. Women homeworkers sewing *khols* (patchwork quilts) out of *chindi* (small scraps of waste from the textile mills) first came to SEWA in 1977 because they had heard that SEWA helped poor women. They were getting less than 40 paise (net of the cost of thread) to sew a khol requiring about one-and-a-half hours of labour, and decided to demand that the rate be raised to Rs 1.25. The traders refused to consider their demand, but SEWA filed a complaint in the State Labour Court and the labour commissioner arranged a series of meetings between workers' representatives and traders. Negotiations continued for over a month, during which the women maintained a strike, and the traders finally agreed to pay one rupee per quilt.

After the agreement, however, the traders victimized some of the women by refusing to give them work. The other women at first tried to help the victims by sharing work with them, but then came to SEWA suggesting it could set up a small production unit for these women. SEWA obliged, and after some teething problems succeeded in setting up the Sabina Chindi Workers' Co-operative, which was registered in 1982. The fact that they were paying better rates than the traders put pressure on the latter to keep up the rate, although even then they paid only 70 to 80 paise per quilt, not the rate they had agreed to. Since the quilts were sold to very poor rural consumers who could not afford to pay more than a few rupees per quilt, Sabina could maintain the piece-rates paid to workers only by running at a loss. They therefore decided to train younger members in patchwork production of bed-covers, cushion covers, skirts, kurtas, table-mats and tea-cosies for middle- and upper-middle-class markets. The surpluses earned by this part of their production compensated for losses on khol production.

SEWA is a very diverse and broad-based organization, and this has been its strength. The combination of bank, union and co-operatives has given it a great deal of flexibility, enabling it to offer credit, union organization or income generation to its members as the need arises. In particular, the combination of union and co-operatives seems to be a potent one for workers in the informal sector, strengthening the bargaining power of the union by providing a fall-back source of income if workers lose their employment. The formation of service co-operatives is also a novel and potentially powerful idea; performing the functions usually done by housewives and mothers, it offers them a low-cost service which helps to reduce their double burden. At the same time, a co-operative would be in a stronger position to obtain better remuneration and working conditions for its members than isolated domestic helpers or contract workers performing these same services.

However, the very low level of earnings continues to be a problem. For example, in 1995 the members of Soundarya, the cleaning co-operative, were earning only Rs 150 per month for part-time work of two hours a day for six days a week; members of Trupti, the catering co-operative, were earning Rs 600 per month for working eight hours a day, six days a week. The women themselves complained that the income was inadequate, and some even joined other unions in order to bargain with their own organization for better pay!

PROBLEMS AND POSSIBILITIES

Surplus labour, insecurity and victimization

Both SEWA and SSA set up production units in which women workers could earn a livelihood. These experiments provided an environment in which women could have some control over their own working conditions, and the experience of SEWA showed that they also enhanced the bargaining power of workers in employment. By contrast, the beedi workers, despite their militancy, suffered chronic insecurity and extreme vulnerability to victimization. In a labour market where extremely high levels of unemployment and under-employment constantly exert a downward pressure on wages and conditions, it makes sense to try and create alternative sources of livelihood through workers' co-operatives. This requires an elaborate and sophisticated support structure, especially to cope with the difficult task of marketing.

It is noteworthy, however, that the incomes of the women in these co-operatives remained at the extremely low levels characterizing the informal sector. This is highlighted if we compare their incomes with those of women workers of comparable seniority in the formal sector at the same period (the mid-1990s), who were earning five to ten times as much. One answer to this problem is to enhance the technological level of the production units. Although the argument that advanced technology is not suitable for surplus-labour societies is widespread, the experience of the chindi workers' co-operative shows the inherent limitations of this approach: if you produce cheap goods for poor people, you run at a loss, and the only alternative is to produce for the more affluent in order to break even. Only one production unit of SSA was trying to break out of this dilemma by adopting more advanced mass-production technologies.

The main problem, however, is that these co-operatives compete with sweated labour in the rest of the informal sector: the members of Soundarya, for example, are competing with contractors who can offer cleaning services at a lower rate because they pay their workers even more abysmal wages. The only solution, of course, is regulation. There is no way of tackling this difficulty unless the whole rationale of the existence of an unregulated informal sector where workers have few or no rights is challenged. The ostensible justification for not regulating it is that it creates more employment, but the example of the beedi industry shows (and other studies confirm) that the consequence, rather, is to shift production from the formal to the informal sector. In any case, we have to question the morality of a policy that seeks to expand employment by a *de facto* denial of the most basic rights of the vast majority of workers. The large sums of government money spent in subsidizing these enterprises would surely be better spent assisting workers to form and run their own co-operatives.

The example of the beedi workers, as well as the entire formal sector, shows that where protective legislation exists, workers have used it to their advantage. Winning equal rights for women workers in the informal sector would require a co-ordinated challenge to the existing system of virtual industrial apartheid, not only from organizations in the informal sector, but also from formal sector unions. The formation in 1995 of the National Centre for Labour, an umbrella federation of informal sector workers' organizations with a strong representation of women in the leadership, was a step in the right direction, but it has yet to formulate such a policy and press for it within the wider trade union movement. At the international level, while SEWA played a major role in pushing through the ILO Home Work Convention, 1996, which safeguards the rights of homeworkers, getting the government to ratify and implement this convention is a much more difficult task. Given the determined opposition of employers in India to any extension of workers' rights, and their demand, on the contrary, for the curtailment of existing rights, it is not likely that this struggle will succeed unless it becomes part of a common strategy of the international trade union movement for the defence of workers' rights globally.

Unions and the gender dimension

But the possibilities of such a strategy will clearly be very limited unless the gender dimension—in its fullest sense—is front and centre. Even among the examples we have examined here, only the beedi union took up cases of domestic violence and attempts to control women by husbands and in-laws, but these instances show how important it is to tackle such problems. It was very clear that patriarchal authority within the family worked in tandem with employer resistance to prevent many women from playing an active part in the union, and in some ways reinforced the putting-out system by discouraging women from going out to work. Most of the women were quite ready to work outside the home, and older ones who had worked in beedi factories regretted their demise. They felt they could produce and earn more if their children were cared for in a work-place creche while they concentrated on their work. But this option was not available to them, and it was not only the employers who wanted them at home.

Sexual harassment was not mentioned explicitly, but could have been the reason why some women in Self Help who had previously worked in mixed sweatshops said so emphatically that they preferred an all-women work-place. Women in the informal sector, especially if they are non-unionized, are particularly vulnerable to sexual harassment, often faced with the choice of submitting to it or losing their jobs. Gender discrimination was not mentioned either, but was practiced blatantly in beedi production, where the worst-paid workers, rolling beedies at home, were all women, while it was men who did the better-paid packing and labelling jobs in the beedi workshops. Even existing legislation, like the Equal Remuneration Act, is not implemented in the informal sector; but the broader issue of equal opportunities and non-discrimination has not been addressed even in the formal sector.

Both SEWA and SSA had branched out into community activities such as childcare, health care and education, indicating that the working life of women links work-place, home and community. This is, of course, especially true of homeworkers, for whom the work-place *is* their home. It appears from these examples that organizing women successfully involves taking up gender issues which are not usually considered to be trade union issues. Yet if they are not taken up, women workers—even in the formal sector—tend to play a marginal role in their organizations, or even drop out altogether.

These cases of women organizing in the informal sector are not isolated ones. There are other examples of relatively large-scale organizations, like the Working Women's Forum in Chennai and Annapurna in Mumbai, as well as a plethora of smaller community-based efforts like Jeevan Nirvaha Niketan in

Mumbai, which includes producer co-operatives, child care, health care, and shelter from domestic violence. In addition, women are also members of mixed informal sector unions of construction workers, agricultural workers, fish workers, and so on. While the proportion of women in India's informal sector who are organized still remains small (the exact numbers are not known), these successes show what can be achieved by determined efforts in this direction. Women who were interviewed said they felt empowered by their membership of an organization, not only in relation to employers, but also within their families. The more activist elements appreciated their knowledge of 'the system' and ability to confront and deal with officials and the police, while those who were less active enjoyed the sense of community and solidarity with other women. What the organization of women workers in India's informal sector shows is that, while the obstacles to organizing are formidable, the unions in this sector, once formed, can be extremely strong. There is a lesson here for the working classes globally.

NOTES

1.   The *Economic Survey 1997–98* estimated that the total labour force in 1997 was 397.2 million, while the workforce in the organized (regulated) sector was 27.94 million. The informal sector is defined in various ways, but for the purposes of this paper, I have used it to refer to all workers, both urban and rural, who are not covered by basic labour legislation, including informal workers (e.g. contract workers, temporary and casual workers) in large-scale production.
2.   See United Nations Development Programme *Human Development Report 1995* for an assessment of India's poor performance in bringing about gender equality.
3.   These case studies were carried out in 1994–5 by staying for a while in the place where the organization was located, collecting any documentation available on it, and interviewing the organizers as well as several women workers. Where the organization covered different communities (e.g., Hindus, Muslims, etc.), members from the different communities were interviewed.

'A RACE STRUGGLE, A CLASS STRUGGLE, A WOMEN'S STRUGGLE ALL AT ONCE': ORGANIZING ON THE BUSES OF L.A.

ERIC MANN

In Los Angeles today, the Labor/Community Strategy Center is carrying out a difficult Left experiment in the age of the omnipresent Right. The center is an explicitly anti-racist, anti-corporate, and anti-imperialist think-tank focusing on 'theory-driven practice'—the generation of mass campaigns of the working class and oppressed nationalities, in particular the black and Latino workers and communities. These campaigns are historically relevant on their own terms, but also have real relevance to any transition to an uncharted socialist future. Despite Clinton/Blair-style refinements on neoliberalism, imperialism's infliction of massive human suffering and its moral and ethical deterioration has never been more apparent; there is an enormous opening for an anti-capitalist, anti-imperialist Left, as there is now no viable progressive liberalism or social democracy even trying to co-opt radical Left ideology and organizing.

The work of the Strategy Center is reflected in several interrelated organizational forms: a staff that initiates mass campaigns and establishes the political policies and priorities of the organization; a National School for Strategic Organizing that recruits and trains ideologically-oriented college and working-class activists who often rapidly become front-line leaders of the mass campaigns (i.e., the development of cadres along the lines theorized in Lenin's *What is to be Done*, and emulated in every successful U.S. Left organization from the CPUSA to SNCC to SDS to the Black Panthers); AhoraNow, a bilingual political magazine, that focuses on raising practice to the level of theory and has generated a target audience of 1,000 key organizers, activists, and intellectuals—

with a growing international readership. At center stage is the Bus Riders Union/Sindicato de Pasejeros (BRU): a multi-racial mass organization of the transit dependent, the front-line mass campaign that extends the political influence of the center, tests its anti-imperialist theories, and generates a militant struggle to improve the public transportation system and the lives of 400,000 overwhelmingly minority, female, and low-income members of the urban working class.

The BRU, formed in 1993, is known for its yellow T-shirted, militant, multi-racial band of on-the-bus organizers, taking over the bus and contesting public space, as they organize bus drivers and bus riders in a moving site of struggle—exemplified by its 'No Somos Sardinas/No Seat No Fare' campaign in which tens of thousands of bus riders refused to pay their fare as a protest against bus overcrowding. The union's explicitly ideological approach to organizing, reflected in its slogans on posters, leaflets, and T-shirts throughout the city—'Fight Transit Racism', 'Stop the Corporatization of Government', 'Mass Transportation is a Human Right'—explicitly challenges the accommodation to neoliberal globalization of many former socialists and communists who are now pro-corporate labor union officials, community organizers, and powerful Democratic Party liberal operatives.

Organizing the bus riders has involved recognizing the strategic centrality of public services for the urban working class. For most of the twentieth century, communists, social democrats and even Keynesian liberals, have all argued that the market system and the trade union struggle cannot provide a living wage. In a capitalist system, the working class needs both a wage from the employer and a supplemental wage, a 'social wage' from the state in the form of publicly funded medical care, transportation, housing, education, culture, and recreation. The present mantra of privatization works for the upper classes who can purchase on the market any services they desire, but for the low-wage working class low-cost, efficient public transportation is an urgent need. Moreover, for transit dependent workers in sprawling areas like Los Angeles, Atlanta, and Chicago public transportation takes a very significant part of their day. While suburban auto commuters complain about gridlock, they can turn on the air conditioning and CD-player, contact clients on their cell phone, and suffer in style. For the working class, with increasingly dispersed employment and education centers, the one- and two-hour commutes each way on filthy, overcrowded buses, the long waits, the missed transfers, the constant fear of being fired for being late for work, the intrusion into any leisure time generates a rage that can be directed at a clear enemy—the powerful Metropolitan Transportation Authority (MTA) with a U.S.$ 3 billion a year budget that if captured and redirected towards a first-class bus system, could dramatically improve life for the working class.

ORIGINS: THE VAN NUYS LABOR/COMMUNITY COALITION

The Strategy Center was initiated in 1989, but its formative experience was the UAW Campaign to Keep GM Van Nuys Open, launched in 1982 to challenge General Motor's efforts to shut down L.A.'s last remaining heavy industrial plant with a workforce of more than 5,000. (I was the primary organizer of that campaign, situated as an assembly line worker in United Auto Workers Local 645, one of the most militant, progressive, and powerful locals in the U.S. labor movement at the time.) The campaign built a powerful in-plant movement led by Latino, black, white, and women workers, in strong alliance with L.A.'s large black and Latino communities. For a decade, from 1982 to 1992, that movement forced General Motors, the largest transnational industrial corporation in the world, to keep the plant open. The campaign achieved significant visibility and national impact through its unexpected tenacity in the age of Reagan and UAW concessions, as well as its ties to the New Directions Movement (a vibrant national insurgency to change the UAW at the time), the constructive, essential role of communist organizers in the plant (including me) and the determined efforts we made to document the struggle for a wider audience.

In the realm of Left politics the campaign broke new ground. It challenged management's rights theories by arguing that workers and communities, in particular black and Latino communities, had countervailing and special rights to restrict capital flight. It went beyond 'colour blind' approaches to working–class unity by highlighting the special rights of black and Latino workers to jobs. This was done in a way that went beyond contractual arguments. It asserted the obligations to the black working class created by centuries of slavery and segregation; it located the just demands of Chicano workers in terms of California's common colonial past with Mexico; and it drew attention to GM Van Nuys as the last provider of heavy industrial jobs for black and Latino workers. The campaign also argued for the special rights of women workers, who had just fought their way into heavy industrial jobs after decades of exclusion, and who had to fight for federal laws and programmes just to be able to be exploited on the shop floor.

The movement to challenge GM's 'management rights' provision in the collective bargaining contract and to boycott the cars of the very company for whom we worked put our local union on a direct collision course with the international leadership of the UAW. They defended GM's contractual right to close the plant, urged the workers instead to elect Democrats and oppose Japanese imports, and attacked the local for its 'self-destructive militancy' at a time when, according to the international union bureaucracy, the workers' obligation was to help the company regain greater profitability and competitiveness internationally. Against this explicitly pro-imperialist stance, the campaign gave explicit content to 'independent Left politics' through its main confrontational tactic, a pre-emptive boycott of GM products in the Los

Angeles new car market, and its insurgent form of organization, the Labor/Community Coalition, an independent forum explicitly designed to link the union local with powerful community forces in order to challenge the collusion and repression of GM and the UAW.

The long-term strategic significance of the campaign lay in how it addressed the complexities of working-class social formation in terms of class, race and gender. It was rooted in an analysis of the specific and controversial disposition of forces in an anti-racist anti-imperialist united front—the strategic alliance of the multi-national working class with the oppressed nationality workers in the U.S. The analysis evolved from specific events in the campaign. At the first major strategy meeting in late 1982, attended by more than 250 active GM Van Nuys workers and community allies, we broke into small groups in which each worker was asked to make an inventory of their own organizational, neigh-bourhood, racial, and other affiliations. Several women talked about being graduates of shelters for battered women, and issues of male alcoholism and battery, and the life and death face of women's liberation were brought into the open. Out of these discussions the first Women's Committee was organized in the local and contacts were made with the Coalition of Labor Union Women and other women's groups. The Mexicano workers talked about their problems as immigrants, and formed a vibrant Spanish language organizing committee—reaching out to Chicano students, immigrants' rights groups, and to the predominantly Latino Catholic Archdiocese. Many black workers focused on their ties to the Baptist and First African Methodist Episcopal churches. We learned that some workers (including several laid-off auto workers from other plants already closed) were black pastors running very small 'storefront' churches, while holding full-time working-class jobs.

The campaign helped clarify both the racialized nature of class and the class structure of racially oppressed groups. There is a tendency among some Leftists, even while acknowledging some racial and ethnic contradictions, to discuss the working class as fundamentally unified; by implication, this means accepting the dominant white identity of the U.S. working class. There is also a tendency to collapse oppressed nationalities—very complex multi-class formations—into uniformly classless black or Latino or other 'communities'. In reality, it is impos-sible to build an effective united front without giving great attention to the racial contradictions and white racism inside the working class, and the class contra-dictions within oppressed nationalities. In the Van Nuys campaign, the multi-national working class was 50% Latino (about one-third of whom were immigrants), 15% black, and 15% female. It was understanding the multiple and dynamic identities of the workers, and in particular taking up the demands of the black and Latino workers, that allowed us to energize the local working class as an actor. Explicitly addressing difference and contradiction were essential for unity of action. Similarly, while the support of Latino and black college students and clergy was pivotal, it was the black and Latino GM workers—who were parishioners in the churches, and whose kids went to the community colleges and state universities—who had both the strategic positioning in the factory and the moral authority in the community to push the clergy and the elected local officials into the united front against GM. In the Van Nuys Labor/Community Coalition, it was the oppressed nationality workers who were the main force inside labor, and also the main force inside the black and Latino communities. That pivotal and dual role has continued in the work of the Bus Riders Union.

By 1987, as the union local and the Labor/Community Coalition increased its pressure on GM (having already forced GM to issue a five-year stay of execution from its original intention to close the plant in 1982), the UAW counterattacked. It imposed a 'team concept' of labor management co-operation on the local union, suppressed any UAW militants who refused to co-operate, colluded in the firing of Pete Beltran and Mike Velasquez, the president and vice president of the local who had led the movement against the 'team concept', and ushered in a Right-wing pro-company faction. This faction, armed with thugs and the threat of more firings of militant workers, openly repudiated the campaign, embraced the attack on the Japanese, and physically prevented the Left from using the union hall.

Under these conditions, we formed the Strategy Center, with the following objectives: (1) Continuing the Van Nuys campaign: the center became the new home for the Labor/Community Coalition and the 'union hall in exile' for militant UAW workers trying to recapture the local. (2) Recruiting and training a new group of organizers to initiate community based campaigns. (3) Focusing on 'environmental justice' campaigns in which the most impacted low-income minority communities, suffocating with industrial and auto toxins, would challenge large-scale industrial polluters and state regulatory agencies in big-picture, test-case campaigns. (4) Functioning as a strategic think-tank for organizers and activists, situated in local labor unions and oppressed nationality communities, who were trying to create an independent base, separate from and in contradiction to the trade union bureaucracy and Democratic Party.

CONTEXT: THE POLITICAL FACE OF LOS ANGELES

The initiation of the Strategy Center took place none too soon. By 1991 the Left wing of the local was completely crushed and by 1992 the plant was closed, with no organized resistance. With fitting irony, in 1994 the UAW West Coast Region was closed altogether, for lack of membership. So much for the benefits of labor/management co-operation. The consequences of such a strategy were increasingly visible, moreover, throughout the megacity of Los Angeles. In a development mirrored in every advanced capitalist country, and many Third World countries as well, where many former revolutionaries have become the most militant apologists for the imperialist world order, virtually all the leading figures in what used to be called the 'progressive' and Left trade union and minority movements are now firmly entrenched in the corporate orbit. Our initial tactic of the GM boycott in Los Angeles county, and the subsequent work on regional air quality and mass transportation issues, demanded a greater understanding of the political economy of Los Angeles.

Los Angeles is a major ruling-class city in the U.S.—a 'world city' of media, manufacturing, banking and ruling-class politics, with national and international impact. The growing importance of L.A.'s international position has taken place over a few short decades, coinciding with the historic election of Tom Bradley, a liberal black former policeman, as mayor in 1973. Bradley's election involved the construction of a powerful liberal black/Jewish alliance and the defeat of the old reactionary white regime that had shaped L.A. since its inception. Bradley's initial focus on anti-racism and curtailing police brutality moved rapidly into a corporate makeover, which rationalized the local state as a more sophisticated instrument of downtown development. Some have called this the Manhattanization of L.A.: it involved co-opting the AFL–CIO (through contracts for building trades construction unions) and the black bourgeoisie (through the transformation of black churches into 'community development corporations').

Bradley was elected mayor for four terms—he was the FDR of Los Angeles, the true corporate liberal. During his reign, it was the black and Latino working class who suffered the most. The downtown high-rise office developers destroyed the black janitorial unions, subcontracting to non-union, low-wage employers. Los Angeles became the new center of U.S. garment manufacture as sweatshop owners realized that the city had all the advantages of a Third World labor market and a First World consumer market for high-end goods. Bradley upheld the mobility of capital by refusing to challenge the many industrial plant closings of the time (including giving GM a green light to close both of its L.A. plants). More than 35,000 high-paying industrial jobs were eliminated, the recently-created well-paid working class of colour was decimated, while the labor bureaucracy, Democratic Party and black bourgeoisie stood mute, content with their piece of the action.

Fittingly, the last year of Bradley's last term was punctuated by an anti-racist rebellion. His efforts to curtail the paramilitary LAPD had failed: the videotaped beating of Rodney King, and the subsequent Simi Valley jury's defiant acquittal of the police, vividly highlighted the structural role of police repression and white suburban support in the continued subjugation of blacks. The acceleration of urban poverty, low-wage industry, and changing urban demographics sparked the first large-scale black/Latino street action, expanding the racial composition and geographic area of any previous urban revolt. In 1993, the venture capitalist, Richard Riordan, rode the white backlash against the 'riot' and the Latino backlash against Bradley's chauvinist exclusion of them into a mayoral victory. Riordan pledging to hire 2,000 more cops and to 'run the city like a business.'

From Bradley to Riordan the government of L.A. has come to play a far more central role in corporate development, moving massive amounts of federal, state, and local funds into massive construction projects with guaranteed profits and cost overruns that benefit a complex alliance of corporate forces. In the early years of the Bradley administration the city purchased 2,000 new buses to modernize and expand the fleet—to deliver low-wage labor to the increasingly dispersed L.A. capitalists and in anticipation of the 1984 Olympics (the crowning jewel of Bradley's efforts to display L.A. as a world city). In 1980 and 1984 L.A. voters passed two half cent sales taxes—with bus riders having been promised a reduced 50 cent bus fare and a network of fast, clean buses. But this was linked to a new MTA plan for a vast array of subway and light rail lines. This plan was driven by corporate development objectives—rail construction as a publicly funded boondoggle for contractors and monuments to developers, real estate speculators, politicians, and their contributors. It was clear from the outset that there was no way they could afford to construct an even minimally viable mass transit plan if rail construction was prioritized over expanding the bus system. L.A. county, with 4,000 square miles, does not have the density for rail; only bus can compete with the auto. Moreover, rail construction costs are prohibitive—$350 million per mile for subways, $150 million a mile for light rail, whereas the cost of a first-class bus system that could serve 500,000 daily riders would be less than three miles of subway construction. As the MTA rail lines came in at 350% above cost, and attracted less than 50% of their projected ridership, the subsidy for each suburban passenger (mostly white) rose to as much as $5 to $10 a ride—for only 6% of all mass transit riders. It was the city's 500,000 bus riders, mostly black and Latino (94% of all mass transit riders) who paid the bill. By the early 1990s, despite a 15% increase in population, the MTA bus system had deteriorated. A once brand new 3,000 bus fleet was down to 2,000 dilapidated ones, as old buses were not replaced and ridership declined by 20%.

The BRU's challenge to what it called 'transit racism' has led it to a frontal challenge to the fiscal priorities of the local capitalist state, posing the central political question: which class should government subsidize? The BRU demanded 'Billions for Buses', a carefully-developed programme for replacing 2,000 dilapidated diesel buses with 2,000 new clean-fuel (compressed natural gas) buses, expanding the bus fleet by an additional 500 buses to reduce over-crowding and another 500 buses for new service to medical, employment, and educational centers. This would require hiring more than 2,000 bus drivers and an additional 750 mechanics and maintenance people. This plan would get the working class to work, attract many auto drivers as well, but would offer no kickbacks, no monuments, and no sacrifices to the gods of corporate urbanism.

In 1992, when we initiated the 'Billions for Buses' mass transportation campaign, we understood we would have to challenge virtually every organized force in the city. No 'anti-corporate united front' was possible at the time; we had first to initiate an anti-corporate center of gravity. But we were also aware that the BRU's efforts at anti-racist organizing were taking place in a context of heightened racism and xenophobia. Throughout the 1990s, California, the alleged cutting edge political laboratory for U.S. politics, has seen right-wing, pro-corporate reactionaries, armed with sophisticated Republican electoral tactics, engage in bi-annual rites of racial political sadism in which substantial majorities of white working class and middle class voters are organized into referenda crusades to strip every last civil right and civil liberty from minority communities. For more than a decade they have spent millions to place on the ballot repressive measures with demagogic slogans: 'The Taxpayers Revolt' to reduce property taxes and reduce funding for public (that is, black and Latino) education; 'Three Strikes and You're Out' to legalize putting minority youth in prison for the rest of their lives; 'Save our State' which would deny medical benefits and education to undocumented immigrants; and even the notorious 'Civil Rights Initiative' to eliminate affirmative action for university admissions and government contracts. As each initiative passes, it whets the public's appetite for more racism and reaction—sentencing youth as adults, banning gay marriage. In this context, the Strategy Center has tried to use mass campaigns such as the Bus Riders Union to construct an 'anti-racist united front' focusing on the urgent needs and legitimate demands of the working class of colour. The fight against national oppression and racism is the central 'class' question in a structurally racist society.

The BRU's work has focused heavily on the class nature of national oppression—talking about 'class-based racism' and 'race-based poverty'. We have highlighted the many overtly material manifestations of discrimination and racism—the substandard services and the discriminatory use of public funds in order to subsidize white suburban commuters. We have also elaborated the ideological reflection of racism, which is also a material force: the massive overcrowding, sometimes more than 40 people standing, bodies pushed together, with every seat taken on a 43-seat bus; the bus drivers' often contemptuous screaming at bus riders to 'get back', as if they have any place to go; the despair of watching bus after bus pass you by as if your time and your life are worth nothing; the constant fear of being late for work, with the assumption you are lazy or unreliable, when in fact you must get up an extra hour early for work or school to compensate for the many times buses break down or pass you by; the two-hour bus rides from South Central and East L.A. by domestic workers to clean white wealthy people's homes; and the sexually threatening pushing, grabbing and touching that many male passengers inflict on women to add insult to injury on the overcrowded buses. Humiliation, degradation, devaluation—the bus system reflects and replicates racist policies. The 'No Somos Sardinas' campaign struck a chord—'we are not sardines, goddamn it.' As BRU leader Norma Henry angrily told the MTA board, 'If the bus system was carrying 400,000 white males, no matter how rich or how poor, there is no way you would tolerate those disgusting conditions.' For the working class of colour this is a race struggle, a class struggle, and a women's struggle all at once, but the struggle against national oppression for working-class black and Latino bus riders clearly is what used to be called the 'primary contradiction': placed at the center of the strategy it has the potential to unlock and unleash all the other struggles.

ORGANIZING BUS RIDERS:
THE CLASS STRUGGLE IN MOTION

The buses are an exciting arena of organizing for the Left—a site of social and structural formation of the multi-lingual, multi-cultural urban proletariat. The generalized concept of 'people of colour' stands in for a new working class whose complex character challenges even the best organizers. Like the factory, the bus system forces together working-class people of different nationalities, races, ethnicities, genders, and strata, who share a common proximity and oppression. Over time, and through the organizing work of the BRU, many bus riders are coming to understand their own experience in more systemic terms, seeing the MTA as a mechanism of the capitalist state, exploiting their time and money to subsidize the wealthy and the corporate class. The bus creates the structural possibility of breaking through the parochialism and ethnic balkanization of the neighbourhoods. If you live in East L.A. (Chicano) but have a job on the West Side the bus rides take you through Pico Union (Central American) Koreatown, Crenshaw (black) and Fairfax (white, Jewish, elderly) before you get to work. The bus is what we call a factory on wheels, carrying the Korean restaurant worker, the Thai woman garment worker, the Latino hotel worker, the black department store worker, the black and Latino domestic workers, high school kids with their boom boxes, the black and Latino parolees—and the cruellest new growth industry of all, black and Latino security guards, minimum wage workers asked to risk their lives and at times take the lives of others to protect private and corporate property. Like the former heavy industry factory, the bus system creates one of the multi-racial contexts in which an appeal to a common destiny and a common enemy can be made—the objective conditions into which the organizers attempt to inject the subjective factor—strategy, tactics, agitation and propaganda.

Bus riders are a powerful numerical force in the city. L.A. has 400,000 daily bus riders taking 1.3 million daily trips. Several major urban bus lines, the Wilshire, Pico, Vermont Western, and Third St. lines, carry more than 20,000 riders a day each, more than any heavy or light rail line, and the MTA has 77 high density bus lines. This is a mass constituency that if organized could repre-sent an important power bloc in the politics of a megacity. At present, the BRU reaches as many as 50,000 bus riders each month—through flyers, on-the-bus discussions, agitations and theatre presentations, BRU members talking to other riders on the way to work, massive media campaigns and high visibility feature stories, television shows, and films about our work.

Moreover, Bus riders have many organizational affiliations. This is impor-tant to solving the complex questions of how to win our demands. Given the powerful coalition of forces that benefit from the rail juggernaut—construction companies, building trades unions, elected officials of every persuasion and nationality, how can we build a countervailing force to pressure the federal courts and the MTA board to prioritize the bus system? As the BRU recruits members on the bus, we learn that, like the Van Nuys workers, they have multiple organizational affiliations with the Hotel and Restaurant Union, the clothing and textile workers' union UNITE, Justice for Janitors, Los Angeles City College, NAACP, churches, disability rights groups. Even trade unions who have strongly disagreed with our politics are careful as to how they handle us, because many of their own members are also members of the BRU. As Ricardo Zelada, a Salvadorian immigrant with long ties to the Left agitated, 'I wear two hats for two unions—UNITE, for my workplace, and the Sindicato de Pasejeros for my civil rights and my transportation.' This tactic of organizing the industrial and service working class through a city-wide struggle over public services allows us to re-enter the trade union movement through a new form of working-class union.

In 1993, when BRU organizers began their work, the only material expression of a unified or even nascent class or race struggle was in their brain cells. The bus riders and the bus drivers began with only one thing in common— they were pissed off at each other, alone in their experience and consciousness, thinking and speaking in different languages, with no sense of a common destination or destiny. This is the multi-racial working class doing its own spontaneous thing. The first steps involve commandeering the space—sending organizers on to the bus, militantly engaging the passengers, distributing leaflets, making loud speeches when many bus riders were yelling and screaming anyway. The aggressiveness of the BRU organizers is legendary. They often include young recruits from our National School for Strategic Organizing along with our most developed members. But how to shape the bus into an effective arena for organizing? To begin with, the BRU focuses heavily on the written word; agitational flyers that are very hard to write, because the story is so complex—the history of transit racism, the complex corporate and political forces, the specificities of our legal case, and the endless series of parliamentary manoeuvres at the monthly MTA board meetings that require a level of specificity and at times technicality that would drive away all but the most committed. Still, we target 'the opinion leaders of the oppressed', those who are attracted to, even fascinated by, our protracted, and highly conceptual approach to long-term political struggle. Then we learn to refine our agitation, speaking at times to the whole bus, then settling in for one on one conversations, most leading nowhere, but again, looking for the attentive eyes, the open and inquiring minds.

Equal attention needs to be paid to the language of organizing. All of our leaflets are in Spanish and English, most of our organizers, Latino, black, Asian, and white are bilingual English/Spanish, and every team is always bilingual. We have had one Korean organizer, Carol Song, and when she was with us the involvement of Korean people on the bus was radically expanded. Our inability to find an effective replacement has been a major setback. The strong presence of black organizers—Kikanza Ramsey and Sean McDougall, who speak fluent Spanish—is as educative for the blacks on the bus as the Latinos, seeing a model of blacks who are aggressively challenging the reactionary anti-Latino sentiment prevalent among members of the black political establishment. The multi-racial, multi-lingual team of organizers is often as compelling as the demands for more buses and better mass transit—people want buses, but they want to join a movement as well. The unapologetically Left, internationalist, expansive anti-racist politics of the BRU helps recruit and retain new members.

The bus really comes alive when organizers challenge people to act and do so in a way that unleashes class, race, and gender dynamics. In the summer of 1997 the Bus Riders Union organized a 'No Seat No Fare' campaign, asking bus riders to refuse to pay their fare to protest the MTA's refusal to reduce overcrowding to agreed-upon levels and to demand that the MTA purchase 500 additional buses. Out of the 400,000 daily bus riders, we estimate the BRU/Sindicato has about 3,000 dues-paying members and 30,000 self-identified members—so when we go on the buses we often begin with at least one or two out of 60 to 80 passengers who know who we are and who see themselves as supporters or members.

We began the campaign with a commissioned poster from well-known guerrilla artist Robbie Conal, a full colour can of sardines with the slogans, 'No Somos Sardinas, We Won't Stand for It.' Several thousand posters were plastered on bus shelters throughout the city and got a great reception. We spent the entire summer doing mass leafleting on the buses, carrying out militant actions such as stopping dilapidated buses at their stops, putting yellow homicide tape around the buses, labelling them 'dead on arrival'. This expanded street presence led to many confrontations with the LAPD including several arrests for 'defacing property' and resisting arrest. Several BRU members were roughed up by the police.

This is not to say the bus riders are, as a group, very militant—certainly not spontaneously. Many are very poor, with no history of political struggle and, at first, worried that not paying their fare would be like stealing or cheating. Over time, we educated many bus riders that this was not individual free-loading, but instead, group resistance, a politically symbolic act of defiance to signal the media, the courts, and the MTA that the bus riders were angry as hell, and clearly identified with the BRU. While even at its height the campaign was very much driven by the initiative of the BRU staff and active members, more than 30,000 passengers participated in the 'No Seat No Fare' campaign. This mass militancy was reinforced by very sympathetic press coverage, and a federal court decision, several months later, ordering the MTA to purchase 350 additional buses and to hire as many drivers as necessary—estimated at more than 700—to operate them.

From the inception of our organizing work, we gave high priority to trying to enlist and organize the support of the bus drivers. We theorized that the drivers and riders had a common material and class interest. Overcrowded buses were terrible for the riders, but what driver wanted to be faced with the daily war games between him or herself and a busload of angry passengers?

Moreover, the BRU's demands to reduce overcrowding and develop service to new areas would require as many as 1,000 additional buses, creating as many as 2,000 new jobs. But building working-class unity between the more privileged and the more super-exploited sectors of the working class is far more difficult than logical argument of common interests. The drivers, significantly black and Latino, with as many as 20% of them female, are represented by the United Transportation Union (UTU), a conservative AFL-CIO craft union. The drivers work alone, and often do not experience the passengers as fellow workers but rather see them as the main 'problem' in their working conditions. While many drivers are courteous and even solicitous of the passengers, many treat the largely Latino and Asian immigrants with contempt. Conversely, many bus riders see the drivers as 'the MTA' and when we talk about 'transit racism' many angry riders say, 'the main problem is the arrogant drivers who pass me by, yell at us to step back like we are cattle, and won't learn my language to give me instructions.'

The work with the drivers has included efforts to help them build a rank-and-file caucus. This got off to a good start but collapsed under pressure from the UTU leadership. We have continued our daily conversations with the drivers, and we put out open letters to the drivers about a common programme at least every six months. On every bus, one BRU organizer talks to the driver while the others talk to the passengers. We have also made many overtures to the UTU leadership, and have met with them on several occasions, but they have never expended any of their limited influence on behalf of bus riders or even a better bus system. The UTU has made significant concessions to the MTA on issues of subcontracting, privatization, and a two-tiered wage system. Several MTA drivers have told us that the union leadership is threatened by the BRU because our militant stance against privatization exposes their own deals with the MTA. Many drivers say 'the BRU even fights harder for our jobs than our own union.'

This patient work was tested during the 'No Seat No Fare' campaign when most drivers offered at least passive support—adhering to a narrow contractualism by simply 'quoting the fare' and refusing to call MTA police. A significant minority of drivers went further, chanting into their microphones 'Support the BRU' and putting their hands over the fare box, informing passengers, 'No Asiento, No Pago'. Given the growing privatization and police control of public space, making it increasingly difficult for Left organizers to even reach mass constituencies, the driver/rider alliance, no matter how tenuous, has been a critical breakthrough in our work—not the least of which is allowing us the physical space in which to do it.

Through six years of organizing we have recruited and retained a core of several hundred active members. The BRU holds regularly scheduled monthly membership meetings that average 75 to 100 participants, elects an executive board/planning committee that meets weekly to set all major polices and objectives of the organization, creates multiple structures for membership participation and leadership such as the Action Committee and the newly formed Teatro whose members write political skits and perform them at bus stops and on the buses. Again, all of this work is carried out and performed in Spanish and English, facilitated by professional translators and the use of headsets.

ACHIEVEMENTS AND DILEMMAS

The Strategy Center, in the absence of a Left political party or other national organization, has created an organized center of resistance and large-scale campaigns to challenge the powerful L.A. and U.S. ruling class. Using racial oppression as a fulcrum, we are slowly unlocking the complex dynamics of class, race, gender, disability, age, and using the most oppressed sectors of society to impact the politics of a megacity of nine million people. From that base, we are reaching out to make new alliances with activists and social movements in other major urban centers—Atlanta, New York, San Francisco/Oakland, Toronto, and Johannesburg.

In 1994, the center initiated an aggressive civil rights law-suit Labor/Community Strategy Center and Bus Riders Union vs. Los Angeles Metropolitan Transportation Authority, charging the MTA with establishing a racially discriminatory separate and unequal mass transit system in violation of the 1964 Civil Rights Act and the 14th amendment to the U.S. Constitution. The suit resulted in a precedent-setting ten-year Consent Decree, whose provisions included: the reinstatement of the unlimited use bus/rail pass and its guaranteed existence for ten years; the creation of a low-fare affordable transit system, with a $42 monthly bus pass and a first-ever $11 weekly bus pass; the first national standard to restrict overcrowding—an enforceable limit of no more than 15 people standing on a 43-seat bus by 1998 and no more than 8 people standing by 2002; a 'New Service' bus plan to combat transportation segregation in which the MTA and the Bus Riders Union will jointly develop an integrated county-wide transit plan to new centers of education, medical services, and jobs; and the establishment of the Bus Riders Union as 'class representative', i.e., as the official representative of 400,000 bus riders. And after three further years of organizing since that victory, the BRU has pushed the MTA to order more than 1,200 new Compressed Natural Gas clean-fuel buses, at a cost of more than $400 million, to phase out more than 1,200 diesel buses, and to agree to the complete conversion of the fleet to clean fuel buses by 2003, as well as hiring more than 1,000 new bus drivers and an additional 500 mechanics and maintenance workers.

In the realm of sustained mass organizing and struggle, the BRU is by far the most vital organization in the city. Since the 'No Seat No Fare' campaign the BRU has initiated an every-Thursday fare strike—Juelga de Jueves—to create low-level but constant pressure on the MTA. The BRU sends grassroots lobbyists to Sacramento and Washington D.C. to challenge MTA's budget allocations. It has invented on-the-bus masked heroine Superpasajera, and initiated the on-the-bus theatre group that carries out counterhegemonic 'actos' in transit. In a recent campaign, confronting the Latino political elite that is attempting to push through a new billion-dollar rail line in direct violation of the Consent Decree with funds that are urgently needed for bus service, the Sindicato has organized high school students, built large-scale puppets caricaturing the powerful elected officials, and taken the campaign deep into the housing projects and low-income communities that will suffer the consequences. In all of this work the BRU continues to reinvent its tactics and sustain impressive media coverage—with major features on National Public Radio, ABC World News Tonight, *Christian Science Monitor, New York Times, Washington Post,* and the influential minority media, *La Opinion, Korean Times, Rafu Shimpo, Watts Times.* A recently released feature documentary film, B*us Riders Union* by academy-award cinematographer Haskell Wexler, hopes to bring the movement and its message to 'a theatre near you'. The BRU is organizing a national tour with the film, having already had major events in New York, Atlanta, and Boston, a 600-person film showing at the L.A. Director's Guild, and now scheduled showings in Vancouver, Toronto, and Johannesburg.

Despite these achievements, the future challenges to the movement are more difficult than ever. The MTA has launched a major legal counter-attack, appealing the court orders requiring it to expand its bus fleet by 350 buses. While the BRU has been able to force the MTA to replace its existing dilapidated fleet of 2,000 buses, we cannot exert enough political or legal muscle to force them to expand the fleet, which is the biggest ticket item, and would require the suspension of every other rail project. After the federal district courts ordered the MTA to purchase the first 350 of those additional buses, the MTA counterattacked by challenging the entire legal basis of the Consent Decree. The Ninth Federal Circuit Court will hear a wide-ranging MTA appeal based on 'states' rights' theories that the federal courts do not have the authority to compel a state agency, even one that voluntarily entered into a contract with the BRU, to reallocate funds based on racial equality. At a time when the scope and enforceability of civil rights laws are being abrogated by the Supreme Court, the Labor/Community Strategy Center case becomes even more historically significant. If a government agency can enter into a legally binding Consent Decree with a grassroots organization, in this case the Strategy Center and BRU, and then go back to the federal courts to have it abrogated, then there is virtually no legal tactic in the realm of challenging racial discrimination that has the slightest chance of bringing any tangible relief.

There are times when the political landscape looks bleak and foreboding. The Strategy Center and Bus Riders Union try to carry out a dual strategy—trying to 'unite all who can be united' to create the broadest possible united front, even on a tactical level, such as all those who would benefit from a first-class bus system regardless of political philosophy and larger objectives, as well as carrying out 'independence and initiative in the united front' to make sure an independent Left voice can try to shape the larger debate. But often, after months and years of organizing, the united front still seems very narrow. Most of the organized forces in the city are so tied to either the rail juggernaut itself or the main political forces who are driving it that there is very little possibility of winning over powerful tactical allies. The establishment is playing winner take all, and punishing those who would break with them on even one issue.

In that context, the reforms won by the BRU, however impressive, need to be seen in terms of whatever significance it will have on the future form and content of working class organization. The challenge for all Leftists at this point in history is figure out how to construct independent institutions (Left organizations, trade union caucuses, black, Latino, Asian, women's organizations, that are independent of the Democratic party, the trade union bureaucracy, the civil rights establishment) and to theorize and attempt to carry out an independent working-class programme that rejects imperialism, racism, and xenophobia. The Los Angeles Strategy Center's assessment of current conditions leads it to conclude that the best form for such struggles is the creation of similar Left centers for organizing and the initiation of city- and county-wide campaigns that challenge corporate policies and the capitalist state. It used to be felt that building Left caucuses in the trade unions and moving from that base into a city-wide and national Left politics was the best allocation of resources and the most productive trajectory. But the debate about where to situate the Left is far less important now than the political goals that define our work, for the situation of one's forces, one's cadre, if such an organization even exists, is a question of tactics, whereas programme, reflected in demands, is the most concrete reflection of one's strategy and ultimate aims.

After almost 20 years of work in Los Angeles, from the demands of the GM workers to the environmental demands of low-income residents in the Strategy Center's Watchdog Project to the present work of the Bus Riders Union, the challenge of constructing and maintaining an anti-capitalist, anti-imperialist consciousness in the minds of leaders of the working class has been at the heart of how we have defined the challenge of the socialist project. With all its many limitations, and its own dilemmas in going beyond 'bus consciousness' (which is an analogy to trade union consciousness), the BRU has exhibited a surprising resiliency and an evolving world view that is taking the discussions of the struggle against national oppression and neoliberal state policies in Los Angeles into larger national and international arenas—the Democratic National Convention and the militant protests against the World Trade Organization, the World Bank and International Monetary Fund. The effort of L.A.'s bus riders to become the drivers of their own history is a work in progress. Like Haskell Wexler's film about the Bus Riders Union, there is no ending to this story, just a finite time when the narrative has to be arbitrarily 'freeze framed' while the movement and the debate continues.

PEASANT STRUGGLES AND INTERNATIONAL SOLIDARITY: THE CASE OF CHIAPAS

JUSTIN PAULSON

When the Zapatista National Liberation Army burst on to the global stage in 1994, the initial reaction was one of surprise, coming so soon after the much-touted End of History and the world-wide triumph of the market. The assumption of anachronism soon faded, however, into a kind of condescending sympathy for the Indians' plight. Liberal common sense today has the insurgency pegged as the inevitable, reactionary response of an ignorant but justifiably angry indigenous peasantry to the new global economy. The Zapatistas, in this view, simply do not realize that they have no choice but to tie on what Thomas Friedman calls the 'golden straightjacket' of neoliberalism and change with the rest of the world, come what may.[1] But while neoliberals may see the 'backlash' as something of a residual side-effect of structural adjustment predestined to be swept away, many peasant and campesino movements in this situation have demonstrated an increasingly effective ability to frame the terms of the debate such that they, too, are in favour of moving forward into a 'globalized' world—albeit of a different kind. The Zapatista struggle in particular advances the very notions of autonomy, collective action, and dignity that are denied under neoliberalism, and in doing so it demonstrates that its movement 'against the tide' is in fact progressive rather than merely one of putting on the brakes. It also conceives the scope of its movement to reach well outside Chiapas, understanding that it is fighting against the momentum of global capital as well as the national state, and fighting alongside other movements similarly disaffected or with similar goals. Thus, while—as Henry Bernstein points out elsewhere in this volume—globalization does not lead to the inevitable end of the peasantry or of peasant-based struggles, it does lead to a 'globalized' solidarity between these and other struggles against neoliberalism.

Precisely because of the enormous stakes involved, it is crucial that socialists soberly examine these struggles—and the solidarity networks built around them. Judith Adler Hellman's critique of the Zapatista solidarity movement ('Real and Virtual Chiapas: Magic Realism and the Left', *Socialist Register* 2000) was an important and insightful intervention in what will probably be a growing debate on the merits of 'cyberactivism', and of solidarity more generally, over the next several years. I agree with several of Hellman's basic points concerning technology and activism: that vicarious participation in an Internet 'community' does not substitute for real community (or real activism); that oversimplifications of the struggle will in the end hinder rather than help the movement; that there is unequal access to the Internet; and that fetishism of 'new' technology is simply the wrong way to approach the possibilities offered to us by that medium (a position I've never hesitated to express since I first brought the *¡Ya Basta!* Web-page online in 1994).

Yet, despite these points of agreement, I feel that many of Hellman's specific criticisms miss their mark. In insisting on the complexity of what is too often taken to be a simplistic struggle between good and evil, Hellman aims to show that foreign activists have, in general, been subjected to a 'flattened' version of events in Chiapas; that the appeal of Zapatismo in fact has more to do with the 'appeal of the events as seen from a great distance' than with Zapatista proposals *per se;* and that Zapatista rhetoric, particularly concerning the issues of land tenure and autonomy, is too simplistic and reductionist to match the realities of life in Chiapas. In what is intended as a friendly response to Hellman's essay, I shall attempt to show that this judgement is too harsh. An appreciation of Zapatismo, and of solidarity activists' relationship to it requires a fuller contextual setting than Hellman's essay provides. Apart from specific disagreements to be raised below, my first concern is to show that the strategies of the Ejército Zapatista de Liberación Nacional (EZLN) need to be understood in terms of the centrality to the movement of neoliberalism. Such an understanding is needed if we are to appreciate that the international support for the EZLN has actually resulted from a *real* resonance of the Zapatista struggle rather than from knee-jerk solidarity.

DIGNITY, CLASS AND NEOLIBERALISM

'Durito', the small beetle serving as the economically-astute alter-ego of Subcomandante Marcos, has made something of a name for himself by coining concise sound-bites about neoliberalism: for example, 'neoliberalism isn't in crisis—neoliberalism *is* the crisis itself'; and 'the trouble with globalization is that all the *globos* end up popped.'[2] The idea that neoliberalism is inherently unstable and ultimately self-destructive underlies most of Durito's diatribes against capitalism. The message is that the destructive force of neoliberalism hinders its own capacity for reproduction on a global scale, while simultaneously engendering a global explosion of discontent—and this discontent can quickly become resistance.

Judy Hellman alludes to the fact that Zapatismo exists against the backdrop of neoliberalism; she suggests that the preconditions for the struggle were in fact provided by 'rapid penetration of capitalist relations' merging with existing oligarchies and racism to stimulate 'a new militancy and consciousness' in Chiapas. Yet, perhaps too wary of 'reductionist' analyses which frame Zapatismo around narrow economic considerations and 'neoliberal predations', she underestimates the *centrality* of neoliberalism to Zapatista aims and discourse, and thus the importance it attaches to building networks of resistance against neoliberalism. As Henry Veltmeyer et al. have put it, it is 'the extension of capitalism toward all parts of Mexico, through privatization, deregulation and the "free market" that has provoked the rebellion.'[3] Indeed, Chiapas offers a window on any 'forgotten' or 'inconsequential' region in which resources (the resources, of course, are not forgotten) are exploited for consumption by both a domestic elite and the 'information societies' of the First World, while entire populations are rendered *surplus* in numbers far beyond the reserves historically necessary to keep capitalism's gears greased through its various cycles and surges.

Ana Esther Ceceña and Andrés Barreda have even called Chiapas 'an illustration of the contradictions of capitalism', suggesting that one can, in that state, 'catch a glimpse of the redefinition of hegemonies, geo-economic integration, and the rebuilding of a world-wide proletarian army.'[4] When 'proletarian' is understood to mean not simply one whose labour-power is immediately exploited for the extraction of surplus-value, but anyone whose existence is in an antagonistic relationship with capitalism, this is not a far-fetched idea. As the ranks of the dispossessed, the unemployed and the redundant grow more numerous globally, the conditions are created in which a rural state in southern Mexico that seemed inconsequential to most observers before 1994 comes to give the lie to the bourgeois promise of a 'levelling up' via the world market. Ceceña rightly notes of Chiapas:

> What is indisputable is that in the collective imaginary, neoliberalism, if only intuitively, begins to be perceived as a mode of social organization that transcends the strictly economic and which determines and causes the deterioration of the many aspects that make up our daily lives. And to this recognition of the omnipresence of neoliberalism are added the evidence of diverse forms of violence that are essential to it: the violence of unemployment, of impunity, of racism, of competition.[5]

The Zapatista notion of dignity perhaps provides the best framework for understanding the significance of Zapatismo for the contemporary Left, and this also helps explain its mass popularity. 'Dignidad' for Zapatismo is quite different from the concept of dignity many North American and European scholars are used to; as John Holloway has recently shown, the fight is not for a 'dignity-based society' with all citizens' civil rights enshrined in a liberal constitution (with economic and cultural rights largely ignored); nor can it be directly equated with the struggles of identity-based 'new social movements'. Rather, dignity is a radical, open-ended class category that is the subject of the Zapatistas' struggle against neoliberal capitalism, at a time when the latter threatens to become a totalizing social order—and at a time when the old industrial proletariat and its parties are not leading the fight. In explaining the differences between the Zapatista concept of dignity and the imperfectly defined traditional revolutionary subject (the narrowly-defined 'proletariat'), Holloway notes that the way the Zapatistas speak of 'dignity' is not only more inclusive, but involves an understanding of capitalism 'not based on the antagonism between two groups of people but on the antagonism in the way in which human social practice is organized.' And this antagonism is by no means limited to Chiapas; rather, it is the foundation for contemporary class struggle on a global scale. On this basis, let me now turn to my disagreements with Hellman's account of specific aspects of Zapatista strategy before turning to her critique of the 'cyberactivism' of the international solidarity activists.

THE LAND QUESTION

In Chiapas, the 'surplus' populations aren't merely put out of work (or, more precisely, idled by structural adjustment policies and international treaties that ensure their corn won't sell), but many are also physically displaced—some to be driven into more 'efficient' industries (such as *maquiladoras*) as the neoliberal model requires, others to be simply driven from one place to another. As such, land tenure, as Hellman points out, has been an important rallying cry for the movement. Of course, land has been a central concern of every Mayan uprising since the 'Conquest',[7] and the class dimension was always present as the crux of the issue (despite various religious or ideological overtones).[8] Adolfo Gilly put this concisely, explaining that 'la *ley de la tierra*' has historically counterposed itself to and resisted 'la *ley del dinero*':

> Such rebellions ... beneath their many forms, reveal a common basis that is often ignored by their own protagonists: the resistance to accept that the land can be converted into merchandise; the refusal to send to the world of market exchanges between things that which, within the community, is the cultural and historical substrate of the direct exchanges between people; and opposition to the external world interfering in the order of such exchanges, which are understood as part of the natural order.[9]

Recognizing the importance of 'the land' does not mean that we concur with presenting those who have joined the rebellions as 'country people who did not want to move and therefore got into a revolution'—as the opening line of John Womack, Jr's classic work on Zapata puts it.[10] This implies a static history of settlement that doesn't match up with the more complex reality. The history of South-east Mexico, for the past half-millennium, has been one of constant movement, upheaval, and displacement. Carlos Montemayor notes that 'the concentration of land in Chiapas ... is a permanent source of social imbalance',[11] and it is this imbalance that created the early conditions for Zapatismo.

Hellman, however, takes the view that the 'agrarista dream' of large-scale land redistribution cannot be realized in the regions of Zapatista influence in Chiapas, because 'there is almost no "distributable" land left in large haciendas.'[12] She notes the accelerated breakup of the regions' *latifundios* beginning in the 1950s, citing in particular agrarian reform programmes that set aside small *ejido* distributions, as well as a larger programme in the 1980s that set aside 80,000 hectares of land for 159 communities. But the lack of substantial *latifundios* in eastern Chiapas is not sufficient reason to conclude that there is no redistributable land at all left in the area—unless one is to confuse *legal* redistribution with *possible* redistribution. Left out of Hellman's description of the 1980s was the signing of 7,646 'certificates of inaffectability' (i.e., non-distributability) in Chiapas during those years; these certificates protected *1,142,881* hectares of quality agricultural land across Chiapas—far more than the 80,000 redistributed in the eastern region—from legal expropriation, thus ensuring the land would remain permanently in the hands of the ranchers, *caciques*, and private landowners.[13] The land may not have been tied up in a small number of large *latifundios*, but neither was it made available to the campesinos. By contrast, the 80,000 redistributed hectares was a beneficial gesture toward the 159 affected communities—but not a realization of all that could be done, and certainly not a solution to the problem of land concentration.

Also important to keep in mind are the specific historical roots of the land disputes in the South-eastern jungle region, since many of the present conflicts there, as Hellman notes, date from 'colonization schemes' instituted under the administration of President Echeverría in the early 1970s. Yet perhaps the most pertinent of these schemes was neglected by Hellman: a 1972 decision by President Echeverría to grant 660,000 hectares of the jungle to just 66 families of the Lacandón Maya, an act which on paper displaced more than 3,000 Chol and Tzeltal families who had migrated to the region since the 1950s. As Neil Harvey explains: 'Behind the decree was an agreement between the representatives of the Lacandon Indians and the state-owned forestry company (COFOLASA), which allowed for the latter to exploit 35,000 cubic metres of mahogany and cedar for a period of ten years.'[14] The first independent, radical campesino organizations in southeast Chiapas—several of which later merged into the EZLN—were created as a direct response to this government decree, in an attempt to prevent the forced expulsion of the affected families. Since that time, the struggle for land in eastern Chiapas has been about both *expropriating* land from large landholders and *keeping* the land of indigenous and campesino communities in their own hands in the face of encroachment by loggers and ranchers.

By 1992, the Mexican Constitution's Article 27, the revolutionary clause guaranteeing land to peasants who were willing to work it, had been reformed beyond recognition, and available legal avenues for securing small parcels of land were sharply curtailed not just in Chiapas, but across the country. Much of the land was, and still is, in government possession (such as the Montes Azules bioreserve) or private holdings of various sizes; but effective expropriation would, after 1992, have to take extra-legal means. The EZLN saw its ranks surge after the constitutional reforms, and the EZLN's own Revolutionary Agrarian Law, established at the end of 1993, declared expropriatable any private (non-collective) holdings of more than 100 hectares of poor-quality land, or 50 hectares of good-quality land.[15] While there may not be many large *latifundios* to break up in the jungle region, many private landowners did find their holdings (of various sizes) taken by the Zapatistas at the beginning of the war, and many other private and government holdings remain outside the areas of direct Zapatista control. The '*agrarista* dream' in question is not a naïve one of redistributing non-existent large estates; it is about securing the concentration of land in communal *ejidos* and co-operatives rather than in private holdings, and establishing permanent collective *rights* to land and to the means of agricultural production.[16] This goal is a realistic one, not to be dismissed simply because the *Porfirista* estates have become scarcer.

THE INDIGENOUS QUESTION

Hellman also argues that the 'indigenous question' is more complicated than foreign supporters of the Zapatistas realize. Her interviews show there are critics in Mexico who claim autonomy is 'not the answer', and one of them even rhetorically suggests that those supporting the Accords of San Andrés Sakamch'en de los Pobres might actually be employing essentialized notions of 'el indio', or that they might believe gambling casinos (*à la* indigenous 'autonomy' in the United States) will solve the problems in Chiapas. While some such people may exist, this critique once again seems misplaced.

While explicitly a 'fundamental' demand, indigenous autonomy is not, and never was, *the* singular goal of the Zapatista movement, nor of the indigenous movement (spearheaded by the National Indigenous Congress) in which the EZLN plays a significant role. The San Andrés Accords marked the completion of the *first* stage of the peace talks, which were divided into four thematic areas with the 'easiest' ('Indigenous Rights and Culture') taking place first; the other sessions were to be 'Democracy and Justice' (begun but halted after a short time due to non-implementation of the indigenous rights agreement), 'Social Welfare and Development', and 'Rights of Indigenous Women'. Reading Hellman, one could come away with the mistaken impression that the Zapatistas and their supporters are simply fighting for a weak form of autonomy, and that the struggle would be over if only the San Andrés Accords—or even some watered-down version of them (or worse, the reservation system that Hellman seems to think is on the table)—were fulfilled.

The desire for autonomy from (and subsequent coexistence with) the state is not a recent quest among the indigenous people of the Americas.[17] The Zapatistas certainly didn't begin the debate in Chiapas, where it has been a longstanding demand among many of the Maya but never granted.[18] Ceceña and Barreda argue that a new relationship of autonomy is such a pertinent issue today because what is '*also involved is the capacity of the population to rebel against the capitalist depredation of human beings and to open the way for liberating alternatives.*'[19] Therefore, they assert, the issue is not merely one of land *per se,* but of 'territoriality and sovereignty'. If the state cannot provide alternatives, the demand must then be for the *space* to create those alternatives; if without state support, then at least without interference as well.

The negotiations on indigenous autonomy leading to the San Andrés Accords were not straightforward and uncomplicated, and the meaning of autonomy was the subject of much detailed public debate throughout 1995 and 1996. The EZLN sought the advice of a great many intellectuals, activists, and community leaders in staking out a position on autonomy; and the negotiated agreements, in which these representatives of civil society were able to take part at the negotiating table itself, reflect the attention paid to such voices. As may be seen by reading the Accords in detail (all the pertinent documents are readily available online), both sides agreed that the most effective way to guarantee respect for indigenous rights and culture was through autonomy, and the document explicitly states that, as part of the 'new relationship between the indigenous people, the state, and the rest of society',[20] national and state legislation (including the federal constitution) should 'recognize the indigenous people as subject to the right to self-determination and autonomy'.[21] Such autonomy would involve, among other things, considerations of territory (though not as separate 'states within a state'), an increased voice for indigenous communities in local economic development and in the use of natural resources found on their lands, and the use of traditional means of election and representation for participation in state and national political bodies (e.g., voting by community assembly rather than by secret ballot). Additional constitutional changes were to include remunicipalization, indigenous education that is bilingual and intercultural, guarantees of fair access to both the judicial system and means of communication, and rights to the use and promotion of language and culture. (Neither casinos nor Reservations were part of the equation.) The fact that many of the documents are framed in very general terms, and serve as statements of intention, reflects the recognition that there are many different groups of indigenous people with varying interests, needs, and desires; the Accords suggest that the concrete manifestations of autonomy need to be defined at a local level.

The EZLN accepted the Accords with several reservations; the government accepted them as written. Vigorous discussions continued, and the Accords' promise of bringing these issues to the forefront of national debate was achieved, with an emphasis on *how* to implement the autonomy agreements, not whether or not to do so. But the government stopped short of making the promised constitutional and legislative changes. The EZLN suspended peace talks in frustration in September 1996, but it certainly wasn't a lone voice crying for autonomy. The broad-based National Indigenous Congress, whose constituent members played an important role in creating the agreements to begin with, wholly endorsed them and demanded at the time an 'immediate and complete compliance with the Accords'.[22] Despite the EZLN's effective participation in further multi-partisan discussions and proposals that same fall, President Zedillo changed his mind and rejected the San Andrés Accords themselves, preferring to wage a public relations campaign against the very concept of autonomy.

In short, indigenous autonomy, and particularly the San Andrés version of it, has become such an important issue not because anybody believes it would solve all the problems of the indigenous people of Mexico, but because the future of negotiations rests on the implementation of what was signed at San Andrés Sakamch'en de los Pobres. Those agreements constitute one step in the right direction, and they *must* be implemented. If this were to happen, it might clear the way for a resumption of the peace talks. However, if implementation continues to be stalled, with calls for 'more debate' or renegotiation, the future of Chiapas will be a dark one. The Mexican government has been trying to renegotiate the accords from square one and desperately wants people to forget that the earlier meetings at San Andrés ever happened. Such rewriting of history is an important element of the struggle Subcomandante Marcos has characterized as 'between the forgetting of those above and the memory of those below'.[23] The EZLN does not have a simplistic view of autonomy; if its supporters seem to, it's because autonomy has *already* been debated, negotiated, and an agreement signed. If as foreigners we now choose to argue against those agreements, *that* would be a far more interventionist stance than militating for the implementation of what was already agreed upon.

VIRTUAL ZAPATISMO?

Let us now turn to the question of 'foreign activists'. One of the most troubling aspects of Hellman's analysis is that, in her critiques of foreign Zapatista activists for their tendency to oversimplification, she levels her criticism at broad, unspecified categories of people and media. 'Virtual Chiapas' and 'the Internet' themselves have little descriptive meaning (and even less explanatory or analytical capacity); and Hellman lumps together activists, 'Internet junkies', Web-pages, archives, organizations and mailing lists to the point of effacing their differences and assigning all of them the worst characteristics of a few (about whom the criticisms may certainly be justified). At one point Hellman even slips into giving the Internet itself agency ('the Internet does make constant generic reference ...')[24]—which is precisely what those of us working through that medium but arguing against fetishization are determined not to do.

The Internet is a *medium* that enables a fairly disparate set of transmissory and receptive activities to take place; to take all Zapatista-support activities on the Internet and lump them together for critique is akin to making claims against 'the press' when one's real concern is with particular instances of yellow journalism. At one point Hellman locates the problem of partiality and bias in the news distributed outside Chiapas—in 'the way that material is selected and distributed and edited for Internet distribution'—claiming that 'most of what we read about Chiapas, and civil society in general in Mexico, has been selected and transmitted by Harry Cleaver or a couple of other people';[25] and yet there are literally scores of Web-pages, dozens of mailing lists and archives—not to mention dozens of 'mainstream press' sources that now report regularly from Chiapas and are available online—that spread information over the Internet. Every one of these has different standards for distribution of information, fact checking, and so on. While Cleaver has probably done more than any single other person to promote the Internet as a medium for activists, he is not responsible for what the Zapatistas say, what *La Jornada* prints, what Reuters reports, or what I put online; there isn't one person (Cleaver or anybody else) who oversees what gets printed on each Web-page or what information gets spread around and what doesn't get 'selected or distributed'.

Hellman states that 'careful examination of the material that is translated, summarized and distributed through a variety of networks reveals that almost all of this material is drawn from the Mexican leftist daily, *La Jornada*, which is published in Mexico City.'[26] This is misleading in that it greatly overplays the influence of *La Jornada*, and it is unfortunate that I was in fact cited to bolster such a claim in Hellman's article. I stated to Lynn Stephen and others, and I have written on the *¡Ya Basta!* Web-page, that many EZLN communiqués that I distribute are first faxed to *La Jornada* and converted to hypertext for their Web-page, after which I collect them and put them online on *¡Ya Basta!*; historically, most communiqués sent out on the electronic e-mail lists and those that show up on other Web-pages have also been gleaned from the pages of *La Jornada*. But the context of my statements was an attempt to debunk myths about 'cyberguerillas' with cellular modems in the Lacandon Jungle—not to assert that any relevant information comes only from *La Jornada*. It is true that activists have relied extensively (although rarely exclusively) on *La Jornada* as a regular news source, but even this is less true now than it was several years ago; the Frente Zapatista (FZLN), Enlace Civil, and the Congreso Nacional Indígena (among many others)[27] are all 'Internet-savvy' and have been taking an increasing role in rapid electronic distribution of communiqués, action alerts, and so on—and each of these has at least as great a role to play in the struggle (and usually a far more proactive one) as *La Jornada*.

But Hellman's critique of *La Jornada* goes further. She also quotes a Chiapanecan activist as saying 'they [*La Jornada*] report things in a very partial way', and asserts that the paper takes a consistent stance on the left somewhat critical of the Democratic Revolutionary Party (PRD), and that this leads to a simplistic, pro-Zapatista bias.[28] Yet, editorially, *La Jornada* remains very close to the PRD, and has never wavered in its *perredista* leanings. The Founding Director, Carlos Payán, is now a PRD Senator, and when Carmen Lira took over the reins *La Jornada* swung even further toward support of the PRD, not away from it. The newspaper developed a reputation for printing news from Chiapas because it was one of the only 'independent' newspapers with a national circulation, and the only one that was willing to routinely cover events pertaining to the uprising. (It was also the first Mexican newspaper to achieve free international distribution on the Internet, making it a very popular source of information among both Mexicans living abroad and sympathizers of the EZLN.) While it is true that many of *Jornada's* articles and editorials have tended to express sympathies for Zapatismo in general, the paper has nevertheless maintained a consistent opposition to armed struggle in Chiapas (which the EZLN has, of course, never renounced). In short, *La Jornada* is a much more complex paper than Hellman portrays it to be.

Hellman's discussion of the role of *La Jornada* leads her into a discussion of the media coverage surrounding the 1995 elections in Chiapas, which she claims was biased toward the EZLN boycott and perhaps contributed to the 66% abstention rate in that state. In the eyes of the left-wing PRD, a large portion of those 66% would likely have voted for the PRD had they not abstained, and so the party was (understandably) quite distressed that they did. After offering a critique of the Zapatistas' anti-electoral strategy, Hellman recommends that 'foreign activists concerned with the future of Chiapas would at least want to think through and debate these assertions' from the PRD's point of view.[29] Two critiques are actually at work here: a critique of foreign activists who supported the boycott, and the critique of the Zapatista boycott itself, which I believe to be the fundamental issue.[30]

While admitting it may be 'easy to understand the EZLN's decision,' Hellman nonetheless chooses to argue against it, perhaps as devil's advocate. Fair enough. Yet, the Zapatistas made a political decision not to support the electoral process due both to the state of siege in which its communities were living, and, just as importantly, the fact that none of the parties campaigning in Chiapas adequately represented its interests. Why ought the EZLN to subordinate itself to the PRD and help legitimate an election process that it doesn't trust, or, worse, support a party that simply has quite different goals? Before the similarly-boycotted elections of 1997, the EZLN declared: 'It is easy to see that the PRD's proposal to "smooth away the sharpest spines of neoliberalism" will run into a hedgehog whose embrace wounds and kills.'[31] This is not exactly a ringing endorsement of the party, and it reflects the fact that there are very substantive *political* differences between the EZLN and the PRD. Hellman also quotes from a single Chiapanecan PRD activist, who asserts that the PRD 'would have been able to form a majority in the Chamber of Deputies.'[32] But this rests on the assumption that the election *would* have been fair and that the results would have been accepted. Hellman herself makes clear the problem that fraud has historically posed in Chiapanecan elections, and there was little reason to believe things would have been any different this time.

In a communiqué issued shortly before the 1997 elections, the EZLN provided an explanation of the Zapatista abstention from elections in general:

> In electoral moments or outside of them, our political position is and has been clear. It is not in favour of any political party, but neither is it against them; it is not electoral, but neither is it anti-electoral. It is against the State-party system, it is against presidentialism, it is for democracy, liberty and justice, it is of the left, it is inclusive, and it is anti-neoliberal.[33]

The crux of the issue here is that 'democracy' means something quite different for the EZLN than it does for the parties. As far as the EZLN is concerned, liberal-democratic electoral politics (with or without blatant fraud) have no necessary connection to *democracy*, which Zapatismo equates with the principle of *'mandar obediciendo'*, the horizontal exercise of power among the population itself. The EZLN is an armed revolutionary movement; the parties are not. The fact that both the EZLN and the PRD are 'of the Left' should not lead us to think in terms of the PRD—*even if* the particularities of its platform were more palatable—being *owed* EZLN electoral support in a process that in many respects is irrelevant to Zapatismo.

INTERNATIONAL ACTIVISM

At stake in the debate over international activism are not only questions of how much (and what kind) of information one needs or is obligated to ingest before taking a stand and acting on a particular issue, but also broad issues of what constitutes legitimate struggle and who one is fighting for in a movement of 'solidarity'. These are fair issues to bring up; yet one should also be wary of the trend toward paralysis and inaction that comes with not acting unless one is 'fully informed' of all the complexities of an issue (an impossible, if desirable, task).

Nor should one accept the view that those who do act in solidarity thereby reflect a preference for embracing revolution elsewhere rather than struggling at home, as Hellman suggests in the introduction of her essay. Indeed, the global character of neoliberalism, and the fact that Zapatistas stress this, helps explain why people can feel that they're struggling *both* in solidarity *and* at home by supporting the EZLN. The Zapatistas know full well, as do most of their supporters, that the struggle isn't just about Chiapas or Mexico; they know that whether they stand or fall will depend on events around the world, just as what happens in Mexico can have a profound effect on the spread or collapse of neoliberalism as a global strategy. Is there any significant meaning to a 'struggle at home' when neoliberalism has placed internationalism back on the agenda, both for capitalism and those opposed to it (if they hope to have any effect)?

I won't argue that there aren't any foreign activists trying to 'revolt vicariously' through the Zapatistas; but for many EZLN supporters abroad, the Zapatistas' appeal to dignity strikes a chord that resonates well with their own experiences of the global economy. When Subcomandante Marcos speaks of different oppressions (for which he lays much of the blame on capitalism), he speaks to the material, lived experiences of a great many people throughout the world today, and it should come as no surprise then that the EZLN has become so popular internationally. It is not unusual, in Zapatista pronouncements, to see such statements as:

> In our voice shall travel the voice of others, of those who have nothing, those condemned to silence and ignorance, those thrown off their land and from history by the arrogance of the powerful, of all those good men and women who walk these lands of pain and anger, of the children and

aged dead of abandonment and solitude, of humiliated women, of little men. Through our voice will speak the dead, our dead, so alone and forgotten, so dead and yet so alive in our voices and in our footsteps.[34]

Is this some kind of megalomania? Or, rather, can the Zapatistas really be so inclusive in their discourse and their activities that they might awaken these others' own dreams and struggles? If so, when the latter do become active, if they claim to be supporting Zapatismo, are they *avoiding* the 'struggle at home' in favour of solidarity with an indigenous uprising in Chiapas? Or have they perhaps come to the recognition that *it is part of the same struggle*? While the EZLN does have a great number of 'local' concerns, it takes great pains to not limit itself to those, nor to concerns based solely on an indigenous identity; and though the EZLN *is* indigenous, it strives to show that its struggle is *not just* an indigenous struggle.

Hellman's conclusion, suggesting that we need to be as informed as we can be about Chiapas because 'to do otherwise compromises the crucial role that foreigners can play in protecting the human rights of people at risk',[35] is a good point—but a limited one. The struggle, for Hellman, seems to be restricted to Chiapas; 'they' are struggling, 'we' are supporting. This is part of the truth, and intuitive or casual support for the Zapatistas would only hinder a movement operating from such a perspective. But what the EZLN has tried desperately to make clear over the past several years is that its battle is only one of the many being waged in the larger struggle for dignity, against capitalism; with this in mind, activists who have an intuitive sympathy for Zapatismo because of their own experiences or political leanings can be perfectly justified in their support for the Zapatistas—even if they've only seen a couple of Web-pages and a brief TV news story. When someone claims to be pro-Zapatista in Canada, France, Japan, or South Africa , he or she is not abandoning local politics, nor even— necessarily—flattening the image of a 'true' Chiapas, but rather is taking a side in (to use the EZLN's term) World War IV: a war not between the EZLN and the Mexican government, but between neoliberalism and a dignified existence. It is *this* war that needs support and struggle from all sectors, and if the international Zapatista movement is to be faulted it should be, more than anything else, on the basis of a failure to recognize the strategic implications of the unity of the struggle at home and the struggle in Chiapas, sometimes imagining that the world-wide anti-neoliberal army is going to march out of *Chiapas* rather than—more effectively—marching out of every corner at once.

It may well be that the ability of Zapatismo to stir up support around the world has less to do with oversimplification of the message, and much more to do with the vitality and resonance of the message itself. As the 'global proletariat' shows an enduring but changing face in the twenty-first century, so the old leftist tropes of solidarity and internationalism take on new significance. The networks we have built are far from perfect, but they have nonetheless demonstrated—so far—a capacity to endure and evolve within the struggle.

NOTES

I would like to thank Barbara Epstein and Joshua Paulson for commenting on early drafts of this paper.

1. Cf. Thomas Friedman, *The Lexus and the Olive Tree: Understanding Globalization*, New York: Farrar, Straus & Giroux, 1999.
2. This is a play on words; 'globo' serves as both the root of 'globalización' and the word for a party balloon.
3. Henry Veltmeyer, James Petras, and Steven Vieux, *Neoliberalism and Class Conflict in Latin America*, New York: St. Martin's Press, 1997, p. 201.
4. Ana Esther Ceceña and Andrés Barreda, 'Chiapas and the Global Restructuring of Capital', in John Holloway and Eloina Peláez, eds., *Zapatista! Reinventing Revolution in Mexico*, London: Pluto Press, 1998, p. 39.
5. Ana Esther Ceceña, 'Neoliberalismo e insubordinación', *Chiapas*, 4, 1997, p. 34. (Translation mine.)
6. John Holloway, 'Dignity's Revolt' in Holloway and Peláez, 'Zapatista!', p. 183.
7. In fact, no group in Chiapas was ever 'conquered' with any sense of finality: the best study is probably Antonio García de León, *Resistencia y Utopía. Memorial de agravios y cronica de revueltas y profecias acaecidas en la provincia de Chiapas durante lo ultimos quinientos años de su historia*, Mexico, D.F.: Era, 1985, 2 vols.
8. See esp. Carlos Montemayor, *Chiapas: la rebellion idigena de Mexico*, Mexico, D.F.: Joaquin Mortiz, 1997, p. 72.
9. Adolfo Gilly, *Chiapas: la razón ardiente*, México, D.F.: Era, 1997, p. 19. (Translation mine.)
10. John Womack, Jr, *Zapata and the Mexican Revolution*, New York: Vintage, 1968, p. ix. See also Enrique Rajchenberg and Catherine Héau-Lambert, 'History and Symbolism in the Zapatista Movement', in Holloway and Peláez, 'Zapatista!', pp. 30–31, for a more in-depth critique of this statement.
11. Montemayor, 'Chiapas', p. 40. (Translation mine.)
12. Judith Adler Hellman, 'Real and Virtual Chiapas: Magic Realism and the Left', *Socialist Register 2000*, p. 167.
13. Montemayor, 'Chiapas', p. 101; Gilly, 'Chiapas', p. 58. See also Neil Harvey, 'Peasant Strategies and Corporatism in Chiapas' in Joe Foweraker and Ann Craig, eds., *Popular Movements and Political Change in Mexico*, Boulder: Lynn Rienner Publishers, 1990, p. 191.
14. Neil Harvey, *The Chiapas Rebellion: The Struggle for Land and Democracy*, Durham: Duke University Press, 1998, p. 80.
15. EZLN, *El Despertador Mexicano: Organo Informativo del EZLN*, 1 (December) 1993, p. 14. (Some copies of the *Despertador Mexicano* indicate the maximum allowable holdings to be 50 hectares and 25 hectares, respectively.)
16. *El Despertador Mexicano*, pp. 14–16.
17. See Hector Díaz-Polenco, *Indigenous Peoples in Latin America: The Quest for Self-Determination*, Boulder: Westview Press, 1997. Also cf. Gilly, 'Chiapas', p. 27.
18. It is worth noting in this respect that the EZLN has learned enough from history not to wait for autonomy to be granted from above; rather it has taken the initiative to create several dozen autonomous regions of its own after the government backed away from the San Andres agreements. The status of these municipalities is bitterly contested, and both the army and right-wing paramilitary groups have been involved in violent (sometimes fatal) attempts to dismantle them over the past

two years.

19. Ceceña and Barreda, 'Chiapas and the Global Restructuring', pp. 57–8 (italics mine).

20. Acuerdo de San Andrés. 'Documento 1: Pronunciamiento Conjunto que el Gobierno Federal y el EZLN enviarán a las Instancias de Debate y Decisión Nacional', 16 January 1996. Online: http://spin.com.mx/~floresu/FZLN/dialogo/documento1.htm. (Translation mine).

21. Acuerdo de San Andrés. 'Documento 3.1: Compromisos para Chiapas del Gobierno del Estado y Federal y el EZLN', 16 February 1996. Online: http://spin.com.mx/~floresu/FZLN/dialogo/documento3.htm. (Translation mine.)

22. Congreso Nacional Indígena, 'Resolutivos del Congreso Nacional Indígena', 8–11 October 1996. Online: http://www.laneta.apc.org/cni/d-961011.htm.

23. EZLN, 'La Mesa de San Andrés: Entre los Olvidos de Arriba y la Memoria de Abajo', 27 February 1998. Online: http://www.ezln.org/archive/ezln980227.html

24. Hellman, 'Real and Virtual Chiapas', p. 169.

25. Ibid., p. 177.

26. Ibid., p. 174.

27. Despite Hellman's assertion to the contrary (and her valid point that access to communication media remains uneven notwithstanding), even the EPR has at least two affiliated Web-pages, and it has also been sending its communiqués via a dedicated e-mail list for over a year now. Unlike those of the EZLN, I've also seen Web-page and e-mail addresses on the EPR's communiqués themselves, casting doubt on Hellman's conclusion that 'as a consequence [of having neither an articulate spokesperson nor a Webmaster], their perspectives are not before us on our screens, and their activities are rarely reported' (Hellman, 'Real and Virtual Chiapas', p. 177). In this case, Hellman may have—inadvertently—assigned more power to the Internet medium than was warranted, given that the mass international popularity of the EZLN, far beyond that of the EPR, must be attributed to something other than whether or not they have an affiliated webpage.

28. Hellman, 'Real and Virtual Chiapas', p. 175.

29. Ibid., p. 176.

30. With regard to the foreign activists' attitude toward the Zapatista boycotts, in fact there was discussion among them about the strategy regarding the elections (I particularly recall those of 1997)—although most people involved in such discussions, as I remember them, preferred to defer to those living in Chiapas as to what attitude those most affected should take toward the political system there. I generally agree with this; although no policy ought to be supported with a knee-jerk response, there's nonetheless no compelling reason that foreign activists should be telling the Zapatistas who they can and cannot trust.

31. EZLN, communiqué, 1 July 1997. Online: http://www.ezln.org/archive/ezln970701-eng.html.

32. Hellman, 'Real and Virtual Chiapas', p. 176.

33. EZLN, communiqué, 1 July 1997.

34. English translation from Carlos Monsiváis, Mexican Postcards, New York: Verso, 1997, p. 146.

35. Hellman, 'Real and Virtual Chiapas', p. 181.

VIRTUAL CHIAPAS:
A REPLY TO PAULSON

JUDITH ADLER HELLMAN

O n reading Justin Paulson's thoughtful critique of my article I am struck by how much of what he says reinforces the case I have made. To be sure, the first section of the essay doesn't address my work at all, but rather offers Paulson's own interpretation of the nature of globalization, neoliberalism and the Zapatista response. But once he turns to my ideas, Paulson argues that I am mistaken in my assertion that the agrarista dream cannot be realized in the conflict zone in Eastern Chiapas because the situation is not a simple case of poor landless peasants facing off against traditional large landowners, i.e. haciendados. Yet the material he offers to refute my view, the aspects of agrarian history he says I neglected to detail, in fact provide further evidence for my reading of the situation which is that it is very complex, often pits one group of indigenous people against another, and frequently degenerates into a 'war of the poor' against one another.

Indeed, the particular case that he emphasizes, the displacement of 3,000 indigenous families of Chol and Tzetal settlers by a 1972 federal decree that reserved the land for the aboriginal people of the selva, the Lancandon Indians, is an excellent example of what I have argued. I assert that there is a problem with taking an essentialized view of Chiapanecan Indians in which all indigenous people are posed as living in harmony with nature and one another and that problems only arise with the intrusion of the 'bad guys', variously understood as the dominant society, neoliberal policy makers, the Mexican state, the Mexican military, the Chiapanecan state, the Chiapanecan bourgeoisie, public and private lumber companies, the landlords and their henchmen and so forth. In reality, much of the conflict in Chiapas plays out as territorial and religious disputes within and between indigenous communities and between indigenous and poor mestizo peasant communities. If we don't understand these deep-seated conflicts and how they are reinforced and exploited by the array of outsiders listed above, then it becomes impossible to see any way out of the stalemate in Chiapas. Moreover, I stick by my assertion that there is nothing progressive about the seizure of the private land holdings that are minifundia (i.e., sub-family farms) or family farms—i.e., land sufficient to employ and sustain a single family—and that minifundismo and family farms constitute the forms of land tenure that predominate through almost all of the disputed area.

Moving on in his critique from the Land to the Indigenous Question, Paulson insists that 'indigenous autonomy is not, and never was, the singular goal of the Zapatista movement.' I have to point out that nowhere in my writings do I claim it was. Rather, I discuss the difference of opinion among progressive people working in Chiapas (Mexicans and foreigners, and above all, feminists) on whether gaining greater autonomy would represent a step forward for indigenous people. I, myself, do not know whether it would be, and it was neither out of coyness nor lack of conviction that I did not take a position on the issue in my article—let alone assert, as Paulson has me saying, that foreigners should take a stand against autonomy! Rather I offered the debate—or, more to the point—the lack of debate on the left as an example of the 'flattening' of information which has the effect of silencing diverse progressive opinion. This is particularly true with respect to some feminist opinion which argues that greater autonomy would not necessarily improve the condition of indigenous people in Chiapas and, in particular, would not improve women's condition.

Moreover, while Paulson expresses the fear that readers would 'come away [from my article] with the mistaken impression that the Zapatistas and their supporters are simply fighting for a weak form of autonomy', I never suggest anything of the kind. Rather, I pose the entire discussion of the autonomy issue as one example of the lack of full information available electronically. If, for example, one goes to Paulson's website, one finds more of what he has written here on the push for autonomy, the San Andrés accords, and the EZLN communiqués on the subject. One would never guess from a visit to that site that there are progressive people in Mexico—both indigenous and non-indige-nous—who think that autonomy could turn out to be a dead end.

Alas, these are not the only words that Paulson puts in my mouth. Paulson has me claiming that the EZLN should subordinate itself to the PRD. Nowhere do I say this. Indeed I wouldn't think of sitting in Toronto and recommending anything to the EZLN. The whole idea is preposterous and comes out of a concept of distance politics in which I do not believe nor engage. Moreover, like almost any reader of *Socialist Register* who has closely followed the development of the PRD since the late 1980s, I harbour all the same doubts that socialists within the PRD do about the capacity of that party to offer a left alternative in Mexico.

Rather, what I argue is that the PRD is an important actor on the left and that it would have been nice if those who rely on the Internet to stay informed about the situation in Chiapas had had available to them the arguments of people like Gilberto Gómez Maza who is not, as Paulson describes him, simply 'a single Chiapanecan PRD activist', but as I make clear, head of the PRD in the state of Chiapas. Moreover, he is someone who, in my view, has a legitimate claim on our attention as a consequence of his thirty years of political activism on the left and decades of work as the only paediatrician serving the indigenous people in Los Altos. If Paulson doesn't agree with my notion that 'foreign activists concerned with the future of Chiapas would at least want to think through and debate [Gómez Maza's] assertions' regarding the viability of the electoral option in Chiapas, he might choose not to join me in this activity. But it is quite another thing to claim that I am sitting around telling the Zapatistas what to do, or uncritically embracing the PRD's positions, let alone suggesting that everyone should engage in this discussion 'from the PRD's point of view'!

Indeed, the caricature that Paulson draws of someone like me who believes that there could be multiple and diverse points of view on the left regarding events in Chiapas or the efficacy of the electoral road says more than any picture I could sketch of the one-dimensional nature of the perspectives provided on websites like his.

Ironically, on 19 June 2000, just two weeks before the elections that ended the PRI's stranglehold on political power in Mexico, Marcos issued a new communiqué in which he observed that 'while the political left is broader than Cardenism and the PRD,...we believe that for millions of people elections represent a dignified and respectable space for struggle.' Thus the EZLN called for 'respect for this form of civil and peaceful struggle' and endorsed the participation of their own people in the process in any way they might choose. Sadly, the fact that the EZLN's articulation of a new, more tolerant position on voting and its dissemination by Chiapas web masters came only days before the elections had unfortunate consequences. When compared with the 1994 presidential contest, a striking aspect of the July 2000 election was the precipitous decline in the number of foreigners who registered to work as observers and the very modest presence of leftists among them. While foreigner poll watchers recruited by the PRI were thick on the ground, many on the left were caught flat-footed because the new EZLN position came too late for foreign Zapatistas to apply for observers' visas in time to travel to Mexico to witness or discourage electoral fraud.

Finally, readers of *Socialist Register 2000* can confirm for themselves that in the introduction to the article I ask—polemically, to be sure —if attachment to the Zapatista cause represents 'involvement with people's struggles elsewhere in place of participation and personal investment in the struggle at home' (p. 162) and I then go on to answer that question by emphasizing that, in fact, 'many foreign Zapatista solidarity groups are explicit on the need to support the effort in Chiapas by pursuing struggles closer to home.' (p. 163). Under the circumstances, I am surprised to see Paulson attribute to me the view that 'those who do act in solidarity thereby reflect a preference for embracing revolution elsewhere rather than struggling at home.' I am particularly perplexed that he would make this claim when he, himself, acknowledges that foreign solidarity groups comprise a quite mixed lot and he says, 'I won't argue that there aren't any foreign activists trying to "revolt vicariously" through the Zapatistas'. In this respect, I believe we are actually in substantial agreement.

I would love to be wrong in my assertions about the narrow range of progressive opinion available to those who can only follow events in Chiapas electronically. Justin Paulson cites 'literally scores of webpages, dozens of mailing lists and archives' that are available online. Inspired by these assurances, I have resumed my electronic quest for more varied perspectives on Chiapas. However, although I can't exclude that my problem springs from the limits of my skills in surfing the web, what I find in July 2000 is, if anything, a narrower range of ideas than when I first sat down to write about this problem in December 1998.

This is particularly regrettable in light of the outcome of the recent Mexican election whose significance is such that it deserves a great deal of debate on the left, and not only in Mexico. A breakdown of the votes cast on 2 July indicates that the PRI—to be sure, only with the help of its customary fraudulent practices in the countryside—substantially held the base of support that it enjoyed in the 1997 elections. The avalanche of urban votes that carried the right-wing candidate, Vicente Fox, to the presidency and his party, the PAN, to its largest-ever representation in the legislature, appears to have come overwhelmingly from Mexicans who had previously supported Cuaúhtemoc Cárdenas and the PRD. While the preference for PAN among the urban poor and working classes has been offered by conservative observers as evidence of popular support for Fox's frankly neo-liberal program and his commitment to remove anti-clerical restraints on the Church, in reality, the shift of the anti-PRI vote from the PRD to the PAN more likely represents the pragmatic decision of millions of protest voters to go with the candidate who was most likely to wrest power from the official party. As the left attempts to analyze and rebound from the effects of the defection a significant portion of the Cardenista base to a right-wing candidate, the need for more open discussion about left alternatives in Mexico should be very clear.

THE POLITICS OF LABOUR MIGRATION: CHINESE WORKERS IN NEW YORK

PETER KWONG

M ost socialists have always embraced the concept of proletarian internationalism. Indeed, organizations like the International Working Men's
Association and the Second and Third Internationals were established to forge
alliances among working people of all countries. This kind of alliance was necessary to fight the capitalist form of accumulation, which is global. To counter this,
as Marx and Engels pointed out, it is necessary to 'bring to the front the
common interests of the entire proletariat, independently of all nationality.'[1]

But in practice proletarian internationalism has meant the working class of
one country supporting the working-class struggle of another; the spirit of
internationalism has not often extended to immigrant workers. Clearly,
popular sentiment has not favoured immigrants. Native workers have been
wary of newcomers, seeing them as competitors who increase the labour
supply, reduce wages and cause unemployment. Resentment against them has
been typical in America. Irish immigrants, arriving poor and Catholic, incurred
the wrath of Americans in the form of the mid-nineteenth-century 'Know-
Nothings'. Yet decades later an Irish leader expressed a thought common
among his peers: 'There should be a law ... to give job to every decent man
that's out of work. And another law ... keep all them I-talians from comin' in
and takin' the bread out of the mouths of honest people.'[2] Native workers built
institutional shells around their jobs to exclude immigrant competition. Engels
noticed that the American native worker took on 'an aristocratic attitude and
wherever possible leaves the ordinary badly paid occupations to the immigrants,
of whom only a small section enter the aristocratic trades.'[3] Even progressive
labour leaders have considered immigrants, like racial minorities, as serious

obstacles to organizing the working class, and their anti-immigrant feelings have been openly expressed.[4] They sometimes considered the immigrants as lacking class consciousness and being willing to conspire with the employers, and thus unfit to be organized; or if immigrants wanted to be included in the unions, they feared their improved conditions would only attract more immigrants and thus nullify their organizing efforts.

Hostility towards immigrants has usually been expressed in ugly chauvinistic ways. During the second half of the nineteenth century virtually every labour newspaper and organization in the U.S. supported the exclusion of Chinese immigrants. The progressive Knights of Labour, who organized everyone, including farmers, unskilled labourers, women and Negroes, invited them all into the local assemblies—except the Chinese,[5] who were some of the first 'coloured' immigrant groups to arrive. Members of the organization claimed that the Chinese were 'inassimilable elements' who should be barred from immigration, and urged that those already in the country should be expelled from the labour force and prevented from 'competing' with whites. Even the International Workingman's Association passed a resolution to exclude Chinese immigration only one year after it had called for 'complete political and social equality for all, without distinction of sex, creed, colour or condition.'[6] Its leaders claimed that the Chinese were slaves and willing to work under any conditions and that American free individuals could not compete with them.

The historical lessons are clear. By excluding immigrants, organized labour leaves them defenceless, and they become easy victims of employers for use, as cheap and docile labour, and as strike-breakers. Their presence ensures the perpetuation of xenophobic anti-immigrant sentiments which further accentuate divisions within the working class. The result is that the immigrants cannot benefit from the gains achieved by the labour movement, while the movement itself is weakened. In effect, capital is able to use immigrants to blackmail the whole of the working class.

Today, more than ever, the left needs a unified position, accepting and insisting that immigrant workers are fully part of the working class. This does not mean that we need to take a moralistic point of view, by insisting that immigration issues should 'not start from economic consequences but from rights and freedom',[7] or by defending the immigrants' absolute right of movement across national borders to seek better opportunities. The problem with this position is that it places immigrants' desire to migrate as the central determining factor of migration. True, migration has always been part of human experience—people choose to move to places where there are better conditions for survival. However, wanting to get to places of higher wages does not mean they'll get there. In the modern era, large-scale and sustained migration waves have been the result of the uneven development of capital. It is capital's initiative that in large part determines migration. Migrations are never indiscriminate flows of people looking for a better future. They do so from very specific areas and towards equally specific destinations—drawn to serve capital's need for labour. Most importantly, capital encourages and manipulates labour migration to maximize its leverage over the working class.[8]

It is clear that a central challenge for socialists is to turn the issue of international workers' migration to their advantage in the struggle against global capitalism. As it is, the inability to incorporate immigrants politically has been the weakest link of most labour movements around the world. In this essay, I will use the experience of Chinese workers in the U.S. as an example to show that immigrants are indispensable strategic partners in the building of a powerful labour movement for socialist transformation.

IMMIGRANTS AND CAPITALIST RESTRUCTURING

In today's 'global economy' capitalist markets have permeated the globe more thoroughly than any time in the past, drawing more zones of the world and a growing portion of its population directly into capitalist social relations. The result is more uneven development and greater social disruption worldwide. This makes the issue of international migration more important than ever.

The pressure to emigrate to the advanced countries is great, but the demand from these countries for Third World labour is also great. A recent conservative estimate suggests a total migration of 'well over 100 million for post-war migrations to the OECD countries, with the majority of those movements taking place in the thirty years between 1965 and 1995—more than triple the great transatlantic migrations of the 1880s to the 1920s.'[9] The driving force behind the current globalization is the need to maintain a high rate of profit, by means of the capitalist restructuring process that began in the 1970s. To overcome the accumulation crisis of that decade it was necessary to invest in new technology and to increase efficiency through reorganization, particularly by dismantling inefficient industries and moving them abroad. But in addition to moving production overseas, to wherever labour is cheaper and less organized, businesses also subcontracted work to smaller domestic production sites whose operations remained more flexible because they employed unregulated labour. To accomplish the last objective, it was and still is critical to break down domestic labour opposition to it.

In the United States, this required a readjustment in the balance of power between labour and capital established since the 1930s. The destruction of the powerful labour movement that organized many immigrant workers and was able to make significant gains in collective bargaining, higher wages, health and retirement benefits, unemployment compensation, and other social welfare safety nets has been a chief objective of the new business order in the U.S. One of the best ways to achieve this is by hiring the least organized and most vulnerable labour available—new immigrants and, preferably, undocumented ones who have no protection at all.

There is a paradox in the role played by undocumented immigrants in all this. Cognizant of concerns for equality and human rights, most states have gotten rid of discriminatory ethnic and racial restrictions. They have also accepted the right to family unity and the right to appeal for political asylum. The central question on immigration has shifted to defining who can be 'legal immigrants' and who should be excluded as 'illegals'. Employers are usually not satisfied with the flow of legal immigration to supply the number and the kind of workers they wish to employ. They often induce the state to modify the laws and relax their execution, sometimes to the point of not enforcing them at all. The result is a persistent influx of 'illegals'.

In the U.S., the 1965 Immigration Act made no provision for a continued inflow of unskilled labour unless would-be immigrants could claim a close blood relationship to an American citizen. The new act ended the Bracero programme, which had found temporary jobs (largely as migrant farm workers) for some four million Mexicans between 1942 and 1960.[10] The termination of the programme, however, had little impact on the demand for such labour. Workers who in the past came 'legally' under the Bracero programme now infiltrated the border 'illegally'. Other governments confronted with similar situations often enforce the law ambivalently, in order to appease capital's need for labour. So as long as illegals continue to come, the employers are satisfied; in fact, their 'illegal' status, hence their greater vulnerability, may serve the interests of the employers even better.

These developments run counter to the expectations of those who argue that advanced nations like the U.S. are moving towards high-tech, high-income service and information economy. They predict that low-wage jobs will be exported and that immigrant labour will no longer be needed. The opposite has happened in the U.S. At the precise period of economic restructuring from the late 1970s to the 1990s, as American family incomes were stagnating, America experienced its highest influx of legal and illegal immigrants. Normally we should expect low immigration in times of economic hardship. Yet, in the 1990s over one million legal immigrants arrived in the U.S. each year, not counting those who came in illegally or those who overstayed their non-immigrant visas—which some estimate as amounting to an additional 1 to 1.5 million per year.[11] Such a high rate of influx has only ever been surpassed at the beginning of the twentieth century.

Modern capital, then, just as in the past, imports immigrants to cut costs. With very few exceptions immigrant labour in the advanced countries has created a 'third world' within them. These immigrants play a part in the efforts of the advanced countries to hold on to their industries by providing a local source of cheap labour to counter the lower labour standards in competing countries. Globalization thus enables employers to pit workers from different countries against one another. They seek to compete by having the lowest possible labour standards; immigrants promise a low-cost, disciplined, and unorganized workforce. They force governments to try to secure these conditions by repressing the workers' movement everywhere. This is very different from the general belief that sweatshops only exist outside of the rich countries. The virtual indentured servitude of the Chinese illegal immigrants in the U.S. is a very instructive example of this phenomenon.

CHINESE ILLEGAL MIGRANTS UNDER INDENTURED SERVITUDE

On 6 June 1993, a Honduran-registered steamer named the *Golden Venture* ran aground just outside New York Harbour. The ship carried 286 illegal immigrants, most of whom were rural farmers from Fujian Province in southern coastal China. This was the first time the problem of Chinese illegal immigrants came to public attention, though they began arriving in the U.S. and other advanced industrial countries as labourers soon after Deng Xiaoping's 'liberalization' programme in China in the late 1970s. What is unusual about this traffic is the conditions under which they arrived—by using the service of sophisticated international smuggling networks, paying exorbitant fees which require the newly arrived workers to work for many years before paying them off.

The current price of a clandestine trip to New York from Wenzhou or Fuzhou, where most of the Chinese illegals are from, ranges from U.S. $33,000 to $50,000. Individuals who intend to make it have to raise $1,500 to pay a snakehead (human smuggler) in China. The rest is to be paid upon arrival in the U.S., usually by the relatives already in the country. If the relatives make the payment, the new arrival pays them back, normally within three to five years at 3 percent interest.

In the last ten years, so many people have been coming that their relatives can no longer help because they are already burdened with the debts of others who came earlier. In that case, the new arrivals are forced to borrow from loan sharks or the snakeheads themselves, at 30 percent interest. New immigrants, without any knowledge of English, can only get menial jobs, often earning less than $1,000 a month. That is just enough to pay the interest portion of the loan, not counting money needed for survival. But the debts must be paid, lest the snakeheads hire 'enforcers' to beat the money out of the debtors. One favourite tactic is to threaten the victim's relatives with his/her imminent execution, to convince them to come up with quick cash. In some cases, the snakeheads simply make the debtors their virtual slaves. During the day, the victims work at restaurants affiliated with organized crime. At night, after they are brought back to prison-like dormitories, hand over all their money and are locked up until the next day. These immigrants, in virtual indentured servitude, are forced to accept practically any job just to keep up with their debt payments.

With the flood of desperate undocumented aliens willing to work, Chinese-American employers are in the position to depress labour conditions to the limit. Chinatown wages, already low by American standards before the arrival of the Fuzhounese, have declined even further. Testifying in 1995 at a Senate hearing for anti-sweatshop legislation, Mrs Tang, once a schoolteacher in Guangdong Province who had immigrated ten years earlier to Brooklyn, recalled that in the early 1980s she worked eight hours a day and earned

$40–$50. Today, with competition from the Fuzhounese, she slaves twelve hours a day to make a paltry $30.[12] In her case, she has to work almost twice as long to make the same amount of money. It is common for workers to work seven days a week, twelve hours a day, at an average hourly wage of $3.75.[13]

Competition from the illegals is thus forcing documented Chinese workers to settle for less if they want to maintain steady employment. Thus the employers have effectively erased the distinction between legal and illegal immigrant workers. They all line up outside the factory long before the doors open in order to be the first ones to begin work. At night, they refuse to quit even after ten, just to get a few more pieces done for a few more dollars. Some of the seamstresses on sewing machines are known not to drink anything during the day lest they interrupt their work, calculated by piece rate, by going to the bathroom. One Cantonese garment worker has testified to a Congressional committee that Fuzhounese illegals work until two in the morning, sleep in the factory, and start again right after sunrise. If they are not able to complete a given order, they ask their children to come in to help.[14]

Undocumented immigrants have given employers leverage that enables them to force workers to accept many obviously illegal labour practices. Homework, thought to have disappeared in America 50 years ago, is a common phenomenon in Chinatown, as is child labour. The most egregious practice at both non-unionized and unionized Chinese garment factories in New York is withholding workers' wages. Previously, the normal withholding period was three weeks; now anything under five weeks is considered good. Of course, there is never a guarantee; after the employment starts, the employer can claim cash-flow problems or manufacturers' non-payments to postpone his own wage payments. After a few weeks, the workers are faced with the difficult decision of whether to hope against hope and work for another week, or quit and cut their losses.

After several years of working like machines, at the rate of eighty-four hours a week, some workers begin to develop physical ailments. Restaurant workers complain of pinched nerves, back and shoulder pains, swollen feet, stomach cramps and insomnia. Kitchen help can be temporarily blinded by the sudden rush of steam to the eyes from pots or dishwashers. Some have even developed 'battle fatigue' syndrome, unable to move at all. Seamstresses complain of sore arms, headaches, dizzy spells, and rapid heart palpitation. Bronchial asthma is common, caused by exposure to the chemicals used in treating fabrics. The worst problems develop from working with polyester, whose shredded fibres, if inhaled over a long period of time in the dry, unswept conditions of most work places, can cause nose bleeds and asthma. Many such health problems, like repetitive stress syndrome, can be avoided by taking regular breaks and working shorter hours; as for back and shoulder aches, a change in the construction of the chairs workers sit on could minimize their problems. Of course, the employers will do none of this.

Illegal Chinese workers have also been used for union busting. In 1994, the owners of Silver Palace Restaurant—one of Chinatown's largest restaurants, which was unionized in 1980—locked out all their union workers, claiming that their wages were too high. The owners saw that it made no sense to pay union wages when there was such a large supply of cheap labour to be had. The locked-out union workers picketed the restaurant for more than seven months. 'If the owners win this one,' the leader of the picketing workers stressed, 'employers all over Chinatown could impose any kind of conditions they want on the working people, no matter whether they are legal or undocumented. We are then nothing but slaves.'

The issue is no longer just the treatment of illegals. In Chinatown, by using illegals to depress wages for all workers, employers have simply aggravated the class struggle between labour and management. It should be added that most Americans see the Fuzhounese as an aberration—an isolated ethnic phenomenon at the margin of society. But in the past ten years, undocumented Fuzhounese have penetrated the garment, construction, and restaurant trades all over New York City. Non-Chinese-owned small electronics factories and vegetable farms in New Jersey, construction companies specializing in pricey loft renovation in the fashionable Manhattan neighbourhood of Soho, and Long Island farms use Chinese employment agencies to find Chinese labour contractors who will take care of the selection, transportation, payment and management of their workers.

Moreover, Chinese illegal immigrants are not the only group paying high fees for their passage to enter this country. This 'contract labour' phenomenon has spread to other immigrant groups as well. Mexicans are paying $5,000, Poles $8,000 and Asian Indians up to $28,000 for their passages. Thai women were discovered in Elmonte, California, working and living in a locked and fenced-in factory because they could not repay their transportation fee. They were routinely abused, and told that if they escaped their captors would 'go to their homes in Thailand to burn their houses down.'[15]

THE ROLE OF THE STATE

How is it possible that this most advanced nation has these nineteenth-century immigrant and labour conditions? Why does the U.S. government not crack down on the smuggling networks and sweatshop labour practices?

Saskia Sassen argues that economic internationalism, the formation of transnational economic space, and the emergence of an international human rights regime have changed the 'substantive nature of state control over immigration.'[16] Moreover, states are increasingly becoming part of a web of rights and regulations that are embedded in supra-national entities, from the European Union (EU) and the World Trade Organization (WTO) to international courts defending the human rights of immigrants and refugees. States no longer have the technical or administrative capacity to control their borders, nor the ability to set labour standards in their work places.[17] But states are the guarantors of the capitalist mode of production. On immigration, they have shown their willingness to use their power to benefit the business community in a number of ways. First of all, states have the power to select and determine who can enter, allowing only able-bodied healthy individuals in and screening out others and not permitting immigrants to bring their families. Once inside the country, states may have laws that restrict immigrants' access to housing, education, health care, and business and land ownership. Before the mid-nineteenth century, the U.S. government even enforced 'legal' contracts that placed immigrants in indentured servitude.[18] In the twentieth century capitalist states keep immigrant workers in a special legal category. Non-citizen immigrants are placed in a transitory status as guest or non-resident temporary workers who enjoy limited social benefits and legal protection. If they appear to be the least bit political they can be removed. Illegals are not allowed at all. But if the state does not deport them, and at the same time ignores their labour conditions, illegals have no means to object to abuse by their employers.

In the case of Chinese illegals, while labour violations and abuses by employers continue, U.S. law-enforcement authorities are passive and slow to respond to their complaints. Workers find that taking legal action against employers almost never succeeds. To begin with, employers do not believe that illegal workers will dare to file complaints against them. But even when they do, scarcely anything happens; there are currently hundreds of complaints filed with the New York State Labor Department against Chinese employers for back wages, but so far there have been only two convictions.[19]

In New York State, the State Apparel Industry Task Force is supposed to be the watchdog of the industry but it has just five inspectors to monitor more than 4,000 clothing factories. Moreover, the majority of the cases that have been cited for violations involve the failure to register, which is the absolute minimum level of compliance with industry regulations. Nevertheless, these labour departments blame their inaction on lack of funding, while reproaching the victims, the immigrant communities, for not coming forward with incriminating information. This typical official response does not address the criticisms, that the slow and passive response by officials endangers the lives of those who do come forward. The result is a stalemate between law-enforcement officers and the employers with the latter free to operate at will, treating the immigrant communities in the U.S. as foreign territory.

At the same time, the flow of illegal immigration into this country has not slowed, even with the passage of the harsh 1996 Immigration Reform Act. What has happened is only a dramatic increase in the fees charged by human smugglers and a new sophistication in the methods used by the smuggling networks. For the Chinese, prices that were $33,000 at the time of the Act's passage have now reached $50,000. In addition to the original sources of illegal migration—the southern cities of Fuzhou and Wenzhou—Chinese today come illegally from Shanghai, Beijing, Tianjin, and many other cities in the north. To avoid detection by American authorities along America's Pacific coast, the snakeheads have developed dozens of alternative routes through the Caribbean Islands. But these days fewer illegal immigrants come in by ship or cross the U.S. borders by land. They are increasingly coming in by air. These illegals, holding stolen or counterfeit passports, are allowed to board U.S.-bound planes by unsuspecting airline officials or by the paid-off ground security personnel.

The problem is, however, not shortcomings in the labour department, the immigration office or the Border Patrol, that could easily be fixed by increased budgetary appropriations. It is the misdirected supply-side illegal immigration policy which ignores the fundamental factor behind illegal immigration—namely, American employers' demand for cheap and vulnerable labour. In fact, the U.S. is so addicted to immigrant labour that without it many businesses in agriculture and the garment and meat packing industries would not survive. Americans have become so used to immigrants working in the restaurant, service and domestic-help trades that they are not even conscious of their presence in their midst. So long as the employers are willing, or prefer, to hire illegals, the human smugglers can be assured of an income.

The American approach to attacking illegal immigration from the demand side is contained in the 'employer sanctions' provision of the Immigration Reform and Control Act (IRCA) of 1986. The act treats 'knowingly' hiring illegals as a crime, but not employers' exploitation of illegals. 'Employer sanctions' were the best compromise Congress could come up with after long years of debate and controversy. In the end, the opponents of 'employer sanctions' from the business community succeeded in getting Congress to make the Act easy for employers to comply with; by doing so, they also made violations easy. Before the passage of the IRCA, it was not against the law for an employer to hire illegals; they simply followed a 'don't ask, don't tell' policy. However, since the IRCA was passed employers have to inquire about the legal status of their workers in order to protect themselves. If an employer still hires an illegal worker after checking, it means that he has leverage over that worker.

Wing Lam, the executive director of the Chinese Staff and Workers' Association, an immigrant rights group in New York City, refers to the 'employer sanctions' legislation as 'the slave law'. According to him, if workers have proper papers, many bosses will tell them that there is no work available. From the bosses' perspective illegals make a much better workforce; they are usually young, compliant, and willing to work long hours. If a worker cannot produce documentation, the boss says he will do him a favour. Since the boss is doing the worker such a big favour, the worker is expected not to mind being paid less—say, 20–30 percent less,[20] nor working very long hours. Wing believes that in the end employer sanctions hurt all workers, legal or illegal, in that 'before the law, few people worked a seven-day week, but now it's very common. They have nowhere to go. It's like on [a] plantation.'[21] Employer sanctions have helped employers to create a larger army of surplus labour and to keep *all* workers' wages down—which is exactly the opposite of what the IRCA had intended, and exactly what employers hoped for. The 1996 laws against immigrants have to be seen as a political ploy to win votes from a public shaken by the media images of the Golden Venture and World Trade Center bombing incidents.

The American pattern is no different from that of the states of the EU who, since the end of the cold war, have been building a 'Fortress Europe' to deter illegals from their region. These anti-immigrant measures will not work as long as the need for immigrant labour continues. Employers, on their part, just assume to see the states establishing ineffective punitive restrictions depriving immigrants of protection for easier exploitation. The society in the end gets the worst of both worlds—unchecked immigration and impoverished immigrants.

LABOUR'S FAILURE TO ORGANIZE CHINESE GARMENT WORKERS

The fact that the U.S. Congress can pass laws detrimental to the interest of American workers shows the absence of powerful organized labour to oppose them. In fact, the American labour movement is suffering from a steady decline. It has had trouble developing an adequate response to capital's aggressive tactics of outsourcing, leveraged buyouts, relocations, and casual employment.[22] The white ethnic labour leadership inherited from the past is getting out of touch with the rank-and-file membership. Many unions, no longer engaged in militant crusades against large corporations like those that dominated the 1930s, have themselves become led by well-paid and powerful bureaucracies. They shunned organizing in the secondary labour market in the past for a simple cost-benefit reason: to unionize low-income workers in small separate workplaces costs more and requires more organizing effort than to unionize large, centralized plants. The bureaucratized union leaders have lost the fire in their bellies to do the tough work that is necessary to rebuild union membership by 'organizing the unorganized'. Besides, union bureaucrats are interested in maintaining themselves in power. They are often fearful of low-ranking organizers who become successful by being close to the rank-and-file.

The problem is aggravated by the absence of union democracy. Most unions keep their members at a distance from real decision-making. Only a handful give members the opportunity to vote for their representatives. In most unions the rank-and-file are treated as 'clients', not as active participants in their own struggles.[23] Chinese immigrants' experience with ineffectual unions reflects the present crisis of the American labour movement.

Chinese immigrants entered the American labour market in significant numbers just when the American economy was being restructured. Much domestic manufacturing had been subcontracted to firms located in ethnic immigrant neighbourhoods under the management of co-ethnic subcontractors. New Chinese immigrants, with limited education and without English language skills, end up working inside Chinese ethnic enclaves like New York's Chinatown in either restaurants or garment trades. The Chinese entered New York's garment industry just at the time of its decline because of competition from Southern states and Third World countries. Between 1969 and 1982, the number of jobs in New York's garment industry fell by almost 40 percent. This decline, however, has been reversed since the influx of the Chinese. During this same period, the number of Chinese working in New York's Chinatown garment factories increased from 8,000 to 20,000 (a rise of 250 percent).

American organized labour has not at all been interested in organizing Chinese restaurant workers, but the first Chinese immigrant workers to be organized by American unions inside their ethnic enclaves were those who worked in the garment industry. Most of the Chinatown garment shops were organized in the mid-1970s, when Chinese contractors agreed to unionization by the International Ladies Garment Workers Union (ILGWU) in exchange for a promise that the union would help commit large clothing manufacturers to providing Chinese contractors with a steady supply of job orders. From the beginning, Chinatown factories were unionized from the top down, without the ILGWU ever having to mobilize the Chinese in the factories; today, 90 percent of Chinatown's garment workers in Manhattan's Chinatown, both legal and illegal, belong to the ILGWU, now renamed UNITE (Union of Needletrades, Industrial and Textile Employees). Yet even with their importance to the industry and the fact that they are unionized, their wages and conditions remain deplorable.

The ILGWU has made very little effort to involve the workers on the shop floor, even though most of them are new arrivals, unfamiliar with the laws of this country. Many factories have no shop representative to whom workers can report their grievances. Without a shop representative, business agents—the union's overseers of individual shops—become the only union presence in the factories. The most common complaint among the Chinese seamstresses is expressed in a labour newsletter: 'The business agent rarely visits our shops, and when he/she does come, he/she never talks to the workers.'[24] This is not surprising, since the success of the union is based on its ability to maintain dues-paying membership, and that depends more on the co-operation of Chinese owners than on the rank-and-file. This being the case, the owners' power is dominant in the factory, and workers cannot be expected to speak up and risk retaliation from their bosses and betrayal by union officials.[25]

The union's strategy of 'organizing from the top' worked as long as the manufacturers wanted a steady, stable supply of labour. After the manufacturers adopted flexible production, the ILGWU still continued to tie its survival to its co-operative relationship with the manufacturers. It watched as production moved to the South, to Third World countries, and to non-unionized shops, powerless to stop the process, and blamed cheap foreign imports for its inaction. One of the ILGWU campaigns consisted of asking members to attend 'Buy American' rallies in order to induce Congress to pass restrictive import legislation. It is ironic for the union's Chinese members to be picketing against their fellow workers in China and Hong Kong. The prevailing wage in Hong Kong stands at $3.50 an hour—comparable to sweatshop rates in America.

After a number of embarrassing exposés of sweatshop conditions in unionized shops, the union has currently embarked on 'A Partnership for Responsibility' campaign to stop sweatshops. Its literature proposes a programme to urge American consumers not to purchase sweatshop-made goods.[26] Notably, their targets of sweatshops are in Third World countries like China, Bangladesh and Guam, not in New York or Los Angeles.

The union implicitly justifies its weak enforcement of contracts by appeal to the fear that strict enforcement would put Chinese-American owners out of business, although there is no indication that the threat is real. Plenty of 'help wanted' ads appear on factory gates and in Chinese-language papers every day. Beginning in the mid-1980s, Mr K. L. Lin, a Hong Kong-born American citizen and a one-time 1960s radical, got involved in the profitable business of importing garments manufactured in China to the United States. By the mid-1990s, he decided to move his operations back to America, because contractors in New York who ten years ago asked $3.75 for one piece of sewing now offer to do the same job *plus* cutting the garment before sewing for just $1.75. 'It's actually cheaper to do it in New York,' he says, 'because the labor cost in New York has come down, if you add the cost of transportation, purchasing of the U.S. import quota, insurance and all sorts of taxes imposed by the Chinese government, it's not worth doing it in China anymore.' Besides, he adds, 'you get a much faster turnover rate in New York.'

While calling for corporate responsibility and consumer boycotts, the union thus itself shows neither the ability nor the willingness to organize the unorganized, or at least to do so effectively in so far as those it has organized are not protected from substandard conditions. The call for public vigilance is reflective on the union's inability to mobilize its own membership. This, however, is not because the Chinese women workers are not militant. The ILGWU stereotype image, that Chinese women are docile and tied to Chinatown's political and social structure, was shattered in the summer of 1982 during negotiations for a new contract. The negotiations involved the renewal of a three-year-contract and called for the standard wage increase. The manufacturers signed the contract; in fact, the same contract had already been signed to cover 120,000 non-Chinese garment workers on the East Coast. But the Chinese subcontractors balked. They were angry because even though 85 percent of the firms affected by the contract in ILGWU Local 23–25 were Chinese-owned, there were no Chinese on the negotiating team. The subcontractors expected the community to rally behind them, particularly in this clear case of 'racial discrimination'. The contractors said to the workers: 'We are all Chinese and should be able to settle this in our own house; there is no need to go to the white man's union.'[27]

The union had to head off the confrontation and called for a demonstration by its membership in Chinatown. Within the union, the officials had no idea how the Chinatown women would react, since their staff had not been close to the membership. Some even doubted that the Chinese would turn out at all.

But they did. The rank-and-file ILGWU union members quickly mobilized. Hundreds of women volunteered to operate phone banks to contact individual members, urging them to turn out. Others produced bilingual leaflets, banners, and propaganda material. On the day of the demonstration 20,000 workers turned out, making it one of the largest union demonstrations in the city's history. After the demonstration, the Chinese contractors backed off, and the workers won a new contract.

This militant demonstration showed that the Chinese workers were more class- than race-conscious on issues relating to their work, and that this would show itself if they were given a chance to participate and take a stand in the American labour movement. Unfortunately, the union did not take advantage of the workers' activism to build a strong rank-and-file power base, but just co-opted the most active members into management positions. It continues to treat the rest of its membership as 'clients', not as the fount of its power.

In 1997, during the new three-year contract negotiation between UNITE and Chinese contractors, the union, trying to put pressure on the contractors, revealed the results of its own membership survey, which asked union members to list their greatest grievances on their jobs. The number-one complaint, according to the survey, was working extremely long hours, including Sundays, without overtime pay.[28] UNITE members in the United States, under union contracts, have been working over sixty-hour weeks without overtime pay. Did the union need a membership survey to come up with this information? Where was the union after all? The institutionalization of the labour movement has robbed the workers of their strength to fight. Wing Lam, the executive director of the Chinese Staff and Workers Association, describes this as a profoundly 'dehumanizing process'.

Of course, this lack of commitment to organizing is not limited to UNITE, nor does it affect only the Chinese. This same attitude of passivity has long plagued organized labour nation-wide. Not surprisingly, union member-ship among American workers dropped from 35 percent in 1955 to 11 percent in 1995.[29] Unions lost membership even though the American workforce continued to expand, especially in the service industries. Contrary to the oft-heard assertion that the American working class is shrinking in this high-tech 'information age', the labour force in fact grew from 82.3 million in 1970 to 131 million in 1994. But even with declining membership, organized labour still hesitated to organize the unorganized, the immigrants and especially the illegals. Yet, Latinos and Asian immigrants have been the fastest-growing segment of the American population. It was clear for a long time that the unions' justification of their passivity by blaming the Republicans and the conservative climate in the U.S. had been wearing very thin. So was the excuse that American workers cannot be organized until the wage levels of the Third World workers catch up.

MIGRATION PRESSURE IN CHINA

Illegal immigrants from China come mainly from the cities of Fuzhou and Wenzhou, or rather from the rural outskirts of these cities. They are two of the fastest-growing economic regions in China, fuelled by foreign investment. The village outskirts of the two cities have always been highly productive, supplying food produce for city-dwellers. The residents of these villages commanded a favourable position even during the days of the People's Commune. Deng Xiaoping initiated his economic reforms first in rural China, allowing the farmers to break up the collectives and sell their produce in free markets. The farmers accumulated wealth quickly. They then invested their earnings in hand-icraft and small-scale manufacturing industries, such as making shoes and clothing. Thus, Deng's reforms initially brought remarkable gains in rural productivity. Between 1978 (the beginning of the reform) and 1984, gross output in the countryside grew at an impressive annual rate of 9 percent. In a very short time these rural farmers became wealthy relative to urban residents who worked for state enterprises on fixed salaries.

By the middle of 1980s the Chinese government loosened its external controls, permitting foreign firms to set up factories in special industrial zones. This policy was intended to gain cash reserves from these enterprises, and to use this to modernize state industries. Immediately, multinationals like NIKE and K-Mart set up production plants to take advantage of China's cheap labour. Much of China's most dynamic expansion has occurred in sectors predicated on export, and their development was mainly financed by foreign investors often under the management of subcontractors from Taiwan and Hong Kong. Most of this growth is concentrated in the southern coastal areas in places like Fuzhou and Wenzhou.

With new high-wage jobs available in these cities, people's expectations rose. Migrants from rural areas and interior regions where there had not been such development rushed there looking for jobs. China's internal migration is also encouraged by factory owners, including the foreign ones, who prefer out-of-province workers as 'being less demanding and working harder'. Some factories recruit only young out-of-province girls who live in barracks and work in sweatshop conditions. Still, workers are competing for these jobs because whatever they make there is far more than they can make at home. In many of these foreign investment zones the 'out- of-province' population even surpasses the local population. This rural-to-urban, north-south migration has brought inflation, over-crowded housing, open sewage, street congestion, depressed wages, high unemployment, petty crime and general social disorder to the cities. Unaccompanied young girls and boys sleep in the open air and sell their labour and bodies in city markets to anyone willing to pay. Some of them become street urchins, barefoot and dressed in rags, scabby-headed, with flies gathering in the corners of their eyes. Their presence recalls the human depri-vation of pre-1949 China.

On the other side of the coin, the consequence of foreign investment is the destruction of newly-established domestic industries. Village enterprises simply could not compete with the newer, urban ventures equipped with modern machinery and backed by foreign investment. As one small rural entrepreneur, a relative of one of the 'Golden Venture' human cargo, put it in an interview: 'As increasing numbers of people got into making shoes and clothing like ours, the profit margins declined and the markets dried up.' This individual, who had prospered earlier in shoe manufacturing, explained: 'We are left to fend for ourselves in a highly risky business,' and concluded that 'without government connections, we cannot get into the more lucrative export markets. Where can we sell our products?'

Around 1985 rural output slowed down noticeably in contrast to the growth in the urban areas. Some analysts suggest that once peasants abandoned grain production for the more profitable cash crop and rural industries, they soon fell victim to the cyclical process that begins with heated market competition and leads to the shortage of raw materials, price inflation, and finally overproduction and glut.[30] Certainly, those individuals who had the opportunity to taste the fruits of free enterprise have grown resentful of the new development and blame the corrupt political system for their troubles. Chinese Communist Party officials are using their positions to monopolize the most lucrative enterprises for themselves. It is a common complaint that party officials allocate public funds to invest in their private business ventures. During China's 8th National People's Congress 5th Plenary Session held in Beijing in March 1997, delegates castigated the government for its failure to halt the massive exodus of $100 billion stolen government funds since 1979. An estimated $17.8 billion left in 1995 alone. The culprits are top managers of national enterprises and sons and daughters of high-ranking officials—known in China as princelings—who use their privileged positions to channel state funds to private savings accounts outside the country.[31]

Members of the Communist Party have, in effect, arranged for themselves and their children to be first in line to benefit from China's transition to capitalism. The corrupt environment is so suffocating that ordinary Chinese feel that they have no future in China. They also believe that continued government corruption and the increasing polarization of classes will inevitably lead to another political upheaval, much worse than the Tienanman massacre of 1989. You don't have to be poor and at the bottom of the social strata in China to want to leave.

So the pressure of emigration is still building. China has a rural workforce of approximately 440 million. At the current rate of growth in agricultural production, only 200 million farmers are needed.[32] The newly sprouted village and township enterprises alleviated this unemployment temporarily. Even so, by the end of 1995, village and township enterprises were providing work for only 126 million former farmers. This leaves China with millions of unemployed. In one 1999 study, China's rural and urban unemployment was estimated to have reached 130 million people, many of whom are roaming around the country in search of work.[33] China's economic growth, impressive as it has been, is not likely to absorb all this vast mass of surplus manpower. The Chinese leadership had to look for Western help. But in order to get it, it had to agree on 'privatization programmes', more specifically to liquidate all unprofitable state enterprises in three years.[34] The result of this was to add five million more unemployed per year, at a time of economic slowdown in Asia.

This is a risky situation. Already in the first nine months of 1996 there were 1,520 reported incidents of mass demonstrations by threatened and laid-off workers in 120 cities. They marched under unofficial, unsanctioned banners, reading 'Unemployment Workers Alliance', 'Anti-Capitalist Restoration Association', or simply, 'Chinese Labour Association'.[35] In the rural countryside there is also a great deal of unrest due to the imposition of heavy and arbitrary taxes by local officials. When the peasants cannot pay, officials resort to confiscation of property and imprisonment. These harsh measures have led to violent revolts in half a dozen provinces, including Fujian. The worst reported incident happened in one county of Hunan Province where the peasants, angered by a variety of unreasonable taxes, demonstrated in front of the county government building. More than ten thousand gathered and sacked the government offices. Eventually thousands of police and militia were called in from other regions to quell the uprising.[36]

The Chinese leadership is thus facing an immediate crisis of survival, which explains its anxiety to join the WTO; yet in joining the WTO, while China gains trade and tariff benefits, it has to open its most lucrative insurance, banking and communication markets to foreign ownership. In a way, the leaders are counting on the Western powers to pull the country out of its economic crisis, in order to stay in power. In this sense the Chinese Communist leadership may be in danger of becoming no less comprador in nature than the Nationalist Party leadership, which it overthrew fifty years ago.

The government is also encouraging emigration. The labour department has intensified its efforts to export workers to wealthy nations. The government makes money out of these transactions. The government's desperation can be seen from the way it tries to please its clients. A local court in Sichuan Province recently sentenced an individual to a two-year prison-term for his leadership role in organizing a strike in Kuwait, where he had worked. The strike by Chinese labourers was against Kuwaiti construction companies forcing them to work over thirteen hours a day, in violation of their contract which set a maximum of nine hours a day.

In this global economy, Chinese workers have no escape, either inside their country or as immigrant labour elsewhere. Globalization has strengthened the hand of capital and weakened workers everywhere. To reverse the situation there has to be an organized international opposition. The building of such an opposition, however, has to start from the working-class movement in each country, just as Marx and Engels had spelled out that workers 'first of all settle matters with its own bourgeoisie.' Today, the well-being and living standards of workers even in the richest countries depends on a successful labour movement that advances beyond its past to encompass the entire working class: including people of colour, immigrants and illegal aliens.

THE POLITICAL POTENTIAL OF CHINESE IMMIGRANT WORKERS

Are the Fuzhounese illegals in the United States ready to be part of such a struggle? Is their kinship loyalty too strong? True, Chinese immigrant workers are mainly from rural farming backgrounds, hoping to move up to property ownership in the new land. As immigrants they are dependent on kinship loyalty to sustain their migration chain. Therefore, their sense of ethnic solidarity is likely to be strong. In the Chinese American community the strength of kinship loyalty is seen in the formation of clan, family, village, fraternal and trade associations. These associations, transplanted from China during the feudal period of the nineteenth century, remain important to assist new immigrants to adapt to this country.

Before the 1960s Chinese immigrants, without English language and professional skills, could not find jobs in the American labour market because of strong objections by whites to working alongside them. They had to survive by self-employment in small businesses like laundries, restaurants and the grocery trade. To start these businesses, they needed sums of money beyond the reach of most individual immigrants, and relied on district and kinship connections to help them find business partners and pool their resources together. Now, the decentralization of American industry has changed the situation—manufacturing jobs and service firms have come to the ethnic communities to tap their cheap labour resources. Chinatown has, in effect, been transformed from a small-business ghetto into an ethnic manufacturing centre. The majority of the Chinese in Chinatown today are no longer self-employed but employees in factories and restaurants that retain dozens to a couple of hundred people. They are workers.

This is true of Fuzhou and Wenzhou immigrants as well, except that initially they are even more dependent on kinship networks to help them to pay off their exorbitant smuggling fees. However, as the number of illegals entering the U.S. grows, the kinship networks are overburdened with debts and no longer able to handle further kinship demands. The usefulness of kinship networks has declined. In fact, those Fuzhounese who came earlier use the networks to prey on the newcomers, so it has become increasingly clear to illegal immigrants that their future lies with other workers. They may have petty bourgeois aspirations, but the oppression against them is so intense that they have to accept their class position to save themselves. The indications are that Fuzhounese illegals are fighting back.

In the late 1980s, Wai Chee Tong and Stanley Chang opened a garment factory in Brooklyn's Sunset Park district. The employees were mainly illegal workers—Fuzhounese, Malaysians and Hispanics—approximately seventy in all. Around September 1990, when the shop was particularly busy, the owners stopped paying wages, even though the factory was turning out an average of 15,000 garments per week. After a few months, the owners of Wai Chang owed one female worker $3,000; another $6,000, one year's back pay; a couple a total of $10,000; and a seventy-year-old male worker $1,900. The situation was becoming critical, and a number of workers could no longer hold on. They organized a work stoppage, and the partners brought a nasty-looking gangster on to the factory floor to threaten them. The owners also threatened to report the workers to the Immigration and Naturalization Service.

When the workers went to the U.S. Labor Department for help its investigation quickly halted when department officials 'could not locate the owners'. By then, the partners had closed the factory, transferred their accounts out of the corporation, liquidated their properties and disappeared. But the workers did not give up. At a news conference open to the Chinese and English language press, two undocumented workers contended that because the partners knew that they had no green cards they thought that they could get away with not paying wages. The two workers vowed to pursue the case to get back their hard-earned pay, *even if it meant deportation*, and offered to testify in court against the owners to achieve that objective.

The workers filed criminal charges with the New York State Attorney General's Office. After four months of investigation the owners, Wai Chee Tong and Stanley Chang, were charged on forty-one misdemeanour counts of failing to pay wages and keep accurate payroll records. The judgement stipulated that Tong and Chang pay $80,000 in unpaid wages, making it the largest suit ever won in New York's garment industry. The prosecution, however, could not move forward because the two owners 'disappeared' again. Wai Chang workers organized a rally in the Chinese community, seeking help in locating the owners. They also encouraged others in the community who had suffered from the same type of mistreatment to come forward. The workers spent weeks and stayed up for nights and finally spotted Stanley Chang walking out of his hiding place and had him arrested. He was convicted and imprisoned for nine months. Again, the imprisonment of an employer for holding back wages was the first in New York State history. Unfortunately, after he got out Chang claimed bankruptcy and still refused to pay the workers.

But the Wai Chang workers' action has served as an inspiration to many others, showing them that they can fight even if they are undocumented aliens. Thousands of workers employed in hundreds of Chinatown factories and restaurants have experienced similar problems with unpaid back wages. The employers count on the fact that labour laws on this issue are lenient and never enforced, and on the assumption that Chinese workers, particularly the undocumented, will not fight back. But one Chinese community organizer now describes the issue of back wages sprouting like 'green grass after a spring rain.' Soon dozens of garment workers in other factories came forward to demand return of back wages. Employees of a number of Uptown Manhattan Chinese restaurants also went on strike to demand back wages.

Chinese workers, the undocumented included, are clearly ready to fight for their rights despite having to confront the co-ethnic business owners, the threat of gang violence, pro-business labour laws, indifferent labour officials, and even the possibility of deportation. Their problem is the reluctance of the organized labour to mobilize them. Chinese illegals saw themselves as workers and wanted to fight for the enforcement of 'American labour standards', to challenge the unlawful practices of the traditional Chinese pro-business superstructure, and demolish Chinese employers' efforts to split ethnic Chinese labour into legal and illegal immigrants, in order to better super-exploit them both.

Yet in view of the current economic changes taking place in the U.S., what is going on in Chinatown is not at all marginal to the American labour movement. Fuzhounese immigrant workers are not that different from the rest of American working people—they only happen to be on the breaking edge of the crumbling working class structure. The presence of Fuzhounese and other kinds of indentured servitude is an indication of the decline in the American labour movement. Capital counts on labour's traditional racism and exclusionary practices, recruiting precisely those whom organized labour excludes. Today, the well-being and living standards of all Americans depends on a successful labour reform movement that rises from a broad, bottom-up mobilization campaign encompassing the entire working class including people of colour, immigrants and illegal aliens. The inclusion of Fuzhounese immigrants in the ranks of American labour will be a test of organized labour's viability in the future. Protecting the most vulnerable segment of the working class from brutal exploitation is necessary both to save American workers from a downward slide into the primitive conditions of the nineteenth-century capitalism, but also to create the strength to build an international working movement capable of sustaining an advance to socialism.

NOTES

1. Eric Hobsbawm, ed., *The Communist Manifesto: A Modern Edition*, New York: Verso Books, 1998.
2. Quoted in David Montgomery, *The Fall of the House of Labor*, New York: Cambridge University Press, 1977, p. 82.
3. Engels, letter to Schluter, 30 March 1892, in *Marx and Engels on the Trade Unions*, Kenneth Lapides, ed., New York: International Publishers, 1987, p. 143.
4. Montgomery, *The Fall of the House of Labour*, p. 82.
5. Alexander Saxton, *The Indispensable Enemy*, Berkeley: University of California Press, 1971, p. 40.
6. Stuart Crighton Miller, *The Unwelcome Immigrant: The American Image of the Chinese, 1785–1882*, Berkeley: University of California Press, 1969, p. 196.
7. Bob Sutcliffe, 'Freedom to Move in the Age of Globalization,' in D. Baker, G. Epstein and R. Pollin, eds., *Globalization and Progressive Economic Policy*, Cambridge: University of Cambridge Press, 1999.

8.   To take just one historical example: in the 1880s, Flemish-speaking Belgian immigrants were recruited to work in the textile factories of the Roubaix region in France, to break a strike and discourage resistance to mechanization by native French workers. Belgian worker's desire to work in places with relative high wages obviously was a 'necessary' condition for migration; however, it was French employers' interest in hiring workers who were docile and culturally distinct from French workers, and resented by them, that was the decisive factor in paving the way for these immigrants to come to France. See Roger Magraw, *Workers and the Bourgeois Republic*, London: Blackwell, 1992, p. 71. Magraw recounts (p. 42) that, in a similar fashion at the turn of the century, Italian immigrants were recruited to work in the French coal-mines. They lived and worked in a world apart from the native workers. Their accident rate was three times higher than that of French coal-miners.

9.   David Held et al., *Global Transformations*, Stanford: Stanford University Press, 1999, p. 311.

10. Thomas Muller, *Immigrants and the American City*, New York: New York University Press, 1993, p. 51.

11. Held et al., *Global Transformations*, pp. 312, 318–19.

12. *World Journal*, 26 September 1996, p. B4.

13. Rachel X. Weissman, 'Reaping What they Sew,' *Brooklyn Bridge*, vol. 2, no. 9, May 1997, pp. 52–53.

14. Lin Baoqing, *World Journal,* 26 August 1996, p. B1.

15. *The New York Times*, 4 August 1995, p. A1, A18.

16. *Saskia Sassen, Losing Control? Sovereignty in an Age of Globalization*, New York: Columbia University Press, 1996, p. 72.

17. Saskia Sassen, *Guests and Aliens*, New York: The New Press, 1999, p. 133.

18. Patricia Cloud and David W. Galenson, 'Chinese Immigration and Contract Labor in the Late Nineteenth Century', *Exploration in Economic History*, 24, 1987, pp. 22–42.

19. Peter Kwong, *Forbidden Workers*, New York: The New Press, p. 178.

20. *Chinese Staff and Workers' Association Newsletter*, May 1988, p. 6.

21. Aurelio Rojas, 'Border Guarded, Workplace Ignored,' *San Francisco Chronicle*, 18 March 1996, p. A6.

22. Ibid., pp. 100–102.

23. See the excellent editorial, 'Towards a New Unionism,' *Social Policy*, vol. 25, no. 2 (Winter) 1994, p. 2.

24. Quoted in *Chinese Staff and Workers' Association Newsletter*, 1988 issue.

25. Peter Kwong and JoAnn Lum, 'How the Other Half Lives Now,' *The Nation*, 18 June 1988, pp. 899.

26. Pamphlet issued by UNITE's Research Department.

27. Altagacia Ortiz, 'Puerto Rican Workers in the Garment Industry of New York City, 1920–1960', in Robert Asher and Charles Stephenson, eds., *Labor Divided: Race and Ethnicity in United States Labor Struggles, 1835–1960*, Albany, N.Y.: State University of New York Press, 1990, p. 152.

28. *China Daily News*, 1 April 1997.

29. Robert Kuttner, *Everything for Sale: the Virtues and Limits of Markets*, New York: Knopf, 1997, p. 100.

30. Maurice Meisner, *The Deng Xiaoping Era: An Inquiry into the Fate of Chinese*

Socialism 1978–1994, New York: Hill and Wang, 1996, p. 239.

31. *Apple Daily*, Hong Kong, 16 March 1997.
32. Cathy Chen, 'China Seeks End to Rural–Urban Divide', *Asian Wall Street Journal*, 25 April 1994.
33. Jack A. Goldstone, *A Tsunami on the Horizon?: Potential for International Migration from the People's Republic of China*, paper presented at Conference on Asian Migrant Trafficking, sponsored by the Pacific Forum-CSIS, Honolulu, Hawaii, 26 July 1966, p. 19.
34. *Duoweinews*, Chinesenewsnet.com, 27 November 1999.
35. *Cheng-min Monthly*, Hong Kong, no. 230 (November) 1996, p. 11.
36. *Dongfong Daily*, Hong Kong, 11 November 1996, also in World Journal, 4 March 1997.

THE 'MISTRESS' AND THE 'MAID' IN THE GLOBALIZED ECONOMY

BRIGITTE YOUNG

Most accounts of economic restructuring concentrate on global culture, the hypermobility of capital, and the power of transnationals. But in neglecting the sites of material production of advanced information and communications technology, we overlook the capital that is at least still partly embedded in national territories. If we focus on the practices that provide the infrastructure for the production and reproduction of global capital, we uncover a multiplicity of work cultures involving real people in real places. These include secretaries, pizza delivery persons, cleaning crews, truck drivers, dog walkers, industrial service workers, maids, child-care workers, and a host of other low-skilled, mostly 'blue-collar' workers who have become invisible in the narrative of hypermobile capital. As Saskia Sassen properly reminds us, the corporate work culture with its emphasis on specialized information services is overvalued while other kinds of work cultures are devalued. This is especially true of the work of women and immigrants.[1]

Globalization also differentiates women's work in new ways. The flexibilization of the labour market has produced greater equality between educated middle-class women and men while creating greater inequality among women. High value is placed on the integration of professional women into the formal economy while the 'paid' reproductive work of women in the informal economy (the household) continues to be undervalued; women's 'paid' work outside the home is not equal to women's 'paid' work inside it. Globalization and the process of individualization (i.e., social differentiation) are complementary processes which are restructuring both the private and the public arenas.[2]

These changes have produced two categories of women within the household: professional women and maids. The growing participation of professional women in the labour market is accompanied by the largely 'invisible' development of paid work in the private household. Growing numbers of migrant women are employed in undeclared jobs in the household-oriented service industry, in cleaning, and as child caretakers, allowing more women to have professional careers. An invisible link has thus emerged between women's increasing participation in the formal labour market and the informal labour market roles of migrant and immigrant women.[3]

It is important to recognize, however, that this development is directly linked to the neoliberal character of globalization as this is reflected in state policy. As long as most welfare states are reluctant to provide, and are in the process of scaling back, the support structure for working women, the conditions upon which women enter 'male work structures' are not just gender but also class and race specific. Professional women have the advantage of falling back upon mostly cheap, often undocumented migrants, to perform household tasks and child-rearing. Without adequate public child-care services, and without being able to fall back on the services of women from developing and transitional countries, educated women would not be able to climb professional ladders that demand great personal mobility and flexibility. Whether these activities are performed by (mostly) over-qualified East European women in Germany, or by African-Americans or Latin and Central American immigrants in the United States, or Filipina women in Italy and Canada, they involve a new international division of labour. On the one side is the 'mistress' and on the other stands the 'maid', separated by different racial, ethnic, class and national belongings and backgrounds.[4]

GENDER REGIMES IN THE GLOBALIZATION ERA

In the new decentralized 'flexible accumulation' processes[5] of the global economy the organization of work has changed. We witness a polarization between the 'feminization of work' with the creation of 'cheap-wage zones' even in highly industrialized countries,[6] and the emergence of a new professional class of global 'workers' that includes well-educated women. In Europe, women have filled more of the new jobs created in the last two decades than have men, and not all of these have been low-paid, insecure 'McJobs';[7] in the USA 52 percent of all the jobs created between February 1994 and February 1996 were in the top three deciles of classification by pay and only 32 percent were in the lower-paid categories.[8] In the 'global cities' young well-educated females have succeeded in entering the middle and upper echelons of the finance and business world,[9] although this comes with the caveat, as Saskia Sassen has again pointed out, 'that notwithstanding the growing number of top level women professionals in global economic activities and in international relations, both these worlds can be specified as male-gendered in so far as each in its distinct way has the cultural properties and power dynamics that we have historically associated with men and power'.[10] As a result of these labour market changes, the gender order associated with the industrial Fordist regime is being radically transformed.[11]

1. The end of the Fordist family breadwinner model

Globalization has eroded the material conditions for the male breadwinner and his dependent wife and family. The rise in the number of dual wage-earners since the 1970s is a product of this. One group of dual wage-earner families consists of relatively well-off professionals who are part of the formal economy. A much larger group can be found in the medium and lower level of the economy, relying on the additional wages of women to maintain or improve the family's living standard. Another category that has occupied the space vacated by the Fordist male breadwinner model are single parents (mostly female), whose numbers have increased dramatically.

Even in West Germany, which lags behind its European neighbours in regard to female employment, the number of working-age women employed has risen from around 40 percent in 1970 to 60 percent just before German unification. Despite Germany's inadequate child-care infrastructure, 81 percent of the women in one-parent households are active in the work-force force and 61 percent of married women of all ages are employed (in the 18–40 age group the number increases to 70 percent).[12] If we extrapolate from recent trends, by the year 2008 women in the US will have the same labour force participation rate as men (at a level of 84 percent), and women in the European Union will reach it by the year 2014 (at a level of 67 percent).[13]

The integration of women into the labour market has led to new definitions of gender roles and to changes in the social value-system. The Fordist norm of women dependent on the male breadwinner is being replaced by the increasing individualization of women. A woman from Mexico, living in the United States, puts it as follows: 'Before, if you worked, everybody knew it was to help your husband but it was his obligation [to support the family]. Now it's your obligation; people expect women to work [outside the home] whether they like it or not'.[14]

2. The reconfiguration of the public/private and production/reproduction

The flexibilization of the labour market has also undermined the separation between the productive and reproductive economy that was once the hallmark of the Fordist gender order.[15] The conceptual separation between private and public cannot deal with the fact that the daily work of many women is done in a 'triple shift'[16] in both the formal and informal sectors and in family activities. Whether this work is done by women in the Caribbean, in Asia, or in the 'global cities', its common feature is that women's work is a combination of activities in formal transnational production, in informal sector work, and in the subsistence economy of the family. The borders of this 'triple shift' are quite fluid for women, but relatively rigid for men. Women often spend up to sixteen hours in this 'triple shift' in order to survive. In contrast, males do comparatively little work in the household economy and work either in the formal economy or as subcontractors or workers in the informal economy.[17]

These new forms of work are also redefining gender identity. While the woman was identified with the family and subordinated to the male in the Fordist period, she is 'individualized' in the global economy. Whether they are engaged in the formal economy as well-paid professionals, or employed in the informal economy of the Free Export Zones or in the global sweat-shops, or work as domestic servants, these women have in common the fact that combining productive with reproductive work is becoming ever more difficult. Neoliberal discourse is silent about how to reconcile the need for a job with the demands of raising children. From an economic standpoint, reproductive activities are 'invisible'. In the Fordist era reproductive work was at least socially recognized, despite its private seclusion. With the flexibilization of the labour market, child-rearing has again become an economic and social externality, and the dialectical relation between market and non-market activities has disappeared from the neoliberal discourse of the global economy.[18]

3. Increasing inequality among women

The rising integration of women in the labour force has also meant a greater disparity between women of different classes, races and nationalities. Although the new members of the new 'club society' are mostly 'new boys', as Wendy Larner calls the new players in the global job-market,[19] professional women are no longer a rarity in the upper echelons of the knowledge and information industries. At the other end of the spectrum are the low-skilled service jobs that are not just an important part of the infrastructure of the formal economy, but essential to permit professional women to enter the job market. Women domestic servants are the key to permitting middle-class women to pursue their careers. Here we meet the new 'mistress' and her 'maid'; one cannot do without the other.[20] It is important to point out that this new dependency between 'mistress' and 'maid' is a structural problem of western capitalist societies and not a 'woman's problem'. As long as child care and care responsibilities remain privatized in the home, and as long as males do not contribute significantly to the unpaid labour in the home, professional women are forced to reinstitutionalize the system of housemaids of the last century.

In their triple dependence on the welfare state (as social workers, clients, and consumers), women are particularly hard hit by the social welfare crisis. The reduction in social services places the burden of caring for the elderly and the sick, and providing a range of needed inputs into education, once more on the shoulders of women. Moreover, the privatization of these and other social services destroys the very conditions that made the integration of women in the labour market possible. Particularly for women in less-skilled jobs, publicly provided child-care services often make the difference between seeking employment or staying at home. And the social service jobs generated by the

Keynesian welfare state, and which were often largely filled by women, disappear too.[21]

Globalization has thus fundamentally challenged the very notion of what is public and what is private. In the process, it has worsened gender-specific social division. Re-privatization of the domestic, as Janine Brodie argues, has elevated and revitalized the hetero-patriarchal family.[22] It rests on the dubious assumptions that the family is responsible for social reproduction, and that a family still consists of the male 'breadwinner' and his dependants. Aside from the conservative and ideological premise of these assumptions, they neglect to take into account the changing reality of the family. The Fordist gender order no longer exists. Today's reality is that women—even if they wanted to—no longer have the 'luxury' of remaining as caretakers in the home.

WHO IS DOING THE HOUSEWORK? THE GERMAN CASE

The discourse around this question has changed since the beginning of the feminist movement in the 1970s. The initial demand was to call on men to share equally in the burden of the housework and child care. The much hoped-for redistribution of household work has been disappointing. Virtually all studies show that despite the increasing integration of women into the labour force, men have not equally shared in the burden of domestic work—especially in Germany, where married men and fathers are, by comparison with the rest of Europe, almost the least willing to share household duties. Together with men in countries like Luxembourg and Ireland the average man in Germany continues to believe that household and family duties are the responsibility of the wife.[23]

Gøsta Esping-Andersen came to the same conclusion about men's contribution to unpaid labour in the home, noting that men's unpaid hours have changed little and show little variation internationally, typically being in the range of 10–15 hours. In contrast women's hours of unpaid labour vary a good deal, from 25 percent per week in Denmark to 45 in Spain.[24] The call for equal burden sharing of women and men in the domestic sphere thus seems to have failed. We are witnessing in virtually all industrial countries a new redistribution of housework and caring work which no longer counts on males to change their behaviour. The problem of sharing the new burdens is resolved by *other* women doing the daily household work for professional women (and of course, also for men).

This reliance by women on other women to do the housework is not new. But in Germany, as in other industrialized countries, the dismal working conditions of maids in the domestic sphere and the new job opportunities for women in industry and the service industry after 1945 led to a drastic decline of female servant workers.[25] What we are seeing now is a new version of what went before. The new 'maids' are often from a variety of foreign backgrounds. Many are undocumented migrants with insecure legal status. Another significant difference from the past is that while domestic workers in the nineteenth century were invariably from the lower classes, today they include unemployed professionals—especially academics—from Eastern Europe.

To get reliable data on the number of people working in the domestic sphere, and the types of households that employ them, is a difficult task in all countries. Many of today's 'maids' are afraid to come out into the open for fear of being deported and thus endangering their economic survival. The 'employers' are equally reluctant to endanger the benefits they derive from 'black market' arrangements. Germany is no exception in this respect. The official number of socially insured domestic workers in the private household in 1994 is listed as 35,000.[26] Beyond these, 732,000 part-time workers were employed in private households in 1992. This number is mainly made up of women: 677,000 women (92.5 percent) versus 55,000 men.[27] In contrast to these official numbers, unofficial estimates of women working in German households tell a different story. It is estimated that 9 percent of households regularly employ help which translates to around 2.65 million households for 1994. This does not include the 1.4 million households (4.6 percent) which rely on household or cleaning help on an irregular basis. Which are the households employing domestic help? Not surprisingly, Munz estimates that 17 percent of families with incomes of more than DM 5,000[28] per month regularly employ help. By contrast, only 8 percent of all households rely on paid help.

If we compare the official data on socially insured domestic workers with the estimates of maids actually employed in the German household sector, we can assume that the discrepancy is the result of a flourishing 'black market'. In the past, the German tax system actually subsidized the black market for married German women who wanted to earn something 'on the side' by engaging in part-time household work. Since wives are covered by the social insurance of the husband, they have little incentive to get individual coverage. Their main interest is the net salary they can earn without jeopardizing the tax allowance husbands receive for wives who are participating in the labour market ('Ehegattensplitting').[29]

But the present demand for outside help in the private home can no longer be met by German housewives wanting to earn some money on the side. Both demand and supply side factors have contributed to a changing domestic labour market. Changes on the demand side include the increasing integration of women in the labour market; the flexibilization of the working time of spouses; the increase in single-parent homes; the absence of a social infrastructure permitting women to combine work with family life; the rising number of older single people with relatively high incomes; the refusal of men to share in the burden in the domestic sphere. Changes on the supply side are: the high unemployment rate among women; the increasing 'new poverty', particularly among women; the availability of cheap migrant labour from Yugoslavia and Turkey, and now also from Eastern Europe, as well as asylum seekers and refugees from the developing world.

In Germany, as well as in many other industrial countries, we are confronted with a 'scissors' phenomenon: an increase in the number of households with ever more income and little time and of others with little income and more time. These two factors, in combination with scaling back the social infra-structure for family assistance, have led to two different, but complementary labour markets for women: one cannot do without the other. 'Current occu-pational class structure produces two groups (of women) in relation to domestic work and child care: those who have not got the time to do it and those who have no alternative but to do it'.[30]

THE SOLUTION:
OUTSOURCING OF DOMESTIC PRODUCTION

Gøsta Esping-Anderson has taken the unchanging level of men's burden-sharing and given it a positive twist with the provocative suggestion that women should stop 'nagging' their mates and instead bring household produc-tion to the market. His advice for men and women is to stop producing these services in the home and obtain them on the market instead.[31] This would create jobs, decrease poverty, and help resolve the welfare-state crisis. Instead of creating a women-friendly welfare state, we should head for a collective welfare state.

Since increasing household demand for outside provision of domestic services is basically the result of rising income levels, favourable costs of such services, and shortage of time, Esping-Andersen concludes that the problem must lie in the currently high market prices for goods and services that substi-tute for household-produced services (e.g., private child care, domestic labour). High market prices lead to low market demand, since these services can be self-produced at a lower cost in the home. Yet Esping-Andersen does not question the class, race and gender aspects of external services that would ensure that their costs were 'favourable'.

If domestic services are to be obtained via the market, then we also have to accept large wage differentials—i.e., low wages for the workers providing them. Otherwise this development will be hampered by Baumol's 'cost disease'. Baumol has shown that the assumption of price inelasticity of demand for services is not justified in cases where the consumer can switch to substitution.[32] Simple services in the home have always competed with 'self-service'. The productivity of such service work increased over time through industrially produced household machines, tools, and other mechanical and electronic gadgets. If as a result of economic development the relative prices for industrial goods decreased while the price of domestic labour increased, then one could expect that 'self-production' would expand at the expense of the demand for services on the market. This conclusion led Fritz Scharpf to suggest that we are not on the road to a service-economy. Instead we are witnessing the rise of a 'self-help society'.[33]

If we want to avoid the 'cost disease' there are three solutions to the problem. The first is to have the state provide and subsidize personal and household services. This is done in Sweden, Denmark and Norway where taxes are high and consequently the share of privately supplied personal and household services is low. At the same time, wage differentials are relatively low in the Nordic states. Second, we can accept high wage differentials and provide personal and household services via the private market. In the United States, the share of private domestic services is the highest of any industrial country while at the same time the wage differentials are also high. The third group of countries (Germany, Austria, France, Belgium and Holland) do not have large private nor public service sectors. Not surprisingly, these countries have the lowest share of people as a percentage of the working population working in the service economy. We are faced with three models: state subsidized care, services that are privatized and available at 'favourable cost', and domestic work which continues to be mainly done by the family itself (i.e., the woman).

These models have in common that they are gender-, class-, and race-blind. Esping-Andersen starts from the assumption that dual-earner families are income rich but short of time. Thus outsourcing domestic work is the answer. But in this calculation, the supply side is completely absent. Who are the 'workers' who are forced to sell their labour at a 'favourable price' and what level is considered 'favourable'? First, we know that the suppliers of such services are overwhelmingly women and not men. Second, they are mostly working-class women and their income is often crucial to the survival of their families. Third, many of these women are migrant domestic workers lacking many basic citizenship rights. Advocating low market prices for household services, as Esping-Andersen suggests, in order to increase the demand for such labour, means that we create at the household level a new ethnically defined female underclass that lacks political rights and legal rights.

Whether we look at female migrant workers in Italy, in Canada, the United States, England or Germany, studies show that they overwhelmingly find work in the domestic sphere. For Germany there are no available data on the number of non-Germans involved. However, various researchers have learned from interviews with representatives of labour administration, labour unions, welfare associations, organizations for foreigners and other such agencies that a large part of the paid work in the home is done by non-Germans. They include economic migrants, asylum seekers, expatriates from the former Eastern Europe, but also language students, women on tourist visas, as well as 'foreigners' of the second generation.[34] Rerrich suggests that a higher proportion of foreign women is found in cleaning homes than in caring for children. This has to do with the increasing number of foreign women pressured to find a job in the informal economy. They often do not possess a work permit and do not speak the language sufficiently to qualify for work in the formal economy. Given their insecure residence status and the need to find a paid job, migrant women are often forced to take the low-paid and little-valued domestic work.

While migrant women have often little choice but to take the cleaning jobs in the private German households, immigrant women with a more secure residence status face the problem of higher unemployment rates in contrast to both German women and foreign men. Thus they too are available for these domestic jobs. Germany has an immigrant population of 11 percent. The biggest number comes from Turkey. The increase of immigrant women who seek hourly paid work in the informal and black labour markets is a reflection of the general unemployment situation and the difficulty of finding regular work. There are, as Kaj Fölster emphasizes, no figures of the ratio of immigrants to non-immigrants in household services, as these workers are not part of the unemployment statistics.[35]

Refugees or expatriates of German origin from the East European countries are not included in the immigration statistics because they are registered as German citizens as soon as they enter the country. But their problems on the labour market are not much different from other immigrants. They often lack sufficient qualifications and do not have a sufficient command of German. Polish women are also increasingly entering the black market of paid domestic work in Germany. They invariably enter on a three-month tourist visa, and then return home. Often a relative or friend secures the replacement position at the work-place. The work is thus often shared among persons who know each other, and these work arrangements can be flexible enough to satisfy the employer. Employment on a tourist visa is illegal but their status as a tourist permits them to move about freely in Germany and their income is seldom checked. Polish women have an advantage over other immigrants, as they are culturally similar to Germans. Newspaper announcements that read: 'German, French, Russian and Polish-speaking woman, 40 years old, with educational training, undertakes child care and domestic work, live-in lodging desired' are no longer a rarity in Germany.[36]

Women asylum seekers, migrants, immigrants, expatriates of German origin who work in the domestic sphere in Germany reinforce women's position as hidden workers with peripheral problems. Whether they have to contend with sexual harassment, long hours of work, arbitrary treatment by their employers, insecurity or even the loss of the job and the right to stay in the country, these problems remain 'hidden' and do not precipitate a response from the state. Moreover, while 'paid housework' was initially sought as a short-term strategy by most immigrant women, it generally turns into long-term employment. This has two consequences. These jobs do not provide any kind of promotion or career prospects that will permit movement out of the domestic arena. In addition, a well-hidden fact is that many of these migrant women cannot take their children to the country of employment. We not only need to ask the question 'Who is doing the housework?' But also 'Who is doing the child care for the domestic worker?'

CONCLUSION

Globalization has increased flexibilization and individualization in the labour markets. These global processes perpetuate old patterns of segregation and create new forms of marginality. The globalization literature has largely focused on the information technology revolution with its new ways of producing, communicating, managing, and living. Less attention has been paid to the formation of new social patterns which have arisen at the level of the household. As the trend toward women professionals increases we also witness, in the absence of public and communal child and domestic care facilities, the need for paid household workers. The much hoped for redistribution of caring work between men and women has not materialized. Instead we witness a new international division of labour between women of different ethnicity, class, generation, and citizenship. The new class of domestic servants are often migrant women who do not have independent legal status, nor are they counted as part of the official migrant population. In countries without security of residence, migrant women are at constant risk of deportation and abuse.

This development points to a new power relationship at the level of the household *between women*. We are witnessing the rise of a privileged professional class of women and the growth of an ethnically-defined female underclass. Increasingly, the career of middle-class women intersects with the position of immigrant women. Both sides are mutually dependent on the other. As Marianne Friese points out, there are risks for both sides that are not part of the traditional sexual contract between married men and women. While a husband is able to 'purchase' life-long freedom from domestic work through marriage, a wife with a professional job can only gain limited security from the services of a 'maid'.[37] More important, 'the occupation that brought women of different class backgrounds together in the women's sphere is now bringing race relations into the middle-class homemaker's home'.[38] In this struggle, majority and minority women's interests intersect, despite different social realities and origins.[39] The increasing equality among middle-class men and women of the same class and ethnic background is accompanied by a new kind of inequality among women of different ethnic and class backgrounds.

To avoid the creation of a new ethnically defined female underclass, the common struggle has to be fought at several levels. First, it is essential to 're-politicize the private'. The privatized nature of the household hides the class and race dynamics that are embedded in the new domestic service economy. At the same time, employing other women to do the caring work in the homes of professionals reproduces the gendered aspect of responsibility for the household. As long as state policies in most advanced capitalist countries adhere to the outdated 'breadwinner doctrine', deficiencies in social support systems and welfare state provisions are the logical result. The dismantling of the ideology of the male breadwinner model doctrine is a first step in the much needed discourse on how men and women can combine family and work without exploiting women from other class and ethnic backgrounds. Feminist scholarship is also challenged to reveal and make visible the new inequities that arise in response to the neoliberal reprivatization discourse. Bakan and Stasiulis conclude that 'only by revealing how systematic practices render some relatively privileged women complicit in the reproduction of racial, ethnic, and other forms of inequities for other women that the real structural boundaries of oppression can be revealed, understood, and challenged'.[40] Finally, we need to focus more strongly on the 'feminization of migration' that ends for many women as undocumented domestic servants in the 'host' country. The newer discourses on citizenship stress that citizenship reflects the asymmetrical state relationships in the global economy. However, we also need to take into account that citizenship interacts with ethnic, gender, and class differences.

NOTES

1. Saskia Sassen, 'Toward a Feminist Analytics of the Global Economy', *Indiana Journal of Global Legal Studies*, Fall 1996, pp. 7–41.
2. Brigitte Young, 'Genderregime und Staat in der globalen Netzwerkökonomie', *Prokla,* 111, 1998, pp. 175–198.
3. Wuokke Knocke, 'Migrant and Ethnic Minority Women: The Effects of Gender-neutral Legislation in the European Community', *Social Politics*, 2(2), 1995, pp. 225-38.
4. Marianne Friese, 'Modernisierungsfallen im historischen Prozeß. Zur Entwicklung der Frauenarbeit im gewandelten Europa', *Berliner Journal für Soziologie,* 2, 1995, pp. 149–162, also Birgit Mahnkopf, 'Die "Feminisierung der Beschäftigung"—in Europa und Anderswo', *Weibblick* 718, 1997, pp. 22–31, and Jacqueline Andall, 'Women Migrant Workers in Italy', *Women's Studies Int. Forum,* 15(1), 1992, pp. 41–48.
5. David Harvey, *The Condition of Postmodernity,* Oxford: Blackwell, 1989.
6. Mahnkopf, 'Die "Feminisierung der Beschäftigung"', pp. 22–31.
7. Commission of the European Community: Soziales Europa. Chancengleichheit für Männer und Frauen, 3/91, p. 24.
8. Jennifer Hunt, Presentation at the Conference on the US-Labour Market, Berlin, 17 June 1998.
9. Linda McDowell, *Capital Culture. Gender At Work in the City*, Oxford: Blackwell, 1997.
10. Sassen, 'Toward a Feminist Analytics of the Global Economy', p. 10.
11. We use the concept of gender orders to refer to the aggregate of gender regimes (institutionalized practices and forms of gendered system of domination) at the level of macro-politics; see Robert W. Connell, *Gender and Power. Society, the Person and Sexual Politics*, Stanford: Stanford University Press, 1987.
12. Kaj Fölster, 'Paid Domestic Work in Germany. Report on the legal reforms and the different Initiatives in order to create more regular employment in domestic work in Germany', paper for the Conference *Labour Market and Social Policy—Gender Relations in Transition*, Brussels, 31 May–2 June 1999.
13. Günther Schmid, 'Enhancing Gender Equality by Transitional Labour Markets', paper presented for the workshop *Labour Market and Social Policy—Gender*

Relations in Transition, in Brussels on 31 May–2 June 1999.

14. M. Patricia Fernández Kelly and Saskia Sassen, 'Recasting Women in the Global Economy: Internationalization and Changing Definition of Gender', in: Christine E. Bose and Edna Acosta-Belén, *Women in the Latin American Development Process*, Philadelphia, 1995, p. 113.

15. Brigitte Young, 'Globalization and Gender: A European Perspective', in: Rita Mae Kelly, Jane Bayes, Mary Hawkesworth, and Brigitte Young, *Gender, Globalization and Democratization*, New York: Rowman and Littlefield Publ., 2000.

16. Karin Hossfeld, '"Their Logic against Them": Contradictions in Sex, Race, and Class in Silicon Valley', in: Kathryn Ward, ed., *Women Workers and Global Restructuring*, Ithaca: Cornell University Press, 1990.

17. Kathryn Ward and Jean Larson Pyle, 'Gender, Industrialization, Transnational Corporations, and Development: An Overview of Trends and Patterns', in: Bose and Acosta-Belén, ed., *Women in the Latin American Development Process*, pp. 37–64.

18. Diane Elson, 'Micro, Meso, Macro: Gender and Economic Analysis in the Context of Policy Reform', in: Isabella Bakker, ed., *Strategic Silence. Gender and Economic Policy*, London: Zed Books, 1994.

19. Wendy Larner, 'The "New Boys": Restructuring in New Zealand, 1984–94', *Social Politics*, 3(1), 1996, pp. 32–56.

20. Fölster, 'Paid Domestic Work in Germany', p. 3.

21. Elisabeth Hagen and Jane Jenson, 'Paradoxes and Promises. Work and politics in the post-war years', in: Jane Jenson, Elisabeth Hagen and Ceallaigh Reddy, eds., *Feminization of the Labor Force*, New York: Oxford University Press, 1988.

22. Janine Brodie, 'Shifting the Boundaries: Gender and the Politics of Restructuring', in: Bakker, ed., *The Strategic Silence. Gender and Economic Policy*, p. 57.

23. Federal Ministry of Work and Social Regulation, *Arbeitsplatz Privathaushalt—Dienstleistungszentren*, Bonn, 1998.

24. Gøsta Esping-Andersen, 'Summary of the speech by Prof. G. Esping-Andersen', Conference Report *Out of the Margin 2/IAFFE Conference*, University of Amsterdam, Amsterdam, 5 June 1998.

25. Simone Odierna and Karin Baumann, 'Die Rückkehr der Dienstmädchen durch die Hintertür. Empirische Befunde und theoretische Vorarbeiten zur Analyse bezahlter Arbeit in Privathaushalten', im Auftrag des Sonderforschungsbereich 333 *Entwicklungsperspektiven von Arbeit*, Universität München, Juni 1992.

26. Sonja Munz, 'Beschäftigungspotentiale im Bereich privater Haushalte', *IFO–Schnelldienst*, 17–18, 1996, pp. 38–45.

27. Claudia Weinkopf, 'Beschäftigungsförderung im Bereich haushaltsbezogener Dienstleistungen', in: Ute Behning, *Das Private ist ökonomisch*, Berlin: Edition Sigma, 1997, p. 134.

28. The present US $ equivalent is around $2,500 which reflects the undervalued Euro. The real equivalent is more like $5,000.

29. Notburga Ott, 'Eigenproduktion versus Dienstleistung im Haushalt. Zum ökonomischen Wert der Hausarbeit' in: *Hausarbeit als Erwerbsarbeit*, eine Berliner Fachtagung zur Europawoche 1997, Berlin: Zukunft im Zentrum, 1997, pp. 27–37.

30. Maria S. Rerrich, 'Neustrukturierung der Alltagsarbeit zwischen Lohn und Liebe—Überlegungen zu möglichen Entwicklungspfaden bezahlter häuslicher Dienstleistungen', Presentation in Bremen, 5 February 1999, p. 8.

31. Esping-Andersen, 'Summary of the speech', June 1998.
32. William J. Baumol and Wallace E. Oates, 'The Cost Disease of the Personal Services and the Quality of Life', *Skandinaviska Enskilda Banken Quarterly Review*, 2, 1972, pp. 44–54.
33. Fritz W. Scharpf, 'Strukturen der post-industriellen Gesellschaft oder: Verschwindet die Massenarbeitslosigkeit in der Dienstleistungs- und Informations-Ökonomie?' *Soziale Welt*, 37, 1986, pp. 3–24. Also Traute Meyer, 'Wider "Selbstbedienungsökonomie" und "Brotverdienermodell"? Beschäftigungspolitische Chancen der Subventionierung haushaltsnaher Dienstleistungen in Deutschland', in: Behning, ed., *Das Private ist ökonomisch*, pp. 189–205, and Weinkopf, 'Beschäftigungsförderung', pp. 133–151.
34. Maria S. Rerrich, 'Auf dem Weg zu einer neuen internationalen Arbeitsteilung der Frauen in Europa? Beharrungs- und Veränderungstendenzen in der Verteilung von Reproduktionsarbeit', in: Bernhard Schäfers, ed., *Lebensverhältnisse und soziale Konflikte im neuen Europa*. Verhandlungen des 26. Deutschen Soziologentages in Düsseldorf 1992, Frankfurt/New York: Campus Verlag, 1993, pp. 93–102, also Odierna and Baumann, 'Die Rückkehr der Dienstmädchen durch die Hintertür', and Friese, 'Modernisierungsfallen im historischen Prozeß', pp. 149–162.
35. Fölster, 'Paid Domestic Work in Germany', p. 11.
36. Friese, 'Modernisierungsfallen im historischen Prozeß', p. 158.
37. Ibid, p. 158.
38. Mary Romero, *Maid in the U.S.A.*, New York: Routledge, 1993, p. 69.
39. Knocke, 'Migrant and Ethnic Minority Women, p. 236.
40. Abigail B. Bakan and Daiva K. Stasiulis, 'Making the Match: Domestic Placement Agencies and the Racialization of Women's Household Work,' *Signs*, Winter 1995, pp. 303–335.

FEMINISM'S CHALLENGE TO UNIONS IN THE NORTH: POSSIBILITIES AND CONTRADICTIONS

Rosemary Warskett

In most advanced capitalist societies, the feminist challenge to labour unions began well over twenty-five years ago. This essay examines the history of the ambivalent relationship between women and unions and assesses the difference feminism has made in terms of the structure, practices and overall vision of unions' role and goals. Has feminism helped to renew union movements across the capitalist world and moved them at all towards socialism? The answer to this is complex and involves assessing both the different strands of feminist influence and the way these were interwoven with the attack on unions and working people that occurred in the 1980s and 1990s.

From the perspective of the end of the twentieth century there have been three distinct influences on the formation of union feminism. Socialist-feminism that developed during the 1970s; working class feminism that emerged from the largely economic struggles of union women, starting in some countries as early as the 1960s and continuing through to the present; and mainstream gender politics, generally going under the rubric of 'equal opportunity', that sprung up in many liberal-democracies in the late 1970s and 1980s. All three influences remain in tension within labour movements today, interwoven together to produce important changes.

The overall argument of the essay is that feminism's contribution to legal and collective bargaining gains is real and substantial; that the ideological separation between home and work has been effectively challenged by feminist insights; that how democracy works in some unions has been changed under the influence of feminist democratic processes; and that women are more visible at the leadership level. All of this, however, has not changed in any fundamental way labour unions' vision of what the work-place, community and society could be. Indeed it can be argued that union feminists, like their male counterparts, have pushed an agenda that is both economistic and reformist and that the sources of this lie as much in mainstream feminism as in male-dominated business unionism. In this respect the vision of socialist-feminism has not succeeded in changing labour movements, despite the positive changes that have been wrought by the conjuncture of feminism and unionism. This essay mainly draws on examples from Canadian feminism. While it is difficult to say how representative these are, nevertheless, they are indicative of developments over the last fifty years.

THE EMERGENCE OF SOCIALIST-FEMINISM

Feminism re-emerged within capitalist liberal-democratic societies at a critical moment for socialist movements. In most of these societies, by the end of the 1960s, the state was experiencing challenges from progressive movements of workers and students demanding radical changes in politics, society and the work place. In this context feminism re-emerged as part of the widespread challenge to the political and social hegemony of the period. This manifested itself in a multitude of ways; in student unrest and defiance of traditional authority; in trade union militancy that in certain places joined forces with student radicals; in New Left community activism and politics that questioned the power of developers; in international solidarity struggles and 'in the assertion of the power of women and the demand for transformed personal and sexual politics'.[1] Until then the struggle for socialism had had very little to do with changing the subordination and oppression of women, either within society generally or within socialist organizations themselves. Within these movements women were active but generally not seen, relegated to backroom work, serving as secretaries, organizers, tea and coffee makers. Ideas about human liberation during the 1960s had not done much to change this. Women for the most part were condemned to a subordinate position within the Left. Patriarchy within socialist movements was just as strong as it was within conservative institutions. In this context socialist women began to organize to change themselves and their respective parties and groups.[2]

There were a number of possibilities open to women on the Left in the late-1960s and early-1970s. Some took up the challenge within the socialist groups they already belonged to. Some, tiring of the attempt to change the patriarchal relations and authoritarian processes of sectarian groups, decided to leave and join with other women in the small groups that constituted the women's liberation movement. Others kept a foot in both camps. Still others made the labour movement the locus of their political activity. In Britain *Beyond the Fragments* by Sheila Rowbotham, Lynne Segal and Hilary Wainwright defined the debate from the perspective of the late 1970s' disillusionment with the Labour Party and other Left parties and groups.[3] Their view was that the experiences of the women's liberation movement had much to contribute to overcoming the problems which had held back the creation of 'a more democratic, more truly popular and more effective socialist movement than was possible before'.[4]

For women who considered themselves socialist-feminist, working with other women—whether in Left groups, the union movement, or the women's movement in general—resulted in an experience which led them to demand democratic participation. Not only did this raise questions and criticism about vanguardism and the sectarian Left, but in later writings, when reflecting on this experience, socialist-feminists argued that the process of women working together developed collective capacities both to live their everyday experience democratically and also to struggle for radical change.[5] One of the most important insights of 'second wave' feminism was the need for women to develop self-activity, to free themselves from subordination where they experienced it, to rid themselves of passivity, deference and lack of confidence. In this respect working-class men had much to gain by applying the lessons of the women's liberation movement. But of course at that time they were incapable of hearing the message.

Developing women's self-activity involved consciousness-raising through analysis and discussion; developing processes for communicating democratically and rejecting hierarchical and bureaucratic structures. In this respect Johanna Brenner's argument that feminism is 'a rich resource for the renewal of Marxism—for recapturing and developing its radically democratic liberatory vision',[6] accurately captured the perspective of socialist-feminists who never claimed that the women's movement was a complete model on which the Left should base itself, but rather that, as Hilary Wainwright says, it 'has made an absolutely vital achievement—or at least the beginnings of it—which no socialist should ignore'.[7]

Socialist-feminists also thought that feminism had the potential to democratize unions by including and encouraging the education and participation of those who have been traditionally subordinated within unions; by changing authoritarian and bureaucratic structures and practices; and by reducing hierarchy and encouraging equalitarianism. Socialist-feminists carried these ideas into the union movement and met up with union women who were in the process of confronting the reality of low pay and low status in the work-place, and of subordination and invisibility in the unions that represented them.[8]

THE RISE AND GROWTH OF WORKING-CLASS FEMINISM

The issues for women of the dominant classes revolve around the possibilities of transforming the internal gender relations of class without transforming class itself. Clearly those for working-class women confront a more fundamental contradiction, particularly as the ambiguous local patriarchal forms of the family are eroded by changes in the bases of the family economy.[9]

The changing material conditions of working-class women's lives contributed to a growing militancy by union women in many capitalist economies. While in most countries women—especially married women—flooded into the paid labour force from the late 1960s to the 1980s, a significant number of working-class women had always been there.[10] They did not leave the paid labour force once they had children, but remained in jobs which were segregated from men. This was particularly the case in France where from the early part of the century significant numbers of working-class women were employed in industrial production. It is not surprising, therefore, that in France militancy by union women predated the re-emergence of a women's movement.[11]

In Britain, Canada and the United States the experience of working-class women was somewhat different. Between the 1960s and 1980s there was a rapid increase in labour force participation and, as a consequence, in the numbers of women organized into unions. This occurred mainly in the public sector. In these countries working-class feminism grew out of strikes and militant struggles waged by unionized women in the 1970s and 1980s.[12] At the time these were not characterized as women's strikes. It was only later as women within unions became more acquainted with the language of feminism that these strikes were seen as the beginnings of their struggle for equality. In nearly all the cases the main issue was low pay or the need for equal pay (later constructed in socialist-feminist terms as women as a source of cheap labour).[13] Coupled with the demand for more pay, however, was a focus on women's low status in the work-place and the need for respect and dignity on the job.

For women with working-class experience the movement for women's liberation seemed a luxury they could ill afford. The much-publicized image of North American women burning their bras and demanding sexual liberation seemed indulgent to women who worried each week about stretching the family wages to cover basic needs. As Dorothy Smith points out, patriarchy was not as visible to working-class women as those in the intermediate classes because it is found '… in the same set of institutional processes which organize class hegemony' and for this reason '… its patriarchal practices are not easily distinguishable from its class rule'.[14]

Socialist-feminists made sense of the changed material reality of union women's lives through the analysis that they brought into the unions. In informal groups, and later in formal education courses and workshops, the material and ideological bases of women's oppression were debated. In a number of countries feminists from outside the union movement turned up on picket lines to support women during strike action and demonstrate their solidarity with their union sisters.[15] In Italy as well as France 'collectivities' of women unionists were formed during the 1970s with initiatives taken by women from the New Left. They demanded and won autonomous sections of women inside unions.[16] These networks placed their emphasis on political activism rather than employment demands. This was in contrast to the informal women's committees that started to be formed in the mid-1970s in the US and Canada, which mainly emphasized changing male-dominated collective bargaining and politics within unions.[17]

One of the most contentious issues for labour unions concerns women separately organizing inside them. Informal women's committees started in Canada and the United States in the mid-1970s and were succeeded by formal women's committees, education courses, workshops and conferences. As noted earlier, one of the most significant insights of feminism is the necessity for women to confront their passivity and subordination and become active participants. Because of women's propensity to remain silent and invisible, either being unable to prevent men's dominance or allowing them to take over, union women pushed for separate forums where they could discuss, debate and analyse their subjection together,without the presence of men. Developing from the early ideas of consciousness-raising, this kind of separation allowed women to develop the skills, knowledge and confidence needed to take their full place in their unions. Furthermore, within these forums attempts were made to develop democratic feminist process, rejecting the authoritarian and hierarchical processes found in traditional union meetings. Separate women's committees are also the forums where union women can strategize about getting their demands on to the bargaining table and the convention floor.[18]

While socialist-feminists have argued that in the final analysis separate organizations for women strengthen unions overall, there is the problem that marginalization of women can result, in terms of both process and their demands.[19] In the case of France, Jane Jenson argues that the establishment of autonomous groups of women within unions resulted in their being seen as marginal workers who were not part of the unions' main business, so that they were not treated equally as regular workers either in the unions or the labour market.[20] Clearly there is a need for women to maintain a balance between autonomy and integration if they are to strengthen their power within unions. Women and other subordinated groups have been in many cases hived off into separate committees, set apart from the 'serious' business of unions and thus marginalized.

Furthermore, women have been marginalized as wives in their attempts to have input into union policy that directly affects them. In this sense committees of union wives have been constructed by unions as being separate and marginal to union decision-making. Two examples of this stand out: in Britain 'Women Against Pit Closures' in 1984 and, in Canada 'Wives Supporting the Inco Strike' in 1978. Both groups were formed to promote solidarity between the unions and the community. Both organized activities that resulted in the private realm of the home being merged with the realm of work, into a community of defence and action. Both groups attempted to ask crucial questions regarding the separation of the work-place from the community. Did not the community have as much of their lives tied up in the mines as the men that worked there? Should they not have a say, or even a vote,about the decisions to be made? In this sense both groups raised fundamental questions concerning working-class democracy, and the rights of both those who produce and those who *reproduce* to debate and contribute to decisions that affect the entire working-class community.[21]

By the early 1980s union feminists debated and started to develop strategies and policies aimed at changing women's subordination in the work-place, in their unions and at home.[22] This involved addressing women's 'triple day' (as workers, parents and union activists), and devising policies which relieved women of their duties in the home, such as the provision of paid child care during union events. This emphasis on the relationship between home, the work-place and the subordination of women in both spheres also had the effect of questioning the traditional goals of industrial unionism. Should unions be concerned only with work-place problems or also with social issues generally? In Canada, by the end of the 1980s union feminism effectively challenged the narrow vision of industrial unionism to include policies on abortion, child care, sexual and racial harassment and other equality issues.[23] It is now well established in Canada that collective bargaining demands should address the needs of women and other discriminated groups, and more generally that the union movement should move beyond work-place issues to deal with social concerns that reflect the relationship between work and the community as a whole.

Union-feminism has to this extent played a fundamental role in breaking down the ideological separation of paid and unpaid work, home and work, the economy and the community. Challenging the idea of work as a separate sphere from that of the community has raised fundamental questions concerning the private/public divide and increased the union movement's potential to broaden its vision of the relationship between work and society. For example issues such as reduced working time were reconceptualized by feminists, so as to broaden the demand, linking it with issues in the home and community and the need for more time for the reproduction of labour power and for developing a culture of community activity.[24]

RESTRUCTURING ECONOMIES AND INSTITUTIONALIZING FEMINISM

After the heady days of the women's liberation movement, the development of socialist-feminism and the flourishing of working-class feminism, the women's movement settled down and became institutionalized in advanced capitalist societies by the 1980s and 1990s. Indeed its institutionalization is a mark of how successful the second wave of feminism really was. The formalizing of the movement started in most countries in the late 1970s with the introduction of equal opportunity and anti-discrimination programmes by governments. 'Status of Women' offices were established and staffed by women, the 'femocrats' who made a career out of equal opportunities initiatives.[25] Such initiatives followed from International Women's Year in 1975, the

United Nation's symbolic attempt to promote women's equality in its member countries. With the institutionalization of feminism within various states, mainstream feminism became more acceptable within unions. In Canada and the United States unions established equal opportunity committees along the lines found within state bureaucracies. Frequently positions on these committees were held by women who could be trusted by the unions' male-dominated executives 'not to rock the boat'.

The main emphasis in equal opportunity policies is the removal of barriers to women's advancement within work places and other economic and political institutions, with declarations of gender equality and guarantees that women and men will receive equal treatment. This was all well and good, but for working-class women, condemned to a narrow range of low-paying job ghettos, 'equal opportunity' had little impact on the everyday double burden of unpaid work in the home and low pay in the work place. The influence of equal opportunity policy on unions resulted in bringing more women into leadership positions, challenging sexist practices and supplementing labour's traditional agenda with women's issues. In other words, equal opportunity policies set out to modify union structures and practices so women can be accommodated; they do not, by themselves, question bureaucratic and hierarchical decision-making. The equal opportunity approach also fostered a dependence on legal processes rather than on collective, militant action.[26] Equal opportunity recognized women's subordinate status within the union movement and the work-place but could not by itself change it.

The concept of equal opportunity was extended and developed into notions of pay and employment equity. Women, especially in unions, demanded that their low pay and status be addressed, and equal opportunity programmes had little to say about this. Equity has been interpreted as being about members of subordinate groups, including women, gaining the benefits, the status, the positions that white males already have. This is in profound contradiction with a more radical conception of equity as meaning a reduction in inequality in pay and status generally, a goal not satisfied by distributing the places in an unequal hierarchy more evenly.[27]

At the same time that equal opportunity policies were being put in place, economic restructuring and the move to the right were occurring. Eventually by the 1990s all liberal-democratic and social-democratic economies were deeply affected by the restructuring of capital, the work-place and social-welfare provisions. Economic restructuring in general produced a marked increase in non-standard and precarious forms of work—historically associated with women. In many labour movements the loss of male-dominated industrial jobs and the expansion of the service sector provided an opening for feminist initiatives because women workers became the 'paradigmatic trade unionists'.[28] Because unions were experiencing a dramatic loss of male members, the need became apparent to organize women in the service sector and to try to address their specific needs at the bargaining table.

The move to the right also occurred with respect to feminism and was reflected in the undermining of social welfare states and the marketing of state functions. Johanna Brenner points out that 'the new right has been so successful a counter to feminism', because '… without the capacity to construct personal dilemmas as political issues, feminism is necessarily on the defensive …'.[29] Of course, mainstream feminism remains alive. In the United States it is institutionalized in a vast network of organizations which operate as pressure groups on politicians to bring about legislative and juridical change.[30] And in Europe as well as Canada there has also been an increasing tendency to take up equity issues through legislative and court processes.[31] This has resulted in some outstanding successes in terms of wage settlements for women even in a neoliberal era. For instance, in Canada—after a long and costly process for the union in terms of legal representation—the largest sum ($4.5 billion) in the entire of history of equal value/comparative worth was awarded in 1999 to the members of the Public Service Alliance of Canada (PSAC), the union that represents most federal government workers who occupied female-dominated positions.

Swedish women also have been demanding pay equity. In the 1930s Swedish unions accepted women's right to be in the paid labour force and later in the post-war period took special measures to help them to be active members of unions. Also women in general benefitted from the labour movement's wage solidarity strategy. With the erosion of collective bargaining in the 1990s, however, and the breakdown of wage solidarity, the wage gap between men and women began to widen. This provided an opening for feminists in unions to demand equal pay for work of equal value. In LO this resulted in the creation of a special women's 'pot' of money, instead of special pots for the lower paid whether they are men or women. What this means is that women are separated out from the rest of the working-class, and the special 'pot' now also benefits higher-paid women. While agreeing to the women's 'pot', LO has resisted juridification of equity issues, largely due to its tradition of centralized bargaining.[32]

There are often good arguments for such resistance, above all that juridification of union struggles inevitably results in a loss of mobilization and a reliance instead on legal experts and legal arguments. Yet this is not always the case and was not entirely the case in the PSAC's struggle for pay equity in Canada. The sixteen-year-long legal process was paralleled by strikes, sit ins, demonstrations and education sessions. The union spent considerable resources educating and mobilizing the membership in support of its conception of the equal value principle, so the struggle was far from being a mere legal battle controlled entirely by legal experts. Yet there are contradictory outcomes for unions in allowing the courts to be the main forum in which conflicts are decided. In the case of the PSAC, despite the mobilization of the membership around the issue of equal value, the fact that the main battle was fought in the courts means that the issue has not become embedded in the collective bargaining experience and practice of the union. Future collective bargaining cannot build on the experience and learning that might have taken place if the whole union had been mobilized to strike over the issue. Will future negotiations revert to the past practice of demanding higher wages for men? Without the experience of struggling for equal pay on picket lines, has the issue really become an embedded part of the 'main business' of the union? It is important for union feminists to develop a clearer vision of law and what it is capable of achieving.[33] Often even successful outcomes have contradictory effects.

Another problem with the equal value approach is that it leads to the view that men's pay and position are the ultimate objective to be achieved. Men's overall higher pay and higher status in the work-place have become the objectives of women's struggle together with the desire to see women equally represented in the hierarchy of jobs and pay. This is in stark contrast to a vision of transforming the hierarchical nature of the work-place, with its authoritarian division of tasks and separation of intellectual and physical labour. The earlier socialist-feminists' vision of changing union organization so as to promote the value of all people's work in terms of self-activity and human liberation is removed from the agenda, and equity, in terms of what white men have, becomes the ultimate objective. Furthermore, in certain sectors during the recent period of restructuring, the wage gap between men and women has declined, not because women's wages have increased but because men's have fallen. The emphasis on equal value has led unionists in some cases away from considering the wage gap between the lowest- and highest-paid workers. Even wages below subsistence level are perceived to be justified if job evaluation plans 'show' them to be only worth that much.[34]

Yet there are instances where these implications of pay equity have been rejected by unionists who have instead fostered a concept of wage justice which rejects bourgeois notions of the market value of skills and labour. In Ontario, which was said to have the 'best' pay equity legislation of any Canadian province, applying to both the private and the public sectors, union locals organized by the Canadian Union of Public Employees refused to allow management's conception of the value of skills to guide the outcome of the pay equity process. Operating with their own conception of justice, union presidents in many cases insisted that pay equity had to mean raising the wages of the lowest-paid workers even though the job evaluation plan did not justify the increase. But in general, because of the use of a range of factors in evaluating skill gradations, job evaluation methodology emphasizes and accentuates the skill differences between workers rather than gathering workers together on the basis of similarities and one common wage.[35] Pay equity and its application through job evaluation therefore is often in contradiction with the need to raise the pay of those in the lowest part of the job hierarchy. This contradiction is frequently not recognized by many union-feminists, who in general do advocate for dramatic increases for those workers, including the unemployed, who receive incomes below subsistence levels.

All this said, it is still the case that while equal opportunities and equity policies carry with them individualizing tendencies focused on achieving a higher place in the hierarchy of jobs and pay for individual women, women in unions have, nevertheless, collectively rallied to support pay equity and in doing so have revealed the systemic, collective nature of women's low pay. In this sense pay equity has been an important, though contradictory, banner behind which union women and men have mobilized and formed alliances with feminist groups.[36]

CONCLUSION

The challenge of feminism to labour unions has varied from country to country, and from union to union, both in its strength and its impact. Some unions remain untouched by feminism's necessary and important influence, while in others men strongly resist sharing their power with women. In general, however, by the end of the twentieth century women are in unions in large numbers and have made themselves and their demands heard. Union women are representatives at all levels of the movement and increasingly they are found in staff positions. New forms of union and working-class solidarity have been forged as a result of feminism that now include, not only women, but also other subordinate groups, and to some extent those outside in other social movements. Feminism has had the effect of broadening the definition of the working-class and work-place struggles and undoubtedly there has been a sea change with regard to the representation by women and collective bargaining issues addressing women's needs.

Economic restructuring and the move to the right in the latter part of the twentieth century had contradictory effects on the feminist challenge. On the one hand, the changes in the economy provided openings for organizing women and responding to their demands, while on the other they emphasized the economistic tendencies of working-class feminism and limited its potential. Improving the economic position of women, other low-paid groups and the working class overall is of utmost importance and helps to strengthen the labour movement in general. An emphasis on economic welfare, however, without examining the underlying labour-market causes of below-subsistence pay and without raising fundamental questions concerning the organization of work and its relationship to the political economy is bound to result in reformist tendencies. In this respect union feminism carries with it the same economistic limitations as those of business unions. In general feminism has been formalized in unions but it tends to be the economist, reformist tendencies that have got the upper hand. Socialist-feminism in the seventies was limited by the absence of working class and non-white women. Joining with union women overcame that limitation but at the same time socialist-feminists' energy has been directed to day-to-day working-class struggles that have attenuated their vision of social transformation. Socialist-feminist tendencies remain present but the transformative vision of socialist-feminism is still struggling in the wings, off the main stage.

NOTES

1. Lynne Segal, *Is the Future Female,* London: Virago Press, 1987, p. 206.

2. This is not to deny the gains made under Communist regimes. Frigga Haug points out that East German women prior to reunification were more independent than West German women because of the social support they received from the East German state. See her *Beyond Female Masochism: Memory—Work and Politics,* London: Verso 1992, pp. 185–217.

3. Sheila Rowbotham described her experience during the 1960s in the Young Socialist group of the Hackney Labour Party where she met young Trotskyists, then later in the1960s she briefly joined the International Socialists (IS). Overwhelmed by the 'energy which erupted in May 1968' she found the subsequent defeat of the broad left movement hard to take. The radical movements of '68 did, however, open her 'political eyes and ears'. The emphasis these placed on human liberation and the rejection of the 'inner hold' of capitalism also made her aware of the limitations of democratic centralism and the 'assumption that the manipulation of people was justified by the supposedly superior knowledge' of the revolutionary leaders. By the early 1970s she had become an 'old leftist', only then did she become involved with the emerging Women's Liberation Movement. See Sheila Rowbotham, Lynne Segal and Hilary Wainwright, *Beyond the Fragments: Feminism and the Making of Socialism,* London: The Merlin Press Ltd., 1979, pp. 26–39.

4. Rowbotham et al., *Beyond the Fragments,* p. 14; also see Hilary Wainwright's arguments in ibid., pp. 231, 252 and in *Arguments for a New Left,* Oxford: Blackwell, 1994.

5. See Rowbotham et al., *Beyond the Fragments,* pp. 211–53; Carolyn Egan, 'Toronto's International Women's Day Committee'; Heather Jon Maroney and Meg Luxton (eds.), *Feminism and Political Economy: Women's Work, Women's Struggles,* Agincourt: Methuen Publications, 1987, pp. 109–18; and Johanna Brenner, 'Feminism's Revolutionary Promise: Finding Hope in Hard Times', *Socialist Register,* 1989, pp. 245–63.

6. From the perspective of the US, Johanna Brenner argued that: 'Feminist theory has helped to undermine the system that Marxist theory had become: its economic reductionism, its productivism and uncritical approach to technology; its narrow definitions of work, worker, and the working-class; its reification of the capitalist split between "public" and "private" and the privileging of the public as an arena for theoretical analysis and political organization; its impoverished understandings of consciousness, particularly its inattention to the way emotional needs shape political understandings, the relationship between gender identities and the construction of political and economic "interests".' Brenner 'Feminism's Revolutionary Promise', pp. 245–6.

7. Rowbotham et al., *Beyond the Fragments,* p. 250. Some of theses ideas form part of the Gramscian vision of educationing the working-class and changing the relationship between leaders and led. The importance of socialist-feminism, however, was the way in which the ideas of educating and activating the masses became part of the debate and practice within women's groups. For a recent discussion of the development of the 'productive forces within capitalism' by building capacities to govern democratically everyday life, the economy, civil society and the state,

including those articulated by socialist-feminists, see Leo Panitch and Sam Gindin, 'Transcending Pessimism: Rekindling Socialist Imagination', *Socialist Register*, 2000, pp. 1–29.

8.   See the important essay by Heather Jon Maroney, 'Feminism at Work', *New Left Review*, 141, Sept–Oct 1983.

9.   Dorothy Smith, 'Women, Class and Family', *Women, Class, Family and The State*, Toronto: Garamond Press, 1985, p. 40.

10. The major exceptions were France and Germany. The female share of the labour force in 1950 was 35.9% for France and 35.1% for Germany, these percentages had increased only slightly by 1982. In Canada and the US in 1950 the female share was 21.3% and 28.9%, and by 1982 these had increased significantly to 40.9% and 42.8%. See Isabella Bakker 'Women's Employment in Comparative Perspective', *Feminization of the Labour Force*, Jane Jenson et al. (eds.), Oxford: Polity Press, 1988, pp. 17–44.

11. Jane Jenson argues that during the mid-1960s 'many women, employed where de-skilling and intensification of production was most important, had emerged on the front line of militant struggle'. 'Legacies of the French Women's Movement: Mobilization of "Difference" in the Labour Movement', Prepared for the Annual Meeting of the Canadian Political Science Association, Winnipeg, June 1986, p. 15. See also Jane Jenson, 'Gender and Reproduction: Or Babies and the State', *Studies in Political Economy*, 20, Summer 1986, pp. 9–46, for a discussion of the difference between Britain and France with respect to women in the paid labour force and the two states' child-care policies.

12. See Rosemary Warskett, 'The Politics of Difference and Inclusiveness within the Canadian Labour Movement', *Economic and Industrial Democracy*, vol. 17, no. 4 (November) 1996. By the 1990s, a catastrophic decline in the numbers of workers organized in the US had resulted in new openings for a different kind of unionism. In Canada the labour movement has not experienced the same kind of decline and women in unions have undertaken the task of changing the old-style business unionism of the 1950s and 1960s. See Julie White, *Sisters in Solidarity: Women and Unions in Canada*, Toronto: Thompson Educational Publishing, Inc., 1993.

13. Heather Jon Maroney in *Feminism at Work* argues that 'the rise of working-class feminism has not, however, been an unmixed blessing'. She goes on to point out that the militant struggles by working-class women has 'reinforced a general tendency in the left to economism'.

14. Smith, 'Women, Class and Family', p. 40.

15. See, for France, Jane Jenson, 'The Limits of "and the" Discourse: French women as marginal workers', *Feminization of the Labour Force*, Jane Jenson, et al. (eds.), Oxford: Polity Press, 1988, p. 17; for Canada, Carolyn Egan, 'Toronto's International Women's Day Committee', p. 114; for Britain, Sheila Rowbotham, *The Past is Before Us: Feminism in Action since the 1960s*, London: Unwin Hyman Ltd., 1989, pp. 225–226.

16. For Italy, see Bianca Beccalli and Guglielmo Meardi, 'When Equal opportunities is not enough: The ambiguous and changing relations between women and unions in Italy', Prepared for the Twelfth International Conference of Europeanists, Chicago, March 30–April 1, 2000.

17. In Ontario, Canada, socialist-feminists formed Organized Working Women (OWW). Organized across union lines and labour centrals, OWW did not win

recognition from the Ontario Federation of Labour (OFL) but had a significant influence on the OFL around a broad range of issues including abortion. For a discussion of separate organizing see Linda Briskin, 'Union Women and Separate Organizing', *Women Challenging Unions: Feminism, Democracy and Militancy,* Linda Briskin and Patricia McDermott (eds.), Toronto: University of Toronto Press, 1993, pp. 89–108. On feminism and union democracy see Miriam Edelson, 'Challenging Unions: Feminist Process and Democracy in the Labour Movement', Canadian Research Institute for the Advancement of Women, 1987.

18. See Debbie Field, 'The Dilemma Facing Women's Committees', *Union Sisters: Women in the Labour Movement,* Linda Briskin and Lynda Yanz (eds.), Toronto: The Women's Press, 1983, pp. 293–303; Julie White, *Sisters in Solidarity,* pp. 123–24.

19. It is interesting to note that in Sweden class solidarity within LO has prevented women from organizing separately. Separation would be seen as a break in class solidarity. See Rianne Mahon, 'Learning to Embrace the Differences Within: Toward the Renewal of Swedish Unions', Prepared for the Twelfth International Conference of Europeanists, Chicago, March 30–April 1, 2000.

20. Jane Jenson, 'The Limits'.

21. See Heather Jon Maroney, 'Feminism at Work'; Lynne Segal, *Is the Future Female,* pp. 202, 233; Rosemary Warskett, 'The Politics of Difference and Inclusiveness'.

22. See Julie White, *Sisters in Solidarity*; Janet Routledge 'Women and Social Unionism' Resources *for Feminist Research,* vol. 10, no. 2, 1981; Debbie Field 'The Dilemma Facing Women's Committees'.

23. See Jane Stinson, 'Window on the North: Women's Issues and Labour in Canada', *Labour Research Review,* no. 11 (Spring, 1988).

24. See Bianca Beccalli and Guglielmo Meardi 'When Equal opportunities is not enough'; for a discussion of Rivalta FIOM women's activity around working-time organization.

25. For a discussion of the construction of women's programmes and anti-discrimination legislation see Suzanne Findlay, 'Facing the State: The Politics of the Women's Movement Reconsidered', Maroney and Luxton (eds.), *Feminism and Political Economy,* pp. 31–50.

26. See Dorothy Sue Cobble (ed.), *Women and Unions: Forging a Partnership,* Ithaca, NY: ILR Press, 1993.

27. Jan Kainer, 'Pay Equity Strategy and Feminist Legal Theory: Challenging the Bounds of Liberalism', *Canadian Journal of Women and the Law,* vol. 8, no. 2, 1985, pp. 440–69. In Canada and Europe pay equity means equal pay for work of equal value. In the United States the term used is comparable worth.

28. See Chris Howell, 'Women as the Paradigmatic Trade Unionists? New Work, New Workers and New Trade Unions in Conservative Britain', *Economic and Industrial Democracy,* vol. 17, no. 4 (November) 1996, pp. 511–43.

29. Johanna Brenner, 'Feminism's Revolutionary Promise', p. 251.

30. The Coalition of Labour Union Women are part of this network. Created in 1974, early on this coalition produced educational materials and had the potential to mobilize union women; see Diane Balser, *Sisterhood and Solidarity,* Boston: South End Press, 1987. The CLUW is now part of the institutionalized women's movement in the US, and does not exhibit the rank and file activism it formerly did.

31. Major exceptions to this are the French labour movements. See Jeanne Gregory, Rosemary Sales and Ariane Hegewisch (eds.), *Women, Work and Inequality: The Challenge of Equal Pay in a Deregulated Labour Market*, London: Macmillan Press, 1999.

32. Rianne's Mahon 'Learning to Embrace the Differences Within: Toward the Renewal of Swedish Unions'. Women secured reforms such as day care and parental leave, and also responding to the challenge of immigration, equality measures and right to Swedish instruction on working-time. But all of these measures were championed in the name of the working-class family rather than equality. Rianne Mahon, *Economic and Industrial democracy*, vol. 17, no. 4 (November) 1996, pp. 545–86.

33. See Carol Smart, *Feminism and the Power of Law*, London: Routledge, 1989. She argues against a totalizing theory of law and outlines a view of law that is refracted rather than unified and has contradictory outcomes: 'It is important to resist the temptation that law offers, namely the promise of a solution', p. 165.

34. See Gillian Cresse, *Contracting Masculinity: Gender, Class, and Race in a White-Collar Union, 1944–1994*, Toronto: Oxford University Press, 1999. She relates the history of the Office and Technical Employees Union (OTEU) at British Columbia Hydro, revealing how male 'breadwinner wages' were embedded in job classification and evaluation systems, and the contradictions in pay equity strategies that do not deal with the entire work organization and hierarchy.

35. See Jane Stinson, 'Ontario Pay Equity Results For CUPE Service Workers in Ontario Hospitals: A Study of Uneven Benefits', Master's Thesis, Carleton University, Ontario, Canada, 1999, p. 84.

36. See Michael McCann, *Rights at Work: Pay Equity Reform and the Politics of Legal Mobilization*, Chicago: The University of Chicago Press, 1994.

TURNING POINTS AND STARTING POINTS: BRENNER, LEFT TURBULENCE AND CLASS POLITICS

SAM GINDIN

Robert Brenner's recent attempt to get a handle on the 'global turbulence' of capitalism's past half-century was soon followed by a more localized turbulence: a highly agitated response from the Marxist left.[1] The hype injected by Brenner's editors at *New Left Review* ('Marx's enterprise has certainly found its successor') may carry some responsibility for the reaction, but great blurbs have rarely aroused Marxists.[2] Brenner's amply justified reputation, and his impressive integration of a mass of economic data, no doubt contributed to the intense interest in his essay but this too falls short of explaining the tempest. His central argument, that the key to the 'turning point' in post-war profits is to be found in the relationship amongst capitalists rather than in the class conflict between capital and labour, is certainly controversial but in itself only resurrects a discussion that seemed to have exhausted itself in the seventies.[3] And his addition to that earlier debate—that the high fixed costs of incumbent firms limited their exit from the world market, leading to excess capacity and pressures on profits—is, as others have emphasized, not entirely novel nor convincing. Why then such attention to, and controversy around, this essay?

The uproar seems to be as much about the political implications of Brenner's work as with the analysis itself; it may be that misgivings over where Brenner's narrative ultimately takes us have led to such a querulous contestation of his starting point. Consider two particularly provocative outcomes of his analysis: the role of the working class and the contradictions of competition. It was one thing to argue in the seventies that workers were not to blame for the downturn. At that time such a position was not generally questioning the relevance of class, but only its role in crises; people who argued then that the crisis was not caused by working-class action were often trying to be supportive (even if misguidedly) of working-class struggles. But in the context of today's relatively demoralized left, to argue that working-class militancy was not particularly relevant even in the sixties, when it was at its peak and expressed some promise, makes a quite different impact. Today—and this isn't about Brenner's intention but the prevailing mood—it seems to reinforce a general inclination to write off the transformative potential of the working class. Since this has always been a question of their capacity for having a direct strategic impact on the economy, not the degree of their victimization, denying the economic relevance of the working class in the dynamics of capitalism seems also to deny their potential political relevance.[4]

As for competition, the conclusion that capitalist competition has system-threatening internal contradictions that are independent of relative class strength may suggest a measure of hope. Yet in the absence of a class that is an integral part of those contradictions, that hope has nowhere to go. Rather, it implicitly tends to leave us with two unpalatable options: either wait passively for capitalism's self-inflicted collapse, or depend—naively and as a diversion from domestic struggles—on the development of an international super-state to stabilize competition.[5]

This 'retreat from class' to the contradictions of competition is part of a deeper sub-text that does exist in Brenner's article: an analytic retreat from historical materialism to a left-economism. This is not to not deny Brenner's obvious commitment to labour or his antagonism to capital, or to ignore his use of categories central to the Marxist tradition—class, property relations, competition, the state, hegemony, and so on. The problem lies in the way he uses these categories, and especially in how he addresses their interrelationships. This in itself does not, of course, mean that Brenner is wrong; that remains to be shown. But if he is right, he has done more than reinterpret the present era of capitalism; he has challenged how Marxists understand capitalism more generally, and this can't help but carry implications for how we approach working-class politics.

Brenner's concept of competition and his notion of high fixed costs are, I will argue, too narrow a base to carry the explanatory burden he places on them. Moreover, as important as it is to get a better understanding of profit trends, this too is not enough.[6] Behind Brenner's long upturn and long downturn lies a more profound *social transition*. That transition involved a historic shift in the overall balance of class forces against labour as well as a shift internal to the capitalist class; the emergence of qualitatively new productive forces; changes in the internal structures and role of states as well as their relationship to markets; and the development of a new kind of imperialism. When these elements are brought properly into view the 'turning point' of our era looks very different than the one identified by Brenner, and implies a different 'starting point' for Left politics.

In saying this, I want to acknowledge the crucial importance of the debate Brenner has generated. Perhaps the real meaning of the reaction to his work is that it reflects a new attitude within the socialist left towards *itself*. For some time now our response to the right's interpretation of the world, and to social democracy's fatalistic adoption of the right's basic framework, has tended to be defensive and moralistic. Perhaps the latest 'Brenner Debate' signals—finally— a return to a focus on our own analytical weaknesses and to the opening up a new period of creative, if stormy, internal debate.

COMPETITION AND CLASS

The centrality of competition has always been a major preoccupation of Robert Brenner. His impressive contribution to Marxism through this emphasis is not in dispute.[7] What is in question, however, is whether, in expecting too much of competition—and an inadequate notion of competition at that—he undermines some of his own otherwise valuable arguments while ignoring or underestimating some of the most important changes in capitalism. In this and the following section, I will concentrate on two specific problems with his notion of competition: the broader problems caused by separating competition from class and the problems caused by seeing competition as being between 'nationally specific groups'.

Brenner sees competition and class as operating in two separate spheres, with competition being privileged a priori in explaining crises and the long-term trajectory of capitalism. As he concludes in one of his replies to critics, '... where the ... direct producers [are] subject to competition, the law of accu- mulation will prevail, even if wage labour is absent'.[8] While this may at some level be true, the issue at hand is not 'the law of accumulation' in the abstract, but the law of *capitalist accumulation*. The latter cannot exclude the process of creating the surplus to be accumulated; workers can never be 'absent' from this.

The point is not to replace an explanation based on competition with one based on class and resistance: it is that posing the question in such terms runs counter to the strength of a Marxist understanding of the world. Capitalist dynamics are about the intersection of competition *and* class, how each— through the economy, culture, and the state—influences, permeates, and is limited by the other.[9] Even the high fixed costs that Brenner emphasizes so strongly are only understandable as a means of controlling and substituting labour in response to both competitive pressures *and* class resistance.[10] The reduction of the role of class to a secondary one cannot help but also lead to a narrowing and distortion of the significance of the class-based state; it thereby tends to build an economistic bias into the theory.

The priority Brenner gives to competition is rooted in his historical argu- ment that the emergence of generalized wage-labour was not a cause, but result of the dynamics of early capitalism. Yet even if, for the sake of argument, we accept that Brenner has accurately captured the essence of how capitalism first emerged, is it not ahistorical to argue, as Ellen Wood has also done in defending

Brenner's current analysis, that the nature of capitalism in its earliest stage remains the same *after* a full-fledged working class has entered history?[11] Why, once *both* competition and class (and the modern state) have arrived, should we continue to privilege one over the other, rather than investigate how they mutually determine each other?

While Brenner does not himself develop the further implications of his analysis along these lines, Wood does.[12] Moreover, sensitive to left arguments that Brenner seems to push the class struggle to the sidelines, Wood has tried to put a radical spin on his analysis: since crises can only occur because of events in the sphere of competition, the class struggle can be conducted without fear that it will undermine itself by *causing* any crisis.[13] This has an obvious and seductive appeal, especially if it is in defence of workers facing wage restraint (as in South Africa, for example), or addressed to a working class whose militancy and confidence has been especially shaken (as in the US). Yet this position, because it implies a too-narrow interpretation of capitalism, runs the danger of promoting a politics (which actually seems uncharacteristic of Wood) that combines adventurist militancy with an abstract call for socialism.

It is one thing to argue that concessions by workers will not solve their problems; it is quite another to argue that workers can ignore the competitive constraints on their actions. Militancy without a context risks isolating workers from communities and, in the aftermath of failed leadership, alienating workers from their organizations.[14] Militancy, even if accompanied by externally-generated socialist ideas, cannot lead to socialism because the problem is not to combine militancy and frustration with a radical discourse, but to develop, through structured struggles, workers' confidence and capacities to move beyond the present. It is through such struggles that workers learn that competitive constraints are real, that they must be addressed, and that addressing them calls for higher levels of collective action—lessons absolutely crucial to politicizing workers (even if that politicization remains far from being socialist).

The tendency to separate the spheres of competition and class shows its strains in linear explanations of specific events and especially in thinking about broader turning points. For example, when Brenner asserts—in defense of his argument that competition and not wage pressures limited profits—that 'aggregate profitability [was] squeezed by reduced prices in the face of downwardly inflexible costs', it is certainly fair to ask why costs, and especially wage costs, were 'inflexible'.[15] That is, were workers too strong relative to the situation capital faced? Isn't the question of labour strength *always* relative to the context? Contrast the post-war and current responses to labour. At the end of the war, a major concern of capital was to turn working-class organizations away from socialist sympathies and work-place militancy to a manageable economism. By the early seventies even that very economism was more than the system could tolerate as the state considered wage demands enough of a potential threat to the recovery of profits to introduce wage controls. What were previously measures of success—decent wages, social programmes, and security—were redefined as barriers to progress.

Brenner's marginalization of class is especially problematic when we look at major social shifts. The very nature of such shifts—they are after all *social* and involve questions of control, of preserving and/or rearranging class relationships—necessitates a more expansive panorama than the contradictions of competition. Something was in fact 'blowin' in the wind' in the late sixties, but the responses of capital cannot be understood by *only* looking at profits, wages, inflation, the accumulated outflow of American capital to Europe, the first American trade deficit in the century, a threatened run on the dollar, or any other economic factors. The impending sense of chaos in elite circles—the spectre of losing control abroad and legitimacy at home—can only be explained if the economic factors are combined with the social resistance and turmoil that came to symbolize the sixties.

This includes the role of labour. In the rebellious context of the late sixties, Brenner's argument that working-class struggles were too localized to have a system-wide impact doesn't wash. Generalized actions were not an unconditional necessity—sporadic actions in a few key countries could and did create a nervousness amongst the ruling classes that went beyond the immediate effect on the class distribution of income. The class momentum of an older generation of American workers may have faded, but a new generation was making it harder for the establishment to sleep peacefully. *Fortune* magazine popularized the phrase 'Blue Collar Blues' as it spotlighted the young militants challenging shopfloor authority structures with wildcat strikes and the turfing out of local officials—both of which said more about what was happening or might happen than trends in real wages and unit labour costs.[16] *Business Week*, sensing that the youth rebellion was not an isolated campus phenomenon, warned that the actions and attitudes of the student movement '... certainly bode ill for industrial discipline [because] if this kind of irrationality spread to industry, the result would be disastrous'.[17]

That social context, affecting the expectations of both workers and corporations, also contributed to the actual lag between the slow-down in productivity growth and the slow-down in wages, thereby increasing unit labour costs and prolonging the profitability crisis. And, as Brenner does acknowledge but fails to integrate into his analysis, whatever the actual explanation of the onset of a serious crisis, the capitalist search for a solution will *always* involve some form of an attack on labour's capacity to influence accumulation. In the aftermath of the sixties, the target was workers' organizational capacities. In Europe this took some time to achieve, but by the eighties rates of unionization were declining throughout the advanced capitalist world. Even in the United States, where unionization had been falling right through the 'golden age', capital felt compelled (and able) to respond in a qualitatively different way. For the first time since the Depression, *reduced* wages and benefits became common among organized workers. In the few sectors where workers had achieved a respectable level of unionization, de-unionization occurred through the movement of jobs to the American south, as in auto parts, or to new domestic competitors, as with smaller mills in steel. And unions themselves accepted, under pressure, the more decentralized structures and inferior contracts that better reflected 'what the market could bear'.

COMPETITION AND THE STATE

Brenner's analysis of competition in the post-war period collapses the distinction between the *units* of competition (independent capitalists), and the set of institutions that frame the *conditions* for competition (national states), into 'nationally specific' groups of capitalists.[18] The image of competition Brenner puts forth is akin to an Olympic-style race between separate teams of runners identified by the flags on their backs (the Americans were once far in the lead but at a particular turn—the late sixties—the others closed in). The problem is that this goes both too far and not far enough.

By passing over what happens at the level of units of capital, Brenner skips over one of the most important developments in the post-war period: the extension of corporate strategies from trade to direct international investment which, together with the financial flows that followed and eventually went beyond that investment, were popularly identified as 'globalization'.[19] With this direct and mutual interpenetration of capital, the flags on the backs of the runners in Brenner's paradigm become blurred; it is no longer clear who is wearing what flag (is Daimler-Chrysler German or American? Which state, American or German—or both—does it depend on? What happens to the notion of a 'national' bourgeoisie?). Moreover, competition occurring by way of direct investment contradicts the core of Brenner's argument. Brenner's case rests on the combination of new entrants (generally via trade) and limited exit (because of high fixed costs) leading to excess capacity and therefore a lowering of average profits. But if a defining element of this period is the overall *mobility* of capital—that is, the increased ability of capital to come *and go*—then, as Carchedi has emphasized, an already weak argument about inadequate exit is further invalidated.[20]

When we turn to setting the conditions for competition, the notion of 'nationally specific' factors—in which Brenner includes the state as only one particular element—underplays the especially significant role of states. It is not only in parts of South-east Asia that we find allegedly strong states directly shaping competition. The European and Japanese states were always more supply-side oriented than Keynesian, and when it came to the erosion of the competitive advantages of its own capital, no state acted more decisively to shape competition than the United States.

In the two decades after 1975 the American state put all its imperial power behind the pressures that led to the doubling of the relative value of the German Mark and tripling that of the Yen. When competition intensified at the end of the sixties and 'the market' implied that a large share of America's productive capacity should be cast aside because it was relatively uncompetitive,who could really have expected the United States to accept that judgement? The American state, partly responding to domestic pressures from capital and labour, acted on a conviction that American global responsibilities were linked to maintaining its strong industrial base; it used its power to limit the competitive destruction of American capacity. Nor was it all that surprising that other states also countered, to the extent they could, to limit the damage on capital—both domestic and foreign—within their own territories. The overall logic of competition was, of course, not challenged, but free competition was attenuated and the boundaries of its impact were, in a sense, negotiated among states.

Brenner's analysis did correctly move from the intensification of competition to the systemic *limit* on competition that was at the centre of the late sixties crisis, but he misplaced its locale and source. In addressing fixed costs, he did return to individual firms (the units of capital) but the actual limit on competition wasn't generated at the level of the firm but at the level of the state, and not because of 'fixed costs' but because of the socio-political determinants of state policy. Whatever the advantages the old state intervention had for short-term domestic stability, its attenuation of competition had, as Brenner emphasizes, a cost in terms of the longer-term dynamics of capitalism. But this was recognized by the American state as well. Neoliberalism emerged as the corrective, restoring and extending the creative winds of capitalist competition. It was—and this is crucial—a *class* response rather than a result of the responses of individual capitalists.

Amongst other things, this involved particular changes in the internal structures and role of the state. The changes in the state's role, as others have emphasized, did not cede state power to markets.[21] The influence of markets increased but this occurred in tandem with equally important changes in the structures of states and with the expansion of (some) technocratic bureaucracies. Restrictions on capital markets were more completely lifted and credit creation was privatized, but only in conjunction with an increase in the power of unaccountable central bankers. Trade and investment were more completely liberalized, but this came with an extension of international property and patent rights and complicated rules made and enforced by distant bureaucrats. The Third World got greater market access to international credit, but the security of the lenders 'necessitated' oppressive, non-market intervention to shape and limit the boundaries on any strategies Third World states pursued. Welfare entitlements were eroded and replaced by the more market-consistent alternative of workfare; but, as if to highlight more clearly the contrast between market freedoms and other freedoms, the new programmes included direct state intervention to legally exclude unionization and to criminalize non-market alternatives such as 'squeegee kids' working to survive on the streets of Toronto and New York.

The operative relationship between markets and state policy, with the

national goal of 'competition' expressing the class goal of profits and accumulation, was bluntly summarized by a prominent Canadian banker (who has since
relocated to Britain):

> We must resolve to make international competitiveness the key driving
> force for all our decisions. ... From now on we must answer a very
> fundamental question: Is this economic proposal or that social
> programme, or this business initiative or that labour demand more or less
> likely to improve our competitive position in the world. If the answer
> is that it is likely to worsen it, we should not do it. Period.[22]

Brenner's underestimation of the general role of states is directly linked to
his particular underestimation of the role of the American imperial state. What
is so significant about the race which Brenner describes in so much detail is that
the Americans were not just leading the race, the American state *was setting the
rules*. The specifics of the competitive challenge to American economic hegemony cannot be understood unless—as I'll later elaborate—they are clearly
located within the larger story of the changing nature of American imperialism.

UNIVERSALIZING CAPITALISM

The problem with Brenner's characterization of the postwar period lies not
just in his theoretical framework, but also in his interpretation of the data. A
closer consideration of this era suggests a quite different view of capitalism's
trajectory: in place of the contradictions of competition sustaining a long downturn, we see the development—unevenly and with its own contradictions of
course—of a re-energized capitalism.

For Brenner '[t]he origins of the long downturn in the advanced capitalist
world are to be found in the US economy after 1965. Between 1965 and 1973,
the rates of profits in the manufacturing and private business sectors fell by
40.9% and 29.3%'.[23] But such numbers are misleading. What Brenner is actually capturing here is a return to trend from a short-term bulge in the
early-sixties.[24] The decline in the rate of profits after 1965 didn't signal a new
direction, but was—as is clear even from the trend lines in Brenner's own
tables—part of a longer-term decline in profits that began in the early-fifties and
continued to the early-eighties.[25] Measured by profit trends, the 'golden age'
seems confined to the short-lived profit boom after the recession of the late-
fifties.[26] After falling for three decades (two, if we exclude the temporary period
of getting Europe and Japan back on their feet), the American rate of profit
subsequently started its slow but steady ascent in the early-eighties. The post-
war trajectory of profits therefore followed—contrary to the imagery of a
rainbow (up then down)—that of a valley (down then up).[27]

This raises quite different questions from Brenner's about what is to be
explained. For example, what accounts for that long decline in the rate of profit
during the golden age 'upturn'? If there was a turning point in the late-sixties,
does it not demand a broader explanation than profit trends? If profits are the

measure, why wasn't the turning point later—in the early eighties when profits began their slow but steady recovery? What is the actual relationship between lower—but still positive—profits and crises?[28]

In periodizing the post-war era, Bretton Woods commonly serves as the institutional moment separating the long upturn from the long downturn, but in light of the above there is good reason to see Bretton Woods in more limited terms. In those first post-war years, the American state came to accept—after some contestation by the financial wing of American capital—certain accommodations to facilitate the rapid reconstruction and further industrialization of what was, at that time, a still relatively agrarian Europe and Japan. This included allowing Europe and Japan the economic, social, and political space for development. While Europe and Japan had open access to US markets and credit, American capital and the American state tolerated their restrictions on imports of US goods, and on capital flows and direct investment. Bretton Woods was the formal dimension of this and, with the benefit of hindsight, should be seen as a temporary regime for recovery, rather than part of a more permanent 'new order'.[29]

By the end of the fifties, this first stage of the post-war period was over and the question shifted to how the US would manage the relationship to a revived Europe and Japan while containing domestic and Third World expectations. At the time, no technical or social fix seemed at hand to resolve the evolving conflict between the US state's imperial and domestic responsibilities, and one measure of that impasse was that profits continued to slide. The eventual solution, along with the reversal of the profit slide, took some two decades to evolve. During that transition, the US dithered between ignoring the need for change in its global role in the early-sixties, refusing to accept economic discipline and limits on its own actions from the late-sixties through the mid-seventies, followed by a period of uncertainty, experimentation and self-conscious debate that finally led to a coherent strategy emerging as the seventies came to an end.

The lack of response in the early-sixties was not surprising; with the left generally subdued after the fifties and the European and Japanese economies experiencing steady growth, there was no pressing urgency for a new direction. Europe and Japan were content to focus on access to the large American market and American technology to close their still extremely large productivity gaps with the US (at the beginning of the sixties, the GDP per capita of Europe-Japan still ranged from one-third to two-thirds of that in the US). At the same time the American state, while increasingly uncomfortable with its growing international economic imbalances, looked to short-term adjustments and could fall back on the leeway provided by the international role of the US dollar.[30] The social rebellions of the late-sixties, combined with the deterioration in economic indicators and the run on the dollar, forced the American state into some kind of response. Its reaction—to retain its domestic autonomy and change the international rules in its favour when necessary—effectively ended

Bretton Woods, but it hardly qualified as the basis of a new regime. On the one hand, this in itself provided no adequate solution to the slowdown in American growth; on the other, any new international order needed *some* semblance of universally applied rules, not least because arbitrariness left even US manufacturing and financial capital nervous.

That American response wasn't just a matter of inertia and arrogance, although these played their part. There was also uncertainty over what was to be done and constraints on what *could* be done; it is only in retrospect that the contingencies that make up historical developments can be read in their ultimate tidiness.[31] The very social forces that had spurred the American elite into action limited its response. A conscious economic slowdown to correct America's domestic and international imbalances was at that point unthinkable.[32] Taxes couldn't be raised to pay for an expensive but unpopular war; housing, welfare and social programmes couldn't be cut while American cities (including sections of the nation's capital) were burning. The American state couldn't cut off the outflow of American capital without aggravating instability in the Third World. Nor was a full-scale trade war with Europe and Japan in the cards, given how internationalized American capital had itself become.

In the decade between the end of Bretton Woods and the resolute move to crush inflation at the end of the decade, Keynesianism was praised (Nixon declaring 'we are all Keynesians now') and then challenged (as monetarist ideas took hold). Freer trade was called for (open up new markets), and then restricted (imposition of 10% surcharge on imports). Free markets were encouraged (let the market set exchange rates) and then undermined (wage controls). But the conditions for a solution were emerging. As the failure of existing alternatives was confirmed and the strength and confidence of finance grew, as the war in Vietnam receded from everyday consciousness and the sixties protests faded, and as the militant wave within the working class came to be seen as a last hurrah rather than a rebirth with broader oppositional potentials, the American state regained a degree of freedom for acting domestically and—especially with the rise of finance—faced both new pressures and new options.[33] A more coherent response began to take shape.

Three interrelated developments stamped the eventual solution. One was the initially slow and then accelerating emergence of a set of new productive forces. This counteracted the apparent exhaustion in capital productivity that was increasingly evident after the mid-sixties.[34] A second was the arrival of neoliberalism as a concerted economic, political and institutional drive to further distance the process of accumulation from that of democracy. That distancing wasn't aimed just at labour's share in accumulation, but involved a direct assault on workers' organizational capacities and the extension of markets alongside, rather than in opposition to, changes in the role of the state.[35] Finance in particular translated this extension of markets and distancing from democracy into the language of capitalist discipline as it came to provide the leadership needed to revive a class in disarray.[36] The third development was the recognition, on the part of American capital and the American state, that its own dynamism and the universalization of American-led capitalism required that they themselves accept the discipline of capitalist markets and internalize neoliberalism. This acceptance—signalled by the imposition of sky-high interest rates and the identification of inflation as enemy number one—was a step that was previously unimaginable, even if it was still qualified and still left the American state with its 'structural power' intact.[37]

As important as the new technologies are, it is the marriage of neoliberalism and American imperialism that defines our times. That marriage has led to an international capitalism under the aegis of an American imperialism that is uniquely powerful in the discipline it imposes. And it is particularly effective in hiding and de-politicizing that discipline behind impersonal market-based rules. Where the crisis of Keynesianism represented the failure of capitalism with a human face, neoliberal imperialism hoped to succeed through hiding behind a capitalism with no face at all (like the Cheshire cat in *Alice in Wonderland*, it revealed only a floating smile).[38]

Capitalism, Marx had pointed out, is a process; it is always incomplete. The 'pure form' exists only in theory while 'in reality there exists only approximation [and] this approximation is the greater, the more developed the capitalist mode of production …'.[39] Some events (downturns, recoveries, upturns) reproduce capitalism as it was, while others raise it to a new stage. By virtue of its impact on minimizing democratically-imposed boundaries to accumulation and on universalizing this relationship across an expanding domain, neoliberal-imperialism represents such a 'more developed' stage of capitalism.

THE NEW IMPERIALISM[40]

Just as competition cannot be understood without class, capitalism cannot be understood without addressing imperialism. In the immediate post-war period, two distinct forms of American imperialism co-existed. In the less-developed countries, colonialism gave way to neo-colonialism as countries whose ties to the international economy had eroded during the Depression and the war were reintegrated. In the advanced capitalist countries ('advanced' in the sense of the stage of development of their internal capitalist institutions and relations), the American state created the space for rapid recovery and economic development. The resulting international division of labour marginalized the less developed countries economically and also in terms of their influence on the evolution of global capitalism. The principal dynamic of imperialism came to depend on America's relationship to the other advanced capitalist countries. That is, the evolution of post-war international institutions, the integration of global manufacturing, the rise of global finance, and the reconstitution of imperialism in its neoliberal form, rested first and foremost on the relationship between the US, Europe and Japan.[41]

This shift in emphasis to the imperialist relationship within the *advanced* capitalist countries, where coherent capitalist institutions already existed and could act as a transmission belt for internalizing imperialist values, structures, and politics, opened the door to an imperialism with a different smell, taste, and colour. This First-World imperialism represented, as Panitch emphasizes (with due credit to Poulantzas),

> ... a new type of non-territorial imperialism which was implanted and maintained not through direct rule by the metropolis, nor even through political subordination of a neo-colonial type, but rather through [what Poulantzas described as] the 'induced reproduction of the form of the dominant imperial power within each national formation and its state'.[42]

Although the old imperialism was far from gone in Europe after the war, that 'induced reproduction' was already emerging.[43] With Marshall Aid came American advisers and 'exchanges' to the United States to 'see how the Americans did it'. This influenced (though it did not completely determine) the technologies used, the forms of work organization, the labour-relations systems, the socializing of unions. Access to American markets affected consumption patterns and values back home, and internalized a dependency on continued access to the US market. The legacy of the accommodation made by the US in the early post-war years had left some space for Europe to modify its integration into global capitalism with nationally-specific variations of the welfare state. But the flow of direct American investment into Europe through the sixties, followed by financial capital, considerably reinforced the trends to 'induced reproduction'. This set in motion the conditions for undermining the national room for a response meaningfully different than that dictated by the American model.

Competition from Europe and Japan certainly pressured American capital into institutional adjustment, and as such was part of the dynamic of the period. But the competitive maturation of Europe and Japan never implied the imminent demise of the United States as an imperial power; the challenge from Europe and Japan was rather an inherent aspect of America's eventual *assertion* of its imperial power. Those earlier economic challenges to the United States were part of a process—often uneven and not always predictable—that integrated Japan and Europe into a world order which reproduced America's *overall* dominance and Americanized its rivals.

Consider, for example, the advent of the 'Japanese model'. In the almost two decades following the energy crisis of the early-seventies, it threatened US economic leadership with a productive system based on decentralized enterprise unionism, in-plant units organized around teams, lean production (internally and *vis-à-vis* suppliers), the promise of jobs-for-life for core workers, and a supportive banking system. Of these factors, the practice of enterprise unionism or company unionism was not at all new; it was in fact the preference of American capital back in the 1920s and never really lost its appeal. What blocked it in the United States was the working-class's achievement of industrial unionism, and what made it possible in Japan was the post-war destruction of Japan's independent labour movement—with the active support of the American post-war administration then posted in Japan. Team production was likewise no more than American Taylorism geared to capturing the synergies (and self-discipline) of group co-ordination. Just-in-time and lean production did include innovative institutional mechanisms for limiting waste; they were soon happily imitated by American producers because they fit so well (and further justified) existing tendencies to rationalize production relations. In spite of the earlier hysteria about corporate America being taking over by the land of the rising sun, at the end of the nineties Nissan's own jobs-for-life policy had given way to an American-style downsizing of some 20,000 workers, the Japanese elite was struggling with how to reform the Japanese banking system along American lines, and long gone were the pilgrimages to discover the secrets of Japanese economic supremacy.

Similarly, Daimler-Benz's highly symbolic take-over of Chrysler, coinciding with the Euro beginning its new life, was at the time commonly cited as another example of the gradual loss of American hegemony. But once we are beyond identifying companies by the nationality of their ownership and focus instead on their role in the international order, things look quite different. The takeover was, in an immediate sense, about getting quick access to the US market and—via the Chrysler name—getting accepted by American consumers as an essentially American company. This included Daimler gaining, in addition to its relationship to the German state, a degree of access to the American state. Equally important, however, was the role of this takeover in reinforcing the introduction into Germany of American production and labour relation methods. Daimler was not bringing back just aspects of Chrysler's technical methods, but also social relationships such as greater corporate expectations of flexibility from its work-force. For this to be successfully transplanted into Germany, modifications in German labour legislation were required. That is, this German 'takeover' of a major segment of American capital tended to Americanize both German capital and the German state.

More generally, while the evolution towards a united Europe was a response to American hegemony, it never contested American power. Playing the game by American rules led, if anything, to the sinking of deeper American social and political roots within Europe. As a recent editorial in *The Economist* trenchantly noted,

> It cannot have escaped notice that, in economics and economic policy, the European model which seems in retreat is giving way to none other than the American kind, with leftist parties narrowing the gap between themselves and America's New Democrats ... Put it this way: what is the point of 'Europe', if Europe is turning out to be just another United States?[44]

Contrast this description with the imperial tensions America faced in the sixties. Between the early-sixties and the early-eighties, the 'space' the US had left open for Europe and Japan, led to a fall in the US share of world manu-facturing from over 40% to under 30%,[45] with a consequent impact on American profits and the American economy. At the same time, the war in Vietnam—waged by the US on behalf of global capitalism—proved far more costly than anyone had expected. Trade deficits threatened a run on the dollar; the American unilateral rejection of Bretton Woods, concerned with defending its own domestic autonomy, alienated American allies; and if inter-imperialist rivalry wasn't in the cards, it seemed that only the exigencies of the cold war stood in the way. Today, on the other hand, the US has managed to construct a world order with both more and stronger competitors than ever *and* strong profits; the trade deficit is higher than ever, yet this is not only tolerated but even welcomed abroad; when the American Treasury intervened to bail out a private speculative fund, at a time when the global watchword for others was 'financial discipline' and avoiding 'moral hazard', there were few accusations of hypocrisy; and though the cold war is over, the likelihood of inter-imperialist rivalry is as remote as ever. What accounts for this sharp difference in the two periods?

The problem for capital in the earlier period wasn't so much the absence of possible solutions, as the existence of social constraints—domestically and abroad—that limited the freedom of capital to develop and apply possible solu-tions. The neoliberal project, led by the American state, was precisely about addressing those constraints and out of that a new strength emerged. With regard to other states, the particular form American imperialism has taken in this era has not just compromised their capacity to fundamentally challenge the US, but also undermined any ambition to do so—success in reproducing American structures and ideology within other social formations has translated into success in limiting the likelihood of a new paradigm.[46] Moreover, the very practical lessons learned over the past period—that global leadership is essential and only the American state can provide it—mean that while the US might occasion-ally be challenged, there is no stomach for risking the implications of defeating it. Domestically, as neoliberalism disciplined labour (and also contributed to disciplining the American state to balance its budget),[47] profits could be restored even with competition being greater than ever before, and American economic leaders were confident that the US could—in contrast to the earlier period—comfortably attract all the capital it needed to offset the trade deficit.[48]

HAS CAPITALISM LOST ITS DYNAMISM?

The assessment of political possibilities is clearly tied to our assessment of the strength and stability of capitalism. For Brenner like many others on the left (including some of his critics), the long downturn is not really over;[49] today's respite is temporary, a lull that obscures '[T]he Looming Crisis of World Capitalism'.[50] As Brenner puts it, 'things are not going smoothly for capi-talism'.[51] Finance, for example, has grown in power through the sixties and especially after the collapse of Bretton Woods; the fact that it is capturing a greater share of the overall surplus means, it is argued, that it is diverting funds from productive investment and therefore harming productivity, growth, and ultimately capitalism's overall strength.

Given the nature of finance, its new power of necessity brings new potential instabilities. Yet we should not be too sanguine about an impending breakdown. What are the dynamic implications of this change in capitalism? What does finance do with its larger share of resources? Do we really understand this? Does their share of profits go into conspicuous consumption or conspicuous investment? And if so, what makes this any different from the waste of potential capital that occurs in other sectors? Are none of its profits recycled into the real economy? Do its services—improved by institutional innovation and technology—not contribute indirectly to the efficiencies of other branches of capital much like efficiencies in transportation? Doesn't its commodification of risk facilitate real world activities in an otherwise overly unpredictable world?[52] Hasn't the increased liquidity created by the deregulation and privatization of finance offset competitive austerity and the dangers of a world depression inherent in neoliberalism? And has financial discipline not pushed the real economy to accumulate more and better, justifying to a significant degree its leadership role?

It is that position of class *leadership* that is so crucial here. The ascension of finance to leadership came with remarkably little internal conflict within the capitalist class. This in itself should lead us to question any too easy notions of fundamental contradictions between productive and financial capital. Capital's general acquiescence to that shift in leadership rested on the loss of momentum on the part of manufacturing as the previous leading sector and, in the ensuing vacuum, on finance's more promising solutions. It wasn't that finance 'invented' those solutions but that finance was, by its very nature, best suited to lead in realizing them.

Finance was the ideal instrument for neoliberalism and American imperialism because of its potential—once it had grabbed and/or been given control over credit and freed from capital restrictions—to act as the enforcer of capitalist discipline.[53] Whereas in the previous era capital had been forced into concessions (social programmes, acceptance of unions) that slowed the process of commodification, financial capital could use the threats implied in its new freedom to move to get things back on track.Where the state had turned to fiscal policy and public debt to support growth and the realization of the surplus, finance offered the alternative of stimulus through the expansion of *private* credit—supporting individual rather than collective consumption and reinforcing rather than moderating existing inequalities. Where that same fiscal stimulus had softened short-term competitive discipline and therefore sacrificed longer- term dynamism—reflecting the more general anxiety of individual capitals (especially smaller capitals) about the impact of what they considered excess competition—financial capital would act in the longer-term interest of capital in general. Being 'indifferent to specific employments' because it is, as

Marx said 'external to production', finance would represent the total 'social capital' and enforce policies that intensified global competition.[54]

When Doug Henwood, in a recent exchange with Brenner, questioned whether capitalism had in fact lost its dynamism, Brenner indignantly replied: 'I am mystified as to how Doug can call an economy "dynamic" which, for nearly a quarter of a century, has been incapable of raising living standards because [it is] unable to raise productivity'.[55] But has capitalism in fact lost its dynamism? To begin with, the measure of capitalism's success is not fairness and 'raising living standards'—unless that affects capitalism's on-going capacity to expand the conditions for, and remove the barriers to, accumulation. To the extent that stagnating incomes reflect working-class defeats, they are hardly a measure of capitalism's weakness. Similarly, any particular crisis in productivity may also be an integral part of a more profound Schumpeterian creative destruction.[56] In the absence of a political movement to challenge the root cause of the crisis-tendencies of the past quarter-century, apparent failures in the economy have only acted as signals for, and been crucial instruments of, capitalism's successful restructuring.

Moreover, and in spite of common perceptions, material living standards in the US as measured by real per capita consumption have actually *doubled* over the past thirty years.[57] There are, of course, well-known and crucial qualifications to this (the quality and distribution of income, the family stress involved in keeping up with consumption, the impact of corporate restructuring on life in the work-place), but its ideological and political importance should not be underestimated. Capitalism has managed to contain wage costs while allowing for the integrative effect of higher private consumption.

The key has been reinforcing the earlier organizational assault on unions with an 'alternative' that shifts the terrain on which workers improve their living standards. Not only has there been a shift from public to private consumption, but private consumption has itself come to depend less on solidaristic struggles for wages and more on private efforts and private credit. This is seen in the growth of overtime and moonlighting, more family members in the work-force and the gradual increase in the working hours of 'secondary' earners, stunning increases in personal debt, greater reliance on the growth of stock market-related assets to compensate for the expected loss of public pensions, and looking to tax breaks to offset stagnant wages. Even where unions have countered social cutbacks with collectively-bargained protections for their own members, this inadvertently contributes to balkanizing and privatizing the welfare state and consequently dividing the relatively stronger and weaker sections of the working class.

As for the 'inability to raise productivity', Brenner himself notes that manufacturing productivity—the focus of his analysis—has generally continued merrily along:

> It remains the case that, during this extended period … manufacturing labour productivity growth actually improved very markedly … Between 1979 and 1990 it averaged 2.9% per annum, just about its

average for the years 1950–73. Between 1990 and 1996, it further increased its momentum …[58]

That momentum has continued. The Left has downplayed the significance of the new digitized productive forces, pointing to their relatively small share of production and reacting against suggestions that it has created anew era of high growth and stability. But one does not have to accept the Panglossian 'new economy' argument to appreciate the very real impact the new informational technologies have had throughout the economy. The rapid rate of growth in the investment in information processing equipment and software may have been misleading in the eighties when its base was so low. But since 1993 it has grown by an astonishing 19% per year in the US and has been driving the overall growth in US private investment in equipment. The latter has increased from 6% of GDP in the early-nineties to 11% at the end of the decade and approximately 80% of that change is due to information-processing equipment and software.[59]

What is special about this technology is its ability to co-ordinate other technologies and its capacity for centralizing control while decentralizing certain functions. It has consequently and significantly also found a place within 'old' sectors. In auto, for example, it took some time for corporations to learn how the new information technology could be modified and applied to facilitate restructuring. Eventually, its integration into the overall production-distribution systems changed both the work-place and broader supplier and client relations—reinforcing and extending lean production, just-in-time delivery, outsourcing of components, and the modular outsourcing of entire subsystems. That outsourcing or decentralization of production represented an exit from certain functions (in contrast to Brenner's arguments on the rigidity of such fixed costs)[60] and the 'fit' between the new technology and neoliberalism raised work-place productivity, stimulated additional and specialized competencies among suppliers, and introduced additional corporate opportunities for de-unionization.[61]

To the extent there *was* an earlier productivity problem in the United States it also reflected the dynamism and strength of American capital. The dramatic outflow of capital that occurred through the sixties into the early-seventies may have negatively impacted the American economy, but it was a key element in maintaining and expanding the hegemony of American capital and the American state.[62] The shift of capital out of the crowded manufacturing sector and into low-productivity private services did lower the overall average growth in productivity, but it also demonstrated the capacity of American capital to find (and then 'rationalize') new sources of capital accumulation.[63]

There is something profoundly disingenuous about cataloguing capitalism's weaknesses without also noting its stunning (and frightening) ongoing proficiency in reshaping labour markets, revolutionizing the forces of production and communication, integrating the world spatially, and generally commodifying every aspect of daily life. There is something too comforting in repeated citations of capitalism's 'contradictions' after almost three decades of experiencing capitalism's powerful (if ominous) capacity to lower the expectations of its citizens to a degree we ourselves never thought possible, and to contain democratic opposition even as capital subordinates the liberal state still more tightly to the priorities of accumulation. Can we really deny the remarkable (if objectionable) dynamism of a system which has—with ourselves as grudging witnesses—so successfully restructured the world, 'after its own image'?[64]

The point is not that any of this has ended the social conflicts and instabilities inherent in capitalism. The stock market will eventually crash, crises will recur, the imposed restructuring and narrowing of people's lives may open new strategic possibilities for the Left. There will be more Seattles. We will have our moments. But what must absolutely be avoided is the analytical and political danger Brenner himself has raised, then just as quickly dismissed: a tempting but false optimism based on underestimating capitalism's persistent structural power, capacity for rejuvenation, and therefore continuing vitality.

> Marxist economists are famous for having accurately predicted seven out of the last one international economic crisis. Perhaps for that reason, many in recent times have been unusually cautious about once again 'crying wolf', even as the evidence of international economic dislocation has mounted around them. ... Today, however, prediction is no longer necessary. The international economy, outside of the United States and Europe—perhaps 50% of the world—is already experiencing an economic downturn that is worse than any that has occurred since the 1930s. To make matters worse, the US economy, which has provided the main motor for the nascent international cyclical upturn, is in serious trouble.[65]

Brenner's essay opened by observing that the triumphalism of economists and the OECD in the late-sixties 'could hardly have been more ill-timed'.[66] Yet even though Brenner offers us a richer analysis, it seems that his own starting point of imminent collapse is equally 'ill-timed'. Capital, as one major player recently put it, remains as '... convinced as ever that the coming years will be a disappointing time for pessimists'.[67] In retrospect, the relevant 'long downturn' and 'deep crises' of our times seem more applicable to a description of our own politics than to capitalism's dynamism. Capitalism has entered the new century with a smile on its face.

CONCLUSION: WIPING THEIR SMILE AWAY

For Brenner, the golden age of capitalism ended some three decades ago and we are living through an age of capitalism in crisis. The reading in this essay suggests, in contrast, that from the perspective of capital the golden age is *now*. In Brenner, capital's self-assurance will collapse under the contradictory logic of competition; in this essay's alternative reading, only a movement directed at challenging the essence of capitalism at its peak can erase the smile on capital's face. The particular form capitalism's dynamism exhibits in its current phase—economic strength alongside extreme unevenness and overbearing commodification—suggests the potential both for revived economic militancy and for building new movements to challenge capitalism's capacity to meet human needs.

What is so exciting about the post-Seattle politics is not just the energy and creativity that signals a new generation of activists, but that this movement has grasped capitalism as a totality and has dared to question its legitimacy. The issue is not this or that inequality, failure, or abuse, but the amorality of capitalism, its narrow commodification of humanity and nature and therefore negation of our collective potential, its centralization of economic, social, and political power—nationally and internationally—and consequent corruption of any meaningful popular democracy. And yet the very breadth of such anti-capitalist sentiments has its inherent limits. To sustain its momentum and to move beyond protest towards one day implementing an alternative vision, this new politics will have to move beyond symbolic attacks on global capitalism. It will have to develop its oppositional foundation locally without narrowing its goals, and its strategies will need to combine the spectacle of 'events' with the more mundane self-education that reaches to understand the full implications of what we are up against. What is now an anti-capitalist movement will, in other words, have to struggle afresh with the same questions and issues the socialist movement has always had to address.

This demands a link with the working class—a link that doesn't romanticize the current potentials within the labour movement. Without the resources of labour and its strategic clout (the police can organize to protect conferences; they cannot defend against massive refusals to provide the services that keep society functioning) the new movement cannot be sustained. At the same time, when the bubble in the stock market does burst (and depending on the effect that has on the rest of the economy), the question is whether working people will limit their sights on restoring the 1990s or join the challenge to capitalism's legitimacy. The struggle to establish such connections between the new activism and labour is therefore part of collectively figuring out how to relate immediate demands to ultimate goals, how to join the global and cultural to the local and economic, and how to address all the difficult questions of developing our capacities to organize, educate, communicate, and act at a level that matches capitalism's universalism with a universalism of our own. The question of taking state power remains distant; what we must place on the agenda is how, in Ariel Dorfman's beautiful phrase, we can '... build a second and invisible country' in the midst of their turbulent and dynamic capitalist world.[68]

NOTES

1. Robert Brenner, 'The Economics of Global Turbulence', *New Left Review*, May–June, 1998.
2. Editorial introduction, *New Left Review*, p. v.
3. Ben Fine, et al., referred to the latest Brenner debate as an 'exercise in nostalgia' ('Addressing the World Economy: Two Steps Back', *Capital & Class,* Spring, 1999).
4. 'Those who are ideologically disposed to blaming the working class for inflation will do so with or without benefit of our analysis, while Marxists will see the crisis from the perspective of the underlying conflictual basis of the capitalist system itself. The fundamental point is that we locate class conflict not only as a potentially revolutionary force, but as the basis for understanding the past and present.' Leo Panitch, 'Profits and Politics: Labour and the Crisis of British Capitalism' (1977) in *Working Class Politics in Crisis, Essays on Labour and the State*, London: Verso, 1986, p. 90.
5. As Mike Lebowitz puts it, '... in so far as Brenner's analysis of the slump is essentially that of a market failure, another direction is already implicit in that description—to substitute for the anarchy of capital a way to co-ordinate the actions of capital ... on a world scale.' ('In Brenner, Everything is Reversed', *Historical Materialism*, Summer, 1999 p. 127).
6. On both these points see Fine, et al., as well as various responses to Brenner in the Summer, 1999 issue of *Historical Materialism*.
7. Fine, et al., note that Brenner has, over the past three decades, managed to insert himself into the eye of the most significant storms in Marxism (ibid, pp. 73–4). The same may be said of Ellen Wood, whose defence of Brenner will be taken up below. In addition to the controversies over the origins of capitalism, they have been at the centre of polemics around monopoly capital, structuralism, regulation theory, postmodernism, and now the interpretation of the late-sixties 'turning point'. In each case, the concept of competition played a prominent if not central part. The polemical context of this and previous debates has perhaps been a factor in their one-sided exaggerations of the role of competition.
8. Brenner, 'Competition and Class: A Reply to Foster and McNally', *Monthly Review*, Dec, 1999, p. 43. See also Wood, 'The Politics of Capitalism', *Monthly Review*, Sept, 1999, p. 22–24.
9. Orthodox Marxism—in contradistinction to Brenner—tends to brush competition aside, arguing it only determines the distribution of the surplus. On this point, I'm sympathetic to Brenner's emphasis on the relevance of competition in affecting the overall surplus. For example, if—as I'll argue later—states (especially hegemonic states) respond to competition in a way that affects class relations, intensified competition *may* affect the surplus. Or such intervention may affect the realization of the surplus (and hence investment and future profits) through either the negative impact of competitive austerity or a dramatic increase in liquidity following the ascension of a new financial regime.
10. David McNally, 'Turbulence in the World Economy', *Monthly Review*, June, 1999, p. 43.
11. Wood argues that even if class is removed and replaced by worker-co-ops, as long as competition remains the driving force we do not have a socialism worthy of the name. True, but this hardly proves the pre-eminence of competition over class. Wood would surely make the same ultimate judgement about a 'socialism' that

ended competition by merging all companies into a central plan but put bureaucrats in control rather than the working class. Limiting the discussion to maintaining or ending competition, with no reference to class, is simply inadequate. Wood,'The Politics', pp. 22–24.

12. Ellen Wood, ibid., pp. 24–26 (originally an address to workers in South Africa).

13. Wood's point is actually contradicted by Brenner, since he argues that localized or sectoral squeezes on profit caused by worker struggles can't be sustained because they will ultimately bring about '*compensatory* economic, political, and social mechanisms that are set off, more or less automatically, precisely as a consequence of a squeeze by labour or the citizenry on profits'. Brenner, *New Left Review*, p.23.

14. Martijn Konings, 'Globalization and Class Politics: Preparing the Ground for an Argument', p. 24, unpublished, York University, Political Science.

15. Brenner, *New Left Review*, p.24.

16. *Fortune*, January, 1969. *Life Magazine* had already devoted a special issue (August 26, 1966) to the impact of the US strike-wave in the growing public sector.

17. *Business Week*, 3 May 1969.

18. 'I make no apology for attempting to bring out the ways in which *nationally specific* [author's italics] conditions including labour markets and movements, exchange rates, financial institutions, forms of government intervention, trade protection and the like influenced competitiveness', Brenner, *Monthly Review*, p.38.

19. Fine, et al, ibid., pp. 67–73.

20. Carchedi, 'A Missed Opportunity: Orthodox versus Marxist Theories of Crises', in *Historical Materialism*, ibid., p. 53. For other persuasive critiques of Brenner's argument on fixed costs see Fine, et al., as well as Simon Clarke, 'Capitalist Competition and the Tendency to Overproduction: Comments on Brenner's "Uneven Development and the Long Downturn"' *Historical Materialism*, ibid., p. 70.

21. Greg Albo, David Langille, Leo Panitch, *A Different Kind of State: Popular Power and Democratic Administration*, Toronto: Oxford University Press, 1993; see also Stephen K. Vogel, *Freer Markets More Rules*, New York: Cornell, 1996.

22. Matthew Barrett, then CEO Bank of Montreal, *The Globe and Mail*, April 9, 1992.

23. Brenner, *New Left Review*, p. 95.

24. Gerard Dumenil and Dominique Levy, 'Brenner on Distribution' in *Historical Materialism*, Summer, 1999, p. 83.

25. Brenner, *New Left Review*, p. 7 (figure 3), p. 8 (figure 4), p. 103 (figure 8), p. 186 (figure11).

26. Weber and Rigby see the 'golden age' in the US as extending slightly longer but still limit it to the years 1958–65. (*The Golden Age Illusion*, New York: Guilford, 1996, p. 19.).

27. Brenner has argued that for the G-7 as a whole, 'Between 1970 and 1990, the manufacturing rate of profit...was, on average, about 40% lower than between 1950 and 1970'. This creates the false impression that the break was in 1970, whereas such numbers are also consistent with a *steady* decline from the early fifties to the early eighties—as was the case for profit rates in both the US and Germany (i.e., if profits are falling, any average for a group of earlier years will necessarily be higher than for a later group of years). Japan does conform to a break in the early-seventies but it is the clear exception in his chart. See Brenner, *New Left Review*, p. 7, text and Figure 3.

28. Fine, et al., (ibid., p. 56) make the point that there is no reason for lower profits to

cause a crisis. Note that during the slide in profits, investment as a share of GDP continued to rise through the seventies.

29. 'It was a naïve illusion of the crafters of the post-war regime that the goals of expanding international trade, restoring currency convertibility and fostering foreign direct investment could be realized without the eventual resurgence of international finance, restrained only by the weak capital controls permitted under Bretton Woods.' Leo Panitch, 'The New Imperial State', *New Left Review*, 2, March–April, 2000, p. 11.

30. The boom in the early-sixties was the result of monetary and fiscal stimulus combined with a new corporate aggressiveness against labour. See Brenner, *New Left Review*, p. 49.

31. A credible case for a more 'conspiratorial' reading of this period is made by Peter Gowan in *The Global Gamble*, London, Verso, 1999.

32. '... such a course would mean stumbling into recession and slack, losing precious billions of dollars of output, suffering rising unemployment, with growing distress and unrest. It would be a prescription for social disaster as well as for unconscionable waste.' *Economic Report to the President, 1969*, Washington, January, 1969, p.10.

33. For a discussion of the ascent of finance, see Randall Germaine, *The Internationalization of Credit*, Cambridge: Cambridge University Press, 1997, pp. 118–136.

34. While labour productivity was doing fine, relatively more capital was needed to sustain that success. See Dumenil and Levy, *Historical Materialism*, p. 83.

35. Brenner does address the 'powerful across-the-board-assault on [American] workers and their institutions' which resulted in a 'fundamental shift in the balance of class forces' (p. 58). But he dates this a decade earlier than the attack on labour I've emphasized. My quarrel is not with the importance of that earlier attack; what marks the assault I'm addressing is that: (a) the general rollbacks of past gains after the mid-seventies represented something qualitatively different than anything previously seen in the US; (b) it was part of a specific response to the militancy of the late sixties; (c) it was part of a broader process of economic and political change (neoliberalism and the new imperialism); and (d) it was international in scope, with the status of US labour affecting, if not driving, the pressures on labour elsewhere.

36. Dumenil and Levy place this on a larger historical canvass in 'Costs and Benefits of Neoliberalism: A Class Analysis' MODEM-CNRS and CEPREMAP-CNRS, September, 1999. They put finance at the centre of their analysis, defining neoliberalism as '... the ideological expression of the reassertion of the power of finance' (p. 1). My argument, while agreeing that finance is crucial, places finance in the broader context of neoliberal imperialism (see below). The overall work of Dumenil and Levy, impressively combining theoretical clarity, empirical rigour, and an historical-institutional context is a must for anyone interested in any of the issues raised by Brenner's essay; it is available through the Internet at www.cepremap.cnrs.fr.

37. Susan Strange, *States and Markets*, Oxford: Blackwell, 1988, pp. 24–25. America's structural power rested on the size of its market, the strength of its economic base especially in higher-tech sectors, the dominance of its financial institutions, the role of the American dollar, and its special status as a safe haven for capital when the system itself is threatened (all backed by its pre-eminent military position).

38. Capital's attempt to constitutionalize its achievements through international agree-

ments has, as we saw in the campaign against the MAI and then in Seattle, made neoliberalism more visible and therefore re-politicized the changes going on.

39. Karl Marx, *Capital, Volume 3*, London: Penguin, 1981, p. 275.

40. The section draws heavily on Leo Panitch's important essay, 'The New Imperial State', pp. 5–20.

41. A recent newspaper headline captured the coexistence in some of the developing countries of aspects of both the new imperialism and the old: 'A War Vets Return to Offer Vietnam Capitalist Skills', *Globe and Mail*, 25 April, 2000.

42. Leo Panitch, 'The New Imperial State', p. 9. The new imperialism, whatever its ultimate meaning, could not be defined in terms of such standard categories as the outflow of value and surplus or measured in trade, capital flows, and growth—the US had sustained periods of both trade surpluses and trade deficits with Europe and Japan; it went from being a creditor to a debtor; and it generally grew at a slower rate than they did.

43. In Germany and Japan the US remained an essentially occupying force in the early post-war years and directly influenced the shape of the labour movements. In France and Italy the US blocked the participation of Communists in government in spite of their widespread working-class support.

44. Editorial, *The Economist*, 12 February, 2000.

45. Weber and Rigby, *The Golden Age Illusion*, p. 43.

46. Panitch, *New Left Review*, pp. 8, 20. The interaction of US and domestic capital within the same territory may not erase an identifiable Japanese, German, or European bourgeoisie. But it certainly erodes, as Panitch argues, their coherence as a distinctly nationalist force with any inclinations to a radical anti-American challenge. This also fundamentally questions the viability of strategies based on any cross-class nationalist alliances.

47. The difference between a budget deficit and a trade deficit is class-based and tied to the perspective on globalization. The former is associated with the public sphere and the social wage. It is therefore defined as 'bad' because it indicates a lack of capitalist class control. To the extent a trade deficit 'only' reflects the global allocation of production it can be tolerated as long as, in capitalist eyes, there is confidence in the ability to pay (i.e., it becomes, to some degree, comparable to the trade deficit between California and Texas).

48. Ironically, if we imagine a serious threat to American stability, funds may be as likely to come in as leave. The reasoning might be that if the US economy collapses, the global economy will be expected to be not too far behind; amidst the chaos, the US might consequently be the safest place to be because of the strength of the American state and weakness of oppositional forces (talk about 'moral hazard'!). That this didn't happen in 1929 reflects, in part, the inability or unwillingness of the US state to play the role of imperial power at that time.

49. For example, Callinicos (and he is not alone) refers to 'the extent to which, despite the massive restructuring of the past two decades, the most powerful capitalism in the world has failed to overcome its structural problems'. Alex Callinicos, 'Capitalism, Competition, and Profits: A Critique of Brenner's Theory of Crisis', *Historical Materialism*, 4, p. 21.

50. Robert Brenner, 'The Looming Crisis of World Capitalism: From Neoliberalism to Depression?', *Against the Current*, October, 1998. p. 1.

51. Brenner, *New Left Review*, p. 235.

52. Corporations cannot get rid of the overall level of risk in global operations (all the more so in the context of floating exchange rates). What they can however do is pay others to carry the risk. A market for risk therefore includes a degree of 'functional speculation' on the part of those buying the risk. This inevitably opens the door to a degree of wilder, 'unproductive speculation' (the distinction between the two dimensions of speculation is, of course, not always easy to discern).

53. For a very rich Marxist overview of the role of finance see David Harvey, *The Limits to Capital*, London: Verso, 1999, Chapters 9 and 10.

54. Marx, *Capital, Vol. 3*, p. 490.

55. Unpublished e-mail from Brenner in response to Henwood's comments in *Left Business Observer*, September 27, 1998.

56. As Simon Clarke noted in his critique of Brenner, '… the dynamism and the crisis-tendencies of capitalist accumulation are necessarily two sides of the same coin', 'Capitalist Competition', p. 70. Mike Lebowitz similarly emphasizes the need for a more nuanced sense of capital's strength by not mistaking the apparent weakness of capital at the national level with its actual dynamism overall. See his 'Trade and Class: Labour Strategies in a World of Strong Capital', *Studies in Political Economy*, 27, 1988, pp. 137–148.

57. Source: *Economic Report to the President*, February, 2000, Appendix B, Table B-29.

58. Brenner, *New Left Review*, p.199, Brenner's emphasis. In fact, productivity in durable goods and especially in machinery (industrial and electrical) has grown very much faster between 1979 and the mid-nineties than during the long boom.

59. Source: *Economic Report to the President*, p. 29 and Appendix B, Table B-16.

60. The outsourcing and restructuring led to a massive exit of capacity during the late-seventies' recession which continued through the nineties. Over this period, for example, UAW members at the American operations of General Motors fell from 450,000 to under 150,000 (and are expected to fall to 100,000 in the next few years).

61. Sectoral unionization might increase exit by blocking weak firms from surviving by way of lowering wages. As unionization falls, overcapacity might therefore be expected. (I tend, however, to think that the issue of capacity is dominated by other factors.)

62. In the decade before 1973 an amazing 20%–30% of manufacturing investment by American capital went abroad. See Brenner, *New Left Review*, p. 55, Figure 5.

63. McDonald's wages and its treatment of its workers are desultory, but that is not inconsistent with its 'dynamism' in terms of marketing innovations or removal of barriers to global growth. At a meeting discussing the future of General Motors, one executive raised '… continuing concerns and problems with [GM's] dealerships' and used McDonald's as an example of the ability 'to implement high standards of achievement in customer satisfaction areas'. ('A Report to the GM Team', February, 1992, transcripts, p. 15).

64. Karl Marx, *The Communist Manifesto*, London, Merlin Press, 1998, p. 5.

65. Brenner, *Against The Current*, p. 1.

66. Brenner, *New Left Review*, p. 2.

67. Merrill Lynch advertisement in *The Economist*, 24 October, 1998.

68. Ariel Dorfman, 'Matter of Time', *Rethinking Marxism*, Spring 1990, p. 12.

REFLECTIONS ON STRATEGY FOR LABOUR

Leo Panitch

To speak of strategy *for labour* needs some justification today. Class analysis went out of intellectual fashion almost two decades ago; and class politics has been increasingly displaced as the pivot of party political discourse and electoral mobilization. Class, as we have been so often reminded, is not everything.

But nor is class nothing, and the costs of the marginalization of class in the intellectual and political arena are becoming increasingly severe, especially in the context of 'globalization'—which is another word for the reach of American imperialism, the power of financial markets, the spread of capitalist social relations, the intensification of exploitation and a vast growth in social inequality. An extensive process of what looks like classic proletarianization is taking place in many countries of the so-called 'developing' world; and in the advanced capitalist world the decline in the size of the traditional industrial labour force is accompanied by the proletarianization of many service and professional occupations and the spread of more unstable, casual and contingent employment. These are developments that can only be comprehended through a revival of class analysis; and they may also provide the grounds for new strategies for labour which transcend the limits of the old forms of class politics.

The discourse of 'civil society' has made a strong bid to displace the discourse of class on the left. It is intended to present a more inclusive and pluralist approach than the old class politics in terms of identifying those social forces which are the fount of political freedom and progressive change. But one of the ironies of this discourse's claim to inclusivity is that it has often left labour out, having afforded almost no vantage point for observing that arena of non-freedom within civil society, the work-place, where most people, in selling the right to determine what they do with their time and abilities, enter an authoritarian relationship with an employer within which freedom of speech and assembly are considerably attenuated.[1] Moreover, despite the central importance which the discourse of civil society properly gives to associational autonomy from the state, there has been a remarkable silence in most of the civil society literature regarding state attacks on trade unions over the past two decades—making organizing harder and decertification easier, restricting or removing the right to strike, and so on. It sometimes even appears that trade unions have a better appreciation of what is entailed in securing freedom of association than many contemporary NGOs: contrast the financial dependence on government grants of so many NGOs with the trade unions' traditional sensitivity (famously articulated even by such non-radical labour leaders as Samuel Gompers) to the danger posed by state funding for associational autonomy.

To be fair, the labour movement's capacity to collect dues (often institutionalized in collective bargaining arrangements) is not open to the NGOs and new social movements. Yet this very fact has made some of these movements rely on the labour movement for the funding of various campaigns. It is unfortunately the case that trade unions often use their financial clout to narrow or moderate these campaigns; but this precisely speaks to the need for a new strategy for labour. It is now obvious—it always should have been—that there is nothing inevitable about the working class becoming a transformative agency. Not only reformist and revolutionary, but even reactionary practices have issued from the working classes. But what is also true is that, unless a very substantial part of the labour movement becomes involved, no fundamental socio-economic change is realizable.

This is why even as harsh a critic as Andre Gorz, despite having famously bid 'farewell to the working class' at the beginning of the 1980s, had returned by the 1990s to thinking again about a 'strategy for labour'—as he had originally done in his famous book of that name in 1964. The very success of the new social movements—whose specific campaigns were not only 'mould[ing] the consciousness of a growing number of people' but contained the promise of 'a wider, more fundamental struggle for emancipation'—had brought out the necessity for this:

> The fact that the trade-union movement is—and will remain—the best organized force in the broader movement confers on it a particular responsibility; on it will largely depend the success or failure of all the other elements in this social movement. According to whether the trade-union movement opposes them or whether it seeks a common alliance and a common course of action with them, these other elements will be part of the left or will break with it, will engage with it in collective action or will remain minorities tempted to resort to violence.[2]

A new strategy for labour would mean altering labour movements themselves in fundamental ways, but what Gorz came to see was that the trade unions' indifference or hostility to the new social movements was neither foreordained nor unchangeable. As he put it: 'The attitude towards the other social movements and their objectives will determine [the labour movement's] own evolution'.

That this may be an opportune moment to address new strategies for labour is suggested not only by the strikes in so many countries in recent years (as this volume was finalized, in May/June 2000, there were general strikes in Argentina, India, Korea, Nigeria and South Africa); or by recent surveys that show rising class awareness even in the USA where working-class self-identification has historically been very low.[3] What is much more important than these instances of conflict and consciousness is the fact that *labour is changing in ways that make it a more inclusive social agent*. The main developments here have been women's massive (re)entry into the labour force and changing patterns of migration, both of which have recomposed the working classes of many countries and made them into very different classes in both objective and subjective terms than they were even a quarter-century or so ago. Working classes have, of course, always been made up of many diverse elements: what is significant is the way the old labour movements are being changed by the recomposition of the working classes in our time.[4]

The image many people, including many on the left, have of labour is outdated. Feminism and environmentalism, even gay rights activism, have had a visible effect within the labour movement, and the discourse and, in many cases, the practice of unions reflects this. Of course, these changes are very uneven around the globe, and there is substantial variation even within each national labour movement, and sometimes even within each union. Sexism, racism and homophobia continue to be serious problems and hostility to environmental issues among those unions whose members' jobs are directly affected remains strong. Even among those which have learned to 'talk the talk', there is often far to go in terms of the issues to which unions actually assign priority— and tensions can be severe when change goes so far as to induce a clash of priorities. Yet, it is also true, as many of the essays in this volume have demonstrated, that there is far more pluralism in today's working classes than is allowed for in the perspectives of those who find it convenient to essentialize labour as male, white and straight. This new pluralism is one of the main reasons why new strategies for labour are needed.

The case to be argued here for a new strategy for labour in no way implies that what the new social movements do is somehow 'less important'. On the contrary, if we concentrate on strategy for labour it is only because, with Gorz, we think the enormous potential of the new social movements for social transformation will only be realized if labour finally takes enthusiastically on board the key emancipatory themes raised by the other movements. But at the same time, the new social movements themselves can hardly ignore their own need for strategy for labour. Many of the essays in this volume have addressed the experience and possibilities of feminism in relation to labour, and the challenge that this entails not only for unions but also for a feminist movement that wants to speak to immigrant 'maids' as well as their professional 'mistresses'. Nor can the issue of strategy for labour in the environmental movement be ignored: this is seen in the internal debates that go on within environmental groups over whether the priority often attached to high profile campaigns as necessary for fund-raising among the well-to-do comes at the expense of addressing the environment as a matter of public health in working-class communities.

If the working classes of every country have always been diverse, then the fact that they are becoming more so in our time ought to be a source of strength—and it will be the task of new strategies for labour in unions as well as political and social movements to unleash that strength. The notion of solidarity would never have made any sense if the working classes were homogeneous to begin with. Solidarity as process has always been about, not ignoring or eliminating, but *transcending* working-class diversity—and this has meant gaining strength via forging unity of purpose out of *strategies of inclusiveness* rather than repressing diversity. At the core of all the failures of past labour strategies lay the inability to build solidarity in this sense as effectively as possible.[5] The organization within unions of caucuses, conferences, committees among women or minority members is a healthy development precisely because it allows additional space within the union for capacity-building among those who have suffered most from discrimination or marginalization. The challenge is to discover (and to overcome resistance to attempts to discover) how to build fully inclusive labour movements which are democratically structured in such ways as to encourage the development of the capacities of *all* members of the working class in as many facets of their lives as possible.

II

But to say new strategies are needed, does not get us far in determining what they should be. Social movement activists have rightly been wary that many traditional labour attitudes and old strategies are recipes for failure and that the labour movement's clinging to them, even if sometimes clothed in new language, is a major factor in blocking social change. The most favoured labour strategies have indeed turned out be failures, partly due to changing conditions represented under the symbol of globalization, but also partly due to fundamental flaws in the strategies themselves, flaws which were already visible under the old conditions.

In speaking of this, one should not only count the obvious failures of the Communist parties and the insurrectionary left; or the no less obvious limitations of the American 'service' model of trade unionism. Many people on the left today take as their benchmark of success the European social democratic labour movements, especially in building the democratic 'mixed economies' in the post-war era. But the latter's own failures, if less immediately obvious, are perhaps for that very reason the most important to come to understand. From today's perspective of the defeat of the mixed economy by neoliberalism, these failures need to be measured above all in terms of the long-run effects of social democratic labour movements having lulled themselves into ideological stupor and organizational inertia for three decades with illusions of the humanization of capitalism. In the wake of the post-war settlement and cold war, unions took little or no responsibility for the education of their supporters on the nature of capitalism as a system or for the development of popular democratic capacities for challenging that system and for collective self-government in every walk of life. It was in good part because of this that the neoliberal restoration proved possible in the face of the impasse of the Keynesian welfare state in the last quarter of the twentieth century. The ruthless competitive dynamism of capitalism reasserted itself in the form of free trade and foreign direct investment, the ascendancy of financial capital, and 'lean' production through job 'flexibility' and casualization. Labour movements were unprepared for all this—and, worse, had not prepared their members and supporters with the organizational and intellectual resources to readily understand what was happening; nor had they been encouraged to imagine any alternative. No wonder the bourgeoisie at the end of the twentieth century has once again been able 'to make the world in its own image'.

This is not a matter of hindsight being easy. These failures were evident enough even in the heyday of the 'mixed economy'. They were uppermost in Gorz's mind when his *Strategy for Labour* was first published in France in 1964. Gorz took direct aim against those predominant labour strategies which offered

> no other perspective than that of increased *individual consumption*. In other words, they place the workers as a class on the tail end of the "consumer society" and its ideology; they do not challenge the model of that society, but only the share of the wealth which the society accords to the salaried consumer. They consciously bring into question neither the workers' condition at the place of work, nor the subordination of consumption to production; not even ... the diversion and confiscation of productive resources and human labour for frivolous and wasteful ends ... [It] is not that struggles over wages are useless; rather, it is that their effectiveness, in so far as mobilization, unification, and education of the working class are concerned, has become very limited. These struggles by themselves, even if they sometimes succeed in creating a crisis within capitalism, neither succeed in preventing capitalism from overcoming its difficulties in its own way, nor in preparing the working class sufficiently to outline and impose its own solutions ... On the contrary, the working class runs the risk of provoking a counteroffensive ... an attack levelled not only in the economic, but in the ideological, social and political realms; and the working class, because it did not also wage a fight in these spheres, would be unable to respond with the necessary alertness and cohesion.[6]

With the inflationary dynamic which undid the post-war order already on the horizon, Gorz also warned against union adhesion to corporatist incomes policies, whereby they restrained their members' wage demands to try to stave off the crisis: 'The incomes policy merely expresses the political will of organized capitalism to integrate the union into the system, to subordinate consumption to production, and production to the maximization of profit. The union cannot defend itself against this political will except by an opposite and autonomous political will which is independent of party and state ...'. Corporatist partnerships with capital and the state foreclosed strategies directed at 'the socialization of the investment function', and without being able to challenge the determination of what was produced and how, the main effect of these corporatist arrangements could only be to subordinate union autonomy to social democratic governments which left 'the power of the capitalist state intact'. By virtue of not taking up 'structural reforms' to challenge and change the structure of power in the capitalist order, the post-war nationalizations and welfare reforms would not only be absorbed by the system but increasingly undermined: 'The only way the socialized sector can survive is by limiting capital's sphere of autonomy and countering its logic, by restraining its field of action, and bringing its potential centres of accumulation under social control ... (socialized medicine must control the pharmaceutical industry, social housing must control the building industry, for example), or else be nibbled away and exploited by the private sector'.[7] Gorz clearly foresaw the main contours of the strategic failures of the labour movement that opened the way to the neoliberal restoration.

Yet as the 'new world order' represented by neoliberal globalization began to take shape, many of those who had earlier showed some indication of appreciating the problems Gorz had identified in European corporatism and social democracy now rushed to defend them as the only actually-existing alternatives to neoliberalism. A great deal of ink was spilled extolling the virtues of the Swedish or German or Austrian 'models' even as unions in these countries were themselves increasingly internally divided by corporatism's effects in terms of unevenly applied wage restraint and the loss of union autonomy. More significant still, given the real structure of power, even these 'models' of corporatism were being abandoned by employers, bureaucrats and politicians who had already redefined the parameters of economic management. In making the containment of inflation, not unemployment, the prime goal of economic policy, they had already given up on the strategy of securing the wage moderation of unions through corporatist negotiations on incomes policies, and had given priority instead to winning the confidence of financial markets with monetary policies designed to break union militancy through unemployment and job insecurity.

Nevertheless, the advocacy of 'social partnerships' between capital and labour has remained the main leitmotif of most 'pragmatic' and 'moderate' labour leaders and liberal and social democratic intellectuals in the new era. Sometimes this has been boldly put forward in terms of 'making capitalism an offer it cannot refuse' whereby unions have been urged to present themselves in terms of 'being able to solve problems for capitalists which they cannot solve on their own'.[8] This attempt to revive a social partnership strategy in the context of globalization was generally guided by the argument that the one thing unions could offer that capital wanted was higher productivity. This 'supply-side' form of corporatism—what has been termed 'progressive competitiveness' in *The Socialist Register*—had at its core what Bienefeld called the 'cargo-cult' of training ('if we train them, the jobs will come'): partnerships between unions, capital and state designed to 'train' workers to become so productive that they could compete with low-paid labour abroad, or at least so innovative that they could sustain the search for 'niche' markets .[9]

The problems with this as a strategy for labour were manifold. First of all, there were the obvious ethical ones. It is as though, seeing a man on the street, hungry and homeless, you perceive his problem only in terms of his not being motivated enough, entrepreneurial enough, skilled enough to get a job, rather than seeing that something must be wrong with the system. This kind of logic is applied, in the progressive competitiveness framework, to whole sectors, regions and economies. Even if such a strategy of export competitiveness were successful, its effect would be to export unemployment to the regions that are less successful. But the problems with such a strategy were also practical, embedded in the over-production that must attend a global system where everyone tries to increase their exports and limit their imports through domestic austerity, and in the financial instability that attends capital movements in such a system.

In so far as social democracy by the early 1990s still had any distinctiveness in terms of economic strategies, it was reduced to advocating an active role for states and unions in advancing the export competitiveness of this or that particular capitalist economy. This strategy exaggerated considerably what national capital was willing to do, or could do, to achieve competitiveness, even while, as with the old corporatist strategy, this new one also sacrificed the autonomy of labour to this end. For this reason, the 'supply-side' attempt to revive the corporatist approach, masquerading as a new strategy for labour, proved a dead end. With wage militancy and inflation having been broken by monetarism, and with the competitive dynamic of capitalism having already asserted itself in 'free' capital flows as well as free trade, the offer of a deal that couldn't be refused was now usually met with a shrug or a blank stare. And when social democratic governments were elected, usually even before the new measures to implement corporatist 'training' strategies were put in place, let alone could have much effect, these governments were quickly overwhelmed by the problems of short-term economic management. Since everything hinged on the goal of co-operating with capital, they invariably placated financial markets by limiting imports and stabilizing the currency through fiscal austerity. Where social democracy went so far as to accede to capital's insistence that the price of its co-operation was that social democracy jettison its own partnership with the unions what we had left was Blairism—which prides itself on not conceiving its project as a strategy *for* labour at all, but rather a strategy for explicitly distancing itself from the labour movement.

It is worth noting, especially given this denouement, that Gorz's original *Strategy for Labour* proceeded from the exact opposite premise from that of offering capital a deal it could not refuse—'one which does not base its validity and its right to exist on capitalist needs, criteria and rationales'. The 'structural reforms' he advanced were 'determined not in terms of what can be, but what should be', and he based his strategy on 'the possibility of attaining its objectives on the implementation of fundamental political and economic changes'. These changes could be gradual, but the measure of structural reforms was that they effected 'a modification of the relations of power'—strengthening workers' capacities to 'establish, maintain, and expand those tendencies within the system which serve to weaken capitalism and to shake its joints'.[10] In this way, a continuity could be 'established between the objectives of present mass struggles and the prospect of a socialist society'. The point was to build the kinds of organizations and to engage in the kinds of struggles through which workers might feel—'on all levels of their existence'—that elements of a desirable socialist society were actually discernable within their own world in the here and now. Compromises would still have to be struck, but this needed to be 'understood explicitly for what it is: the provisional result of the temporary relationship of forces, to be modified in future battles'.[11]

Of course, this was not the approach most unions adopted in the face of globalization. Yet some did: I am aware of no better example of the distinction between offering capital 'a deal it cannot refuse' and Gorz's opposite strategic principle than that adopted by the Canadian Auto Workers union in the early 1980s—just as Gorz was (temporarily) bidding 'farewell to the working class'. The strategic principle the CAW adopted in the face of the big three auto companies demanding concessions from workers to meet the new global competition (leading to its break with its American parent 'international' union, the UAW) was straightforward: 'Competitiveness is a constraint, but it is not our goal'.[12]

III

Even if the 'progressive competitiveness' strategy is more clearly recognized today as a misguided response to globalization, it is nevertheless the case that no adequate new strategy for labour can evolve unless what is to be done about globalization is seriously addressed. It is first of all necessary to clear up some misconceptions. Globalization is not an objective economic process which labour needs to 'catch up to', as so many seem to think. It is a political process advanced by identifiable interests for clear purposes. The failure to see the strategic political nature of globalization reflects an economism which needs to be overcome. Nation states are not the victims of globalization, they are the authors of globalization. States are not *displaced* by globalized capital, they *represent* globalized capital, above all financial capital. This means that any adequate strategy to challenge globalization must begin at home, precisely because of the key role of states in making globalization happen. But labour's traditional goal of securing a progressive alliance with their 'national bourgeoisie' under the aegis of the state is increasingly *passé;* for 'the state' more and more represents a set of (domestic and foreign) internationally-oriented capitalist classes.

What then is to be done? In order to answer this question we can usefully begin by looking again at the approach Gorz adopted in the mid-1960s to the European Community (as it then was), since it presented problems for European unions that in many ways anticipated those now facing all unions under full globalization. Indeed, one the most fascinating things about reading Gorz's *Strategy for Labour* now is to see how relevant his analysis of the European Common Market at the time remains to the development of labour strategies in the context of globalization today. Gorz saw the Common Market in the first years of its existence—with its 'yearly average of 1,000 "mergers and agreements" between companies of different nationalities'—as a prerequisite of a new kind of 'monopoly expansion', whereby the nature of competition among big private corporations had shifted to the penetration of each others' interior markets. This entailed rationalization within and across sectors, but it also gave rise to over-investment and over-production, leading in turn to a further 'thrust of industrial and especially financial concentration'. Each state supported or sponsored its own big corporations, and as the financial risks entailed in this competitive mutual penetration of interior markets escalated, a degree of supranational planning at the European level was needed. Such planning, however, 'obviously has nothing to do with real economic planning' since it was designed only to smooth out the contradictions of the competitive process in which 'the capitalists' freedom of action remains untouched'. If labour's goal was to attach union representatives to such supranational planning, it 'would obviously make a fool's bargain ... Cut off from the working masses ... the workers' representatives are under strong pressure to become technocrats, working out summit compromises which win a great deal less than mass action could have'.[13]

The recent history of European economic integration chillingly confirms this. Capital's room for manoeuvre has been greatly expanded, and so has the 'democratic deficit', embedding even further in the European Central Bank what each state's central banks had already represented in this respect. But as Andrew Martin and George Ross have demonstrated, what the European Trade Union Congress (ETUC) saw as its 'breakthrough, beyond anything it could have reasonably expected' when it was suddenly embraced as a negotiating partner under Maastricht's Social Protocol, turned out to be only a breakthrough for the union bureaucracy in Brussels. The embrace 'turned out very different from what enthusiasts had foreseen in the heady days of 1985 to 1990' and left the ETUC 'essentially excluded from more fundamental matters of economic governance'. This was reflected in the sheer weakness of the Social Protocol actually negotiated under Maastricht (especially in so far as matters concerning pay or the rights to organize and strikes were entirely excluded).

Even the much-vaunted subsequent protocol mandating European Works Councils in MNCs (which covered only some ten percent of the European work-force in any case) left so much leeway to employers that it produced 'less than a handful of agreements [which] provide for consultation more meaningful ... than an "exchange of views" after the fact'. Despite some modest success in the area of parental leave benefits, there can be no escaping the fact that 'the EMU macroeconomic policy regime has squeezed social policy between unemployment and convergence/stability pact criteria' to such an extent that capitalist 'supply-side' strategies for greater labour market 'flexibility' have come to take precedence over any positive new strategy for labour.[14]

Above all, what is confirmed in Gorz's prognosis is that labour's involvement in European integration has been 'largely a top-down process'. As Martin and Ross put it: 'The ETUC has so far developed largely by borrowing resources from European institutions to gain legitimacy with its own national constituents ... ETUC, in other words, has developed from the top rather than as a mass organization built from below out of a broader social movement'. Moreover, since the promise of substantial gains from elite bargaining within European institutions has not materialized, the result has been that the European unions' position of 'critical support' for Economic and Monetary Union 'has so far put them in an excruciating political bind. It ties them to the particular version of the economic approach to political integration that has been pursued despite its social costs and rising popular disenchantment, including among union members'.[15] Not surprisingly in this context, unions have relied on national collective bargaining and political structures to protect themselves as best they could. But the 'competitive corporatism' they are still oriented to at this level, seen in various new 'social pacts' that have been struck with employers and the state, has mainly to do with competitive adjustment (via the sacrifice of earlier labour market and welfare state reforms as well as wage moderation) to the neoliberalism embedded in European integration.

It is indeed significant that strategies for transnational collective bargaining have made so little headway since Charles Levinson made the case for it thirty years ago in the context of the rise of the multinational corporation.[16] The reasons for this may partly be laid at the door of national-level trade unions bureaucrats, but much more important has been that the very purpose of globalization, from the perspective of business and the capitalist state, has been to bring about competition among workers, not foster centralized bargaining at a higher level. Notably, Gorz, unlike Levinson, did not advocate working 'toward the unification and the centralization of a labour strategy ... besides being impossible at present, [this] would only result in bureaucratic sclerosis'. While it was necessary to try to 'co-ordinate among the various sectoral, regional, or national strategies so they complement, not contradict each other', one had to primarily let each national struggle 'develop according to its own particular qualities' since it was from struggles at this level 'that the labour movement principally draws its strength'. This did not mean the class struggles ought to be isolated from the international arena; Gorz believed, rather, that it was increasingly possible to 'trust in the contagious effect of each national victory'. Isolated national victories would not be possible any longer, because in the context of the new international competitiveness, each national government, once forced by its labour movement to undertake a structural reform, would have to advance its adoption at the European level to ensure that the policy labour imposed in one state did not remain 'a national peculiarity'.[17]

IV

These considerations are very germane to the question of how labour should respond to further efforts to extend globalization today. It is time to question strategies—often borrowed from superficial accounts of the European Social Protocol—for securing the inclusion of labour rights in international trade treaties. Along the lines of the NAFTA labour and environmental 'side agreements', this strategy is designed to 'constitutionalize' minimum labour standards, as well as secure a place for labour representatives in the negotiation and administration of these treaties. Such a strategy may be useful for bringing terrible labour conditions and anti-union policies into public discussions of globalization, but at the same time, the very idea of attaching labour rights to such treaties also means endorsing the free trade and capital flows which these treaties are all about securing. Moreover, apart from what ideological effect they have, the difficulties of enforcing labour rights articulated in such side agreements are notorious.

What is most disturbing about this response to globalization, however, as Gerard Greenfield has especially pointed out, is how often it is used both by the International Confederation of Free Trade Unions (ICFTU) and national union leaders

> to justify the abandonment of collective action locally, and even nationally, as ineffective or irrelevant. Based on what they see as the inevitability of capitalist globalization and the weakness of organized labour, they are instead seeking a new set of compromises with global capital. Or to put it more accurately, they are seeking a continuation of the old compromises with national capital at a global level.[18]

In so far as this new strategy of global compromise 'displaces rather than supports militant workers struggles', Greenfield argues, it is not only misguided, but positively harmful. This is not to say that the institutions of globalization don't have to be engaged with by unions; the question is what priority they assign to this and what they seek from such engagement. In a discussion document prepared for developing union strategy for the WTO's round of multilateral negotiations that was supposed to have begun in Seattle at the end of 1999, Greenfield articulated, in direct contrast with the ICFTU's 'strategy for inclusion', a new 'strategy for exclusion'. This meant that, in terms of the content of international economic treaties, unions and their allies could follow the principle of immunity ('freedom from') rather than of rights ('freedom to') along the lines of those labour law regimes which established that organizing attempts or strikes were protected from punishment or legal prosecution by the employer. This would take the form of demanding the exclusion of particular sectors, or particular bio-resources (such as seeds), from WTO agreements, and would go along with demands for the immunity of workers' and farmers' organizations from repression when their states face unfair trading practices through the WTO's complaint mechanisms. This defensive aspect of the strategy, designed to limit the damage caused by such agreements, can accompany a more general strategic challenge to the whole process entailed in these negotiations, above all to the secrecy of the negotiations which 'reflects an inherent hostility towards democracy and democratic processes among WTO technocrats, government advisers and the powerful corporate interests they represent'. Greenfield goes on:

> This problem is not simply resolved by getting unions a chair at the negotiating table. Whatever is decided will still be decided behind-the-scenes anyway ... Past experience has shown that getting a seat at the table sometimes places far too much emphasis on representing labour, rather than organizing labour ... More important is the task of breaking down walls to these behind-the-scenes deals in a way that organizes and mobilizes our members along with a broader alliance of democratic forces. Clearly this requires a public education and mobilization campaign to achieve what WTO technocrats and TNCs do not want— a critical awareness among working people of *what is being done to them*.[19]

The negotiated exclusion strategy advanced by Greenfield was thus explicitly conceived as secondary and subsidiary to a primary strategy of mobilization against the institutions of globalization themselves. This is what actually came to the fore at Seattle, where the initiative was taken away from those trying to get a seat at the table in a such a surprising and stunning fashion that it may be counted as a turning point. To be sure, what happened on the streets of Seattle was not spontaneous combustion—a lot of planning was involved by a great many NGOs and unions. And it followed on the impressive activities already undertaken in the same year by People's Global Action, a new alliance formed in February 1998 by some 300 delegates from movements in 71 countries on the basis of their common rejection of the WTO and other trade liberalization agreements. Their self-described 'confrontational attitude' was based on the perception that lobbying cannot 'have a major impact in such biased and undemocratic organizations [as the WTO], in which transnational capital is the only real policy-maker'. The Global Day of Action they sponsored in the world's financial centres on 18 June 1999 was an important, if much less noticed, prelude to what took place in Seattle six months later.

The sight of steelworkers declaring solidarity with anarchists on the streets of Seattle was a heady one. The multiplicity of voices and slogans was bewildering and frustrating to those 'progressive' negotiators, whether from the 'Third' World or the 'First', whose main priority is the strategy of global compromise. 'Its not clear what they want—they want so many different things', was the complaint often heard. The mutterings of officials in the French royal court in 1789 must have been much the same. One measure of the truly radical nature of these kinds of protests is just this—they aren't putting forward a series of demands that can be negotiated within the given institutional frameworks of globalization: they really are building critical awareness among people of 'what is being done to them'—and are galvanizing a great deal of attention and support as a result.

Unfortunately, immediately after Seattle the political initiative against globalization within the USA swung back to the negotiators in the American labour movement who, by the time of the anti-IMF and World Bank protests in Washington, D.C., four months later, had narrowed the issue down to whether or not the US Congress should endorse China's inclusion in the WTO. The problem was not so much that of 'protectionism' *per se* (any serious attempt to challenge globalization entails 'protection' for local and national communities); it was rather what can only be called the *chauvinist* protectionism and *imperial* condescension that lay behind the demand that the American state should not be giving the Chinese masses the 'benefit' of access to its markets until 'labour rights' were enforced in China. The whole discourse was framed in terms of appealing to the American state to play its 'proper' world role as a democratic and benevolent good guy against the Chinese state. The absence of a strong alternative vision, and the danger of not having one, was revealed in the astonishing support which key American NGO leaders gave to the AFL/CIO's narrowly-conceived campaign against China's inclusion in the WTO.[20] They contributed in this way to legitimating the WTO as something really worth getting into, even as they mobilized for the Washington demonstration against the other institutions of globalization, the IMF and World Bank.

Lost in the rhetoric in the debate on China after Seattle were two main things: first, the enormous concessions China is making to foreign capital to get into the WTO;[21] and second, the fact that the struggle for labour rights is not external to China but is being conducted within it (as it is in all developing countries), including by the millions of Chinese workers who, by official estimates, undertook over 120,000 strikes in 1999 alone.[22] If the AFL/CIO really wants to help Chinese workers, it will campaign for the exclusion of those provisions in the WTO that will result in tens of millions of Chinese workers losing their jobs when public enterprises are robbed of their 'subsidies'; and it will take direct action itself by providing the level of resources and support to those struggling to build independent trade unions in China that it once provided to Solidarity in Poland (of course it was encouraged in this at the time by the American state—as it will not be regarding Chinese independent unions now).

But can much better be said of those Third World elites who themselves employed the charge of imperialism against those who called for labour rights to be included in the WTO? We should have no illusions either about Third World leaders and their technocratic advisers who are ready and willing to set aside labour rights in their anxiety to ensure at all costs that foreign capital comes their way rather than leaves them marginalized in the new world capitalist order. It is misleading to speak, as Samir Amin does today, of the 'political authorities in the active peripheries—and behind them all of society (including the contradictions within society itself)—hav[ing] a project and a strategy' for national economic development which stands in 'confrontation with globally dominant imperialism'.[23] He includes in the 'active peripheries' China, Korea and India as well as unnamed others in Southeast Asia and Latin America and contrasts these with 'marginalized peripheries' which are 'the passive subjects of globalization'. But while the ruling classes and political elites of India, Korea and especially China are definitely not merely the 'passive subjects' of globalization as they actively manoeuvre for a place in the new global order, it is also patently clear that only a major transformation in class relations in each of these countries will lead to anything like a 'confrontation with globally dominant imperialism'. For Third World leaders who really want to take an anti-imperial stand, a good place to start, rather than clamouring for a seat at the table of the imperium, would be to stop their repression of domestic class struggle and their denial of freedom of association.

A sustained mobilization against the institutions of globalization will have to eventually offer a strategic vision for a different order. Until such a vision gains some currency, legitimacy will continue to be lent to the institutions of globalization by many labour, NGO and Third World elites who see no practical alternative to them. No such vision has not yet emanated from the mobilizations that gave us Seattle. Andrew Ross previously noted that 'the capacity to organize dissent and resistance on the international scale' has been considerably enhanced by the 'undeniable asset' of the Internet, but the 'new informational landscape' has also 'magnified the gulf between the temporality of activists—based on urgency around mobilization—and the temporality of intellectuals—based around the slower momentum of thought and theoretical speculation. Many forms of radical thought require a patient process of germination that is antipathetic to the new speed of information circulation'.[24] To be sure, the contribution that even left intellectuals see themselves as making is mostly limited to offering narrow-gauge policy advice to their states which internalizes the politics of compromise (as such, left intellectuals bear some responsibility for the dead end to which competitive corporatism and progressive competitiveness have led). The seeds of an alternative vision have more often been planted by the activist groups themselves, such as by the People's Global Action organizational philosophy of 'decentralization and autonomy' which implies inward-oriented development strategies ('localization') rather than export competitiveness. But for this glimmer of an alternative to make sense to people it needs to be made much clearer what this can mean, and what its implications are for strategy.

V

The key long-term condition for an alternative to globalization is democratic investment control within each state—the opposite goal to that of today's multilateral international negotiations. This must mean going beyond the type of quantitative controls on the inflow and outflow of capital allowed under Bretton Woods, let alone beyond the Tobin Tax on capital flows now being advanced by many on the left. A campaign for qualitative democratic capital controls is required, one which puts on the agenda what international investment is for and should be for, rather than governments themselves either taking a piece of the action (the Tobin Tax is a version of tobacco and alcohol taxes) or just managing short-term capital flows in relation to currency stability, as they did prior to globalization. Nor can we pretend that controls over foreign investment can be divorced from the need for democratic control over private *domestic* investment. This will not be adequately addressed by notions of 'pension fund socialism' or labour investment funds which offer tax breaks to the workers that put their money in them.[25] Far from giving the labour movement control over jobs and the direction of the economy, such funds as now exist generally lack even the capacity to control any particular project, and many of them adopt no investment criteria other than profitability, or even require that the jobs created include unionization. Moreover, at the same time as shifting the risk of investment to workers' savings, these schemes envelop workers in the world of the stock markets and tax accountants (investors *should* be taxed and regulated, not subsidized, which is what accountants seek to achieve). And perhaps most important, approaching the issue of control over investment in this narrow way reinforces the conventional notion that the money in the banks is legitimately the capitalists' to do with as they please.

But how does the notion of democratic investment control get on the agenda in a world where even pension fund socialism sounds radical? We should not initially approach this in terms of getting it on the *state's* policy agenda. We need to recognize that the *first step in a new strategy* is to get labour movements to think again in terms that are not so cramped and defensive, *to think ambitiously again*, and then, once mobilized in such frame of mind, to make radical demands on the state of this kind. I have found the following argument effective in talks with trade unionists and social movement activists.[26] We now have in Canada directly elected local school boards which are vested with the statutory responsibility of providing everyone under eighteen in their catchment area with a place in the school system; and they are provided by higher levels of government with the funds, or the means of taxation, to accomplish this. Why do we not have directly elected 'job development boards' or 'economic planning boards' at the local level which are vested with the statutory responsibility of providing everyone in their catchment area with gainful paid employment? They wouldn't have to provide the jobs directly but could vet and fund proposals for *new projects* (to avoid displacing other workers). They would have to be given, like the school boards are, the funds, or the taxing powers, to accomplish this. There is no question it would be very costly if it were to be done properly. So how to fund it? The only really effective way to fund it would be to establish such control over the banks and other financial institutions as would allow for a considerable portion of the surplus that passes through their hands (*our own money*) to be designated for distribution to the elected local boards. This should be done centrally and the money distributed by higher levels of governments to each planning board to ensure regional parity.

When I present this argument, because it begins with a democratic reform related to job insecurity, there is usually strong assent by the time I get to the control over the financial system as being the condition for making this happen. It is necessary to make it clear that this is not a matter of 'socialism in one city'—it is a structural reform (political as much as economic) which needs to implemented across the board. And there is no sense ignoring the likelihood that unless the mobilization capacity of the labour movement and other social movements is enhanced considerably, it will be real estate agents and property developers who will get elected to the local boards. Moreover, such a municipal scheme for the democratic control of investment would have to be synchronized with sectoral councils bringing together workers and consumers in all industrial and service sectors (in contrast to the notion of industrial democracy at the level of single companies which would leave workers balkanized and sustain competition between them). In the public sector, such councils would include public employees and their 'clients', involving thereby the democratization of the services that meet social needs, but are now bureaucratically decided and provided.

At this stage, this proposal is mainly about getting labour movements and working people generally to think about how to develop their capacities to the point where this kind of structural reform could be meaningfully put on the political agenda. This brings us to *the second dimension of a new strategy for labour*— the need for a strategy for *transforming labour itself*. Nor is it only new radical demands, like democratic investment control, that bring this to the fore. Even reforms that are currently on the agenda, such as the reduction of work-time, face limits that are internal to labour. The 35-hour legislation passed in France, for instance, quickly ran into the type of agreement struck in the engineering sector with the bulk of the unions. The goal of job creation was frustrated by offsetting the loss of four hours a week by 'annualizing' and raising the ceiling of 'normal' time worked over a full year as well as by doubling the limit on annual overtime. In doing this, this agreement not only reduced the likelihood of companies having to hire more workers or pay more overtime as a result of the 35-hour law, but also met employers' demands for 'flexibility'—and this aspect of the agreement was incorporated into the second round of legislation, as a way of accommodating capital.[27]

This only shows that the scandal of work polarization—whereby at one end 'full-time' employees are working over 50 or 60 hours a week, while at the other end, 'casual' employees are working under 20 hours—also cannot be overcome without the transformation of unions themselves, from the local level to that of national confederations to the ICFTU. This must partly involve the shift in the balance of union activity more towards 'organizing' than 'servicing' that many people in the American labour movement are now talking about (although the ability to 'service' can never be divorced from any serious organizing drive); and it partly must involve the spread of 'social movement unionism' along the lines articulated in Kim Moody's important book, *Workers in a Lean World*.[28] In both respects, the goal must be to make unions more inclusive not only in terms of their members' racial, ethnic and gender identities, but also in terms of being more inclusive of their members full life experiences as more than 'just workers'. This will need to be reflected in collective bargaining priorities, but it will also mean thinking hard about the limits of unions in relation to all the spaces and places working people currently interact outside of work, and interrogating the degree of democracy and developmental capacity-building that they might enjoy if such centres of working-class life could be appropriately restructured.[29] Unions have a major role to play in this, but this is also where movements conceived in broader social and political terms are still so badly needed, and could still have enormous potential if only they were ambitious and committed enough.

To speak of a strategy for labour, then, is not initially about laying out a detailed set of policies for democratizing the economy and the state but for *refounding, reorganizing and democratizing the labour movement itself* in order to make clear what new capacities workers and their unions need to develop to start to change 'the structure of power'. In his essay in this volume, Greenfield speaks to the irony of mass mobilizations of workers for militant protests and strikes in East Asia which 'articulate political demands for democracy and democratic reform in society at large but without promoting democratic processes within the collective action or organization itself'. The same point needs to be made about unions in the advanced capitalist countries, like the American, which have rediscovered the importance of putting more resources into organizing drives, and even active 'rank and file' involvement in recruiting new members, but don't connect this with the issue of internal union democracy. As Mike Parker and Martha Gruelle have put in their Labour Notes handbook, *Democracy is Power*:

> The organizing model is a big step forward from the servicing model, but it can have limitations. In practice, some union leaders encourage member *involvement* without member control. They expect to turn member involvement on and off like a faucet. That way, leaders can keep tighter control of a possibly volatile situation. When the rank and file await their marching orders from clever staffers or officials, there's less likelihood they'll undertake tactics that step outside conventional boundaries, or threaten deals made elsewhere.[30]

Of course, there is a deeper union culture involved here—a dialectic between 'rank and file' deference and pride in the leader who can talk tough with an employer (or a president or a party leader or a media talk-show host) and the paternalism of even a radical reform leadership which, as Parker and Gruelle put it, 'may genuinely have the members' interests at heart, but believe the ranks are best served if the leaders maintain control'.[31] Which precise constitutional mechanisms are technically best in terms maximizing accountability and democratic decision making is not the issue here; the point is to measure these mechanisms in terms of the contribution they make to developing democratic capacities whereby members overcome deference, leaders pass on expertise (rather than hoard it like their personal capital), and more frequent changes of leadership are made possible. Above all, debate needs to be encouraged, rather than avoided, even over the most potentially divisive issues. The problem of avoiding debate—whether due to impatience, intolerance or avoidance of tough questions—once again emerges out of a dialectic in which members attitudes as much as leaders' inclinations are entwined. As Bill Fletcher (the most creative and radical staff member brought into the AFL/CIO under the new Sweeney regime) has put it:

> The emphasis on dialogue is essential. The aim is not to talk *at* workers, but rather to encourage debate. The object of debate is to promote the consciousness of workers. But here we come up against some fundamental problems. Some in the labour movement argue that workers must come to understand their economic interests as workers and must therefore not be distracted by 'wedge issues', i.e., divisive issues around race, gender and the like. Others argue that while economic interests are of critical importance, the working class does not see things only through the narrow prism of economics. Class itself is configured racially, ethnically, and by gender in the United States. So workers cannot be inoculated against divisive or wedge issues. Class consciousness cannot be built unless they deal with such issues and take a position on them. History demonstrates time and again the folly of attempting to live in denial of their centrality to class struggle.[32]

This relationship between democracy and class consciousness is, in other words, especially important in terms of those changes in the working class that are turning labour into a more inclusive social agent. Similarly, the most effective way to extend union organization to the unorganized is to identify democratic capacity-building among old as well as new members as the main goal. And what matters for this is the development of leadership just as much as the development of membership. Katherine Sciacchitano, drawing on a wealth of organizing experience, has recently expressed this:

> For frontline organizers, then, the crucial link between union campaigns and movement building is not just militancy. As one organizer said, you can take workers through mobilization after mobilization—but if they

play no role in building and debating strategy they won't necessarily learn anything. Movement building requires understanding how learning and organization takes place at the bottom. This means frontline organizers, educators and labour intellectuals alike beginning a process of open reflection about failures as well as successes ... Most of all, it means paying attention to workers'—not just organizers'—accounts of organizing ... It also suggests we need to develop and train staff ... not just to educate leaders and committee members to mobilize co-workers, but to educate them to develop the group as a whole. The development of staff and leaders as educators is the missing link needed to support democratic decision making, participation, and organizing by members.[33]

Of course, the type of radical strategy for labour articulated by Gorz, and echoed here for our own time, is unmistakably a socialist one. This is appropriate at a time when the label 'anti-capitalist' is not only commonly attached by the establishment media to demonstrations like those in Seattle and Washington, but is openly embraced by the participants themselves. There is indeed a growing sense of the need to think not only in terms of class once again, but also to think about the question of socialist political organization again. This is heard not just among political activists in the labour movement as well as the other social movements, most of whom have worked together for years in coalition campaigns, but especially among the new generation of young activists who have emerged in the anti-corporate branding and sweat-shop campaigns as well as in the burgeoning protests against the institutions of globalization.[34] The alienation from party politics remains, but there is an oft-heard lament that something more than coalitions and campaigns is needed, some sort of organization within which to discuss and develop what an anti-capitalist strategy would seriously amount to. This is the *third necessary element in a new strategy for labour.*

In Canada this has given rise to discussions followed by some tentative moves towards what is being called a 'structured movement' that has clearly touched a nerve among many activists.[35] It would not be a party, but it would be more than the kind of coalition among movement activists on a specific issue that we have become familiar with in recent years. Its immediate emphasis, sensitive to this historical moment of uncertainty on the left, would be transitional: to create the spaces and processes for collectively working out how to combine daily activism with the need for a broader alternative politics; and to increase the likelihood, through organizing the impressive commitments to radical change that already exist, that such energies will be organizationally cumulative rather than dissipated. The 'structured movement' would neither take people away from the broad-based coalitions and organizations that concentrate on campaigns against the institutions of globalization, nor would it seek to undermine social democracy's electoral project. It would have a different project, a much longer-term one oriented to developing a genuinely alternative vision and programme to neoliberal globalization—and a genuinely alternative practice, especially in terms of the kind of leadership qualities and democratic and capacity-building processes discussed here. Social democratic parties today seem incapable of doing this—but the question of whether new ones will be needed or old parties might yet somehow be changed is something best left to the future when some measure of the progress made by the structured movement may be taken. One of those measures will have to be whether the type of strategy for labour sketched here gets enriched and developed and taken up in the unions as well as the other social movements. But no less important a measure will eventually be how many trade-union activists will be prepared to join such a new 'structured movement'. There was a time when local and even national labour leaders were prepared to risk trying to bring those whose confidence they had earned in the industrial arena with them into socialist political organizations; a significant change in labour movement culture among both leaders and members would have to take place in Canada before this would be likely to happen again on any scale. But there is no alternative but to try.

Of course, in each country the landscape of political culture and organization is different. Those of us trying to build a 'structured movement' in Canada will have much to learn from those places like Brazil where the landscape was already such two decades ago that labour leaders could carry many of their members with them in building a party of a new type. The time-scales within which strategies for change are conceived in the North and South may, of course, be very different. For example, in El Salvador after the end of the civil war, one of the main leaders, Fecundo Guardado, expressed his worry that the FMLN had too short a time horizon, regarding the elections that were to take place at the end of the decade (for which Guardado himself would eventually be chosen as the FMLN's presidential candidate) as the long-term goal for which the party had to prepare itself. In Guardado's view, this was a mistake. This period up to the next election was really the short-term, and the most the FMLN could hope for was to hold on to the activist base it developed during the civil war and effectively turn it into the membership of a mass party. The medium-term was 2010, when the party might hope to develop that membership politically and gather within it such additional new elements as would establish it as the strongest political force on the Salvadoran political stage. The long-term was 2020, by which point it might be hoped that the FMLN would have established such a hegemonic presence in Salvadoran society that it could get elected with the expectation of really doing something. Notably, however, Angela Zamora, director of the FMLN's educational programme at that time, reacted to the idea of such a patient strategy with dismay. Indeed, she indicated she would have to think about leaving the party if it adopted such a time-scale. After the sacrifices the people she had worked with had made through the long civil war, they needed immediate reforms and she felt she couldn't look them in the eye and tell them they'd have to wait another two decades, as Guardado's strategy implied they would.[36]

The strategy for labour as discussed in this essay has been conceived, as was Gorz's, in the context of experience in the North. The kind of patient time-horizon outlined by Guardado makes a great deal of sense for the new 'structured movement' in a rich country like Canada, but one can certainly see why by no means everyone would agree it makes sense for El Salvador. Yet at the same time, as Guardado's long-term strategy suggests, and so many of the essays in this volume on working classes in the South also make clear, many of the same problems faced by labour in the North, and which will require a long-term patient strategy to change, are by no means exclusive to it. Sexism, intolerance, fragmentation, undemocratic mobilization processes, the hierarchy built into 'labour aristocracies' in every country, organizational dialectics that reinforce member deference on the one hand and leader egotism on the other—all these problems are as common, and will take as long to change, in the labour movements of the South as in those in the North. To take another important 'southern' example: even in the midst of the general upsurge of working-class militancy and self-confidence that accompanied the liberation from apartheid and the democratic election of the new government in South Africa, the fragmentation in the labour movement was notable. This was seen in the lack of contact—and to some extent even concern—on the part of activists in the metal workers union, NUMSA, not only with the 7,000 black nurses in the Eastern Cape who were fired (by a Communist provincial prime minister) in 1995 for going on strike, but even with the municipal workers on strike in Johannesburg the same year.[37] Such fragmentation between public and private sector unions is, of course, notorious in the North; but it is also very significant that it was so evident at such a historic moment even in the labour movement which perhaps more than any other in our time was living proof that solidarity was a viable practice not just a song.

These sobering reflections are appropriate to the conclusions we need to come to about the *fourth strategic dimension of a new strategy for labour: a new internationalism.* But what exactly does internationalism mean for labour in this era of globalization? There is no sense pretending that problems that are deeply embedded in, and reflect the weaknesses of, each national movement will somehow magically be resolved through transnational collective bargaining with the multinationals and international campaigns against the political institutions of globalization. Sam Gindin is right when he says that international labour bodies can

> make constructive contributions to our struggles. They are useful vehicles for exchanging information and analysis and mobilizing acts of solidarity and support. But here, too, we should be clear about their limits. Strategic international co-ordination is dependent on the strength of national movements. For example, what kind of internationalism can we expect among the United States, Mexico, and Canada if the American labour movement can't yet organize its own South; if the

Mexican labour movement doesn't yet have a common union across work-places within a single company like GM; if the Canadian labour movement hasn't yet been able to achieve major organizing break-throughs in its own key private service sectors?[38]

Nor is there any sense pretending that, in the South as much as in the North, anything other than class struggles of the most trenchant kind at the level of each state can shift the global political terrain. Certainly the notion that without a major shift in the balance of class forces in the leading capitalist states, campaigns to reform the IMF or World Bank or even the ILO can amount to anything significant is nonsensical. The importance of shedding the illusion that globalization displaces the nation state is that we are then able to perceive how states have become responsible for taking charge of the complex relation of international capital to the domestic bourgeoisie; and to appreciate that states do this in ways that still reflect the specific features of class struggle and polit-ical and ideological forms that remain distinctively national even as they are increasingly influenced by, and express themselves within, conjunctures deter-mined on a global basis. Hugo Radice correctly notes that 'the asymmetry between labour and capital in their degree of transnationalization makes workers more a passive object of globalization than an active contestant'.[39] But if this is so, it is mainly because of the asymmetries of power between capital and labour at the *national* level, and can't be changed without change at this level. Radice also contends that the dead end of 'progressive competitiveness' is yet another instance of 'the failure of progressive nationalism itself'. But here again the main answer can only lie in transformations in the class relations at the national level. In so far as labour remains satisfied with being—and capable of being no more than—a subsidiary partner of a national bourgeoisie, nation-alism can be no more progressive than this, as Radice discerns. But in the context of the increasing inability, indeed with very few exceptions the increasing lack of interest, on the part of domestic bourgeoisies to chart a course of development beyond that determined by globally dominant imperialism in this conjuncture, such a partnership is no longer on offer in any case. This is precisely why a new strategy for labour has such importance and promise today.

If internationalism is conceived in a way that is an alternative to, or a substi-tute for, changes that are necessary at the national level the results can only be negative, if not disastrous. There can be little tolerance for the kind of invoca-tions of global working-class unity that, as was first made so tragically clear in 1914, has always produced more rhetorical heat than effective transnational soli-darity and understanding. The most effective internationalism at this stage is for each labour movement to try to learn as much as possible from others about the limits and possibilities of class struggles that are still inevitably locally based. When Mayor of Porto Alegre comes to Toronto to talk about the democratic 'popular budget' the Workers Party runs in that Brazilian city,[40] we need to see less of the glossy brochures that are designed to convince Coca-Cola to invest there, and to be given more detail on how it is that workers and not real estate agents and property developers predominate at the community meetings that compose the popular budget process: this is something that we do not know how to ensure in Canada. And when Canadian trade unionists and left intellectuals go abroad and talk about the union and social movement coalitions that organized the successive one-day general strikes across Ontario's cities, they need to be candid about the tensions and divisions that soon brought this exciting mobilization to an end with a whimper.[41]

What is needed is the kind of internationalism that reinforces the space for, and that contributes to building the strategic and material resources for, working-class struggles in each country. In this respect labour movements in the North were much indebted to the Workers Party in Brazil and COSATU in South Africa, among others, in the last two decades of the twentieth century for the inspiration and guideposts they provided in developing new strategies for labour. Those of us in the North can try to repay this political debt by throwing all our weight behind campaigns that would commit each leading capitalist state to a policy of cancellation of third-world financial debt: this is the most practicable immediate reform that can be won from the institutions of globalization today. We can repay our political debt even more by working towards a long-term transformation of working-class culture in each of the rich capitalist countries, so that unions can really do more than 'place workers as a class on the tail end of the consumers' society', to use Gorz's formulation. Apart from ecological sanity, what is at stake here is the possibility of developing the kind of internationalism that alone will allow for the massive material redistribution from the rich countries to the poor ones that any progressive alternative to global capitalism must entail.

The world's working classes have changed and the world's labour movements will change with them. There can be no doubt that the greatest challenge will be to learn how to 'reinvent solidarity' in this era of globalization. Winning international support for local struggles is as important, or indeed more important, than ever. But the most open and trenchant discussion of each movement's weaknesses and ongoing problems must also be the focus of transnational strategic discussions. This is especially needed now because advances made—and defeats suffered—by labour and its allies in any one state will have a greater exemplary effect than ever. In this era of globalization, it will be through converging and co-ordinated national pressures that successful new strategies for labour will have significant effects at the international level. A new labour internationalism that appreciates this is what is needed if working people are to develop the confidence and capacity to build a better tomorrow out of the great many popular struggles in evidence around the world today.

NOTES

1. Some of the 'associational democracy' literature does explicitly try to marry the concerns of community groups and unions, although usually in a manner that would tie this 'third sector' to the state in neo-corporatist 'social capital' and 'stake-holding' arrangements. See Alan Zuege, 'The Chimera of the Third Way', *Socialist Register 2000*, esp. pp. 102–105.

2. Andre Gorz, *Critique of Economic Reason*, London: Verso, 1989, pp. 231–3. Cf. *Farewell to the Working Class*, Boston: Southend Press, 1982. Gorz's original *Strategy for Labour: A Radical Proposal*, Boston, Beacon: 1967 was originally published as *Strategie Ouvriere et Neocapitalisme*, Editions du Seuil, 1964. Gorz's 'socialist strategy for structural reform' was set out in his 'Reform and Revolution' *Socialist Register 1967*.

3. For instance, a *New York Times* poll in 1996 found that 55% of Americans defined themselves as working class while only 36% defined themselves as middle class; while Gallup found that the number of people who thought 'there is a class struggle' in Britain rose from around 60% in the early 1960s to 81% in the mid-1990s. Colin Leys and I earlier discussed these indications of growing class awareness in our essay, 'The Legacy of the Manifesto' *Socialist Register 1998*.

4. A personal anecdote may exemplify some of what I mean by this. About 10 years ago, while on a flight returning to Toronto, I struck up a conversation with the young woman seated beside me. We chatted amiably about the differences in growing up in Winnipeg in her time and mine, but when I ventured to ask her what she did for a living, she said 'I'd rather not tell you'. When I assured her that I was quite broad-minded, she eventually laughed and relented, telling me that she was a postal worker, but that she was reluctant to tell strangers about it because it usually led to recriminations about the strikes her union had been engaged in. Since she supported these, she would either get into a fruitless argument with a stranger or have to suffer the recriminations in silence. She then proceeded to tell a fasci-nating story about how she got active in her union. She had been hired by Canada Post straight out of high school and had been put to work on the 'docks' of the central postal terminal where the bags of mail arrive and are shifted to various sorting stations. She was one of the first women to be assigned this kind of heavy manual work, but she felt comfortable with it, except for the fact that there were no women's toilets in the docks area and she had to make a very long trek to the other side of the terminal whenever she needed to go to the bathroom. She mentioned this to the foreman one day, who responded: 'Well, you'll just have to learn to stand up and pee at the urinal like the rest of the guys'. To this point, she had nothing to do with the union; indeed she came from an anti-union family and refused to go to the union's orientation session for new workers. But this comment from her foreman led her to seek out her shop steward, whose positive support began a transformation in her attitude to the union. She was now chief steward of the Winnipeg local of the Canadian Union of Postal Workers.

5. There is wealth of outstanding labour history on this: see, most recently, Paul Buhle, *Taking Care of Business: Samuel Gompers, George Meany, Lane Kirkland and the Tragedy of American Labour*, New York: Monthly Review Press, 1999.

6. Gorz, *Strategy for Labour*, p. 26.

7. Gorz, *Strategy for Labour*, pp. 17, 99.

8.   See Joel Rodgers and Wolfgang Streeck, 'Productive Solidarities: Economic Strategy and Left Politics' in David Miliband (ed.), *Reinventing the Left*, Cambridge, Polity: 1994, p. 134.

9.   Fred Bienefeld, 'Capitalism and the Nation State in the Dog Days of the Twentieth Century', *Socialist Register 1994*, p. 115; 'Is a Strong National Economy a Utopian Goal at the End of the Twentieth Century', in R. Boyer and D. Drache (eds.), *States Against Markets*, London: Routledge, 1996, pp. 429–31; on 'progressive competitiveness', see also the Panitch and Albo essays in *Socialist Register 1994*.

10. Gorz, *Strategy for Labour*, pp. 7–8.

11. Gorz, *Strategy for Labour*, p. 181.

12. See Sam Gindin, 'Notes on Labour at the End of the Century' in Ellen Wood et al. (eds.), *Rising from the Ashes*, Monthly Review Press: New York, 1998; and his *The Canadian Auto Workers*, Lorimer: Toronto. 1995.

13. Gorz, *Strategy for Labour*, pp. 152–3.

14. 'The Europeanization of Labour Representation' in Andrew Martin and George Ross, (eds.), *The Brave New World of European Labour*, New York: Berghahn Books, 1999, pp. 312–39.

15. Ibid., pp. 352, 358.

16. Charles Levinson, *International Trade Unionism*, Allen & Unwin: London, 1972.

17. Gorz, *Strategy for Labour*, pp. 187–9.

18. Gerard Greenfield,'The ICFTU and the Politics of Compromise' in Ellen Wood et al. (eds.), *Rising from the Ashes? Labour in the Age of 'Global' Capitalism*, New York: Monthly Review Press, 1998, pp. 180–1. Cf. Peter Waterman, 'International Labour's Y2K Problem', A Contribution to the ILO/ICFTU Conference on Organized Labour in the 21st Century, 15/11/99, unpublished but available on the Internet at <http://www.antenna.nl/~waterman/>

19. Gerard Greenfield, 'Union Responses to Negotiations on the WTO Agreement on Agriculture: A Strategy of Exclusion', Discussion paper, May 7, 1999.

20. Including Lori Wallach, Director of Public Citizen's Global Trade Watch campaign: see Moses Naim, 'Lori's War', *Foreign Policy,* Spring 2000, and John Nichols, 'Now What? Seattle is Just a Start' *The Progressive,* January 2000.

21. Within China, an important critique of the negative effects of entry to the WTO in terms of increased unemployment, economic dependence on foreign companies, American 'hegemony' and 'double standards' has been put forward by Dr Han Deqiang. His book, *Collision,* with a print run of 10,000 copies, has reputedly attracted significant attention from concerned officials and academics across China. Another important and influential critique, focusing on the enormous social inequalities that will be generated, has been set out by Shaoguang Wang of the Chinese University of Hong Kong in his unpublished paper, 'Openness, Distributive Conflict, and Social Insurance: The Social and Political Implications of China's WTO Membership', March 2000.

22. See John Pomfret, 'China Reports Big Surge in Labour Unrest during 1999' *The San Francisco Chronicle*, April 24, 2000.

23. Samir Amin, 'The Political Economy of the Twentieth Century', *Monthly Review*, June 2000, p. 9.

24. Andrew Ross, *Real Love: in pursuit of cultural justice*, New York: New York University Press, 1998, pp. 26–7. See also Naomi Klein's very perceptive examination of the mode of organizing these types of protests: 'The Vision Thing', *The*

Nation, July 10, 2000.

25. See Henry Jacot's critique of Robin Blackburn's proposals in this vein in 'The New Collectivism?' *New Left Review (II)*, 1, Jan/Feb 2000. For the definitive critique of labour investment funds in Canada, see Jim Stanford, *Labour Investment Funds*, Toronto: CAW, 1999; and his *Paper Boom*, Lorimer: Toronto, 1999, esp. ch. 15.

26. I first set out this argument in 'A Socialist Alternative to Unemployment', *Canadian Dimension*, 20:1, March 1986.

27. See Robert Graham, 'Unions split over 35-hour week', *Financial Times*, Oct. 14, 1998, and 'Turning Back the Clock', *Financial Times*, July 29, 1999. For a perceptive look at the complex union politics behind work-time reduction in Germany as well, see Stephen J. Silva, 'Every Which Way But Loose: German Industrial Relations Since 1980' in Martin and Ross, *Brave New World*, pp. 99–100.

28. See Kim Moody, *Workers in a Lean World: Unions in the International Economy*, New York: Verso, 1997.

29. See my essay with Sam Gindin, 'Transcending Pessimism: Rekindling Socialist Imagination', *Socialist Register 2000,* for a fuller discussion.

30. Mike Parker and Martha Gruelle, *Democracy in Power: Rebuilding Unions from the Bottom Up*, Detroit: Labour Notes, 1999, p. 26.

31. Ibid., p. 2.

32. Bill Fletcher, Jr.,'Labour Education in the Maelstrom of Class Struggle' in Wood et al., *Rising from the Ashes*, p. 119.

33. Katherine Sciacchitano, 'Unions, Organizing, and Democracy: Living in One's Time, Building for the Future', *Dissent*, Spring 2000, pp. 75–81.

34. See Naomi Klein, *No Logo: Taking Aim at the Brand Bullies*, Knopf: Toronto, 2000.

35. See Sam Gindin 'The Party's Over', *This Magazine,* Nov–Dec 1998, and the subsequent debate in various issues of *Canadian Dimension* through the following year.

36. Both these statements were made as personal communications to me when I was in El Salvador in January and February 1995 to help the FMLN inaugurate a new intra-party educational programme.

37. These observations are based on discussions with NUMSA activists while I was in South Africa in October 1995 to participate in a series of joint CAW/NUMSA educational seminars.

38. Sam Gindin, 'Notes on Labor at the End of the Century' in Wood et al., *Rising from the Ashes*, p. 202.

39. Hugo Radice, 'Responses to Globalization: A Critique of Progressive Nationalism' *New Political Economy* 5:1, March 2000, pp. 14–15.

40. For an account of this visit, and of the popular budget process, see Judy Rebick, *Imagine Democracy*, Stoddart: Toronto, 2000, ch. 2.

41. For sober assessments, see Marcella Munroe, 'Ontario's "Days of Action" and strategic choices for the Left in Canada", *Studies in Political Economy* 53, Summer 1997; Marsha Niemeijer, 'The Ontario Days of Action—the beginning of a redefinition of the labour movements' political strategy?' Paper presented to the Fourth International Working Conference of the Transnational Information Exchange (TIE) on 'The Building of a Labour Movement for Radical Change', Cologne, March 16–19, 2000; and Janet Conway, 'Knowledge, Power, Organization: Social Justice Coalitions at a Crossroads', *Studies in Political Economy* 62, Summer 2000; see also 'Forum: Assessing Seattle' in the same issue of *SPE* (pp. 5–43).